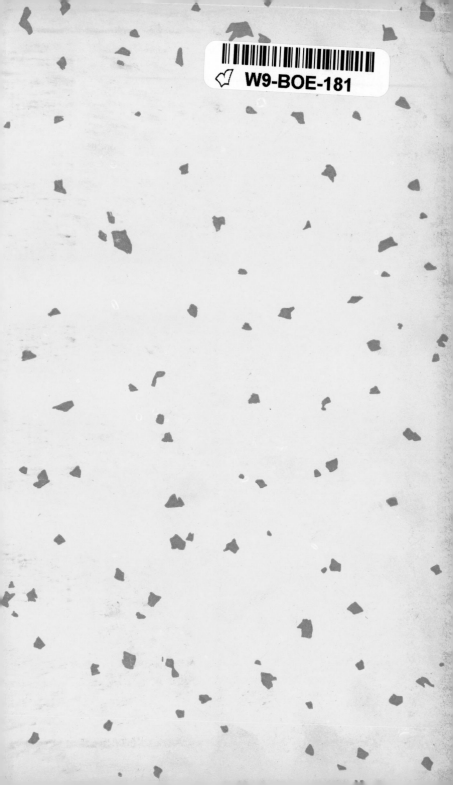

A DREAM OF
RED MANSIONS

A DREAM OF RED MANSIONS

Volume II

TSAO HSUEH–CHIN
and KAO HGO

FOREIGN LANGUAGES PRESS BEIJING

First Edition 1978
Third Printing 1995

Translated by
YANG HSIEN-YI and GLADYS YANG

Illustrated by
TAI TUN-PANG

ISBN 7-119-01547-8
© Foreign Languages Press, Beijing, 1978

Published by Foreign Languages Press
24 Baiwanzhuang Road, Beijing 100037, China

Distributed by China International Book Trading Corporation
35 Chegongzhuang Xilu, Beijing 100044, China
P.O. Box 399, Beijing, China

Printed in the People's Republic of China

CONTENTS

CHAPTER 41

Pao-yu Sips Tea in
Green Lattice Nunnery
Granny Liu Succumbs to Wine
in Happy Red Court

Granny Liu's gestures and response, "A huge pumpkin forms when the flowers fall," caused a fresh gale of mirth. After tossing off the cup of wine, in the hope of raising another laugh she observed:

"To tell the truth, I'm clumsy. And now that I'm tipsy, unless I'm very careful, I may smash this porcelain cup. If you'd given me a wooden one it wouldn't matter even if I dropped it."

Once more everybody laughed.

"If you really prefer wooden cups I'll fetch some," offered Hsi-feng. "But first I must warn you that the wooden cups aren't like porcelain ones; they come in a set, and you must drink from every cup in the set."

The old woman thought: I was only trying to raise a laugh, but it seems they really do have them. When I've dined with the village gentry I've seen plenty of gold and silver cups, never any made of wood. I know! These must be wooden bowls that the children use. She just wants to fool me into drinking more. Never mind, this wine's no stronger than mead anyway, so I needn't be afraid of drinking a bit extra.

So she said, "Fetch them, and we'll see."

Hsi-feng told Feng-erh: "Bring that set of ten cups carved out of bamboo root on the bookshelf in the inner room."

The maid assented, but as she was about to go on this errand Yuan-yang put in with a smile:

"I know that set, it's too small. Besides, you just said wood and it won't look right if now you produce bamboo. Better

1

fetch from our place that large set of ten cups made out of boxwood roots. Let her drink from those."

Hsi-feng thought this a better idea, so Yuan-yang sent someone to fetch them. These cups when brought filled Granny Liu with amazement and admiration. Amazement because all ten fitted into each other, the largest being the size of a small basin and even the smallest as big as the cup in her hand. Admiration at the fine landscapes, trees and figures carved on them, as well as the seals and inscriptions.

"Just give me that small one," she said hastily. "I can't use so many."

"No, you can't just have one," chuckled Hsi-feng. "None of our family has ever ventured to use this set, not having a big enough capacity for it. As you asked for it, granny, and we went to all the trouble of fetching it, you must drink from each cup in turn."

"I daren't!" exclaimed Granny Liu in consternation. "Dear madam, do let me off."

The Lady Dowager, Aunt Hsueh and Lady Wang, knowing that she was too old to stand this, made haste to intervene.

"She mustn't drink too much," they said. "It'll do if she just empties the biggest cup."

"Amida Buddha!" cried the old woman. "Let me use the small one, and put that big one aside. I'll take it home to drink up little by little."

All Yuan-yang could do was to have one large cup filled, and Granny Liu raised this in both hands to her lips.

"Go easy," warned both the Lady Dowager and Aunt Hsueh. "Mind you don't choke."

Aunt Hsueh urged Hsi-feng to give her some food with the wine.

"What would you like, granny?" Hsi-feng asked. "Just name it and I'll feed you some."

"How can I tell what these dishes are?" said Granny Liu. "They all look good to me."

"Give her some fried egg-plant," proposed the Lady Dowager with a smile.

Hsi-feng did so, picking up the food with her chopsticks and putting it into Granny Liu's mouth.

"You must eat egg-plant every day," she remarked. "Taste this of ours and see how you like it."

"Don't try to fool me," cackled Granny Liu. "If egg-plant tasted like this, we'd stop growing other crops — just stick to egg-plant."

"It really is egg-plant," they assured her. "We're not fooling you."

"Really egg-plant, is it?" marvelled the old woman. "All this time I'd no idea. Give me some more, madam, to chew more carefully."

Hsi-feng accordingly fed her another mouthful.

After savouring it slowly Granny Liu said, "It does taste a little like egg-plant, but still it's quite different. Tell me how you prepared this, so that I can cook some for myself."

"It's quite simple," replied Hsi-feng, twinkling. "Pick some early egg-plant and peel it, keeping only the best part, which must be cut into small pieces and fried with chicken fat. Then get some chicken breast, fresh mushrooms, bamboo shoots, dried mushrooms, spiced dried beancurd and various kinds of preserved fruit. Dice these too and boil them with the egg-plant in chicken soup, then add sesame oil and pickles and store it in a tightly-sealed porcelain jar. That's all."

Granny Liu shook her head and stuck out her tongue in amazement.

"Gracious Buddha! No wonder it tastes so good, cooked with a dozen chickens."

While talking she had slowly finished the wine and now she started examining the cup.

"You haven't drunk enough yet," said Hsi-feng. "Have another cupful."

"Not on your life! It would kill me. It's just that I admire pretty things like this. What workmanship!"

"Now that you've finished drinking from it," put in Yuan-yang, "tell us what wood it's made of."

"I'm not surprised you don't know, miss." Granny Liu

smiled. "Living behind golden gates and embroidered screens, what should you know about wood? But we hobnob with wood all day long, sleep on wooden pillows, rest on wooden stools and even eat the bark of trees in time of a famine. Seeing it and hearing and talking about it all the time, I can naturally tell good wood from bad and true from false. Well now, let me see what this is." She was scrutinizing the cup carefully as she spoke. "Such a family as yours would certainly have nothing cheap, nor would you use any wood that's easily come by. Judging by the weight of this, it can't be fir, it must be pine wood."

The whole party had exploded in fits of mirth when a serving-woman came in to tell the old lady:

"The young actresses have all gone to Lotus Fragrance Anchorage and are waiting for Your Ladyship's instructions. Should they start their performance now or wait a while?"

"Yes, we'd forgotten them," chuckled the Lady Dowager. "Tell them to start."

Soon after the serving-woman left on this errand they heard the lilting strains of flutes and pipes. The breeze was light, the air clear, and this music coming through the trees and across the water refreshed and gladdened their hearts. Pao-yu could not resist filling his cup with wine, which he tossed straight off. He had just poured himself another cup when he saw his mother, who also wanted a drink, send for freshly-heated wine. He promptly took his cup over and held it to her lips. She took two sips.

When presently the heated wine arrived, Pao-yu returned to his place while Lady Wang rose from her seat, holding the wine-pot. At this all the rest, including Aunt Hsueh, stood up. At once the Lady Dowager told Li Wan and Hsi-feng to take the pot.

"Make your aunt sit down," she said. "Let's not be so formal."

Lady Wang relinquished the pot then to Hsi-feng and resumed her seat.

"How pleasant it is today," remarked the Lady Dowager

cheerfully. "Let's all have a couple of drinks." Having urged Aunt Hsueh to drink she said to Hsiang-yun and Pao-chai, "You two must drink a cup too. And even though your cousin Tai-yu can't take much, we won't let her off either."

With that she drained her own cup so that Hsiang-yun, Pao-chai and Tai-yu had to follow suit.

Now the music, on top of the wine, set Granny Liu waving her arms and beating time with her feet for sheer delight. Pao-yu slipped across to whisper in Tai-yu's ear:

"Look at Granny Liu!"

"When the sage king of old played music, all the hundred beasts started dancing," quipped Tai-yu. "Today we've just this one cow."

The others tittered.

Presently the music stopped and Aunt Hsueh rising from her seat suggested, "We've all had enough to drink, haven't we? Let's go for a stroll before sitting down again."

As this suited the Lady Dowager, they all got up and she led the way outside. In the hope of some fresh diversion, she took Granny Liu to a grove at the foot of a hill and led her to and fro, telling her the names of the different trees, flowers and rocks.

After digesting all this information the old woman remarked, "Fancy, in town it's not only the people who have class, the birds are high-class too. Why, when they come to this place of yours, they grow so clever they can even talk."

Baffled by this the others asked, "What birds have grown so clever they can talk?"

"I know that green bird with the red beak on the golden perch in the corridor," she said. "He's a parrot. But how come that black crow in the cage has grown a phoenix-like crest and learned to talk too?"

This provoked a fresh burst of laughter.

Soon some maids came to ask if they would take some refreshments.

"After all that wine, we're not hungry," replied the Lady

Dowager. "Still, bring the things here and those who want to can help themselves."

The maids fetched two teapoys and also two small hampers. These when opened were seen to contain two different confections each. In one were cakes made of ground lotus-root flavoured with fragrant osmanthus, and pine-kernel and goose-fat rolls. In the other were tiny fried dumplings no more than one inch long.

"What's the stuffing in these?" asked the Lady Dowager.

Some servants told her, "Crab-meat."

The old lady frowned. "Who wants anything so greasy?"

The other confection, small coloured pastries fried with cream, did not appeal to her either. Aunt Hsueh took a roll when she was pressed, but after one bite she handed it to a maid.

Granny Liu was struck by the daintiness and variety of the small pastries. Selecting one shaped like a peony she said:

"The cleverest girls in our village couldn't make scissor-cuts as good as this. I'm longing to try one, but it seems a shame to eat them. It would be nice to take some back as patterns for the folk at home."

Everyone laughed.

"When you go," promised the Lady Dowager, "I'll give you a jarful to take back with you. First try some while they're hot."

The others simply picked out one or two titbits which took their fancy, but Granny Liu had never tasted anything of the sort before. It hardly seemed possible that these small dainty objects could be very filling, and so she and Pan-erh sampled some of each until presently half were gone. Hsi-feng had the remainder put on two plates and sent in a hamper to the actresses.

Now Ta-chieh's nurse brought her along and they played with her for a while. The child was amusing herself with a pomelo when she noticed Pan-erh's Buddha's-hand and wanted it. Although the maids promised to fetch her one too, she was unwilling to wait and burst into tears. At once they gave the pomelo to Pan-erh and induced him to part with his Buddha's-hand. He had played with it long enough by then and now had both hands full with the cakes he was eating; besides, this fragrant round pomelo seemed more amusing; so, kicking it about like a ball, he cheerfully relinquished the Buddha's-hand.

As soon as they had finished this collation the Lady Dowager took Granny Liu to Green Lattice Nunnery. Miao-yu promptly ushered them into the courtyard, luxuriant with trees and flowers.

"It's those who live the ascetic life, after all, who have time to improve their grounds," observed the Lady Dowager. "These look better-kept than other places."

As she spoke, they were walking towards the hall for meditation on the east side, and Miao-yu invited them to go in.

"We've just been having wine and meat," said the old lady. "As you've an image of Buddha inside, it would be sacrilege. We'll just sit in the outside room for a while and have a cup of your good tea."

Miao-yu at once went to make tea.

Pao-yu watched the proceedings carefully. He saw Miao-yu bring out in her own hands a carved lacquer tea-tray in the shape of crab-apple blossom, inlaid with a golden design of the "cloud dragon offering longevity." On this was a covered gilded polychrome bowl made in the Cheng Hua period,[1] which she offered to the Lady Dowager.

"I don't drink Liuan tea," said the old lady.

"I know," replied Miao-yu smiling. "This is Patriarch's Eyebrows."

"What water have you used?"

"Rain-water saved from last year."

The Lady Dowager drank half the bowl and passed the rest with a twinkle to Granny Liu, urging her to taste the tea. The old woman drank it straight off.

"Quite good, but a bit on the weak side," was her verdict, which made everyone laugh. "It should have been left to draw a little longer."

---

[1] 1465-1487.

All the others had melon-green covered bowls with golden designs of new Imperial kiln porcelain.

Having served tea, Miao-yu plucked at the lapels of Pao-chai's and Tai-yu's clothes and they went out with her, followed surreptitiously by Pao-yu. She invited the two girls into a side room, where Pao-chai sat on a couch and Tai-yu on Miao-yu's hassock, while the nun herself fanned the stove and when the water boiled brewed some fresh tea. Pao-yu slipped in then and accused them teasingly:

"So you're having a treat here in secret!"

The three girls laughed.

"What are *you* doing here? There's nothing here for you."

Miao-yu was just looking for cups when an old nun came in bringing the used bowls.

"Don't put away that Cheng Hua bowl," cried Miao-yu hastily. "Leave it outside."

Pao-yu knew that because Granny Liu had used it, she thought it too dirty to keep. Then he saw Miao-yu produce two cups, one with a handle and the name in uncial characters: Calabash Cup. In smaller characters it bore the inscriptions "Treasured by Wang Kai of the Tsin Dynasty" and "In the fourth month of the fifth year of the Yuan Feng period[1] of the Sung Dynasty, Su Shih of Meishan saw this cup in the Imperial Secretariat." Miao-yu filled this cup and handed it to Pao-chai. The other, shaped like a small alms-bowl, bore the name in the curly seal script: "Rhinoceros Cup." Having filled this for Tai-yu, she offered Pao-yu the green jade beaker that she normally drank from herself.

"I thought that according to Buddhist law all men should be treated alike," said Pao-yu with a grin. "Why give me this vulgar object when they get such priceless antiques?"

"Vulgar object!" retorted Miao-yu. "I doubt if your family could produce anything half as good, and that's not boasting either."

"As people say, 'Other countries, other ways.' Here with a

---

[1] 1082.

person like you, gold, pearls, jade and jewels must all count as vulgar."

Very gratified by this remark, Miao-yu produced a huge goblet carved out of a whole bamboo root which was covered with knots and whorls.

"Here's the only other one I have," she said. "Can you manage such a large one?"

"Of course I can!" declared Pao-yu delightedly.

"Even if you can, I've not so much tea to waste on you. Have you never heard the saying: 'First cup to taste, second to quench a fool's thirst, third to water an ox or donkey'? What would you be if you swallowed such an amount?"

As the three others laughed, Miao-yu picked up the pot and poured the equivalent of one small cup into the goblet. Pao-yu tasted it carefully and could not praise its bland purity enough.

"You've your cousins to thank for this treat," observed Miao-yu primly. "If you'd come alone, I wouldn't have offered you tea."

"I'm well aware of that." Pao-yu chuckled. "So I'll thank them instead of you."

"So you should," said the nun.

"Is this made with last year's rain-water too?" asked Tai-yu. Miao-yu smiled disdainfully.

"Can you really be so vulgar as not even to tell the difference? This is snow I gathered from plum-blossom five years ago while staying in Curly Fragrance Nunnery on Mount Hsuanmu. I managed to fill that whole dark blue porcelain pot, but it seemed too precious to use so I've kept it buried in the earth all these years, not opening it till this summer. Today is only the second time I've used it. Surely you can taste the difference? How could last year's rain-water be as light and pure as this?"

Tai-yu, knowing her eccentricity, did not like to say too much or stay too long. After finishing her tea she signalled to Pao-chai and the two girls left, followed by Pao-yu.

As he was leaving he said with a smile to Miao-yu, "That bowl may have been contaminated, but surely it's a pity to throw it away? I think you'd do better to give it to that poor woman, who'd make enough by selling it to keep her for some time. Don't you agree?"

After a little reflection Miao-yu nodded.

"All right," she said. "It's a good thing I'd never drunk out of it, or I'd have smashed it. But I can't give it to her myself. If you want to give it to her, I've no objection. Go ahead and take it."

"Of course," he chuckled. "How could you speak to the likes of her? You'd be contaminating yourself. Just let me have it."

Miao-yu sent for the bowl and had it handed to him.

As he took it he said, "After we've gone, shall I send a few pages with some buckets of water from the stream to wash your floors?"

"That's a good idea." She smiled. "Only make them leave the buckets by the wall outside the gate. They mustn't come in."

"Of course not."

He withdrew, the bowl in his sleeve, and entrusted it to one of his grandmother's small maids with the instruction, "Give this to Granny Liu to take home tomorrow."

By this time the Lady Dowager was ready to leave, and Miao-yu did not press her hard to stay but saw them out and closed the gate behind them.

The Lady Dowager, feeling rather tired, told Lady Wang and the girls to go and drink with Aunt Hsueh while she herself had a rest in Paddy-Sweet Cottage. Hsi-feng ordered a small bamboo sedan-chair to be brought. The old lady seated herself in this and was carried off by two serving-women, accompanied by Hsi-feng, Li Wan and all her own maids and older serving-women.

Meanwhile Aunt Hsueh had taken her leave too. Lady Wang, having dismissed the actresses and given what was left in the hampers to the maids, was free to lie down on the couch vacated by her mother-in-law. She told a small maid to lower the portière and massage her legs.

"When the old lady wakes, come and let me know," she

ordered the servants. With that she settled down for a nap, and the rest of the party dispersed.

Pao-yu, Hsiang-yun and the other girls watched the maids put the boxes of titbits on the rocks. Then, some sitting on the rocks or grass, some leaning against trees or strolling by the lake, they made very merry.

Yuan-yang arrived presently to take Granny Liu for a stroll, and the rest of them tagged along to watch the fun. When they reached the arch erected for the Imperial Consort's visit home, Granny Liu exclaimed:

"My word, what a big temple!"

She plumped down to kowtow, making everyone double up with laughter.

"What's so funny?" she asked. "I know the words on this arch. We have plenty of temples like this where I live, all with arches like this one here. The characters on it are the name of the temple."

"What temple is this?" they demanded.

Granny Liu looked up and pointed at the inscription.

"Splendid Hall of the Jade Emperor, isn't it?"

They laughed and clapped and would have gone on teasing her, but Granny Liu's stomach suddenly started to rumble. Hastily asking one of the younger maids for some paper, she set about loosening her clothes.

"No, no! Not here!" they cried, nearly in hysterics.

An old nurse was told to take her to the northeastern corner. Having shown her the way, the old servant took the chance to amble off to have a rest.

Now the yellow wine which Granny Liu had been drinking did not agree with her; and to quench her thirst after eating all that rich food she had drunk so much tea that her stomach was upset. She remained squatting for some time in the privy. When she emerged the wine had gone to her head, and squatting so long had left the old creature too dizzy to remember the way she had come.

She looked round. Trees, rocks, towers and pavilions stretched on every side, but having no idea how to reach these different places she could only hobble slowly down a cobbled path until she came to a building. After searching for a long time for the gate, she saw a bamboo fence. So they have bean-trellises here too, she thought. Skirting the hedge, she reached a moon-gate and stepped through it. Before her was a pool five or six feet across, its banks paved with flag-stones, a clear green brook flowing through it, and lying across it a long slab of white stone. She crossed over this stone to a cobbled path which, after a couple of bends, brought her to a door. The first thing she saw as she entered it was a girl, smiling in welcome.

"The young ladies ditched me," said Granny Liu hastily. "I had to knock about till I found this place."

When the girl did not answer, the old woman stepped forward to take her hand and — bang! — bumped her head painfully on a wooden partition. Looking carefully at it, she found it was a painting. Strange! How could they make the figure stick out like a real person? Touching it, however, she found it was flat all over. With a nod and couple of sighs of admiration she moved on to a small door over which hung a soft green flowered portière. She lifted this, stepped through and looked around.

The four walls here were panelled with cunningly carved shelves on which were displayed lyres, swords, vases and in-cense-burners. They were hung moreover with embroidered curtains and gauze glittering with gold and pearls. Even the green glazed floor-tiles had floral designs. More dazzled than ever she turned to leave — but where was the door? To her left was a bookcase, to her right a screen. She had just dis-covered a door behind the screen and stepped forward to open it when, to her amazement, her son-in-law's mother came in.

"Fancy seeing *you* here!" exclaimed Granny Liu. "I suppose you found I hadn't been home these last few days and tracked me down here. Which of the girls brought you in?"

The other old woman simply smiled and did not answer.

"How little you've seen of the world," chuckled Granny Liu. "The flowers in this garden are so fine, you just had to go picking some to stick all over your own head — for shame!"

Again the other made no reply.

Suddenly Granny Liu recalled having heard that rich folk had in their houses some kind of full-length mirror. It dawned on her that this was her own reflection. She felt it with her hand and looked more carefully. Sure enough, it was a mirror set in four carved red sandalwood partitions.

"This has barred my way. How am I to get out?" she muttered.

Then the pressure of her fingers produced a click. For this mirror had western-style hinges enabling it to open or shut, and she had accidentally pressed the spring which made it swing back, revealing a doorway.

In pleased surprise Granny Liu stepped into the next room, where her eye was caught by some exquisite bed-curtains. Being still more than half drunk and tired from her walk, she plumped down on the bed to have a little rest. But her limbs no longer obeyed her. She swayed to and fro, unable to keep her eyes open, then curled up and fell fast asleep.

Meanwhile the others outside waited in vain for her till Pan-erh started crying for his grandmother.

"Let's hope she hasn't fallen into the cesspool of the latrine," they said jokingly. "Someone should go and see."

Two old women were sent but came back to report that there was no sign of her. So they searched in all directions but still could not find her.

She must have lost her way because she's drunk, thought Hsi-jen, and may have followed that path to our back yard. If she passed the hedge and went in by the back door, even if she knocked about blindly the girls there must have seen her. If she didn't go that way but headed southwest, let's hope she's found her way out. If not, she may still be wandering around there. I'll go and have a look.

Thinking in this way, she went back to Happy Red Court and called for the younger maids who had been left to keep an eye on the place. But they had seized this chance to run off and play. Going in past the latticed screen she heard thunderous snores and, hurrying into the bedroom, found the whole place reeking of wine and farts. On the bed, sprawled out on her back, lay Granny Liu. Hsi-jen was shocked. She ran over and shook her hard until Granny Liu woke with a start. At sight of Hsi-jen she hastily scrambled up.

"It was wrong of me, miss," she cried. "But I haven't dirtied the bed." She was brushing it with both hands as she spoke.

Hsi-jen signed to her to keep quiet, not wanting to disturb others for fear Pao-yu should come to hear of this. Hurriedly she thrust several handfuls of incense into the large tripod and replaced the cover, then straightened things a little in the room. It was lucky at least that the old woman hadn't been sick.

"It's all right," she whispered quickly. "I'll see to this. Just say you were so tipsy that you fell asleep on one of the rocks outside. Now come along with me."

Granny Liu assented readily and followed Hsi-jen out to the young maids' room where she was told to sit down. Two bowls of tea sobered her up enough to ask:

"Which of the young ladies' room was that? So elegant and beautiful! I thought I was in heaven."

"That?" Hsi-jen smiled. "That's Master Pao's bedroom."

Granny Liu was too shocked to utter another word. Hsi-jen took her out the front way to find the rest of the party.

"Granny Liu fell asleep on the grass," was all she told them, "Now I've brought her back."

Then the others thought no more of the matter, and there it rested.

To know what the sequel was, read the next chapter.

CHAPTER 42

The Lady of the Alpinia Warns Against Dubious Tastes in Literature
The Queen of Bamboos' Quips Add to the General Enjoyment

Presently the Lady Dowager awoke and the evening meal was served in Paddy-Sweet Cottage. But the old lady, too listless to eat, had herself carried back in the small bamboo sedan-chair to her own apartments to rest. She insisted, however, that Hsi-feng and the others should dine, and so they returned to the Garden. After the meal they went their different ways.

Now Granny Liu took Pan-erh to see Hsi-feng.

"I must go home first thing tomorrow," she announced. "I've not stayed here long, only two or three days, yet I've seen things, eaten things and heard tell of things I never even knew existed. The old lady and you, madam, as well as the young ladies and the girls in the different apartments, have all been kindness itself to a poor old woman. I've no way to show my gratitude when I get back except by burning incense every day and praying hard to Buddha to grant that all of you live to be a hundred."

"Don't look so pleased," replied Hsi-feng with a smile. "All because of you, the old lady's in bed with a chill and our Ta-chieh has caught cold too and is running a fever."

"The old lady feels her age, and she isn't used to exercise," observed Granny Liu with a sigh.

"She's never been in such high spirits as yesterday," Hsi-feng assured her. "Though she likes a jaunt in the Garden, she usually only sits a while in one or two places before coming back. With you here to show round yesterday, she covered more than half the Garden. As for Ta-chieh, Lady Wang gave her a cake while she was crying for me, and eating it in the wind has made her feverish."

"I don't suppose the little dear goes much into the Garden or places she doesn't know. Not like our children, who as soon as they can walk are scampering all over the graveyards. She may have caught a chill in the wind, or being a clear-eyed innocent she may have met some spirit. If I were you I'd look up some book of enchantments, just so as to be on the safe side."

Acting on this advice, Hsi-feng asked Ping-erh to find *The Records of the Jade Casket* and told Tsai-ming to look up the relevant passage. After leafing through it Tsai-ming read, "On the twenty-fifth of the eighth month, illness may be caused in the southeast by meeting a flower spirit. The cure is to carry forty coloured paper coins forty paces southeast, offering one at each step."

"There you are!" exclaimed Hsi-feng. "There must be flower spirits in the Garden. Probably the old lady has run into one too."

She sent for two lots of paper money and two servants to exorcise these spirits for the Lady Dowager and her own small daughter. Then sure enough Ta-chieh fell into a sound sleep.

"Yes, after all, it's the old who are the most experienced," observed Hsi-feng. "Can you tell me, granny, why our Ta-chieh is always ailing?"

"It's natural enough. The children of wealthy families are too delicate to stand any rough handling. Being too pampered isn't good for kiddies either. She'll do better, madam, if you don't spoil her too much."

"I think you're right," agreed Hsi-feng. "By the way, she has no name yet. You give her one so that she can share your good fortune and live as long as you. Besides — I hope you won't mind my saying this — you country folk aren't so well off, and a name given by someone poor like you should act as a counterbalance."

"When was she born?" asked Granny Liu after some thought.

"That's the trouble: the seventh of the seventh month."

"Why, that's good! Call her Chiao-ko[1] then. This is what is known as 'fighting poison with poison and fire with fire.' If you agree to this name, madam, she's sure to live to a ripe old age. And when she grows up and has her own family, if anything untoward happens, her bad luck will turn into good all because of this 'happy coincidence' in her name."

Hsi-feng was naturally pleased and said gratefully, "I hope it will turn out for her as you say."

She called Ping-erh then and told her, "Tomorrow we'll most likely be busy. Sort out our presents for granny now that you're free, so that she can leave as early as suits her tomorrow."

"You mustn't spend any more on me," protested Granny Liu. "I've imposed on you for several days already, and if I take presents too I shall feel even worse."

"It's nothing much, nothing special," replied Hsi-feng. "But good or bad you must take it. That will look better to your neighbours — you'll have something to show for your trip to town."

Just then Ping-erh returned and said, "Come and have a look, granny."

She led the old woman to the other bedroom, where the *kang* was half covered with things. Ping-erh picked them up one by one to show them to her.

"This is the green gauze you admired yesterday," she said. "And here is some pale grey gauze from our mistress for a lining. These two rolls of raw silk would do well for tunics or skirts, and the two lengths of silk in this wrapping will make clothes for New Year. Here's a hamper of all sorts of cakes from the Imperial kitchen; some you've tasted, others you haven't; they're better to offer to visitors than any you can buy outside. One of these two sacks you brought vegetables in has two pecks of rice in it from the Imperial fields, which makes an excellent porridge; the other is full of fruit and nuts from our Garden. In this packet are eight taels of silver. All these are presents

---

[1] *Chiao* means "happy coincidence," *ko*, "boy." It flattered a girl in old China to call her *ko*.

from our mistress. These two packets of fifty taels each, a hundred in all, are a present from Lady Wang who wants you to start a small business or buy some land with it, so that in future you don't have to appeal to friends for help." Then, smiling, she said in a low voice, "These two tunics and this skirt, four headscarfs and packet of embroidery silks are from me, granny. The clothes may not be new, but they haven't been worn much. Still, if you turn up your nose at them, I shan't complain."

Granny Liu had exclaimed "Gracious Buddha!" at each item mentioned, until she must have invoked Buddha hundreds of times. Now, finding Ping-erh so generous and so modest too, she protested with a smile:

"How can you say such a thing, miss? Who am I to turn up my nose at such fine things? Things money wouldn't buy, even if I had any. I just feel ashamed to take so much, and yet since you're so generous, miss, I must."

"Don't talk as if we were strangers," chuckled Ping-erh. "I wouldn't presume like this if we weren't good friends. So don't have any scruples about accepting. I've a favour to ask you too. Next New Year I want you to bring us some of your dried vegetables — cabbage, string-beans, lentil, egg-plant and gourds. All of us here, high and low, enjoy such things. That'll be quite enough, don't trouble to bring anything else."

Granny Liu agreed to this with a thousand thanks.

"Off to bed with you now," Ping-erh urged her. "I'll pack everything up for you and put it here. First thing tomorrow I'll get some boys to order a carriage and load this on for you, so that you don't have to worry about a thing."

More grateful than ever, Granny Liu went back to thank Hsi-feng effusively and take her leave of her. She spent the night in the Lady Dowager's apartments, meaning to say goodbye to the old lady as soon as she was up the next day.

But since the Lady Dowager was unwell, the whole family came the next morning to ask after her health, and a doctor was sent for. Soon a maid announced his arrival and an old nurse stepped forward to draw the bed-curtains.

"I'm an old woman," said the Lady Dowager.   "Old enough to be his mother.   Why should I be afraid of his laughing at me?   Leave the curtains as they are, he can see me like this."

The maids moved a small table up to the bed, put a tiny cushion on it and sent to invite the doctor in.   Presently Chia Chen, Chia Lien and Chia Jung led Doctor Wang over.   Not presuming to walk up the central ramp, he took the side steps up the terrace behind Chia Chen.   Two serving-women had the portière raised and two others ushered him in, while Pao-yu came out to greet him.

The Lady Dowager in a blue silk tunic lined with a curly sheepskin was seated on the couch.   On either side stood two short-haired young maids holding whisks, rinse-bowls and the like, while ranged beside them were half a dozen old nurses; and behind the green gauze screen the doctor glimpsed other figures wearing gay silks and trinkets set with precious stones and pearls.   Lowering his head, he advanced to pay his respects. The Lady Dowager saw from his robes of the sixth official rank that this was one of the Imperial physicians.

With a smile she greeted him, then asked Chia Chen: "What is this gentleman's honourable name?"

"Wang."

"In the old days," she said, "the director of the Academy of Imperial Physicians, Wang Chun-hsiao, was an excellent diagnostician."

Wang bowed and, his head lowered, rejoined with a smile, "He was my great-uncle."

"So our families are old friends."   With these words she slowly placed one hand on the cushion.   An old nurse put a low stool slightly to one side of the table and Doctor Wang, sitting respectfully on the edge of the stool, bent one knee to lean over the couch.   He felt both her pulses in turn for some length of time, his head inclined meditatively, after which he rose with a bow, his head lowered, to take his leave.

"Thank you for your trouble," said the Lady Dowager. "Chen, take the doctor to the study and see that he gets some tea."

Chia Chen and Chia Lien, quick to obey her instructions, conducted the doctor to the study outside.

There he told them, "There is nothing wrong with the old lady except a slight chill. She need not take any medicine. A light diet and keeping warm will put her right. However, I'll make out a prescription and if she likes the old lady can take one dose. If she feels disinclined, it's of no consequence."

He sipped some tea then and wrote out the prescription. Just as he was about to leave, Ta-chieh's nurse carried her in and asked with a smile:

"Will Doctor Wang look at us too?"

The doctor at once stood up. Supporting the child's hand with his own left hand as she nestled in the nurse's arms, with his right hand he felt her pulse. Then he felt her forehead and made her show him her tongue.

"This young lady may scold me for what I'm going to say," he told them with a smile. "She will be all right if she just goes without two meals. There's no need to dose her with medicine. I'll bring some pills for her to take dissolved in ginger-water before sleeping."

With that he left, seen off by Chia Chen and the others. They went back to report his diagnosis to the Lady Dowager, then laid the prescription on her desk and withdrew. Lady Wang and the younger women and girls had emerged from behind the screen once the doctor had gone, and Lady Wang sat there a little longer before returning to her own apartments.

When Granny Liu knew that the old lady was free, she came in to say goodbye. The Lady Dowager urged her to come again and told Yuan-yang:

"See Granny Liu out. I'm not well enough to see her off myself."

Then with final thanks Granny Liu took her leave and withdrew with Yuan-yang to the maids' room. Yuan-yang pointed at a bundle on the *kang*.

"Those are two sets of clothes given to the old lady on previous birthdays," she said. "She never wears anything made outside, and it's a pity to keep them stored away, but she's never once put them on. Yesterday she told me to choose two sets for you to take back — you can either give them away or wear them at home. In this hamper are the pastries you asked for. In this packet the medicines: plum-blossom powder, purple-gold pills, tonic for the blood and restorative pills, each kind wrapped up with directions for its use. Here are two embroidered pouches you can wear for fun." She loosened the strings of these and took out two silver ingots. Showing her the device "May your wishes come true," she suggested with a smile, "You take the pouches, granny, and leave these to me."

Granny Liu, in such raptures already that she had invoked Buddha several hundred times, at once agreed, "Of course, you keep them, miss."

Yuan-yang smiled to see that the old woman thought her in earnest. Replacing the ingots she said, "I was only teasing. I've plenty of these. Keep them to give the children at New Year."

And now a young maid stepped forward to hand Granny Liu a porcelain bowl made in the Cheng Hua period.

"This is a present from Master Pao," she announced.

"Well, imagine that!" cried Granny Liu, taking the bowl. "I must have done good deeds in some past life to have all this happen today."

"Those clothes you changed into when I asked you to have a bath the other day were mine," Yuan-yang told her. "If they're any use to you keep them, and here are a few others."

As Granny Liu hastily thanked her, she produced two more sets of clothing and wrapped them up for her. The old woman wanted to go to the Garden to say goodbye to Pao-yu, the young ladies and Lady Wang, but Yuan-yang prevented her.

"There's no need. They don't see people at this hour. I'll tell them later. You must come again when you've time."

An old serving-woman was dispatched to get a boy from the inner gate to help Granny Liu with her things. Then they went to Hsi-feng's apartments to fetch the gifts there, which the page carried out through the side gate and loaded on to the carriage they had hired. Finally, the old serving-woman escorted Granny Liu to the carriage and saw her off.

After breakfast, Pao-yu and the others paid their respects again to the Lady Dowager, after which they returned to the Garden. Where their ways parted Pao-chai said to Tai-yu:

"Come with me. I've something to ask you."

So Tai-yu accompanied her to Alpinia Court.

As soon as they arrived, Pao-chai sat down and announced teasingly, "You must kneel down. I'm going to try you."

"The girl must be mad!" exclaimed Tai-yu in amazement. "What am I to be tried for?"

"A fine young lady you are, a sheltered, innocent girl!" Pao-chai snorted. "Yet the things you *say*! Confess now."

Tai-yu, who had not the least idea what she meant, was amused but beginning to be worried too.

"What have I said wrong?" she asked. "You're just trying to pick fault. Tell me what you mean."

"So you're still playing the innocent." Pao-chai smiled. "What were those lines you quoted yesterday when we played the drinking game? I couldn't think where they had come from."

Tai-yu remembered then that, the day before, she had been careless enough to quote two lines from The Peony Pavilion and The Western Chamber. Her cheeks flaming, she threw her arms round Pao-chai and giggled:

"Dear cousin, they slipped out inadvertently. Now that you've scolded me, I promise not to say them again."

"They were new to me but I was so struck by them I'd like to know where they're from."

"Don't tell anyone, dear cousin! I won't do it again."

She was blushing in such confusion and pleading so hard that Pao-chai had not the heart to question her further. Instead she made her sit down and have some tea.

"You may not believe it, but I used to be a madcap too," she said gently. "At seven and eight I was a real handful. Our family could be considered a scholarly one, and my grandfather's chief delight was collecting books. There were a lot of us in those days, boys and girls together, and we all hated serious books. Some of my boy cousins liked poetry, others librettoes. We had books like *The Western Chamber*, *Tale of the Lute* and *A Hundred Dramas of the Yuan Dynasty* — a whole collection of that sort. They used to read them in secret, and so did we girls. When the grown-ups later found out, we were beaten or scolded and the books were burnt, which put a stop to that.

"So it's best for girls like us not to know how to read. Even boys, if they study to no good purpose would do better not to study at all, and that's even truer in our case. Poetry-writing and calligraphy are not required of us, nor of boys either for that matter. If boys learn sound principles by studying so that they can help the government to rule the people, well and good; but nowadays we don't hear of many such cases — reading only seems to make them worse than they were to start with. And while study leads them astray, the books they read are debased too. So it's worse than taking up farming or trade, for in those professions they could do less damage. As for us, we should just stick to needlework. If we happen to have a little education we should choose proper books to read. If we let ourselves be influenced by those unorthodox books, there's no hope for us."

Tai-yu had lowered her head to sip tea during this lecture and, rather impressed by it, she now simply murmured, "Yes."

Just then Su-yun came in to announce, "Our mistress wants you both to go and discuss some important business. All the other young ladies are there with Master Pao."

"What can this be?" wondered Pao-chai.

"We'll know when we get there," said Tai-yu.

They went to Paddy-Sweet Cottage, where they found all the others assembled.

Li Wan told them gaily, "Before we've got our club going, someone's trying to wriggle out. Here's Hsi-chun asking for a whole year's leave."

"That's all because the old lady told her yesterday to paint a picture of the Garden," said Tai-yu. "She's glad of the excuse to ask for leave."

"You can't blame it on the old lady," countered Tan-chun. "It was Granny Liu who started it."

"That's right," rejoined Tai-yu promptly. "It's all owing to her. Whose granny is she anyway? Old Mother Locust would be a better name for her."

Everybody laughed.

"Hsi-feng knows all the usual run of smart talk," said Pao-chai. "Luckily she hasn't had too much education, so all her jokes are the vulgar talk of the town. But now our sharp-tongued Tai-yu is using the method of the *Spring-and-Autumn Annals*[1] to condense such talk, extract its essence and colour it with metaphors so that every phrase tells. How graphically the name Old Mother Locust conjures up everything that happened yesterday. What a ready wit!"

"Your commentaries are quite up to their standard too," cried the others, laughing.

Li Wan interposed, "I asked you here to decide how much leave to allow her. I said a month, but she thinks that's too short. What do you say?"

"Actually a year isn't too long," replied Tai-yu. "Since this Garden took a year to build, painting it will naturally require two, what with grinding the ink, spreading out the paper, dipping the brushes in the colours and then. . . ."

Before she could finish the others, knowing that she was poking fun at Hsi-chun, asked, "And then what?"

Unable to hold back her laughter, Tai-yu went on, "Then slowly painting the whole thing in detail. It will surely take two years."

This sally was greeted with hilarious applause.

"Marvellous!" cried Pao-chai. "Especially that last bit about 'slowly painting.' Painting is the crux of the business,

---

[1] A chronicle of the Kingdom of Lu from 722 to 481 B.C. compiled by Confucius (551-479 B.C.) to praise or censure historical figures, passing judgement by implication.

isn't it? That's why all those jokes yesterday seemed funny at the time, not when you look back on them; but when you consider what she's just said, though there seems nothing to it, it's so funny in retrospect that I can't move for laughing."

"You're egging her on to show off," complained Hsi-chun. "And at my expense this time."

Tai-yu caught hold of her arm. "Tell me, are you just painting the Garden or us as well?" she asked.

"The idea at first was just the Garden," said Hsi-chun. "But yesterday the old lady objected that that would look like an architect's drawing. She told me to put everybody in, just as in a family outing. I'm no good at the details of buildings or at painting people either, but I can't very well back out now. A fine fix I'm in."

"People are easy," said Tai-yu. "But can you paint insects?"

"You're talking nonsense again," objected Li Wan. "What insects does this painting need? A bird or two, perhaps, would be appropriate."

"We can dispense with other insects," giggled Tai-yu. "But the painting will have no point without yesterday's Old Mother Locust."

This produced a fresh outburst of laughter.

Shaking with mirth and pressing her hands to her heart, Tai-yu cried, "Do start soon. I've even got the title ready for you. Call it *Guzzling in the Company of the Locust.*"

That set them rocking backwards and forwards with laughter until something crashed to the floor. At once all looked round. Hsiang-yun had been leaning on the back of a chair and, this being none too steady, her weight on it as she laughed had toppled it over, upsetting both girl and chair. Luckily the partition stopped her from slipping to the ground. This sight convulsed the whole party. Pao-yu hastily helped Hsiang-yun up, and by degrees they regained control of themselves.

Pao-yu then shot Tai-yu a glance. Taking the hint she went into the bedroom and took the cover off the mirror to have a look. Seeing that the hair at her temples was dishevelled, she smoothed it with a hair-brush from Li Wan's dressing-case, then put the brush away again and rejoined the party.

Wagging one finger at Li Wan she demanded, "Are you teaching us needlework and sound principles, or are you getting us here to romp and have fun?"

"Just listen to her!" protested Li Wan. "She takes the lead in sending you into hysterics but puts the blame on me. What a terror she is! Well, I just hope, when you marry, you'll get a fierce mother-in-law and several really vicious sisters-in-law. We'll see if you can go on being so cheeky then."

Tai-yu, flushing, caught hold of Pao-chai. "Let's grant her one year's leave."

"I'll make a fair proposal," countered Pao-chai. "Listen, all of you. What Hsi-chun's best at is impressionistic sketches, whereas for a painting of this Garden one needs to have the whole lay-out in mind. As a matter of fact, this Garden itself is exactly like a painting with just the right number of rocks, trees, pavilions and villas near and far, some scattered, some grouped together. If you put all that on paper as it is, the result can't possibly please. You must consider the spacing on the paper, how much to present in the background, how much in the foreground, what to play up and what to play down. Certain things should be added, others left out; certain things should be hidden, others revealed. And you must study your draft carefully to produce a good composition.

"The second essential thing is that in order to get the proportions of the buildings right you'll have to use a ruler. The least carelessness may result in crooked balustrades, collapsing pillars, lopsided windows and doors, steps out of line, or even tables squashed into the walls and flower-pots perched on top of screens. Then the whole thing would be a joke.

"The third thing is to make sure that the figures put in are suitably spaced and at different heights. Then the folds of their clothes, their girdles, their fingers and the way they walk are especially important. One slip of the brush and you'll get swollen hands and deformed feet which will look worse than dirty faces or tousled hair.

"So it seems to me a very difficult job. One year's leave is too long, but one month is too short. I suggest allowing her half a year and asking Cousin Pao to help her. Not that he can teach her anything about painting — he'd only hold her up — but if she has any problems or difficulties he can help solve them by consulting those gentlemen in the study outside who are good at painting."

"That's a good idea," cried Pao-yu eagerly. "Chan Tzu-liang paints excellent pavilions in the meticulous style and Cheng Jih-hsing does superb beauties. I can go and consult them right away."

" 'Much Ado About Nothing' — that's you," observed Pao-chai. "I say one word and off you go to consult them. At least wait till we've reached a decision. First let's discuss what materials we'll need."

"We've some big sheets of *hsueh lang* paper[1] at home which absorbs ink well," put in Pao-yu.

"I knew you'd be no use." Pao-chai smiled mockingly. "That *hsueh lang* paper absorbs the ink and gives good shading effects for calligraphy, ink sketches or landscapes of the Southern School. But if you used it for this, the colours wouldn't stand out and would easily run. You'd ruin the picture and simply waste the paper.

"So let me make a suggestion. When this Garden was built there was a detailed architect's drawing, and though it was done by craftsmen the lay-out and directions are accurate. Ask Lady Wang for that and Hsi-feng for a piece of heavy weight silk of the same size, then get the secretaries outside to have the silk prepared and make a draft according to the drawing with some additions or omissions; and once you've put in the figures there's your painting. Ask them to prepare the green and blue colours and the gold and silver too. In addition you'll need portable stoves to melt and extract the glue, as well as to heat water to clean the brushes. A big varnished table with a felt cover will be needed too. You haven't enough

---

[1] Presumably a kind of painting paper produced in Hsuancheng, Anhwei.

paint-saucers or brushes either. You'd better buy new sets."

"I haven't all that equipment," exclaimed Hsi-chun. "I just paint with my writing-brushes. And the only pigments I have are red-ochre, indigo, gamboge and rouge. Apart from that, all I have is a couple of colouring brushes."

"Why didn't you tell me earlier?" scolded Pao-chai. "I've got all that paraphernalia, more than you'd need — you couldn't have used it all if I'd sent it over. I'll keep it for you, and let you have whatever you want when you need it. But these things are only good for painting fans; it would be a pity to use them on a painting this size. I'll make out for you now a list of materials you can ask the old lady for. In case you don't know everything that's required, I'll list them and Cousin Pao can write them down."

Pao-yu, not trusting his memory, had already got brush and ink ready and at this he picked up the brush with alacrity.

"Four large brushes for drawing outlines, four of the medium size and four small ones," Pao-chai began. "Four large colouring brushes, four medium and four small ones; ten large brushes for painting fine lines and ten small ones; ten beard-and-eyebrow brushes; twenty large and twenty small brushes for colour washes; ten brushes for painting features; twenty willow brushes.

"Then you'll need four ounces each of 'arrow-head' cinnabar, southern ochre, orpiment, azurite, malachite and gamboge; eight ounces of indigo; four boxes of white lead; ten sheets of rouge; two hundred sheets each of red gold-foil and green gold-foil; four ounces of glue and four ounces of pure alum — that's not counting what's used to prepare the silk, but you can leave that to the secretaries when you get them to do it. Once these pigments are properly rinsed, ground, mixed with glue and shaken, I guarantee you'll have enough to play about with and last you a lifetime.

"Then you must prepare four fine silk filters; four sieves; four feather-dusters; four large and small mortars; twenty large coarse bowls; ten five-inch saucers; twenty three-inch coarse white saucers; two portable stoves; four large and small earthenware cooking pots; two new porcelain jars; two new buckets; four white cloth bags one foot long; twenty catties of soft charcoal; one catty of hard charcoal; one chest with three drawers; ten feet of plain gauze; two ounces of ginger; half a catty of soy sauce. . . ."

"And one pan and frying-slice," put in Tai-yu.

"What are they for?" demanded Pao-chai.

"Since you want things like ginger and soy sauce, I may as well get you a pan to fry those colours and eat them."

Everyone laughed.

"You don't understand," rejoined Pao-chai with a smile. "Those coarse saucers can't stand too much heat. The fire would crack them if you didn't first smear ginger and soy sauce on the bottom."

"Yes, that's right," agreed the others.

Tai-yu had another look at the list, then nudged Tan-chun and whispered, "Look at all the pots and chests she wants just for one painting. She must have mixed things up and put in the list of her dowry as well."

Tan-chun exploded in a fit of laughter.

"Cousin Pao-chai!" she cried. "Why don't you pinch her lips? Ask her what she just said about you."

"I don't have to ask," retorted Pao-chai. "One doesn't expect ivory from a dog's mouth."

As she spoke she pushed Tai-yu down on the *kang* to pinch her cheeks.

"Forgive me, dear cousin," pleaded Tai-yu giggling. "I'm too young to know the right way to talk; but you, dear as an elder sister to me, can teach me. If you won't forgive me, who else can I turn to?"

The others did not know what lay behind this exchange.

"How pathetic she sounds," they teased. "Our hearts bleed for her. Do let her off!"

Pao-chai had only been joking, but catching this reference to her earlier lecture on reading improper books, she stopped teasing and let Tai-yu go.

"What a good girl you are," observed Tai-yu. "If it had been me I shouldn't have been so forgiving."

Pao-chai pointed a finger at her. "No wonder the old lady's so fond of you and everybody loves you. I declare I'm growing quite fond of you myself now. Come here and let me do your hair for you."

Tai-yu, complying, turned round and Pao-chai arranged her dishevelled hair for her. Pao-yu, watching, decided that this way of dressing her hair was an improvement and regretted having sent her to comb her hair before — the job should have been left for Pao-chai. His reverie was cut short by Pao-chai remarking:

"If you've finished that list, you can show it to the old lady tomorrow. We may have the things at home; if not, they can be bought. I'll help you with the preparations."

Pao-yu put the list away then and they chatted. That evening after dinner they went as usual to pay their respects to the Lady Dowager. As she had been suffering from nothing more serious than a slight chill caught when she was tired, a day in bed and a dose of medicine had set her right by the evening.

What happened the day after is told in the next chapter.

CHAPTER 43

To Kill Time Money Is Raised
to Celebrate a Birthday
Incense Is Burned on the Ground
to Undying Love

The Lady Dowager was not really ill but had simply caught a chill that day in the Garden. Knowing that a visit from the doctor and some medicine had set her right, Lady Wang stopped worrying and sent for Hsi-feng whom she told to prepare some things to be taken to Chia Cheng. While they were discussing this, the old lady summoned them and they both hurried over.

"Are you feeling better, madam?" asked Lady Wang.

"Much better," replied the Lady Dowager. "Just now I tried some of that quail soup you sent, and found it tasty. I ate a few mouthfuls of the flesh too, and enjoyed it."

"That was a filial offering from Hsi-feng," said Lady Wang. "It shows a proper respect for her elders and due gratitude for all your kindness to her."

"It's good of her to be so thoughtful." The old lady nodded. "If there's any left not yet cooked, I'd like a few slices fried, because being salty it goes well with porridge. The soup doesn't, although it's good."

Hsi-feng promised to see to this at once and had the order passed on to the kitchen.

Meantime the Lady Dowager told Lady Wang, "I'll tell you why I sent for you. The second of next month is Hsi-feng's birthday. Last year and the year before that I meant to celebrate it, but each time something urgent cropped up and I let matters slide. This year everyone's here and nothing's likely to happen, so let's all have some good fun."

"Just what I was thinking," replied Lady Wang. "If that's what you want, madam, why not settle on it?"

"For birthdays in the past we've always sent our presents separately, which is stereotyped and rather formal. Now I've thought of a new, informal way which should be fun."

"We'll do whatever you think best, madam."

"Well then, why don't we copy those poorer families in which everybody chips in, and however much is collected goes for a treat. What do you say? Wouldn't that be fun?"

"Very good. But how shall we go about it?"

Hearing this, the Lady Dowager in high spirits at once gave orders to invite over Aunt Hsueh, Lady Hsing, the girls and Pao-yu, as well as Chia Chen's wife Madam Yu from the other mansion, and the wives of the chief stewards such as Lai Ta. The maids, infected by the old lady's good humour, bustled off cheerfully to deliver her invitations; and in less time than it takes for a meal the room was packed with people, old and young, high and low.

Aunt Hsueh and the Lady Dowager had the seats of honour; Lady Hsing and Lady Wang had two chairs by the door; Pao-chai and five or six other girls sat on the *kang*; Pao-yu sat at his grandmother's knee; and the rest stood, crowding the floor.

The Lady Dowager ordered stools to be fetched for Lai Ta's mother and a few of the older and most highly thought of nurses; for it was the family custom to show more respect to domestics who had served the older generation than to the sons and daughters of the house. Hence Madam Yu and Hsi-feng remained standing while, after a show of declining, Lai Ta's mother and three or four other old nurses sat down.

Then the Lady Dowager, beaming, announced her plan. All fell in readily with the novel suggestion. Those on good terms with Hsi-feng liked the idea, those afraid of her were glad of a chance to please her; and since everyone could afford it they agreed with alacrity.

The Lady Dowager made the first contribution, promising to give twenty taels.

"I'll follow suit," said Aunt Hsueh, "and give twenty too."

"We dare not rank ourselves with the old lady," disclaimed Lady Hsing and Lady Wang laughingly. "Since we're one grade lower, we'll give sixteen apiece."

"We're naturally one grade lower still," put in Madam Yu and Li Wan. "We'll give twelve taels each."

"You're a widow with no means of support," objected the old lady to Li Wan. "We can't milk you like this. I'll pay your share."

"Don't get carried away, madam," warned Hsi-feng with a chuckle. "First count the cost. You still have two more shares to pay, yet now you're offering to give twelve taels for her. You're in a good mood at the moment, but presently you may regret it and complain, 'So much spent on that minx Hsi-feng!' Then you'll play some clever trick to make me part unknowingly with three or four times the amount."

"What do you propose then?" asked the Lady Dowager amid general laughter.

"My birthday hasn't come yet," said Hsi-feng, "but already I'm quite overwhelmed. Here I am, not paying a cent myself but imposing on all of you — it's really too bad. So why not let me pay for my sister-in-law? Then I'll eat more on that day and enjoy myself better."

Since Lady Hsing and the others approved, the old lady gave her consent.

"I've something else to say," continued Hsi-feng. "It's quite fair, I think, for our Old Ancestress to give twenty herself plus Tai-yu's and Pao-yu's shares, and for Aunt Hsueh to give twenty herself plus Pao-chai's share. But it's not very fair for the two mistresses to give less themselves, only sixteen each, and not to pay for anybody else either. This is too hard on our Old Ancestress."

The Lady Dowager laughed heartily. "So this hussy Hsi-feng takes my side, and quite right too," she crowed. "They'd have cheated me if not for you."

"Just turn Pao-yu and Tai-yu over to them," urged Hsi-feng. "Make them pay one extra share each."

"Yes, that's only fair," the old lady approved. "We'll do that."

Lai Ta's mother rose to her feet in mock indignation.

"This is too bad! I can't bear to see Their Ladyships treated this way. One is Madam Lien's mother-in-law, the other's her father's sister; yet instead of taking *their* side she sides with someone less close. What's become of her family feeling?"

This set the whole party laughing.

Then Lai Ta's mother said, "Twelve taels each from Madam Yu and Madam Chu. Of course we're a grade lower, aren't we?"

"No, you can't reckon that way," replied the old lady. "It's true you're one grade lower, but I know you're all rich. You've much more money than they have. So though you rank lower, you must pay the same amount."

The stewards' wives readily agreed to this.

"As for the girls," continued the old lady, "they can simply make a gesture by each giving the equivalent of her monthly allowance." She turned then and called, "Here, Yuan-yang! A few of you get together and decide on your contributions."

Yuan-yang assented and went out, coming back presently with Ping-erh, Hsi-jen, Tsai-hsia and a few other younger maids. Some said they would give two taels, others one.

"Why are *you* in on this?" the old lady asked Ping-erh. "Shouldn't you give your mistress something special for her birthday?"

"I have my own present ready," replied Ping-erh gaily. "But I want to give my share to the general fund too."

"That's a good girl," approved the Lady Dowager.

"That accounts for everyone here," remarked Hsi-feng. "Just to be polite, though, we'd better ask the two concubines whether they'd like to join in or not. Otherwise they may feel slighted."

"Of course. Fancy my forgetting them! I don't suppose they're free to come. Send a maid to ask them."

One of the girls went and after some time brought back the answer, "They'll give two taels each too."

The Lady Dowager was pleased. "Get a brush and ink and see how much it comes to," she ordered.

"You greedy bitch," whispered Madam Yu to Hsi-feng. "So many in-laws and nurses chipping in for your birthday, yet you're still not satisfied. You must needs drag in those two poor wretches too."

"Nonsense!" countered Hsi-feng softly. "Get away with you! Who says they're poor? They throw their money away on other people. We may as well take some and have a good time."

By now the contributions had been counted and they totalled just over a hundred and fifty taels.

"That's more than enough for one day's theatricals and feasts," observed the Lady Dowager.

"As we're not inviting guests, the feasting won't cost much," remarked Madam Yu. "This sum should be enough for two or three days. Besides, the theatricals won't cost anything. We can save on that."

"We must get whatever troupe Hsi-feng wants," insisted the old lady.

"We've heard our own actresses so many times," said Hsi-feng, "let's spend some money and get in a troupe from outside."

"I'm entrusting all the arrangements to Chen's wife," announced the Lady Dowager. "We mustn't make Hsi-feng work. She's just to have fun that day."

Madam Yu agreed to this. And they went on chatting till the old lady was tired, when the party slowly dispersed.

After seeing Lady Hsing and Lady Wang off, Madam Yu called on Hsi-feng to discuss what arrangements to make for the party.

"Don't ask me," said Hsi-feng. "Just watch the old lady's reactions and do whatever she wants."

"You minx, you don't deserve such luck," Madam Yu teased. "I couldn't think what we were being summoned for. So it was just for this. And as if paying up weren't bad enough,

I've got to go to so much trouble too. How are you going to thank me?"

"Don't talk rubbish," chuckled Hsi-feng. "*I* didn't ask you to help, why should I thank you? If you think it too much trouble, go and ask the old lady to give someone else the job."

"See how this has gone to your head!" Madam Yu laughed. "Take my advice and be a bit more modest. If you're so full of yourself you'll spill over!"

After some further conversation she left.

The next morning Madam Yu was still making her toilet when some silver was delivered to the Ning Mansion.

"Who brought this?" she asked.

Her maids told her the wife of the steward Lin Chih-hsiao. She sent to have her fetched from the maids' room. Madam Yu offered her a stool and still combing her hair inquired:

"How much is there in this packet?"

"It's the money from the staff which we've brought over first," was the answer. "The old lady's and the mistresses' isn't here yet."

At this point the maids announced, "People have come with chips from Madam Hsueh and the mistress in the other mansion."

"You wretches," scolded Madam Yu, smiling. "You only remember words of no consequence. Yesterday, for fun, the old lady decided to copy the way poor families chip in to raise money; but you keep solemnly repeating the word. Bring the silver in at once. And see that the messengers have some tea before they go."

With a cheerful assent the maids brought in two packets of silver, including the shares of Pao-chai and Tai-yu.

"Whose is still missing?" asked Madam Yu.

"The old lady's, Lady Hsing's and the shares of the young ladies and their maids," replied Mrs. Lin.

"How about Madam Chu?"

"You'll get hers from Madam Lien when you go over there, madam. It's all there."

Madam Yu, having finished her toilet, ordered her carriage and drove to the Jung Mansion. She called first on Hsi-feng, who had already wrapped the silver up ready to be delivered.

"Is it all here?" asked Madam Yu.

"Yes." Hsi-feng smiled. "Hurry up and take it away. I won't be responsible if anything's lost."

"I don't quite believe you." Madam Yu laughed. "I must count it here in your presence." She did so, and found that Li Wan's share was missing. "I knew you were up to one of your tricks," she scolded. "Where's your elder sister-in-law's contribution?"

"Haven't you got enough with all the rest? What does it matter if you're one share short? I'll make it up later if your funds run out."

"Yesterday in front of everyone you played the Lady Bountiful; now you want to get out of it, but I won't let you. I'll have to apply to the old lady now for the money."

"What a terror you are," protested Hsi-feng, smiling. "Don't complain next time you're in trouble if I put on the screws."

"So you can be frightened too! I wouldn't let you off if you weren't usually so dutiful to me." She took out Ping-erh's share then, saying, "Here, Ping-erh, take this back. I'll make it up for you if we haven't enough."

Ping-erh understood and replied, "Do keep it, madam. If there's any left over, you can give it back to me later just the same."

"So your mistress is allowed to cheat, but I'm not allowed to bribe you," teased Madam Yu.

Then Ping-erh had to take the money back.

"Your mistress is so thrifty," continued Madam Yu, "I wonder what she does with all her money. If she can't spend it all, she'll have to take it and spend it when she's in her coffin."

With this she set off to pay her respects to the Lady Dowager, and after a little conversation with her adjourned to Yuan-yang's room to ask her advice about the party and how best to please the old lady. When their plans were made and she was ready to leave, Madam Yu returned Yuan-yang's two taels with the explanation:

"I shan't be needing these."

She went on then to Lady Wang's apartments to chat, and when Lady Wang withdrew to her Buddhist shrine she gave Tsai-yun her share back too. Next she took advantage of Hsi-feng's absence to reimburse the two concubines Chou and Chao as well. When they dared not take the silver she insisted:

"You're not well off enough to afford this. If Hsi-feng hears about it, I'll take the blame."

Then the two women accepted with effusive thanks.

In no time it was the second of the ninth month. All the inmates of the Garden knew that Madam Yu had arranged for a grand party with not only operas but acrobatics and blind story-tellers too, both men and women. They were looking forward to a delightful time.

Li Wan reminded the girls again, "Don't forget, today is the day for our club meeting. I suppose Pao-yu's not here because he's forgotten this refined gathering in his eagerness to join in the fun." She sent a maid to see what he was doing and ask him over.

The maid returned after some time to report, "Sister Hsi-jen says he went out first thing this morning."

"Surely not!" they exclaimed in surprise. "This girl's muddled up the message."

So Tsui-mo was sent to ask again, but on her return she confirmed that Pao-yu had gone out, saying that a friend of his had died and he must go to offer condolences.

"Impossible," cried Tan-chun. "Nothing could have induced him to go out today. Fetch Hsi-jen and let me ask her."

But even as she was speaking, Hsi-jen walked in.

"Whatever business he had, he shouldn't have gone out today," said Li Wan and the others. "In the first place, how could he run off on Madam Lien's birthday, when the old lady's in such good spirits and high and low in both mansions are going to join in the fun? In the second, this is the day for our first club meeting, yet he sneaks off alone without even asking leave."

Hsi-jen explained, "Last night he told me he'd important business first thing this morning and must go to the mansion of the Prince of Peiching, but he'd hurry back. I tried to dissuade him, but he wouldn't listen. When he got up today he asked for a suit of mourning. It looks as if some lady of consequence in the prince's household has died."

"If that's so, he did right to go," observed Li Wan. "Still, he should be back by now."

They discussed what to do.

"Let's just go ahead with our poems," said some. "We can punish him when he comes back."

But just then the Lady Dowager sent for them, and they all went to her apartments. The old lady was displeased when Hsi-jen reported Pao-yu's absence. She ordered him to be fetched back.

Pao-yu, with something preying on his mind, the previous day had given Ming-yen some instructions. "I'm going out first thing tomorrow, so have two horses waiting at the back gate. I don't want anyone else to come with us. Tell Li Kuei that I'm going to call on the Prince of Peiching, and that he must stop anyone going out to look for me. He can say I've been kept by the prince and will soon be back anyway."

Ming-yen had no idea what was afoot but had to carry out his orders. The next morning, sure enough, he had two horses ready saddled outside the back gate of the Garden.

At dawn Pao-yu, in full mourning, came out of the side gate, mounted his horse without a word and, bending low in the saddle, cantered off down the street. Ming-yen could only mount the other horse and whip it on to catch up, shouting after him:

"Where are we going?"

"Where does this road lead?"

"It's the main road to the North Gate. There's nothing amusing outside, it's quiet and deserted."

Pao-yu nodded. "A quiet spot is what I want to find."

He whipped his horse on and after a couple of turns it sped through the city gate. More puzzled than ever, Ming-yen followed close behind. They rode straight on for seven or eight *li* until the houses were few and far between. Then Pao-yu reined to a halt and turned to ask:

"Can I buy some incense here?"

"I suppose so," said Ming-yen. "What kind do you want?"

Pao-yu replied thoughtfully, "Other kinds are no good; it must be made of sandalwood, rue or laka-wood."

"Those are difficult to get," Ming-yen told him, grinning. When Pao-yu looked worried he asked, "What do you need incense for, sir? I've noticed that you often carry bits of incense in your pouch. Why don't you use that?"

Thus reminded, Pao-yu reached for the pouch inside his lapel and was pleased to discover two bits of eaglewood in it. He thought, "This seems a bit lacking in respect. Still, something I have on me should be better anyway than anything I can buy." He asked then where he could get hold of an incense-burner.

"An incense-burner!" exclaimed Ming-yen. "Where would we find one out in the open country? If you wanted these things why didn't you tell me before? I could easily have brought them."

"Don't be a fool," retorted Pao-yu. "I wouldn't have been riding so hard if it was so simple."

Ming-yen thought for a while then suggested, "I have an idea you might consider, sir. I imagine you'll be needing other things too, so why not go on another couple of *li* to River Goddess Convent?"

"Is River Goddess Convent near here? So much the better. Come on, then."

With a crack of his whip Pao-yu set off again, calling over his shoulder to Ming-yen, "The nuns in that convent often come to our house. If we ask them for the loan of an incense-burner, they're bound to let us have one."

"Of course, we're patrons of theirs. Even in a temple we

didn't know they could hardly refuse. Only I don't understand why you're so pleased to go there today, sir. I always thought you had a special dislike for this River Goddess Convent."

"It's those vulgar fools who worship gods and build temples for no reason that I hate. Those rich eunuchs and ignorant women who have too much money to spend hear of some god and build a temple to him without knowing the least thing about him, on the strength of some legend or romance they've heard, which they take as the truth. In this River Goddess Convent, for example, they worship the Goddess of the River Lo. That's how the convent got its name. But of course in ancient times no such goddess existed. She's Tsao Tzu-chien's invention.[1] Yet some fools had to make an image and worship her. Still, this happens to suit my purpose today, so I'll make use of it."

They had now reached the convent gate. The old abbess was as astonished by this visit as if a live dragon had swooped down from the sky. She made haste to welcome them and told an old serving-man to see to their horses. Pao-yu, going in, did not bow to the image of the goddess but simply stared at it in admiration. For though made of clay it really had the grace of "a startled swan or drifting dragon" and the charm of "a lotus rising from green water or sun shining through morning mist."[2] Unwittingly, he shed tears.

When the old abbess offered him tea he asked if he might borrow an incense-burner. She went to fetch one, finally returning with incense and sacrificial paper to burn as well, but these Pao-yu declined. He told Ming-yen to find a clean spot at the back of the garden for the incense-burner. Failing to find one, his page asked:

"How about the coping of the well?"

Pao-yu nodded and went with him to the well. Having put down the incense-burner, Ming-yen stepped aside. Pao-yu produced and lit his eaglewood, bowed to it with tears in his

---

[1] Tsao Chih (192-232), Tsao Tsao's son and a noted poet, wrote a poem on the Goddess of the River Lo.

[2] These are lines from Tsao Chih's poem.

eyes, then turned and ordered Ming-yen to return the incense-burner. The page assented, but instead of doing as he was told he fell on his knees, kowtowed several times and then prayed:

"I, Ming-yen, have served our second master for several years now and known all his affairs; but he didn't tell me about today's sacrifice, and I dared not ask. Though your name, oh spirit to whom he is sacrificing, is unknown to me, I am sure you must be a girl with no peer on earth or in heaven, of incomparable intelligence and beauty. As my master can't tell you what it is he wants, let me pray to you in his place.

"If your fragrant spirit has feeling and compassion, although separated from the world of men do come and visit our young master from time to time, since he longs for you so much. And do help him in the nether world too, so that in his next life he may be reborn as a girl and enjoy himself with the rest of you, never again becoming a filthy man with a beard and shaggy eyebrows."

This prayer ended, he gave several more kowtows before scrambling to his feet. While he was still holding forth, Pao-yu could not help bursting out laughing. Now he kicked him over and swore:

"Shut up, or people will laugh."

Ming-yen rose then and picked up the incense-burner. As they walked away he said, "I told the abbess you'd come out without any breakfast, sir, and asked her to prepare a simple meal. So do try to eat something. I know you've come out to avoid the big feast and the racket at home today. Spending a quiet day here you'll have anyway observed the proprieties; but it would never do if you eat nothing."

"If we cut the feast, I don't mind if we have a vegetarian snack here."

"Good. But there's another thing: people are bound to be worried by our absence. If not for that, it wouldn't matter going back late. But since they'll be worrying, you ought to start back to town soon, sir, and go home. For one thing, that will relieve the minds of the old lady and Lady Wang; for another, you've already paid sufficient respect to the dead. That's all there is to it. If you go home to drink and watch the shows, it won't be because you want to but simply out of respect for your parents, sir. If you're so set on staying here, regardless of how upset the old lady and Lady Wang are, even the spirit you've just sacrificed to will feel uncomfortable. What do you think, sir?"

"I know what's on your mind." Pao-yu grinned. "You're the only one to have come out with me, and you're afraid of a dressing-down when we get home — hence all this high-sounding advice. But I've not been here long, and I only came to make a sacrifice before going to the feast and watching the show. I never said I'd stay out here all day. Now that I've done what I came for, we can hurry back and stop them worrying. That's best both ways, isn't it?"

"That's more like it," said Ming-yen.

They entered the hall where the abbess had indeed prepared a vegetarian meal for them. Pao-yu ate a little and so did Ming-yen, after which they mounted their horses and rode back the way they had come.

Ming-yen behind kept warning, "Steady on, sir. That horse hasn't been ridden much. Keep a good grip on the reins."

In no time they re-entered the city and returned home through the back gate, then Pao-yu hurried over to Happy Red Court. Hsi-jen and the other girls had gone, leaving only a few old women there in charge. They beamed with joy at sight of Pao-yu and exclaimed:

"Amida Buddha! Here you are at last. You had Miss Hsi-jen worried frantic. The feast is just starting. Do hurry, Master Pao."

Pao-yu hastily changed his mourning for splendid robes and asked where the feasters were.

The old women told him, "In the new hall in the small garden."

He headed straight for the place, hearing in the distance the faint sound of singing and fluting. When he reached the entrance hall he saw Yu-chuan sitting alone on the porch, in tears. She stopped crying at sight of him.

"Here comes the phoenix!" she cried. "Go in, quick. If

you'd been any later, I can't think what would have happened."

"Guess where I've been," he said with a sheepish smile.

But she did not answer, simply wiping her eyes.

He hurried into the hall and paid his respects to his grandmother and mother. Everyone was as delighted as if they had indeed got hold of a phoenix. Then Pao-yu greeted Hsi-feng and offered his congratulations.

"You must have taken leave of your senses," scolded the Lady Dowager and his mother. "How could you run off without telling anybody? Disgraceful! If you ever do such a thing again, we shall tell your father when he comes home and he'll give you another beating."

Then the Lady Dowager rounded on the servants. "Why do you all do as he says?" she stormed. "You let him go wherever he pleases without reporting it. And just where *did* you go?" she asked Pao-yu. "Have you had a meal? Did anything frighten you?"

"Yesterday one of the Prince of Peiching's favourite concubines died," said Pao-yu. "I went to offer condolences. He was weeping so bitterly, I hadn't the heart to leave him. So I stayed for a while."

"If you go out again without letting me know," she warned, "I really shall tell your father to beat you."

Pao-yu promised to do as she said. She threatened, then, to have his servants beaten; but the others pleaded:

"Don't take it to heart, madam. Now that he's back we should stop worrying and have some fun."

As the old lady's fit of temper had been caused by anxiety, her delight at his return now restored her good humour. She stopped reproaching Pao-yu and started making much of him instead, afraid he had had a bad time, missed his breakfast or been frightened on the road. Hsi-jen had come to wait on him too, and they all went on watching the opera.

The opera performed that day was *The Tale of the Thorn Pin,* which so moved the old lady and Aunt Hsueh that they shed tears. The others laughed at or cursed the characters.

If you want to know what followed, read the next chapter.

Hsi-feng, Taken by Surprise,
Gives Way to Jealousy
Ping-erh, Unexpectedly Gratified,
Makes Her Toilet

Pao-yu was sitting with the girls as everybody watched *The Tale of the Thorn Pin*. When it came to the scene in which the hero sacrifices to his drowned wife, Tai-yu remarked to Pao-chai:

"What a fool this Wang Shih-peng is! Surely he could offer a sacrifice anywhere. Why must he rush off to kneel beside the river? The proverb says: Things have their associations. But water the whole world over in the last analysis comes from the same source. He could have ladled out a bowl of water anywhere and wept over it to work off his feelings."

Pao-chai refrained from answering, while Pao-yu turned away to ask for some heated wine to toast Hsi-feng.

As this was a special occasion, the Lady Dowager was determined that Hsi-feng should have a whole day of unalloyed pleasure. Feeling unequal to joining the feasters herself, she reclined on a couch in the inner room to watch the opera from there with Aunt Hsueh, from time to time nibbling some of her favourite titbits set out on the teapoy beside her as they chatted. The two tables of food prepared for her she made over to the maids and serving-women who had no share in the feast, with instructions not to stand on ceremony but to sit in the verandah outside and eat and drink as much as they pleased.

Lady Wang and Lady Hsing sat at the high table in the old lady's room, the girls at tables in the outer room.

The Lady Dowager reiterated to Madam Yu, "Hsi-feng must take the seat of honour. And mind you play hostess well for me to show our appreciation of her hard work all the year round."

"I'll do my best, madam," promised Madam Yu. "But she says she's not used to sitting in the seat of honour. She feels out of place there and won't drink anything."

"If *you* can't make her drink," chuckled the old lady, "I'll go out presently and toast her myself."

Hsi-feng hurried in to protest, "Don't believe her, Old Ancestress. I've had quite a few cups already."

The old lady jokingly ordered Madam Yu, "Drag her out, quick, and force her on to her seat, then take it in turns to toast her. If she still refuses to drink, I shall really come out."

Madam Yu gaily carried out these instructions and ordered a mug to be filled.

"From one end of the year to the other you've been dutifully filial to the old lady, Lady Wang and me," she told Hsi-feng. "I've no gift for you today, so I'll offer you a mug of wine with my own hands. Drink up now like a good girl."

"If you really want to show appreciation you must kneel down, then I'll drink," was Hsi-feng's laughing retort.

"Don't be carried away by all the compliments paid you. I can tell you, such good luck is very rare. Who knows if a day like this will ever come again? So make the most of it, and now drink two cups."

Hsi-feng had no choice but to do as she was told. Next, all the girls presented cups and she had to sip from each. Then Lai Ta's mother, seeing the Lady Dowager in such high spirits, decided to join in the fun and led some old serving-women in to toast Hsi-feng, who again could not refuse them. By the time Yuan-yang and the younger maids came to drink her health, she had really had all she could take.

"Good sisters, let me off," she begged. "I'll drink with you some other time."

"So we have no face, is that it?" protested Yuan-yang. "Why, even the mistress condescends to drink with us. You usually show us more consideration, but now in front of all these people you're putting on the airs of a mistress. Well, it's my fault for coming. If you won't drink, we'll leave you." She turned to go.

Hsi-feng hastily stopped her, crying, "All right, good sister, I'll drink."

She picked up the winepot, filled her cup to the brim, and tossed it off. Then Yuan-yang withdrew with a smile.

After seating herself again, Hsi-feng felt the effects of the wine. Her heart was beating so fast that she decided to go home for a rest. As the jugglers had just come in, she asked Madam Yu to see about tipping them while she went and had a wash.

Madam Yu nodded and, since no one else detained her, Hsi-feng left the table and slipped out the back way. Watchful Ping-erh quickly followed her and took her arm. They were just approaching the covered walk when they noticed one of their young maids standing there, but at sight of them she turned and ran. This made Hsi-feng suspicious. She called to her to stop. At first the girl pretended not to hear, but when Ping-erh called to her too she had to come back.

Hsi-feng, more suspicious than ever now, stepped with Ping-erh into the entrance hall and told the maid to join them and close the partitions. Seating herself on the steps leading to the small courtyard, she made the girl kneel down.

"Get two boys from the inner gate to bring ropes and whips," she sharply ordered Ping-erh. "We'll give this impudent little bitch a good flogging."

The girl, frightened out of her wits, burst into tears and knocked her head on the ground as she begged for mercy.

"I'm not a ghost," snapped Hsi-feng. "Why didn't you stand to attention when you saw me? Why run away?"

"I didn't see you, madam," sobbed the maid. "I ran because I remembered there was no one in our apartments."

"If so, why did you come here in the first place? Even if you didn't see me, we called you at the top of our voices a dozen times, but that only made you run the faster. We weren't far off and you're not deaf. How dare you answer back?"

She slapped the girl so hard on the face that she staggered, then gave her another slap on the other side. At once the girl's cheeks began to swell up and turn purple.

"Mind you don't hurt your hand, madam," urged Ping-erh.

"Hit her for me then. Make her say why she ran away. If she won't, tear her lips!"

The maid went on protesting her innocence until Hsi-feng threatened to brand her mouth with a red-hot iron. Then she confessed with tears:

"The master's home. He sent me here to watch out for you and let him know as soon as I saw you coming, madam. He didn't think you would be back so soon."

Hsi-feng guessed that there was more to it than this. "Why did he ask you to do that?" she demanded. "Why should he be afraid of my return? There must have been a reason. If you tell me straight out, I'll be good to you; but if you won't talk, I'll get a knife this instant and carve you up." She drew a pin from her hair as she spoke and jabbed viciously at the maid's mouth.

Shrinking back in fright the girl sobbed, "I'll tell you, madam. But please don't let the master know that I told."

Ping-erh, trying to pacify Hsi-feng, urged the maid to hurry up.

"The master came home not long ago and had a short nap," she said. "After he woke up he sent someone to see what you were doing, madam. She reported that you'd just started the feast and wouldn't be back for some time. Then the master opened a case and took out two pieces of silver, two hairpins and two bolts of satin. He told me to take them secretly to Pao Erh's wife and ask her to come over. She took the things and came; then the master told me to watch out for you, madam. What happened after that I don't know."

Trembling with rage, Hsi-feng sprang to her feet and hurried towards her compound. Another young maid was stationed at the gate, and at sight of Hsi-feng she ducked back and ran. Hsi-feng called her by name to stop, and this girl had more sense: seeing that there was no escape, she came running out instead.

"I was just coming to report to you, madam," she said with a smile. "But luckily here you are."

"What were you coming to report?"

"Our master's back. . . ." She went on to repeat the story told by the other.

Hsi-feng spat in disgust. "And what have you been doing all this time?" she cried. "You're only trying to clear yourself because I caught you."

She dealt the maid a blow which made her stagger, then tiptoed into the courtyard and up to the window to listen.

She heard the woman inside say laughingly, "If only that hellish wife of yours would die!"

"What if she did?" replied Chia Lien. "I'd marry another who might be just as bad."

"When she dies, you can promote Ping-erh and make her your wife. She should be easier to handle."

"Nowadays she won't even let me touch Ping-erh," said Chia Lien. "Ping-erh resents it too, but she dares not complain. What a fate, being saddled with a hell-cat like her!"

Hsi-feng was convulsed with fury, convinced by their praise of Ping-erh that the latter must have been complaining about her behind her back too. By now the wine had quite gone to her head and, not stopping to think, she rounded on Ping-erh and slapped her. Next she kicked open the door and burst into the room. Without a word she caught hold of Pao Erh's wife and pummelled her, then posted herself at the door to cut off Chia Lien's retreat.

"Dirty whore!" she cursed. "You steal your mistress' husband and plot to murder your mistress. And Ping-erh, you come here! You whores and bitches have ganged up against me, yet you make such a public show of trying to please me."

With that she struck Ping-erh again. Having no one to whom to complain of this injustice, Ping-erh holding back her tears nearly choked with rage.

"Can't you wallow in the muck by yourselves without dragging me in for no reason at all?" she stormed. She started scratching and slapping Pao Erh's wife too.

Chia Lien, coming home in high spirits after drinking, had allowed himself to be caught off his guard so that when his wife burst in he was quite at a loss. Now that Ping-erh was making a scene too he flew into a drunken passion. When Hsi-feng beat Pao Erh's wife he could only look on furiously and sheepishly, but as soon as Ping-erh joined in he charged forward and kicked her.

"You slut! Who are *you* to raise your hand against her?"

Ping-erh fearing that he would beat her promptly left off, protesting tearfully, "When you talk behind our backs, why drag me in?"

Ping-erh's fear of Chia Lien made Hsi-feng angrier than ever. She rounded on her and struck her again, insisting that she go on beating Pao Erh's wife. In desperation, Ping-erh ran out of the room to find a knife with which to kill herself, but the serving-women and maids outside hastily stopped her and tried to dissuade her.

When Hsi-feng saw Ping-erh bent on suicide, she rammed her head against Chia Lien's chest and screamed, "You've all ganged up to do me in, and when I find out you all try to frighten me. Strangle me and have done with it!"

In a towering rage Chia Lien snatched a sword from the wall.

"She needn't kill herself," he bellowed. "I've had all I can take. I'll kill the lot of you and pay with my life. Make a clean sweep!"

This uproar was at its height when Madam Yu and some others arrived on the scene.

"What does this mean?" they exclaimed. "A moment ago all was well. What's the row about?"

Their presence emboldened Chia Lien, half drunk as he was, to bluster even more wildly and swear to kill Hsi-feng. For her part, at their arrival she had stopped storming and slipped away tearfully to enlist the support of the Lady Dowager.

By this time the opera was over. Hsi-feng ran to the old lady and threw herself into her arms.

"Save me, Old Ancestress! Lien wants to kill me."

The old lady, Lady Hsing and Lady Wang immediately asked what had happened.

"When I went home just now to change," Hsi-feng sobbed, "I heard him talking to someone. Not liking to intrude if he had a guest, I listened outside the window. It was Pao Erh's wife there, and the two of them were plotting to poison me because I'm a shrew and put Ping-erh in my place. Angry as I was, I dared not quarrel with *him*; I just gave Ping-erh a couple of slaps and asked her why she should want to murder me. He flared up then and threatened to kill me."

The Lady Dowager and the others believed her story.

"How monstrous!" exclaimed the old lady. "Bring the wretch here."

That same moment Chia Lien rushed in with his sword, followed by a crowd of people. Counting on the Lady Dowager's usual indulgence and the helplessness of both his mother and aunt, he ranted and raged with a great show of bravado.

Lady Hsing and Lady Wang angrily barred his way. "Have you gone mad, you degenerate?" they scolded. "How dare you behave like this in the old lady's presence?"

He cast them a sidelong glance. "It's the old lady who's spoiled her," he retorted. "So now she even has the nerve to swear at me."

Lady Hsing wrathfully snatched away his sword and ordered him out of the room. But he simply went on blustering and storming.

"I know you have no respect for *us*," snapped the Lady Dowager. "Send someone to fetch his father, and see if he'll go then."

Then Chia Lien slunk off. Too angry to go home, he went to his outside study.

Meanwhile Lady Hsing and Lady Wang had been remonstrating with Hsi-feng.

"Don't take it so seriously," said the old lady, smiling. "He's only a boy and as greedy as a cat. This sort of thing can't be helped. All young men go through such stages. It's my fault for making Hsi-feng drink so much — the wine's turned to vinegar."

At this everybody laughed.

"Don't worry," the old lady told Hsi-feng. "Tomorrow I'll make him come here to apologize to you. Don't go back today to embarrass him. As for that wretch Ping-erh, I thought she was a good girl — how could she turn out so sly?"

"Ping-erh's not to blame," put in Madam Yu soothingly. "Hsi-feng was just making a whipping-boy of her. Husband and wife couldn't very well fight each other, so both worked off their temper on her. Ping-erh feels most terribly wronged. Don't you go blaming her too, madam!"

"So that's how it is," said the Lady Dowager. "Yes, I never thought the child was one of those vamps. Well then, poor thing, her mistress stormed at her for no reason. Here, Hu-po! Go and tell Ping-erh from me: I know she's been unfairly treated and tomorrow I'll get Hsi-feng to apologize; but she mustn't make a scene today because it's her mistress' birthday."

Long before this Li Wan had led Ping-erh into Grand View Garden, but she was still sobbing too much to speak.

"You're an intelligent girl," reasoned Pao-chai. "You know how well Hsi-feng's always treated you. Today she just happened to have too much to drink and whom could she vent her anger on if not you? People are laughing at her for getting drunk. If you go on taking it so much to heart, it'll look as if all your good qualities are a pretence."

Just then Hu-po arrived with the Lady Dowager's message which vindicated Ping-erh and made her feel rather better. She did not go back, however, to Hsi-feng's apartments.

After resting for a while, Pao-chai and the others rejoined the Lady Dowager and Hsi-feng. Then Pao-yu invited Ping-erh to Happy Red Court, where Hsi-jen came out to welcome her with a smile.

"I was going to ask you over," she remarked, "but Madam Chu and the young ladies got in first."

Teh period[1] containing ten sticks of four-o'clock-seed powder. He handed one to her.

"This isn't white lead. It's made of the seeds of purple four-o'clock ground fine and mixed with aromatics."

Ping-erh holding it on her palm found it light, pinky white and fragrant, delightful in every respect. Brushed over her cheek it was easy to spread smoothly and felt moist, having much finer grains than the usual powder which was bluish-white and sticky. The rouge too, in its small white-jade box, she observed, was not in the usual sheets but looked more like rose salve.

"The rouge sold in the market isn't clean, and the colour's faint," explained Pao-yu. "This is made from the essence of the very best safflower, which is steamed after all impurities have been extracted and attar added. You need only take a little on a pin, rub it on the palm of your hand, then dilute it with a drop of water and apply it to your lips. What's left on your palm will be enough for your cheeks."

Ping-erh carried out his instructions and did indeed find the rouge extraordinarily vivid and fragrant.

Then, with a pair of bamboo scissors, Pao-yu cut a spray of double autumn flowering orchid that was growing in a pot for her to pin on her hair. Just then, however, Li Wan sent a maid to fetch her, and Ping-erh hastily left.

It distressed Pao-yu that he had never shown much attention to Ping-erh before, though she was such an intelligent, good-looking girl, altogether superior to the common run of stupid, vulgar creatures. He had been grieving all day because this was Chin-chuan's birthday, till this chance to show Ping-erh some attention — a chance he had never expected in a lifetime — had brought him a quite unlooked-for happiness. He therefore curled up on his bed feeling very pleased with himself.

"Chia Lien's only interested in sex but has no consideration for girls," he reflected. "Here's Ping-erh, all alone, with no parents, brothers or sisters, waiting on Chia Lien and Hsi-feng

[1] 1426-1435.

and coping so well with his vulgarity and her vindictiveness; yet she still gets into this dreadful trouble today. How unkind fate is to her! She's even worse off than Tai-yu."

These reflections upset him again, reducing him to tears, and as Hsi-jen and the others had left the room he indulged in a fit of weeping. Noticing that the alcohol sprayed on Ping-erh's clothes was now almost dry, he pressed the clothes with the iron and folded them neatly. He saw she had forgotten her handkerchief. As it was still stained with tears, he washed it in the basin and hung it up to dry in a mood of pleasurable melancholy. Then, growing bored, he went off to Paddy-Sweet Cottage to chat with the others until it was time to light the lanterns and part.

Ping-erh spent the night with Li Wan and Hsi-feng with the Lady Dowager. Thus Chia Lien, going home that evening, found the place uncannily quiet. But since he could hardly fetch them he had to spend that night alone. The next morning, too late, he regretted the scene he had made. So when Lady Hsing came over early, distressed by his drunken behaviour the previous day, he accompanied her to the old lady's apartments. Going in sheepishly, he fell on his knees before the Lady Dowager.

"Well?" she asked.

With an apologetic smile he said, "Yesterday I drank too much and disturbed you, madam. I've come now to be punished."

She spat in disgust and swore, "You degenerate! After swigging you might at least stretch out on your bed quietly like a corpse instead of beating your wife. Hsi-feng's a regular saucebox and likes to lord it over everyone, but how you frightened the poor thing yesterday! If not for me you might have killed her. What do you intend to do now?"

Chia Lien had to accept this reproach, much as it rankled, and did not venture to vindicate himself.

"Aren't Hsi-feng and Ping-erh both beauties? Aren't they enough for you?" the old lady demanded. "You never stop philandering, dragging every stinking bit of filth to your room. Fancy beating your own wife and concubine for a whore like that! How can the son of a good family behave so disgracefully? If you've any respect for me, get up. I'll forgive you on condition that you apologize to your wife and take her home. That's the way to please me. Otherwise just take yourself off, I won't have you kneeling to me."

During this lecture Chia Lien saw Hsi-feng standing there, not in her usual finery but with her eyes swollen from weeping, her pale face unpainted and unpowdered, looking more pathetic and lovely than ever before. He thought, "I may as well apologize and make it up. That will please the old lady too."

He therefore replied with a smile, "To hear is to obey, madam. But I'm afraid this will only make her more headstrong."

"Nonsense," retorted the Lady Dowager. "She has the strongest sense of what's fitting, I know, and won't burst out like this again. If she offends you in future, of course I'll give you permission to make her submit to your authority."

Chia Lien rose to his feet then and bowed to Hsi-feng.

"It was my fault, madam," he said. "Please forgive me."

At that the whole company laughed.

"Don't make a scene now, Hsi-feng," said the old lady smiling. "If you do, I shall be cross."

Next she sent for Ping-erh and ordered Chia Lien and Hsi-feng to make their peace with *her*. This Chia Lien was very ready to do. He promptly stepped forward and said:

"I'm the one to blame for the unjust way you were treated yesterday, miss, and because of me your mistress wronged you too. So let me apologize for myself as well as for your mistress." With that he bowed again, making the Lady Dowager and Hsi-feng laugh.

Then the old lady told Hsi-feng it was her turn, but already Ping-erh had kowtowed to her mistress.

"I deserve death, madam," she said, "for offending you on your birthday."

Hsi-feng was thoroughly ashamed of having drunk so much the previous day that she had forgotten their long friendship and lost her temper, humiliating Ping-erh quite groundlessly just because of something a third party had said. Seeing the maid kowtow now, she hastily raised her to her feet, shedding tears of contrition and distress.

Ping-erh was weeping too. "In all the years I've served you, madam, you've never laid a finger upon me," she said. "I don't blame you for striking me yesterday. It was all the fault of that bitch. How could you help being angry?"

The Lady Dowager ordered attendants to escort the three of them to their own apartments.

"If anyone raises the subject again," she said, "report it to me at once. And no matter who it is, I'll take my cane and give him a good beating."

The three of them, having kowtowed once more to the old lady, Lady Hsing and Lady Wang, were seen back by some old nurses.

As soon as they were alone Hsi-feng demanded, "Just why am I hellish? A hell-cat? When that bitch cursed me and wished me dead, you joined in. In a thousand and one days I must be good at least one day; yet it seems, after all this time, I'm less to you than a whore. How can I have the face to go on living now?" By now she was weeping again.

"What more do you want?" cried her husband. "Just think a bit who was most to blame yesterday? Yet today it was *I* who knelt down and begged your pardon in front of all those people. You've got quite enough face, so stop nagging now. Do you expect me to kneel to you *again*? It's no good going too far."

This silenced Hsi-feng and she giggled.

"That's better." He grinned. "I honestly don't know how to cope with you."

Just then a serving-woman came in to report that Pao Erh's wife had hanged herself. They were both shocked to hear this. But after her initial fright Hsi-feng put on a bold face.

"If she's dead, she's dead," she retorted. "What's all the fuss about?"

Presently, however, Lin Chih-hsiao's wife came in and whispered to her, "Pao Erh's wife has hanged herself, madam. And her people are threatening to sue you."

"That's fine." Hsi-feng gave a scornful laugh. "I've been waiting for a chance to go to court."

"We've all been trying to talk or frighten them out of it," said Mrs. Lin. "They're willing to drop the matter if you'll give them a few strings of cash."

"I haven't a cent, and I wouldn't give it to them if I had. Let them go ahead and arraign me. Don't try to talk them round or scare them away. Just let them go ahead. But if they lose their case I shall sue them for blackmail."

Mrs. Lin was in a quandary when Chia Lien glanced at her significantly and, catching on, she withdrew to wait outside.

"I'll go and see what can be done," he told Hsi-feng.

"You're not to pay them anything," she warned.

He went to talk the business over with Lin Chih-hsiao, then sent people to negotiate and finally hushed the matter up by paying two hundred taels. To give them no chance to change their minds, however, Chia Lien also sent stewards to ask Wang Tzu-teng for some runners and sergeants to help with the funeral. When the dead woman's family knew this, they dared make no further move but simply had to swallow their resentment.

Chia Lien also told Lin Chih-hsiao to deduct the two hundred taels from their housekeeping funds, under cover of various items in their daily expenditure. In addition he gave Pao Erh some money too, and promised to find him a good wife later on. Pao Erh raised no objection, naturally, having received both money and consideration. He continued in Chia Lien's service as before.

As for Hsi-feng, although inwardly uneasy she pretended outwardly to be unconcerned. When no one else was about she took Ping-erh's hand and said gently:

"Yesterday I was drunk. You mustn't hold it against me. Where did I hurt you? Let me have a look."

"It's nothing," Ping-erh answered. "You didn't hit hard."

Then someone outside announced, "Madam Chu and the young ladies have come."

To know the reason for their visit, read on.

CHAPTER 45

Two Girls Pledge Friendship After
a Heart-to-Heart Talk
A Plaintive Poem Is Written One Windy,
Rainy Evening

As Hsi-feng was comforting Ping-erh the young people called. They were offered seats and Ping-erh handed round tea.

"Well, you've come in force," chuckled Hsi-feng. "Anyone would think we'd issued invitations."

"We've come about two things," Tan-chun announced. "One is Hsi-chun's business; and we've also brought you a message from the old lady."

"What is it that's so urgent?" demanded Hsi-feng.

"We've started a poetry club," Tan-chun explained, "but not even the first meeting was fully attended — all because we're too soft to keep order. So it occurred to me that we must rope you in too as our supervisor — we need someone strict and impartial. Then Hsi-chun needs more materials of every kind for her painting of the Garden. We told the old lady, and she says there may be some left-over materials in the downstairs store-room at the back, which we can have if we can find them. If not, we can send out to buy more."

"I'm no hand at versifying," Hsi-feng answered. "All I can do is come and join in the eating."

"You wouldn't have to write anything," said Tan-chun. "Your job would simply be to watch out for truants or slackers and punish the offenders as you think fit."

"Don't try to fool me." Hsi-feng laughed. "I can guess what you're after. It's obviously not a supervisor you want but a mint-master to supply you with cash. You must take it in turns to play host in this club of yours, and because your monthly allowances aren't enough you've thought up this scheme to rope me in so that you can milk *me*. Isn't that the idea?"

The others laughed.

"There's true perspicacity for you!" cried Li Wan.

"What an elder sister-in-law you are!" scolded Hsi-feng. "You're supposed to be in charge of these girls' studies and of teaching them good manners and needlework. If they do wrong you ought to remonstrate with them. Now they've started this poetry club which shouldn't cost much, but you refuse to take charge. The old lady and Lady Wang have their titled status of course, but your ten taels a month is twice as much as *we* get, and yet the old lady and mistress still pity you as a poor widow with no means of support. So you get an extra ten taels for your son, which means getting as much as *they* do, and on top of that you've been given land in the Garden farm and are paid rent, apart from the largest share in the annual bonuses. There are less than ten in your household, counting the servants, and your food and clothing still come from the common fund. Your income adds up to four or five hundred taels a year. Then why not use one or two hundred a year to keep these girls amused? After all, it won't be for long. When they marry, *you* won't be the one to provide their dowries. Yet here you are, so afraid of spending a cent, you've put them up to coming to pester me. I've a good mind not to take the hint but just go and eat up everything you've got."

"Listen to her!" cried Li Wan laughingly. "I say one word and the crazy thing spews out two cartloads of shameless talk like a real dirty swindler and tight-fisted money-grubber. This creature was lucky enough to be born the daughter of a family of scholar-officials and to marry into a family like that too, yet she still carries on in this way. If she'd been the son of a poor family, there's no knowing what dirty language she'd have used. She'd have tried to swindle everyone on earth.

"How could you strike even Ping-erh yesterday? For shame! You behaved like a dog drunk on yellow wine. I was so

furious, I'd have taken up the cudgels for Ping-erh if not for
the fact that it was the dog's birthday and I didn't want to
upset the old lady either.   But I'm still simmering with indignation. And now you're challenging *me*! You aren't good
enough to pick up Ping-erh's shoes.   The two of you ought
to change places."

The girls burst out laughing.

"I see," Hsi-feng retorted. "You honoured me with this
visit, not because of your poetry club or the painting either,
but simply to avenge Ping-erh.   I didn't know she had such
a champion.   If I'd known, I should never have struck her —
not even if some devil were forcing my hand.   Here, Miss
Ping-erh, let me apologize to you in front of Madam Chu and
the young ladies for my wild behaviour in my cups."

The others laughed again.

Li Wan asked Ping-erh, "Well? Didn't I promise to help
you get your own back?"

"It's all very well for you ladies to have your fun, but I
can't take it," was Ping-erh's reply.

"Nonsense," said Li Wan. "I'll back you up.   Hurry up
and fetch the key now, and ask your mistress to open the
storeroom for us."

"My dear sister-in-law," put in Hsi-feng, "do take these
girls back to the Garden first.   I was just going to check this
rice account, and then I've got to see Lady Hsing who sent
for me on some business, and give instructions for the clothes
everyone needs for New Year."

"Never mind those other things," rejoined Li Wan.   "Just
settle my business first so that I can go home and rest and
these young ladies will stop bothering me."

"Give me a little time, dear sister," countered Hsi-feng.
"Why should you, who are usually so good to me, be so hard
on me today just because of Ping-erh?   You used to say,
'However busy you are, you must take good care of your health
and find time to rest.'   Yet now you want to kill me with
overwork! Besides, it doesn't matter if other people's clothes
are late, but you're responsible for these young ladies' being

ready on time. If they're not, the old lady will scold you for not seeing to it or at least reminding me. I'd rather take the blame myself than get *you* into trouble."

"Listen, the rest of you, to this fine talk!" Li Wan smiled. "What a clever tongue! Tell me, are you going to take charge of our club or not?"

"What do you think? If I don't join your club and fork out some money, I'll be looked on as a traitor to Grand View Garden. How could I go on living here then? First thing tomorrow I shall proceed to my post, respectfully accept the seal of office, and then straightway give you fifty silver taels to spread over for several months for your club's refreshments. And as I can't write poems or essays — being just completely vulgar — whether you call me supervisor or not, a few days after I've paid up you can still drive me away."

Amid general laughter she went on, "I'll open the storeroom presently and tell them to fetch out all the painting materials for your inspection. If there's anything of use to you, you can have it; and if you'll make out a list of what's still missing, I'll send people to buy it. I'll supply you with the silk for the painting too. The drawing of the Garden isn't with the mistress, Lord Chen still has it. I'm telling you this to save you a trip for nothing. I'll have it fetched and sent with the silk for the secretaries to work on. How about that?"

Li Wan nodded. "Thank you. If you'll really do that I'll let bygones be bygones. All right, let's go. If she doesn't send the things, we can come and pester her again."

As she started off with the girls Hsi-feng remarked, "There's only one person who could have put you up to all this, and that's Pao-yu."

Li Wan turned back with a smile.

"Oh yes! I'd forgotten. It was Pao-yu we came about. He was the one who didn't turn up at our first meeting; but we were too soft with him. What should his punishment be?"

After a second's thought Hsi-feng replied, "The only thing I can think of is to make him sweep all your floors for you."

They approved laughingly and were on the point of leaving

when Granny Lai came in, leaning on a young maid's arm.

Hsi-feng and the others hastily rose, urged her to sit down and offered her congratulations. Seating herself on the edge of the *kang* she said:

"Our masters and mistresses are rejoicing over our good fortune, and we owe it all to your kindness. Yesterday when you sent Tsai-ming over with presents too, madam, my grandson kowtowed his thanks at the gate."

Li Wan asked, "When will he be leaving to take up his post?"

Granny Lai sighed. "I pay no attention to their affairs, they do just as they please. When he kowtowed to me at home the other day, I gave him a piece of my mind. I said, 'Child, don't start throwing your weight about now that you're an official. You're thirty this year and, though you were born in bondage, our masters were kind enough to give you your freedom the moment you came out of your mother's womb. Thanks to the generosity of your masters above as well as your parents below, you were able to study like a young gentleman, cossetted by maids and nurses as if you were a phoenix. Though you've reached this age I doubt if you even know how the word "slave" is written. All you know is how to enjoy yourself.'

"'It doesn't occur to you,' I said, 'that you owe your present position to the generations of hardship your grandfather and father had to go through.

"'You've had one trouble after another since you were a boy, and the money we've spent on you would make a silver statue bigger than you are. When you were twenty our masters were kind enough to help you purchase an official post, although plenty of real gentlefolk go hungry. You were born a slave, so watch out — don't tempt fortune too far. After having an easy life of it for ten years you managed somehow — Heaven only know how — to get our masters to have you selected for this post. A district magistrate may not rank too high yet he has a lot of work to do as the father and mother of everyone in the district. If you don't behave properly as a loyal servant of the state to be worthy of your masters' kindness, Heaven and Earth will surely condemn you.' "

"You worry too much," Li Wan and Hsi-feng told her with a smile. "We're sure he will do all right. He called occasionally some years ago but hasn't been here for quite a few years now — we only saw his visiting-card at New Year or on birthdays. The other day, though, when he came to kowtow to the old lady and Lady Wang we caught a glimpse of him in the old lady's compound. He cut quite an impressive figure in his new official robes, and seemed to have put on weight too. You should be pleased by his appointment instead of worrying like this. If he doesn't do well, that's his parents' look-out; you should just concentrate on enjoying yourself. When you've time you must come by sedan-chair for a day of card-playing or a chat with the old lady. No one would dream of treating you shabbily. You've fine big buildings at home too, where of course everybody must respect you like a lady of quality."

Ping-erh brought in tea at this point and at once Granny Lai stood up to take it.

"You should have let one of the younger girls do this, miss," she said. "You're doing me too much honour."

Sipping the tea she continued, "You don't understand, madam, all children need a firm hand. Even then, the way they still make trouble on the sly causes us endless worry. Those who know us say: Boys will be boys. Those who don't may talk of our relying on wealth and influence to bully other people, and that would damage even the masters' reputation. When I get too provoked, I often call in his father and give him a good dressing-down, to make them behave a bit better for a while."

She pointed then at Pao-yu. "You won't like what I'm going to say, but your father isn't strict enough with *you*, and the old lady always shields you. Who didn't see, in the old days, how your grandfather beat your father when he was a boy, though he never ran wild the way you do, fearing neither Heaven nor Earth. And Lord Sheh in the east courtyard, though he was naughty, never buried himself at home the way you do; yet he got beaten every day. As for your cousin Chen's grandfather in the East Mansion, he had such a fiery temper he'd flare up at a word, grilling his son as if he were a brigand. From all I've seen and heard, Lord Chen seems to follow his grandfather's method of disciplining his son, only he's erratic. And as he doesn't mind how he behaves himself, you can't blame his cousins and nephews for not being afraid of him. If you've any sense, you should be glad of this warning. If not, you may not like to say anything but I dare say you're cursing me in your heart."

Lai Ta's wife came in just then followed by the wives of Chou Jui and Lin Chih-hsiao to make their reports.

Hsi-feng remarked with a smile, "The daughter-in-law has come for her mother-in-law."

"That's not why I came," said Lai Ta's wife, "but to ask if you ladies would honour us with your presence."

"How stupid of me to forget what I really came for and just to maunder on!" exclaimed Granny Lai. "Now that my grandson's appointed to this post, we've got to give a feast at home for all the relatives and friends who want to congratulate him. I didn't want to invite some people, not others. Besides, I thought, it's sharing our masters' good fortune that's brought us this undreamed-of honour, so I don't mind even if it bankrupts us. That's why I told his father to make it a three-day affair. The first day we shall have a few tables of guests and an opera in our humble garden, and invite the old lady, the mistresses, and all you other ladies and young ladies to come and have some fun; at the same time we'll ask the gentlemen to honour us with their presence at another feast with an opera in the hall outside. On the second day, we'll entertain relatives and friends; on the third, our fellow servants from these two mansions. This will be a great occasion for us, these three days of excitement, and we owe it all to our masters."

"When is it to be?" asked Li Wan and Hsi-feng. "We'll certainly come, and quite likely the old lady will be happy to come too, but we can't say for sure."

"We've chosen the fourteenth," said Lai Ta's wife promptly. "Do give mother face by coming."

"I can't answer for the others, but I promise to come," said Hsi-feng. "First let me warn you, though, I've no presents or tips to bring, so mind you don't laugh at me if after eating I just up and leave."

"What a thing to say, madam!" Lai Ta's wife smiled. "Why, if you felt like it, you could give us twenty or thirty thousand taels."

Granny Lai put in, "Just now I went to invite the old lady, and she's promised to come too, so it seems I really have face."

After pressing the invitations she was rising to leave when the sight of Chou Jui's wife reminded her of something.

"Oh, there's something else, madam," she said to Hsi-feng. "What has Mrs. Chou's son done wrong that you want to dismiss him?"

"Yes, I meant to tell your daughter-in-law, but I was so busy I forgot," said Hsi-feng. "When you go home, Mrs. Lai, tell your husband that neither mansion is to keep Chou Jui's son. He must go."

While Mrs. Lai had to agree to this, Chou Jui's wife fell on her knees to beg her son off.

"What happened?" asked Granny Lai. "Tell me what he did, and I'll be judge for you."

"On my birthday yesterday, he got drunk before the feasting even started," said Hsi-feng. "And instead of seeing to the presents my parents' family sent, he sat there swearing and wouldn't bring them in. Only after the two serving-women delivering the things came in themselves did he at last get some pages to help him carry them in. The boys did all right, but he went and dropped a hamper so that dumplings started rolling all over the courtyard. After the two women had gone, I sent Tsai-ming to tell him off, and he had the nerve to swear at *him*. How can we keep on such an insolent, lawless young bastard?"

"Is that all?" Granny Lai smiled. "I thought it was something serious. Take my advice, madam, and if he's done wrong, beat him, reprimand him and make him mend his ways, but don't dismiss him — that would never do. He can't be treated like one of *our* children, as his mother came here with the mistress at the time of her marriage; so dismissing him would reflect badly on Her Ladyship. Keep him on, I say, madam, and give him a good beating to teach him a lesson. If you've no consideration for his mother, at least have some for Lady Wang."

Hsi-feng turned to Lai Ta's wife. "In that case give him forty strokes, and see to it that he doesn't get drunk again."

Lai Ta's wife assented and Chou Jui's wife kowtowed her thanks. She would have kowtowed to Granny Lai too, but Lai Ta's wife stopped her. Then these three women left and Li Wan and the girls returned to the Garden.

That evening Hsi-feng was as good as her word. She had servants get out all the painting material in the storeroom and send it to the Garden. Pao-chai and the rest went through it and found only half what they wanted. They made out a list of the other things they needed for Hsi-feng to purchase. But no more of this.

Soon the silk had been sized with alum outside, and the draft drawing was delivered. Pao-yu went to help Hsi-chun every day, while Tan-chun, Li Wan, Ying-chun and Pao-chai often forgathered there to watch her painting and to be together.

As the weather was chilly now and the nights were lengthening, Pao-chai asked her mother for some sewing to do. Every day she paid two courtesy calls on the Lady Dowager and Lady Wang, and could not but keep them company for a while if they seemed so inclined; and from time to time she felt obliged to drop in for a chat with the girls in the Garden; thus her days were so fully occupied that she sewed every night by lamplight, not going to bed till the third watch.

Tai-yu, who suffered from a bad cough around every spring and autumn solstice, had overtaxed her strength this year by going out more than usual, because of the Lady Dowager's good spirits, and had recently started coughing again worse than ever. She therefore stayed in her own rooms to rest. Sometimes she grew bored and wished the girls would drop in for a chat to while away the time; yet when Pao-chai and the rest called to see how she was, a short conversation was enough to exhaust her. Knowing how delicate and hyper-sensitive she was, they all made allowances for her, overlooking any lack of hospitality and courtesy.

Today Pao-chai came to visit her and turned the conversation to her illness.

"Though the doctors who come here aren't bad, their pre-scriptions don't seem to be doing you much good," said Pao-chai. "Why don't you ask a real authority to come and examine you and see if he can't cure you? You can't go on like this, having trouble every spring and summer. After all, you're not an old woman or a child."

"It's no use," was Tai-yu's reply. "I have a hunch I shall never get over this. You know how poorly I am at the best of times, let alone when I'm ill."

"That's true." Pao-chai nodded. "The ancients said, 'Food is life,' yet what you normally eat doesn't give you energy or strength, and that's a bad sign."

"Life and death are determined by fate, rank and riches decreed by Heaven," quoted Tai-yu with a sigh. "It's beyond the power of man to alter fate. It seems to me my illness is worse this year." This short speech had been punctuated by several bouts of coughing.

"I saw your prescription yesterday," said Pai-chai. "It struck me there was too much ginseng and cinnamon in it. Although they stimulate the vital forces, you shouldn't have anything too hot either. To my mind, the first essential is to calm your liver and improve your digestion. Once the fire in your liver is quelled so that it can't overcome the 'earth' element your diges-tion will be better and you'll be able to assimilate your food. When you get up each morning, you should take an ounce of the best quality bird's-nest boiled into a gruel with half an ounce of crystal sugar in a silver pot. Taken regularly, this is a better tonic than any medicine."

"How good you always are to others!" Tai-yu exclaimed with a sigh. "I'm so touchy that I used to suspect your motives. I really began to appreciate you that day when you warned me against indiscriminate reading and gave me such good advice. I can see now I'd misjudged you all along. My mother died early and I've no sisters or brothers so, come to think of it, in all my fifteen years no one ever advised me as you did the other day. No wonder Hsiang-yun speaks so highly of you. I used to be sceptical when she sang your praises, but not after my own recent experience. For instance, when you said anything I always answered back, but instead of taking offence you offered me good advice. That showed that I'd been wrong. If I hadn't realized this the other day, I wouldn't be confiding in you now.

"You just said I should eat bird's-nest. Bird's-nest is easy to buy, but my health is so poor that I fall ill every year and while it's nothing serious I've already caused plenty of trouble, what with sending for doctors and preparing medicine with ginseng and cinnamon. If I started demanding bird's-nest now, the old lady, Lady Wang and Hsi-feng wouldn't say anything, but those below would be bound to think me too pernickety. Look how jealous these people are and how much gossip there is here because the old lady favours Pao-yu and Hsi-feng. In *my* case, they'd resent it even more. After all, I'm not a daughter of the house, I'm here because I've nowhere else to go. They resent me enough as it is. If I should push myself forward, they'd all start cursing me."

"Well, in that case I'm in the same position as you."

"How can you compare yourself with me? You have your mother and your brother too; you have shops and land here as well, not to mention all your property at home. You're just staying here to be close to your relatives, not spending a cent of their money on anything, free to leave whenever you please. But I have nothing. Yet all I eat, wear and use, down to the least blade of grass or sheet of paper, is the same as their own girls get. Naturally those petty-minded people dislike me."

"It only means providing one extra dowry in future," Pao-chai chuckled. "And it's too early to worry about that yet."

Tai-yu flushed red. "I confide my troubles to you, thinking you'll take them seriously," she said, "but instead you make fun of me."

"I was only joking, but it's quite true. Don't worry. As long as I'm here I shall keep you company. Just tell me any complaints or troubles you have, and I'll help as far as I can. As for my brother, though, you know what *he*'s like. My only advantage over you is that I have a mother. Fellow-sufferers can sympathize with each other. Why should an intelligent girl like you lament your lack of a brother? Of course, you were right just now in saying that it's better not to put people to too much trouble. Tomorrow when I go home, I'll ask my mother for some of the bird's-nest I fancy we still have, and bring you a few ounces. You can get your maids to prepare some every day. It won't cost anything and you'll not be putting anybody out."

"It's a small thing, but I appreciate your kindness," said Tai-yu gratefully.

"It's not worth mentioning. I'm afraid I'm often lacking in consideration. Well, you must be tired, I'll go now."

"Do drop in again this evening for a chat."

Pao-chai promised to do this and left.

Tai-yu sipped two mouthfuls of rice gruel, then lay down to rest again.

The weather changed unexpectedly before sunset and it began to drizzle. Autumn is a capricious season of many showers and as dusk fell it grew very dark, while the rain pattering on the bamboo leaves made the place seem unusually lonely. Knowing that Pao-chai would not come out in this weather, Tai-yu picked up a book at random under the lamp. It was an anthology of *Yueh-fu*, containing lyrics such as *Autumn Sorrow in a Girl's Chamber* and *The Pain of Parting*. Tai-yu was moved to write a poem about separation herself entitled *A Windy, Rainy Evening by the Autumn Window* in the style of *A Night of Flowers and Moonlight by the Spring River*. This was her poem:

Sad the autumn flowers, sear the autumn grass,
Autumn lamps flicker through the long autumn night;
Unendurably desolate by the autumn window,
In the wind and rain autumn seems infinite.
The wind and rain speed autumn on its way,
By the window shattering her autumn dream;
And the girl with autumn in her heart cannot sleep
But trims the candle by her autumn screen.
Guttering on its stick, the candle sheds tears of wax,
Evoking the grief of separation, its pain,
As through each autumn courtyard gusts the wind
And on each autumn window beats the rain.
The autumn wind, through silken quilts strikes chill,
Her water-clock the autumn rain spurs on.
All night the pelting rain and soughing wind
Accompany her tears for one now gone.
Chill mist enwraps the court in loneliness,
Bamboos drip by the lattice without pause;
None can tell when the wind and rain will cease,
But already tears have soaked her window's gauze.

Having read this through, she had just put down her brush and was about to go to bed when Pao-yu was announced. And in he walked, in a large hat of plaited bamboo leaves and a coir cape.

"Where does this fisherman come from?" she greet him laughing.

"Do you feel better today? Have you taken your medicine? How is your appetite?" As he made these inquiries he took off his cape and hat and picked up the lamp, shading it with one hand, to examine her face intently.

"You look a little better today," was his verdict.

She saw that he was wearing a red silk coat, no longer new, with a green girdle, green silk trousers embroidered with flowers, cotton socks embroidered with gold thread, and slippers with butterfly and flower designs.

"Why did you only protect your head and clothes from the rain, not your footwear?" she asked. "Not that your shoes and socks are dirty either."

"I've got a complete set of rain-wear," he told her gaily. "I came here in pyrus-wood pattens, which I left outside on the verandah."

She noticed then that his cape and hat were not the usual sort sold in the market, but extremely finely made.

"What plant are they woven of?" she asked. "You don't look like a hedgehog in that cape, for a wonder."

"These three things are all presents from the Prince of Peiching. When it's raining he wears a similar outfit at home. If you like them, I'll get you a set. The best thing is the hat as it's adjustable — the crown can be detached. So men or women alike can wear it in winter in the snow. I'll get you one for when it snows this winter."

"No thank you," Tai-yu chuckled. "If I wore one of those, I should look like the fisherman's wife in paintings and operas."

As these words left her lips she remembered with dismay that she had just greeted Pao-yu as a fisherman. She flushed scarlet and leaned forward over the table, coughing as if she could never stop. Pao-yu, however, appeared not to have noticed. Catching sight of the poem on the table, he picked it up, read it through, and exclaimed in involuntary admiration. Tai-yu hearing this instantly snatched the paper from him and burned it over the lamp.

"Too late! I know it by heart," he said cheerfully.

"I'm better now. Thank you for coming so often to see me, even in the rain," she said. "Now it's late and I'd like to sleep. Please go now. Come again tomorrow."

At this he took from his pocket a golden watch the size of a walnut. Its hands, he saw, showed that it was after nine. Replacing the watch he agreed:

"Yes, it's time to turn in. I've disturbed you too long again." He put on the cape and hat and took his leave, turning back at the door to ask, "What would you like to eat? Let me know and I'll tell the old lady first thing in the morning. I'm a better messenger than those old women."

"I'll think about it during the night, and let you know early tomorrow. Listen, how it's pouring outside. You'd better go quickly. Have you anyone with you?"

Two serving-women answered, "Yes, they're waiting outside with umbrellas and a lantern."

"A lantern? In this weather?" she asked in surprise.

"That's all right," said Pao-yu. "It's a horn lantern, and it's rain-proof."

She took an ornate glass lantern from the bookcase, ordered a small candle to be lit in it, and handed it to him.

"This is brighter, just the thing to use in the rain."

"I have one like that too," he said. "I didn't bring it for fear they might slip and break it."

"Which is more valuable, lamp or man? You're not used to wearing pattens, so get them to carry the horn lantern in front and take this one yourself, since it's handy and bright and meant to be used in the rain. Wouldn't that be better? You can send it back later. And even if you drop it, it won't matter. What's come over you suddenly that you want to 'cut open your stomach to hide a pearl'?"

Pao-yu promptly took the lantern. Two serving-women led the way with an umbrella and the horn lantern, while two young maids with umbrellas followed behind. He made one of these hold the glass lantern and rested a hand on her shoulder.

Scarcely had he gone when a woman, also with an umbrella and a lantern, arrived to deliver a big package of the best quality bird's-nest and a packet of fine plum-petal snow-white sugar from Alpinia Park.

"This is better than any in the shops," she said. "Our young lady hopes you will use it, and when it's finished she'll send some more."

Tai-yu thanked her and asked her to sit down in the outer room to have some tea.

"I won't stay," the woman replied. "I've got other things to do."

"I know what keeps you busy," rejoined Tai-yu laughingly. "Now that it's turning cold and the nights are long, this is the time for evening gambling parties."

"I'll confess, miss, my luck has been very good this year," said the woman with a smile. "There are always a few of us on night duty, and we mustn't sleep during our watch; so gaming helps to keep us awake and pass the time pleasantly.

Tonight it's my turn to be banker. Now that the Garden gates are closed it's time to start."

"Thank you very much for bringing these things in the rain. I'm sorry if I've kept you from making more money." She ordered her maids to give the woman a few hundred cash for wine to keep out the chill.

"Thank you, miss, for treating me again." The woman kowtowed and, having gone to the outer room to take the money, went off with her umbrella.

Tzu-chuan put away the packages, moved aside the lamp and lowered the curtains, then helped her mistress to bed.

Tai-yu's thoughts turned to Pao-chai as she lay on her pillow, and again she envied her for having a mother and a brother. Then she reflected that, good as Pao-yu was to her, there was still a certain distance between them. Moreover, the rain drumming steadily down on the bamboos and plantains outside wafted a chill through her curtains and made her shed tears again. Only towards the end of the fourth watch did she finally fall asleep.

If you want to know the sequence, read the next chapter.

CHAPTER 46

An Old Reprobate Makes an Unseemly Proposal
Yuan-yang Vows Never to Marry

Tai-yu did not fall asleep till nearly dawn. But let us leave her now and turn back to Hsi-feng, who received a mysterious summons from Lady Hsing and after hastily changing her clothes went off in her carriage to the east court.

Lady Hsing sent her maids away then confided to Hsi-feng, "The Elder Master has given me a difficult task, and I am at a loss, so I want your advice as to how to handle it. He's taken a fancy to the old lady's maid Yuan-yang and wants to make her his concubine. He's told *me* to go and ask the old lady for her. I know this is quite commonly done, but I'm afraid the old lady may not agree. What would you advise me to do?"

"If I were you, I wouldn't run my head against a brick wall," replied Hsi-feng promptly. "The old lady can't even eat without Yuan-yang; how could she part with her? Besides, when we're chatting I've often heard her remark that the Elder Master, at his advanced age, shouldn't be taking concubines left and right. For one thing, he's spoiling those girls' chances of marriage; for another, he's injuring his health and neglecting his official duties by spending all the time drinking with his concubines. You can judge from that, madam, that she's not particularly partial to the Elder Master. He'd do better to try to avoid offending her further instead of 'tickling the tiger's nose with a straw.' Please don't be annoyed, madam, but *I* haven't the courage to approach her. As far as I can see, it would be useless and just cause unpleasantness. The Elder Master's behaviour *is* rather unbecoming for a gentleman getting on in years; you should talk him out of it. It wouldn't matter if he were young; but when a man has such a flock of younger brothers, nephews, children and grandchildren, doesn't it look bad to go on fooling around like this?"

"Other noble families often have three or four concubines, so why shouldn't we?" retorted Lady Hsing coldly. "I doubt if I can talk him out of it. Even if Yuan-yang is the old lady's favourite maid, when her elder son, a grey-bearded official wants her for his concubine his mother can hardly refuse him. I invited you over simply to ask your opinion, but at once you trot out all these reasons against it. Did you think I'd send *you* on this errand? I shall go myself, of course. You blame me for not dissuading him, but surely you know your father-in-law better than that. He'd ignore my advice and fly into a temper."

Hsi-feng knew that her mother-in-law was a stupid, weak-minded woman who, to save herself trouble, always humoured Chia Sheh, finding her sole pleasure in life in amassing property and money. All decisions great or small in their household she left to her husband; but when money passed through her hands she was extraordinarily tight-fisted, alleging that she had to economize to make up for *his* extravagance. Not one of her children or servants did she trust, nor would she listen to their advice. It would be futile to reason with her now, seeing that she was so stubborn.

So with a pleasant smile Hsi-feng replied, "You're quite right, madam. What can I know, young as I am? After all, she's his mother and would surely never refuse him the rarest treasure, not to say a maid. Whom else would she give her to if not the Elder Master? I was silly to take what she said in private so seriously. Even in Lien's case, for instance, the master and you may threaten to beat him to death when he displeases you, but the moment you see him your anger melts away and you still give him things you treasure. Of course, that's how the old lady will treat the Elder Master. As she's in high spirits today, it seems to me now's the time to make this request. Would you like me to go first to coax her into a good humour? Then when you come I'll make some excuse to leave, taking everyone else there with me, so that you can broach the subject.

If she agrees, so much the better. If she doesn't, no harm will be done as no one else will know."

Mollified by this, Lady Hsing told her, "My idea was not to approach the old lady first, for if she refused that would be the end of the matter. I was thinking of telling Yuan-yang first in private. She may be bashful, but when I've explained it all to her she naturally won't say anything. And that can be taken to mean consent. Then I'll go and ask the old lady, and she'll find it difficult to refuse even though she doesn't want to part with the girl. For as the proverb says, 'There's no holding someone who wants to leave.' It's sure to work out all right."

"After all, you know best, madam." Hsi-feng smiled. "This is bound to work. Every girl, not to mention Yuan-yang, wants to rise in the world and become someone of importance. Who would refuse to become a semi-mistress and remain in service instead, with no prospect but that of marrying some servant in the end?"

"That's what I think," agreed Lady Hsing. "Not to say Yuan-yang, even those senior maids in responsible positions would jump at the chance. All right, you go over first, but don't let a word leak out. I'll come over after dinner."

Meanwhile Hsi-feng had been thinking, "Yuan-yang is a sharp customer. Still she may refuse. If I go back first and Yuan-yang agrees, all right; but if she refuses my mother-in-law's so suspicious she's sure to think I told her and encouraged her to hold out. Seeing me proved right and herself made to look a fool, she may vent her temper on me and that would be no joke. Better if the two of us go over together, for then whether Yuan-yang agrees or not no suspicion can fall on me."

So she said cordially, "As I set out just now, my maternal uncle's house sent over two baskets of quails which I told the kitchen to have deep-fried and sent over for your dinner. And as I came through your main gate, I saw some pages carrying off your carriage for repairs — they said it was cracking up Why don't you come back now, madam, with me in mine? Then we can go together."

Lady Hsing called for her maids to change her clothes,

assisted by Hsi-feng, after which they both mounted the carriage.

Then Hsi-feng said, "If I accompany you to the old lady's place, madam, she may ask what I've come for and that would be awkward. Suppose you go first, and I follow after changing my clothes?"

Lady Hsing thought this reasonable, and went on first to call on the Lady Dowager. After chatting with her for a while, she left on the pretext of going to see Lady Wang. Instead, however, she slipped out through the back door to Yuan-yang's bedroom. The girl, who was sitting there doing some needlework, hastily rose to her feet at her approach.

Lady Hsing asked with a smile, "What are you making? Let me have a look. I'm sure you're doing finer work than ever." So saying she entered the room, inspected the embroidery and praised it loudly. Putting it down then, she subjected Yuan-yang to a careful scrutiny.

The maid was wearing a light purple silk tunic, none too new, a black satin sleeveless jacket with silk borders, and a pale green skirt. She had a supple wasp-waist, slender shoulders, an oval face, glossy black hair and a finely arched nose, while her cheeks were slightly freckled. This close inspection embarrassed and puzzled her.

"What brings you here at this hour, madam?" she asked with a smile.

Lady Hsing signed to her attendants to leave, then sat down and took Yuan-yang's hand. "I've come specially to congratulate you," she announced.

This gave Yuan-yang some inkling of what was afoot. She blushed and lowered her head without a word.

"You know, the Elder Master has no one reliable to wait on him," Lady Hsing continued. "He could buy a girl, of course, but those one gets through brokers aren't clean and there's no knowing what mayn't be wrong with them; besides, after two or three days they're liable to get up to monkey-tricks. So he's been trying to choose one in our household. At first there seemed to be no one suitable. One was ugly, another bad-tempered, and some had certain good points but other shortcomings. After keeping his eyes open for the past six months, he's decided that of all the girls here you're the best — pretty, well-behaved, dependable and sweet-tempered. So he wants to ask the old lady to let him take you into his chambers.

"Your position will be quite different from that of a girl bought from outside, for as soon as you enter our house we shall go through the ceremonies and give you the rank of a secondary wife, treated with all respect and honour. Besides, you're a girl with a will of your own. As the proverb says, 'True gold will find its price.' Now that the Elder Master has picked you, you'll be able to realize your highest ambitions, and this will stop the mouths of those who dislike you. So come along with me to tell the old lady."

She took Yuan-yang's hand to lead her out, but the girl coloured and shrank back.

"What's there to be so bashful about?" asked Lady Hsing, seeing how embarrassed she was. "You won't have to say a word. Just come with me."

Yuan-yang simply hung her head and would not budge.

"Don't tell me you're unwilling!" cried Lady Hsing. "You're a very silly girl if that's the case, turning down the chance to be a mistress and choosing to remain a maid instead. All you can look forward to then is marrying some servant in two or three years' time — you'll still be a slave. Far better come to us. You know I'm much too good-natured to be jealous, and the Elder Master will treat you well. In a year or so, when you give birth to a child, you'll be on the same footing as me with the whole household at your beck and call. If you let slip this chance to better yourself, you're going to regret it — but then it'll be too late."

Still Yuan-yang simply hung her head and said nothing.

"You've always been a straightforward girl," persisted Lady Hsing. "Why are you being so sticky about this? What's worrying you? Just tell me, and I'll see that your wishes are met."

Yuan-yang remained silent.

"I suppose you're too shy to say 'yes' yourself and would prefer to leave it to your parents." Lady Hsing smiled. "Quite right and proper too. I'll speak to them and get *them* to speak to you. You can be frank with them." This said, she went off to find Hsi-feng.

Hsi-feng had long since changed her clothes, and since no one else was in the room but Ping-erh she disclosed this news to her.

Ping-erh shook her head. "I don't see this working out," was her verdict. "From the way she's spoken when we were chatting on our own, she's not likely to consent. But we shall soon see."

"The mistress may bring Yuan-yang here to discuss it," said Hsi-feng. "If Yuan-yang's willing, all right; if not, she'll be feeling put out, and it would be embarrassing for her to have you others here. Tell the rest to go and deep-fry some quails and prepare a few other dishes to go with them. Then you can go off and amuse yourself somewhere else till you think she'll have gone."

Ping-erh passed on these instructions to the other servants, then sauntered off to enjoy herself in the Garden.

Meanwhile Yuan-yang had guessed that Lady Hsing would be going to discuss this business with Hsi-feng, and that other people were sure to come to sound her out again. Thinking it wisest to make herself scarce, she told Hu-po:

"If the old lady should ask for me, tell her I'm not feeling well and I had no breakfast. I've gone for a stroll in the Garden but shan't be long."

Hu-po agreed to this, and Yuan-yang went out. While walking in the Garden, to her surprise she met Ping-erh, who seeing that they were alone cried teasingly:

"Here comes the new concubine!"

Yuan-yang flushed scarlet. "So that's it!" she exclaimed. "You're all in league against me. Wait till I go and have this out with your mistress."

Ping-erh hearing this regretted her tactlessness. Drawing Yuan-yang over to sit on a rock under a maple, she told her frankly all that Hsi-feng had said since her return.

Still blushing, Yuan-yang answered bitterly, "What good friends we were, the dozen or so of us — Hsi-jen, Hu-po, Su-yun, Tzu-chuan, Tsai-hsia, Yu-chuan, Sheh-yueh, Tsui-mo, Tsui-lu who went with Miss Hsiang-yun, Ko-jen and Chin-chuan who've died, Chien-hsueh who's left, and the two of us. We worked together from the time we were young and never had any secrets from each other. Now that we've grown up we've gone our different ways, but *I* haven't changed — I don't hide anything from you. So I'll confide something to you, but mind you don't tell Madam Lien. Quite apart from the fact that the Elder Master only wants to make me his concubine, even if Lady Hsing had died and he sent matchmakers in style to make me his principal wife, I wouldn't agree to it."

Before Ping-erh could reply they heard laughter behind the rock.

"For shame!" someone cried. "Such talk's enough to set one's teeth on edge."

Startled, they jumped to their feet to see who was there. It was Hsi-jen, who emerged laughingly from behind the rockery.

"What's up?" she asked. "Let me into the secret."

The three of them sat down again and Ping-erh retold her story.

"Of course, we shouldn't say this, but what an old lecher the Elder Master is!" was Hsi-jen's comment. "He can't keep his hands off any girl who's not bad-looking."

"Since you're unwilling," said Ping-erh, "I'll tell you an easy way to fob him off."

"What's that?" asked Yuan-yang.

"Simply tell the old lady you've already given yourself to Master Lien." Ping-erh giggled. "The father can hardly take what belongs to his son."

Yuan-yang spat in disgust. "What rubbish! Your mistress was raving the other day. How can you go repeating that today?"

"If you don't want either of them," teased Hsi-jen, "get the old lady to tell Lord Sheh you're already promised to Pao-yu. Then he'll have to give up."

Frantic with rage and embarrassment, Yuan-yang swore, "You two bitches, you won't come to a good end! I turn to you in trouble, thinking you'll have the decency to help me, but instead you take it in turns to make fun of me. You think your own futures are assured and you'll both end up as secondary wives. I'm not so sure. In this world, things don't always turn out the way you want. So don't start counting your chickens before they're hatched."

Seeing how frantic she was, the two others did their best to soothe her.

"Don't take it the wrong way, dear sister," they cried. "We've been like real sisters since we were small and were only having a joke among ourselves. But, seriously, tell us your plan, so that we can stop worrying."

"Plan? What plan do I have? I just refuse to go."

Ping-erh shook her head. "Then he may not give up. You know what Lord Sheh's like. Though he won't dare do anything now while you're with the old lady, you won't be in her service all your life, will you? Some day you'll be leaving. If you fell into his clutches then, that would be worse."

"Pah! As long as the old lady lives, I shan't leave this house. If she passes away, he'll have to observe three years' mourning anyway: he can't take a concubine the moment his mother dies. And in those three years anything might happen. Time enough to worry then. If the worst comes to the worst, I can shave my hair off and become a nun. Failing that, I can kill myself. I don't care if I *never* get married. Then life would be simpler."

"What a shameless slut!" laughed Ping-erh. "The wild way she runs on!"

"Things have gone too far for modesty," Yuan-yang retorted. "If you don't believe me, wait and see. Lady Hsing said just now she means to speak to my parents. She'll have to go to Nanking for that."

"Your father and mother are looking after properties in the south," said Ping-erh. "So even though they're not here, they can still be found. Besides, your elder brother and sister-in-law are here. It's too bad you're a house-born servant. It's worse for you than for us who are here on our own."

"What difference does it make? You can't force an ox to bend its head to drink. Would he kill my parents if I refuse?"

Just then they saw her sister-in-law approaching.

Hsi-jen remarked, "As your parents aren't on the spot, they must have spoken to your sister-in-law."

"That whore!" swore Yuan-yang. "She's a regular camel-dealer. She won't let slip this chance to suck up to them."

By now her sister-in-law had come up to her.

"I've been looking for you everywhere," she said smiling. "So this is where you'd run off to. Come with me. I want to have a word with you."

Ping-erh and Hsi-jen asked her to sit down.

"No thank you. Don't stir," said the woman. "I just want to have a word with my sister-in-law."

"What's the hurry?" they asked, pretending not to know. "We're guessing riddles here and making bets. We must hear her answer to this one before she goes."

"What do you want?" demanded Yuan-yang. "Out with it."

"Come with me," the other insisted. "I'll tell you over there. It's good news for you, anyway."

"You mean what Lady Hsing told you?"

"If you know, why keep putting me off? Come along, and I'll give you the details. It's simply the most wonderful piece of good fortune."

Yuan-yang sprang up and spat hard in her face. Pointing an accusing finger at her she swore.

"Shut your foul mouth and clear off, if you know what's good for you. What's all this talk of 'good news' and 'good fortune'? No wonder, though. You've always envied those families who start throwing their weight about once their daughters are concubines, as if every one of them was a concubine too. You can't wait to pitch *me* into that fiery pit. Then if I get given face you can bully people outside, calling yourselves relatives of the Chia family; if I lose face and land in trouble, you turtles can shrink back into your shells and leave me to my fate."

She wept and stormed while Ping-erh and Hsi-jen restrained her and tried to calm her.

Her sister-in-law was goaded to retort, "Whether you're willing or not, you might at least explain properly instead of slinging mud at other people. The proverb says, 'One doesn't talk about midgets in front of dwarfs.' Your abuse of *me* I won't presume to answer. But these girls haven't offended you, why embarrass them with all this talk about concubines?"

"That's no way to speak," protested the other two. "She wasn't referring to us. *You're* the one trying to drag us into this. Which master or mistress has made us concubines? Besides, we've no parents or brother in service here who could make use of our position to bully others. There *are* people of that kind. Let her swear at them — it doesn't worry *us*."

"I put her to shame and she didn't know how to cover up," said Yuan-yang. "That's why she tried to provoke the two of you. It's a good thing you understand. Being carried away, I didn't choose my words carefully enough; then she saw her chance and grabbed it."

Her sister-in-law flounced off in a huff while Yuan-yang went on fulminating against her. When at last they had calmed her Ping-erh asked Hsi-jen:

"Why were you hiding there? We didn't see you."

"I went to Miss Hsi-chun's apartment to fetch Master Pao, only to be told I'd just missed him — he'd gone back. I doubted that, for in that case I would have seen him. I decided to see if he was with Miss Lin, but I ran into some of her people who told me he wasn't there either. It had just occurred to me that he might have left the Garden, when you happened to come along. I dodged out of sight, and then Yuan-yang came along too. I slipped from behind that tree to behind this rockery; but you were so busy talking that even with two pairs of eyes you didn't see me."

"Even with two pairs of eyes they didn't see you?" Someone

behind them laughed. "Even with *three* pairs of eyes you didn't see *me*!"

With a start they turned and saw Pao-yu approaching them.

"What a chase you've led me," Hsi-jen exclaimed with a smile. "Where have you been all this time?"

"After I left Hsi-chun, I spotted you coming and guessed you were looking for me, so I hid myself to tease you. I watched you sail straight past into the courtyard, then come out again and question everyone you met. I was laughing up my sleeve, ready to pop out and frighten you when you reached me. But then I saw you dodge into hiding too and knew you were playing a trick on someone else. I peeped out and saw these two. So I crept behind you, and after you came out I hid where you'd been hiding."

"We'd better go and have another look in case another couple's hiding there," proposed Ping-erh with a laugh.

"No, there's no one there now," he assured her.

Aware that Pao-yu must have overheard everything, Yuan-yang laid her head on her arms on the rock and pretended she was dozing off.

"It's cold on that stone. Come back to my place to rest," he suggested, nudging her.

Helping her up, he invited Ping-erh too for a cup of tea. Pressed by both Ping-erh and Hsi-jen, Yuan-yang acquiesced and the four of them went together to Happy Red Court. The conversation Pao-yu had overheard had naturally depressed him. He simply lay down quietly on his bed, leaving the three girls to chat in the outer room.

To return to Lady Hsing, she had learned from Hsi-feng that Yuan-yang's father Chin Tsai and his wife were acting as caretakers in Nanking and seldom came up to the capital. However, her elder brother Chin Wen-chiang was a buyer for the Lady Dowager, and her sister-in-law was chief laundress in her apartments.

Lady Hsing promptly sent for Wen-chiang's wife and told her what she proposed. Young Mrs. Chin was of course only too pleased and went off jubilantly to find Yuan-yang, sure that her mission would meet with instant success. Instead, she was denounced to her face by Yuan-yang and snubbed by Hsi-jen and Ping-erh into the bargain.

She returned, angry and discomfited, to report to Lady Hsing, "It's no use, she just swore at me." Since Hsi-feng was present she dared not mention Ping-erh, but she added, "Hsi-jen joined in her attack on me and talked a whole lot of other nonsense too, which doesn't bear repeating. You had better persuade Lord Sheh to buy another girl, madam. That little bitch isn't cut out for such great fortune, nor are we for such good luck."

"What has this to do with Hsi-jen?" asked Lady Hsing. "How did she come to hear of it? Who else was there?"

"Miss Ping-erh was there too."

Hsi-feng promptly interposed, "Why didn't you slap her face? Every time I go out, off she goes to amuse herself. When I got home today there was no sign of her. I suppose she took Yuan-yang's side too?"

"Miss Ping-erh wasn't there on the spot," replied Mrs. Chin. "It looked like her from a distance, but I may have been mistaken. That was just my guess."

Hsi-feng ordered a servant, "Go and fetch Ping-erh, quick. Tell her I'm back and Her Ladyship is here too. She's wanted for something."

Feng-erh hastily stepped forward to put in, "Miss Lin sent a maid with a note several times to invite her over, so finally she went. As soon as you came back, madam, I went to fetch her, but Miss Lin asked me to tell you she'd like to keep her for a little, madam."

"Every day she seems to want her for something or other," remarked Hsi-feng, then let the matter drop.

As there was nothing more Lady Hsing could do, she went home after dinner and told her husband that evening what had happened. Chia Sheh thought the matter over, then summoned Chia Lien.

"We have other caretakers besides the Chins in Nanking," he said. "Send at once to have Chin Tsai recalled."

"According to the last letter from Nanking, Chin Tsai has had a stroke, sir," replied his son. "Money for his coffin has already been issued there, and for all we know he may already be dead. Even if he's still living he'll be in a coma, so it wouldn't be any use sending for him. And his old wife is deaf."

Chia Sheh swore. "You scurvy scoundrel!" he fumed. "Quite a know-all, aren't you? Get out!"

In consternation Chia Lien promptly withdrew. Soon he heard the order given to fetch Chin Wen-chiang. He himself remained on call in the outside study, daring neither to go home nor to confront his father.

Presently Wen-chiang arrived and some pages ushered him through the inner gate. He was with Lord Sheh for the space of five or six meals, and after he left Chia Lien did not venture to ask what had been said. Not until late that evening, having ascertained that his father was asleep, did he finally go home where Hsi-feng cleared up the whole mystery for him.

As for Yuan-yang, she passed a sleepless night. The next day her brother came and asked the Lady Dowager's permission to take her home for a rest. The old lady agreed and told her to go. This was not what Yuan-yang wanted, but she complied reluctantly in order not to arouse the old lady's suspicions. Her brother told her what Lord Sheh had said and what dignity she would have as his secondary wife. However, Yuan-yang refused to consider it. Unable to change her mind, he had to go back and report this to Chia Sheh.

Chia Sheh flew into a rage. "Tell your wife to tell her this from me," he fumed. "Tell her these are my own words. 'From of old, young nymphs have preferred youth to age. She must think me too old for her. I daresay she has set her heart on one of the young masters, most likely Pao-yu or possibly my son. If that's her scheme, tell her to forget it. For if she refuses me, who else will dare take her later? That's the first thing.

" 'The second is this: if she's counting on the old lady's partiality to her to find some decent husband outside, she'd

better think again. For no matter whom she marries she'll still be within my reach, unless she dies or remains single all her life, in which case there is nothing I can do. Otherwise, the sooner she changes her mind the better for her.' "

Wen-chiang had expressed agreement after each sentence of this diatribe. Now Chia Sheh added:

"And don't you try to cheat me. Tomorrow I shall send the mistress to her again. If you've really told her and she still refuses, I won't hold you responsible. But if when we ask her again she agrees, you'll have to watch out for your head!"

Chin Wen-chiang agreed hastily and withdrew. Upon his arrival home, without waiting to get his wife to pass on this message he told Yuan-yang himself, reducing her to a state of speechless anger.

After some reflection she said, "Well, supposing I agree, you'll still have to take me back to report this to the old lady."

Her brother and his wife were overjoyed by this apparent change of heart. Her sister-in-law at once took her to the Lady Dowager, who happened to be chatting with Lady Wang, Aunt Hsueh, Li Wan, Hsi-feng, Pao-chai and the other girls, as well as a few of the chief stewards' wives, all of whom were doing their best to amuse the old lady.

Delighted by this opportunity, Yuan-yang drew her sister-in-law forward and threw herself on her knees before her mistress. Sobbing, she told the old lady what Lady Hsing had said to her, what her sister-in-law had told her in the Garden, and how her brother had threatened her today.

"Because I wouldn't agree, the Elder Master says I've set my heart on Pao-yu. He swears I'll never escape him, not even if I marry someone outside, no, not even if I go to the ends of the earth — he'll have his revenge in the end. Well, my mind's made up. Everybody here can bear witness. I shall never marry so long as I live, neither Pao-yu with his precious jade, nor someone born with silver or gold, not even a Heavenly King or Emperor!

"If Your Ladyship tries to force me, I'll kill myself rather than marry. If I'm lucky, I shall die before you, madam.

Otherwise I mean to serve Your Ladyship till the end of your life; then, rather than go back to my parents or to my brother, I shall commit suicide or shave my head and become a nun. If you think I'm not in earnest and this is just empty talk which I'll go back on later, may Heaven, Earth, all the deities and the Sun and Moon who are my witnesses choke me with an ulcer in my throat so that I rot away into a pulp!"

Before coming in, she had hidden a pair of scissors in her sleeve, and while uttering this oath she let down her hair with her left hand and started cutting it with the scissors in her right. Maids and serving-women hurried over to stop her. She had cut off one lock already but, luckily, her hair being so thick, it was difficult to cut much. They lost no time in dressing it for her again.

The Lady Dowager was trembling with rage.

"The only girl left I can trust, and they want to get her away from me," she quavered. Her eye falling on Lady Wang beside her, she cried, "So you're all deceiving me, putting on a show of being dutiful but plotting against me in secret. Whenever I have anything good you come and demand it from me. And my best servants too. Now I've only this one girl left, and seeing how partial I am to her naturally infuriates you. You're trying to get her away from me, so as to get me under your own thumb."

Lady Wang had risen to her feet but did not venture a word in self-defence. And Aunt Hsueh being her sister, could not try to shift the blame from her. Li Wan had quietly taken the girls outside when Yuan-yang began her story.

Tan-chun, however, had sense enough to see that it was not for Lady Wang to clear herself of these false charges, nor for Aunt Hsueh to defend her sister, nor for Pao-chai to defend her aunt, while Li Wan, Hsi-feng and Pao-yu were in no position to protest either. It was now up to one of the girls to speak. But Ying-chun was too naive, Hsi-chun too young. So after listening for a while outside the window, she entered the room with a smile.

"What has this to do with Her Ladyship?" she asked her grandmother. "Just think, madam, how could a younger sister-in-law know that her elder brother-in-law was going to get a concubine? Even if she did, could she say anything?"

At once the old lady chuckled. "I'm losing my wits with age," she exclaimed. "Don't laugh at me, Madam Hsueh. This elder sister of yours is a very good daughter-in-law, not like my elder son's wife who's so afraid of her husband she only makes a show of compliance to me. Yes, I was wrong to blame your sister."

Aunt Hsueh murmured agreement, then added, "I wonder if you're not, perhaps, rather partial to the wife of your younger son, madam?"

"No, I'm not partial," the old lady declared. She continued, "Pao-yu, why didn't you point out my mistake and prevent me from blaming your mother so unfairly?"

"How could I stick up for my mother at the expense of my elder uncle and aunt?" he countered. "Anyway, someone's done wrong; and if mother here won't take the blame, who will? I could have said it was *my* fault but I'm sure you wouldn't have believed me."

"Yes, that's right," chuckled the Lady Dowager. "Now kneel to your mother and ask her not to feel hurt, but to forgive me for your sake on account of my old age."

Pao-yu stepped forward and knelt to do as he was told, but his mother instantly stopped him.

"Get up," she cried with a smile. "This is absurd. How can you apologize for your grandmother?"

As Pao-yu rose to his feet the old lady said, "And Hsi-feng didn't pull me up either."

"I haven't said a word against you, madam," retorted Hsi-feng laughingly, "but now you're trying to put the blame on me."

All the others laughed and the old lady cried, "This is strange! Let's hear what you have to say against me."

"Who told you, madam, to train your girls so well? If you bring one up as fresh as a sprig of young parsley, you can't blame people for wanting her. It's lucky I'm a grandson's wife. If I were a grandson I'd have grabbed her long ago. I shouldn't have waited till now."

"So it's all my fault, is it?" the old lady chortled.

"Of course it is," agreed Hsi-feng.

"In that case I won't keep her. You can take her away."

"Wait till I've done enough good deeds in this life to be reborn as a man. Then I'll marry her."

"You can take her and give her to Lien. See if that shameless father-in-law of yours still wants her then or not."

"Lien doesn't deserve her," said Hsi-feng. "He'll have to make do with scarecrows like Ping-erh and me."

They were all laughing at this when Lady Hsing was announced, and Lady Wang went out to greet her.

If you want to know what followed, read the next chapter.

CHAPTER 47

A Stupid Bully Is Beaten Up
for His Amorous Advances
A Cool Young Gentleman Leaves Home
for Fear of Reprisals

Lady Wang hurried out to greet Lady Hsing who had come in the hope of news, unaware that the Lady Dowager knew all about her proposal to Yuan-yang. Only as she stepped into the courtyard was she quietly apprised of this by some serving-women; but it was too late to retreat now that her arrival had been announced and Lady Wang had come out to meet her. She had no choice but to go in and pay her respects.

The old lady received her without a word, to her great mortification. Hsi-feng had already left on the pretext of some business, while Yuan-yang had retired to her room to sulk. Now Aunt Hsueh, Lady Wang and the others withdrew one by one to spare Lady Hsing embarrassment. She herself dared not leave, however.

Once they were alone the Lady Dowager sneered, "I hear you've been doing some matchmaking for your husband. Quite a model of wifely submission and virtue, aren't you? Only you carry this obedience too far. You have children and grandchildren now, yet you're still afraid of him. Instead of giving him a little good advice you let him carry on just as he pleases."

Blushing all over her face Lady Hsing replied, "I have reasoned with him several times, but he pays no attention. You know how it is, madam. I had no choice."

"Would you commit murder too if he insisted? Have some sense! Your sister-in-law is a simple soul and, for all her poor health, she has to worry about high and low in this household. Though your daughter-in-law helps her, her work is never done.

93

So I don't make too many demands on them, and when the two of them overlook certain things, that child Yuan-yang is thoughtful enough to attend to my wants. She sees I get what I need, and tells them in time what wants replenishing. If not for her, in all their press of business the pair of them would be bound to forget this or that. Do you expect *me* to see to everything? To work out every day what I need to ask for? She's the only maid left me who's not just a child and knows something of my ways and temperament. In the second place: she gets on well with the older and younger mistresses alike here, and never tries in my name to ask this mistress for clothes or that for money. So during the last few years the whole household old and young, starting with your sister-in-law and daughter-in-law, all trust her. It's not just that *I* rely on her, she saves them trouble too. As long as I've someone like her, I don't have to worry about going short of anything even if my daughters-in-law or my grandsons' wives forget it. But who would you give me in her place if she left now? Even if you managed to produce a girl of her size made of pearls but unable to talk she'd still be no use to me.

"I was just on the point of sending to tell your husband: I've money here for him if he wants to buy someone, and I don't care if it costs eight or even ten thousand taels; but he can't have *this* girl. If she can be left to wait on me for a few years, that'll be the same as him waiting on me day and night himself like a dutiful son. It's a good thing that you've come. It's more fitting that he should hear this from you."

She called for her maids then and told them, "Ask Madam Hsueh and the young ladies to come back. We were having fun together, why have they all left?"

The maids made haste to carry out her orders.

Everyone hurried back except Aunt Hsueh, who objected, "I've just got home, why should I go over again? Tell her I'm sleeping."

"Do us a favour, dear madam, good ancestress!" pleaded the maid. "Our old lady's in a bad temper. If *you* won't go, we shall never manage to soothe her. Just do it for our sake. If you're tired, madam, I'll carry you there on my back."

"You little imp!" Aunt Hsueh chuckled. "You've nothing to fear except a taste of her tongue." None the less she felt constrained to go back with the maid.

The Lady Dowager made her sit down and suggested, "What about a game of cards? You must be rather rusty, so let's sit together to make sure that Hsi-feng can't cheat us."

"That's right, you must help me, madam," agreed Aunt Hsueh. "Shall we have a foursome or rope in one or two others?"

"Yes, there are just four of us," observed Lady Wang.

"One more would be more fun," put in Hsi-feng.

"Then send for Yuan-yang," directed the old lady. "Tell her to sit on my left. Your aunt's eyesight isn't good; she can help us both with our cards."

Hsi-feng sighed and remarked to Tan-chun, "With all your education, it's too bad you haven't learned to tell fortunes too."

"What an odd thing to say!" exclaimed Tan-chun. "Why not concentrate on winning some money from the old lady instead of thinking about fortune-telling?"

"I want some fortune-teller to predict how much I'll be losing today. How can I hope to win? Look, before the game even starts they've laid ambushes right and left."

The Lady Dowager and Aunt Hsueh laughed.

Presently Yuan-yang arrived and took a seat between the Lady Dowager and Hsi-feng. The red felt cloth was spread and the cards were shuffled and drawn. After the five of them had played for a while, Yuan-yang noticed that the old lady needed only a "two of circles" to win the game, and she signalled this to Hsi-feng whose turn it was to discard. Hsi-feng deliberately hesitated.

"I'm sure Aunt Hsueh has the card I want," she said. "If I don't play *this* she'll never part with it."

"I haven't anything you want," said Aunt Hsueh.

"I won't believe that till I've seen your hand."

"You can have a look if you like. But first discard and let's see what that card is."

Hsi-feng put down the "two of circles" in front of Aunt Hsueh.

"*I* don't want that," chuckled the latter. "I'm only afraid the old lady is going out."

"I've thrown the wrong one!" cried Hsi-feng hastily.

But the Lady Dowager, beaming, had already laid down her hand.

"Don't you dare take it back," she crowed. "Who told you to throw the wrong card?"

"You see why I wanted to consult a fortune-teller," said Hsi-feng. "But this time it was really my own fault."

"That's right." The old lady laughed. "You should slap your own face and blame yourself." She turned to Aunt Hsueh. "It's not that I'm miserly and out to win; I play for luck."

"Of course, madam," replied Aunt Hsueh with a smile. "Who's so foolish as not to know that?"

Hsi-feng, who was counting out the cash she had lost, strung the coins together again on hearing this. "That's fine," she cried with a twinkle. "If the old lady only plays for luck, not for money, I needn't count my cash in this miserly way. I'll put it away at once."

The Lady Dowager always made Yuan-yang shuffle the cards for her, but now as she chatted with Aunt Hsueh she noticed that the girl had made no move.

"What's the matter?" she asked. "Won't you even shuffle for me?"

Yuan-yang picked up the cards then, asking, "Isn't Madam Lien going to pay?"

"Not going to pay? Paying up will bring her better luck!" cried the old lady.

She ordered a young maid to bring Hsi-feng's whole string of cash and put it by her pile. The girl did as she was told.

"Give that back," pleaded Hsi-feng. "All right, I'll pay the amount I owe."

"Hsi-feng really is stingy," laughed Aunt Hsueh. "This is only a game, after all."

At this Hsi-feng left her seat and, taking Aunt Hsueh by the arm, turned and pointed at the wooden chest in which the Lady Dowager kept her money.

"Look there, aunt," she said. "Goodness knows how much of my money has been swallowed up by that. It's less than an hour since we began, and already the money in that chest has beckoned to this string of cash. As soon as this string's gone in too we shan't have to play any more, and our Old Ancestress will have got over her temper. Then she'll send me off to attend to my duties again."

The whole company was laughing uproariously when Ping-erh arrived with another string of cash, for fear her mistress might not have enough.

"There's no need to put that in front of *me*," cried Hsi-feng. "Just put it on the old lady's pile. That will save the money in her chest the trouble of beckoning twice."

The Lady Dowager laughed so much at this that she scattered the cards in her hand all over the table as she nudged Yuan-yang and told her to pinch Hsi-feng's mouth.

Ping-erh put the money down as she was told and, having joined in the laughter, left. By the courtyard gate she met Chia Lien.

"Where's my mother?" he asked. "Father sent me to fetch her."

"She's been standing stock-still all this time before the old lady. You'd better clear off, quick. It's taken our mistress a long time to coax the old lady into a better temper."

"I've come over just to ask whether she's going to Lai Ta's feast on the fourteenth or not, so that I can have her sedan-chair ready," he replied. "What's wrong with fetching my mother and pleasing the old lady at the same time?"

"Take my advice and steer clear." Ping-erh smiled. "The whole family, Lady Wang and Pao-yu too, have had a dressing-down. But here you come asking for a share in it."

"It's blown over now. Why should I have to make up for

something past and done with? Besides, this business had nothing to do with *me*, and my father himself ordered me to fetch my mother. If he discovered that I'd sent someone else, in the temper he's in now he'd vent his anger on me."

With that he walked in. And since there was reason in what he said, Ping-erh followed. Once in the hall, Chia Lien tiptoed to the door of the inner room and peeped inside. He had just seen Lady Hsing standing there when Hsi-feng with her sharp eyes spotted him. She signalled to him to keep out and threw a meaning glance at Lady Hsing; but the latter, afraid to go without taking her leave, poured a cup of tea for the Lady Dowager. As the old lady turned to take it, she caught sight of Chia Lien who had not stepped back in time.

"Who's that in the hall?" she demanded. "It looked like some young fellow peering in."

"Yes, I thought I saw someone too," said Hsi-feng. "I'll go and have a look." She got up and started out.

At once Chia Lien came in with a conciliatory smile.

"I've come to ask whether the old lady means to go out on the fourteenth," he announced, "so that I can have her chair ready."

"Why didn't you come in, then, instead of skulking outside?" asked the Lady Dowager.

"I didn't like to disturb you at your game, madam. I was hoping to get my wife to come out so that I could ask *her*."

"Why couldn't you wait for her to go home where you can ask her all the questions you want? Since when have you been so attentive? Or are you spying for someone, acting in this hole-and-corner way? You gave me quite a fright, you sneaky devil. Your wife is playing cards with me and won't be free for some time. Better go home and plot against her again with that wife of Chao Erh's."

Amid general laughter Yuan-yang put in, "Pao Erh's wife, not Chao Erh's wife, Old Ancestress."

"That's right." The old lady smiled. "How do you expect me to remember their names, whether they mean 'carried in the arms or on the back'?[1] Talking of that business I can't help but be angry. I came to this house as the bride of a great-grandson, and now I have great-grand-daughters-in-law myself. In my fifty-four years first and last here, I've had plenty of shocks and frights and seen all manner of amazing happenings — but never such scandalous carryings-on as yours. Off with you now. Out of my sight!"

Without venturing to say a word, Chia Lien beat a hasty retreat.

"Well," whispered Ping-erh, standing outside the window, "you wouldn't take my advice and now you've caught it." Just then Lady Hsing came out and Chia Lien complained, "It's all the master's fault, but *we* are the ones to suffer for it, madam."

"May lightning strike you, you unfilial wretch," scolded Lady Hsing. "Other sons would die for their fathers; but you, you start complaining just because of a little talking-to. You'd better watch your step. He's in a bad mood these days — mind he doesn't beat you."

"Please go home quickly, madam," he urged. "It's some time now since I was sent to find you."

He then accompanied his mother out and across to the other courtyard.

When Lady Hsing gave her husband an abbreviated version of what the Lady Dowager had said, Chia Sheh felt at a loss and bitterly mortified too. After this, on the pretext of illness he stopped calling on his mother, being actually afraid to face her, sending his wife and son instead to pay their respects every day. None the less he made his men scout around and finally, for the sum of eight hundred taels, bought a seventeen-year-old girl called Yen-hung to be his concubine. No more of this.

The card game in the Lady Dowager's rooms went on until dinner time, and the next couple of days passed uneventfully.

---

[1] The surname *pao* (鮑) has the same pronunciation as *pao* (抱) meaning "to carry in the arms," which is contrasted with *pei* (背) — "to carry on the back."

Soon it was the fourteenth, and almost before it was light Lai Ta's wife came to invite them over. The Lady Dowager, being in a good humour, took Lady Wang, Aunt Hsueh, Pao-yu and the girls to spend half a day in Lai Ta's garden. Although it could not compare with Grand View Garden, the grounds were extensive and neatly laid out with pleasant streams, rocks and trees, as well as some splendid lodges and fantastic pavilions.

Hsueh Pan, Chia Chen, Chia Lien, Chia Jung and some other close relatives of the Jung and Ning households were entertained in the outer hall. Their distant relatives did not come, however, and neither did Chia Sheh.

A few officials and sons of good families had also been invited to keep them company. Among these was a certain Liu Hsiang-lien, whom Hsueh Pan had been longing to meet again ever since he first made his acquaintance; for the report that Liu was fond of acting in romantic operas about young scholars and beauties had made him mistake him for a homosexual. Eager as he was to make closer acquaintance, he was overjoyed by this chance meeting today.

The others also knew Liu Hsiang-lien's reputation, and Chia Chen, emboldened by wine, persuaded him to perform in two operas, after which he came and sat down next to Liu, chatting with him for a while on various subjects.

Now this Liu Hsiang-lien was the son of a good family who had lost both parents early. No great scholar but frank, chivalrous and unconventional in his ways, he was a good spearman and swordsman addicted to gambling and drinking, fond of the company of singsong girls and quite a musician himself. His youth and good looks led many who did not know him to mistake him for an actor; but he had been invited today because he was a friend of Lai Ta's son Shang-jung. The other guests behaved decently enough after drinking; but Hsueh Pan got up to his old tricks again, which so disgusted Liu that he would have slipped away had not Lai Shang-jung most earnestly detained him.

"Just now Master Pao told me he'd noticed you as soon as

he came in, but there's too much of a crowd here to talk in comfort," said Lai Shang-jung. "He hopes you'll stay on after the party breaks up, as he has something to ask you. If you insist on going, let me fetch him first. Then I shan't be responsible for your leaving without having seen him."

He ordered some pages, "Go in and get one of the old women to have a quiet word with Master Pao and ask him to come out."

This was done, and in less time than it would take to drink a cup of tea they were joined by Pao-yu.

"I leave Hsiang-lien to you, my dear uncle," said Lai Shang-jung with a smile. "I must see to our other guests." With that he left them.

Pao-yu led Liu Hsiang-lien into a small study at one side of the hall and, when the two of them were seated, asked, "Have you visited Chin Chung's grave at all recently?"

"Yes, I have," Hsiang-lien told him. "Some time ago a few of us were flying falcons near his grave. For fear it might not have stood up to the heavy rain this summer, I rode over on my own to have a look and, sure enough, found it slightly damaged. So after coming home I got together a few hundred cash and went out three days later with two men I'd hired to repair it."

"That explains it," said Pao-yu. "Last month when the lotus seed-pods in our pool in Grand View Garden ripened, I picked ten and sent Ming-yen out to offer them at his grave. When he came back, I also asked if the grave had been damaged by the rain; but he said that on the contrary it looked in better condition than before. I guessed, then, that some friends must recently have restored it. My trouble is that I'm cooped up at home all the time and am not my own master. Every move I make is known, and there's always someone trying to stop me or dissuade me, so whatever I say, I can't do a thing. Though I've money, I can't spend it as I want."

"You don't have to worry about that," Hsiang-lien assured him. "I'll see to anything that you can't do outside. So long as you remember him, that's what counts. It will soon be the first of the tenth month, and I've put by some money to sacrifice at his grave. You know how hard up I am, with no property of my own, and any money I get slips straight through my fingers. It seemed better to set this sum aside so as not to be caught empty-handed when the time comes."

"That's why I was meaning to send Ming-yen to look for you; but you're so seldom at home, floating about free as duckweed every day, one never knows where to find you."

"There was no need to look for me. Each of us must simply do what he can. But soon I shall be setting out on a long journey. I don't expect to be back for three or four years."

"Why should you stay away so long?"

"You don't know what's been on my mind." Hsiang-lien gave a bitter smile. "You'll find out all in good time. Now I must take my leave."

"It's so rarely we have a chance to meet, can't you stay until the party breaks up this evening?"

"That honourable maternal cousin of yours is up to his old tricks again. If I stay, there may be trouble. I'd better keep out of his way."

"I see," said Pao-yu after a thoughtful pause. "Well, you may be right to keep out of his way, but you mustn't really go off on a long journey without letting me know beforehand. Whatever happens, don't just slip away." He was shedding tears as he spoke.

"Of course I'll say goodbye to you," promised Hsiang-lien. "Only don't tell anyone else." As he stood up to leave he added, "Go on in, there's no need to see me out."

He left the study and had just reached the main gate when he saw Hsueh Pan there bawling, "Who let that lad Liu get away?"

Liu Hsiang-lien's eyes flashed with anger. He longed to strike Hsueh Pan dead with one blow of his fist. Only the thought that a drunken brawl would embarrass Lai Shang-jung made him control himself.

Hsueh Pan catching sight of him was as overjoyed as if he had found some treasure.

"Where are you going, brother?" he chortled, staggering forward to catch him by the arm.

"I'll be back soon," said Hsiang-lien.

"If you go, dear fellow, it won't be any fun. Do stay a bit longer to show you care for me. Any pressing business you have, just leave it to me — your elder brother — only don't hurry off. Do you want an official post? Want to make money? Your elder brother can easily fix it for you."

Angered and humiliated by this outrageous talk, Hsiang-lien hit on a plan. He pulled Hsueh Pan aside.

"Do you mean that, about wanting to be my friend?"

Hsueh Pan could hardly contain himself for excitement.

"How can you ask such a question, dear brother?" he leered. "If I'm not in earnest may I drop dead!"

"Very well, but we can't talk here. After staying a little longer I'll leave first, and you can follow me presently to my place. We may as well make a night of it. I've two marvellous boys there, absolutely virgin; so there's no need for you to bring a single servant. I've people to wait on you."

Hsueh Pan was so overjoyed that he half sobered up.

"Do you really mean it?"

"Now, come, come!" Hsiang-lien chuckled. "Why turn sceptical when someone's sincere with you?"

"I'm no fool." Hsueh Pan grinned. "I trust you. But I don't know where you live. If you go on ahead, how am I to find you?"

"I live outside the North Gate. Do you mind spending a night outside, away from your family?"

"If I've got you, I shan't miss my family."

"In that case, I'll wait for you on the bridge outside the North Gate. Now let's go back to the feast. Once you see I'm gone, you can slip out and no one will notice."

Hsueh Pan promptly agreed. They went back to their table then and drank another round. Hsueh Pan could hardly sit still. As he feasted his avid eyes on Hsiang-lien he grew more and more jubilant, until soon he was tossing off whole pots of wine without waiting to be urged. When he was nine-tenths drunk, Hsiang-lien rose to leave and slipped away unnoticed. Outside the gate, he ordered his page Hsin-nu to go home while he paid a call out of town.

Then he mounted his horse and rode straight out of the North Gate to wait on the bridge for Hsueh Pan. In less time than it takes for a meal, he saw a solitary horseman approaching. It was Hsueh Pan, his mouth open, his eyes gaping, his head turning right and left like a pedlar's rattle as he gazed wildly around. So intent was he on staring into the distance that he missed what was close at hand and rode right past Hsiang-lien's horse. Amused and disgusted, Hsiang-lien cantered after him. Riding on, Hsueh Pan observed that the houses now were few and far between. He turned back then to make another search and was overjoyed by the sight of Liu Hsiang-lien.

"I knew you'd keep your word," he chortled.

"Ride on, quick," said Hsiang-lien. "We don't want people to see us and follow us."

He spurred on his horse and Hsueh Pan followed close behind. At a lonely spot near a marsh overgrown with reeds, Hsiang-lien dismounted and tethered his horse to a tree.

"Down you get," he said. "First we must take an oath. Cursed be he who has a change of heart or betrays our secret."

"Right you are!" Hsueh Pan slithered eagerly down from his saddle. Having made fast his horse he fell on his knees to swear: "If ever I have a change of heart or betray our secret, may Heaven and Earth destroy me. . . ."

Before he had finished, wham! He was struck from behind by what seemed like an iron hammer. Everything went black before him, then he saw a riot of golden stars as he flopped to the ground.

Hsiang-lien stepped forward to have a look at him and, knowing the oaf to be unused to beatings, gave him only a few light punches in the face which instantly turned all the colours of a fruit stall. When Hsueh Pan tried to struggle to his feet, Hsiang-lien tripped him with one foot a couple of times and sent him sprawling again.

"We did this by mutual consent," complained Hsueh Pan.

"If you didn't want to, you could simply have said so. Why fool me into coming out here and then beat me up?" He let loose a flood of abuse.

"You must be blind not to know your master," cried Hsiang-lien. "Now instead of asking my pardon you insult me. There's no point in killing you, I'll just teach you a lesson."

He fetched his horsewhip and gave him a few dozen strokes all over his back till Hsueh Pan, pretty well sober now, yelped with pain.

"You coward," sneered Hsiang-lien. "I thought you could take a beating." As he spoke he dragged him by the left leg through the mud into the reeds, bedaubing him with slime. "Now do you know who I am?"

Hsueh Pan said nothing, just lay face downwards, groaning. Hsiang-lien tossed away the whip to pummel him with his fists. Hsueh Pan rolled over and over frantically howling:

"You've broken my ribs. I know you're straight. I shouldn't have believed other people's talk."

"Don't drag anyone else into this. Just stick to the point."

"What more do you want me to say, except that you're straight and I was wrong?"

"You'll have to do better than that to be let off."

Hsueh Pan whined, "Dear younger brother. . . ."

Once more Hsiang-lien punched him.

"Ouch!" he yelled. "Dear elder brother. . . ."

Hsiang-lien struck him twice again.

"Mercy, kind master, spare me! I was blind. From now on I'll respect and fear you."

"Drink two mouthfuls of that water," ordered Hsiang-lien.

Hsueh Pan wrinkled his brows. "It's too foul. How can I drink it?"

Hsiang-lien raised a threatening fist.

"I'll drink it, I'll drink it."

Bending his head he lapped up a mouthful of the water at the base of the reeds; but before he could swallow it, he retched and spewed up everything he had eaten.

"Filthy swine!" swore Hsiang-lien. "Lick up that vomit and I'll let you off."

Kowtowing frantically Hsueh Pan begged, "Have a heart! Do a good deed and let me off. I can't stomach that, not if you kill me."

"This stench is making me sick!" declared Hsiang-lien.

With that he left Hsueh Pan, untethered his horse and, mounting it, rode away. When Hsueh Pan saw with relief that he had gone, he regretted his blunder in mistaking his man. He tried to struggle to his feet, but the pain was too much for him.

When the absence of the two of them from the feast was suddenly noticed by Chia Chen and others, they searched high and low for them but could not find them. It was rumoured, though, that they seemed to have gone out of the North Gate. Hsueh Pan's pages were too afraid of him to follow him against his orders; Chia Chen, however, was so worried that he sent Chia Jung with some men to track them down. The search party rode out of the North Gate for more than two *li* along the road from the bridge, until they saw Hsueh Pan's horse tethered to a tree beside the marsh.

"Thank goodness!" they exclaimed. "If the horse is here, the rider can't be far off."

Going up to the horse, they heard groaning in the reeds and hurrying forward discovered Hsueh Pan there, his clothes tattered and torn, his face swollen and bruised, covered from head to foot with mud like a sow.

Chia Jung had a shrewd idea of what had happened. Quickly dismounting, he ordered some men to help Hsueh Pan to his feet.

"So today Uncle Hsueh's pursuit of love has brought him to this swamp," he joked. "I suppose the Dragon King was so impressed by your romantic spirit that he wanted you to be his son-in-law; but then you knocked into the dragon's horn!"

Hsueh Pan wished he could sink through the ground for shame. As he could not ride, Chia Jung sent to the North Gate to hire a small chair for him, after which they all returned to

the city together. Chia Jung threatened to carry him back to
Lai Ta's feast, and Hsueh Pan had to plead hard not to have
this business made public before he was allowed to go back
home.

Then Chia Jung returned to Lai Ta's house to tell Chia Chen
what had happened. Hearing of the beating Hsiang-lien had
given Hsueh Pan, Chia Chen observed with a laugh:

"A lesson like this should be good for him."

After the party had broken up that evening he went to inquire
after Hsueh Pan's health, but the latter sent word from his
bedroom that he was too unwell to receive anyone.

To return to the Lady Dowager and her party, after they all
went back to their own quarters Aunt Hsueh and Pao-chai
noticed that Hsiang-ling's eyes were swollen from weeping.
Having learned the reason they hurried in to see Hsueh Pan.
They found that, although badly bruised on both face and body,
he had broken no bones. Aunt Hsueh, torn between maternal
affection and anger, abused her son and Liu Hsiang-lien by
turns. She wanted to complain to Lady Wang and have Hsiang-
lien arrested.

"This isn't all that serious," Pao-chai demurred. "They were
simply drinking together, and drunken brawls are common
enough. A man often gets a thrashing too when he's drunk.
Besides, everyone knows how wild and headstrong Pan is. I
understand why your heart's bleeding for him, mother, and
it won't be hard to get even. In three days' or five days' time,
when my brother's well enough to go out again, Cousin Chen,
Cousin Lien and the others over there won't let the matter drop.
They'll invite that fellow to a feast to make a public apology to
Pan. If you make such an issue of it and spread the news,
everyone will think you spoil your son and encourage him to
make trouble and that once he's beaten you raise a big rumpus,
relying on your powerful relatives to bully humble folk."

"You're right as usual, child," replied her mother. "I was
muddled for the moment by anger."

"In fact, this is all to the good," continued Pao-chai with a smile. "He's not afraid of you, mother, and won't listen to other people's advice either. He's growing more and more headstrong. Coming a few croppers should cure him."

Hsueh Pan was still raging at Liu Hsiang-lien from his *kang*, ordering his servants to go and pull down Liu's house, beat him to death, or take the case to court. Aunt Hsueh stopped them however, saying:

"Liu Hsiang-lien ran riot after a bout of drinking, but now that he's sobered up he's filled with remorse. He's run away for fear of the consequences."

Hsueh Pan, hearing this, gradually got over his rage.

To know the outcome, read on.

CHAPTER 48

A Rebuffed Reprobate Decides
on a Journey
An Aspiring Maid Racks Her Brains
to Write Poetry

After he was told that Liu Hsiang-lien had fled, little by little Hsueh Pan's anger abated. In a few days he was over his pain and simply pretending to be ill, being ashamed to see relatives or friends till his bruises had disappeared.

In no time the tenth month arrived, and as some of their shop managers were to go home to settle their annual accounts, the Hsueh family had to prepare a farewell feast for them.

One of those leaving was Chang Teh-hui, a man of over sixty who had managed the Hsuehs' pawnshop since he was young and was now worth two or three thousand taels. Not wanting to return before spring he said:

"This year sacrificial paper and aromatics are in short supply, which means that next year the price is bound to rise. I propose to send my eldest son here to see to the shop after New Year and on my way back purchase sacrificial paper and scented fans to sell before the Dragon-Boat Festival. After deducting taxes and expenses, we should still net a profit of several hundred per cent."

When Hsueh Pan heard this he reflected, "Since my beating I've been ashamed to show my face, wishing I could disappear for a year or so; but I have nowhere to hide. I can't go on shamming illness indefinitely. Besides, all these years I've never taken to books or soldiering, and although I'm in business I've never handled a balance or abacus and know nothing either about local customs and different parts of the country. I may as well take some capital and travel around with Chang Teh-hui for a year. It doesn't matter whether I make money or not; I can at any rate hide my face for a while and enjoy some sight-seeing at the same time."

Having made up his mind to this, he took Chang aside after the feast, explained his plan, and asked him to wait a couple of days so that they could travel together.

That evening he told his mother. But though pleased in a sense, she was also afraid he might get into trouble outside — the loss of capital was immaterial. So she withheld her consent.

"I don't worry too much so long as you're with me," she said. "And it's not as if we needed *you* to handle business or were short of money. If you'll stay quietly at home that's worth more to me than a few hundred taels."

But Hsueh Pan, once his mind was made up, was stubborn.

"You keep complaining every day of my lack of worldly wisdom, my ignorance and failure to learn," he protested. "Yet now that I've resolved to stop fooling around, come to grips with life and establish myself by learning to run the business, you won't let me. What do you expect me to do? I'm not a girl to stay cooped up at home all the time. You'll have to let me out *some* day. Besides, Chang Teh-hui is well on in years, a moral character and an old family friend. What could go wrong if I'm with him? He'll naturally point it out if I make the least blunder. And he knows the market so well that his advice will be most useful to me. Yet you won't let me go! All right, I'll slip away some day without telling you, and come back next year with my fortune made. Just wait and see if I don't!"

He went off to bed in a huff. Then Aunt Hsueh discussed the matter with her daughter.

"If my brother's really serious about working properly, that's good," said Pao-chai. "But if he's just saying this to talk you round, once away from home he may slip back into his bad old ways and it will be even more difficult to restrain him. Still, it's no use worrying too much. If he truly reforms, so much the better for him; if he doesn't, there's nothing you can do about it, mother. It depends half on what one can do for him, half on his own fate. He's no longer a boy, and if you keep him at home this year for fear he's too inexperienced to travel or do business, it'll be just the same next year. As his arguments sound reasonable, you may as well send him off to have a try — at worst it only means wasting eight hundred or a thousand taels. After all, he'll have assistants who can't very well cheat him. Besides, once he's gone there'll be no one to egg him on or to back him up, and he won't be able to throw his weight about. If he has food, he can eat; if not, he'll just have to go hungry. And for all we know, seeing that he's on his own, he may cause less trouble than at home."

Aunt Hsueh thought this over for a while.

"You're quite right," she said at last. "It's worth a little money if he'll learn to behave himself better."

Having agreed on this they retired for the night.

The next day Aunt Hsueh invited Chang Teh-hui to a meal in the study at which Hsueh Pan presided, and standing in the back corridor she urged Chang very earnestly through the window to take good care of her son. Chang promised to do so.

After the meal as he took his leave he said, "The fourteenth is an auspicious day to start a journey. Please get your luggage ready, sir, and hire mules. On the fourteenth we can make an early start."

Hsueh Pan was overjoyed and passed on this message to his mother, who promptly set to work with Pao-chai, Hsiang-ling and two old nurses to prepare his things. An old steward, the husband of Hsueh Pan's wet-nurse, was to accompany him with two other experienced old bondsmen as well as two of the pages who usually attended him, making a party of six. Three carts were hired for the luggage, and four sturdy mules. Hsueh Pan himself would ride a large black mule from the family stable, in addition to which a horse was provided for him too. When all these preparations had been made, his mother and sister went on to give him good advice and warnings which we can pass over here.

On the thirteenth, Hsueh Pan went to take his leave first of his maternal uncle, then of other members of the Chia family;

but we need not dwell on all the farewell banquets offered by Chia Chen and the rest.

On the fourteenth, first thing in the morning, his mother and sister saw him out of the ceremonial gate and with tears in their eyes watched until he was out of sight before turning back again.

Aunt Hsueh had brought to the capital only four or five families of servants apart from a few old nurses and young maids. Now that five of the men had gone with her son, only one man-servant was left. That same day, accordingly, she had all the ornaments, curtains, and other furnishings of the study stored away and ordered the wives of two men who had accompanied Hsueh Pan to move into the inner quarters. She also told Hsiang-ling to clear up and lock her room and to share her own bedroom.

"You already have quite a few people to keep you company, mother," observed Pao-chai. "Why not let Sister Hsiang-ling move in with me? We've plenty of space in the Garden, and now that the nights are getting longer and I sew every evening, wouldn't it be better if I had one more companion?"

"Of course." Her mother smiled. "That had slipped my mind or I should have suggested it. Only the other day I was telling your brother that Wen-hsing's too young to do much, and Ying-erh can't wait on you properly all on her own. We must buy you another maid."

"A girl bought outside is a dark horse," objected Pao-chai. "If she turns out badly the money will be wasted, but that's a small matter compared with the trouble she may cause. We'd better take our time making inquiries, and not buy a girl until we know her record."

She urged Hsiang-ling to pack up her bedding and toilet things, and ordered an old nurse and Chen-erh to take them to Alpinia Park. Then she went back to the Garden with Hsiang-ling.

"I thought of asking our lady's permission to stay with you after your brother left," Hsiang-ling confided. "I was afraid, though, she'd think I just wanted to play about. I'm so glad you suggested it."

"I know how long you've admired this Garden without ever having time really to enjoy it," Pao-chai answered. "There's no fun in hurried visits every day. So if you take this chance to stay here for a year, I'll be glad of your company and you'll get your wish too."

"Can you take this opportunity, dear miss, to teach me to write poetry?"

"The more you get, the more you want!" chuckled Pao-chai. "As this is your first day here, I advise you to start by paying your respects to all the ladies in the different apartments outside the Garden's east gate, beginning with the old lady. You needn't tell them specially that you've moved into the Garden; but if anyone askes, just say I've brought you to keep me company. Then after you come back you ought to call on all the young ladies here."

Hsiang-ling agreed and was about to set out when Ping-erh hurried in. Hsiang-ling greeted her, and Ping-erh returned her greeting with a strained smile.

"I've brought her here to keep me company," Pao-chai told Ping-erh. "I was just going to send someone to report it to your mistress."

"What a way to talk, miss!" cried Ping-erh. "How do you expect me to answer?"

"No, this is only right. 'Hostels have their hosts, abbeys their abbots.' It's a small matter, but still I should notify her so that the night-watch will know whom to expect here before locking the gates. Will you report this for me when you go back? That'll save me sending someone."

Ping-erh agreed readily, then asked Hsiang-ling, "Why don't you call on your neighbours now that you're here?"

"Just what I was saying to her," remarked Pao-chai.

"But you'd better leave us out," advised Ping-erh. "Master Lien is at home, ill in bed."

Hsiang-ling did as she was told, going first to call on the Lady Dowager. As soon as she had left, Ping-erh took Pao-chai's arm.

"Have you heard the latest news in our family, miss?" she whispered.

"Not a word," rejoined Pao-chai. "These last few days we've been so busy getting my brother off, I've heard nothing of what's been happening in your apartments. I haven't even seen my cousins for a couple of days."

"Then you haven't heard of the beating Lord Sheh gave Master Lien? It's quite laid him up."

"I heard something vaguely this morning but didn't believe it. If you hadn't come, I'd have gone to call on your mistress. What did he beat him for?"

"It's all the fault of that upstart Chia Yu-tsun — the bastard deserves to starve to death!" fumed Ping-erh, grinding her teeth. "In the less than ten years that we've known him he's stirred up endless trouble. This spring Lord Sheh happened to see a few old fans somewhere, which made him so dissatisfied with all our best fans at home that he sent men out at once to search for better ones. A wretched crank they call the Stone Idiot had twenty old fans as it happened, but though so poor that he'd hardly a bite to eat, he'd sooner die than part with them. Master Lien had to pull a lot of strings just to meet him. Then, after much urging, the idiot invited him home and let him have a look at a few of these fans. According to Master Lien they were quite unique, all made of rare varieties of bamboo. And the calligraphy and paintings on them were by genuine old masters.

"When he came back and reported this, Lord Sheh determined to buy them at any price. But the Stone Idiot swore, 'I'll die of cold and hunger sooner than sell, even if you offer me a thousand taels apiece.'

"There was nothing Lord Sheh could do, except storm at Master Lien every day. Even when the fellow was promised five hundred taels in advance, he still refused. 'I'd sooner die than part with my fans,' he insisted. So, really, miss, what could be done?

"Then that black-hearted scoundrel Chia Yu-tsun heard about it and hatched a scheme. He had the idiot taken to his

yamen on a charge of owing the government some money, and
ordered the default to be made good by the sale of his property.
So the fans were seized, paid for at the official price and
brought to our house. As for that Stone Idiot, who knows
whether he's alive or dead?

"Lord Sheh, once he had the fans, asked Master Lien, 'How
did *he* succeed where you failed?' Master Lien simply answered, 'It's nothing to boast of, if somebody is willing to ruin
a family for such a trifling reason.' Then his father flew into
a passion, and accused him of trying to put him in the wrong.
That was the main reason.

"There were a few other things too, so insignificant that I
can't remember them exactly. Together, anyway, they got our
young master a beating. Instead of being held down and flogged
with a cane or stick, he was beaten where he stood — with just
what, nobody knows — so that his face was cut open in two
places. We heard that Aunt Hsueh had a cure for cuts of that
kind. Could you send for a pill now, miss, for me to take to
him?"

Pao-chai promptly despatched Ying-erh to fetch a pill, and
handed this to Ping-erh, "I won't call just now, under the
circumstances," she said. 'Please give my regards to your
mistress."

Ping-erh assented and left.

Let us return to Hsiang-ling, who had paid her courtesy
calls. After dinner, when Pao-chai had gone to see the Lady
Dowager, she went to Bamboo Lodge. And Tai-yu, now in
better health, was delighted to learn that she had moved into
the Garden.

"I shall have more free time here," remarked Hsiang-ling.
"If only you'd teach me to write poems, how lucky I'd count
myself!"

"If you want to write poetry you must acknowledge me as
your tutor," replied Tai-yu teasingly. "I'm no poet myself, but
I dare say I could teach you."

"Of course I'll be only too glad to be your pupil. But you must be patient with me."

"It's quite simple really. There's hardly anything to learn," Tai-yu told her. "In regulated verse[1] it's just a matter of opening, developing, changing and concluding; and the developing and changing couplets in the middle should be antithetical. A level tone should be contrasted with a deflected one, an abstract word with a concrete one. But if you've got a really fine line, the rules can be disregarded."

Hsiang-ling said, "No wonder, then, that whenever I steal time to read a couple of old poems, I find some lines have very neat parallelisms while others have none. And I understood there was a rule that the first, third and fifth characters of a line needn't follow the tone pattern, but the second, fourth and sixth must abide strictly by it. Yet I found that in some old poems even the second, fourth and sixth characters break the rules. This has always puzzled me. From your explanation it seems one needn't bother with these rules, provided the line is fresh and original."

"That's right. The rules of prosody are secondary, the main thing is to have original ideas. For if there's feeling, a poem is good even if the lines are unpolished. This is what we mean by 'not letting the words interfere with the sense.' "

Hsiang-ling gushed, "I simply love those lines by Lu Yu:

> The heavy hangings, unrolled, retain the scent of incense;
> The old inkstone, slightly concave, brims with ink.

That's so true and so quaintly put."

"You mustn't on any account read poems of that kind," warned Tai-yu. "It's because you don't understand poetry that you like such superficial lines when you come across them. Once you get into that habit you'll never cure yourself of it. Now, listen to me: If you really want to write poetry, take my copy of the complete poems of Wang Wei and study a hundred of

---

[1] Regulated verse, originating in the Tang Dynasty, is a pentasyllabic or heptasyllabic eight-line verse form, with the third and fourth lines and the fifth and sixth lines forming two antithetical couplets.

his pentasyllabic poems in regulated verse until you know them well. Then read one or two hundred of Tu Fu's regulated heptasyllabics, and one or two hundred of Li Po's[1] heptasyllabic quatrains. After digesting these and laying a foundation with these three poets, go on to read Tao Yuan-ming, Ying Yang, Hsieh Ling-yun, Yuan Chi, Yu Hsin and Pao Chao.[2] In less than a year's time, with your intelligence, you can count on becoming a poet."

"That's fine, miss." Hsiang-ling smiled. "Please give me that book then to take back with me, and I'll read a few poems tonight."

Tai-yu told Tzu-chuan to fetch Wang Wei's *Regular Pentasyllabics* and give it to Hsiang-ling.

"Just read those I've marked with red circles," she told her. "Read all the ones I've chosen. If there's anything you don't understand, ask your young lady. Or I can explain it to you next time I see you."

Hsiang-ling took the book back to Alpinia Park and, oblivious of all else, read poem after poem by lamplight, ignoring Pao-chai's repeated reminders to go to bed. Seeing her so much in earnest, Pao-chai finally let her be.

One morning, Tai-yu had just finished her toilet when a radiant Hsiang-ling came in to return Wang Wei's poems and ask for Tu Fu's *Regulated Verse*.

"How many poems have you memorized?" asked Tai-yu.

"I've read all those marked with red circles."

"Do you appreciate them better now?"

"I think so, but I'm not sure. I'd like your opinion."

"Go ahead. We can only make progress by talking things over."

"To my mind, the beauty of poetry lies in something that can't be put into words yet is very vivid and real when you

---

[1] Lu Yu (1122-1210), a patriotic Southern Sung Dynasty poet. Wang Wei (699-760), Tu Fu (712-770) and Li Po (701-762) were famous Tang Dynasty poets.

[2] Chinese poets of the third to the sixth centuries.

think about it. Again, it seems illogical, yet when you think it over it makes good sense."

"There's something in that. But what grounds have you for saying so?"

"Well, take that couplet in the poem on the northern borderland:

> In the great desert a single straight plume of smoke;
> By the long river at sunset a ball of flame.

Of course the sun's round, but how can smoke be straight? The first description seems illogical, the second trite. But when you close the book and think, the scene rises before your eyes, and you realize it would be impossible to choose any better words. Or take the couplet:

> As the sun sets, rivers and lakes gleam white;
> The tide comes up and the horizon turns blue.

The adjectives 'white' and 'blue' seem illogical too; but when you think about it no other words would be so apt, for read aloud they have all the savour of an olive weighing several thousand catties! Again, take the lines:

> The setting sun still lingers by the ford,
> A single plume of smoke ascends from the village.

It's the choice of 'lingers' and 'ascends' that I admire. On our way to the capital that year, our boat moored by the bank one evening. There was nobody about, nothing but a few trees, and the smoke from some distant cottages where supper was being cooked rose up, a vivid blue, straight to the clouds. Fancy, reading those lines last night carried me back to that place."

Meanwhile Pao-yu and Tan-chun had also arrived and sat down to listen to this disquisition on poetry.

"Actually, you don't need to read any more poems," remarked Pao-yu with a smile. " 'True understanding need not be sought far away.' Judging by the little I've heard you say, you've already grasped the gist of the matter."

Tai-yu put in, "You've praised that expression 'a single plume of smoke ascends' without realizing that it's taken from an earlier poet. Have a look at this line, which is even more evocative and natural."

She found and showed her Tao Yuan-ming's lines:

> Misty the distant village,
> Smoke dawdles up from the hamlet.

Hsiang-ling read this and nodded her appreciation. "So 'ascends' is derived from 'dawdles up,' " she said.

"You've got it," cried Pao-yu laughing. "No need for further explanations. In fact, more might lead you astray. Just start writing poetry yourself now, and you're bound to produce something good."

Tan-chun said, "Tomorrow I'll prepare some refreshments and invite you formally to join our poetry club."

"Don't laugh at me, miss," cried Hsiang-ling. "It's just out of admiration for you that I'm learning this for fun."

"Who's not doing it for fun?" countered Tan-chun and Tai-yu. "We don't write seriously either. If we really set up as poets, people outside the Garden would split their sides laughing."

"Don't be too modest," said Pao-yu. "The other day, when I was discussing our painting with those secretaries outside and they heard we'd started a poetry club, they begged me to show them some of our poems. I wrote out a few for them, and they were so genuinely impressed that they copied them all out to have them printed."

"Is that true?" demanded Tan-chun and Tai-yu.

"I'm not a liar like that parrot there on the perch."

"You really are the limit!" they exclaimed. "In the first place they aren't proper poems, and even if they were you shouldn't circulate our writings outside."

"What does it matter?" he argued. "We'd never have heard of the poems by ladies of old if they hadn't been made public."

At this point Hsi-chun's maid Ju-hua arrived, and at her request Pao-yu went to see her mistress.

Hsiang-ling again urged Tai-yu to lend her Tu Fu's poems, and begged her and Tan-chun to set her a subject.

"Let me try my hand and you can correct it," she said.

"Last night there was a fine moon," rejoined Tai-yu. "I was meaning to write a poem on it but didn't get round to it. Take that as your subject, and choose as your rhymes any characters in the fourteenth group rhyming with *han* ('cold')."

Hsiang-ling went back in high delight with the poems. After cudgelling her brains she wrote a few lines, then read a couple more of Tu Fu's *Regulated Verses* which she could not bear to put down. She was so engrossed that she forgot food and sleep.

"Why torture yourself?" asked Pao-chai. "This is all Tai-yu's fault. I must settle scores with her. You were always a bit weak in the head, and now this has crazed you completely."

"Please don't distract me," begged Hsiang-ling.

With that she finished her verse and showed it to her.

Pao-chai read it and commented with a smile, "This isn't the way. Don't be shy, though. Just show it to her and see what she has to say."

So Hsiang-ling took the poem to Tai-yu, who read as follows:

> The moon hangs in mid-sky, cold is the night;
> Round its reflection, limpid white its light,
> Inspiring poets to let their fancies roam,
> But travellers, sick at heart, cannot bear the sight.
> By emerald pavilion hangs a mirror of jade,
> A disc of ice outside pearl screen displayed;
> No need for silvery candles this fine night —
> Its bright splendour lights up the painted balustrade.

Tai-yu commented with a smile, "You've no lack of ideas but the language lacks elegance, because you're restricted by having read so few poems. Scrap this one and write another. Just let yourself go."

Hsiang-ling went away in silence. She did not go back to her room but strolled by the pool and under the trees, sat lost in thought on the rocks or crouched down to scribble on the ground, to the amazement of all those who passed by.

When Li Wan, Tan-chun, Pao-chai and Pao-yu heard of this, they climbed a slope some way off and stood there laughing as they watched her, now frowning, now smiling to herself.

"The girl's bound to go mad at this rate," giggled Pao-chai. "She sat up all last night muttering to herself, and didn't go to sleep till nearly dawn. In less time than it takes for a meal it was daybreak, and I heard her get up and make a hurried toilet before rushing off to find Tai-yu. She came back to spend the whole day in a daze; but since the poem she wrote was no good, now of course she's writing another."

Pao-yu chuckled. "This is a case of 'a remarkable place producing outstanding people.' So Heaven has endowed her with more than good looks. We were always regretting that such a girl lacked polish, but now see what's happened! This shows there is true justice in the world."

"I only wish *you* would work as hard." Pao-chai smiled. "Then you'd succeed in your studies."

Pao-yu let this pass.

They now saw Hsiang-ling set off exuberantly to find Tai-yu again.

"Let's follow her," suggested Tan-chun. "I want to see if she's done any better this time."

So off they trooped together to Bamboo Lodge, where they found Tai-yu discussing Hsiang-ling's poem with her.

"What's it like?" they asked.

"A creditable effort but still poor," was Tai-yu's verdict. "This one is too arty. She'll have to try again."

They asked to see the verse, which read:

> Neither silver nor liquid this chill light on the window;
> A jade disc hangs above in the limpid sky;
> Pale the plum-blossom steeped in fragrance,
> Slender the willow slips, their dew half dry.
> Golden steps appear coated with powder,
> Marble balustrades seem lightly frosted over;
> Waking in West Pavilion, no trace of man,
> But some vestiges still behind the screen we discover.

Pao-chai remarked pleasantly, "This doesn't read like a poem about the moon, but it would do if the subject were changed to *The Colour of the Moon*, for almost every line seems to deal with colour. Never mind, all poetry starts with meaningless talk. In a few days you'll do better."

Hsiang-ling, who had preened herself on this poem, was discouraged again by these comments. She refused to give up, however, and once more started racking her brains. Leaving the others to chat, she strolled into the bamboo grove before the steps and concentrated on thinking, deaf and blind to everything going on around her.

Presently Tan-chun called to her through the window, "Do have a rest, Hsiang-ling!"

" 'Rest' belongs to the fifteenth group of rhymes — you've got the wrong rhyme," she answered absently.

Everybody laughed.

"She's really become a demoniac poet!" said Pao-chai. "It's all Tai-yu's fault for egging her on."

"The Sage says 'tireless in teaching others,' " quipped Tai-yu. "Since she consulted me, I had to tell her what I knew."

"Let's take her to see Hsi-chun," proposed Li Wan. "It'll wake her up to look at the painting."

No sooner said than done. They dragged Hsiang-ling off past Lotus Fragrance Anchorage to Warm Scented Arbour, where Hsi-chun was having a siesta on her couch. The painting, propped against one wall, was covered by a piece of gauze. Having woken Hsi-chun they removed the gauze, disclosing that the painting was only about one-third finished. Hsiang-ling saw some beautiful girls in it. Pointing at two of them she said with a smile:

"This is our young lady, and that's Miss Lin."

Tan-chun laughed. "If all who can write poems are to be painted there, you'd better hurry up and learn."

After a few more jokes the party dispersed.

Still Hsiang-ling's whole mind was occupied by poetry. That evening she sat up facing the lamp lost in thought, only going to bed after midnight and lying there open-eyed, not getting off to sleep till nearly dawn. When presently day broke and Pao-chai woke up, she found her sleeping soundly.

"She's been tossing and turning all night," thought Pao-chai. "I wonder if she's finished her poem? She must be tired out. I'd better not wake her."

Just then Hsiang-ling laughed in her sleep and cried, "Ah, now I've got it! She'll hardly be able to find fault with *this*."

Amused and touched, Pao-chai woke her up to ask, "What have you got? Your single-mindedness should move the gods to pity. But you may fall ill if you can't write good poems."

Having finished her toilet she went off with the other girls to pay her respects to the Lady Dowager.

Now Hsiang-ling had been so determined to learn to write poems, giving her whole mind to it, that although she had failed to finish this new poem the previous day she had suddenly hit on eight lines in her dreams. As soon as she was dressed she wrote them out. And as she could not tell whether they were good or not, she went to find Tai-yu again. She reached Seeping Fragrance Pavilion as Li Wan and the girls, just back from Lady Wang's apartments, were laughing at Pao-chai's account of how Hsiang-ling had been versifying and talking in her sleep. When they looked up and saw her, all clamoured to see her new poem.

If you want to know what it was like, read the next chapter.

CHAPTER 49

White Snow and Red Plum-Blossom Make
the Garden Entrancing
Girls Enjoy Rustic Fare at
a Venison Barbecue

When Hsiang-ling discovered the others talking about her, she went up to them with a smile.

"Read this," she said. "If it's any good, I'll persevere; if not, I'll give up trying to write poetry."

She handed Tai-yu her poem and they all read:

> Hard, surely, to hide such splendour,
> A form so fair, a spirit so cold, so withdrawn;
> Washing-blocks pound in an expanse of white,
> Only a crescent is left when cocks crow at dawn;
> In green coir cape on the river he listens to autumn fluting,
> In red sleeves she leans over her balustrade at night.
> Well might the goddess Chang Ngo ask herself:
> Why cannot *we* enjoy endless, perfect delight?

"Not only good but original and ingenious," was the general verdict. "As the proverb says, 'All difficulties on earth can be overcome if men but give their minds to it.' You certainly must join our poetry club."

Hsiang-ling, hardly able to believe her ears, was questioning Tai-yu and Pao-chai to make sure they were not teasing when some maids and old nurses hurried in.

"A party of ladies, old and young, have arrived," they announced. "We don't know them, but they're your relatives. Please go quickly to welcome them."

"What are you talking about?" asked Li Wan. "You must explain more clearly. Whose relatives are they?"

"Two of them are your younger cousins, madam. Two young ladies, one of them is said to be Miss Hsueh's cousin, and

124

there's a young gentleman who's Master Hsueh's cousin. We're on our way now to invite Madam Hsueh over. You and the young ladies had better go first."

As these messengers left Pao-chai exclaimed joyfully, "Can it be our Hsueh Ko and his sister?"

Li Wan said gaily, "It sounds as if my aunt has come to the capital again. But how odd that they should all arrive together."

Going in some mystification to Lady Wang's reception hall, they found it crowded with people. Lady Hsing's brother and sister-in-law had brought their daughter Hsiu-yen to stay with her; and they had travelled with Hsi-feng's elder brother Wang Jen, who was coming to the capital too. Half way there, when their boats moored, they had happened to meet Li Wan's widowed aunt making the same journey with her daughters Li Wen and Li Chi; and having found out in the course of conversation that they were related, these three families had proceeded on their way together. Then there was Hsueh Pan's cousin Hsueh Ko, coming to arrange for the marriage of his younger sister Pao-chin who had been betrothed to the son of Academician Mei when their father was in the capital. Learning of Wang Jen's trip, he had followed with his sister and overtaken him. In this way they had arrived together today to visit their respective relatives.

The Lady Dowager and Lady Wang welcomed these guests most warmly.

"No wonder our lamp wicks kept forming snuff and sputtering last night!" remarked the old lady with a smile. "It was a sign of this reunion today."

While exchanging family news and accepting the gifts brought, she ordered a meal. Hsi-feng, it goes without saying, was busier than ever, for Li Wan and Pao-chai were naturally chatting with their relatives about all that had happened since they parted. Tai-yu enjoyed the general excitement too until it came home to her that she alone had no family but was all on her own, and at this thought she shed tears. Pao-yu, well aware how she felt, finally succeeded in consoling her, after which he hurried back to Happy Red Court.

"Go and have a look, quick!" he urged Hsi-jen, Sheh-yueh and Ching-wen. "Pao-chai's boy cousin looks and behaves quite differently from Hsueh Pan, more as if he were her real brother. And there's something even more amazing. You always insist that nobody can rival Pao-chai's looks, but you should just see her girl cousin and my elder sister-in-law's two cousins — words fail me to describe them! Old Man Heaven, what fine essences and subtle spirits you must have used to produce such exquisite creatures! Why, I've been like the frog at the bottom of a well, imagining that our girls here were unmatched; but now, without searching far afield, here on this very spot I see others who surpass them. We certainly live and learn. Does this mean there are still others like these?"

He had been laughing and exclaiming so wildly that Hsi-jen refused to go. Ching-wen and the others had done as he said, however, and now they ran back smiling.

"You must go and have a look," they urged Hsi-jen. "Lady Hsing's niece, Miss Pao-chai's cousin and Madam Chu's two cousins are as pretty as four fresh young shallots, they really are!"

While they were speaking, Tan-chun came to find Pao-yu. "This is a fine thing for our poetry club," she told him.

"That's right," he agreed. "You had the bright idea of starting the club, so now all these people turn up as if by magic. We don't know, though, whether they can write poems or not."

"I asked them just now," said Tan-chun. "Though they disclaimed modestly, they all seem as if they can. Even if they can't, they can learn — look at Hsiang-ling."

"Miss Hsueh's cousin sounds the best of them all," put in Hsi-jen. "Is that your impression, miss?"

"Yes," said Tan-chun. "I shouldn't be surprised if she surpasses even Pao-chai and all the rest of us here."

"It will be strange if she does. I shouldn't have thought it possible to find anyone better than *her*!" exclaimed Hsi-jen, much impressed. "I must go and have a look."

"The old lady lost her heart to her as soon as she set eyes on her," Tan-chun continued. "She's already told Lady Wang to adopt her as her daughter, and means to bring her up as her own grandchild. It's just been decided."

"Is that true?" demanded Pao-yu joyfully.

"Since when have I lied to you?" retorted Tan-chun. "Now that the old lady has this good grand-daughter she'll forget you, her grandson."

"I don't mind. It's only right to love girls more. Tomorrow's the sixteenth — our club ought to hold another meeting."

"Tai-yu's just out of bed and Ying-chun's ill again. There's always someone missing."

"Ying-chun doesn't write much, so we can manage without her."

"Wouldn't it be better, though, to wait a few days till the newcomers have settled down and then invite them? Our elder sister-in-law and Pao-chai naturally won't be in a poetizing mood just now either. Besides, Hsiang-yun's not here and Tai-yu's only just recovered. It wouldn't suit anyone. Let's wait till Hsiang-yun comes. By then the new arrivals will know us, Tai-yu will be completely well, Li Wan and Pao-chai will have less on their minds, and Hsiang-ling will have made further progress; then we can have a better meeting. Come on now, let's go and see what's happening in the old lady's place. We don't have to worry about Pao-chai's cousin — it's settled that she's to stay here. If the other three aren't, we can beg the old lady to invite them to stay in the Garden too. The more the merrier."

Pao-yu's face lit up. "That's a splendid idea," he cried. "I'm such a fool, I was so carried away by their arrival, I never thought of that."

The two of them went together then to the Lady Dowager's quarters. Sure enough, the old lady was so delighted with Pao-chin that she had made Lady Wang adopt her as her god-daughter. And overjoyed by this, she would not even hear of Pao-chin staying in the Garden — the girl was to sleep with *her*. Hsueh Ko was to be put up in Hsueh Pan's study.

The Lady Dowager then told Lady Hsing, "Your niece needn't go home for a few days either. Let her enjoy herself in the Garden first."

As Lady Hsing's elder brother was poorly off, he and his wife had counted on her providing them with accommodation and financial assistance during this visit to the capital; so Hsiu-yen was entrusted to Hsi-feng. Now there were many girls, temperamentally different, in the Garden; and as Hsi-feng considered it unnecessary to open up another house for Hsiu-yen, she decided the best thing would be to put her up with Ying-chun; for then if later Lady Hsing heard that her niece was dissatisfied, no blame would attach to Hsi-feng. And not counting the time she chose to spend at home, each month that she stayed in Grand View Garden Hsi-feng would allocate her the same monthly allowance as Ying-chun. Dispassionately appraising Hsiu-yen's character and behaviour, she found her unlike both Lady Hsing and her parents, being extremely gentle and lovable. So Hsi-feng gave her preferential treatment out of pity for her poverty and hard life, whereas Lady Hsing paid little attention to her.

Because the Lady Dowager and Lady Wang appreciated Li Wan's good qualities and her admirable conduct since her husband's untimely death, they would not hear of her widowed aunt staying anywhere but in their house. So although most reluctant to impose on them, on the old lady's insistence Li Wan's aunt had to move into Paddy-Sweet Cottage with her two daughters.

Barely had the newcomers settled in than Shih Ting, Marquis of Paoling, was transferred to a provincial governorship. In a few days he would be taking his family to his new post. Not wanting to part with Hsiang-yun, the Lady Dowager kept her and had her fetched to their house, directing Hsi-feng to give her a separate establishment. This Hsiang-yun resolutely declined, however, and at her insistence they let her move in with Pao-chai instead.

Things were livelier in Grand View Garden now that thirteen people, counting in Hsi-feng, lived there. In addition to Li Wan who had senior status there were Ying-chun, Tan-chun, Hsi-chun, Pao-chai, Tai-yu, Hsiang-yun, Li Wen, Li Chi, Pao-chin and Hsiu-yen, as well as Hsi-feng and Pao-yu. Apart from the two married women, the other eleven were all about the same age — fifteen, sixteen or seventeen. Some of them had been born in the same month, on the same day or at the same hour, with the result that they themselves often confused their ages. Thus the terms "elder sister," "younger sister," "younger brother" and "elder brother" were bandied about at random.

Hsiang-ling's whole heart was nowadays set on writing poetry, but she did not like to trouble Pao-chai too much. For her, talkative Hsiang-yun's arrival was a stroke of luck, as the latter was only too glad to be consulted on poetry and would cheerfully hold forth on the subject at all hours of the day and night.

"You're deafening me with this noise," protested Pao-chai jokingly. "Real scholars would laugh to hear a girl discussing poetry so seriously. They'd say you'd forgotten your place. One Hsiang-ling is more than enough without a chatterbox like *you* joining in and spouting about 'Tu Fu's profundity, Wei Ying-wu's quiet distinction, Wen Ting-yun's brilliance and Li Shang-yin's recondite obscurity.' All these are *dead* poets; why harp on them without any mention of our two *living* poets?"

"Which two living poets? Do tell me, dear sister," begged Hsiang-yun.

"The hard-working eccentric Hsiang-ling and the garrulous lunatic Hsiang-yun," answered Pao-chai.

Hsiang-ling and Hsiang-yun were laughing uproariously when Pao-chin arrived. She was wearing a glittering green and gold cape made of some fabric they did not recognize.

"Where did this come from?" asked Pao-chai.

"The old lady got it out for me because it was beginning to hail," replied her cousin.

Hsiang-ling examining it more closely remarked, "No wonder it's so pretty; it's made of peacock feathers."

"Not peacock feathers," Hsiang-yun corrected her. "The feathers from wild ducks' heads. That shows how fond of you the old lady is. Fond as she is of Pao-yu, she never gave *him* this to wear."

"As the proverb says, 'The fortune of each is predestined,'" put in Pao-chai. "I never thought she'd come here at this time or that, having come, the old lady would take such a fancy to her."

Hsiang-yun told Pao-chin, "There are two places here where you can enjoy yourself just as you please: the old lady's apartments or here in the Garden. When you call on Lady Wang, if she's at home it's all right to stay and chat with her for a while; but if she's out, don't go in. They're a nasty lot there who'd all like to do us in."

Pao-chai, Pao-chin, Hsiang-ling and Ying-erh all laughed.

Pao-chai said, "That's good sense from a flibbertigibbet like you, but you still talk too bluntly. Our Pao-chin is rather like you. You're always saying you wish I were your sister; but now I think you'd better take my cousin as your younger sister."

With another glance at Pao-chin, Hsiang-yun said, "She's the only one here fit to wear this cape. It's too good for the rest of us."

As they were chatting Hu-po came in with the message, "The old lady doesn't want Miss Pao-chai to be too strict with Miss Pao-chin, because she's still very young. Just let her do as she pleases and ask for whatever she wants, and don't interfere."

Pao-chai rose to give her assent, after which she nudged Pao-chin and said mischievously, "I wonder where such good luck as yours comes from. Better leave us now before we start bullying you. I don't see in what way I'm worse than you."

As she was teasing, Pao-yu and Tai-yu arrived.

"You're only joking, cousin," said Hsiang-yun, "but some people are really jealous."

"If anyone is, it must be him," said Hu-po laughingly, pointing at Pao-yu.

"Oh, no, not him," Pao-chai and Hsiang-yun retorted in unison.

"If not him, then her." Giggling, Hu-po pointed at Tai-yu.

Hsiang-yun kept silent but Pao-chai cried, "You're even wider of the mark this time. She treats my cousin like her own sister; in fact she's even fonder of her than I am. So how could she be jealous? Don't believe that nonsense Hsiang-yun talks. You can never take anything she says seriously."

Pao-yu knew very well how narrow-minded Tai-yu could be, and having as yet no idea of what had recently passed between her and Pao-chai he was really afraid she might resent the Lady Dowager's partiality for Pao-chin. Her reactions to Hsiang-yun's remark and Pao-chai's answer were not what they would once have been but tallied with what Pao-chai had said, and this puzzled him. He thought, "The relationship between these two has changed, they now seem ten times better friends than the others." And then he heard Tai-yu address Pao-chin as "younger sister" without mentioning her name, as if they were real sisters.

Pao-chin was young and warm-hearted, intelligent too, and well-educated from an early age. After a couple of days there she had formed a general impression of the Chia family. And since the girls gave themselves no airs but were all good to her cousin, she tried likewise to make herself agreeable to them. Noticing too that Tai-yu stood out from the rest, she treated her even more affectionately. Pao-yu observed all this with secret surprise.

Presently Pao-chai and her cousin rejoined Aunt Hsueh, Hsiang-yun went to the Lady Dowager's apartments, and Tai-yu returned to her own rooms to rest.

Pao-yu followed her there and said with a smile, "Although I've read *The Western Chamber* and annoyed you by quoting some lines from it in fun, a line has occurred to me which I can't understand. I'll recite it now and see if you can explain it."

Sensing something behind this she said archly, "Go on."

"In that scene 'Trouble Over the Billet-doux' there's an excellent line:

> Since when did Liang Hung and Meng Kuang become so intimate?

Isn't that superb! The reference to Liang Hung and Meng Kuang is just an ordinary classical allusion, but turned into a question it's rather neat. So, *since when*? Can you explain?"

Unable to suppress a laugh she replied, "That's a good question. Well asked in the play, and well asked by you too."

"You wouldn't take my word for it before. Now you two are getting on fine, but I'm left out in the cold."

"I never knew how truly good she was, but used to think she had ulterior motives."

Tai-yu proceeded to give him a full account of all Pao-chai had said to her when she pulled her up for her gaffe in the drinking game, and her gift of bird's-nest during her illness.

This explained matters to Pao-yu. "I was wondering since when Liang Hung and Meng Kuang started to hit it off so well," he said. "So it all came of her 'being young and talking too freely.' "[1]

Then Tai-yu spoke of Pao-chin, and wept because she had no sister of her own.

"There you go again, upsetting yourself for no reason," scolded Pao-yu. "Just see, you're thinner this year than last, yet you won't look after yourself. Every day you work yourself up for no reason at all, and aren't satisfied until you've had a good cry."

Wiping her tears she answered, "I've been feeling sick at heart, but I don't seem to cry as much as before. Though my heart aches, I haven't many tears to shed."

"You just imagine that because you're so used to crying," he objected. "How can anyone's tears dry up?"

At this point one of his maids brought him a scarlet woollen cape and the message, "Madam Chu just sent to say that, as

---

[1] This and the previous line are from *The Western Chamber*. Liang Hung, a poor scholar of the Eastern Han Dynasty, married swarthy 30-year-old Meng Kuang but paid her little attention for seven days on end though she decked herself out in her best finery. Then the bride changed into homespun clothes and busied herself with household chores, and Liang Hung praised her, saying: "This is how my wife should be." In *The Western Chamber*, the heroine Tsui Ying-ying feigned annoyance when her maid Hung Niang tried to bring her and the young scholar Chang together, as they were secretly in love. Learning that Ying-ying had already arranged a meeting with Chang, the maid taunted her mistress by using the classical allusion about Meng Kuang and Liang Hung. "Being young and talking too freely" is here quoted by Pao-yu to tease Tai-yu for previously repeating lines from *The Peony Pavilion* and *The Western Chamber*, both considered improper books.

it's started to snow, she wants to consult you about calling a meeting of the poetry club tomorrow."

While she was still speaking a maid arrived from Li Wan with an invitation for Tai-yu, and Pao-yu urged her to go with him to Paddy-Sweet Cottage. Having put on red boots lined with lambskin and with a gold-thread cloud-design appliqué, a crimson silk cape lined with white fox-fur, a green and gold plaited belt with double rings, and a snow-hat, she walked with him through the snow to Li Wan's apartments. There they found the other girls assembled, most of them in red capes of wool or satin. Li Wan, however, had on a gown of blue velvet buttoned down the middle, Pao-chai a pale purple woollen cape embroidered with flower designs, and Hsiu-yen her ordinary indoor clothes without any outer garments to keep off the snow.

Presently Hsiang-yun arrived wearing an ermine coat lined with grey squirrel given her by the Lady Dowager, a scarlet woollen hood with a gosling-yellow appliqué of cloud designs and a golden lining, and a big sable collar.

"Look, here comes the Monkey King!" exclaimed Tai-yu laughing. "She's got a cape too, yet she's dressed herself up like a saucy little Tartar."

"You should see what I'm wearing underneath," chuckled Hsiang-yun.

Taking off the coat she revealed a narrow-sleeved, none too new greenish yellow satin tunic lined with white squirrel, with fur-lined cuffs and collar, which was embroidered with dragons in gold thread and coloured silks. Her pink satin breeches were lined with fox fur. A long-tasselled coloured butterfly belt was fastened tightly round her waist. Her boots were of green leather. With her slender build she looked thoroughly neat and dashing.

"She loves dressing up like a boy," they teased. "And that costume suits her better than a girl's."

"Hurry up and discuss the poetry meeting," urged Hsiang-yun. "I want to know who's to be host."

"It was my idea," said Li Wan. "We should have met yesterday, and the next date isn't due for quite some time; so

I thought, as it happens to have snowed, why shouldn't we get together for a meeting to welcome the newcomers and to write some poems? What do the rest of you think?"

"That's a good idea," responded Pao-yu promptly. "But it's too late today, and tomorrow if the weather clears it won't be such fun."

"The snow may not stop," said the others, "Even if it does, this evening's fall is big enough to enjoy."

"There's nothing wrong with this place, but Reed Snow Cottage would be even better," remarked Li Wan. "I've already sent people there to heat the flues under the floor, and we can sit round the fire and write poems. I don't suppose the old lady will be in the mood to join us. And as we're just going there for a romp, we need only let Hsi-feng know. Each of you can send one tael of silver here, and that ought to be enough." Indicating Hsiang-ling, Pao-chin, Li Wen, Li Chi and Hsiu-yen, she continued, "We'll leave these five newcomers out, as well as Ying-chun who's poorly and Hsi-chun who's asked for leave. If you four send your share, I guarantee that five or six taels will be ample."

Pao-chai and the others readily agreed, then asked what the subject and the rhyme would be.

"I've already decided, but all in good time," replied Li Wan with a smile. "You'll hear what I've chosen tomorrow."

After chatting a little longer they went to see the Lady Dowager. And nothing more of consequence happened that day.

Too excited to sleep soundly, Pao-yu got up the next day as soon as it was light to draw the curtains. Although the blinds were down, it was so bright outside that he concluded regretfully that the weather must have cleared and the sun had come out. When he raised the blinds, however, to look through the glass window, he discovered that this brightness was not sunlight. It had been snowing hard all night so that the snow lay over a foot deep, and it was still falling in great flakes like cotton-wool.

In high delight he called for someone to help him with his toilet. Wearing just his purple velvet gown lined with fox-fur and an otter waistcoat and belt, with a fine coir cape over his shoulders, a rattan hat on his head and pattens on his feet, he set off without delay for Reed Snow Cottage.

Once outside his own gate he gazed round. All was white except for some green pines and emerald bamboos in the distance, so that he had the sensation of being in a crystal bowl. As he rounded the foot of the slope he smelt a cold fragrance and, looking over his shoulder, saw a dozen or so crimson plum trees in Green Lattice Nunnery where Miao-yu lived, their blossom, red as rouge, reflected in the snow and remarkably vivid against it. He stopped there awhile to enjoy the sight. As he was about to continue on his way, on Wasp-Waist Bridge he saw a messenger with an umbrella sent by Li Wan to invite Hsi-feng over.

Outside Reed Snow Cottage, maids were sweeping the snow from the path. This cottage was built on the bank of a stream by a hill. Its adobe rooms with their thatched roofs and bamboo windows were surrounded by a wattle-fence, and it was possible to fish through the windows. All around grew clumps of reeds, through which a path meandered to the bamboo bridge of Lotus Fragrance Anchorage.

When the maids saw Pao-yu approaching in his rattan hat and coir cape, they burst out laughing.

"We were just saying we needed a fisherman, and here you are to fill the bill," they cried. "The young ladies won't be coming till after breakfast. You're too impatient."

Pao-yu had to go back then, and he had just reached Seeping Fragrance Pavilion when he saw Tan-chun in a hooded scarlet woollen cape emerging from Autumn Freshness Studio leaning on the arm of a maid, followed by a serving-woman with a black silk umbrella. Guessing that she was on her way to see their grandmother, he waited for her by the pavilion and they left the Garden together.

In the Lady Dowager's inner room, Pao-chin was doing her hair and changing her clothes. Soon all the girls arrived and

Pao-yu set up a clamour, urging them to hurry breakfast because he was hungry. When finally the tables were laid, however, the first dish was a lamb embryo steamed in milk.

"This is a tonic for us old people," said the Lady Dowager. "It's a creature that's never seen the sky and the sun, so I'm afraid you children mustn't eat it. There's some fresh venison which you can have presently."

They all agreed to this except Pao-yu, who was too impatient to wait. He steeped a bowl of rice in hot tea, added some diced pheasant and hastily swallowed this down.

"I know you're busy again today and can't be bothered to eat," said his grandmother. "Keep the venison for him for this evening," she told the maids.

Only when Hsi-feng assured her that there was plenty, did she say no more about saving it for him.

Hsiang-yun whispered to Pao-yu, "If there's fresh venison, let's ask for some to cook ourselves in the Garden. That would be fun."

Pao-yu promptly passed on this request to Hsi-feng, who ordered a serving-woman to take some venison to the Garden.

Presently they left the Lady Dowager and trooped back to the Garden and to Reed Snow Cottage to hear what subject and rhyme Li Wan had chosen. But at this point Hsiang-yun and Pao-yu disappeared.

"It's no good when those two get together," remarked Tai-yu. "Whenever that happens, there's trouble. They must have slipped off because they have designs on that venison."

Li Wan's aunt came in now to watch the fun. She told her niece, "That boy with the jade and the girl with the golden unicorn are fine handsome young people who must have plenty to eat, but there they are planning to eat raw meat — and talking as if they meant it. I can't believe it!"

The young people laughed and exclaimed, "What an idea! Somebody fetch them, quick!"

"This is all Hsiang-yun's doing," said Tai-yu. "What did I tell you?"

Li Wan hurried out to find the two of them. "If you want to

eat raw meat, I'll take you to the old lady's place," she said. "I shan't care then if you eat a whole deer and fall ill — it won't be *my* responsibility. Look how it's snowing and how cold it is. Don't go making trouble for me."

"We're not eating it raw," countered Pao-yu. "We're going to grill it."

"That's all right then," said Li Wan, eying the barbecue and spits which some old servants had brought. "Be careful now, and don't cry if you cut your fingers!" With that warning she went in again with Tan-chun.

Now Ping-erh arrived, sent by Hsi-feng to explain that she was unable to come as she was busy distributing the New Year allowances. Hsiang-yun insisted that Ping-erh must stay with them, and the maid was only too willing, for she was naturally playful and always up to endless pranks with her mistress. Seeing the fun they were having, she took off her bracelets to join Pao-yu and Hsiang-yun by the barbecue, and suggested grilling three pieces first to try. Pao-chai and Tai-yu, being used to a barbecue, were not surprised by this; but to Pao-chin and Li Wan's aunt it seemed very strange.

By now, Li Wan and Tan-chun had fixed the subject and rhyme.

Tan-chun said to Li Wan, "Just smell that venison! If it smells so good even from here, I must try some too."

She joined the party outside and Li Wan followed.

"All your guests are here," she protested. "Won't you stop eating?"

Hsiang-yun, still munching, replied, "It's only after eating this that I feel like drinking, and I need wine to give me inspiration. Without this venison I couldn't possibly write a poem today." Her eye fell on Pao-chin in her wild duck cape, who was standing there smiling at them. "Come here, silly!" she cried. "Come and try some."

"How dirty it looks," laughed Pao-chin.

"Go and taste some," urged Pao-chai. "It's really delicious. Cousin Tai-yu's so delicate, it would give her indigestion. If it weren't for that, she'd like some too."

Pao-chin went over then to try a morsel, and finding it good she helped herself to more.

Presently a young maid came from Hsi-feng to fetch Ping-erh.

"Miss Hsiang-yun won't let me go. You go back first," Ping-erh told her.

Not long after the maid had left, Hsi-feng came in person, a cape over her shoulders.

"So you have such a treat without telling me!" she scolded, joining the group around the barbecue.

"Where did all these beggars come from?" cried Tai-yu. "Well, well! Reed Snow Cottage is out of luck today, all messed up by Hsiang-yun. My heart bleeds for it."

"A lot you know," retorted Hsiang-yun. "A real scholar can afford to be eccentric. You pretend to be so refined and pure, it's disgusting! Stuffing ourselves now with this venison will inspire us presently to produce some fine lines."

"If you don't make good that boast," threatened Pao-chai, "you'll have to pay the penalty by bringing up that meat and swallowing some of those reeds under the snow!"

When they had finished eating, they washed their hands and rinsed their mouths. Ping-erh, looking for her bracelets, found one missing. She searched everywhere but there was no trace of it, to everyone's surprise.

"I know where it's gone," said Hsi-feng with a smile. "There's no need to look for it now. Just get on with your poems. I guarantee you'll get it back within three days." Then she asked, "What are you writing today? The old lady says it will soon be New Year, and we should make some lantern riddles to amuse ourselves in the first month."

"That's right," they agreed. "We'd forgotten. We must hurry up and make up a few good ones to guess in the first month."

They went into the room with the heated floor, where refreshments and drinks were ready. Pasted on the wall was the subject on which they were to write, and the rhyme and metre. Pao-chai and Hsiang-yun, going over to have a look, saw that they were to compose a collective poem on the scenery in five-character lines using rhymes from the *hsiao* group of rhymes. The order in which to write was not stipulated.

Li Wan proposed, "As I'm a poor hand at versifying, let me just do the first three lines. Whoever's quickest can go on from there."

"We should arrange some sort of order," protested Pao-chai.

If you want to know the upshot, read the next chapter.

CHAPTER 50

In Reed Snow Cottage Girls Vie in Composing
a Collective Poem
In Warm Scented Arbour Fine Lantern Riddles
Are Made

"We must have some sort of order. Let me write out the numbers," proposed Pao-chai.

She made them draw lots. And Li Wan, as it happened, drew first place.

"If that's how it is, I'll give you the first line," volunteered Hsi-feng.

"Better still," responded the others laughingly.

Pao-chai put down "Phoenix" before "Old Peasant of Sweet Paddy," while Li Wan explained the subject to Hsi-feng. The latter thought for a while.

"You mustn't laugh!" she warned. "I have only one line — rather a crude one, too — but I wouldn't know how to go on from there."

"The cruder the better," they replied. "Let's hear it, and then you can go off and attend to your own business."

"I suppose when it snows the north wind must blow," said Hsi-feng. "At any rate I heard it all last night. So my line is:

The north wind blew hard all night.

Will that do?"

The others exchanged smiling glances.

"It may be crude but it doesn't show what is to follow, and that's the proper way to start a poem," was their verdict. "So besides being good, it leaves plenty of scope for the others. Let's start with this line. Hurry up and write it down, Old Peasant of Sweet Paddy, then complete the couplet and begin a new one."

Hsi-feng, Aunt Li and Ping-erh drank a few more cups of wine with them, then went off on their own business. Meanwhile Li Wan wrote:

Hsi-feng:

> The north wind blew hard all night....

After this she went on to write down the following lines composed by herself and others:

Li Wan:

> The door opens on a flurry of snow.
> Pity the pure white mingling with the mud....

Hsiang-ling:

> Jade scattered on the earth below.
> Fain would it revive the dead grass....

Tan-chun:

> But no veil on withered plants throw.
> The village brew, matured, is costly now....

Li Chi:

> With a good crop the granaries overflow.
> Ash flying from the pipe shows the change of season....

Li Wen:

> The Dipper turns and longer the nights grow.
> Cold hills have lost their vivid green....

Hsiu-yen:

> In frozen creeks no tide is heard to flow.
> The snow hangs lightly on sparse willow boughs....

Hsiang-yun:

> But slides off tattered plantain leaves drooped low.
> Musk-ink is melted in the precious tripod....

Pao-chin:

> Rich sables hide the silken sleeves below.
> Brightness the mirror by the window catches....

Tai-yu:

> Scent clings to walls with pepper dye aglow.
> A side wind blows and blows incessantly....

Pao-yu:

> While the clear dream lingers slow.
> Whence comes the sound of the plum-blossom flute?...

Pao-chai:

> Who is it that on green jade pipe doth blow?

> The giant turtle fears the earth may sink. . . .

Li Wan interposed at this point, "I'll go and see about getting some wine heated for you."

Pao-chai urged Pao-chin to go on; but before she could do so, Hsiang-yun stood up boisterously.

Hsiang-yun:

> Dragons fight, the cloud-wrack billows to and fro.
> A lone boat puts back to the lonely shore. . . .

Pao-chin, standing up too, continued:

Pao-chin:

> A whip points at the bridge, the poet must go.
> Fur coats are issued to the garrison. . . .

Hsiang-yun could never bear to take second place. And being more quick-witted than the others, arching her eyebrows now she straightened up and declaimed:

Hsiang-yun:

> Cotton-padded clothes to conscripts in the snow.
> Hard the going through gullies and hills. . . .

"Well done!" cried Pao-chai, and continued:

Pao-chai:

> They must not shake the branches hanging low.
> Soft and gleaming swirls the snow. . . .

Tai-yu cut in:

Tai-yu:

> In swaying dance, now swift, now slow.
> Fresh taros are steamed for a treat. . . .

She nudged Pao-yu, but he was too intent on watching Pao-chin, Pao-chai and Tai-yu compete against Hsiang-yun to be bothered to join in himself. Prompted by Tai-yu, however, he improvised:

Pao-yu:

> To "scattered salt" the song compares the snow.
> The boatman is fishing still in his coir cape. . . .

"You're no good!" cried Hsiang-yun with a laugh. "Keep out of this. You're only holding us up."

Pao-chin took over.

Pao-chin:

> Silent the woodman's axe, unheard each blow.
> Hill after hill like crouching elephants....

Hsiang-yun struck in:

Hsiang-yun:

> A single snake-like path winds to and fro.
> Congealed by cold these flowers of ice....

As Pao-chai and the others exclaimed in admiration, Tan-chun went on:

Tan-chun:

> Beauty no frost can blight or overthrow.
> In the deep courtyard chilly sparrows take fright....

As Hsiang-yun was thirstily gulping down some tea, Hsiu-yen took this chance to join in.

Hsiu-yen:

> In lonely hills an old owl hoots its woe.
> Snow dances up and down the courtyard steps....

Hsiang-yun hastily put down her cup to interject:

Hsiang-yun:

> Drifts at will on the lake below.
> Glittering bright in dawn's clear light....

Tai-yu:

> Setting the whole night aglow.
> Truly the cold of three feet of snow is forgotten....

Hsiang-yun hastily continued:

Hsiang-yun:

> Its promise clears the sovereign's gloomy brow.
> Who cares for the one lying frozen....

Pao-chin cut in gleefully:

Pao-chin:

> While merry-makers, feasting, toast the snow.
> A white silk belt from the heavenly loom is broken....

Hsiang-yun:

> Whiter than mermaid's silk from sea-market below.

Before she could start a new couplet, Tai-yu put in:

Tai-yu:

      Deserted pools are locked in loneliness....

Hsiang-yun swiftly rounded this off.

Hsiang-yun:

      Back to his humble lodge the poor scholar would go.

Again Pao-chin cut in:

Pao-chin:

      The ice to make our tea is slow to boil....

Hsiang-yun who was having great fun, laughed and went on:

Hsiang-yun:

      The leaves to warm the wine will hardly glow.

With a giggle Tai-yu continued:

Tai-yu:

      Snow covers the broom of the monk up on the hill....

Pao-chin gaily capped this:

Pao-chin:

      It hides the boy's lyre below.

Hsiang-yun, doubled up with mirth, now babbled something so quickly that the others had to ask her to repeat it. She gasped:

Hsiang-yun:

      On the stone tower sleeps an idle crane....

Hugging herself to stop her sides from splitting, Tai-yu fairly shouted:

Tai-yu:

      And silken quilts are warm, the fond cats know....

They rattled off the next lines between fits of laughter.

Pao-chin:

      From the moon cave roll silver waves....

Hsiang-yun:

      Cloud ramparts hide the crimson glow....

Tai-yu:

> One can almost taste the scent of wet plum-blossom. . . .

"A fine line!" exclaimed Pao-chai, and capped it:

Pao-chai:

> And from the dripping bamboos sweet melodies flow.

Pao-chin:

> Snow-flakes wet the belt with a design of love-birds. . . .

Hsiang-yun:

> Or congeal on emerald hairpins in a row. . . .

Tai-yu:

> They hang in the air although there is no wind. . . .

Pao-chin:

> And though there is no rain still hiss down slow. . . .

Hsiang-yun had collapsed by now in a fit of laughter. The rest of the party had long since opted out to enjoy watching these three rivals compete. Tai-yu urged Hsiang-yun to go on.

"So even *you* can run out of ideas," she teased. "Let me hear if you can't rattle on a bit longer."

Hsiang-yun, lying in Pao-chai's lap, was shaking with laughter.

Pao-chai made her sit up, declaring, "If you can use all the rhymes in this category, then I'll admit you've won."

"Call this versifying?" she spluttered, getting up. "I'm fighting for my life!"

"Whose fault is that?" they retorted laughingly.

Tan-chun, having decided earlier on that she could not compete, had been writing down their lines. She told them now, "This still requires an ending."

Li Wen took over and added:

Li Wen:

> These lines record this happy day. . . .

Li Chi added the concluding line:

Li Chi:

> And praise on this sagacious reign bestow.

"That's enough," said Li Wan. "Even if we haven't used up all the rhymes, to do that would sound forced and awkward."

After a careful reckoning they found that Hsiang-yun had made up the most lines.

"The credit should go to that venison!" they quipped.

"It hangs together quite well when you read it through," observed Li Wan. "Only Pao-yu flunked again."

"I'm no good at collective poems," he rejoined. "You'll just have to make allowances for me."

"We can't make allowances every time," she retorted. "You complain either that the rhyme's too difficult, the judge too unfair, or that you're no good at collective poems. Today you'll have to pay the penalty. I was struck just now by the red plum-blossom in Green Lattice Nunnery, and wanted to pick a spray for this vase; but because I can't stand Miao-yu's ways, I never have anything to do with her. Now we'll punish you by sending you to fetch a spray."

"A good penalty, refined and amusing," was the general verdict.

Pao-yu agreed readily. He was starting out when Hsiang-yun and Tai-yu both spoke up together.

"It's very cold outside. Have some hot wine before you go."

Hsiang-yun picked up the wine pot and Tai-yu filled a large goblet.

"After drinking our wine, if you don't carry out your mission we'll redouble your punishment," Hsiang-yun threatened him.

Having tossed off the wine he went out into the snow. Li Wan told some servants to accompany him, but Tai-yu stopped them.

"There's no need," she said. "If other people go with him, he won't get it."

"Yes, you're right." Li Wan nodded and ordered a maid to fetch a tall vase with a narrow neck and sloping shoulders, and fill it with water in readiness. "Presently we should write some poems on red plum-blossom," she suggested.

Hsiang-yun promptly volunteered to do the first one.

"Oh no, you don't," laughed Pao-chai. "You've done quite enough for today. It's no fun if you hog everything and leave the rest of us idle. Pao-yu has got to be punished when he comes back. He says he's no good at collective couplets. All right then, we'll make him write a poem on his own."

"Quite right," agreed Tai-yu. "And I've another idea. Just now we didn't make enough couplets. We should get those who contributed least to write on red plum-blossom."

"That's an excellent idea," approved Pao-chai. "Hsiu-yen, Li Wen and Li Chi had no chance to shine although they are, after all, our guests, because Pao-chin, Tai-yu and Hsiang-yun were so greedy. This time, the rest of us should keep out of it and let just the three of them write."

"Chi's not too good at poetry," said Li Wan. "Let Pao-chin take her place."

Pao-chai had to accept this. She added, "Let's choose the three characters 'red plum flower' as rhymes. Each of them can write a heptasyllabic regulated verse, Hsiu-yen using the rhyme 'red,' Wen 'plum' and Pao-chin 'flower.'"

"That's all very well," said Li Wan. "But we mustn't let Pao-yu off."

"I've another good subject for him," put in Hsiang-yun quickly. Asked what it was, she replied, " 'Calling on Miao-yu to Beg for Red Plum-Blossom.' Wouldn't that be fun?"

They were voicing their approval when Pao-yu came back, beaming, holding a branch of red blossom. The maids at once took it and put it in the vase, while all the others expressed their appreciation.

"Go ahead and enjoy it," said Pao-yu. "You don't know the trouble it cost me."

Tan-chun handed him another cup of hot wine, and maids came to take his cape and hat and shake off the snow. Maids from different apartments had brought extra clothing for all their young mistresses, and Hsi-jen had sent Pao-yu an old jacket lined with fox-fur. Li Wan ordered a dish of steamed taros and two plates of tangerines, oranges and olives to be sent back to Hsi-jen, while Hsiang-yun told Pao-yu the subject just chosen for him and urged him to hurry up and write.

"Do let me choose my own rhymes, good cousins," he begged. "Don't set the rhymes for me."

The rest agreed, "All right. Do as you like."

Meanwhile they were looking at the plum-blossom bough. Only about two feet in height with a side branch nearly five or six feet long, it had branchlets coiling like dragons or worms, others pointed like brushes, or densely twigged as a forest; and the petals, red as rouge, were fragrant as orchids. As the others were admiring this, Hsiu-yen, Li Wen and Pao-chin composed and wrote out their poems. The rest read them in the order of the rhymes as follows:

RED PLUM-BLOSSOM
Rhyming "red"

Braving the cold it blossoms for the east wind
Ere peach trees bloom or apricots turn red;
In a dream, rosy clouds bar the way to Mount Lofu,
But to Yuling's eternal spring my soul has fled.
Green sepals, rouged, blend into brilliant torches,
Tipsy snow-sprites over shattered rainbows have sped;
We can see this is no ordinary beauty
That in the snow and ice blooms pink and red.

Hsing Hsiu-yen

Rhyming "plum"

What loveliness assails my drunken eyes?
'Tis not the white I sing, but the red plum.
Its frozen cheeks are stained with tears of blood,
Its heart though free from misery is numb.
Transformed by an elixir wrongly swallowed,
Down it slips, its old guise cast off, from Elysium.
Magnificent the spring north and south of the Yangtze;
Bees and butterflies who doubt this — do not come!

Li Wen

Rhyming "flower"

Like rich girls in spring finery competing,
Stark boughs burst into flower.
Still courts, winding balustrades, with no white plum;

Stream and lonely hills glow with sunset at this hour.
Like fairy bark on red stream floating free,
Fluting drifts chill in the dreaming maiden's bower.
It must have sprung from seeds in paradise;
Past doubting this, though changed in form the flower.

Hsueh Pao-chin

They praised all these poems delightedly, pointing out that the last was the best. Pao-yu was amazed that Pao-chin, although the youngest, had the quickest wit; and Tai-yu and Hsiang-yun poured a small cup of wine to congratulate her.

"All three poems have their merits," said Pao-chai. "You two have grown tired of making fun of *me* every day, so now you're picking on *her*."

Li Wan asked Pao-yu, "Are *you* ready?"

"I did concoct something," he replied. "But their poems so overawed me that I've forgotten it. Let me think again."

Hsiang-yun struck her hand-stove with a copper poker. "I'm starting to 'beat the drum,'" she warned. "If you're not ready by the time I stop, you'll have to pay another forfeit."

"I'm ready," he answered.

"Dictate it to me." Tai-yu picked up a brush.

Hsiang-yun struck the hand-stove, crying, "One!"

"All right," agreed Pao-yu. "Take this down." He declaimed:

"Before the drinking starts, ere poems are made. . . ."

Tai-yu shook her head as she wrote. "A nondescript opening."

"Hurry up!" ordered Hsiang-yun.

He continued:

"He goes to the Fairy Isles in search of spring, asking a boon."

Tai-yu and Hsiang-yun nodded. "That's more like it." He proceeded:

"Not in quest of dew from the Bodhisattva's *kundi*,
But to beg a plum branch by the fence of the Goddess of the Moon."

Once more Tai-yu shook her head as she wrote this down. "Too arty."

Hsiang-yun hastily struck the stove again.

Pao-yu went on:

> "He returns to earth with a load of cold red snow,
> A fragrant cloud cut far from the dusty world;
> Its forked boughs resting on the poet's slim shoulders,
> His clothes by moss from the nunnery still purled."

When Tai-yu had finished writing this out and the others were discussing it, some maids ran in to announce:

"The old lady's coming!"

All hurried out to meet her, commenting, "What a good mood she must be in!"

She could be seen in the distance wearing a big cape with a grey squirrel-fur hood, seated in a small bamboo sedan-chair sheltered by a black silk umbrella, and surrounded by her maids, each holding an umbrella. Li Wan and the young people were hastening to meet them when the Lady Dowager sent word that they should stay where they were.

Upon reaching them she announced, "I've given Lady Wang and Hsi-feng the slip. Though the snow lies so deep, I'm all right in this chair; but I didn't want *them* to come traipsing through the snow."

Calling out greetings, they pressed forward to take her cape and help her out of the chair.

Her first remark on entering the room was, "What beautiful plum-blossom! You certainly know how to enjoy yourselves. I've come at the right time."

Li Wan had already ordered maids to spread a big wolf-skin rug in the middle of the *kang* for the old lady.

"Go on with your fun, and don't stop eating or drinking," she said when she had sat down on the rug. "Now that the days are shorter I've given up taking a nap after lunch. I was playing cards when I suddenly thought of you, so I came to join in your fun."

By now Li Wan had passed her a hand-stove, and Tan-chun

brought over clean chopsticks and a cup and poured some warm wine for her.

The old lady took a sip.

"What's on that plate there?" she asked.

They brought it over and told her, "Quails cured in wine."

"That will do nicely," she said. "Pull off some bits of the leg meat for me."

Li Wan assented and did so, after first calling for water to wash her hands.

"Just sit down as you were and go on chatting," urged the old lady. "I like listening." She told Li Wan, "You must sit down too as if I weren't here, or else I shall go away."

All resumed their seats then, except Li Wan, who moved to the lowest place.

"What were you doing?" the Lady Dowager asked. When informed that they had been writing poems she said, "You'd do better to make up some lantern riddles for all of us to enjoy after New Year."

They agreed to this.

After some more conversation she remarked, "It's damp here. You mustn't stay too long or you may catch cold. Hsi-chun's place is warmer than this. Let's go and see how she's getting on with her painting, and whether it will be ready by New Year."

"By New Year?" they exclaimed. "Not likely! It probably won't be ready till the Dragon-Boat Festival."

"Well I never! Is it going to take her longer to paint the Garden than it took the workmen to build it?"

She mounted her chair again then, and the whole party accompanied her past Scented Lotus Pavilion and along a covered walk with at either end an archway, both sides of which were inset with stone tablets. They passed through the western arch, which on its outer side bore the inscription "Through the Clouds," on the inner side "Across the Moon," and entered Hsi-chun's compound by the front northern gate. By the time the Lady Dowager alighted, Hsi-chun had come out to meet her and lead them all along the verandah to her bedroom. Above its door was the inscription "Warm Scented Arbour," and perfumed air struck warm on their cheeks as attendants lifted the red felt portière. As soon as they were inside, before even sitting down, the Lady Dowager asked to see Hsi-chun's painting.

Hsi-chun explained that it was difficult to mix colours in such cold weather, as they congealed. "I was afraid of spoiling it, so I've put it away," she concluded.

"I want it for New Year, so don't be lazy!" teased the old lady. "You must fetch it out at once and go on with it."

As she was speaking, Hsi-feng, in a purple woollen gown, made a smiling entrance.

"What a dance you've led me, Old Ancestress!" she cried. "Coming here without a word to anyone."

The Lady Dowager was pleased to see her.

"I didn't want you to come out in the cold; that's why I wouldn't let them tell you," she replied. "You're an artful puss to have found me after all. There's no need to show your dutifulness in this way."

"I didn't come out of any sense of duty," countered Hsi-feng laughingly. "When I found your place so quiet and questioned the maids, they wouldn't tell me where you were, just suggested I try the Garden. I was puzzling over this when a few nuns turned up. I realized they must have come with an alms list, or to make their annual requests for donations or incense money. So many people apply to our Old Ancestress just before New Year, I knew you'd run away to avoid being dunned. Now I've come to report to our Old Ancestress: Your duns have gone, you can come out of hiding. I've some very tender pheasant ready. So please come back for dinner. If you leave it any later, it'll be overcooked."

Amid the general merriment that followed, and before the old lady could make any retort, Hsi-feng ordered her sedan-chair. The Lady Dowager mounted it with Hsi-feng's help, in smiling acquiescence, and was carried through the east gate of the covered walk, chatting with the rest of the party.

All about lay snow, soft as powder, bright as silver. And

suddenly, at the top of a slope, they saw Pao-chin in the cape of wild ducks' down, with a maid behind her carrying a vase of red plum-blossom.

"So there she is!" they cried laughingly. "No wonder two people were missing. She's got herself some plum-blossom as well."

"Just look!" exclaimed the old lady in delight. "This snowy slope matched with a girl like her, in that costume too, and with plum-blossom in the background — what does it remind you of?"

"It's like Chiu Ying's[1] painting *The Beauty in Snow* which hangs in your room, madam," some of them answered.

The Lady Dowager shook her head.

"No, the girl in that painting hasn't a costume like hers, and she isn't a patch on Pao-chin for looks, either."

Even as she spoke, someone in a red felt cape stepped out from behind Pao-chin.

"Which of the girls is that?" asked the old lady.

"All the girls are here," they told her. "That's Pao-yu."

"My eyes are failing," she sighed.

While talking they had drawn level with Pao-yu and Pao-chin. Smiling, Pao-yu told Pao-chai, Tai-yu and the rest, "Just now I went back to Green Lattice Nunnery, and Miao-yu's given you each a spray of plum-blossom. They've already been sent to your rooms."

As they thanked him for going to such trouble, they left the Garden and made their way to the Lady Dowager's quarters. They were chatting there after dinner when Aunt Hsueh arrived.

"I haven't come over to see you all day because of this heavy snow," she told the old lady. "Are you in low spirits, madam? You should have gone out to enjoy the snowy landscape."

"What makes you think I'm feeling low? I went out and amused myself for a while with the girls."

"Last night I was thinking of asking my sister for the use of the Garden for one day, to invite you to a simple meal so as

---

[1] Ming Dynasty portrait-painter.

to enjoy the snow. But I found you'd gone to bed early, and as Pao-chai told me you weren't feeling too well I didn't like to bother you. If I'd known, I should have invited you."

"It's only the tenth month, and this is the first fall of snow this winter," rejoined the old lady. "You'll have plenty of chances to treat us later on."

"I hope so," said Aunt Hsueh. "That will give me an opportunity to show my respect."

"Mind you don't forget, aunt!" cried Hsi-feng playfully. "Why not weigh out fifty taels of silver now and give it to me to keep? Then as soon as it snows again, I'll prepare the feast. That'll save you trouble and the danger of forgetting."

The Lady Dowager chuckled.

"Yes, just give her fifty taels," she said to Aunt Hsueh, "and we'll take half each. When it snows, I'll excuse myself on the pretext of illness, so as to save you trouble, while Hsi-feng and I reap all the benefit."

Hsi-feng clapped her hands. "Excellent! Just what I was thinking."

General laughter greeted this sally.

"Bah! For shame!" exclaimed the Lady Dowager. "You've always got an eye to the main chance. Aunt Hsueh is our guest and it's *we* who should be inviting her, instead of neglecting her so badly. How can we let her spend money on us? Yet instead of issuing an invitation, you have the nerve to ask for fifty taels. You've no sense of shame at all."

"No one's as shrewd as our Old Ancestress," commented Hsi-feng. "She was just sounding you out, aunt. If you'd really forked up fifty taels, she'd have gone halves with me. Now that her scheme doesn't look like coming off, she turns around to shift the blame to *me*, talking in that high-minded way. All right then, instead of asking Aunt Hsueh for money, I'll let her treat the old lady at *my* expense; and I'll offer our Old Ancestress another packet of fifty taels to make up for my officiousness. How's that?"

By this time all the others were prostrate with laughter.

The Lady Dowager then reiterated that Pao-chin, with the

plum-blossom in the snow, had looked prettier than a picture. She asked her age as well as the hour, day and month of her birth, and wanted to know all about her family. Aunt Hsueh guessed that she wished to arrange a match between Pao-chin and Pao-yu, and she would have been quite wiiling had the girl not been promised already to a son of the Mei family. But as the old lady had made no direct proposal, she could not say so outright. She answered therefore in a roundabout way:

"It's a pity this poor child has had no luck. Before her father died two years ago, she saw a good deal of the world and travelled to all sorts of beauty spots with her parents. Her father knew how to enjoy life. And as he owned shops everywhere, he used to take his family to stay in different provinces for several months or a year at a time, until they'd visited more than half the country. Last time he was here he betrothed her to Academician Mei's son; but the year after that he died. And now her mother is a victim to asthma. . . ."

She was interrupted at this point by Hsi-feng, who heaved a long sigh.

"Too bad!" she exclaimed. "I was on the point of proposing a match for her, but she's already engaged."

"Whom were you going to propose?" asked the old lady with a smile.

"Never you mind, Old Ancestress. I was convinced they'd make an ideal couple. But as she's engaged it's no use bringing it up. I'd better hold my tongue."

The Lady Dowager knew very well whom Hsi-feng had in mind, but in view of Pao-chin's engagement she said no more. After a little more chat the party broke up, and the night passed without further incident.

The next morning the sky had cleared. After breakfast the old lady told Hsi-chun, "Never mind the weather but get on with your painting, and try to finish it before New Year. Of course, if you really can't, it doesn't matter. The main thing is to lose no time in painting in Pao-chin and her maid with the plum-blossom, just the way they looked yesterday."

This was a tall order, but Hsi-chun had to agree. When the others went to see how she was getting on, they found her lost in thought.

"We can chat while she's thinking," Li Wan told the rest. "Yesterday the old lady asked us to make up some lantern riddles; so when I went home with Chi and Wen, and we couldn't sleep, I made up two using quotations from the *Four Books*, and they thought up two each as well."

"Yes, we ought to get to work on those riddles," the others agreed. "Let's hear yours first and see if we can guess the answers."

" 'Kuan Yin (Goddess of Mercy) lacks a chronicle,' " said Li Wan. "The answer should be a line from the *Four Books*."

Hsiang-yun promptly guessed, " 'The end is supreme goodness.' "

Pao-chai smiled. "First think about 'chronicle.' "

"Try again," urged Li Wan.

"I'll make a guess," said Tai-yu. "Is it 'though good there is no documentation'?"

"That must be right," cried the others.

Li Wan continued, " 'A poolful of plants — what are they?' "

" 'Just flags and reeds,' " responded Hsiang-yun promptly. "I must be right this time."

"Yes, good for you," said Li Wan. "Here is Wen's riddle: 'The water flows cold by the rocks.' And the answer is the name of a man of old."

"Shan Tao?"[1] asked Tan-chun.

"That's right," said Li Wen.

"Chi's riddle is the word 'glow-worm,' " Li Wan went on. "And the answer is a single word."

They cudgelled their brains for a long time. Then Pao-chin said, "This one's deep. Is the answer 'flower'?"

"You've hit the nail on the head," Li Chi told her.

"What has 'glow-worm' got to do with 'flower'?" some of them demanded.

---

[1] Name of a Tsin Dynasty eccentric. *Shan* means mountain and *Tao* torrent.

"Most ingenious," remarked Tai-yu with a smile. "Doesn't grass turn into glow-worms?[1] The character for 'flower' consists of the 'grass' radical and the character for 'metamorphosis,' doesn't it?"

The others laughed when they caught on and said, "Very good."

"They're all good, but they're not the sort of riddle the old lady wants," observed Pao-chai. "We'd better make up some about everyday objects, which everyone can enjoy."

All agreed to this.

After a moment's thought Hsiang-yun volunteered, "I've got one written after the melody *Tien Chiang Chun,* about something very common. See if you can guess the answer." She recited:

> "Parted from his valleys and streams,
> He fools about midst mankind
> In utter futility.
> Fame and profit are vanity,
> And nothing is left behind."

For a long time they failed to guess the answer. Some suggested a monk, others a Taoist, yet others a marionette.

"You're all wrong," declared Pao-yu, who had been chuckling to himself for a while. "I've got it. It must be a monkey in a circus."

Hsiang-yun confirmed that he was right.

"The first part makes sense," said the others. "But what does the last line mean?"

"Is there any performing monkey that hasn't got its tail docked?" asked Hsiang-yun.

All the others protested laughingly, "Even when making riddles, she's full of monkey-tricks!"

Li Wan now turned to Pao-chin. "Aunt Hsueh was telling us yesterday that you've travelled a good deal, and seen lots of sights. Do try your hand at some riddles. And since you write such good poems, why not make them in verse?"

---

[1] The *Book of Rites* says: "Rotting grass turns into glow-worms."

Pao-chin nodded cheerfully and went off to rack her brains. Meanwhile Pao-chai was ready with a riddle which she recited:

> "Tier upon tier of carved cedar and sandalwood,
> By no craftsmen was it reared;
> Even when the sky is swept by wind and rain
> No holy bells are heard."

While the rest were trying to solve this, Pao-yu chimed in:

> "Vanished from heaven and the world of men,
> The bamboo frame bids us beware!
> Gaze up to catch the message from the phoenix,
> And sigh your answer to the azure air."

By now Tai-yu had one ready too and she declaimed:

> "No need to tether these fine steeds with ropes,
> Galloping round the walls how fierce they seem!
> At their master's bidding they speed fast as lightning;
> Only three fairy isles on the giant turtle's back have left
>   a name."

Tan-chun now had one ready too, but before she could tell it to them Pao-chin came back.

"I've visited many places of historical interest since I was small," she said. "So I've made ten verses about ten of them. They're very crude, but at least they recall the past and the answers are everyday objects. I hope you'll guess them."

"How ingenious!" exclaimed the others. "Won't you write them out for us?"

If you want to know more about this, read the next chapter.

CHAPTER 51

Pao-chin Composes Poems
Recalling the Past
An Incompetent Physician Prescribes
Strong Medicine

Pao-chin told the others that she had written ten riddles in the form of quatrains, about famous places she had visited in different provinces.

"How original!" they cried.

They crowded round to read the poems, which were as follows:

RED CLIFF[1]

Wrecked by Red Cliff, choking the stream,
Nothing remains in the empty hulks but names;
Yet countless gallant souls are roaming there
Where cold winds sough and fan the leaping flames.

COCHIN CHINA[2]

His rule is strengthened by great bells of bronze,
Whose sound has spread to tribes beyond the seas;
Ma Yuan assuredly achieved great deeds,
And the iron flute of Chang Liang[3] needs no praise.

---

[1] Red Cliff is on the south bank of the Yangtze, northeast of Chiayu, Hupeh. In A.D. 208 Tsao Tsao led an army of over 500,000 men to launch an attack on Sun Chuan. The latter, in alliance with Tsao Tsao's antagonist Liu Pei, mustered 30,000 men. Knowing that Tsao Tsao's army was weakened by epidemics and unaccustomed to action afloat, the allied forces of Sun Chuan and Liu Pei set fire to Tsao Tsao's fleet and crushed his army.

[2] Emperor Kuang-wu of the Han Dynasty sent his general Ma Yuan (14 B.C.-A.D. 49) to suppress the people of Cochin China in A.D. 42.

[3] Chang Liang (?-189 B.C.), one of the advisors and generals of Liu Pang, the founding emperor of the Han Dynasty, laid siege to Hsiang Yu, the Conqueror of Chu, at Kaihsia (present-day Linpi, Anhwei). Chang Liang made his men play iron flutes and sing Chu folksongs every night, making the Chu troops so homesick that their morale was undermined and they were finally defeated by the Han troops.

MOUNT CHUNGSHAN[1]

Fame and profit have never kept you company,
Abruptly haled into the dusty world;
To sever all the strings attached is hard;
Don't murmur, then, if taunts at you are hurled.

HUAIYIN[2]

Even the brave must guard against savage hounds;
He was made Prince of Chi and died straightway;
But let not the worldly despise him —
He remembered the gift of a meal till his dying day.

KUANGLING[3]

Cicadas chirp, crows roost, in a flash they are gone;
How looks the landscape by Sui Dyke today?
T'was the emperor's romantic reputation
That was to blame for so much calumny.

PEACH-LEAF FORD[4]

Flowers bloom in idleness by the shallow pool,
Peach-Leaf must part company at last with the bough;
Many mansions stood here in the Six Dynasties,
Only a portrait hangs on the bare wall now.

THE GREEN TOMB[5]

The dark stream is stagnant, choked,

---

[1] This poem is about Chou Yu of the Southern Chi Dynasty (479-501), who lived as a hermit on Mount Chungshan, Nanking, and once summoned to court abandoned all pretence of being high-minded and unworldly. His contemporary Kung Chi-kuei wrote an essay exposing his hypocrisy.

[2] Han Hsin, a native of Huaiyin, was so poor in his early days that he asked a washerwoman to share her meal with him. He later helped Liu Pang defeat Hsiang Yu and was entitled Prince of Chi, but then he was killed for plotting against Liu Pang.

[3] Kuangling was the ancient name for Yangchow, Kiangsu, where the Grand Canal built in the Sui Dynasty flowed to the Yangtze. The canal banks, flanked with willow trees, were made into imperial highways and named the Sui Dyke.

[4] This was by Chinhuai Creek, Nanking, where the famous calligrapher Wang Hsien-chih (344-386), saw his concubine Peach Leaf off and wrote a song to her. The portrait in the poem is that of Peach Leaf.

[5] This is the tomb of Wang Chao-chun in Huhehot, Inner Mongolia, which was said to be covered with evergreen grass. A palace maid, she was sent by the Han Emperor Yuan-ti (reigned 48-33 B.C.) to marry a Hunnish chieftain in order to pacify the borderland tribesmen. When Chao-chun passed the Great Wall, the sad note of her lute was said to have stopped the flow of the stream.

The icy strings of the lute all her grief proclaim;
How absurd they were, the rules of the House of Han;
Wood the carpenter scorns should feel eternal shame.

MAWEI SLOPE[1]

Lonely traces of rouge and perspiration remain,
But with the flowing water her beauty has gone;
Yet some vestiges of her charm still linger on,
And even today a fragrance clings to her gown.

PUTUNG MONASTERY[2]

A young maid, low-born and flippant,
By stealth brings a couple together;
Though caught out at last by her mistress,
She has induced her young lady to join her lover.

PLUM-BLOSSOM NUNNERY[3]

Not by plum trees but by willows,
Who will pick up the beauty's portrait here?
It is no use longing for a reunion in spring,
Autumn means parting for another year.

They all admired the subtlety of these riddles, Pao-chai,
however, commented, "The first eight deal with authenticated
incidents in history, but it's harder for us to understand the last
two fictitious ones. I think you ought to write two others
instead."

Tai-yu at once objected, "Don't be so sanctimonious and
strait-laced, dear cousin. The last two incidents may not
appear in historical records, and not having read the romances

---

[1] In Hsingping County of present-day Shensi, where Lady Yang, favourite
of the Tang Emperor Hsuan-tsung who reigned from 713 to 756, hanged herself
on the demand of the Imperial Guards who were escorting the emperor from
the capital Changan, where a rebellion was raging, to Chengtu.

[2] According to *The Western Chamber*, this monastery in Puchow, Shansi,
was where the young scholar Chang first met Ying-ying. They fell in love
and her maid Hung Niang arranged for them to meet every evening.

[3] The tomb of Tu Li-niang, heroine of *The Peony Pavilion*, was said to
be in this nunnery in the Tayu Mountains, Kiangsi. The first line of this
poem was written by Li-niang on her portrait which was picked up by Liu
Meng-mei, the young scholar who later married her.

from which they come we may not know the details; but we've surely all seen the operas based on them. Why, even three-year-olds know them, not to say us."

"That's quite right," agreed Tan-chun.

"Besides," Li Wan added, "these poems are about places she's visited. What if these two stories are fictitious? Plenty of legends have come down from ancient times, and well-meaning busybodies have even faked relics to fool men. For instance, that year we came to the capital we passed three or four tombs on the way said to be Lord Kuan's. Well, there's historical evidence for Lord Kuan's life and actions, but how could one man have so many tombs? They appeared, of course, as often happens, because later generations admired him and wanted to show their respect. I've since learned from a book of geography that Lord Kuan isn't the only one to have several tombs — so do most famous men of old. As for legendary sites, there are even more of them. So though the stories referred to in these two riddles are fictitious, they're mentioned in ballads and operas, even in temple oracles. The whole world knows them. Each one is a household word. Besides, it's not as if we ourselves had read *The Western Chamber* and *The Peony Pavilion*, which are licentious works. So it doesn't matter if these two verses are kept."

Then Pao-chai did not insist, and they tried for a while to guess the answers, but with no success.

In winter the days are short, it was soon dinner-time, and they went to the mansion for a meal. Then a maid reported to Lady Wang that Hsi-jen's brother Hua Chih-fang had brought word that their mother was ill and wanted to see her daughter. He had come to beg permission to take her home.

"Of course we can't keep her if her mother wants her," was Lady Wang's reply. She sent for Hsi-feng and told her to see to the matter.

Hsi-feng agreed and went back to her apartments. She asked Chou Jui's wife to break the news to Hsi-jen, and gave her these instructions:

"You must get another matron beside yourself and a couple

of young maids to go with Hsi-jen. Four older attendants are to escort her carriage. Take a big one yourselves and a smaller one for the girls."

As Mrs. Chou was leaving to carry out these orders, Hsi-feng added, "Hsi-jen is a sensible girl. Tell her from me to dress smartly and to take a big bundle of good clothes in a handsome wrapper, as well as a good hand-stove. She must come and let me see her before she leaves."

Mrs. Chou assented and went off.

After some time, sure enough, Hsi-jen arrived, having changed her clothes, accompanied by Mrs. Chou and two maids who were carrying her hand-stove and bundle. Hsi-feng saw that she had some fine gold pins ornamented with pearls in her hair, and was wearing an ermine-lined peach-red silk tapestry jacket with a hundred-beads design, a yellowish-green padded skirt embroidered with coloured silk and gold thread, and a black satin coat lined with squirrel.

"These three garments which your mistress gave you are of good quality," acknowledged Hsi-feng with a smile. "But the coat's on the drab side. It's not warm enough either. You need one with thicker fur."

"The mistress gave me this squirrel, and the ermine too," Hsi-jen replied. "She promised to give me a fox-fur as well at New Year."

"Well, I have a fox-fur, but I don't care for the way the fringe hangs and was meaning to have it altered," said Hsi-feng. "You may as well have that for the time being. When the mistress orders a coat for you for New Year, I'll have it made for myself instead. That'll compensate me for the one I'm giving you."

Everybody present laughed.

"We know your way of talking, madam," they said. "You give with both hands the whole year round, privately giving away all sorts of things to make up for the presents that the mistress forgets. There's really no saying how much you've given. And you never charge the mistress for them, of course. Yet you talk in this stingy way to raise a laugh."

"How can the mistress remember all these things, which aren't important anyway?" Hsi-feng retorted. "But if no one saw to them, it would reflect badly on the family; and I'm quite willing to put my hand in my pocket to keep everyone decently dressed — for the sake of my *own* good name. I'm in charge of the household, after all, and if everyone here looked like scarecrows I'd be blamed for fitting you out in such a beggarly way."

This impressed them all. "No one else can hold a candle to you, madam," they said. "So considerate as you are to Her Ladyship, and kindness itself to those of us beneath you."

Ping-erh had been sent to fetch Hsi-jen the fox-fur-lined coat of slate-blue silk tapestry with eight circular designs which Hsi-feng had worn the previous day. Now, seeing that Hsi-jen's wrapper was of black and white silk gauze, lined with pink silk, and in it she had only two worn silk-padded jackets and one fur jacket, Hsi-feng told Ping-erh to bring her own jade-coloured velvet wrapper with a silk lining, as well as a cape for the snow. Ping-erh brought two capes, one of worn crimson felt, the other a rather newer one of red satin.

"One is already too much," Hsi-jen demurred.

"The felt's for you," chuckled Ping-erh. "I've brought the other at the same time to send to Miss Hsiu-yen. Yesterday, in that heavy snow, the others were all wearing felt, camlet or satin, and it was really a splendid sight — a dozen or so red capes against the snow. She was the only one in a shabby cape, all hunched up with cold, poor thing! So we'd better give her this."

"See the way she gives away my property!" cried Hsi-feng. "As if I'm not spending enough myself without her help. A fine thing!"

"It's *your* fault, madam, for being so dutiful to Her Ladyship and so good to us servants," they retorted, smiling. "If you were the stingy sort that hoards things up with no consideration for those below you, she wouldn't dare do such a thing."

"That's because she's the only one with some inkling of my character," rejoined Hsi-feng. She told Hsi-jen, "Let's hope your mother is better. If not, you'll just have to stay there; but send me word, and I'll have your bedding sent over. Don't use their bedding or combs." She turned to Mrs. Chou. "You all know our rules, of course. I don't have to remind you."

"We know, madam," replied Mrs. Chou. "When we get there, we'll ask the others to keep their distance. If we stay, we'll insist on a couple of inner rooms."

She went out then with Hsi-jen and ordered the servant-boys to light the lanterns. Mounting their carriages, they drove to Hua Chih-fang's house.

Meanwhile Hsi-feng had summoned two old nannies from Pao-yu's quarters.

"Hsi-jen probably won't be back today," she told them. "You know which of the older girls have most sense. Get a couple of them to keep watch at night in Pao-yu's rooms. You must see to things too. Don't let Pao-yu run wild."

The two nannies assented and left, returning presently to report:

"We've told Ching-wen and Sheh-yueh to attend Master Pao. The four of us will keep watch at night in turn."

Hsi-feng nodded.

"See that he goes to bed early and gets up early."

They promised to do this and went back to the Garden.

Before long Chou Jui's wife sent word that Hsi-jen's mother was dying, and Hsi-jen could not come back. Having reported this to Lady Wang, Hsi-feng sent to the Garden for Hsi-jen's bedding and dressing-case. Pao-yu looked on while Ching-wen and Sheh-yueh got these ready and sent them off. This done, the two maids changed their clothes for the night, and Ching-wen sat down on the big openwork bronze clothes-warmer over the brazier.

"Stop putting on such ladified airs," Sheh-yueh teased. "Do something, can't you!"

"I will after all the rest of you are gone," retorted Ching-wen. "So long as you're here, I mean to take it easy."

"I'll make the bed, dear sister, but you must let down the

cover over the mirror and hook back the clasp above — you're taller than I am." She then went to make Pao-yu's bed.

"I was just nicely warm and you had to disturb me!" Ching-wen gave a mock sigh.

Pao-yu had been sitting brooding, wondering whether Hsi-jen's mother would recover or not. Hearing this exchange between the girls, he got up and went out to cover the mirror and hook back the clasp himself.

"You can stay in the warm," he said as he came in again. "I've seen to everything."

"I can't toast myself here *all* the time," replied Ching-wen smiling. "That reminds me, I've not fetched your pewter bed-warmer."

"How thoughtful you suddenly are!" remarked Sheh-yueh. "He never uses a bed-warmer. And we shall be snugger here on the clothes-warmer than on the cold *kang* in the other room. There's no need for a bed-warmer today."

"If you both sleep on that clothes-warmer, I'll be all alone out here," objected Pao-yu. "I'd be too scared to get a wink of sleep."

"*I* mean to sleep here," declared Ching-wen. "You sleep in his room, Sheh-yueh."

By this time it was already the second watch. Sheh-yueh who had by this time drawn the curtains, removed the lamp and added incense to the burner, now helped Pao-yu to bed. Then the two girls slept too, Ching-wen on the clothes-warmer above the brazier, Sheh-yueh outside Pao-yu's alcove.

After the third watch had sounded, Pao-yu called Hsi-jen in his sleep. He called a couple of times but no one answered, and it dawned on him as he woke that she was away, at which he laughed at himself.

Ching-wen, awake too now, called to Sheh-yueh, "You really sleep like the dead! He's even woken me, over here; but you right next to him didn't hear a thing."

Sheh-yueh turned over, yawning.

"It was Hsi-jen he called. What's that to do with me?" She asked Pao-yu what he wanted.

He told her, "Some tea."

She got up at once then, wearing nothing over her night clothes but a padded red silk jacket.

"Slip on my fur before you go out to the other room," he advised. "You mustn't catch cold."

So she put on the warm sable jacket he used as a dressing-gown, then washed her hands in the basin and took Pao-yu a cup of warm water and a large rinse-bowl, so that he could rinse his mouth. Next she fetched a bowl from the cupboard, warmed it with hot water and half filled it with tea from the warm pot for him to drink. She then rinsed her own mouth and drank half a bowl of tea too.

"Bring me a drop too, dearie!" called Ching-wen.

"You're getting above yourself, aren't you?" Sheh-yueh retorted.

"Good sister, tomorrow night you needn't stir, and I'll dance attendance on you. How about that?"

Then Sheh-yueh gave her water to rinse her mouth and poured her half a bowl of tea.

"Don't go to sleep just yet, you two," she said. "You can have a chat while I slip out for a moment."

"Beware of the ghost out there waiting for you," teased Ching-wen.

"The moon's bright tonight," said Pao-yu, clearing his throat. "We'll be talking. Just run along."

Sheh-yueh opened the back door then and, raising the felt portière, found that it was indeed a bright moonlit night. As soon as she had gone, Ching-wen felt tempted to give her a scare for fun. As she was stronger than the other girls and did not feel the cold, she slipped quietly down from the clothes-warmer wearing nothing but a light tunic, and tiptoed after Sheh-yueh without putting on any wraps.

"Don't go out like that," warned Pao-yu. "It'll be no joke if you catch cold."

Ching-wen motioned to him to keep quiet and slipped out of the door. Once outside the room, however, a breath of wind chilled her to the bone and set her shivering.

"No wonder they say you shouldn't expose yourself to the wind when you're warm," she thought. "This cold really cuts like a knife."

Just then, before she had time to frighten Sheh-yueh, Pao-yu called loudly from inside, "Ching-wen's gone out!"

She turned back and went in again at once.

"Did you think I was going to scare her to death?" She giggled. "What a fuss-pot you are — a regular old woman!"

"That wasn't what worried me," Pao-yu explained. "For one thing, I didn't want you to catch cold. For another, if she'd been caught by surprise and screamed that might have woken the others; and instead of seeing the joke they'd accuse us of getting up to mischief as soon as Hsi-jen was away. Now, come and tuck in my bedding for me, will you?"

Ching-wen did so, putting her hands inside his quilt to warm them.

"Your hands are *icy*!" he exclaimed. "I warned you you'd catch cold."

He noticed that her cheeks were as red as rouge, and feeling them found them as cold as ice as well.

"Hop inside my quilt, quick, and warm up!" he urged.

That same instant the door was flung open. Sheh-yueh burst breathlessly in.

"Goodness me! I've had such a fright," she cried laughing. "I thought I saw someone crouching in the dark, behind the rocks. I was just going to scream when I realized it was only that big pheasant — it flapped out into the light at the sight of me, and then I saw it clearly. If I'd screamed, it would have woken all the others." Washing her hands then she remarked, "So Ching-wen's gone out, has she? How come I didn't see her? She must have been meaning to scare me."

"Here she is," chuckled Pao-yu. "Thawing out under my quilt. If I hadn't called out quickly, she'd have given you a fine fright."

"She didn't need *me* for that. The wretch took fright herself," retorted Ching-wen, returning to her own bed.

"Surely you didn't slip out like that, in that tight-fitting horse-thief's outfit?" asked Sheh-yueh.

"Oh yes, she did," said Pao-yu.

"You deserve to catch your death!" exclaimed Sheh-yueh. "What a day to choose! Why, just standing outside for a minute would chap your skin."

She took the copper guard off the brazier to shovel some ash over the glowing charcoal, then put in two slabs of incense before replacing the guard. After that, stepping behind the screen, she trimmed the lamp and lay down to sleep again.

Ching-wen, warm now after being chilled, gave a couple of sneezes.

"What did I tell you?" Pao-yu sighed. "Now you've caught cold."

"She complained of not feeling well this morning," Sheh-yueh told him. "And she hasn't eaten anything all day. Yet instead of taking proper care of herself she tries to scare me. If she's ill tomorrow it will serve her right."

"Do you have a fever?" asked Pao-yu.

"It's nothing." Ching-wen coughed. "I'm not all that delicate."

Just then the clock on the shelf in the outer room struck two. The old nanny on night duty outside coughed warningly.

"Go to sleep now, young ladies," she said. "There'll be plenty of time for chattering tomorrow."

"We'd better stop talking before they start to nag," whispered Pao-yu.

And so the three of them settled down to sleep.

The next morning, sure enough, Ching-wen woke feeling listless. Her nose was stopped up and her voice was hoarse.

"Let's say nothing about this," suggested Pao-yu. "If the mistress heard, she'd want you to go home and rest; and though you might enjoy being back with your people, it would be colder there. Better stay here. Just lie down in the inner room. I'll have a doctor fetched through the back gate and he can take a look at you on the quiet."

"That's all very well," said Ching-wen. "But at least let

Madam Chu know. Otherwise, how will you explain it when people ask what the doctor's doing here?"

Pao-yu saw sense in this and called in one of the old nannies.

"Go and tell Madam Chu that Ching-wen has a slight cold, nothing serious," he said. "But if she goes home to rest I'll have nobody here, as Hsi-jen's away just now. Ask her to send for a doctor and have him come here quietly through the back gate. There's no need to tell the mistress."

The nanny returned in due course to announce, "I've told Madam Chu. She says if a couple of doses will cure her, all right; otherwise she should be sent home. The weather now is treacherous. Infecting other people doesn't matter much, but we mustn't let the young ladies in the Garden catch anything."

Ching-wen heard this as she lay coughing in the alcove.

"She talks as if I had the plague!" she cried crossly. "Whom am I going to infect? All right, I'll leave this place. But after this none of you must ever complain, as long as you live, of so much as a headache!"

She started getting up.

"Don't be angry," begged Pao-yu, making her lie down again. "She's only doing her job, afraid the mistress may scold if she hears about this. She doesn't mean it seriously. You lose your temper far too easily, and of course being ill today makes you extra fractious."

Just then the doctor was announced. Pao-yu hid hurriedly behind a bookcase while a few matrons from the back gate ushered him in. The young maids had withdrawn, leaving three or four older women to let down the embroidered red curtains in front of the alcove, and Ching-wen put her hand out through the curtains. The doctor hastily averted his eyes at the sight of two nails a good two to three inches long, stained crimson with balsam; and at once an old nanny covered the hand with a handkerchief. After feeling the patient's pulse for a while, the doctor rose and withdrew to the outer room.

"The young lady is suffering from a cold aggravated by indigestion," he told the nannies. "The weather has been trying recently, and this is a mild attack of influenza. Luckily she is a young lady who normally eats and drinks with moderation, and the trouble isn't serious; but as she is rather delicate she has succumbed to a slight infection. A couple of doses of medicine will set her right." He then followed the matrons out again.

Since Li Wan had sent to order the attendants at the back gate and the maids in the various apartments to keep out of sight, the doctor could only feast his eyes on the Garden — not a single young woman did he see on his way out. Upon reaching the back gate, he sat down in the gatehouse used by the pages on duty to make out his prescription.

The old nannies asked him not to leave at once.

"Our young master is most particular," one of them explained. "He may want to ask you some questions."

"Young master!" exclaimed the doctor. "Wasn't that a young lady I examined just now? Surely it was a young lady's boudoir. And the curtains were let down too, so how can it have been a young gentleman?"

"Why, sir," chuckled the nanny, lowering her voice, "I see now why the boys told me they'd invited a new doctor. You don't know our family. That was our young master's room, and your patient was one of his maids, one of the more senior ones, true, but no young 'lady.' You wouldn't have gained admission so easily to one of our young ladies' boudoirs."

With that she took the prescription back to the Garden.

Pao-yu examined it and found it listed such herbs as *perilla, platycodon, siler* and *nepeta*, as well as *citrus trifoliata* and *ephedra*.

"Confound the fellow!" he swore. "He's prescribing for her just as he would for a man. How could she stand such strong medicine? Even if she had bad indigestion how could she take *citrus trifoliata* and *ephedra*? Who sent for this fellow? Get rid of him, quick, and fetch some doctor we know."

"How were we to know what his prescriptions would be like?" retorted the nanny. "We can easily send for Doctor Wang, but we'll have to pay for the hire of this other man's

sedan-chair, as we didn't send for him through the chief
steward."

"How much will it be?"

"It wouldn't look well to give too little," she answered.
"A family like ours, in such a case, should pay at least a tael."

"How much do we usually pay Doctor Wang?"

"Doctor Wang and Doctor Chang, who come so often, aren't
paid for each separate visit. Our rule is to give them a lump
sum at the chief festivals every year. Since this new man's
only coming this once, we should give him one tael."

Pao-yu then ordered Sheh-yueh to fetch some silver.

"I don't know where our Mistress Hsi-jen keeps it," she
answered laughingly.

"I often see her getting money from that small inlaid
cabinet," he told her. "I'll help you find it."

They went together into the storeroom and opened the
cabinet. The top compartment was full of brushes and sticks
of ink, fans, incense slabs, multi-coloured pouches, sashes and
the like. On the lower shelf lay a few strings of cash. But
upon opening one of the drawers, they discovered a small
wicker basket containing some silver ingots, as well as a balance
for weighing them with.

Sheh-yueh picked up the balance and one ingot of silver.

"Which is the one-tael mark?" she asked Pao-yu.

"Are you asking *me*?" he chuckled. "You should know
better."

She smiled too and started out to consult someone else.

"Just pick one of the biggest pieces," urged Pao-yu. "We're
not shopkeepers — why be so finicking?"

Setting down the balance, Sheh-yueh picked up another ingot
which she weighed in her hand.

"This is probably about one tael," she remarked. "We'd
better be on the generous side, so as not to have that poor devil
laughing at us. It would never occur to him that we don't
know how to use a balance. Instead, he'd call us misers."

The woman standing on the steps outside the door put in,
"That's half a five-tael bar, it must weigh at least two taels.

As you've nothing here to cut it with, you'd better put it away, miss, and pick something smaller."

By now, however, Sheh-yueh had closed the cabinet.

"I can't be bothered," she laughed. "If it's too much, you can pocket the difference yourself."

"Just go and fetch Doctor Wang here fast," ordered Pao-yu. The woman took the silver and went to do as she was told.

Before very long Ming-yen brought Doctor Wang, who first examined the patient then made a diagnosis very similar to the previous one. But instead of such ingredients as *citrus trifoliata* and *ephedra*, his prescription called for angelica, orange peel and white peony; moreover the dosage was smaller.

"*This* is more like medicine for girls," observed Pao-yu approvingly. "Although we want to drive out the cold, drastic methods are no good. Last year when I had a chill and a bilious attack, and Doctor Wang examined me, he said I couldn't take strong drugs like *ephedra*, *gypsum* and *citrus trifoliata*. When I compare myself with you girls, I'm like a big poplar scores of years old in the graveyard, while you're like that white begonia in bud which Chia Yun gave me last autumn — how can *you* take medicines too potent even for me?"

"Are poplars the only graveyard trees?" Sheh-yueh countered. "What about pines and cedars? Personally, I can't stand poplars. They have so few leaves for their size, and they keep up that maddening rustling even when there's not a breath of wind. How low-class to compare yourself to such a tree!"

"I wouldn't venture to compare myself with the pine or cedar," chuckled Pao-yu. "Even Confucius said, 'When winter comes, we realize that the pine and cedar are evergreen.' You see, they're so magnificent, only really thick-skinned people would compare themselves with *them*."

As they were chatting, a serving-woman brought in the drugs. Pao-yu ordered them to fetch the silver medicine-pot and brew the decoction over the brazier.

"Why not let the kitchen do it?" asked Ching-wen. "You don't want the whole place reeking of medicine, do you?"

"The smell of medicine is sweeter than any flower or fruit," asserted Pao-yu. "What could be finer than these herbs which immortals, as well as hermits and recluses, pick to decoct as medicine? I was thinking only just now that we lack nothing here except the fragrance of herbs; but now it will be perfect."

With that he had the medicine brewed. He also made Sheh-yueh prepare some things to send by an old nanny to Hsi-jen, with a message begging her not to grieve too much. After having seen to all this, he went to pay his respects to his grandmother and mother and to have his meal.

Just then Hsi-feng was saying to the Lady Dowager and Lady Wang, "Now that it's so cold and the days are shorter, wouldn't it be better for the girls to have their meals with my elder sister-in-law in the Garden? They can come here to eat again once it is warmer."

"That's a good idea," said Lady Wang. "Especially if there's a high wind or snow. Exposure to cold after eating isn't good; neither is breathing cold air on an empty stomach. Some maids are always on duty in those five large rooms inside the back gate of the Garden, and we can send two women from our kitchen there to cook for the girls. They can get their share of fresh vegetables and any money or things they need from the chief steward's office. And when we have game like pheasant or roebuck, we can send them a share."

"The idea did occur to me too," said the Lady Dowager. "But I was afraid it would mean more work, setting up another kitchen."

"It won't," Hsi-feng assured her. "They'll get their usual share. More in one place means less in another. And even if it causes a little more trouble, it will prevent the girls from being exposed to the cold. The others might stand it all right, but not Tai-yu, or even Cousin Pao for that matter. In fact, none of the girls is really strong."

"Quite so," approved the Lady Dowager. "I would have proposed this myself, but saw you were all so busy, even if you didn't complain of the extra work you might well feel that I only care about my younger grandchildren, with no consideration for those of you who run the household. I'm glad you suggested this."

It so happened that Aunt Hsueh and Aunt Li had called, while Lady Hsing and Madam Yu were still there paying their respects.

"I'm going to say something today which I've been keeping back for fear of giving Hsi-feng a swelled head or causing jealousy," the old lady told them. "All of you have been sisters-in-law yourselves, before and after your own marriages. So tell me — have you ever known a sister-in-law as thoughtful as she is?"

Aunt Hsueh, Aunt Li and Madam Yu agreed.

"She's one in a thousand!" they said. "Other young married women do no more than politeness requires, whereas she has genuine feeling for her husband's younger relatives and is truly dutiful to you as well, madam."

The Lady Dowager nodded.

"But fond as I am of her, I'm afraid she may be too clever for her own good," she sighed.

"You're wrong there, Old Ancestress," laughed Hsi-feng. "It's said that the cleverest people don't live long. It's all right for everyone else to say that and believe it. But you're the last person who should subscribe to that. Our Old Ancestress is at least ten times more intelligent than I am, and since *you're* enjoying both good fortune and long life, I ought to do even better. I may live to be a thousand, not dying until our Old Ancestress has ascended to the Western Paradise."

"What fun would that be, pray?" the Lady Dowager parried. "Everybody else dead and only we two old hags left?"

The whole party burst out laughing at this retort.

What followed is related in the next chapter.

CHAPTER 52

Tactful Ping-erh Conceals the Theft of Her Gold Bracelet
Plucky Ching-wen Mends a Peacock-Feather Cape in Bed

After the rest had left, Pao-chai and the other girls dined with the old lady. The meal at an end, Pao-yu went back first to the Garden as he had Ching-wen on his mind. His rooms were filled with the pungent scent of herbs and Ching-wen was lying all alone on the *kang,* her face flushed with fever, her forehead hot to his touch. After hastily warming his hands over the brazier, he felt her body beneath the quilt and found it burning too.

"I don't mind the others going off," he said, "but how could Sheh-yueh and Chiu-wen have the heart to leave you?"

"I made Chiu-wen go for her meal, and just now Ping-erh called Sheh-yueh out to have a word with her. Goodness knows what they're being so secretive about — my staying here although I'm ill, I suppose."

"Ping-erh's not like that," he assured her. "Besides, she'd no idea you were ill. She must have come to talk to Sheh-yueh about something else and, happening to find you in bed, said she'd come to ask after you. That's only common politeness. If any trouble comes of your staying here, it has nothing to do with her. And the two of you normally get on so well, she'd never risk spoiling your friendship over something that is no concern of hers."

"You're probably right," agreed Ching-wen. "But why are they suddenly hiding something from me?"

"I'll slip out by the back door and listen outside the window, then let you know what it's all about," he told her with a grin.

He did in fact go out to eavesdrop and heard Sheh-yueh ask softly, "How did you recover it?"

"When I missed it that day after washing my hands, my mistress told me not to make a fuss," replied Ping-erh. "Once out of the Garden, however, she ordered the matrons in all the Garden apartments to investigate carefully. It was Miss Hsiu-yen's maid whom we suspected. We thought that, being poor and never having seen such things before, the child might have picked it up. We never dreamed it would turn out to be one of *your* girls. Luckily Madam Lien was out when Mrs. Sung brought the bracelet back to me saying she'd seen young Chui-erh take it, and she'd come to report it to Madam Lien. I was very glad to get my bracelet back.

"I couldn't help thinking then how considerate Pao-yu is to you girls, and how proud of you as well. Yet two years ago Liang-erh stole a piece of jade, which is still making idle tongues wag, and now another of your girls has stolen a gold bracelet — from one of his neighbours, too! It's a shame that Pao-yu of all people should be disgraced by his own maids in this way. So I hurriedly asked Mrs. Sung on no account to tell him but just to forget it, and to say nothing to *anyone* about it. For if this came to the ears of the old lady and Lady Wang, how angry they'd be! It would reflect badly on Hsi-jen and the rest of you as well.

"So I simply told Madam Lien that the clasp of my bracelet was loose and so I'd dropped it in the grass on the way to Madam Chu's place, when the snow was too deep to find it. Today after the snow had melted and it lay glinting in the sun, I picked it up where I'd dropped it. And she took my word for it. The reason I'm telling you this is so that you'll take precautions in future and not send Chui-erh out on any errands. When Hsi-jen comes back, you can talk it over with her and cook up some excuse for dismissing the girl."

"It's not as if the little bitch hadn't seen plenty of things of that sort," exclaimed Sheh-yueh. "Why did she have to steal it?"

"There's not too much gold in that bracelet, though the pearl on it is a good size," remarked Ping-erh. "It's one that

Madam Lien gave me. She called it her 'shrimp-beard bracelet.'
I haven't told Ching-wen because she's as hot-tempered as
crackling charcoal. She'd be bound to flare up and start
beating or cursing the girl; then the whole story would get out.
That's why I'm just warning *you* to be on your guard." This
said she took her leave.

Pao-yu had overheard this with mixed feelings: pleasure at
Ping-erh's consideration for him, anger at Chui-erh's dishonesty,
and regret that such an intelligent girl should do something so
underhand.

He went back to Ching-wen and told her all that Ping-erh
had said, concluding, "She didn't want you to know till you
were better, because you take things so much to heart that this
news might make your illness worse."

Indeed, Ching-wen's eyebrows had shot up and her eyes were
round with rage. She wanted to summon Chui-erh then and
there.

"All Ping-erh's consideration for us would be wasted if you
make a scene," he warned. "As she's been so thoughtful, let's
do as she suggested and get rid of Chui-erh later."

"It's all very well for you to talk," cried Ching-wen. "But
I can't stand it — I'm so angry!"

"It's not worth flaring up about. Just concentrate on getting better."

Ching-wen took some medicine then and that evening had
the second infusion. She sweated a little that night, but not
enough, and awoke the next morning with a fever, headache,
a stopped-up nose and sore throat. Doctor Wang called again
and made certain alterations in the prescription; but although
her temperature went down a little, her head continued to ache.

"Bring her some snuff," Pao-yu told Sheh-yueh. "She'll feel
better after a few good sneezes."

Sheh-yueh accordingly brought him a small flat, golden-
starred glass case with gilt double-catches, and Pao-yu opened
it. Inside the lid, in Western enamel, was a picture of a naked
girl with yellow hair and fleshy wings. The case contained

some genuine *Wangchia* foreign snuff; but instead of taking it, Ching-wen just pored over the picture.

"Do hurry up and take some," Pao-yu urged her. "It's not good to expose snuff to the air too long."

She promptly dipped one finger-nail into the snuff, put it to her nose and inhaled. As she felt no effect, she tried a larger amount. At once her nose tingled and the smarting spread right up to her cranium. She sneezed so violently, five or six times in succession, that her nose and eyes started to run.

"My, that's better!" she exclaimed, closing the case. "Fetch me some paper, quick."

One of the younger maids had a stack of fine soft paper ready, and Ching-wen took sheet after sheet to blow her nose.

"Well, how's that?" asked Pao-yu.

"Better. But my temples still ache."

"We may as well try some other Western medicine to set that right too." He told Sheh-yueh, "Go and ask the Second Mistress for some of that Western ointment she keeps for headaches. *Yi-fu-na*, it's called."

Sheh-yueh assented and went off to Hsi-feng's apartments, returning after a while with some of the ointment. She then fetched a scrap of red satin from which she cut out two round patches, each the size of her finger-tip. Having heated the ointment, she spread it on with a hairpin. Ching-wen picked up a hand-mirror and stuck the patches on her temples herself.

"You were lying there like a tousled ghost," teased Sheh-yueh. "Now with these patches you look rather pretty! We're so used to the Second Mistress wearing these that we hardly notice them on her."

She turned to Pao-yu. "Madam Lien says tomorrow is your Uncle Wang's birthday, and the mistress wants you to go and pay your respects. What will you wear? We'd better get your clothes ready tonight, to save trouble tomorrow morning."

"I'll wear whatever's handy," Pao-yu answered. "I can't keep track of these endless birthdays all the year round."

With that he got up and went out, intending to go and watch

Hsi-chun painting. Just outside his compound, however, he saw Pao-chin's little maid Hsiao-luo passing by not far away. Overtaking her, he asked where she was going.

"Our two young ladies are with Miss Tai-yu," she told him. "I'm on my way there too."

So he changed his mind and went with her to Bamboo Lodge. There, sitting round the brazier and chatting with Tai-yu, he found not only Pao-chai and Pao-chin but Hsiu-yen as well, while Tzu-chuan was sewing in the warm alcove by the window.

"Here comes another!" they cried at sight of him. "There's no place left for you."

"What a delightful picture!" laughed Pao-yu. " 'Beauties in a Winter Chamber!' Too bad I didn't come a bit earlier. Still, this is the warmest room there is and I shan't be cold on this chair."

He seated himself on Tai-yu's favourite chair which was covered with a squirrel-fur rug. And his eye fell on a rectangular marble jardinière in the alcove in which were arranged some single-petalled narcissi and rocks.

"What lovely flowers!" he exclaimed. "The warmer the room, the stronger their scent. How is it I didn't notice them yesterday?"

Tai-yu told him, "The wife of your chief steward Lai Ta sent Pao-chin two pots of winter-plum and two of narcissi. Pao-chin gave me one pot of narcissi and Tan-chun one of winter-plum. I only took it to show my appreciation of her kindness. If you like it, you can have it."

"I've two pots actually in my room, only they're not as good as this," he replied. "How can you possibly give away a present from Cousin Pao-chin?"

"I've medicine simmering on the stove all day; in fact, I practically live on medicine," she countered. "How can I stand the scent of flowers as well? It's too enervating. Besides, the pungent aroma of medicine here spoils the fragrance of the flowers. You'd better take these narcissi to your place where their pure perfume won't get mixed up with other odours."

"How do you know?" he demanded laughingly. "I've a patient taking medicine in my place too now."

"That's a strange way to talk," she retorted. "As if I was hinting at something. How should *I* know what's happening in your apartments? You should have come earlier to listen to our stories, instead of turning up now and raising such a rumpus."

"We've a subject now for the next meeting of our club," declared Pao-yu. "We can write on the narcissus and winter-plum."

"Not I!" cried Tai-yu. "No more versifying for me. One only gets penalized each time, and that's too shameful." She covered her face with her hands.

"Now then!" laughed Pao-yu. "Why make fun of me again? If even *I* don't feel ashamed why should *you* hide your face?"

"Next time I'll call a meeting," announced Pao-chai. "Each of you will have to produce four pentasyllabic *shih* and four *tzu* on different themes. The first *shih* of couplets will be on *The Diagram of the Supreme Ultimate*,[1] and all the words that rhyme with *hsien* will have to be used — not one must be left out."

"You obviously don't really want to invite us, cousin, or you wouldn't make things so difficult," chuckled Pao-chin. "Of course, if one tried, one could manage by filling up the lines with phrases from the *Book of Change* — but where's the fun in that? When I was eight, my father took me to the coast of the western sea to buy foreign goods, and there we saw a girl from the land of Chenchen, who had just turned fifteen, with a face like those beauties in Western paintings. Her long golden hair was plaited, and in it she wore precious stones like coral, amber, cat's-eye and emerald. She had on golden chain-mail and a jacket of foreign brocade, and she carried a Japanese sword inlaid with gold and studded with gems — in fact, she was even lovelier than those beauties in the paintings. It was

---

[1] An exposition of the ancient *Book of Change* by Chou Tun-yi of the Northern Sung Dynasty (960-1127).

said that she was versed in our Chinese classics and could expound the *Five Canons* and write poems; so my father asked, through an interpreter, to see one of her poems written in her own hand."

They all marvelled at this story.

Pao-yu pleaded, "Good cousin, do let me have a look at that poem!"

"I left it in Nanking," said Pao-chin. "I can't lay my hands on it at a moment's notice."

Pao-yu, most disappointed, sighed at not having the luck to see it.

"Don't try to fool us!" chuckled Tai-yu, tugging at Pao-chin's sleeve. "I know you wouldn't leave such things behind. You'd naturally bring them all along. *They* may be taken in by your fib, but not I."

Pao-chin smiled and blushingly lowered her head in silence.

"Trust Tai-yu to say such a thing," put in Pao-chai. "You can't outsmart her."

"If you've brought it, do let us profit by seeing it," urged Tai-yu.

"They've a whole pile of cases and baskets not yet sorted out," explained Pao-chai. "Who knows which one it's in? Just wait until everything's properly unpacked, then she'll let everyone see it." She turned to Pao-chin. "Don't you know it by heart? Do recite it."

"I remember a pentasyllabic regular verse she wrote," said Pao-chin. "It wasn't bad at all for a foreigner."

"Wait a bit," interposed Pao-chai. "Let's get Hsiang-yun here to hear it too." She called Hsiao-luo and told her, "Go to our apartments and tell our mad poetess that we have a foreign beauty here who writes good poems. And tell her to bring the other poetry maniac to see her too."

Hsiao-luo went off on this errand with a smile.

After a while they heard Hsiang-yun demanding merrily, "Where is this foreign beauty?" And in she came with Hsiang-ling.

They teased, "Before you see her, you hear her voice."

Pao-chin and the others hurriedly offered them seats and told them what had been said.

"Hurry up and let us hear the poem," begged Hsiang-yun. Then Pao-chin recited:

> Last night I dreamed in a vermilion mansion,
> Today my songs rise by the sea:
> Clouds from the islands make a haze over the ocean,
> Mist from the hills links the forests' greenery;
> To the moon, past and present are one;
> Men's passions, inconstant, are no counterpart.
> As spring pervades south China,
> How can I but take this to heart?

"Not bad at all!" was the verdict. "Better, in fact, than some Chinese could write."

As they were speaking Sheh-yueh came in to announce, "The mistress has sent to tell Master Pao to call on his uncle first thing tomorrow morning. She wants him to explain that she's not well enough to go herself."

Pao-yu, who had risen to accept these instructions, asked Pao-chai and Pao-chin if they would be going too.

"No," said Pao-chai. "We just sent presents yesterday."

After a little further chat they dispersed.

Pao-yu had told his cousins to go on ahead, leaving him to follow, but now Tai-yu asked him:

"When will Hsi-jen be back?"

"Not until after the funeral, of course," he answered.

Tai-yu had more to say but hesitated, lost in thought for a while.

"Well, go along now," she said finally.

Pao-yu, too, had much in his heart to say but did not know how to put it into words. After a thoughtful pause he rejoined, "We can talk again tomorrow."

He walked down the steps with lowered head, turning back suddenly to ask, "Are you coughing much, now that the nights are longer? How often do you wake?"

"I had a good night yesterday, with only two fits of coughing But I only managed to sleep through the fourth watch — afte that I couldn't get back to sleep again."

"I've just remembered something important." Drawing closer to her he whispered, "I think that bird's-nest Pao-chai gave you. . . ."

He was cut short by the arrival of Concubine Chao, come to ask after Tai-yu's health.

Tai-yu knew that she had only called out of politeness on her way back from Tan-chun's apartments. She made her sit down and remarked, "It was considerate of you to come out on such a cold day."

She ordered tea, glancing at Pao-yu as she did so. Taking the hint, he left to join his mother for dinner, and was there reminded to make an early start the next day. Upon his return to Happy Red Court he saw to it that Ching-wen took her medicine and slept in the warmth inside the alcove, while he remained outside. The brazier was moved closer to the alcove, and Sheh-yueh slept on the clothes-warmer. They passed a quiet night.

The next morning Ching-wen woke Sheh-yueh before it was light.

"Get up!" she called. "You never seem to have had enough sleep! Go and get them to make some tea while I wake him up."

Sheh-yueh scrambled into her clothes.

"Let's get him up and dressed first, and move away this clothes-warmer before we call the others," she proposed. "The nurses said he wasn't to sleep in this room for fear of infection. If we let them see us all crowded together in here, they'll start nagging again."

"Just what I think," agreed Ching-wen.

Pao-yu woke up himself as they were about to rouse him. He got up and dressed without delay while Sheh-yueh called in some young maids to tidy the room. Only when this was done were Chiu-wen and Tan-yun summoned to wait on Pao-yu.

As he finished his toilet Sheh-yueh said, "It's cloudy again and looks like snow, you'd better wear something woollen."

He nodded and changed his clothes, then sipped a little of the lotus-seed and date broth a young maid offered him on a small tray, and took a piece of crystallized ginger from the plate Sheh-yueh brought him. Finally, having urged Ching-wen to look after herself, he went to the Lady Dowager's apartments.

His grandmother was still abed, but hearing that Pao-yu was going out she had him admitted to her bedroom, where he saw Pao-chin lying asleep behind her, her face to the wall.

The Lady Dowager noticed that Pao-yu was wearing, over his brown velvet archer's coat lined with fox fur, a scarlet felt jacket embroidered with gold thread. Its slate-blue satin border was fringed with tassels.

"Is it snowing?" she asked him.

"Not yet, but it looks as if it will," he replied.

"Bring him that peacock-feather cape taken out yesterday," the old lady ordered Yuan-yang.

The maid promptly brought in a cape which shimmered gold, green and blue and was no less magnificent, in a different style, than Pao-chin's cape of wild-duck down.

"This is called 'golden peacock felt,'" his grandmother told him with a smile. "It was woven of peacock feathers in Russia. The other day I gave your cousin one of wild-duck down, so now I'm making you a present of this."

Pao-yu kowtowed his thanks and put on the cape.

"Mind you show it to your mother before you go out," the Lady Dowager charged him with a smile.

He agreed to this and, going out, saw Yuan-yang standing in the passage rubbing her eyes. Since the day on which she had vowed never to marry, she had upset him by ignoring him. At sight of him now she started to slip away, but he stepped forward to greet her.

"Look, dear sister! How does this suit me?"

She flung away from him into the old lady's room.

Pao-yu had to go on then to show the cape to his mother, after which he returned to the Garden and displayed it to Ching-wen and Sheh-yueh. He went back then to the Lady Dowager.

"Mother's seen it and thinks it a pity to wear it," he said. "She told me to be extra careful not to spoil it."

"It's the only one left," replied his grandmother. "If you spoil it, you won't get another. Impossible to replace it." She warned him not to drink too much and to come back early, which he promised to do.

Some old nurses followed him to the main hall where six stewards — Nanny Li's son Li Kuei, Wang Yung, Chang Jo-chin, Chao Yi-hua, Chien Chi and Chou Jui — were waiting for him. With them were his four pages Ming-yen, Pan-heh, Chu-yao and Shao-hung, who were carrying a change of clothes for him and a cushion. A splendidly caparisoned white horse with an embossed saddle stood there in readiness too. When the stewards had received the old nurses' instructions, acting as grooms they helped Pao-yu to mount slowly into the saddle. Then Li Kuei and Wang Yung took the bridle, Chien Chi and Chou Jui led the way, and Chang Jo-chin and Chao Yi-hua followed close behind, one on each side of Pao-yu.

"Let's leave by the side gate, brothers," called Pao-yu to Chou Jui and Chien Chi. "Then I won't have to dismount by my father's study."

"There's no need for that," replied Chou Jui, turning his head with a smile. "His Lordship is away and the place is locked."

"Even so, I still ought to get down," insisted Pao-yu.

"Quite right, sir," chuckled Chien Chi and Li Kuei. "If you were too lazy to dismount and we happened to run into Mr. Lai or Mr. Lin, even if they didn't lecture *you* they'd have something to say about it. And all the blame would be laid on us for not teaching you better manners."

So Chou Jui and Chien Chi led the horse to the side gate. And, sure enough, as they were talking they ran into Lai Ta. Pao-yu promptly pulled up to dismount, but the chief steward hurried forward and clasped his knee. Pao-yu stood up in his stirrups and, taking him by the hand, exchanged greetings with him. Then a page came in at the head of a couple of dozen men with brooms and dustpans. These lined up respectfully by the wall at the sight of their young master, while the page knelt on one knee and paid his respects. Pao-yu, not knowing his name, simply smiled and nodded. Not until he had ridden past did the men move on.

Then Pao-yu and his party passed through the side gate, where some grooms and the boys under the six stewards had some dozen horses ready. Once outside the gate, Li Kuei and the rest mounted these horses. Then the whole troop, escorting Pao-yu on all sides, galloped off.

But let us return to Ching-wen, who was worried because the medicine had done her no good and now started abusing the doctor.

"He's nothing but a swindler and quack," she complained. "His medicine's no use at all."

"You must have patience," urged Sheh-yueh. "Haven't you heard the saying: 'Illness comes as fast as a wall falling down, but goes as slowly as unravelling a cocoon'? He's no Lao Tzu[1] with a magic elixir to cure you overnight. Just rest quietly for a few days and you'll be all right. The more impatient you are, the worse for you."

Ching-wen switched then to lashing out at the younger girls.

"Where have they all buried themselves?" she scolded. "They take advantage of my illness to make off, bold as brass! I'm going to flay each one of them for this when I'm better."

This so frightened Chuan-erh, one of the younger maids, that she hurried in to ask, "Is there anything you want, miss?"

"Are the others all dead?" demanded Ching-wen. "Are you the only one left?"

At this, Chui-erh sidled in.

"Look at that little bitch!" cried Ching-wen. "She won't come unless asked for. But on pay-day or when sweets are shared out, she's always the first to come running. Come over here! Am I a tiger? Are you afraid I'll eat you?"

Chui-erh had to come closer. Then Ching-wen, lunging

---

[1] According to *Pilgrimage to the West*, a 16th-century novel by Wu Cheng-en, the founder of Taoism Lao Tzu became an immortal after his death and distilled elixirs in the Celestial Region.

forward, grabbed one of her hands and began jabbing it with a hairpin from under her pillow.

"What use is this claw?" she swore. "It won't hold a needle or thread, all it's good for is stealing. You with your avid eyes and itching palms, you're the bane of our lives and a disgrace to us all — I'll carve you up!"

Chui-erh screamed with pain until Sheh-yueh pulled her away and made Ching-wen lie down again.

"You'll catch your death after that sweat you were in," she scolded. "Once you're better you can beat her as much as you like. Why raise this rumpus now?"

But Ching-wen ordered someone to fetch Nanny Sung and when she arrived informed her, "Master Pao has told me to tell you that Chui-erh's too lazy. When he gives her a job to do she refuses to stir; and when Hsi-jen asks her to do anything, she even curses her behind her back. She must be sent packing today, and tomorrow he'll report it himself to the mistress."

Nanny Sung knew at once that this was because of the bracelet.

"Even so," she said with a smile, "we'd better wait till Miss Hsi-jen comes back before dismissing her."

"Master Pao was most emphatic," insisted Ching-wen. "Never mind about this 'Miss' or that 'Miss,' we'll answer to her. Just do as I say. Tell her family to come and take her away."

"You may as well," put in Sheh-yueh. "She'll have to go sooner or later. The sooner she goes, the sooner we'll have some peace."

So Nanny Sung had to fetch Chui-erh's mother. And when they had packed up her things, the woman came in to see Ching-wen and Sheh-yueh.

"What's this I hear?" she protested. "If my girl misbehaves, why can't you teach her a lesson instead of throwing her out? At least leave us a little face."

"Save that talk for Pao-yu," snapped Ching-wen. "This has nothing to do with us."

"Ask *him*?" The woman snorted. "He does just what you

young ladies tell him, doesn't he? Even if *he* were willing to keep her, you wouldn't let him. Why, just now, even though you were talking behind his back, you referred to him by name. That may be all right for the likes of *you*, but in our case it would be thought most ill-bred."

"So I called him by his name, did I?" Ching-wen flushed with anger. "All right, go and report me to the old lady. Tell her I've run wild and have me thrown out too."

"Just take your daughter and go, sister," put in Sheh-yueh. "You can have your say about it some other time. This is no place for you to bicker and wrangle. Have you ever seen anyone wrangling with us here? Even Mrs. Lai and Mrs. Lin have to treat us with some respect, not to say you.

"As for using his name, we've done that since he was a child, as well you know, on the old lady's orders. Didn't they have his name written out and posted up everywhere so that everybody would use it, for fear that otherwise he might die young? Why, even water-carriers, night-soil collectors and beggars use it, not to say us. Only the other day, Mrs. Lin was taken to task by the old lady for calling him 'young master.' That's the first point.

"The second is that since we're always in and out reporting things to the old lady and the mistress, we obviously can't refer to him as 'master.' We must use the name Pao-yu a couple of hundred times a day; so it's strange that you should choose this to pick fault. Some day when you have time, you can listen to us using his name to the old lady and Lady Wang; then you'll understand. But of course, it's not to be wondered at that you don't know the rules in the inner apartments, since you don't have any important business that would take you near the ladies of the house — you're mucking about outside the gate all the time.

"And this is no place for you to hang about. If you do, people will be coming to ask you the reason, even if *we* don't say anything ourselves. So first take your girl away. If you're not satisfied, you can complain to Mrs. Lin and ask her to speak to Master Pao about it. There are nearly a thousand people in this household. If you come one day and others the next, how are we to recognize who's who? We can't have everyone running in and out here."

She ordered one of the young maids to fetch a cloth and wipe the floor.

Chui-erh's mother was silenced then and dared stay no longer. Swallowing her anger, she started out with her daughter.

"You really have no manners," expostulated Nanny Sung. "After working here all this time, your daughter should surely kowtow to the young ladies before she leaves. Presents they don't expect, but she should at least kowtow to express her thanks. How can you just walk off?"

At this, Chui-erh had to come in again and kowtow to Sheh-yueh and Ching-wen, then to Chiu-wen and the others. They all ignored her. Her mother, thoroughly discomfited and too cowed to say another word, went off in high indignation.

Ching-wen had caught another slight chill, and this on top of her anger made her feel even more poorly. She tossed about restlessly and did not quiet down until lighting-up time when Pao-yu came back, sighing and stamping his feet. Sheh-yueh asked him what was the matter.

"Today the old lady was in a good mood and gave me this cape," he explained. "But somehow I carelessly burned a hole in the back. Luckily it was too dark just now for my grandmother or mother to notice it."

He took the cape off and Sheh-yueh inspected the damage. There was a hole the size of a finger-tip.

"This must have been done by a spark from a hand-stove," she commented. "It's nothing. We'll smuggle it out at once for some skilled weaver to patch." She wrapped up the cape and told an old serving-woman to take it out. "See that it's done by tomorrow morning," she ordered. "And be sure not to let the old lady or mistress know."

The woman assented and went off, returning some time later with the cape.

"I tried not only weavers and the best tailors but embroiderers and sewing-women too," she said. "But as they'd never seen anything like this before, none of them dared take on the job."

"What's to be done then?" wondered Sheh-yueh. "I suppose you needn't wear it tomorrow."

"Tomorrow is the birthday proper," objected Pao-yu. "The old lady and my mother expressly told me to wear it when I go. But the day before I burn it. What a bad show!"

Ching-wen, who had been following the conversation, could no longer keep silence and now sat up in bed.

"Let me see it," she called. "Maybe it's not in your stars to wear this cape. Look at the state you're in."

"You're right," said Pao-yu, smiling.

He handed the cape to Ching-wen and took her the lamp.

"This is made of peacock feathers and gold thread," she observed after examining it carefully. "If we darn it with the same material it should pass."

"We've peacock feathers and thread," said Sheh-yueh. "But you're the only one here who can do that type of darning."

"There's no help for it then but to try my best, I suppose."

"How can you?" Pao-yu demurred. "You mustn't start working the moment you're a bit better."

"Don't fuss," she retorted. "*I* know what I can do."

With that she sat up to knot up her hair and put on some clothes. At once she felt so dizzy that stars began dancing before her eyes and she was afraid she would collapse; but rather than worry Pao-yu by giving up, she gritted her teeth and stuck it out. Having asked Sheh-yueh to help by twisting the thread, she now took one and compared it with the cape.

"It's not quite the same," she remarked. "Once it's mended, though, the difference shouldn't show."

"That's splendid," said Pao-yu. "Where would we find a Russian tailor?"

Ching-wen first unpicked the lining and slipped a bamboo embroidery-frame the size of a teacup up the back of the cape. Next she scraped away the singed edges with a knife, sewed two threads across at right angles to each other, stitched in the outline in cross-stitch, and then darned the hole to reproduce the original pattern. After a couple of stitches she would stop to examine her work, and after every four or five, feeling dizzy, breathless and faint, she would sink back on her pillow to rest for a while. Pao-yu hovered over her solicitously, offering her hot water, urging her to rest, putting a squirrel cape over her shoulders and sending for a pillow for her back, until she became quite frantic.

"Do go to bed, little ancestor!" she begged him. "If you stay up half the night again, you'll have sunken eyes tomorrow, and that wouldn't do!"

To soothe her he had to lie down, but he could not sleep. He heard the clock strike four just as she finished her task and was fluffing up the down with a small toothbrush.

"That's fine!" exclaimed Sheh-yueh. "If you don't look closely you'd never notice it."

Pao-yu asked to see it too.

"It's really as good as new," he commented.

Coughing after her exertions, Ching-wen said, "I'm afraid the mend still shows. But I can't do any more." She sank back with a groan of exhaustion.

If you want to know the outcome, read the next chapter.

CHAPTER 53

Ancestral Sacrifice Is Carried Out
on New Year's Eve in the Ning Mansion
An Evening Banquet Is Held on the Feast
of Lanterns in the Jung Mansion

Seeing that mending his peacock-feather cape had left Ching-wen exhausted, Pao-yu called a young maid to massage her; and barely had they rested for the time it takes for one meal before the day was light. Then Pao-yu, instead of going out, ordered the doctor to be sent for at once.

Presently Doctor Wang arrived and felt his patient's pulse.

"She was on the mend yesterday — what has caused this relapse today?" he asked in surprise. "Has she been over-eating or tiring herself? Her influenza is better; but after sweating she hasn't had a proper rest. The consequences may be serious."

He withdrew to make out a prescription, then brought it in, and Pao-yu saw that it called for fewer drugs to counteract noxious contagions but more tonics such as *pachyma cocos*, *rehmannia* and angelica.

Pao-yu ordered this medicine to be prepared at once.

"What's to be done?" he sighed. "If anything happens to her, it will all be my fault."

"Run along and mind your own business, young master," scoffed Ching-wen from her pillow. "Is it so easy to fall into a decline?"

Pao-yu had to leave her then. But he returned during the afternoon on the pretext of not feeling well. Although Ching-wen's illness was by no means light, luckily, though hard-working she was not the worrying type, and instead of over-eating she normally kept to a simple diet. The Chia family's cure for a cold or cough, among masters and servants

193

alike, consisted mainly of fasting supplemented by medication. Thus as soon as Ching-wen fell ill she had fasted for a couple of days and been careful to take her medicine, with the result that in spite of her exertions a few days of extra treatment set her right. And because all the girls in the Garden were eating at home now, catering for a patient was simple as Pao-yu could easily ask for soup and gruel. But enough of this.

Upon Hsi-jen's return after her mother's funeral, Sheh-yueh told her in detail of Ping-erh's visit, the part played by Nanny Sung, the reason for Chui-erh's dismissal by Ching-wen and the fact that this had been reported to Pao-yu.

Hsi-jen's only comment was, "You were rather too hasty."

These days Li Wan also had a cold on account of the bad weather; Ying-chun and Hsiu-yen were fully occupied attending to Lady Hsing, who was suffering from an inflammation of the eyes; Aunt Li and her two daughters had been invited by her younger brother to his home for a few days; and Pao-yu was worried by Hsi-jen's depression after her mother's death, as well as by Ching-wen's delayed recovery. So no one was in the mood for poetry gatherings, and several of the appointed dates passed unobserved.

It was now the twelfth month. As New Year was fast approaching, Lady Wang and Hsi-feng had their hands full with preparations. Wang Tzu-teng was promoted at this time to be Chief Inspector of Nine Provinces, and Chia Yu-tsun to the post of Minister of War, to assist with military strategy and advise on state policy. But no more of this.

Over in the Ning Mansion Chia Chen had the Ancestral Temple opened and swept, the sacrificial vessels prepared, the ancestral tablets put in place, and the north hall cleaned in readiness for displaying the ancestral portraits. High and low alike in both mansions were kept hard at work.

One morning in the Ning Mansion, Madam Yu and her daughter-in-law were preparing embroidery and other gifts for those in the other mansion when a maid came in with a trayful of gold New-Year ingots.

"Hsing-erh reports that that packet of loose gold of a mixed quality the other day amounted to a hundred and fifty-three taels and sixty-seven cents, madam," she announced. "It's made two hundred and twenty ingots in all."

She presented them for inspection and her mistress saw that they were of different shapes: plum-blossom, crab-apple-blossom, a writing-brush and an ellipsoid signifying "All Wishes Granted," and "The Eight Treasures of Spring."

Having ordered these to be put away, Madam Yu sent to tell Hsing-erh to hand in the silver ingots without delay. The maid had not been gone long on this errand when Chia Chen came in for his meal, and his daughter-in-law slipped away.

Chia Chen asked his wife, "Have we fetched the Imperial Bounty yet for the spring sacrifice?"

"I sent Jung for it today," was her reply.

"Of course, our family doesn't depend on these few taels," observed her husband. "Still they are a mark of the Imperial favour. We should collect this silver early to show the old lady in the other mansion before using it to prepare the ancestral sacrifice; for this is evidence that we are honoured by the Emperor's favour and benefit from the good fortune of our forbears. Even if we spent ten thousand taels on this sacrifice, it would convey less distinction than the use of this bounty so graciously conferred. Indeed, apart from one or two houses like ours, most poor families of hereditary officials have to rely on this silver for their New-Year sacrifice. Such consideration is truly a sign of the infinite graciousness of the Emperor."

"Exactly what I feel," agreed his wife.

Just then a servant announced their son's return, and Chia Chen ordered him to be admitted. Chia Jung came in, carrying in both hands a small yellow bag.

"Why have you been so long?" demanded his father.

Chia Jung answered with a smile, "I had to go to the Office of Imperial Banquets for the bounty, as it isn't issued by the

Ministry of Rites nowadays. All in that office asked after you, sir, and said they hadn't seen you for a long time but were constantly thinking of you."

"It's not me they're thinking of," laughed his father. "Now that New Year's coming, it's presents they want from me or an invitation to a banquet and opera."

While speaking he examined the yellow bag, which was stamped with the four-word inscription: "Eternal Imperial Favour Granted" and the seal of the Sacrificial Department of the Ministry of Rites. In smaller characters was written: "Two gratuities for the Spring Sacrifice are conferred by the Emperor in perpetuity upon Chia Yen, Duke of Ningkuo, and Chia Yuan, Duke of Jungkuo." The amount and date were specified, together with the name of the recipient Chia Jung, Captain of the Imperial Guard Reserve, while the officer in charge had signed his name in vermilion.

After his meal, Chia Chen washed and rinsed his mouth, then put on his boots and hat to go, accompanied by his son with the silver, to inform the Lady Dowager and Lady Wang and after them Chia Sheh and Lady Hsing that the bounty had been collected. This done, he returned home and took out the silver, ordering the bag to be burned in the large incense-burner in the Ancestral Temple.

After this he told his son, "Go and ask your Second Aunt whether they've fixed on dates or not for their New-Year feasts in the first month. If they have, get the secretaries to write out a detailed list so that our invitations don't clash. Last year we were careless enough to invite several families on the same day, and instead of attributing it to negligence they imagined we'd done it deliberately — to make an empty gesture at no trouble to ourselves."

Chia Jung went off to do as he was told, returning some time later with the list of dates for the feasts and the names of those invited. After running his eye over it Chia Chen said:

"Give it to Lai Sheng. Tell them to avoid asking the same people on those days."

He proceeded then to the hall and was watching the pages

shift screens, clean tables and polish the gold and silver sacrificial vessels, when a boy brought him a card and list.

"Bailiff Wu of the manor in Black Mountain Village has
arrived, sir," he reported.

"The old scoundrel, coming so late!" swore Chia Chen.

Chia Jung took the card and list and held them out while
Chia Chen, his hands behind his back, read them. On the red
card was written:

> "Your servant, Bailiff Wu Chin-hsiao, kowtows to wish the
> master and mistress boundless happiness and good health, and good
> health to the young master and young mistress too. May the New
> Year bring you great happiness and good fortune, wealth, nobility
> and peace. May you be promoted with increased emoluments
> and have all your wishes come true."

Chia Chen chuckled. "They have some sense, these country
folk, eh?"

"Yes, it's not the style," said his son, "but the good wishes
that count."

Next they read the list, which was as follows:

> thirty stags
> fifty deer
> fifty roebuck
> twenty each of three breeds of hogs and pigs
> twenty boars
> twenty wild goats
> twenty each of three breeds of goats and sheep
> two sturgeon
> two hundred catties of other fish
> two hundred each of live chicken, ducks and geese
> two hundred each of salted chicken, ducks and geese
> two hundred brace of pheasants
> two hundred brace of rabbits
> twenty pairs of bear's-paws
> twenty catties of deer-sinews
> fifty catties of sea-slugs
> fifty deer-tongues
> fifty ox-tongues
> twenty catties of dried oysters
> two bags each of hazel-nuts, pine-kernels, peach and apricot-kernels
> fifty pairs of giant lobsters
> two hundred catties of dried prawns
> one thousand catties of first-grade silver-frost charcoal
> two thousand catties of second-grade silver-frost charcoal
> thirty thousand catties of ordinary charcoal

two piculs of rose-rice from the Imperial Farm
five hundred pecks each of three varieties of fine rice
five hundred pecks each of other kinds of grain
one thousand piculs of ordinary rice
one cartload of sun-dried vegetables
two thousand five hundred taels raised by the sale of grain and
    cattle.

In addition, some trifles to amuse the young gentlemen and young
    ladies:

two brace of live deer
four brace of white rabbits
four brace of black rabbits
two brace of live pheasants
two brace of foreign ducks.

Having read this list Chia Chen ordered, "Bring him in."

Soon Wu Chin-hsiao entered the courtyard, kowtowed and offered greetings.

Chia Chen told the servants to help him up.

"So you're still hale and hearty," he remarked.

"Thanks to Your Lordship's good fortune, I can still get about," was the reply.

"Your sons have grown up. You should have sent them instead."

"I'm used to the trip, Your Lordship, and that's a fact. Besides, I was sick and tired of staying at home. Of course they all wanted to come, to see what it's like living at the feet of the Son of Heaven; but they're still young and I was afraid they might get into trouble on the way. A few years from now I shan't worry."

"How long did you spend on the road?"

"There's been heavy snow this year, Your Lordship. The snow's lying four or five feet deep in the country; and a sudden thaw recently made the going so difficult that I was held up for several days. The whole journey took me one month and two days, not that I didn't make the best speed I could, knowing time was running short and Your Lordship might be worried."

"I was wondering why you were so late," replied Chia Chen. "I've just looked at your list, you old scoundrel. So this year you're trying to defraud us again."

Wu hastily took two steps forward.

"May it please Your Lordship, we had a wretched harvest this year," he declared. "It rained steadily·from the third month to the eighth without letting up for five days at a stretch. In the ninth month, hailstones as large as bowls ·fell for one thousand three hundred *li* around, injuring thousands of men and countless houses, to say nothing of cattle and grain. That's why this is all there is. I wouldn't dare lie to Your Lordship."

Frowning, Chia Chen answered, "I counted on your bringing at least five. thousand taels. What use is this paltry sum? In all, we've only eight or nine manors left now, already two of them claim to have suffered from flood or drought. How are we to get through this New Year I'd like to know? And now you default like this."

"Your Lordship's farms haven't done so badly," said Wu. "My brother just a hundred *li* away is much worse off. Those eight farms which he manages for the other mansion are several times bigger than yours, sir; yet he's produced no more than I have this year, apart from just two or three thousand taels extra. They're hard hit too."

"No doubt," replied Chia Chen. "We can just about manage here, with no extra large outlay beyond the normal annual expenditure. If I want to enjoy myself, I spend more; but I can economize if necessary. As for New-Year gifts and entertaining, by not caring about appearances and cutting down I shall get by. It's different for the other house. In recent years they've had so many unavoidable extra expenses, without acquiring any additional income or property, that in the last year or two they've made great inroads into their capital. And whom can they ask for money if not you?"

Wu Chin-hsiao smiled.

"Their expenditure may have increased, but surely it works both ways. Don't they get presents from Her Imperial Highness and His Majesty?"

Chia Chen turned to his son and the rest.

"Did you hear that?" he asked laughingly. "What a joke!"

Chia Jung made haste to explain to Wu, "You people from

the back of beyond don't understand. Can Her Highness make over the Imperial Treasury to us? Even if she wanted to, it's not in her power. Of course she sends gifts at the different festivals, but they're simply brocade, curios and other trifles. As for money gifts, those only amount to a hundred or so gold taels a year — worth little more than a thousand taels of silver. What use is that? The last couple of years, they've had to spend several thousand taels extra each year. Just reckon for yourself how much it cost to build the Garden the first year for the Imperial Visit. A second visit in another couple of years would bankrupt them!"

"These simple country folk don't realize that not all is gold that glitters," chuckled Chia Chen. "Wormwood carved into a drumstick may look imposing, but it's bitter inside!"

"The other house does seem to be in difficulties, sir," remarked his son. "The other day I heard Second Aunt asking Yuan-yang in confidence to smuggle out some of the old lady's things to pawn."

"That's just your Aunt Hsi-feng's trick." Chia Chen laughed. "They're not as poor as all that. You may be sure she does it to make a show of poverty, because she knows they're spending too much and making inroads into their capital, and she wants to cut down on expenditure. I've my own means of reckoning, though. They're not as badly off as they make out."

With that he told the servants to take Wu Chin-hsiao away and entertain him well.

Chia Chen now disposed of this rent in kind as follows: part was kept for the ancestral sacrifice; part delivered by Chia Jung to the other mansion; part kept for family use; and the rest divided into different shares and placed on the terrace of the main hall, where the younger men of the clan were summoned to collect them.

At this juncture the Jung Mansion sent over a variety of sacrificial offerings and gifts for Chia Chen. When he had inspected these and supervised the arrangement of the sacrificial vessels, he changed into his slippers, draped a big raccoon cloak

over his shoulders, and made the servants spread a large wolf-skin rug at the top of the steps by the pillars so that he could sit in the sun watching his junior clansmen collect their gifts. When he saw Chia Chin come to take a portion too, he called him over.

"What are *you* doing here?" he asked. "Who told you to come?"

Standing at attention Chia Chin replied, "I heard you had sent for us to take things, sir. So I came without waiting to be called."

"These things are for your uncles and cousins who have no jobs and no income," Chia Chen told him. "Those two years when you had no job, I gave you a share. But now you're in charge of the monks and Taoist priests in the family temple. Apart from the stipend you receive each month, the allowance for all the monks and priests passes through your hands as well — yet you still show up to take this. You're too miserly. Just look at yourself. Are you dressed like a gentleman of means with a responsible post? You used to complain because you had no income; but now that you have one, you look even shabbier than before."

"I have such a large household, my expenses are heavy."

"Don't hand me that line!" Chia Chen laughed scornfully. "Do you think I don't know what goes on in the family temple? Out there, of course, you're the master and no one dares disobey you. With money in your hands and us at a safe distance, you lord it over everyone, night after night assembling a pack of scoundrels — gamblers, debauchees or queers. And now that your money's squandered you have the effrontery to come here for things. Well, you won't get anything except a good beating. After New Year I shall tell your Second Uncle Lien to dismiss you."

Chia Chin flushed scarlet and dared not reply.

Just then a servant announced that the Prince of Peiching had sent a gift of scrolls and pouches. Chia Chen ordered his son to entertain the messenger and explain that he was out, and Chia Jung, assenting, went off. Chia Chen watched till the distribution of goods was finished, then returned to his rooms to dine with his wife, and the night passed without further incident. The next day there was even more to do, but we need not go into the details.

By the twenty-ninth of the twelfth month all was ready. Both mansions were resplendent with new door-gods, couplets, tablets and New-Year charms. The Ning Mansion's main gate was thrown open, as were the ceremonial gate, the doors of the great hall, the lobby and the inner hall, the three inner gates, the inner central gate and the inner secondary gate — all the gates leading to the main hall. And on both sides below the steps, tall vermilion candles blazed like golden dragons.

The next day all the titled members of the family from the Lady Dowager downwards put on the court costume appropriate to their rank and, led by the old lady in a large sedan-chair carried by eight bearers, went to the Imperial Palace to pay homage and attend a banquet. On their return, they alighted from their chairs by the lobby of the Ning Mansion. All their younger kinsmen who had not gone to court had lined up to wait in front of the main gate, and now ushered them into the Ancestral Temple.

Now as this was Hsueh Pao-chin's first visit here, she took pains to observe the whole place carefully. The temple, a five-frame structure enclosed by a black palisade, stood in a separate courtyard to the west of the Ning Mansion. In large characters on the placard over the gate was the imposing four-character inscription "Chia Family Ancestral Temple." In small characters beside this she read "Written by Kung Chi-tsung, Hereditary Duke Descended from Confucius." The couplet flanking this read:

> The grateful recipients of Imperial Favour will gladly dash
> their brains out on the ground;
> Generations to come will make solemn sacrifice for deeds
> whose fame resounds to Heaven.

This too had been written by the duke descended from Confucius.

Entering this courtyard, the party proceeded along a way paved with white marble and bordered by green pines and cypresses to a terrace on which were displayed ancient bronze tripods and libation cups green with patina. Before the porch hung a placard gilded with the nine-dragon design, and the inscription "Stars Shine on the Assistant," which had been written by the late Emperor himself. The couplet on either side, also in the Imperial calligraphy, read:

> Their achievements outshine the sun and moon,
> Their fame will extend to all their posterity.

The tablet over the entrance to the main hall was engraved with frolicking dragons, and bore the intagliated motto in blue: "Venerate the Departed, Continue Their Sacrifices." The couplet flanking this, also written by the Emperor, read:

> Their descendants succeed to their good fortune and virtue;
> Ning and Jung live in the memory of the black-haired people.

The hall itself, ablaze with candles and lamps, was so brilliant with silk hangings and embroidered curtains that the ancestral tablets, ranged in their places, were hard to make out distinctly.

The members of the Chia family disposed themselves now according to the generations to which they belonged, on the left and right-hand sides. Chia Ching the Master of Sacrifice was assisted by Chia Sheh, with Chia Chen as libationer, Chia Lien and Chia Tsung to present silk, Pao-yu to offer incense, and Chia Chang and Chia Ling to spread a rug for kneeling and tend the incinerator. Black-robed musicians played music while the libation-cup was presented three times and obeisance made. Then the silk was burnt and wine poured.

At the end of this ceremony the music stopped and all withdrew, following the Lady Dowager to the main hall, in front of the portraits. In the middle of the shrine hung with long silk curtains, surrounded by brilliant screens and blazing censers, were portraits of the Duke of Jungkuo and the Duke of Ningkuo in dragon robes with jade belts. On both sides were portraits of other ancestors.

Chia Hsing, Chia Chih and some others had ranged themselves in due order all the way from the inner ceremonial gate to the terrace by the verandah of the main hall, where stood Chia Ching and Chia Sheh outside the palisade, while the ladies stood inside. The family servants and pages remained outside the ceremonial gate. Each time they brought a plate of offerings to this gate, it was taken by Chia Hsing or Chia Chih and passed from hand to hand until it reached Chia Ching on the terrace. Chia Jung, as the eldest grandson of the senior branch, was the only one to accompany the ladies inside. When Chia Ching passed him an offering he handed it to his wife, who passed it on to Hsi-feng and Madam Yu until it reached Lady Wang in front of the altar. She in turn passed it to the Lady Dowager, who set it on the altar. Lady Hsing, posted west of the altar facing east, helped the Lady Dowager.

When all the dishes, rice, soup, cakes, wine and tea had been presented, Chia Jung withdrew to join Chia Ching's group below the steps. Places were assigned according to generations, Chia Ching heading the senior group, Chia Chen the second, and Chia Jung the third; and now they ranged themselves on the two sides, the men on the east and the women on the west. When the Lady Dowager offered incense and bowed, the whole clan knelt down together. Every square foot of the five sections of the hall, the three annexes, the inner and outer corridors, terrace and courtyard, was a mass of rich silks and brocades. And the only sounds to break the solemn silence were the tinkling of gold bells and jade pendants, the rustling of silks and the shuffling of boots and slippers as the worshippers rose or knelt down.

After this ceremony, Chia Ching, Chia Sheh and the other men hurried to the Jung Mansion, where they waited to pay their respects to the Lady Dowager. She, however, now went to Madam Yu's sitting-room, the floor of which was covered with a red carpet where stood a large gilded cloisonné brazier, its three legs in the form of elephant trunks. On the *kang* by the north wall were a new crimson rug and red silk back-rests and bolsters embroidered with "Dragons in the Clouds" designs and the character "Longevity." On it, too, were spread a black fox-skin and a big white fox-skin mattress. When the Lady Dowager had been ensconced here, more furs were spread on both sides and the few other ladies of her generation were invited to sit down.

Then fur rugs were spread on the smaller *kang* behind the partition for Lady Hsing's generation, and twelve carved lacquer chairs covered with grey squirrel-skins and with a large bronze foot-warmer under each were placed in a row on either side for Pao-chin and the other girls.

Madam Yu ceremoniously presented tea to the Lady Dowager while Chia Jung's wife served the other elderly ladies, after which Madam Yu served Lady Hsing's group and Chia Jung's wife the girls. Hsi-feng and Li Wan stood by all this time in attendance.

After sipping some tea, Lady Hsing and the rest rose to wait upon the Lady Dowager, and after a few words to the other old ladies she asked for her sedan-chair. At once Hsi-feng stepped up to her and took her arm.

"We've prepared dinner for you, madam," demurred Madam Yu with a smile. "Why will you never honour us with your company at dinner on this day of the year before you leave? Aren't we as good as Hsi-feng?"

Hsi-feng, supporting the old lady, urged her, "Come on, Old Ancestress. Pay no attention to her. Let's go home to eat."

"You have your hands full here with the ancestral sacrifice," said the Lady Dowager. "How could you put up with more trouble from me? Besides, even though I don't dine here, you send dishes over every year. It's better that way. If there's more than I can eat today, I can save it for tomorrow. That way, don't I get more of your food than by eating here?"

Everyone laughed.

Then the old lady reminded Madam Yu, "Make sure to post reliable people tonight, to see that no fires break out owing to carelessness."

As soon as Madam Yu had promised to see to this, they all went out to the lobby to mount their sedan-chairs. The ladies slipped behind a screen while page boys brought in sedan-bearers to carry them out, Madam Yu and Lady Hsing accompanying the others to the Jung Mansion. As their chairs were borne out of the main gate, they saw the insignia, equipage and musical instruments of the Duke of Ningkuo and the Duke of Jungkuo displayed on the east and west sides of the street, which was closed today to passers-by.

Presently they reached the Jung Mansion and found all its gates, too, open right up to the main hall. But instead of stopping at the lobby this time, they turned west after the main hall and alighted outside the Lady Dowager's reception room. All trooping in after her, they discovered that the place was freshly furnished with embroidered screens and brocade cushions. Fragrant herbs and aromatic pine and cedar-wood were burning in the brazier.

As soon as the Lady Dowager had taken her seat, some old serving-women reported that two or three ladies of her generation had come to offer their congratulations. She rose to welcome them, for they had already entered, and after clasping hands and greeting her they were ushered to their seats and sipped some tea. Then the Lady Dowager saw them out no farther than the inner ceremonial gate. When she had returned and seated herself again, Chia Ching and Chia Sheh led in the younger men of the family.

"I put you to so much trouble the whole year round, don't stand on ceremony now," urged the old lady.

But the men in one group and the women in another paid their respects together, after which they took seats on both sides in order of seniority to receive the salutations of their juniors. When all the men and maid-servants of both mansions had paid their respects according to their degree, there was a distribution of New-Year money, as well as pouches and gold and silver ingots. Then they took their seats for the family-reunion feast, the men on the east side, the women on the west, and New-Year wine, "happy-reunion soup," "lucky fruit" and "wish-fulfilment cakes" were served, until the Lady Dowager rose and went into the inner room to change her clothes, where-upon the party broke up.

That evening, incense and sacrifices were offered at the various Buddhist shrines and to the kitchen god; and incense-sticks and paper effigies were burnt to Heaven and Earth in the main court of Lady Wang's compound. Huge horn lanterns high on both sides of the main gate of Grand View Garden cast a brilliant light, while all the paths were lit with lanterns too. High and low alike were splendidly dressed. And the babel of talk and laughter, punctuated by the explosion of fire-crackers, went on without intermission the whole night long.

The next morning the Lady Dowager and others, rising at dawn, put on their robes of state and went with full pageantry to pay homage at the Imperial Palace as well as to offer the Imperial Concubine birthday congratulations. Upon her return from the Imperial banquet, the old lady went to the Ning Mansion to sacrifice to the ancestors. Then, going back to her own apartments she received the younger generations' New-Year salutations. After these ceremonies she changed her clothes and rested, not receiving any of the kinsmen and friends who came to offer their congratulations but simply chatting with Aunt Hsueh and Aunt Li or playing draughts and card-games with Pao-yu, Pao-chin, Pao-chai, Tai-yu and the other girls.

Lady Wang and Hsi-feng were busy entertaining guests, for an unending stream of friends and relatives attended the New-Year feasts and operas held daily for about a week in their hall and courtyard. And as soon as this was over, both mansions were decked out and hung with lanterns for the approaching Lantern Festival. The Lady Dowager was feasted by Chia Sheh on the eleventh, by Chia Chen on the twelfth, staying with them on each occasion for half a day, while time forbids us to enumerate all the feasts to which Lady Wang and Hsi-feng were invited.

On the evening of the fifteenth, the Lady Dowager had tables spread in the big hall in the small garden, an opera company hired, and gay lanterns of every description displayed at a family feast for her kinsmen in both mansions.

The only one not invited was Chia Ching, who abstained from both wine and meat. After the ancestral sacrifice on the seventeenth he moved back outside the city to live in seclusion; but even during his stay at home he remained quietly in his room, ignoring all the festivities around him.

As for Chia Sheh, after sitting a while at his mother's feast he also asked her permission to withdraw; and this the old lady readily granted knowing that his presence would cause a general constraint. Having his own different pleasures, he went home to enjoy the festival by drinking with his protégés amid a bevy of gaily-dressed girls, to the sound of music and singing.

In the old lady's hall about ten tables were set for the feast. Beside each, on a teapoy, stood an incense-burner burning Palace incense conferred by the Emperor; an incense box and a vase; a miniature garden about eight inches long, four inches wide and two or three inches high, with fresh flowers among small mossy rocks; teacups made in a previous reign; and gay little teapots filled with the finest tea on a small tray of Western lacquerware.

Set out too was a crimson gauze screen in a carved purple-sandalwood frame embroidered with flowers and calligraphy. The embroiderer, a Soochow girl called Hui-niang, had come from a family of officials and literati and been a skilled calligrapher and painter; but occasionally she did some embroidery too — purely for her own amusement, not to sell. All the flowers she embroidered were copied from paintings by famous artists of the Tang, Sung, Yuan and Ming dynasties; thus the compositions and colours were based on excellent models, unlike the stereotyped compositions and garish colours produced by artisans. Beside each spray of flowers there were lines of verse about these flowers from short poems or songs by poets of old, all embroidered in cursive script with black silk thread. And the strokes of these characters, whether light or heavy, continuous or broken, were exactly the same as if written with a brush — a far cry from the grotesquely distorted scripts in the embroidery sold in the market-place.

As Hui-niang was not out to make money from this skill of

hers, although her embroidery was widely known few could procure a specimen of it. Many rich and noble official families were unable to acquire one. It was known as "Hui" embroidery, and some vulgar hucksters had recently started imitating it to fool people and make a profit.

Hui-niang had been fated to die at the early age of eighteen, so that no more of her work could be obtained. Any family which possessed one or two samples only kept them as rare treasures. And then certain admirers of "Hui" embroidery among the literati declared that to call such superb work "embroidery" showed a lack of respect and failed to do justice to its beauty. After discussion they agreed not to call it "embroidery" but "art." Hence it had now come to be known as the "Hui art" and a genuine piece was priceless. Even a wealthy family like the Chias had only acquired three pieces, two of which had been presented to the Emperor the previous year. All they had left now was this screen with sixteen panels. The Lady Dowager prized it so much that she would not display it to guests with her other ornaments. Instead, she kept it in her own apartments to enjoy when in a good mood or entertaining.

There was also a variety of porcelain vases from old kilns filled with flowers symbolizing "The Three Companions of Winter" and "Wealth and Splendour in a Marble Hall."

Aunt Li and Aunt Hsueh took the seats of honour. To their east stood a carved openwork dragon-screen, with below it a low couch spread with cushions, pillows and furs. Beside the pillows, an elegant low table of foreign lacquer with gilt designs was set out with a teapot, cups, rinse-bowls and towels as well as a spectacle-case. Here the Lady Dowager reclined to chat with the others, putting on her spectacles whenever she wanted to watch the performance.

"My old bones are aching," she told Aunt Hsueh and Aunt Li. "Excuse me if I just keep you company lying here." She made Hu-po sit beside her to massage her legs with a small pestle.

In place of a banquet table before the couch, there stood only one tall teapoy on which were a screen, flower-vase and incense-burner, and a small, elegant long-legged table laid with wine-cups, spoons and chopsticks. Pao-chin, Hsiang-yun, Tai-yu and Pao-yu were told to sit at this table to share her feast; for before each dish was served to them it was shown to the old lady and, if she fancied it, left on her small table first for her to taste, then removed to the four young people's table. So they could be regarded as sitting with the Lady Dowager. Lower down sat Lady Hsing and Lady Wang; then Madam Yu, Li Wan, Hsi-feng and Chia Jung's wife; while Pao-chai, Li Wen, Li Chi, Hsiu-yen, Ying-chun and the other girls had tables on the west side.

From the great beams on either side hung crystal, hibiscus-shaped chandeliers with coloured tassels. In front of each table was a candelabrum of Western enamel with a lacquer shade in the shape of an inverted lotus leaf; and this could be turned outwards to shade the coloured candles' light from the feasters and illumine the stage more brightly. The lattices of the windows and doors had been removed and in their place hung gaily-tasselled Palace lanterns. From the eaves of the house, as well as the covered walks on either side, hung lanterns made of horn, glass, gauze, cut-glass or silk and paper with embroider-ed or painted, raised or incised designs. Chia Chen, Chia Lien, Chia Huan, Chia Tsung, Chia Jung, Chia Chin, Chia Yun, Chia Ling and Chia Chang were seated at tables in the corridors.

The Lady Dowager had sent to invite all the members of the clan. But some were too old to enjoy lively celebrations; some had no one to mind the house for them; some were bed-ridden; some envied the rich and were ashamed of their own poverty; some disliked or feared Hsi-feng; some were timid and unused to company — for one reason or another they would not or could not come. Thus, large as the clan was, the only female relative to appear was Chia Chun's mother, née Lou, who brought her son; and the only men were Chia Chin, Chia Yun, Chia Chang and Chia Ling, all of whom worked under Hsi-feng. In spite of their depleted numbers, however, it was quite a merry family feast.

And now Lin Chih-hsiao's wife led in six serving-women carrying three low tables, each covered with red felt and piles of bright copper coins, fresh from the mint, strung together with red cord. Mrs. Lin had two of these tables set before Aunt Hsueh and Aunt Li and the other in front of the Lady Dowager, who told her where to put it. Knowing the family custom, serving-women then untied the coins and stacked them up.

This was towards the end of the scene "Encounter in the Tower" from *The West Tower*,[1] when Yu Shu-yeh flings off in a rage. The girl playing Wen-pao ad-libbed:

"So you're leaving in a huff. Luckily this is the fifteenth of the first month, and the Old Ancestress of the Jung Mansion is holding a family feast. I'm going to ride there as fast as I can on this horse to ask for some goodies now. That's the thing to do."

This set the old lady and the whole party laughing.

Aunt Hsueh exclaimed, "Clever little imp!"

"She's only nine," remarked Hsi-feng.

"That was smart of her," said the Lady Dowager. "Reward the child."

Three serving-women, who had small baskets ready, stepped forward at this command to fill their baskets with coins from the three tables. Then going to the stage they announced:

"Our Old Ancestress, Madam Hsueh and Madam Li are giving this to Wen-pao to buy goodies."

With that they emptied their baskets and the coins scattered, clinking, all over the stage.

Chia Chen and Chia Lien, too, had ordered their pages in secret to bring in several crates of coins.

To know how these were distributed, read the next chapter.

---

[1] By Yuan Yu-lin, a Ching playwright.

CHAPTER 54

The Lady Dowager Debunks Trite Stories
Hsi-feng Clowns to Amuse Her Elders

When Chia Chen and Chia Lien heard the call for largesse
they made their pages scatter the coins which they had prepared
in advance, and the clink and jingle of money on the stage
delighted the old lady. Then, as both men rose from their
seats, a page brought Chia Lien a silver pot of freshly-heated
wine which he carried himself as he followed Chia Chen inside.
First Chia Chen bowed to Aunt Li and, taking her cup, turned
round so that Chia Lien might fill it. He then bowed to Aunt
Hsueh and filled her cup as well.

The two ladies rose protesting laughingly, "Please take seats,
gentlemen. Why be so formal?"

All but Lady Hsing and Lady Wang had risen from their
seats and were standing by them, with their hands at their
sides, to show respect. Now Chia Chen and Chia Lien went
up to the Lady Dowager's couch and, as it was low, knelt
down, Chia Chen holding her cup and Chia Lien, behind him,
the wine-pot. Although only the two of them were proposing
toasts, Chia Huan and the other young men had trooped in
behind them, and when these two knelt the rest fell on their
knees too. Pao-yu made haste to follow suit.

"Why should *you* join in?" whispered Hsiang-yun, nudging
him. "Better offer a toast yourself."

"I will later on," he replied softly. Only when his cousins
had risen after pouring out the wine, did he rise to his feet.

After this toast, Chia Chen and Chia Lien got up to pour
wine for Lady Hsing and Lady Wang.

"How about our cousins?" asked Chia Chen then.

"Get along now and leave them in peace," answered the ladies.

Then Chia Chen and the other young men withdrew.

It was not yet the second watch. Eight scenes from *Eight Gallants at the Lantern Festival* were being performed, and the climax had just been reached when Pao-yu rose to go out.

"Where are you off to?" asked his grandmother. "Watch out for the fireworks outside, or you may get burnt by some of the sparks raining down."

"I'm not going far," he replied. "I'll be back soon."

She ordered some attendants to escort him, and he went out followed only by Sheh-yueh, Chiu-wen and a few young maids.

"Where's Hsi-jen?" asked the Lady Dowager. "She must be getting above herself if she only sends the younger girls out."

Lady Wang rose to explain, "She couldn't very well come, madam, because she's newly in mourning for her mother."

The old lady nodded but commented, "A girl in service can't really afford the niceties of filial piety. If she were still waiting on me, she'd hardly absent herself at this time, would she? This all comes of our leniency. Having enough servants we don't insist on these things, so this seems to be the rule now."

"Even if she weren't in mourning, we need someone in the Garden this evening to keep an eye on the fireworks and prevent accidents," put in Hsi-feng quickly. "Whenever we have operas here all the other maids from the Garden sneak out to watch, but Hsi-jen can be relied on to see to things. Besides, this means that when Pao-yu goes back presently to sleep he'll find everything ready for him. If she'd come too, the others are so thoughtless that he'd find his bedding cold on his return, no tea made and everything at sixes and sevens. That's why I told her to stay there to look after the house and see that everything's ready for his return. Then we here needn't worry, while she can observe the proprieties. Isn't that better all round? But if our Old Ancestress wants her, I'll send for her."

"You're quite right," said the Lady Dowager. "Trust you

to have thought it all out. Don't send for her. But when did her mother die? How is it I didn't know?"

"Have you forgotten, madam?" Hsi-feng smiled. "The other day she came herself to report to you."

The old lady thought back and chuckled.

"So she did. What a memory I have!"

"How can Your Ladyship remember every little thing?" remarked the others laughingly.

"She was only a child when she came to wait on me," recalled the old lady with a sigh. "Then she waited on Hsiang-yun for a time, until finally I gave her to our young demon king, and what a dance he's led her all these years! It's not as if her parents had been our slaves or received any special kindness from us. After her mother died I meant to give her some silver for the funeral, but somehow it slipped my mind."

"The other day the mistress gave her forty taels, and that should have been enough," interposed Hsi-feng.

The Lady Dowager nodded.

"That's all right then. As it happens, Yuan-yang's mother has just died too; but because her home's in the south I didn't send her back for the funeral. Now they can keep each other company." She ordered a serving-woman to take them some refreshments.

"Yuan-yang's gone without waiting to be told," put in Hu-po with a smile.

They went on with their feast then, still watching the opera.

Meanwhile Pao-yu had gone straight back to the Garden. And seeing that he was going to his own quarters, the nurses did not follow him but sat down by the stove in the Garden gatehouse to drink and gamble with the women in charge of making tea there.

Pao-yu found his compound brightly lit but strangely silent.

"Can they all be in bed?" wondered Sheh-yueh. "Let's go in quietly and give them a fright."

Tiptoeing past the full-length looking-glass, they saw Hsi-jen lying opposite someone on the *kang*, with two or three old serving-women dozing on the other side.

Pao-yu thought they were asleep. He was on the point of going in when he heard Yuan-yang say with a sigh:

"There's no telling what will happen in this life. You were on your own here while your parents lived outside and were for ever travelling east and west, so no one would have expected that you'd be able to attend their death-beds. Yet this year your mother died at home and you were able to go to her funeral."

"Yes," said Hsi-jen. "I never thought I'd be able to be there when she breathed her last. And the mistress gave me forty taels too, which was a very handsome reward to her for having brought me up, and more than I dared hope for."

Pao-yu turned to whisper to Sheh-yueh, "I didn't know Yuan-yang was here too. If I go in, she'll leave again in a huff. We'd better go back and leave them to chat in peace. I'm glad she came, Hsi-jen was lonely all on her own."

So they slipped out quietly. Then Pao-yu, stepping behind some rocks, lifted his gown.

Sheh-yueh and Chiu-wen had stopped and averted their faces.

"Don't undo your pants till you've squatted down," they cried, "or you may catch a chill on your stomach!"

When the two younger maids behind knew what he was up to, they hurried to the room where tea was made to get hot water.

As Pao-yu was about to rejoin the others, two of the servants' wives approached.

"Who's that?" they called.

"It's Pao-yu," replied Chiu-wen. "Don't shout like that or you may startle him."

"Sorry, we didn't know," said the women with a smile. "So we've caused you trouble on this festival. You must all be very busy, miss, these days."

As they had drawn level now, Sheh-yueh asked them what they were carrying.

"Some cakes and fruit from the old lady for Miss Chin and Miss Hua."

"They're playing *The Eight Gallants* over there, not *The Magic Box*," quipped Chiu-wen. "So where does this Goddess Chin-hua come from?"[1]

Pao-yu made Chiu-wen and Sheh-yueh open the hampers, and as they did so the two women squatted down. Seeing some of the choicest fruits, sweetmeats, cakes and dishes from the feast there, he nodded and moved on. The two girls hastily closed the hampers and followed.

"Those are friendly, tactful women," remarked Pao-yu cheerfully. "They'll be tired out themselves these days, but they said how busy *you* must be. They're not boastful show-offs."

"Those two are all right," rejoined Sheh-yueh. "Some of the others really have no manners."

"You're intelligent girls," he said. "You should make allowances for those poor coarse creatures."

By now he had approached the Garden gate. The nurses, who had been looking out for him while drinking and gaming, tagged after him as soon as he reappeared and followed him to the corridor behind the feasting hall in the small garden. There the two young maids had been waiting for some time, one holding a basin, the other a towel and a small flask of ointment.

Chiu-wen dipped her fingers in the basin.

"How careless you're growing," she scolded. "Fancy bringing such cold water!"

"It's the fault of the weather, miss," explained the girl. "I took boiling water for fear it might get cold; but it's cooled off all the same."

Just then, as luck would have it, up came a nurse with a kettle of boiling water.

"Please give me some of that, granny," begged the girl.

"This is to make tea for the old lady," retorted the nurse. "Fetch some for yourself, lass. It won't hurt you to walk a few steps."

---

[1] Yuan-yang's family name was Chin and Hsi-jen's Hua. The Goddess Chin-hua was the goddess of water in *The Magic Box*, a mythological opera by an anonymous playwright of the late Ming or early Ching Dynasty.

"Never mind who it's for," put in Chiu-wen. "If you won't give us any, I'll pour water from the old lady's teapot to wash in."

When the woman saw it was Chiu-wen, she hastily poured them some water.

"That's enough," said Chiu-wen. "At your age you should have more sense. As if we didn't know this was for the old lady! But why do you think we asked?"

The nurse smiled and apologized, "My eyes are so dim I didn't see who it was, miss."

When Pao-yu had washed his hands, the girl with the flask poured some ointment over them which he rubbed in. Then Chiu-wen and Sheh-yueh, having rinsed their hands in the hot water and rubbed on ointment too, escorted him back to the hall.

Pao-yu now called for a pot of warm wine to toast Aunt Li and Aunt Hsueh, who both begged him to be seated.

"Let the boy fill your cups," said the Lady Dowager. "And mind you empty them."

She drained her own cup then. And when Lady Hsing and Lady Wang followed suit, Aunt Hsueh and Aunt Li had to drink up too.

"Fill your cousins' cups," the old lady told Pao-yu. "See that you do it properly and make them all drink up."

Pao-yu assented and filled every cup in turn. When he came to Tai-yu she refused to drink but held the cup up to his lips, thanking him with a smile when he tossed it off. He poured her another cup.

"Don't drink cold wine, Pao-yu," warned Hsi-feng. "If you do, your hands will tremble too much to write or draw your bow later on."

"I haven't drunk any cold wine," he protested.

"I know. I'm just warning you."

Having filled all the cups except that of Chia Jung's wife, whose cup was filled by a maid, he went out to the corridor to toast Chia Chen and the other men and kept them company for a while before returning to his seat inside.

Presently soup was served, followed by New-Year dumplings.

"Tell the actresses to rest now," said the Lady Dowager. "Those poor children must have some hot soup and hot food before they go on." She ordered sweetmeats of every kind to be taken to the actresses.

Now that the performance had stopped, one of the matrons brought in two women story-tellers who often visited the house, putting stools for them at one side. They were told to sit down and handed a fiddle and a lute. Then the Lady Dowager asked Aunt Li and Aunt Hsueh what they would like to hear.

"Anything will do," they answered.

She asked the two women what new stories they had.

"One about the end of the Tang Dynasty and the Five Dynasties," they replied.

"What is its name?"

The Phoenix Seeks Its Mate."

"That's a good title," she remarked. "Why is it called that? Let's hear what it's about, and if it sounds good you can tell it."

"It's about a country gentleman named Wang Chung at the end of the Tang Dynasty," said one of the women. "His family came from Chinling. After serving as a minister under two emperors, he retired in his old age. He had an only son called Wang Hsi-feng."

The whole party laughed at that.

"The same name as our minx Hsi-feng," chuckled the old lady.

Some serving-women nudged the story-tellers.

"That's our Second Mistress' name. Be careful," they warned.

"Never mind. Go on," said the Lady Dowager.

The story-tellers rose to apologize.

"We deserve to drop dead. We didn't know it was Her Ladyship's honourable name."[1]

"What does that matter?" asked Hsi-feng cheerfully. "Plenty of people have the same name. Go on."

---

[1] In feudal China, the names of superiors were taboo. If inferiors could not avoid using them, they had to do so in an altered form.

Then one of the women continued, "One year, old Mr. Wang sent his son to take the examination in the capital. Running into heavy rain on the way he took shelter in a village where, as it happened, there lived a gentleman named Li, an old family friend of Mr. Wang's, who put the young man up in his study. This Mr. Li had no son, only one daughter Chu-luan[1] who was thoroughly accomplished in lyre-playing, chess, calligraphy and painting. . . ."

"I understand the title now," interposed the old lady. "You needn't go on. I can guess the rest. Naturally Wang Hsi-feng wants to marry this Miss Chu-luan."

"So you've heard this story before, Old Ancestress." The story-teller smiled.

The others explained, "The old lady can guess the ending, even if she hasn't heard the story before."

"There's a sameness about all these tales," complained the old lady. "And they're so stereotyped — all about talented scholars and lovely ladies. Fancy describing girls who behave so badly as fine young ladies! Why, they're nothing of the sort. They're always introduced as girls from cultured families whose fathers are invariably high officials or prime ministers. In that case, an only daughter would be treasured and brought up as a real fine young lady, well-versed in literature and a model of propriety; yet her first glimpse of a handsome man, whether a relative or family friend, sets her thoughts running on marriage. She forgets her parents then and gets up to all sorts of devilry, behaving quite unlike a fine lady. If she carries on like that she's surely no lady, no matter how her head is crammed with learning. If a man whose head is crammed with learning becomes a thief, does the court spare him on account of his talent? So these story-tellers contradict themselves.

"Besides, not only would the daughter of a good scholar-official family be well-educated and a model of propriety — so would her mother. And even if her father had retired, a big

---

[1] *Chu* means a fledgling, and *luan* a female phoenix, whereas *feng* in Wang Hsi-feng means a male phoenix.

family like that would have plenty of nurses and maids to look after the girl. How is it that in all these stories, when such things happen, no one has any inkling of it except the girl herself and one trusted maid? What are all the others doing, I'd like to know? Isn't that contradictory?"

Everyone laughed.

"The old lady's shown up their lies!"

"There's a reason for this," she continued. "Either the people who spin these tales envy the rank and riches of other families, or ask for help which isn't granted, and so they make up these stories to discredit them. Or else they're so bewitched by reading such tales that they wish they could get a fine young lady themselves, and so they invent these things for their own amusement.

"But what do *they* know about the ways of scholar-official families? Let's not talk about those great families in their stories — even in a middle-rank family like ours such things couldn't possibly happen. They're talking utter nonsense! That's why we never allow such stories here, and our girls have never heard any. Now that I'm growing old and the girls' apartments are some distance away, *I* may listen to a tale or two to pass the time; but as soon as the girls come I put a stop to it."

"That's the rule for a good family, madam," approved Aunt Li and Aunt Hsueh. "Even in our homes we don't let the children hear such frivolous nonsense."

Hsi-feng stepped forward then to pour more wine.

"That's enough," she cried. "The wine's cold but you'd better take a sip, Old Ancestress, to wet your gullet before debunking their lies. This is a story called *Debunking Lies* which is happening in this reign, here and now, in this year, month, day and hour. Our Old Ancestress, with only one mouth, can hardly speak for two families at once. As two blooms grow on separate boughs, let's deal with one first. Never mind whether true or false, let's go back to enjoying the lanterns and opera.[1] Just allow these two relatives to have

---

[1] Here Hsi-feng has been using the introductory patter of professional story-tellers.

a cup of wine and enjoy two more scenes of the show. After that you can go on debunking stories, starting with those of the very first dynasty down to the present one — how about it?"

She had filled everyone's cup, chuckling as she spoke, and by now the whole company was prostrate with laughter. The two story-tellers as well were in fits of mirth.

"What a tongue Her Ladyship has!" they cried. "If she started telling stories she'd soon do us out of a job."

"Don't get too carried away," cautioned Aunt Hsueh. "The gentlemen are outside, this isn't like ordinary times."

"There's only Cousin Chen," retorted Hsi-feng. "We've been like brother and sister since we were small and played naughty tricks together. Since my marriage, of course, I've behaved much more correctly. But even if we hadn't played together as children and were only in-laws, isn't there a story in *The Twenty-four Acts of Filial Piety*[1] about someone dressing in motley and clowning to amuse his parents?[2] *They* can't come and amuse our Old Ancestress, so if I manage to make her laugh and eat a little more, keeping everybody happy, you should all thank me instead of laughing at me."

"It's true that I haven't had a good laugh for the last couple of days," said the Lady Dowager. "Now that she's raised my spirits by her antics I'll have another cup of wine." Sipping her drink, she told Pao-yu to offer Hsi-feng a toast.

"I don't need him," declared Hsi-feng laughingly. "I'll cash in on some of your good fortune, madam."

She took the old lady's cup and drank what was left, then handed the cup to a maid and took another from a basin of hot water. All the cups on the tables were changed then for fresh ones from the basin, and when more wine had been poured they resumed their seats.

"If our Old Ancestress doesn't want to hear this story, shall we play a tune?" asked one of the story-tellers.

---

[1] Compiled by Kuo Chu-ching of the Yuan Dynasty (1271-1368).

[2] Referring to Lao Lai Tzu of the Spring and Autumn Period (770-476 B.C.).

"Yes, play *The General's Command*," ordered the old lady.

The two women tuned their instruments and played until the Lady Dowager asked the time. On being told that it was the third watch, she observed:

"No wonder it's growing so chilly."

Some young maids had already brought warmer clothes.

Now Lady Wang rose to ask, "Why not move to the lobby with the heated floor, madam? Our two relatives needn't be treated like outsiders. We'll keep them company for you."

"In that case why don't we all move inside?" countered the old lady. "That would be cosier."

"There may not be room for us all," demurred Lady Wang.

"I know what. Instead of using all these tables, we'll just join two or three together so that we can sit side by side, cosy and snug."

They all liked this idea and rose from their seats. The servants hastily cleared the feast away, put three large tables together in the lobby, and brought in more refreshments.

"Don't stand on ceremony, anyone," said the old lady when all was ready. "Just sit where I tell you."

She made Aunt Hsueh and Aunt Li take the seats of honour on the north side and took an east seat herself with Pao-chin, Tai-yu and Hsiang-yun beside her. Pao-yu, told to sit by his mother, found a place between her and Lady Hsing. Pao-chai and the other girls sat on the west side, Madam Lou and her son Chia Chun came next, then Chia Lan between Madam Yu and Li Wan, and Chia Jung's wife on the south side.

The Lady Dowager now sent word to Chia Chen, "You can take your brothers away, I shall soon be retiring."

At once all the men came in to take their leave.

"Go along," said the old lady. "No need to come in. We've just sat down and don't want to stand up again. Go and rest now; tomorrow will be a busy day."

"Very good, madam," replied Chia Chen. "But at least let us leave Jung here to serve you wine."

"That's right," she agreed. "I'd forgotten him."

With a word of assent Chia Chen turned to lead Chia Lien

and the others out and, having told servants to see Chia Tsung and Chia Huang home, the two of them went off cheerfully to enjoy the company of some singsong girls. But no more of this.

Meanwhile the Lady Dowager remarked with a smile, "I was just thinking that to make our pleasure complete we ought to have a married couple here. I'd forgotten Jung. Now with him here we've nothing missing. Sit next to your wife, Jung, and we shall have a married pair."

Some matrons announced that another opera was starting.

"We women folk are just having a pleasant chat," said the old lady. "We don't want any more noise. It's so late, those child-actresses must be freezing. Let them rest a while. Go and fetch our girl-actresses here to put on a couple of items on this stage. The troupe from outside can watch."

The women hurried off to send a messenger to Grand View Garden with instructions for the pages at the inner gate. These boys went straight to the changing room to escort all the grown people in the company out, leaving only the young performers. Then the instructor from Pear Fragrance Court brought Wen-kuan and the eleven other girl actresses out through the side gate of the corridor, accompanied by some women carrying bundles. Since there was no time to bring all their stage properties, they had chosen only the costumes for a few operas which they judged the old lady might like. The women led the actresses inside, and when they had paid their respects they stood there at respectful attention.

"It's the first month of the year, why didn't your instructor let you out to enjoy yourselves?" asked the old lady. "What have you been rehearsing lately? The eight scenes from *The Eight Gallants* were so noisy that they've made my head ache. Let's have something quieter. Look, Madam Hsueh and Madam Li here both have opera troupes at home; they've seen countless good performances, and their young ladies have watched better operas and heard better singing than ours. These young actresses we've hired today are from troupes trained by well-known families of opera connoisseurs, better than many older companies, for all that they're only children. We mustn't make a poor showing today, so let's try something new. Fang-kuan shall sing us 'Seeking the Dream'[1] with no accompaniment but a two-string fiddle and a flute."

"Very good," replied Wen-kuan with a smile. "Our performance can't possibly measure up to the standard to which these ladies are accustomed. They can only judge of our delivery and voices."

"That's it," said the old lady.

"What a clever child!" exclaimed Aunt Li and Aunt Hsueh. "You're helping the old lady to make fun of us."

"We just put on shows for fun here, we're not professionals; that's why you won't find us following the usual fashion," said the Lady Dowager. She then told Kuei-kuan, "Sing that aria 'Hui-ming Delivers a Letter'[2] and don't trouble to make up. Just sing a couple of scenes to amuse these ladies with our amateur style. But mind you do your best."

Wen-kuan and the others assented and withdrew to change their clothes. First they staged "Seeking the Dream," then "The Letter Is Delivered." All listened in absolute silence.

"It isn't easy for her. I've seen truly hundreds of companies perform, but never heard an accompaniment of only flutes," observed Aunt Hsueh presently.

"There have been cases," the Lady Dowager told her. "For instance that melody in *The Western Tower* 'Longing by the Chu River' is often sung to a flute accompaniment by the young male actor. It is rare, though, to have a whole scene like this. It just depends on one's taste. This is nothing unusual." Pointing at Hsiang-yun she added, "When I was her age, her grandfather had an opera troupe in which someone performed real lyre music when they played 'Listening to the Lyre' from *The Western Chamber*, 'Seduction by the Lyre' in *The Romance*

---

[1] A scene from *The Peony Pavilion*.
[2] From *The Western Chamber*.

of the Jade Hairpin[1] and 'Eighteen Songs to the Hunnish Pipe' in *The Lute Player's Return*.[2] What do you think of that?"

All admitted that such a thing was even rarer. Then the old lady told servants to order Wen-kuan and her troupe to play with lute and flute *Full Moon at the Lantern Festival*, and they went off to carry out her instructions.

At this point Chia Jung and his wife offered toasts all round. The Lady Dowager was now in such high spirits that Hsi-feng suggested, "While the story-tellers are here, why don't we get them to drum for us while we pass round a spray of plum-blossom and play 'Spring Lights Up the Eyebrows'?"

"That's a fine drinking-game, and this is just the time for it," approved the old lady.

She sent for a black lacquered drum with copper studs which was kept for drinking-games, asked the story-tellers to beat it, and took a spray of red plum-blossom from the table.

"Whoever has the blossom when the drum stops must drink a cup and say something," she decreed.

"The rest of us aren't so smart as our Old Ancestress," objected Hsi-feng. "If we get stuck, it won't be any fun. Let's find something that highbrows and lowbrows alike can enjoy. Suppose the one caught with the blossom tells a joke?"

As Hsi-feng was noted for her jokes and endless fund of original quips, this met with the approval of all the feasters as well as the maid-servants there, both old and young. The young maids hurried out to urge their friends:

"Come quick! The Second Mistress is going to tell a joke." In no time at all the room was crowded with maids.

As soon as the performance ended, the old lady had refreshments sent to Wen-kuan and the other actresses. Then she ordered the drumming to start. The story-tellers, being old hands at this, varied the tempo and the plum was passed from hand to hand to its rhythm. First slow as the dripping of water from a clepsydra, the drumming soon gathered speed like the

---

[1] By the Ming playwright Kao Lien.
[2] By Tsao Yin, Tsao Hsueh-chin's grandfather.

patter of peas being poured into a bowl. Then, after a rapid tattoo like a horse stampeding or sudden flashes of lightning, the sound abruptly broke off just as the plum-blossom reached the old lady's hand. A roar of laughter went up, and Chia Jung at once stepped forward to fill her cup.

"Naturally the old lady's face should light up first," cried the others. "Then we shall be able to share in her happiness."

"I don't mind drinking a cup," she rejoined. "But I can't think of a joke."

"Why, Your Ladyship knows even more and better jokes than Hsi-feng," they expostulated. "Do tell us a good one, madam."

"I've no new jokes, but I'll just have to brazen it out. So here goes," said the old lady. "Well, a family had ten sons and ten daughters-in-law. The tenth daughter-in-law was the cleverest, so smart and so well-spoken that she was the favourite of her father and mother-in-law, who kept finding fault with the nine others. This seemed so unfair that the others put their heads together.

" 'We've been dutiful daughters-in-law,' they said. 'We're just not as smooth-spoken as that bitch, which is why the old couple keep on singing her praises. Who can we complain to about this injustice?'

"The eldest one suggested, 'Let's go tomorrow to the Temple of the King of Hell to offer incense and complain to him. We'll ask why, since we've all been born human, that bitch alone was given the gift of the gab while the rest of us are so dumb?'

"The other eight approved of this idea. They all went the next day to the temple and offered incense, then slept there at the foot of the altar while their spirits waited for the King of Hell to appear. They waited for a long time but nothing happened, and they were growing impatient when they saw Monkey King come somersaulting down through the clouds. At sight of these nine spirits, he raised his magic staff and threatened to beat them. The nine spirits knelt down fearfully to beg for mercy. Then Monkey asked what brought them there, and they told him the whole story. He stamped his foot.

" 'So that's the reason!' he sighed. 'It's a good thing you met *me*. If you'd waited for the King of Hell, he wouldn't have known.'

"The nine spirits pleaded, 'Have pity and tell us, Great Sage. That's all we ask.'

" 'That's easy,' answered Monkey with a smile. 'The day you ten girls were born, I'd gone to visit the King of Hell and happened to piss on the ground. Your youngest sister-in-law lapped it up. If you want the gift of the gab, I've plenty more piss you can drink if you like.' "

The whole company burst out laughing.

"Fine!" cried Hsi-feng. "It's lucky we're all so dumb here. Otherwise people might say we'd drunk monkey's piss."

Madam Yu and Madam Lou joked to Li Wan, "The one who's drunk monkey's piss is playing innocent!"

Aunt Hsueh remarked with a chuckle, "Topical jokes are always the funniest."

The drums started up again then, and some young maids who just wanted to hear Hsi-feng's jokes softly told the story-tellers that they would cough when it was time to stop. The plum-blossom went round twice and had just reached Hsi-feng when they coughed, and silence fell.

"Now we've caught her!" the others exulted. "Drink up quickly and let us have a good one. Just don't make us split our sides laughing."

Hsi-feng drained her cup and thought for a second.

"In the middle of the first month," she began, "during the Lantern Festival a family was having a fine lively time, enjoying lanterns and drinking together. There were the great-grandmother, grandmother, mothers-in-law, daughters-in-law, grand-daughters-in-law, great-grand-daughters-in-law, grand-sons, grand-nephews and a pack of great-great-grandsons, as well as grand-daughters and grand-nieces on the paternal and maternal sides, and grand-nieces on the brothers' and sisters' sides. . . . *Aiya*, it was really lively. . . ."

Already laughing they cried, "Listen to the way she runs on. Who else is she going to put in?"

"If you drag *me* in I'll pinch your lips," warned Madam Yu.

Hsi-fen sprang to her feet to protest, "Here am I hard at work, yet you keep butting in. All right, I won't say any more."

"Go on," urged the old lady. "What happened?"

Hsi-feng reflected before answering, "They sat up together feasting all night, and then the party broke up."

Having said this gravely with a straight face she stopped. The others waited in some mystification for her to go on, but all that followed was an icy silence.

Hsiang-yun stared at Hsi-feng until she said with a smile, "Here's another about the Lantern Festival. A man carried a fire-cracker as large as a house out of town to let it off, and thousands of people followed to watch. One fellow was so impatient that he set light to it on the sly with a stick of incense. Then — Whizz! Bang! — the crowd roared with laughter and dispersed. But the man carrying the fire-cracker complained:

" 'What a sloppy job the cracker-maker did! How could it burst apart before being lit?' "

"Surely he'd heard the bang?" objected Hsiang-yun.

"The man was deaf," Hsi-feng told her.

When this had sunk in, everybody burst out laughing.

Then reverting to the unfinished joke they asked: "What happened afterwards in your first story? Do finish that one too."

"What a question to ask!" cried Hsi-feng, banging the table. "The next day would have been the sixteenth, when the festival would be over and I suppose everyone would be busy clearing up. In that flurry who'd know what happened afterwards?"

At this they laughed again.

"The fourth watch has sounded outside," announced Hsi-feng. "I think our Old Ancestress is tired, and it's time for us to whizz off too like that deaf man's fire-cracker."

All the rest were rocking with laughter, their handkerchiefs pressed to their mouths. Madam Yu wagged a finger at Hsi-feng.

"How this creature does rattle on!" she spluttered.

"The minx is growing perter all the time," chuckled the

Lady Dowager. "She mentioned fire-crackers. We'll let off some fireworks, too, to sober ourselves up."

Chia Jung promptly went out to get pages to set up screens and stands in the courtyard on which to place or hang the fireworks. These had come as tribute from different parts of the country, and although not very large they were most ingeniously made in different colours, ornamented with scenes from stories and fitted with all kinds of fire-crackers.

As Tai-yu was too delicate to stand much noise, her grandmother held her close to her while Aunt Hsueh put her arms around Hsiang-yun, who declared with a smile that *she* was not afraid.

"She likes nothing better than letting off big fire-crackers herself," explained Pao-chai. "Why should she be scared of these?"

Lady Wang had taken Pao-yu on her lap.

"No one cares for poor little me!" Hsi-feng complained.

"*I* do," chuckled Madam Yu. "Come and sit on my knee and don't be afraid. You're behaving like a spoilt brat again. The sound of fireworks has sent you off your head, just as if you'd eaten bees' wax."

"When this party's over let's go and let off fireworks in the Garden," proposed Hsi-feng gaily. "I'm better at that than those page boys."

Meanwhile a pyrotechnical display was going on outside, including sparklers like "A Skyful of Stars," "Nine Dragons Soar to the Clouds," "A Bolt from the Blue," and "Ten Peals in the Air."

After this they ordered the young actresses to perform *Lotus Flowers Fall*, largesse was scattered all over the stage and the little girls scampered round gaily to snatch up the coins.

By the time soup was served the Lady Dowager remarked, "It's been a long night and I feel rather hungry."

"We've prepared some duck congee," Hsi-feng told her.

"I'd prefer something less greasy," was the reply.

"There's date congee too for the ladies observing a fast."

"One's too greasy, the other too sweet," complained the old lady.

"We've almond gruel as well. Only I'm afraid that's sweet too."

"That will do for me."

Then the tables were cleared, fresh delicacies served, and after a small collation they rinsed their mouths with tea and the party broke up.

In the morning of the seventeenth they went to the Ning Mansion's Ancestral Temple to sacrifice once more, after which the temple gates were closed, the ancestral portraits put away, and everybody went home.

That day Aunt Hsueh asked the others over to a New-Year feast. Other feasts were given by the stewards — on the eighteenth by Lai Ta, on the nineteenth by Lai Sheng of the Ning Mansion, on the twentieth by Lin Chih-hsiao, on the twenty-first by Shan Ta-liang, and on the twenty-second by Wu Hsin-teng. The Lady Dowager went to some of these only, staying on till the end if she was in a good mood, otherwise leaving after a short time.

As for relatives and friends who came in person to invite the Chias to a feast or to enjoy a feast given by them, she declined to meet all, making Lady Wang, Lady Hsing and Hsi-feng entertain the callers for her. And Pao-yu, claiming that his grandmother needed him to amuse her, went nowhere but to Wang Tzu-teng's house. So the old lady attended only those stewards' family parties where she could relax and enjoy herself. But enough of this.

Soon the festival was over. To know what happened afterwards, read the next chapter.

CHAPTER 55

A Stupid Concubine Insults Her Own Daughter
in a Futile Squabble
A Spiteful Servant Imposes upon
Her Young Mistress

The Lantern Festival passed. As one of the Dowager Concubines was unwell and the Emperor was known for his filial piety which had brought harmony to the land, all the Imperial Concubines ate and dressed simply, their visits home were cancelled, and there were no New-Year feasts or entertainments in the Palace. Consequently, there was no display of lantern riddles in the Jung Mansion this year.

No sooner was the bustle of New Year over than Hsi-feng had a miscarriage. She had to stop running the household for a month, and two or three doctors attended her every day; but overestimating her own strength, although staying indoors she continued mapping out plans for the household, which Ping-erh was sent to report to Lady Wang. All advice to rest she ignored.

Lady Wang felt as if she had lost her right arm, and simply had not the energy to cope. She decided important matters herself, entrusting lesser domestic affairs to Li Wan for the time being. But Li Wan, being one of those people who have more virtue than ability, inevitably let the servants have their own way; so Lady Wang told Tan-chun to help her out for a month, until Hsi-feng was well enough to take over again.

Hsi-feng had a delicate constitution, however, and as a girl had never looked after her health. In her passion to shine she had overtaxed her strength, with the result that her miscarriage left her very weak. A month after it she was still losing blood. Although she kept this a secret, everyone could see from her pallor and loss of weight that she was not taking proper care of herself. Lady Wang urged her not to worry about family affairs, but just to take medicine and recuperate. And as she herself was afraid that if she fell really ill other people would gloat, she concentrated on getting better as soon as possible. However, she did not start to mend for some time: not until the autumn did she begin to recover and gradually stop losing blood. But this is anticipating.

Meanwhile, seeing that for the time being Tan-chun and Li Wan could hardly be relieved of their responsibilities, and that there were many people in the Garden who needed to be kept in order, Lady Wang enlisted Pao-chai's help as well.

"The old serving-women are no use," she told her. "They drink and gamble whenever they have the chance, sleeping during the day so as to play cards at night. I know all they're up to. When Hsi-feng was up and about there was someone to scare them, but now they'll be taking advantage. You're a good steady girl, my dear. Your cousins are young and I'm busy — do you mind putting yourself out, for a couple of days, to keep an eye on things for me? If there's anything I overlook, come and let me know before the old lady asks and I'm stumped for an answer. If the servants misbehave, just tell them off. If they won't listen, let me know. We don't want to have any trouble."

Pao-chai had to agree to this.

It was now early spring and Tai-yu was coughing again while Hsiang-yun too was under the weather, confined to her bed in Alpinia Park, taking medicine day after day. As Tan-chun and Li Wan lived some distance from each other, now that they were working together it proved so inconvenient sending messages to and fro that they arranged to settle their business every morning in the small three-roomed hall south of the Garden gate. They took to having breakfast there and returning to their own quarters about noon.

This hall had served as the headquarters for the eunuchs in charge at the time of the Imperial Consort's visit, since when it had only been used by some old maid-servants who kept watch there at night. As the weather was warm now no major repairs were needed: a little fixing up made the place fit for the two of them to use. The tablet over this hall bore the inscription "Assisting Benevolence and Discussing Virtue," but members of the household called it the Council Hall.

Now the two young mistresses came here at six every morning and did not leave until noon, after an endless stream of women-servants had reported on the matters entrusted to them. These women had all exulted secretly at the news that Li Wan was to be in sole charge, thinking her too kind-hearted to punish anyone, and obviously much easier to impose on than Hsi-feng. It did not worry them either when Tan-chun later joined her, for they discounted her as a young unmarried girl who had always been most pleasant and easy-going. So they became much slacker than before. After only a few days, however, it dawned on them from the way certain matters were handled that Tan-chun was every bit as alert as Hsi-feng, being simply more soft-spoken and even-tempered.

It happened now that a dozen or so promotions, demotions, marriages or funerals in the families of nobles or hereditary officials related to or friendly with the Jung and Ning houses kept Lady Wang busy for several days in a row, paying visits of congratulation or condolence. This left her less time than ever to attend to affairs at home.

So Li Wan and Tan-chun remained in the hall all day long, while Pao-chai supervised the servants in Lady Wang's apartments until her return; and last thing at night, after doing some needlework, she would make a tour of the Garden in a small sedan-chair accompanied by those on watch. Thus the three of them controlled things even more strictly than when Hsi-feng was in charge.

"We're only just rid of one demon patrolling the sea, and here come three guardian mountain spirits instead!" all the servants started grousing secretly. "We've not even a chance now to drink and play cards at night."

One day, Lady Wang was invited to a feast in the house of

the Marquis of Chinhsiang. Li Wan and Tan-chun rose early to attend her until she left, then went back to the hall. They were sipping tea there when Wu Hsin-teng's wife came in to inform them that Chao Kuo-chi, the brother of Concubine Chao, had died the previous day.

"I reported this yesterday to the mistress," she said. "She told me to let you ladies know."

She made no further comment after this, just stood by at respectful attention.

All the servants who had come to report on business were eager to see how these two would handle the matter. If it was handled correctly they would respect them; if the least mistake was made, not only would they despise them, once out of the inner gate they would start gossiping and making fun of them. Mrs. Wu knew what should be done, and had she been dealing with Hsi-feng she would have made various suggestions to curry favour, quoting precedents for her to decide between. But as she looked down on Li Wan as a simpleton and Tan-chun as only a girl, she said no more, waiting to see what the two of them would do.

Tan-chun consulted Li Wan, who thought for a moment.

"The other day when Hsi-jen's mother died, I understand she was given forty taels," she said. "We can give the same amount."

Mrs. Wu promptly assented, took the tally and was about to go off when Tan-chun stopped her.

"Don't go for the money yet," said Tan-chun. "I've something to ask you. Some of those old concubines in the old lady's apartments came from outside, some from families serving here. There was a distinction. If a relative of one from our household died, how much was given? How much to one from outside? Give us a couple of examples."

When questioned like this, Mrs. Wu could not remember.

"It doesn't matter," she answered with a smile. "Whatever sum's given, who would dare to complain?"

"Nonsense!" retorted Tan-chun pleasantly. "I would just as soon give a *hundred* taels; but if I didn't go by the rules, not only would you laugh at me but I shouldn't be able to face the Second Mistress."

"In that case I'll go and look up the old accounts," offered Mrs. Wu. "I can't for the moment remember."

"You're an old hand at this," Tan-chun pointed out. "Yet you claim to have forgotten, so as to make things awkward for us. Do you have to go and look up the accounts when you report to the Second Mistress? If so, Hsi-feng would count as lenient, not as exacting. Fetch those accounts at once. One more day's delay, and instead of blaming you for negligence people will accuse us of incompetence."

Mrs. Wu flushed scarlet and hurried out, while the other stewards' wives stuck out their tongues in dismay. Then other matters were reported.

Soon Mrs. Wu came back with the old accounts. Tan-chun, taking them, found that two concubines who had been family servants had received twenty taels apiece, and two from outside forty. Two others from outside had received a hundred taels and sixty taels respectively; but it was recorded that this was because the first was allowed an extra sixty to have her parents' coffins moved to another province; the second was allowed an extra twenty to buy a burial ground.

Tan-chun showed these items to Li Wan.

"Give her twenty taels," she ordered Mrs. Wu.

"And leave these accounts here for us to go through carefully." Mrs. Wu assented and withdrew.

Suddenly Concubine Chao burst in. Li Wan and Tan-chun at once asked her to be seated.

"Everyone in this house tramples on my head," she stormed. "I should think *you* at least, miss, should take my side!" She began to sob and snivel as she was speaking.

"Whom are you accusing, madam?" asked Tan-chun. "I don't understand. Who's trampling on your head? If you'll tell me, I'll take your side."

"You're the one — so whom can I complain to?"

Tan-chun hastily rose to protest, "I wouldn't dare."

Li Wan also stood up to act as a peacemaker.

"Sit down, please, and listen to me!" cried the concubine. "I've been treated like dirt in this house all these years, though I've borne you and your brother, and now I rank even lower than Hsi-jen. What face have I got left? Not only me — this makes *you* lose face too."

"So that's it." Tan-chun smiled. "As if I dared take the law into my own hands!"

Sitting down again, she showed Concubine Chao the account books and read out the items to her.

"These are the rules handed down by our ancestors," she declared. "We all have to abide by them — how could *I* change them? Hsi-jen isn't a special case. If Huan takes a concubine from outside later on, she'll naturally rank the same as Hsi-jen. This isn't a question of competing for status, it has nothing to do with face. If someone's in our mistress' service, I can only go by the rules. The sum's given thanks to the kindness of our ancestors and our mistress. If that someone thinks it unfair and is too stupid to know when she's well off, I can't stop her complaining. If our mistress were to give away the whole *house*, I'd get no face from it. If she didn't give a cent, it wouldn't make me lose face either.

"Take my advice and have a quiet rest while the mistress is out. Why work yourself up? The mistress is kindness itself to me, but you've grieved her more than once by the way you make trouble. If I were a boy, able to leave this house, I'd have gone long ago to make my own way in the world, for then of course I'd know what to do. It's too bad that I'm only a girl and mustn't say a word out of turn. The mistress fully understands, and thinks well enough of me to put me in charge; but before I've managed to be of any use you come and start picking on me. If she found out and relieved me of the job so as not to embarrass me, then I'd *really* lose face. And so would you as well." By this time she was sobbing bitterly.

The concubine having no other answer to this retorted, "If the mistress is partial to you, that's all the more reason to lend us a helping hand. But you've quite forgotten us in your eagerness to curry favour with *her*."

"Who says I've forgotten you? How am I to lend a helping hand? You have to ask yourselves: Don't all mistresses like inferiors who make themselves useful? Good people don't need the kind offices of others."

Li Wan put in soothingly, "Don't be angry, madam. It's not her fault. She's only too eager to help you, but how can she say so?"

"Don't be ridiculous, sister-in-law!" cried Tan-chun. "Who do you mean I'm to help? Does the daughter of any house help servants? You should know what they are — their affairs are none of my business."

"Who asked you to help others?" fumed the concubine. "If you weren't in charge I wouldn't have come to you. Now if you say one it's one, if you say two it's two. If you gave an extra twenty or thirty taels for your uncle's funeral, why should the mistress object? Everyone knows how good she is — it's you people who are so stingy. It's too bad she has no chance to show her kindness. But don't worry, miss, it's not your own silver you're saving. I'd always hoped, after you married, you'd show more consideration to the Chao family; but now before your feathers have grown you've forgotten your roots, you're so keen to fly to the very top of the tree."

Before she had finished, Tan-chun's face was white with anger.

Nearly choking with sobs she demanded, "Who's my uncle? My uncle's just been appointed Military Inspector of Nine Provinces. What other uncles do I have? Is this my reward for always observing the rules of propriety — to have all these relatives foisted off on me? If what you say were true, why did Chao Kuo-chi have to stand up whenever Huan went out? Why follow him to school? Why didn't he behave like an uncle?

"Do you have to make such a scene? Everyone knows I'm a child by a concubine, yet you needs must bring it up every few months and rub it in, as if you had to make it plain for fear they didn't know. Who's making the other lose face? It's lucky I've sense enough to remember my manners, or you'd have driven me frantic long ago!"

Li Wan tried desperately to pacify them, but the concubine went on ranting. She did not stop until it was announced:

"Miss Ping-erh has come with a message from the Second Mistress."

Concubine Chao greeted Ping-erh with a smile and urged her to take a seat.

"Is your mistress better?" she asked. "I've been meaning to call on her but haven't yet found the time."

Li Wan asked Ping-erh her business.

"The Second Mistress thought you ladies might not know what the usual allowance would be in connection with the death of Concubine Chao's brother," answered Ping-erh. "The rule is to give only twenty taels, but it's up to you to decide. You can give more if you want."

"Why make an exception in this case?" retorted Tan-chun who had now dried her eyes. "Was he a prodigy who took twenty-four months to be born, or someone who saved his master's life in the army? How clever your mistress is, wanting me to break the rules while she gets the credit, buying herself goodwill at our mistress' expense! Tell her *I* don't dare to increase or cut down amounts for no good reason. If she wants to be charitable and add something, she'll have to wait till she's better."

Ping-erh had sensed as soon as she came in that something was wrong. After this tirade she grasped the situation. And since Tan-chun was glowering instead of replying with one of her usual jokes she waited there in a respectful silence.

At this point Pao-chai arrived too from Lady Wang's apartments. Tan-chun and the others rose to offer her a seat; but before they could enter into conversation another woman came in to make her report. And as Tan-chun's face was tear-stained, three or four young maids brought in a basin, towels and a mirror with a handle. One of them knelt before Tan-chun, who was cross-legged on the couch, and held the basin out to her while two others knelt beside her with the towels, mirror and cosmetics. Seeing that Tai-shu was not there to help, Ping-erh stepped forward to roll up Tan-chun's sleeves, take off her bracelets, and drape a large towel over the front of her clothes. Tan-chun had just dipped her hands into the basin when the woman who had come in announced:

"If you please, my ladies, the family school has sent for this year's allowance for Master Huan and Master Lan."

"What's the hurry?" scolded Ping-erh. "Can't you see the young lady is washing? You should wait outside, not come butting in like this. Would you be so impertinent to the Second Mistress? The young lady may be kind-hearted, but don't blame me if my mistress hears of this and your lack of respect gets you all into trouble."

"How stupid of me!" cried the woman in dismay, then hastily left the room.

Tan-chun, now powdering her face, smiled ironically at Ping-erh.

"You came just too late to see something still more ridiculous," she said. "Even an old hand like Mrs. Wu came without checking up on her facts in order to trip us up. When challenged, she'd the nerve to say she'd forgotten. I asked if that was the way she reported to the Second Mistress. I doubt whether that mistress of yours would put up with it."

"If she tried that just once, I can promise you she'd have her legs broken," replied Ping-erh. "You can't trust these people an inch, miss. They're trying to take advantage, because Madam Chu's a real Bodhisattva and you're such a gentle young lady." Turning towards the door she called to the women outside, "All right, just take all the liberties you like. Wait till Madam Lien's well again, and we'll settle scores with you!"

The matrons outside answered, "You're most understanding, miss. You know the saying: 'If a man does wrong, he alone must take the blame.' *We'd* never presume to deceive Miss Tan-chun. We'd deserve to die and go unburied if we provoked a delicate young lady like her."

"So long as you know that," replied Ping-erh scornfully. Then she turned with a smile to Tan-chun. "You know how busy Madam Lien was, miss. She couldn't cope with everything and is bound to have overlooked certain things. As the proverb says, 'The spectator sees most of the sport.' As a detached observer all these years, you may have noticed cases where she failed to make suitable cuts or additions. If you'll set these right, you'll first of all be helping the mistress in her work and showing your friendship for my lady as well. . . ."

"What a clever girl!" exclaimed Pao-chai and Li Wan, smiling, before Ping-erh could finish. "No wonder Hsi-feng is so attached to you. We'd no intention of making any changes, but after what you've said we shall reconsider one or two cases to show our appreciation."

"I was so furious I wanted to work off my feelings on her mistress." Tan-chun laughed. "But turning up and talking like this she has quite taken the wind out of my sails." She called in the woman who had just come and asked her, "What are these annual allowances for Master Huan and Master Lan for?"

"For a year's refreshments at school and the remainder for stationery," was the reply. "Each gets eight taels of silver a year."

"All the young masters' expenses are covered by the monthly allowances for the different apartments," countered Tan-chun. "Huan's two taels a month are given to Concubine Chao, Pao-yu's to the old lady's maid Hsi-jen; and Lan's to Madam Chu's maid. So why this extra eight taels for the school? Do they go to school for the sake of this eight taels? From now on this will be cancelled. Tell your mistress this from me, Ping-erh, when you go back. Say I think there's no need for it."

"This should have been cut long ago," said the maid with a smile. "Last year my mistress did speak of doing it, but with all the bustle over New Year she forgot."

Then the matron had to assent and take herself off.

Now servants from Grand View Garden brought lunch hampers, and Ping-erh set out the dishes on the small table put ready by Tai-shu and Su-yun.

"You can go and attend to your business now that you've had your say," Tan-chun told her. "You don't have to help out here."

"I'm free now," replied Ping-erh, smiling. "The Second Mistress sent me partly to give you that message, partly to help the girls wait on you if I found you short-handed."

"Where's Miss Pao-chai's lunch?" asked Tan-chun.

Some girls hurried out to notify the matrons, "Miss Pao-chai's lunching here too. Have her food brought over."

Hearing this Tan-chun said loudly, "Don't start ordering them about. They're all the wives of chief stewards, not people you can send to fetch rice and tea! Have you no manners? Ping-erh has nothing to do here. Let her go."

Ping-erh promptly agreed and went out.

The stewards' wives quietly drew her aside and said, "There's no need for you to go, miss. We've already sent someone." They dusted off the steps with their handkerchiefs and urged her to have a rest there in the sun after standing for so long.

As soon as she sat down, two women from the boiler house brought over a mattress.

"That stone's cold, miss," they said. "This is quite clean, do use it."

As she thanked them with a smile, someone else brought her a bowl of good freshly brewed tea.

"This isn't our usual tea but some for the young ladies," she whispered. "Do try it."

Ping-erh inclined her head and accepted it.

Then wagging a finger at them all she scolded, "You've really gone too far. She's only a girl and, quite properly, doesn't like to lose her temper; but that's no reason why you should be rude to her. If you really made her angry, at worst she could be blamed for flaring up but you'd get into big trouble. If she made a scene, even Lady Wang would have to humour her, and there's nothing the Second Mistress could do either. How have you the nerve to slight her in that way? It's like an egg dashing itself against a rock."

"How dare we?" they protested. "It was all Concubine Chao's fault."

"That's enough, my good women," whispered Ping-erh. " 'If

a wall starts tottering, everyone gives it a shove.' Concubine Chao does tend to turn things upside down, I grant you, but when there's trouble you put all the blame on her. I've seen for myself these years the airs you give yourselves and the tricks you play. If the Second Mistress weren't so able, you fine ladies would have got the upper hand of her long ago. Every chance you get, you still try to land her in trouble. Several times she's only just missed falling into your traps.

"People say you're scared of her because she's such a terror," Ping-erh continued. "But I who know her best can tell you she's afraid of you too. Only the other day, we were saying things couldn't go on like this — there were bound to be a couple of rumpuses. Though Miss Tan-chun's an unmarried young lady, you've all misjudged her. She's the only one of the young ladies that my mistress is half afraid of; yet you think you can treat her any way you please!"

They were interrupted by Chiu-wen's arrival. All the matrons greeted her and urged her to rest for a while.

"They're having lunch inside," they explained. "You'd better not go in till they've finished."

"What time have I to wait?" retorted Chiu-wen. "I'm not like you."

She was walking in when Ping-erh called her back. At sight of her Chiu-wen smiled.

"What are *you* doing here? Acting as an extra bodyguard?" she asked, sitting down by her on the mattress.

"What business brings you here?" asked Ping-erh softly.

"We want to know when the monthly allowances for Pao-yu and the rest of us will be issued."

"Very important, I must say! Go back quickly and tell Hsi-jen from me not to try to settle any business today. Every single request you make will be refused."

Chiu-wen asked the reason and all of them promptly told her.

"They're looking for some big issues and someone who counts to make an example of as a warning to everyone," Ping-erh explained. "Why should you bump *your* head against this brick wall? If you go in now, they can hardly make an example of you, out of deference to Their Ladyships; but if they don't they may be accused of bias, of not daring to touch those backed by Their Ladyships and just picking on the weak instead. Wait and see. They're even countermanding a few of the Second Mistress' rulings too — that's their only way to stop gossip."

Chiu-wen stuck out her tongue in dismay.

"Thank goodness you came here, Sister Ping-erh!" she cried. "You've saved me from a snubbing. I'll go straight back and tell them." With that she left.

At this point Pao-chai's meal arrived and Ping-erh went in to serve her. Concubine Chao had now left and the three others were eating on the couch, Pao-chai facing south, Tan-chun west and Li Wan east. The matrons waited quietly outside on the verandah, none but personal serving-maids venturing to go in.

"We'd better watch our step and not try anything on," said the matrons softly. "Mrs. Wu was sent off with a flea in her ear, and do we have more face than she does?" They decided not to go in until lunch was over.

All was quiet now inside, with no clatter of bowls or chopsticks. Presently a maid raised the portière and two others carried out the table. Three girls from the boiler house had brought three basins of water, and as soon as the table was removed they went in, reappearing before long with the basins and rinse-bowls. Then Tai-shu, Su-yun and Ying-erh took in three covered bowls of tea on trays.

When these three came out again Tai-shu instructed the younger maids, "You must see to things here till we come back from our meal. Don't sneak off to have a rest."

Then, slowly, the matrons made their reports in turn, not presuming to behave with their previous impertinence.

Tan-chun, somewhat mollified, remarked to Ping-erh, "I've just happened to remember something important I've been meaning to discuss with your mistress. Come back straight after your meal, will you? As Miss Pao-chai is here too, the four of us can talk it over before asking your mistress whether she agrees or not."

Ping-erh assented and left.

"Why were you away so long?" asked Hsi-feng on her return.

Ping-erh gave her a detailed account of all that had happened.

"Splendid! Good for Tan-chun!" Hsi-feng smiled. "What did I always say? It's too bad she wasn't fated to be the mistress' own daughter."

"So you, too, talk nonsense, dear madam!" retorted Ping-erh. "She may not be the mistress' own child, but everyone has to show her the same respect as the other daughters of the house."

"You don't understand." Hsi-feng sighed. "Though we may *say* they're the same, a girl can't compare with a boy. When the time comes to arrange her marriage, some foolish people will first ask whether she's the daughter of the wife or of a concubine, and most likely refuse her in the second case. Although, not to mention a concubine's child, even one of the maids in our family is better than the daughters of other households. Some unlucky family may lose an excellent daughter-in-law by insisting on the wife's daughter, and some lucky one may do well by not being so choosy."

She changed the subject then, continuing, "You know how hard I've tried to save money these last few years, which must have made the whole household secretly curse me. I'm riding on a tiger's back, and though I'm not clamping down too strictly at present I can't let everything slide. Besides, our expenses have increased while our income's dwindled; yet we still have to manage all affairs large and small according to the ancestors' old rules, in spite of less money coming in every year. If I economize too much, outsiders may jeer and Their Ladyships will feel the pinch, while the rest of the household complain of my stinginess. On the other hand, if I don't devise ways to save money in good time, another few years may see us bankrupted."

"That's very true," agreed Ping-erh. "And there's big expenditure still to come with the marriages of three or four young ladies and two or three young masters, as well as the Old Ancestress' funeral."

"I've taken those into account. We've enough for that. The

marriages of Pao-yu and Tai-yu won't cost the estate anything, as the old lady will pay for them herself. We can count Ying-chun out too, as she belongs to the Elder Master's side. That leaves Tan-chun and Hsi-chun, who will require ten thousand taels each at the most. Huan's marriage shouldn't cost more than three thousand, which we can raise easily by cutting down on other expenses.

"As for the old lady's funeral, all the preparations have already been made, and sundry minor expenses will amount at most to another four or five thousand. So if we economize now we should do all right. It's only the possibility of some unforeseen expenses that makes me anxious, for then we'd really be in serious trouble. Still, it's no use worrying now.

"Hurry up and have your meal, then go back to hear what they're discussing. This is just the chance I wanted: it worried me that I had no assistant. Although there's Pao-yu, he's not cut out for the job — even if I win him to my side he's not much use. Madam Chu's too saintly to be of any use either. And Ying-chun's even worse, apart from the fact that she doesn't belong to our house. Hsi-chun's still too young; Lan's even younger. As for Huan, he's like a kitten half perished with cold, always looking for a stove or heated *kang* to creep under and get his hair singed. It really and truly passes my understanding how one mother could bear two such utterly different children!

"Tai-yu and Pao-chai, now, are both good girls; but not being daughters of our family they can't very well mind our affairs. Besides, one's a lovely paper lantern which a puff of wind will blow out; and it's no use asking the other anything, as she's made up her mind not to open her mouth about matters that don't concern her, but to shake her head in answer to all questions.

"That leaves only Tan-chun, who's quick in the uptake with a ready tongue, a daughter of the house and a favourite with the mistress — she just doesn't show it because of the trouble made by that old bitch Concubine Chao, but at heart she's as fond of her as of Pao-yu. Tan-chun's totally different from

Huan, whom nobody could like. If I had *my* way, he'd have been thrown out long ago. Now that she's made this proposal, we should co-operate and help each other; then I won't be on my own any longer.

"From the point of view of what's fair and right, a helper like her will save us worry and make the mistress' task so much easier. From a selfish point of view, I've made myself so unpopular that it's time for me to back down and look about me; because if I go on being so strict I shall get myself thoroughly hated, and everybody's smiles will hide daggers! You and I have only four eyes and two brains between us: if they once catch us off guard they can do for us. We must make the most of this chance. So long as she's in charge, they'll forget their past grudges against us for the time being.

"And there's another thing I must tell you, as you may not have spotted it for all you're so smart. Young as Tan-chun is she's no fool, only careful how she talks. In fact, with her book-learning, she's smarter than I am. She must know the saying 'To catch rebels first catch the chief.' So to set an example she's bound to start with me. If she reverses any of my decisions, don't argue with her but back her up, the more respectfully the better. On no account protest for fear I lose face."

Long before the end of this speech Ping-erh was smiling.

"What do you take me for — a fool?" she retorted. "That's what I've been doing, and here you are warning me."

"I was afraid you'd forget other people in your concern for me, that's why. If that's what you've been doing, it shows you've more sense than *I* have. Don't get so worked up, though, that you forget yourself and whom you're talking to."

"That's my way," countered Ping-erh. "If you don't like it you can slap my face again. It won't be the first time."

"You bitch!" Hsi-feng laughed. "How many times do you have to harp on that? Why be so provoking when you can see I'm ill? Come and sit down. As we're all on our own let's have our meal together."

Feng-erh and three or four other young maids came in then

with a small table, which they set on the *kang*. Hsi-feng ate nothing but some bird's-nest gruel and two tasty side-dishes, having cancelled her usual food for the time being. Feng-erh set Ping-erh's normal four dishes before her and helped her to rice. Then Ping-erh, half kneeling on the *kang* and half standing, accompanied her mistress. The meal at an end, she helped Hsi-feng wash and rinse her mouth. Then, having given Feng-erh some instructions, she went back to rejoin Tan-chun.

But she found the courtyard quiet and deserted. To know the reason, read the following chapter.

CHAPTER 56

Clever Tan-chun Devises a Scheme to Make
a Profit and End Abuses
Understanding Pao-chai Rounds It Out with
a Small Act of Kindness

After eating with Hsi-feng and waiting on her while she washed and then rinsed her mouth, Ping-erh went back to Tan-chun. She found the Council Hall quiet, with a few maids and matrons waiting outside the windows. As she walked in, the three cousins were discussing family affairs and had just brought up the subject of Lai Ta's garden, where they had feasted shortly before New Year.

Tan-chun offered Ping-erh a foot-stool.

"Here's what I was thinking," she told her. "In addition to our monthly allowance of two taels, our maids have separate allowances; but a few days ago someone reported that each of us gets an extra two taels a month for hair-oil, rouge and powder. This is like that extra allowance of eight taels for the school just now — another duplication. Admittedly it's a small matter, involving very little money, but it doesn't seem right. Why hasn't this occurred to your mistress?"

"There's a reason," answered Ping-erh. "Of course the young ladies should be provided with cosmetics every month, and they're bought by the stewards in charge, then delivered by the matrons to us in the different apartments to be kept ready for when the young ladies need them. That's to save us the trouble of having to send out all the time to buy them. So the stewards get the lump sum for this item, and distribute the cosmetics each month to the different apartments.

"As for the monthly allowance of two taels, that was never meant for this purpose. It was so that you don't have to search for the mistresses in charge, if they're away or too busy to be bothered when you happen to need a little money. In other words, to see that you don't go short. That money obviously isn't meant for cosmetics. But I've noticed that at least half our sisters attending in the different apartments make these purchases with their own money. I suspect it's because the stewards aren't supplying them on time, or because what they buy is of a poor quality."

"So you've noticed that too." Tan-chun and Li Wan smiled. "The stewards supply us all right, they wouldn't dare stop, but always a few days late. When we hurry them they produce something inferior, goodness knows from where, which we can never use. We still have to buy our own with those two taels. We have to ask the sons of other people's nurses or brothers to do this — they get us what we want. But if we send those servants in charge, they buy the same kind, we can't imagine why. Could it be that they just buy us shop-soiled rejects?"

Ping-erh smiled.

"If the stewards get you that kind and they were to buy something better, of course the stewards would be annoyed and accuse them of trying to do them out of a job," she explained. "That's why they have to do this. They'd rather offend you ladies than the stewards. But when you send your nurses, no one can complain."

"It's been worrying me," put in Tan-chun, "because we spend two lots of money but half the purchases are wasted. That means we're spending twice as much as we should. So my first proposal is to stop that monthly allowance to the stewards. I've another idea too. You went with us to Lai Ta's house before New Year. How did you think his small garden compared with ours?"

"It's less than half the size and has far fewer trees and flowers."

"I had a chat with one of their girls," continued Tan-chun. "I learned to my surprise that its annual produce — apart from the flowers they wear and the bamboo shoots, vegetables, fish and prawns they eat — has been contracted for by people who pay them at least two hundred taels a year. That was how I first learned that even a snapped lotus leaf or a blade of withered grass is worth money."

"Truly spoken like a rich young dandy!" laughed Pao-chai. "Though sheltered young ladies know nothing about such things, in the course of your studies you've surely read Chu Hsi's essay *On Not Debasing Oneself*?"[1]

"Of course I have. Just a lot of exhortations and empty talk, I call it. Such things can't really happen."

"So even Chu Hsi's writings are empty talk, are they?" retorted Pao-chai. "No, every word there is true. After just two days of managing affairs you've become so mercenary that you accuse Chu Hsi of empty talk! I suppose if you worked outside, where you'd profit more by cutting down bigger expenses, you'd bring the same accusation against even Confucius!"

"Well-read as you are," countered Tan-chun, "haven't you read *Chi Tzu*?[2] Chi Tzu said, 'Those in a position to seek profit and emolument, or responsible for planning and calculating, may talk like Yao and Shun but disobey the precepts of Confucius and Mencius.'"

Pao-chai smiled as Tan-chun broke off and urged, "Go on."

"That's all I want to quote. Why should I go on to make fun of myself?"

"There's nothing useless in this world, and when something has a use it's worth money. I'd have thought, where a serious matter like this is concerned, you had sense enough to grasp such a self-evident truth."

"You call us here," put in Li Wan, "but instead of talking business the two of you just carry on an academic discussion."

"This academic discussion has a bearing on our business," replied Pao-chai. "If our small tasks aren't guided by principles, they'll get out of hand and sink to the vulgar level of the market-place."

---

[1] From *Commentaries on Mencius* by Chu Hsi, a Northern Sung neo-Confucianist.

[2] An unknown work. It may have been invented by the author.

After this joking they got down to business.

Tan-chun reverting to her earlier question said, "If we consider our Garden just twice the size of theirs, it should bring in double the profit — four hundred taels a year. Of course, it would be petty and unworthy of our family to concentrate solely now on making money. But if a couple of women are assigned to take charge, all the valuable things here won't be squandered — it's a shame to let them go to waste. Better choose a few of the most reliable old women here who know something about gardening, and let them see to things. We needn't charge them or ask for any rent if they send in some presents every year.

"In the first place, with people in charge of the flowers and trees, the Garden will naturally improve as time goes on and we shan't be called on for sudden emergency measures. In the second place, there'll be no waste either. In the third, the old women won't be working hard all year for nothing, but will have a few perks. In the fourth, what we save on the gardeners' and cleaners' pay can be spent on improvements and repairs. How's that?"

"Very good!" Pao-chai, who was standing looking at the scrolls on the walls, nodded approvingly. " 'Within three years an end will be put to famine.' "[1]

"That's an excellent idea," approved Li Wan too. "If we do this the mistress is sure to be pleased. Saving money isn't the main thing, but we shall need fewer cleaners too. If there are people in charge of the Garden's upkeep who are allowed to make something on the side, given the authority and a profit incentive they're bound to do their best."

"This proposal had to come from you, miss," remarked Ping-erh. "My mistress had the same idea, but she could hardly suggest it with all you young ladies living in the Garden. Instead of improving the place, how could she propose putting people in charge to save money?"

Pao-chai stepped up to her and patted her cheek.

"Open your mouth and let me see what your teeth and tongue

---

[1] A sentence from the *Analects of Confucius.*

are made of!" she cried. "From first thing this morning till now you've done so much talking, and you've a different argument each time. You neither praise Miss Tan-chun to her face nor admit that your mistress ever overlooks anything, nor do you agree to whatever Miss Tan-chun says; but each time she makes some proposal you have your answer pat — the same idea occurred to your mistress, too, but there was always some reason why she couldn't suggest it.

"Now you're saying that because *we* live here she couldn't put people in charge so as to save money. Can't you two see what that means? If we really let people make money out of the Garden, they naturally won't want anyone to pick a single flower or fruit. Of course they won't dare deny *us*, but they'll be quarrelling all the time with our maids. How far-sighted and circumspect Ping-erh is! She neither argues back nor flatters you. If her mistress weren't good to us, as in fact she is, hearing Ping-erh talk like this would surely make her repent and mend her ways."

"I was in a bad temper this morning," said Tan-chun. "When I heard *she'd* come I suddenly thought of her mistress and of how insubordinate all the servants have grown under her management. So the sight of Ping-erh made me even angrier. But she came in like a mouse shrinking from a cat, and looked so pathetic all the time she stood there; and then the way she *talked*! Instead of reminding me how good her mistress is to me, she spoke of *my* consideration for her mistress. That not only stopped me being angry but made me so ashamed I felt like crying. I thought: a girl like myself, who's reduced to such a state that nobody cares for me — what can I do for anyone else?" At this point she broke down again and wept.

Her distress reminded Li Wan and the others of all the instances of Concubine Chao's outrageous behaviour, which had involved Tan-chun, making her embarrassed to face Lady Wang. They could not help shedding tears of sympathy.

"Don't talk like that," they urged. "What does it matter? Now that we're free, let's work out a couple of ways to make a profit and get rid of past abuses, so as to prove ourselves worthy of the mistress' trust."

"I understand," put in Ping-erh hastily. "Just trust this business to some reliable people of your own choosing, miss, and that will be that."

"That's all very well, but we must consult your mistress first," insisted Tan-chun. "We've already overstepped our authority, scrimping and scraping, right and left, and I wouldn't suggest this if she weren't so understanding. If she were officious or spiteful, I'd never have dreamed of it either — it would look as if I were trying to show her up. We certainly must consult her."

"In that case I'll go and tell her," said Ping-erh, and with that she went off.

After a while she came back to tell them gaily, "I *said* there was no need to go. It's such a good idea, of course my mistress approves."

Then Tan-chun and Li Wan asked for a list of the names of all the elderly women in the Garden, and after some discussion made a tentative choice of a few. These women, summoned and told the plan in outline by Li Wan, agreed to it readily.

"Just leave that bamboo plot to me," said one. "In a year's time there'll be another plot. Then, apart from supplying the household with bamboo shoots, I can hand in some money too."

Another said, "Let me have the paddy fields. I can keep all the pet birds, big and small, supplied with grain the whole year round without asking the stewards for any, and pay something over and above that too."

Before Tan-chun could reply, it was announced that a doctor had come to the Garden to see a young lady, and the matrons should go to escort him in.

"Even if a hundred of you were to go to meet the doctor it wouldn't look proper," objected Ping-erh. "Surely there are chief stewards' wives to take him in?"

"Yes, Mrs. Wu and Mrs. Shan," the messenger answered. "They're waiting in the southwest corner by the Gate of Embroidery."

Then Ping-erh let the matter drop. And as soon as the women had gone Tan-chun asked Pao-chai her opinion.

"'One who is zealous at the start may grow lax before the finish,'" quoted Pao-chai smiling. "Fine speech may hide a hankering after profit."

Tan-chun nodded her agreement, then selected a few more names from the list for the other three's consideration, whereupon Ping-erh fetched a brush and inkstone.

"Mrs. Chu is a reliable old soul," they said. "Besides, her husband and son have always looked after bamboos, so we may as well put all the bamboos here in her care. And then there's old Mrs. Tien who comes from a farming family. The paddy fields and vegetable plots in Paddy-Sweet Cottage are only for fun and don't need to be cultivated seriously; still, it would be better to have her there in charge during the different seasons."

"What a pity there's nothing we can turn to profit in Happy Red Court and Alpinia Park, large as they both are," remarked Tan-chun.

"Why, Alpinia Park's even better," declared Li Wan. "Isn't it full of the spices and herbs you find sold by perfumers, as well as at all the big markets and temple fairs? I reckon those will bring in the biggest profit of the lot. As for Happy Red Court, not to mention anything else, just think how many roses it has all spring and summer. That fence there is covered with rambler roses and monthly-roses, as well as honeysuckle and other flowers, all of which fetch a good price in tea-shops and pharmacies when they're dried."

"Is that so?" asked Tan-chun with a smile. "We've no one, though, who understands such things."

"The mother of Ying-erh who works for Miss Pao-chai does," Ping-erh informed them. "Have you forgotten that time she gathered and dried some sprigs to make me baskets?"

"I've just been singing your praises, yet now you're laying a trap for me," protested Pao-chai jokingly.

"What do you mean?" asked the other three in surprise.

"This is out of the question," she answered. "All your attendants here with nothing to do will certainly think badly of

me if I bring in someone else.   Let me suggest another woman
instead: Ming-yen's mother, old Mrs. Yeh, in Happy Red
Court.   She's an honest old soul and on good terms with
Ying-erh's mother.   You may as well entrust this to her.   If
there's something she doesn't understand, *we* shan't have to tell
her to consult Ying-erh's mother, she may even leave the whole
job to her — that's up to them.   But if anyone gossips it won't
be our concern.   Handled this way it will look fair and the work
will be properly done."

Ping-erh and Li Wan approved but Tan-chun teased, "I'm
only afraid they may forget friendship for profit!"

"Not they," Ping-erh assured her.   "Only the other day Ying-
erh became Mrs. Yeh's god-daughter and they had a feast to
celebrate.   Those two families are on the best of terms."

Then Tan-chun made no further objection.

By the time they had settled on a few other women who had
won their approval, and marked their names on the list, the
matrons returned to report that the doctor had gone and showed
them his prescription.   Having examined it, the three young
ladies sent for the ingredients and ordered them to be prepared.
Tan-chun and Li Wan then informed the women of the places
entrusted to them.

"Apart from what it's decided the household requires, all the
rest of the year's produce will be yours," announced Li Wan.
"And you must present an account at the end of the year."

"I've thought of something else," put in Tan-chun.   "If the
accounts are made up at the end of the year and you take the
money to the accountants' office in the usual way, there'll be
someone again in control of you.   You'll still be in their clutches,
and they'll be able to fleece you.   As this is *our* idea and we've
bypassed them by entrusting the work to you, they'll resent it
even if they don't say so outright; thus they're bound to squeeze
you if you go to them to settle your annual accounts.   Why,
every year the steward managing each property or estate gets
one-third of the proceeds.   That's how it's always been; it's an
open secret.   That's apart from what else they filch.   Our new
management of the Garden shouldn't go through their hands at

all. So come to us at the end of the year to settle your accounts."

"I don't think accounts need be turned in at all," said Paochai. "Comparisons are so invidious. Better let the woman entrusted with one job be responsible for the expenses of that place. I've worked it out and it doesn't come to much, just what's needed for hair-oil, rouge, powder, scent and toilet-paper for the young mistresses and their maids, as well as for brooms, dustpans, dusters and whisks and food for the poultry, pet birds, deer and rabbits. If they take care of these few items, we needn't draw anything from the accountants' office. Think how much we can save that way."

"These items may be small," agreed Ping-erh, "yet the total saving in a year will amount to more than four hundred taels of silver."

"There you are!" rejoined Pao-chai. "Four hundred a year, eight hundred in two years: enough to buy a few more houses to rent and a few *mou* of not too good land. There'll be more than that, of course; but after working hard for a whole year they should keep some back for themselves. Although our aim is to economize and make a profit, we mustn't be too stingy either. If we saved an extra two or three hundred taels but spoiled our reputation, that wouldn't do.

"In this way, though, the accountants' office can spend four or five hundred less on us each year without anyone feeling the pinch; the people here will benefit, as these women with no special means of livelihood will manage more comfortably; the plants in the Garden will do better from year to year; you'll be more adequately supplied with what you need; and no loss of dignity will be involved. If all we wanted was to economize, of course we could save money and stash all our profits away; but then everyone would start complaining, and that would impair the dignity of a family such as yours.

"Now there are several dozen old married women in the Garden. If we just give jobs to these few, the rest are bound to feel it unfair. For them simply to supply those few items, as I suggested, is letting them off too lightly. On top of that

I think they should also give a few strings of cash each every year, regardless of how much they have left; and this combined sum can be distributed to the other nannies in the Garden. After all, even if they have no special assignments they work here day and night from early to late, running errands and locking or unlocking gates, no matter how bad the weather. They carry the young ladies' sedan-chairs, punt boats, and draw sleighs in winter — in fact, they do all the hard work the whole year round in the Garden. So they should have a small share in the profits too.

"There's another small thing, and I'll put it more bluntly. If you just better yourselves without letting the others share in your good fortune, even if they don't complain openly they're bound to feel resentful; and then if they pick more fruit or flowers ostensibly for their mistresses but actually for themselves, there'll be nobody to whom you can complain. But if they benefit too, they can keep an eye on things for you when you're busy."

The women were delighted with this proposal, which meant they would neither be controlled by the stewards nor have to settle accounts with Hsi-feng — all they needed to do was to pay a few extra strings of cash every year.

"That suits us!" they cried. "This is better than being squeezed by those stewards outside and having to pay them."

Those with no special assignments were also pleased to learn that they would be getting something for nothing.

"If they do the hard work they deserve to make a little money," they said. "How can we sit idle and rake in a profit too?"

"You nannies needn't decline," replied Pao-chai with a smile. "This is as it should be. Just work hard and don't slack or allow any gambling or drinking. This is really none of my business but, as you know, my aunt has urged me repeatedly to help out now that Madam Chu's so busy and my other cousins are still young. I don't like to add to her worries by refusing. Besides, your Second Mistress has poor health and is busy with family affairs, while I've nothing to do. Why, even a neighbour should help out, not to say a niece like myself when specially asked. So I have to overcome my scruples and not mind if everyone thinks me a nuisance. If all I cared about was my own reputation while other people made trouble drinking or gambling, how could I face my aunt? You'd be sorry too, then, and lose face yourselves.

"You're looking after all these young ladies and this big Garden because it's acknowledged that you're the steadiest, most reliable old nannies whose families have served here for three or four generations. So you should behave in a fit and proper way. If my aunt hears you've been giving people a free hand to drink and gamble, she may take you to task; whereas if those stewards' wives learn of it they may lecture you without telling my aunt, and you'll find yourselves being scolded by your juniors! Though they're stewards and in charge, how much better to stand on your dignity and not give them a chance to sneer. That's why I've suggested this bonus for you, so that all of you will work together to take good care of this Garden. When those in charge see you behaving in a serious, responsible way, they won't have to worry about things and will respect you. It's gratifying for us, too, having thought of a way for you to earn a bonus. While you seize power from them and profit yourselves, you'll also be helping to do away with waste and spare them worry. Think it over carefully."

"You're quite right, miss," cried the women jubilantly. "Set your minds at rest, young ladies and madam. If we don't show our gratitude for your goodness, may Heaven and Earth condemn us!"

They were interrupted by the arrival of Lin Chih-hsiao's wife.

"The ladies of the Chen family from south of the Yangtze arrived in the capital yesterday," she announced. "They've gone to the Palace today to pay homage, sending some servants here with gifts and their respects."

Tan-chun took the list of presents from her and read:

> twelve rolls of first-grade Imperial brocade with the serpent design
> twelve rolls of different colours for the Imperial use
> twelve rolls of Imperial gauze in different colours

twelve rolls of Imperial silk
twenty-four rolls of satin, gauze and silk in different colours for
    official use.

Li Wan also looked at the list, then ordered the bringers of
these gifts to be rewarded with the first-grade tip, and sent to
inform the Lady Dowager. The latter summoned Li Wan,
Tan-chun and Pao-chai to her quarters to examine the presents,
which Li Wan then had put aside, telling the servant in charge
of the storeroom not to store them away until Lady Wang had
seen them.

"The Chens are different from other families," observed the
Lady Dowager. "It was right to give their men-servants the
first-grade tip. I expect they will lose no time in sending some
women to pay their respects as well. We must have some dress
materials ready for them."

That same instant, sure enough, it was announced that four
serving-women from the Chen family had come to pay their
respects. The old lady ordered them to be admitted. These
women were all over forty and dressed not very differently from
their mistresses. As soon as they had paid their respects the
Lady Dowager had four foot-stools brought, and with murmured
thanks they seated themselves after Pao-chai and the rest had
resumed their seats.

"When did you come to the capital?" asked the old lady.

"We arrived yesterday," the women stood up to reply. "Today
our mistress has taken our young lady to the Palace to pay
homage. She first told us to come and pay our respects to you,
madam, and to ask after the young ladies."

"It's so long since your last visit, we weren't expecting you
this year."

"Yes, this year we were sent for by the Emperor."

"Has the whole family come?"

"Not the old lady, the young master, the two other young
ladies or the other mistresses. Only our mistress and our third
young lady."

"Is she engaged yet?"

"Not yet."

"Your first and second young ladies' families are on close terms with ours."

"Yes, every year when they write home they say how exceedingly good you are to them, madam."

"Not a bit of it!" The Lady Dowager smiled. "That's how it should be with old family friends and relatives. We see most of your second young lady, who's so very good and modest."

"You're too kind, madam," they replied.

Then she asked, "Does your young master stay with your old lady?"

"Yes, madam, he does."

"How old is he? Has he started school yet?"

"He's thirteen this year," was the answer. "Such a handsome boy that our old lady dotes on him. He's always been very naughty and plays truant every day, but the master and the mistress couldn't be too strict with him."

"It's just the same in our family. What's your young master's name?"

"Because the old lady treasures him so, and he has a fair complexion, she calls him Pao-yu."

The Lady Dowager exclaimed to Li Wan, "Another Pao-yu — fancy that!"

Li Wan half rose to reply, "There have been many people with the same names since ancient times, some living in the same, some in different ages."

"After he was given this pet-name we did all of us, high and low, wonder whether some friend or relative didn't have the same name," volunteered one of the women. "But after some ten years away from the capital, we could none of us remember."

"That's my worthless grandson's name," chuckled the Lady Dowager. She called in her attendants and ordered them, "Go and fetch our Pao-yu from the Garden, so that these good women can have a look at him and see how he compares with *their* Pao-yu."

The maids went off at once, returning presently with Pao-yu, at sight of whom the four women rose to their feet.

"Well, this *is* a surprise!" they exclaimed. "If we'd met

him anywhere else but here, we'd have thought *our* Pao-yu had followed us to the capital."

They went up to Pao-yu, who greeted them with a smile, and taking his hand they asked him a number of questions.

"How does he compare with your boy?" inquired the old lady.

"Judging by what these four nannies just said, the two must look rather alike," put in Li Wan.

"That's no coincidence," rejoined the old lady. "If their faces aren't disfigured in some way, the pampered sons of great houses all look rather handsome. There's nothing strange about that."

"They're the image of each other," declared the four women. "And judging by what you say, madam, both of them have been rather spoilt; but your young master seems to us the better-tempered of the two."

"Why do you say that?"

"We found out by holding his hands just now. Ours would have thought us silly. *We're* not allowed even to touch his things, let alone hold his hands. So all his maids are young ones."

This evoked a peal of laughter from Li Wan and the girls.

"If we sent people to see your Pao-yu, and they took his hand, he'd have to put up with it too," chuckled the old lady. "The thing about boys from families like ours is that, no matter how perverse they may be, they always behave correctly to visitors — otherwise we would never let them be so naughty. We spoil our boy because he looks so engaging, and because his manners to visitors are even better than those of many grown-ups. That's why nobody can help being fond of him and why he has his own way so often at home. If he behaved badly to outsiders too, making us lose face, then no matter how handsome he was he'd deserve to be beaten to death."

"You are quite right, madam," they replied cheerfully. "Though our Pao-yu is so naughty and so wayward, his manners to guests are better than most grown-ups' So everybody takes a fancy to him and can't understand why he should sometimes be beaten. They don't know the way he runs wild at home, saying and doing the most outrageous things which make our master and mistress very angry. It's natural for boys of noble families to be wilful, extravagant and lazy — such faults can be corrected. But what can we do when he was born with such a strange cranky temper?"

As they were talking Lady Wang was announced. She came in to inquire after her mother-in-law, and when the four visitors had paid their respects to her and said a few words the old lady told her to go and rest. This Lady Wang did, having first served her with tea. She was followed by the four women when they had taken their leave of the old lady, and they chatted together for a while about family affairs before she sent them away. But enough of this.

Meanwhile the Lady Dowager was gleefully telling everyone who came in that another family had a Pao-yu just like their own. The others thought little of it, supposing that many official families must use the same names and that it was the general rule, rather than the exception, for a grandmother to spoil her grandson. Only Pao-yu, being a prejudiced simpleton, imagined that the four women had made this up to please his grandmother. He went back to the Garden to see how Hsiang-yun was.

"Now you can be as naughty as you like," she teased. "Before this it was a case of 'A single thread can't make a cord nor a single tree a forest.' But now that there are two of you, next time you're beaten for raising a rumpus you can run away to Nanking to find your double."

"Don't believe such nonsense," he said. "How could there be another Pao-yu?"

"Wasn't there a Lin Hsiang-ju in the Warring States Period and a Szuma Hsiang-ju in the Han Dynasty?" she retorted.

"All right, I'll grant you that. But two people can't possibly look just alike."

"Didn't the men of Kuang take Confucius for Yang Huo?"

"Confucius and Yang Huo looked alike but had different names; Lin Hsiang-ju and Szuma Hsiang-ju had the same name but looked different.   How can I look the same *and* have the same name as someone else?"

Unable to refute him Hsiang-yun said, "You're just quibbling, I refuse to argue with you.   Whether it's so or not, this has nothing to do with me."   Then she lay down to sleep.

Pao-yu started reflecting dubiously, "I may say this can't be, yet I feel all the same it's true.   Yet how can I be sure, when I haven't seen my double with my own eyes?"

Feeling at a loss, he went back to his room and lay down on the couch to think.   Soon he dozed off and dreamed he was in a garden.

"Is there another garden like this apart from our Grand View Garden?" he exclaimed in surprise.

As he was puzzling over this some girls — all serving-maids — approached.

Again he exclaimed in surprise, "So Yuan-yang, Hsi-jen and Ping-erh aren't the only fine girls!"

"What is Pao-yu doing here?" the girls asked each other.

Assuming that they were talking about him he answered with a smile, "I happened to stroll in here, not that I know which of my family's friends this garden belongs to.   Will you show me round it, sisters?"

"Why, this isn't our Pao-yu," cried the girls.   "He's not bad-looking though, and soft-spoken too."

"Do you have another Pao-yu here, sisters?" he asked.

"It was the old lady and mistress who told us to call him Pao-yu, so as to make him live longer and keep him out of danger," they said.   "He likes it when we call him by his name. But how can a stinking young upstart from far away like you start using it at random?   You'd better watch out or we'll beat you to a pulp, you filthy lout!"

"Let's go before Pao-yu sees him," urged another.

"He'd think talking to this stinking wretch had made us stink too."

With that they left.

"Why should they insult me like this?" wondered Pao-yu.

"I've never been treated in such a way before. Can I really have a double?"

Occupied with these thoughts he had wandered into a court-yard.

"Why, this is another Happy Red Court!" he marvelled.

He ascended the steps and walked in. There was someone lying on a couch inside, with a few girls by him sewing or amusing themselves. The young man on the couch sighed.

"Why don't you sleep, Pao-yu, instead of sighing?" asked one of the girls. "I suppose it's your cousin's illness that's worrying you?"

As Pao-yu marvelled at this the young man replied, "I didn't believe the old lady when she told me that in the capital there's another Pao-yu whose character's just like mine. Just now, though, I had a dream. I dreamed I was in a big garden in the capital, where I met some girls who called me a stinking wretch and refused to talk to me. When at last I found his rooms he was asleep. Only his empty form was there — his real self had gone, I don't know where."

Pao-yu hearing this interjected hastily, "I came here to find Pao-yu. So *you're* Pao-yu!"

The other stepped down from the couch and caught hold of him. "So *you're* Pao-yu!" he cried. "This isn't a dream then."

"Of course not. It's absolutely true."

As he said this someone announced, "The master wants Pao-yu."

That threw both of them into a panic. One started out while the other called:

"Pao-yu, come back! Come back!"

Hsi-jen near by heard him calling out in his sleep and shook him to wake him up.

"Where's Pao-yu?" she asked.

Pao-yu, although awake now, was still confused.

Pointing outside the door he answered, "He's just left."

"You've been dreaming," Hsi-jen told him with a smile. "Rub your eyes and look — that's your own reflection in the mirror."

When Pao-yu saw that he was indeed looking at himself in

the big mirror, he also smiled.   By now some maids had brought him a rinse-bowl and some strong tea to rinse his mouth.

Sheh-yueh remarked, "No wonder the old lady keeps warning us, 'There mustn't be too many mirrors in children's rooms.   A young person's spirit is weak, and if he looks at himself too much in the glass he may be frightened in his sleep and have nightmares.'   Yet we've put his couch in front of this big mirror. It's all right when the cover's down, but now that the hot weather's made us sleepy we keep forgetting to lower it.   Just now, for instance, we forgot again.   He must have been lying there amusing himself by looking at his own reflection; then as soon as he closed his eyes he started dreaming foolish dreams. Otherwise he wouldn't have called out his own name.   Tomorrow we'd better move the couch inside."

She was interrupted by the arrival of a messenger from Lady Wang to fetch Pao-yu.   To know why she wanted him, read the next chapter.

CHAPTER 57

Artful Tzu-chuan Tests Pao-yu's Feelings
Kindly Aunt Hsueh Comforts Tai-yu

Pao-yu hurried to his mother as soon as summoned, to find that she wanted to take him to call on Lady Chen. Naturally delighted to go, he changed his clothes hurriedly and accompanied her. The Chens' house struck him as much like the Jung and Ning mansions, if not slightly grander, and by making careful inquiries he learned that they did indeed have a young master called Pao-yu. By the time they had spent the day there, for Lady Chen kept them to a meal, he was quite convinced of this.

On their return that evening Lady Wang ordered a sumptuous feast to be prepared and a celebrated opera company hired to entertain Lady Chen and her daughter, who two days later set off for Nanking without any further leave-taking.

One day, having seen that Hsiang-yun was on the road to recovery, Pao-yu went to call on Tai-yu. She was taking a siesta, and not wishing to disturb her he joined Tzu-chuan who was sewing on the verandah.

"Was her cough any better last night?" he asked.

"A little."

"Amida Buddha! I do hope she soon gets well."

"Really, this is news to me! Since when have you started invoking Buddha?" she teased.

" 'Men at death's door will turn in desperation to any doctor,' " he quipped.

Noticing that she was wearing a thin padded silk tunic with black dots under a lined blue silk sleeveless jacket, he reached out to feel her clothes.

"You shouldn't sit in the wind so lightly dressed," he remarked. "If *you* fall ill too in this treacherous early spring weather, it will be even worse."

"When we talk to each other in future kindly keep your hands to yourself," retorted Tzu-chuan. "You're growing up now and should want people to respect you, but you keep provoking those wretches to gossip behind your back. You're so careless, you still carry on like a little boy. Well, that won't do. Our young lady's warned us many a time not to joke with you. Haven't you noticed recently how she's been avoiding you?"

She got up then and took her needlework inside.

Pao-yu felt as if doused by a bucket of cold water. He was staring blankly at the bamboo grove when Mrs. Chu came to dig up some bamboo shoots and trim the bamboos. Then, stupefied, he went away. Presently, his wits wandering, not knowing what he did, he sank down in a daze on a rock and shed tears. For the time half a dozen meals would take he sat there brooding, but could not think what to do.

It so happened that Hsueh-yen passed here now on her way back from Lady Wang's quarters with some ginseng. Turning her head towards the rock below the peach tree she noticed someone sitting there lost in thought, his face propped on his hands. To her surprise she saw it was Pao-yu.

"What's he doing here all alone on such a chilly day?" she wondered. "Spring's a dangerous time for people in delicate health. Can his wits be wandering again?"

Going over she crouched down beside him.

"What are you doing here?" she asked.

"What do *you* want with me?" countered Pao-yu as soon as he saw who it was. "Aren't you a girl too? To prevent gossip she's ordered you to ignore me, but here you come seeking me out. If you're seen, there will be talk. Hurry up and go home."

Thinking Tai-yu had been scolding him again, Hsueh-yen had to go back to Bamboo Lodge where she gave Tzu-chuan the ginseng, as their mistress was still asleep.

"What's Her Ladyship doing?" Tzu-chuan asked.

"She's been having a siesta too. That's why I've been so long," replied Hsueh-yen. "But let me tell you something amusing, sister. As I was waiting for the mistress and chatting with Sister Yu-chuan in the maids' quarters, who should beckon me out but Concubine Chao. I thought she had some message, but it turned out she was there to ask leave from the mistress to go to her brother's wake tonight and the funeral tomorrow; and she wanted to borrow my pale-blue satin tunic for her little maid Chi-hsiang, who's to go with her too but has nothing decent to wear. Well, I thought, they've clothes of their own, they just don't want to wear them to the funeral for fear of getting them dirty — they'd rather borrow someone else's to soil. Of course, I'm not all that fussy about my clothes, but what kindness has that woman ever done us? So I told her, 'All my clothes and trinkets are kept by Sister Tzu-chuan on our young lady's orders. I should have to tell her first and then report to my young mistress. And as our young lady's not well, it would be a lengthy business and delay you, madam. Can't you borrow from someone else?' "

"You imp!" Tzu-chuan laughed. "You shift the blame for not lending your things to *us*, to stop her complaining about *you*. Is she leaving now or not till tomorrow morning?"

"She was just setting off. I expect she's gone by now."

Tzu-chuan nodded in silence.

"If our young lady's still asleep, who's been upsetting Pao-yu?" continued Hsueh-yen. "He's sitting out there crying."

"Out where?"

"Under the peach-blossom behind Seeping Fragrance Pavilion."

At once Tzu-chuan laid down her needlework.

"Be ready if she calls," she told Hsueh-yen. "If she asks for me, tell her I'll be back in a minute." So saying she left Bamboo Lodge to look for Pao-yu.

Finding him, she told him gently, "I was only thinking of what's best for us all. Why take offence and rush over here to sit crying in the wind? Are you trying to scare me by risking your health like this?"

"I didn't take offence," he answered with a smile.   "You were quite right.   But if everyone feels the way you do, before long nobody will speak to me at all.   The thought of *that* upset me."

Tzu-chuan sat down too then beside him.

"Just now we were talking face to face but you wouldn't stay," he pointed out.   "Why are you sitting right beside me now?"

"You've probably forgotten, but a few days ago you and your cousin had just started talking about bird's-nest when Concubine Chao burst in.   I've just heard that she's gone out, and that reminded me to come and ask you: what more did you mean to say if she hadn't interrupted you that day?"

"Oh, nothing much," said Pao-yu.   "It simply occurred to me that now that she's taking bird's-nest and has to keep it up, it's not right to impose too much on Pao-chai who's only a visitor here.   As it's no use asking my mother, I dropped a hint to the old lady, and I suspect she must have told Hsi-feng.   That was what I started explaining.   I understand an ounce of bird's-nest is being sent over to you every day now, so that's all right."

"So it was you who suggested that, was it?" said Tzu-chuan. "That was very good of you.   We've been wondering what made the old lady suddenly start sending an ounce every day. So that's the reason."

"If she takes it regularly every day, after two or three years her health should be much better."

"She can have some every day here, but where will the money come from to continue the cure when she goes home next year?"

Pao-yu gave a start.

"Who's going to which home?" he demanded.

"Your cousin — back to Soochow."

"Nonsense!"   Pao-yu chuckled.   "Soochow may be her home town, but she came here because there was no one there to look after her after her parents' death.   Whom could she go back to next year?   No, you're obviously fibbing."

"What a poor opinion you have of other people!"   Tzu-chuan snorted.   "You Chias may be a big, wealthy family, but do other families have only a father and mother and no other relatives?

Our young lady was brought here for a few years while she was still only a child, because the old lady felt for her and didn't think her uncles could take the place of her parents. When she grows up to marriageable age, she's bound to be sent back to the Lin family.

"How can a daughter of the Lins stay all her life with you in your Chia family? Even if the Lins were desperately poor, for generations they've been a family of scholars and officials: they'd never expose themselves to ridicule by abandoning a daughter to relatives. So next spring or next autumn at the latest, even if your family doesn't send her back, the Lins are sure to send to fetch her.

"The other evening our young lady told me to ask you for all the little gifts and souvenirs she's given you since you were children. She means to return all yours to you as well."

Pao-yu was thunderstruck. Tzu-chuan waited for him to answer, but not a word could he utter. And just then Ching-wen came up.

"So here you are, Pao-yu!" she cried. "The old lady wants you."

"He's been inquiring after Miss Tai-yu's health, and I've been reassuring him," Tzu-chuan remarked. "But he won't believe me. You'd better take him away." With that she returned to her room.

Ching-wen noticed Pao-yu's distraught look, the hectic flush on his cheeks and the sweat on his forehead. She at once led him by the hand to Happy Red Court where his appearance horrified Hsi-jen, who imagined he must have caught a chill in the wind while overheated. A fever was not too alarming, but his eyes were fixed and staring, saliva was trickling from the corners of his lips, and he seemed in a state of stupefaction. He would lie down if a pillow was put for him, would sit up if pulled, and drink tea if it was brought. His condition threw them all into a panic, but not daring to report this too hastily to the Lady Dowager they first sent for his old nurse, Nanny Li.

Nanny Li, arriving presently, examined Pao-yu carefully. When he made no answer to any of her questions she felt his pulse, then pinched his upper lip so hard that her fingers left deep imprints — yet he felt no pain. At that she gave a great cry of despair and, taking him in her arms, started weeping and wailing.

Hsi-jen frantically pulled her away.

"Is it serious, nanny?" she demanded. "Do tell us, so that we can let the old lady and the mistress know. Don't start carrying on like this."

Nanny Li beat the bed and pillows with her fists.

"He's done for," she wailed. "A life-time of care gone for nothing!"

Hsi-jen had asked the nurse to have a look because she respected her age and experience. So now her words carried conviction. They all started sobbing.

Ching-wen told Hsi-jen then what had just happened, whereupon Hsi-jen dashed off to Bamboo Lodge. There she found Tzu-chuan giving Tai-yu her medicine. Blind to everything else, Hsi-jen flew at her.

"What have you been saying to our Pao-yu?" she demanded. "Go and *see* the state he's in! You'll have to answer for this to the old lady. I wash my hands of it." So saying she threw herself into a chair.

Tai-yu was taken aback by Hsi-jen's furious, tear-stained face and this behaviour which was so unlike her.

"What's happened?" she asked.

Making an effort to calm herself Hsi-jen sobbed, "I don't know what your Miss Tzu-chuan's been telling him, but the silly boy's eyes are staring, his hands and feet are cold; he can't speak, and when Nanny Li pinched him he felt nothing. He's more dead than alive! Even Nanny Li says there's no hope and is weeping and wailing there. He may be dead by now for all I know."

Nanny Li was such an experienced old nurse that Tai-yu could not but believe her gloomy predictions. With a cry she threw up all the medicine she had just taken, and was racked by such dry coughing that her stomach burned and it seemed her lungs would burst. Red in the face, her hair tousled, her eyes distended, limp in every limb, she choked for breath and could not lift up her head. Tzu-chuan made haste to massage her back while she lay gasping on her pillow.

"Stop thumping me," cried Tai-yu at last, pushing her away. "You'd far better fetch a rope to strangle me."

"I didn't say anything," the maid protested with tears. "Just a few words in fun, which he took seriously."

"You should know how seriously the silly boy always takes teasing," scolded Hsi-jen.

"Whatever you said, go and clear up the misunderstanding, quick!" urged Tai-yu. "That may bring him back to his senses."

Tzu-chuan jumped up then and hurried off with Hsi-jen to Happy Red Court, where the old lady and Lady Wang had already arrived. At sight of Tzu-chuan the old lady's eyes flashed.

"You bitch!" she stormed. "What did you say to him?"

"Nothing, madam. Nothing but a few words in fun."

At the sight of her Pao-yu cried out and burst into tears, to the relief of everybody present. The Lady Dowager caught Tzu-chuan's arm, thinking she had offended him, and urged him to beat her. But Pao-yu seized hold of her and would not let go.

"If you go," he shouted, "you must take me with you!"

No one could understand this till Tzu-chuan, when questioned, explained her threat made in fun of going back to Soochow.

"Is that all?" exclaimed the Lady Dowager, the tears running down her cheeks. "So it was because of a joke." She scolded Tzu-chuan, "You're such a sensible girl normally, how could you tease him like that when you know how credulous he is?"

"Pao-yu's always been too trusting," put in Aunt Hsueh soothingly. "And since Tai-yu came here as a child and they've grown up together, they're particularly close. This sudden talk of her leaving would have upset even a hard-hearted grown-up, let alone such a simple, credulous boy. But this disorder isn't serious; you ladies mustn't worry. One or two doses of medicine will set him right."

Just then it was announced that the wives of Lin Chih-hsiao and Shan Ta-liang had come to inquire after the young master.

"Show them in," said the old lady. "It's thoughtful of them."

But on hearing the name Lin, Pao-yu grew frantic again.

"No, no!" he shouted from his bed. "The Lins have come to fetch her. Drive them away!"

Hastily chiming in, "Drive them away!" his grandmother assured him, "They're not from the Lin family. All *those* Lins are dead. Nobody will ever come to fetch her. Don't you worry."

"Never mind who they are," stormed Pao-yu tearfully. "No one but Cousin Tai-yu should have the name Lin."

"There are no Lins here," repeated the old lady. "They've all been driven away." She ordered the attendants, "In future don't let Lin Chih-hsiao's wife into the Garden. And never mention the name Lin again. Mind you all do as I say like good children."

Suppressing their smiles at this, the others assented.

Pao-yu's eye now fell on a golden boat with an engine, a toy from the West, which was on his cabinet.

"Isn't that the boat coming to fetch them?" he shouted, pointing at it. "It's mooring there."

The Lady Dowager ordered its instant removal, and when Pao-yu reached out for it Hsi-jen gave it to him. He tucked it under his bedding.

"Now they won't be able to sail away," he laughed. Seizing tight hold of Tzu-chuan he refused to let her go.

At this point Doctor Wang was announced, and the old lady ordered him to be brought straight in. Lady Wang, Aunt Hsueh and Pao-chai withdrew to the inner room while the Lady Dowager seated herself by Pao-yu. When Doctor Wang found such a company assembled, he paid his respects to the Lady Dowager before taking Pao-yu's hand to feel his pulse, while Tzu-chuan had to stand there with lowered head, to the doctor's astonishment.

Presently the doctor rose and declared, "The trouble with our honourable brother is that some sharp distress has clouded his mind. According to the ancients, 'Disorders of the phlegm take different forms: indigestion owing to a weak constitution, derangement brought on by a sudden fit of anger, and obstruction caused by sudden distress.' This is a disorder of the third kind. It is only a temporary blockage, however, less serious than the other types."

"Just tell us if he's in danger or not," urged the Lady Dowager. "Who wants to hear this recital of medical lore?"

Doctor Wang bowed.

"He is in no danger, no."

"Is that really true?" she persisted.

"There is really no danger, madam, I give you my word."

"In that case, please take a seat in the outer room to make out your prescription. If you cure him, I shall prepare presents to show my gratitude and send him to kowtow to you in person. If you delay his recovery, though, I shall send to tear down the main hall of your Academy of Imperial Physicians!"

The doctor bowed again.

"You are too good, too good!"

For he had heard only the first part of her speech and not the jocular threat with which it concluded. He went on protesting his unworthiness until the old lady and all the rest burst out laughing.

When the medicine had been prepared according to the prescription and Pao-yu had taken it, he did indeed calm down a little. He still refused to let go of Tzu-chuan, however.

"If she leaves here, they'll go back to Soochow!" he cried.

The Lady Dowager and Lady Wang had perforce to let Tzu-chuan stay there. They dispatched Hu-po in her place to look after Tai-yu, who from time to time sent Hsueh-yen over to ask for news and was deeply moved when she learned all that had happened.

As everyone knew how cranky Pao-yu was, and how close he and Tai-yu had been since they were children, they took Tzu-chuan's joke as quite natural and his illness as nothing out of the way either, not suspecting anything else.

That evening, as Pao-yu was quieter, his grandmother and mother returned to their own quarters but sent several times during the night for reports from the sickroom. Nanny Li,

Mrs. Sung and some other matrons nursed the patient devotedly, while Tzu-chuan, Hsi-jen and Ching-wen watched day and night by his bedside. Whenever he slept he had nightmares, and would wake up crying that Tai-yu had gone or that people had come to fetch her. Each time this happened Tzu-chuan had to comfort him.

Now his grandmother had Pao-yu given all sorts of rare medicine — pills to dispel evil influences and powders to clear the mind. And the next day, after more of Doctor Wang's medicine, his condition gradually improved; but although he was in his right senses again, he pretended from time to time to be delirious in order to keep Tzu-chuan with him. As for her, thoroughly repenting the mischief she had caused she served him day and night without a murmur.

Hsi-jen, herself once more, told her, "As you're the one to blame for this, it's up to you to cure him. I've never seen such a simpleton as our young master, the way he catches at shadows. What's to become of him?" But enough of this.

By now Hsiang-yun was better, and she came every day to see Pao-yu. Finding that he had recovered his faculties she mimicked his crazy behaviour during his illness until, lying on his pillow, he had to laugh. Having no idea himself of what had passed, he could hardly believe what was told him.

When no one else was about but Tzu-chuan, he took her hand.

"Why did you frighten me?" he asked.

"I only did it for fun," she replied. "But you took it seriously."

"You made it sound so convincing, how was I to know it was just a joke?" he retorted.

"Well, I made the whole thing up. There's really no one left in the Lin family except for some very distant relatives who no longer live in Soochow but are scattered in different provinces. Even if one of them asked for her, the old lady would never let her go."

"Even if the old lady would let her go, *I* wouldn't."

"*You* wouldn't!" Tzu-chuan laughed. "That's just talk, I'm

afraid. You're growing up now and already engaged; in a couple of years you'll be marrying, and then you'll forget other people."

"Who's engaged?" asked Pao-yu in dismay. "To whom?"

"Before New Year I heard the old lady say she wanted to engage Miss Pao-chin to you. Why else would she make such a favourite of her?"

He laughed.

"People may call me crazy, but you're even crazier! That was just a joke. She's already engaged to the son of Academician Mei. If I were engaged to her, would I be in this state? Didn't you plead with me and say I was mad when I swore that oath and wanted to smash that silly jade? Now you've come to provoke me again just as I'm getting better." Through clenched teeth he added, "I only wish I could die this very minute and tear out my heart to show you. Then all the rest of me, skin and bones, could be turned into ashes — no, ashes still have form — better be turned into smoke. But smoke still congeals and can be seen by men — it would have to be scattered in a flash, by a great wind, to the four quarters. *That* would be a good death." Tears were running down his cheeks as he spoke.

Tzu-chuan hastily put her hand to his mouth, then wiped away his tears.

"You needn't worry," she urged. "I was putting you to the test because *I* was worried."

"You worried? Why?" he asked in surprise.

"You know I don't belong to the Lin family. Like Hsi-jen and Yuan-yang, I was *given* to Miss Lin. And she couldn't have been kinder to me. She treats me ten times better than her own maids brought from Soochow; we don't like being parted for a single moment. I'm worried now because, if she leaves, I shall have to go with her; but my whole family's here. If I don't go, I'll be unworthy of all her goodness; if I do, I shall have to abandon my own people. That's why, in my dilemma, I told you that fib to see how you felt about it. How was I to know you'd take it so hard?"

"So that's what's worrying you," Pao-yu chuckled. "What a goose you are! Well, set your heart at rest. Let me just put it in a nutshell for you. If we live, we shall live together; and if we die, we shall turn into ashes and smoke together. What do you say to that?"

Tzu-chuan was turning this over in her mind when suddenly Chia Huan and Chia Lan were announced. They had called to ask after Pao-yu.

"Thank them for coming," he said. "But tell them I've just gone to bed and they needn't trouble to come in."

The woman who had brought the message assented and left.

"Now that you're better you should let me go back to see my own patient," said Tzu-chuan.

"I know," he replied. "I meant to send you yesterday, but then I forgot. Go along then, since I'm completely well again."

She set about bundling together her bedding and dressing-cases.

"I see several mirrors in your cases," he commented laughingly. "Will you leave me that small one? I can keep it by my pillow to use in bed, and it will come in handy when I go out."

Tzu-chuan had to do as he asked. Having sent her things on ahead, she took her leave of everyone and went back to Bamboo Lodge.

The news of Pao-yu's disorder had made Tai-yu suffer a relapse and brought on many bouts of weeping. Now she asked Tzu-chuan why she had returned and, learning that he was better, sent Hu-po back to wait on the Lady Dowager.

That night, when all was quiet and Tzu-chuan had undressed and lain down, she whispered to Tai-yu:

"Pao-yu's heart is really true to you. Fancy his falling ill like that when he heard we were leaving!"

Tai-yu made no answer to this.

Presently Tzu-chuan went on, half to herself, "Moving isn't as good as staying put. This is a good family anyway. It's the hardest thing in the world to find people who've grown up together and know each other's character and ways."

"Aren't you tired after the last few days?" scoffed Tai-yu. "Why don't you sleep instead of talking such nonsense?"

"It isn't nonsense. I was thinking of you. I've felt worried for you all these years with no father, mother or brothers to care for you. The important thing is to settle the main affair of your life in good time, while the old lady's still clear-headed and healthy. The proverb says, 'The healthiest old people last as long as a chilly spring or a hot autumn.' If anything should happen to the old lady your marriage might be delayed, or else not turn out in the way you hoped.

"There's no lack of young lordlings, but they all want three wives and five concubines and their affections change from one day to the next. They may bring home a wife as lovely as a fairy, yet after four or five nights they cast her off, treating her like an enemy for the sake of a concubine or a slave girl. If her family's large and powerful, that's not so bad; and for someone like you, miss, so long as the old lady lives you'll be all right. Once she's gone, you'll have to put up with ill treatment. So it's important to make up your mind. You've sense enough to understand the saying, 'Ten thousand taels of gold are easier come by than an understanding heart.'"

"The girl's crazy!" exclaimed Tai-yu. "A few days away, and you've suddenly changed into a different person. Tomorrow I shall ask the old lady to take you back. *I* no longer dare keep you."

"I meant well," was the smiling answer. "I just wanted you to look out for yourself, not to do anything wrong. What good will it do if you report me to the old lady and get me into trouble?" With that Tzu-chuan closed her eyes.

Although Tai-yu had spoken so sharply, this talk had distressed her. After Tzu-chuan went to sleep she wept all night, not dozing off until dawn. The next morning she found it an effort to wash herself, rinse her mouth and swallow her bird's-nest broth. Then the Lady Dowager and others called to see her and urged her to take better care of herself.

That day was Aunt Hsueh's birthday. Everyone from the Lady Dowager down gave her presents, and Tai-yu also sent

over two pieces of her own embroidery.   Aunt Hsueh had hired
a company of actresses and at her invitation the old lady, Lady
Wang and the whole family except Pao-yu and Tai-yu went to
watch the performance.   On their way back from it that evening, the Lady Dowager and others dropped in to see the two
patients again.

The next day Aunt Hsueh made Hsueh Ko keep their shop
assistants company at a whole day's feasting.   The celebrations
lasted for three or four days.

Now Aunt Hsueh had been struck by Hsiu-yen's dignity and
refinement; and as the girl was poor, having "only a thorn for
a hair-pin, and plain cloth for a skirt," her habits were frugal.
Thus Aunt Hsueh thought of betrothing her to her son.   After
some hesitation, however, she decided it would not be fair to
the girl to marry her to a profligate like Hsueh Pan, and it occurred to her that Hsiu-yen and Hsueh Ko who was still unmarried would make a perfect match.   She broached the
subject to Hsi-feng.

"You know how crotchety my mother-in-law is, auntie," said
Hsi-feng with a sigh.   "You must give me time to manage it."

When the Lady Dowager called to see Hsi-feng, the matter
was broached to her.

"Aunt Hsueh has something to ask our Old Ancestress, but
doesn't know how to put it."

"What is it?" asked the old lady.

Hsi-feng explained the marriage proposal.

"Where's the difficulty?"   The old lady smiled.   "Nothing
could please me better.   Let me tell your mother-in-law and
she's sure to agree."

Once back in her own apartments, she sent immediately to
ask Lady Hsing over and proposed the match herself.   Since
the Hsuehs came of fairly good stock and were now very wealthy,
while Hsueh Ko was a handsome young man, and the go-
between, moreover, was no less a person than the Lady Dowager, a moment's thought convinced Lady Hsing that this
would be to her advantage.   So she agreed.

The Lady Dowager in high delight promptly asked Aunt Hsueh to come over, and there was the usual exchange of polite formalities between both parties. Lady Hsing lost no time in informing her brother Hsing Chung and his wife; and since they had come there to throw themselves upon her bounty, they were naturally more than happy to give their approval.

"I love meddling in other people's affairs," said the Lady Dowager. "Now that I've fixed this up, how much are you going to pay your go-between?"

"Don't worry about that," replied Aunt Hsueh. "Even if we brought you a hundred thousand taels of silver, I don't suppose it would mean much to you. But since you're the go-between, madam, will you find us someone to take charge of the betrothal ceremony?"

"Whatever else we're short of, we can produce one or two helpers of a sort," the old lady chuckled.

She sent for Chia Chen's wife and daughter-in-law. When they heard the news from her they offered their congratulations.

"You know our family ways," she told Madam Yu. "The two families never squabble over betrothal gifts. You must handle this business for me, neither too stingily nor too lavishly. Report to me when everything is arranged."

As soon as Madam Yu accepted this task, Aunt Hsueh went home overjoyed to write invitation cards for the Ning Mansion.

Madam Yu knew Lady Hsing's cantankerous temper and would have preferred to have nothing to do with the business, but she had to fall in with the old lady's wishes. She did her best to please Lady Hsing, aware that Aunt Hsueh was so easy-going there would be no problem there. But enough of this.

Now that the whole household knew that Hsiu-yen was to marry Aunt Hsueh's nephew, Lady Hsing wanted to move her out of the Garden.

"What does it matter if she stays?" demurred the Lady Dowager. "There's no danger of the two young people meeting, and it shouldn't worry you if she sees Aunt Hsueh and the two cousins of the other family every day. They're all girls, aren't they? They may as well get to know each other better."

Lady Hsing made no further objection then.

Hsueh Ko and Hsiu-yen had met once previously on their way to the capital, and in all probability they were pleased enough with the match; but naturally this made Hsiu-yen more reserved and tongue-tied in the presence of Pao-chai and the rest of the girls. She felt specially shy with Hsiang-yun, who was such a tease. But being a well-brought up girl of some education, she showed no false modesty or silly coyness.

Pao-chai had realized from the start that Hsiu-yen's family was poor, and while the other girls' parents were respectable old people hers were penniless nobodies who cared little for their daughter; Lady Hsing had no genuine feeling for her either, simply making a show of affection. And Hsiu-yen had a sense of self-respect. As Ying-chun was too feeble even to take care of herself, let alone look after her cousin, whenever Hsiu-yen ran short of any daily necessities there was no one to see to it, and she was too unassuming to mention it. Pao-chai accordingly often helped her in secret, not letting Lady Hsing know for fear of giving offence, with the result that now that this un-expected match had been arranged Hsiu-yen felt even more closely bound to Pao-chai than to Hsueh Ko. She often went to chat with her, and Pao-chai continued to address her as "cousin."

One day Pao-chai set out to call on Tai-yu. Happening to meet Hsiu-yen on the way, she beckoned her with a smile and they walked on together. As they skirted the back of a rockery, Pao-chai inquired:

"Why have you changed out of padded clothes into lined ones, when the weather is still so cold?"

Hsiu-yen hung her head and said nothing.

Sensing some reason for this Pao-chai continued, "Don't tell me this month's allowance was held up again? Cousin Hsi-feng really is growing rather thoughtless."

"She issued it on the right date," rejoined Hsiu-yen. "But my aunt sent to tell me I shouldn't need *two* taels a month and must save one for my parents. She said if I was short of any-thing I could borrow from Ying-chun and make do. But, you see, Ying-chun is a simple soul who doesn't always think. *She* wouldn't mind my using her things, but those maids and nannies of hers are all troublemakers — you know what sharp tongues they have. Though I'm staying there, I dare not order them about; in fact, every few days I have to spend money on wine and cakes for them. I can't manage even on *two* taels a month, and now it's been cut to one. So the other day I got someone, on the sly, to pawn my padded clothes for a few strings of cash."

Hearing this, Pao-chai frowned and sighed in sympathy.

"It's too bad that the Mei family have all gone to the new post and won't be back in the capital till the year after next," she said. "If they were here, we could arrange Pao-chin's wedding and then yours. Once you leave here you'll be all right. The trouble is that Hsueh Ko won't consider getting married before his younger sister; yet if you have to put up with two more years of this, I'm afraid it may ruin your health. I must talk to my mother and see what can be done.

"If people bully you, just keep your temper and on no account fall ill. Actually you may just as well give them the other tael too, so that they stop pestering you; then you needn't treat those creatures for nothing. If they make scathing remarks, just pretend not to hear and go about your own business. When you're short of anything just apply to me. Don't be finicky. It's not because you're engaged now to one of our family that I want you to treat me as your relative. Didn't we become friends as soon as you arrived here? If you are afraid of gossip, just send your maid quietly to pass on messages to me."

Hsiu-yen lowered her head and assented.

Then Pao-chai pointed at the green jade pendant hanging from her skirt.

"Who gave you that?"

"It's a present from Cousin Tan-chun."

Pao-chai nodded.

"She must have noticed that you were the only one with no jade to wear; so to stop people laughing at you she gave you this. It shows how thoughtful and observant she is. Still, you should know that trinkets like these are only worn in big official families of rich nobles. Just look at me. Do *I* wear such magnificent ornaments? Seven or eight years ago I did, but not now that our family position's changed. I economize whenever I can. In future, when you come to our family, I daresay you'll find a whole chest of such trash still there. But nowadays our family's not like theirs. We should after all dress more simply, not copy them."

"If that's how you feel, sister, I'll go back and take it off."

"No, that's not what I meant," disclaimed Pao-chai hastily. "Since she was kind enough to give you this, if you don't wear it she'll wonder why. I just happened to mention the matter for you to bear in mind later."

Hsiu-yen assented, then asked her where she was going.

"To Bamboo Lodge," Pao-chai told her. "Slip back and send a maid over to our place with the pawn ticket. I'll have the clothes redeemed quietly and sent to you this evening, so that you have something warm to wear; otherwise you'll catch cold, and that would never do. Which shop is it, by the way?"

"A shop called Heng Shu on the main road west of the Drum Tower."

"It happens to belong to our family." Pao-chai smiled. "If the shop assistants knew they'd say, 'Before the bride is fetched her clothes have arrived.'"

Hsiu-yen blushed when she realized that it was one of the Hsuehs' shops. Making no answer she went away with a smile.

At Bamboo Lodge, Pao-chai found her mother chatting with Tai-yu.

"When did you get here, mother?" she asked. "I didn't know you were coming."

"I've been too busy till today to call to see her and Pao-yu," said Aunt Hsueh. "And now I find both of them are well again."

Tai-yu offered Pao-chai a seat. "Life is certainly full of surprises," she said to her. "Take Aunt Hsueh and my Eldest Aunt, for instance. They're going to be linked more closely still by marriage."

"What do girls like you know about such things, child?" replied Aunt Hsueh. "There's an old saying: 'People a thousand *li* apart may be linked by marriage.' It's all the doing of the Old Man of the Moon. If he's secretly fastened his red thread around the ankles of two young people, not even the ocean or a whole country, or even a family feud for generations can stop them from becoming husband and wife. It always comes as a surprise.

"On the other hand, if the Old Man of the Moon *doesn't* do his part, even if the parents on both sides are willing and the young people have been brought up together and think themselves destined for each other, they'll never be united.

"Take the case of you two girls. We don't yet know whether you'll marry someone close at hand or beyond mountains and seas."

"Mother always drags us in!" protested Pao-chai. Resting her head against her mother's breast she asked laughingly, "Shall we go now?"

"Look at her," teased Tai-yu. "Such a big girl, and when you're not around, aunt, she looks very dignified; but when she's with you she acts just like a baby."

Caressing her daughter Aunt Hsueh told Tai-yu, "This child means as much to me as Hsi-feng does to the old lady. When I've serious business, I consult her; when there's none, she amuses me. When I see her like this all my troubles melt away."

Tears came into Tai-yu's eyes.

"She's doing this on purpose here, to wound me by reminding me that *I've* no mother."

"Look, mother!" cried Pao-chai gaily. "Who's acting like a baby now?"

"You can't blame her for being upset," replied Aunt Hsueh. "She has no parents, poor thing, no one to care for her." She turned then to caress Tai-yu as well. "Don't cry, there's a good child," she urged. "It upsets you to see how fond I am of your cousin, but I love you even more if you only knew it. She's better off than you, because though she's lost her father she at least has me and her brother. I've often told her I can't show how fond I am of *you*, for fear of the gossip it would cause. People like to put the worst interpretation on things. Instead of admitting that you've no one to turn to and behave in a way to make everybody love you, they'd accuse me of being good to you just because you're the old lady's favourite — so as to please *her*."

"If you really love me, aunt, will you be my foster-mother?" pleaded Tai-yu. "If you turn me down, that means you aren't in earnest."

"I'm willing, if you think I'm good enough."

"No, that wouldn't do," put in Pao-chai.

"Why not?" Tai-yu wanted to know.

"Let me ask you a question," retorted Pao-chai with a smile. "Why is Hsiu-yen engaged to my younger cousin before my brother's engaged?"

"Because he's not at home, I suppose. Or because the horoscopes don't match."

"No, it's because my brother has already set his mind on someone, and it'll be fixed up as soon as he returns. I needn't name any names. Why did I say you couldn't take her as your mother? Just work it out for yourself!" She winked at her mother and laughed.

Tai-yu buried her face in Aunt Hsueh's lap protesting, "Aunt, if you don't spank her, I won't let her go!"

Aunt Hsueh put her arms round her and smiled.

"Don't believe a word of it. She's only teasing."

"But honestly!" Pao-chai giggled. "Mother's going to ask the old lady for your hand tomorrow. Why waste time looking elsewhere?"

Tai-yu lunged out at her laughing, "You crazy thing!"

Aunt Hsueh hastily parted them and told Pao-chai, "I think even Hsiu-yen's too good for that brother of yours, that's why I asked for her for your cousin instead. How could I dream of giving your brother this child?

"The other day, the old lady wanted your cousin Pao-chin for Pao-yu; and if she hadn't happened to be engaged it would have been a good match. When I fixed things up for Hsiu-yen the old lady quipped, 'I wanted one of your girls, but you've got one of ours instead.' There's something in that although she was only joking. Pao-chin is engaged and I've no girl for her, but I can make a suggestion. Since the old lady is so fond of Pao-yu and he's such a handsome boy, she'll never agree to a wife from outside for him. Then why not engage him to Tai-yu? Wouldn't that please everyone?"

Tai-yu had been listening intently, but now, at the mention of her own name, she spat in disgust and grabbed hold of Pao-chai.

"I'm going to teach you a lesson!" she cried, her cheeks burning. "Why should you provoke my aunt into rambling on in such an indelicate way?"

"That's strange." Pao-chai laughed. "Why spank *me* for something my mother said?"

Tzu-chuan ran up to them and cried laughingly, "Since you have this idea, madam, why not propose it to the mistress?"

"What's the hurry, child?" asked Aunt Hsueh teasingly. "I suppose the sooner your mistress is married off, the sooner you can find yourself a young husband."

Tzu-chuan flushed and flashed back, "You're presuming on your age, madam!" With that she flung off.

"What has this to do with you?" scolded Tai-yu, and then laughed too at her discomfiture. "Amida Buddha! Serves her right!"

Aunt Hsueh, Pao-chai and all the attendants present joined in the merriment. Then some of the older maids said cheerfully:

"Though it was just said in fun, it's a good idea. We hope, madam, when you have time, you'll discuss this with the old lady. You can volunteer to be the go-between, then this marriage is bound to come off."

"Yes," agreed Aunt Hsueh. "If I make this suggestion, the old lady's sure to be pleased."

As they were talking Hsiang-yun came in, a pawn ticket in her hand.

"What's this certificate for?" she asked.

Tai-yu had a look but did not know what it was.

"It's something marvellous," the matrons laughed. "But we won't teach you for nothing."

Pao-chai took it and saw that it was the pawn ticket Hsiu-yen had mentioned. She hastily folded it up.

"It must be a pawn ticket some old nurse has lost," suggested Aunt Hsueh. "She'll be frantic when she can't find it."

"A pawn ticket? What's that?" asked Hsiang-yun.

Everybody laughed.

"Little simpleton! She doesn't even know what a pawn ticket is."

"That's quite natural," remarked Aunt Hsueh. "As the daughter of a noble house, and still young, how could she know of such things? Where would she have seen one? Even if some one in their household had one, she wouldn't set eyes on it. So don't you go calling her a simpleton. If you showed your young mistresses this, that would make them all simpletons too."

"Just now Miss Lin didn't know it either," agreed the women. "And not only the young ladies. We'd be surprised if Pao-yu ever set eyes on such a thing, though he often goes outside."

Aunt Hsueh then explained to Hsiang-yun and Tai-yu what a pawn ticket was.

"So that's it!" they exclaimed. "How clever people are at making money! Is your family shop the same, aunt?"

"Listen to them!" Everyone laughed. " 'All crows are black the world over.' How could their shop be any different?"

"Where did you find this?" asked Aunt Hsueh.

Before Hsiang-yun could answer, Pao-chai put in, "This ticket has expired. It was cancelled years ago. Hsiang-ling must have given it them for fun."

Her mother, believing this, let the matter drop.

Just then someone reported that the mistress of the other house had called to see Aunt Hsueh, and she went home. When the others had left as well, Pao-chai asked Hsiang-yun where she had found the ticket.

"I saw your future sister-in-law's maid Chuan-erh slip it to Ying-erh, who tucked it between the pages of a book, thinking I hadn't noticed. As soon as they'd gone I took a peep at it, but couldn't guess what it was. Knowing you were all here I brought it along to show you."

"Can she be pawning her things?" asked Tai-yu. "If so, why send you this ticket?"

Realizing that she could no longer hide the truth from them, Pao-chai explained what had happened. Tai-yu exclaimed in distress and sympathy, but Hsiang-yun grew most indignant.

"Wait till I go and take this up with Ying-chun," she fumed. "I shall give those matrons and maids a piece of my mind. Won't that help us to get our own back?"

Pao-chai caught hold of her as she was starting off.

"Are you out of your mind again?" she cried. "Sit down."

"If you were a man, you could go out and right wrongs," teased Tai-yu. "But you're not a Ching Ko or a Nieh Cheng.[1] Don't be ridiculous."

"If you won't let me have this out with them, shall we ask Hsiu-yen to come and stay with us in our apartments?" rejoined Hsiang-yun.

"We can discuss that later." Pao-chai smiled.

Tan-chun and Hsi-chun being announced at this point, they made haste to change the subject. If you want to know the upshot, read the next chapter.

----

[1] Two ancient assassins who attempted to avenge their masters.

CHAPTER 58

Under the Shade of an Apricot Tree
an Actress Mourns Her Stage Lover
The Master of Happy Red Court Sympathizes
with the Girl's Infatuation

The subject of conversation was changed at the arrival of Tan-chun and Hsi-chun. The newcomers having asked after Tai-yu's health, they all chatted for a while before dispersing.

Now the demise of the Grand Imperial Concubine mentioned earlier was announced, and all titled ladies were required to go to court to mourn according to their rank. Nobles throughout the empire were forbidden feasting and music for a year, while common citizens were debarred from marrying for three months.

The Lady Dowager, Lady Hsing, Lady Wang, Madam Yu and her daughter-in-law née Hsu — grandparents as well as grand-children of the Chia family — had to go to court every morning when sacrifice was offered, not returning until two in the after-noon. After twenty-one days of lying in state in the Great Inner Court of the Side Palace, the coffin would be conveyed to the Imperial Mausoleum in the county called Hsiaotzu; and as this was some ten days' journey from the capital, and the coffin would have to wait there for several days before it could be interred in the underground palace, the whole proceedings would occupy nearly one month.

By rights, Chia Chen and his wife of the Ning Mansion should both have assisted at these obsequies; but as that would have left no one in charge at home, after much discussion they decided to beg leave from the court for Madam Yu on the plea that she was with child, so that she could take over the supervision of the two mansions.

Aunt Hsueh, having been prevailed upon to keep an eye on

the girls and maids in the Garden, now had to move in there too. But at this juncture Pao-chai had Hsiang-yun and Hsiang-ling with her; Li Wan, although her aunt and her aunt's two daughters were not staying with her, received visits from them every few days, and she had been entrusted with Pao-chin as well by the Lady Dowager; Ying-chun had Hsiu-yen; Tan-chun's apartments were not convenient either, as she was so occupied with household affairs and the trouble caused by Concubine Chao and Chia Huan; and Hsi-chun's space was limited. Besides, as the old lady had asked Aunt Hsueh to take special care of Tai-yu, for whom she herself felt the deepest sympathy, under the circumstances she naturally moved into Bamboo Lodge where she shared Tai-yu's room and kept a strict eye on the girl's medicine and diet. Tai-yu was more grateful for this than words can tell. She began to treat Aunt Hsueh as her own mother and Pao-chai and Pao-chin as her sisters, feeling closer to them than to all the other girls, to the Lady Dowager's great satisfaction.

Aunt Hsueh simply looked after the girls and controlled the younger maids, however, not interfering with other family business. And though Madam Yu came over every day she dealt only with routine matters, careful not to overstep her authority. In any case she was too busy, for besides being in sole charge of the Ning Mansion she had to see to the daily food and supplies for the Lady Dowager and Lady Wang in the hostel where they were staying.

While those in charge of the two mansions had their hands full in this way, all the chief stewards were busy too — those who had not left earlier to look for lodgings for their masters and mistresses during the funeral ceremonies, either accompanied their masters to court or were busy handling jobs in their hostel outside. And in the absence of proper supervision, the servants of both mansions slacked or ganged up under the provisory chief stewards to abuse their power. The only stewards left in the Jung Mansion were Lai Ta and a few in charge of outside business. Deprived of his usual assistants, Lai Ta delegated authority to some ignorant rogues who proved far from satis-

factory, cheating him and sending in false accusations or rec-
ommendations. But we need not dwell here on all the trouble
they caused.

As other official families were now disbanding their private
opera troupes, Madam Yu and the others decided that when
Lady Wang came home they would suggest dispensing with the
services of their twelve child-actresses too.

"We bought those girls," they told her, "so even if we stop
training them we can keep them on as maids, just dismissing
their instructors."

"We can't treat them as servants," objected Lady Wang.
"They're the daughters of respectable families, whose parents
being unable to make a living sold them into this low trade to
dress up as ghosts and demons for several years. Here's our
chance to give them a few taels of silver as travelling-expenses
and let them go. That's what always used to be done by our
ancestors. To keep them would be unkind, and niggardly too.
We still have a few old actresses here, it's true, but they had
their own reasons for not wanting to leave, which is why we
kept them on as attendants and eventually married them to
our own servants."

"Let's find out which of these twelve girls want to go home,"
proposed Madam Yu. "Then we can send word to their parents
to come and fetch them and give them a few taels of silver as
travelling-expenses. But we must make sure that it's their
parents who come for them, not some scoundrels who pretend
to be their kinsmen and take them off merely to sell them all
over again. For in that case, wouldn't our kindness come to
nothing? Anyone who doesn't want to leave can stay."

When Lady Wang approved, Madam Yu sent to inform Hsi-
feng and ordered the steward in charge to give each of the
instructors an eight-tael gratuity with free permission to leave.
Everything in Pear Fragrance Court was inventoried and put
away, and some servants were appointed to guard the place at
night.

More than half the twelve young actresses, when summoned
and questioned, proved reluctant to go home. Some said that

their parents were only out to make money, and if they went back they would be sold again; others that their parents were dead, and they had been sold by their uncles or their brothers; others that they had nowhere to go; yet others that they had no wish to leave this family which had been so good to them. In all, only four or five elected to leave.

When Lady Wang heard this she had to keep them. The few who chose to leave were instructed to stay with their foster-mothers until their own parents should come for them. Of those who chose to remain, Wen-kuan was kept by the Lady Dowager, most of the rest being sent to different apartments in the Garden. Fang-kuan who played the part of young ladies was assigned to Pao-yu; Jui-kuan who played pert maids to Pao-chai; Ou-kuan who played young gentlemen to Tai-yu; Kuei-kuan who played the chief warriors to Hsiang-yun; Tou-kuan who played lesser warriors to Pao-chin; and Ai-kuan who played old men to Tan-chun. Madam Yu then took Chia-kuan whose role was old women.

Once places had been found for them, they were as merry the whole day long in the Garden as caged birds newly set free; for everyone showed them indulgence, knowing that they had never learned to sew or wait on other people. One or two of the more intelligent, however, were worried by their lack of useful skills now that they had given up acting; so they began to learn sewing, weaving and other tasks expected of girls.

Soon the day came for the great sacrifice at court. The Lady Dowager and her party went at dawn to the hostel, where they had some refreshments before proceeding to court. After breakfast they retired to the hostel for a short rest, returning to court after lunch and a nap for the noon and evening sacrifices, then going back for another rest and not returning home until after dinner. Their hostel, the family temple of a high official, had nuns in residence and scores of cells all of which were scrupulously clean. The Jung Mansion party had the use of the east courtyard, the Prince of Peiching's household that of the west. Since the Princess Dowager and the Princess Consorts also rested there every day, they daily met the Lady Dowager and her party in the east courtyard, and the two families travelled to court and back together, keeping each other company. But these happenings outside need not concern us.

To return to Grand View Garden.   Since the Lady Dowager and Lady Wang were away for the whole month of the state funeral, the maid-servants at home had little to do but amuse themselves in the Garden, whose occupants were increased by several dozen now that the matrons from Pear Fragrance Court were dispersed among the different apartments there. Because Wen-kuan and most of the other actresses, owing to pride or their privileged position, had given themselves airs above their station, treated their inferiors badly, insisted on the best of everything and made cutting remarks, the matrons had always resented them, not that they dared to quarrel with them outright. Pleased by the disbanding of the opera troupe, some of them let bygones be bygones; and though the more narrow-minded still bore a grudge, they were too scattered now to venture to get their own back.

Now the Clear and Bright Festival came round again.   Chia Lien, having prepared the traditional offerings, took Chia Huan, Chia Tsung and Chia Lan to Iron Threshold Temple to sacrifice to the dead.   Chia Jung of the Ning Mansion did the same with other young men of the clan.   Pao-yu, not yet fully recovered, was the only one not to go.

After the midday meal he felt drowsy.

"Why not go out while it's fine?" suggested Hsi-jen. "Sleeping straight after lunch may give you indigestion."

So taking a cane he strolled out in his slippers.

He found the matrons recently put in charge of different parts of the Garden busy at their various tasks, pruning bamboos and trees, planting flowers or sowing beans, while others in boats dredged mud from the lake or planted lotus there.   Hsiang-yun, Hsiang-ling, Pao-chin and several young maids were sitting on the rocks enjoying the sight.

As Pao-yu sauntered towards them Hsiang-yun laughed.

"Drive that boat away, quick!" she cried. "It's come to fetch Cousin Lin."

The general laughter this raised made Pao-yu blush.

"Did I choose to fall ill?" he retorted. "It's not kind to make fun of me."

"Even in illness you had to be unique," she teased. "How can you blame us for laughing?"

He sat down then to watch everyone hard at work.

"There's a wind here and it's cold sitting on the rock," remarked Hsiang-yun presently. "We'd better go indoors."

As Pao-yu was eager to see Tai-yu, he parted company with them and walked on with his cane along the dyke from Seeping Fragrance Bridge. The willows were trailing golden threads, peach-blossom made a red mist, and the big apricot tree behind an artificial mountain was already bare of flowers and covered with thick foliage. The apricots on it were no bigger than peas.

"Just a few days' illness and I missed the apricot-blossom," thought Pao-yu. "Now 'Green leaves make a shade and the boughs are filled with fruit.'"[1]

Lost in contemplation of the tree, he thought of Hsiu-yen and her recent engagement. Though marriage was something everyone must go through with, this would mean one good girl the less; in just a couple of years she would be burdened with children as this tree was with fruit; and just as the apricots would soon be gone, leaving the branches bare, in a few more years Hsiu-yen's hair would be turning silver and she would lose her beauty too. He could not help shedding tears as he gazed at the tree. But as he was sighing, a bird alighting to chirp on one of its boughs set him indulging in foolish fancies again.

"This bird must have visited the tree when it was in bloom," he mused. "Now that there are no flowers left, only fruit and leaves, it's chirping like this by way of lamentation. Too bad

---

[1] Line from a poem by Tu Mu (803-852).

Kungyeh Chang[1] isn't here to tell me what it's saying. Will it come back next year to see the blossom, I wonder?"

As he was occupied with these foolish fancies, a flame sprang up on the other side of the artificial mountain and frightened the bird away.

Startled, Pao-yu heard a voice cry, "Do you want to die, Ou-kuan? How can you burn all this paper money here? I shall report this to the mistresses, so look out for a thrashing!"

Pao-yu hurried in bewilderment to the other side of the rockery. There he discovered Ou-kuan, her face stained with tears, crouching over the ashes of some paper money, a light still in her hand.

"To whom are you making this offering?" he asked. "You mustn't do it here. If it's for your parents or brothers, tell me their names and I'll write them down on paper and get the page boys outside to do it properly for you."

Ou-kuan said nothing to this, not even when Pao-yu repeated his question. Then up came an irate matron to drag her away.

"I've reported this to the mistresses. They're very angry!" she scolded.

Ou-kuan, being only a child, hung back for fear of being put to shame.

"I always said you were riding for a fall," stormed the woman. "You can't fool around here the way you did outside. You have to watch your step." Pointing at Pao-yu she continued, "Even our young master has to observe the rules. Who do you think you are to fool around here? It's no use being afraid. Come along with me."

"She wasn't burning paper coins but waste paper for Miss Lin," put in Pao-yu quickly. "You didn't see clearly and accused her wrongly."

Ou-kuan had been at a loss, and Pao-yu's appearance had frightened her even more; but she took heart when he covered up for her like this and started defending herself.

---

[1] Confucius' disciple and son-in-law who was said to know the language of birds.

"Just look, is this paper money?" she demanded. "Miss Lin spoiled some paper when writing — that's what I've been burning."

The woman, even more provoked by this, stooped to pick up two unburned paper coins from the ashes.

"Still trying to deny it?" she snapped. "Here's the evidence. We'll discuss it in front of the mistresses." She caught hold of the girl's sleeve to drag her off.

Pao-yu quickly pulled Ou-kuan back, knocking the woman's hand away with his cane.

"Take that if you want to," he said. "I'll tell you the truth. Last night I dreamed that the spirit of the apricot tree came to ask me for a string of white paper money, saying that if it was burnt for me by a stranger, not by anyone in my apartments, my sickness would be cured faster. That's why I got this paper, then asked Miss Lin's permission to have her come and burn it for me to make my dream come true. It had to be kept a secret, and I was just beginning to feel better, able to get out of bed. But now, by butting in like this, you've gone and spoiled everything. And do you still mean to report her? Go with her, Ou-kuan, and tell them what I've just said. When the old lady comes back, I'll report her for deliberately spoiling my sacrifice so as to make me die early."

Emboldened by this, Ou-kuan started tugging the woman away. The latter hastily dropped the paper money.

"How was I to know?" she asked Pao-yu meekly. "If you tell the old lady, Second Master, it will be the end of me! I'll go and tell the mistresses that I made a mistake — it was *you* burning sacrificial paper."

"Don't say anything about it and I won't tell her," he promised.

"But I've already reported it, and they ordered me to take her there. How can I say nothing? All right, I'll tell them Miss Lin sent for her."

Pao-yu thought for a while then nodded, and the woman went away.

Then he asked again: "Whom was the offering for? I'm

sure it can't have been for your own people, as in that case you'd have asked others to burn it for you. There must be a story behind it."

Ou-kuan, grateful for his championship, began to feel that they were kindred spirits. Tears sprang to her eyes.

"Only two people know this," she said. "Fang-kuan in your place and Miss Pao-chai's Jui-kuan. As you happened to spot me today and you've just helped me, I shall have to let you into my secret. You mustn't tell a soul though." Then, sobbing again, she added, "I can't bring myself to tell you. If you must know, go back and ask Fang-kuan when no one else is about." With that she went abruptly away.

Pao-yu was very puzzled as he went on to Bamboo Lodge. He found Tai-yu looking more pathetically frail than ever, although she insisted that her health was much better. She saw that he too was much thinner, and could not help shedding tears at the thought of the reason. After a brief chat she urged him to go back and rest, and Pao-yu took her advice, being eager to question Fang-kuan. But it so happened that Hsiang-yun and Hsiang-ling had called and were chatting with her and Hsi-jen. He could not call her aside for fear of arousing their curiosity. All he could do was to wait.

After a while Fang-kuan went out with her foster-mother to have her hair washed. When the woman made her own daughter wash first, Fang-kuan accused her of showing favouritism.

"So I'm to wash with the water your daughter has used, am I?" she complained. "You grab my whole monthly allowance, and on top of taking advantage of me like that expect me to be content with other people's leavings!"

"You don't know when you're well off, you wretch," blustered the discomfited woman. "No wonder everyone says: 'Don't tangle with actresses'; even the best of them go to the bad once they take to the stage. Who do you think you are, you little monkey, to pick and choose like this and give *me* the rough side of your tongue? You're like a mule biting its mates."

Then the two of them started quarrelling in earnest.

Hsi-jen sent a maid to urge them, "Stop that noise. Can't you keep quiet when the old lady's away?"

"Fang-kuan's too fussy," said Ching-wen. "Why should she be so cocky? All she's done is sing in a couple of operas; she's not killed a traitor or captured a rebel chief."

"'You can't clap with one hand,'" quoted Hsi-jen. "The old one's too unfair, and the young one's too tiresome."

"You mustn't blame Fang-kuan," Pao-yu expostulated. "As the proverb says, 'Injustice will cry out.' She has no folk of her own, no one to care for her here; and that woman takes her money yet still treats her so badly. How can you say it's her fault?" He asked Hsi-jen, "How much is her monthly allowance? Why don't you take it and look after her? Wouldn't that save trouble all round?"

"If I want to look after her, I can anyway. Why should I need her bit of money to do it?" replied Hsi-jen. "That would simply set tongues wagging."

She got up and fetched from her room a bottle of scent and pomade, as well as some eggs, soap and hair-ribbons.

"Give these to Fang-kuan," she told one of the matrons. "Tell her to send for some more water to wash her hair. They must stop quarrelling."

This only incensed and humiliated the foster-mother even more.

"You ungrateful slut," she swore at Fang-kuan. "So now you're accusing me of robbing you!" She slapped the girl and set her wailing.

Pao-yu started towards the outer room, but Hsi-jen hastily stopped him.

"Stay where you are," she urged. "I'll see to this."

Ching-wen had already gone out to confront the woman, however.

"Old as you are, you have no sense," she scolded. "We only gave her those things because you don't take proper care of her. But instead of feeling ashamed of yourself, you have the nerve to slap her! Would you dare do such a thing if she were still training in the opera troupe?"

"She accepted me as her mother, so she's my daughter," was the reply. "If she talks back at me, I've the right to beat her."

Hsi-jen told Sheh-yueh, "I'm no good at arguing, and Ching-wen's too hot-tempered. Why don't you go and give her a good scare?"

Sheh-yueh at once went out.

"Stop that noise and answer me this," she said to the woman. "In all the Garden, not just these apartments, which servant have you ever seen reprimand her children in the master's rooms? Even if she were your own daughter, once she's in service here it's up to the master or the senior girls to punish her or scold her. It's not for her parents to meddle with our affairs. If everybody butted in like you, what are we here supposed to do? The older you get, the less you respect the rules.

"You saw Chui-erh's ma make a scene here the other day, so now you're following suit. Well, just you wait! These last few days, with so many people ill and the old lady so busy, I haven't reported this yet. In a couple of days I shall make a full report, and that will take the wind out of your sails. Pao-yu's just getting better, and *we've* all been trying to keep our voices down; yet you raise a rumpus fit to wake the dead. If the higher-ups are away just a few days, you lot run completely wild with no respect for anyone at all. In another day or two, I suppose, you'll be slapping *us* as well. She doesn't need a foster-mother like you to muck her up!"

Pao-yu, in the doorway, pounded the sill with his cane.

"How can these old women be so heartless?" he fumed. "Fantastic! Instead of looking after the girls in their charge, they torment them. If this goes on, what's to be done?"

"What's to be done?" echoed Ching-wen. "Drive all those humbugs out, I say. We don't need such good-for-nothings here."

The woman was too deflated to say a word. Meanwhile Fang-kuan, wearing only a cerise padded jacket and flowered green silk lined-trousers, loose round the ankles, her glossy black hair streaming over her shoulders, had given way to floods of tears.

Sheh-yueh teased, "Miss Ying-ying has turned into Hung Niang after a beating.[1] Although you're not on the stage now, you look just like her. Aren't you going to tidy yourself up?"

"No, she's fine as she is," objected Pao-yu. "She looks completely natural. Why should she spruce up?"

Ching-wen led Fang-kuan away to wash her hair and dry it with a towel for her, after which she fastened it in a loose knot. Then she told her to change her clothes before rejoining them.

The old kitchen-maids now reported that dinner was ready, and asked whether it should be sent in or not. A young maid brought in this message to Hsi-jen.

"With all that racket just now I forgot to listen for the clock," she said. "What time is it?"

"Something's wrong with that silly clock, it needs mending again," answered Ching-wen. Having looked at a watch she said, "Just wait for the time for half a cup of tea."

As the young maid withdrew, Sheh-yueh remarked, "Fang-kuan does deserve a spanking for being naughty. She was playing with the pendulum yesterday; that's how the clock got broken." While speaking she laid the table.

The young maid came back with a hamper for their inspection. And Ching-wen and Sheh-yueh, opening it, found the usual four kinds of pickles inside.

"He's better now, but they keep serving this rice gruel and pickles," grumbled Ching-wen. "Why not send a couple of easily digested dishes instead?"

Just then, however, at the bottom of the hamper, she discovered a bowl of ham-and-fresh-bamboo-shoot soup. She put this before Pao-yu, who took a sip.

"It's too hot!" he exclaimed.

Hsi-jen laughed.

"A few days without meat and you've grown so greedy!"

She took the bowl and blew gently at the film of oil on the

---

[1] Ying-ying was the heroine of *The Western Chamber*, and Hung Niang was her maid. See Note 1 on p. 132.

surface. Then, noticing Fang-kuan standing near by, she passed the bowl to her.

"You can do this," she said. "Time you learned to make yourself useful, instead of acting like a silly goose. Mind you blow gently though. Don't spit into the soup."

Fang-kuan did as she was told, and was managing quite well, when in rushed her foster-mother who had been waiting outside with the rice.

Now when Fang-kuan and the others first arrived they had been assigned foster-mothers outside, who had later accompanied them to Pear Fragrance Court. This woman had originally been a third-class servant in the Jung Mansion, only doing some laundry work and never entering the inner apartments, so that she did not know the rules of the house. Once the actresses were taken into the Garden, however, their foster-mothers had gone with them to the different apartments. After being told off by Sheh-yueh, this woman was afraid that she might not be allowed to remain in charge of Fang-kuan, and that would be very much to her disadvantage. So she was determined now to win them round. Seeing Fang-kuan blowing on the soup, she hurried in.

"Let me do that!" she cried with a smile. "She's so green she may break the bowl." She reached out for it.

"Get out!" shouted Ching-wen. "Even if you make her smash it, this is no job for *you*. How dare you sneak into this room? Out you go at once!" She scolded the younger maids, "Are you all blind? If she doesn't know any better, you should have told her."

"We tried to chase her away but she wouldn't go," they protested. "She didn't believe us. And now she's got us into trouble too." They rounded on the woman. "*Now* do you believe us? Half the places we're allowed in are out of bounds to you, yet here you come bursting in where even *we* are forbidden to go. As if that weren't enough, you start reaching out and opening your big mouth!" They bundled the woman off.

The matrons waiting at the foot of the steps for the hampers greeted her with mocking laughter.

"You should have looked in the mirror before butting in there, sister," one of them sniggered.

The woman, torn between rage and shame, had to control herself as best she could.

By now, Fang-kuan had blown on the soup several times.

"That'll do," said Pao-yu. "Don't tire yourself. Taste it to see if it's cool enough."

Thinking he must be joking, she turned with a smile to Hsi-jen and the other girls.

"Go on, taste it," urged Hsi-jen.

"Let me show you," offered Ching-wen, then took a sip.

Fang-kuan followed her example.

"It's all right," she said.

She passed the soup to Pao-yu, who drank half a bowl and ate a few bamboo shoots with half a bowl of rice gruel. After that they cleared the table, some young maids brought in a basin, and as soon as he had rinsed his mouth and washed it was time for Hsi-jen and the others to have their meal.

Pao-yu signalled at this point to Fang-kuan. And since she was quick in the uptake and had learned a good deal in her few years as an actress, she pretended that she had a headache and had lost her appetite.

"Then you may as well stay here and keep him company," said Hsi-jen. "I'll leave you the gruel, in case you feel like it later." With that the other girls left.

When the two of them were alone, Pao-yu described in detail how he had noticed something burning and spotted Ou-kuan, how he had lied to cover up for her, and how Ou-kuan had told him to ask her, Fang-kuan, for an explanation.

"For whom were those offerings?" he asked.

Fang-kuan heard him out with a smile, then heaved a sigh.

"It's a funny business but pathetic too."

"What do you mean?"

"That offering was for Ti-kuan, who died."

"Why not, if they were friends?"

"They weren't just ordinary friends. Ou-kuan had the fantastic notion that as she used to play young men and Ti-kuan young ladies, and as they were often cast as husband and wife, although it was make-believe they should act the part every day as if they were really in love. So they became so crazy about each other that even offstage they were for ever together. In the end they were so devoted that when Ti-kuan died she nearly cried her heart out, and to this day she's never forgotten her. That's why she burns paper money at all the festivals. When Jui-kuan later took Ti-kuan's place, we found that Ou-kuan was just as attached to *her*.

" 'Has your new sweetheart made you forget the old one?' we asked.

" 'No, but there's a very good reason for this,' she told us. 'I'm like a widower who marries again. If he doesn't forget his first wife, he's still true to her. But if he insists on remaining single all the rest of his life, that's against the rules of propriety too, and how could his dead wife rest in peace in her grave?'

"Don't you call that crazy and senseless? It's really ridiculous!"

However, such foolish talk was precisely the kind to appeal to foolish Pao-yu. He exclaimed in wonder, torn between sadness and joy.

"Since Heaven creates such wonderful girls, what use are we filthy males except to contaminate the world?" he cried.

He took Fang-kuan's hand and urged her, "If that's how things are, you must tell her something from me. I can't very well tell her directly."

"What is it?" asked Fang-kuan.

"In future, she mustn't burn paper coins. That's a later practice and a heretical one, not based on the instructions of Confucius. At all future festivals she need only burn some incense in a censer; and if her heart is pure, Ti-kuan's spirit will know it. Foolish people don't understand and have different sorts of sacrifices for the gods, Buddha and the dead; whereas actually the important thing is just sincerity. Even if you're in a hurry, or away from home and unable to find incense, you can offer a clod of earth or a blade of grass, provided that it's clean. Not only will the spirits of the dead accept such a sacrifice, even the gods will too.

"Haven't you seen that censer on my desk? Whenever I miss some dead friend, whatever the date, I burn incense and offer some fresh water or tea, or maybe flowers or fruit, or even meat or vegetables. As long as your heart is pure, Buddha himself will come to the sacrifice. That's why we say: 'It's the intention that counts, not the empty form.' So go presently and tell her not to burn any more paper money in future."

Fang-kuan promised to do this and then ate the rice gruel.

Just at that moment someone announced that Their Ladyships were back. To know what happened after, read the next chapter.

CHAPTER 59

Ying-erh and Chun-yen Are Scolded
by Willow Bank
And Red Rue Studio Sends
for Reinforcements

Pao-yu put on a coat and went over with his cane to pay his respects to Their Ladyships. Tired out after their recent exertions, they went to bed unusually early and after an uneventful night returned to the court at dawn.

The day for the funeral cortège to set off to the Imperial Tombs was now approaching. Yuan-yang, Hu-po, Fei-tsui and Po-li were busy packing the Lady Dowager's things while Yu-chuan, Tsai-yun and Tsai-hsia packed for Lady Wang, after which they checked through the baggage with the stewards' wives who would be accompanying their mistresses. Six maids and ten stewards' wives in all would be going, in addition to men-servants; but Yuan-yang and Yu-chuan were to stay behind to see to things at home. Horse-borne litters and harness had been made ready. And the curtains and bedding which had been prepared a few days previously were taken on ahead in carts by four of five women and a few men to the hostel, ready for the main party's arrival.

When the day came, the Lady Dowager and Chia Jung's wife took a horse-borne litter, with Lady Wang behind in another, while Chia Chen rode at the head of an escort of servants. There were several big carts too for serving-women and maids which also carried changes of clothing. Aunt Hsueh and Madam Yu, at the head of the rest of the household, saw them off from outside the main gate. And Chia Lien, to smooth their journey for them, having seen his parents off caught up with the litters and followed behind with the escort.

In the Jung Mansion, Lai Ta posted extra night-watchmen and locked the two main gates so that the only way in or out was through the small west side gate; and at sunset he had the ceremonial gate closed, allowing no entrance or exit. The front and back side gates and those to the east and west of the Garden were also locked, except for that leading to the back of Lady Wang's compound, which was used by the girls, and the gate on the east to Aunt Hsueh's compound. These two, being in the inner court, did not have to be locked.

Inside, Yuan-yang and Yu-chuan also closed their mistresses' main apartments, and took the other maids and matrons from there to stay in the servants' quarters; while every night Lin Chih-hsiao's wife brought some dozen old serving-women to keep watch, and all the entrance halls were patrolled by extra pages with clappers. In this way excellent order was maintained.

Early one spring morning when Pao-chai awoke, parted her bed-curtains and got up, she found it rather chilly. She opened the door and looked out. The soil in the courtyard was moist, the moss on it green, for a light rain had fallen at dawn. She then woke Hsiang-yun and the others.

As they were dressing, Hsiang-yun remarked that her cheeks itched. She was afraid she had a spring rash again, and would like some rose-nitric powder to apply to it.

"I gave all I had left the other day to Pao-chin," Pao-chai told her. "Tai-yu had a good deal made and I was meaning to ask her for some, but not having felt any itching this spring I forgot." She ordered Ying-erh to go and fetch some of this powder.

As Ying-erh was about to leave on this errand, Jui-kuan offered to go with her, as that would give her a chance to see Ou-kuan. So the two of them set off from Alpinia Park.

Chatting as they strolled, the girls soon reached Willow Bank. As they walked along it they saw that the willows, now turning green, seemed hung with golden threads.

"Can you weave things out of osiers?" Ying-erh asked.

"What sort of things?"

"Oh, anything — little toys or useful objects. Wait till I've picked a few twigs with leaves and I'll make a basket to fill with different flowers. That should be fun."

So instead of fetching the powder, Ying-erh plucked an armful of tender twigs which she made Jui-kuan carry, and started to weave a basket as on they walked, stopping now and then to pick flowers. The dainty little basket was soon completed. Covered with its own fresh green leaves and filled with flowers, it made a charming and original toy. Jui-kuan was delighted with it.

"Do be a dear and give it to me!" she begged.

"No, this is for Miss Lin. We'll pick more to make some for the rest of us later."

By now they had reached Bamboo Lodge, where they found Tai-yu at her toilet. At sight of the basket she exclaimed with pleasure.

"Who made this pretty thing?"

"I did," said Ying-erh. "It's a present for you, miss."

Tai-yu took it, remarking, "No wonder everyone says you have clever fingers. This is really original." After examining it she made Tzu-chuan hang it up.

Ying-erh, having asked after Aunt Hsueh, disclosed her errand. Then Tai-yu got Tzu-chuan to wrap up a packet of the powder for her.

"I'm better today," remarked Tai-yu. "I mean to go for a stroll. Go back and tell Cousin Pao-chai there's no need for her to come and pay her respects to Aunt Hsueh or trouble to call on me either. As soon as I've done my hair, we're both going over to your place. We shall have our breakfast taken over there too. It will be livelier having it together."

Ying-erh assented, then went to Tzu-chuan's room where she found Jui-kuan unwilling to leave, so engrossed was she in her conversation with Ou-kuan.

"Miss Tai-yu is coming to our place," Ying-erh told them. "Why not come with us, Ou-kuan, and wait for her there?"

"That's a good idea," said Tzu-chuan. "She's just a nuisance here." She wrapped up Tai-yu's spoon and chopsticks in a table napkin and gave it to Ou-kuan saying, "Here's a job for you. Take this along first."

Ou-kuan went off cheerfully with the other two. As they walked along Willow Bank, Ying-erh picked some more twigs, then sat down on a rock to plait them, telling Jui-kuan to deliver the powder first and then come back. But the two other girls were too intrigued by what she was making to leave. To hurry them she threatened:

"If you don't go now, I'll stop."

"I'll go with you," volunteered Ou-kuan. "Then we can hurry back." And with that they went off.

Presently along came Mother Ho's young daughter Chun-yen, who wanted to know what Ying-erh was making. Just at that moment the other girls returned.

"What was that paper you were burning the other day when my aunt spotted you?" Chun-yen asked Ou-kuan. "Before she could report you, Pao-yu gave her such a dressing-down that she went off in a huff and told my mother all about it. What feud did you have with them those few years in the troupe outside the Garden that you're still at loggerheads?"

"What feud?" Ou-kuan snorted. "There's just no satisfying them — they're for ever nagging at us. Not to mention anything else, goodness knows how much they made the last two years out of our daily food allowance outside — more than enough to feed their own families — in addition to their rake-off on purchases. Yet any job we give them, they complain to high heaven. What sort of behaviour is that?"

Chun-yen smiled.

"She's my aunt, so I can't run her down to outsiders. But no wonder Pao-yu says: 'A girl before marriage is a precious pearl; after marriage, she somehow picks up all sorts of bad habits so that the pearl loses its lustre — it's a dead pearl; and as she grows still older, the pearl changes into a fish-eye. What a metamorphosis!'

"That's silly talk maybe, still there's something in it. I don't know about other people, but as for my mother and her sister, my aunt, it's true that the older they grow the madder they get for money. First, at home, the two of them groused that they had no fat jobs; then luckily there was this Garden and I happened to be assigned to Happy Red Court; so apart from saving my keep, the family got four or five hundred cash extra a month. But they still said that wasn't enough. Later both were assigned to Pear Fragrance Court to look after the actresses. My aunt had Ou-kuan as her foster-daughter; my mother, Fang-kuan; so for the last few years they were in clover. Since the actresses have moved into the Garden, they've been living separately, but they're still just as greedy. Ridiculous, isn't it?

"The other day my aunt scolded Ou-kuan; then my mother squabbled with Fang-kuan — wouldn't even let her wash her hair. Yesterday being pay-day, my mother got Fang-kuan's monthly allowance. As she couldn't get out of buying her some things, she told me I could wash first. I thought: I've my own monthly allowance, and even if I hadn't I could wash my hair any time simply by asking Hsi-jen, Ching-wen or Sheh-yueh. Why should I accept this as a favour? How futile! When I refused, she made my younger sister Hsiao-chiu wash before Fang-kuan. Then naturally there was a row. And next she wanted to blow on Pao-yu's soup — it's enough to make you split your sides laughing.

"As soon as she came in here I told her the rules; but she didn't believe me, insisted she knew better. She's simply been asking for a snub. It's a good thing there are so many people in the Garden that no one remembers different relationships clearly. If they did, and it appeared that ours was the only quarrelsome family, I'd feel bad about these squabbles.

"Now you're playing about here where everything's in the charge of my paternal aunt, who's stricter about it, ever since it was put in her care, than about her own property. Apart from getting up early and turning in late so as to watch over it, she makes us keep an eye on things too for fear any damage is done, interfering, I'm afraid, with my own work. Now that they've both moved in here, the two sisters-in-law keep such a careful watch, they won't allow a single blade of grass to be touched;

yet you've plucked all these flowers and twigs! They'll be here any minute now — you'd better watch out!"

"Others may not be allowed to pick what they like, but *I* am," retorted Ying-erh. "After the different places were allotted, each household was assigned its share of the produce. Not counting edibles, just take flowers for example. Those in charge have to send some over every day for the young ladies and maids to wear, as well as to put in their vases. My young lady was the only one who told them not to send any. She said she'd ask for what she needed, but in fact she never once has. So how can they scold me for picking a few flowers now?"

While she was still speaking, sure enough, along came Chun-yen's aunt leaning on her cane. Ying-erh and Chun-yen at once urged her to be seated. The sight of all the willow twigs and flowers which Ou-kuan and the others had picked vexed the woman, but not liking to say anything against Ying-erh, who was making a basket, she rounded on her niece.

"I told you to keep an eye on things, but you take that as a chance to play around and not go back to your apartments. When they want you there, you say you've been working for *me*. Using me as your cover, eh?"

"You order me about yet you're afraid, and now you're scolding me," protested Chun-yen. "I can't be everywhere at once, can I?"

"Don't you believe her, aunt," chuckled Ying-erh. "She was the one who picked all these and asked me to make her a basket. When I tried to chase her away, she wouldn't go."

"Don't talk such nonsense!" cried Chun-yen. "My aunt can't take a joke, she'll believe you."

Indeed, her aunt had been born stupid, and now that age had addled her wits her one interest in life was money: she had no consideration at all for others. Inwardly fuming, she had not known how to retaliate until Ying-erh made this joke. Now, presuming on her seniority, she raised her cane and struck her niece several blows.

"Little bitch!" she swore. "I'll teach you to talk back! Your mother's grinding her teeth, itching to tear you to pieces and chew you up. Yet you still answer me back in that pert way!"

Hurt and humiliated, Chun-yen sobbed, "Sister Ying-erh was only joking, yet you believed her and beat me. Why should my mother be angry? I've not boiled away her water or burned her pan. What have I done wrong?"

Ying-erh, seeing that her teasing had really angered the woman, now caught her by the arm.

"I was only joking," she said soothingly. "By beating her you make *me* feel bad too."

"Don't meddle with our affairs, miss," snapped the other. "Can't we punish our own children just because you're here?"

This stupid gibe made Ying-erh flush with anger. She let go of the woman with a scornful laugh.

"You can punish her any time you please. Why do it just after I make a joke? All right — go ahead."

With that she sat down again and was going on making her basket when who should appear but Chun-yen's mother in search of her daughter.

"Why haven't you fetched water yet?" she called. "What are you doing there?"

"Come and look at this minx!" her sister-in-law chimed in. "She won't obey even *me*. She keeps answering back."

Mother Ho came over to them.

"Now what's the girl up to?" she demanded. "You may have no respect for your own mother, but you should at least show some respect to your aunt."

Ying-erh tried to explain what had happened, but Chun-yen's aunt would not let her get a word in. Pointing to the flower basket on the rock she fumed:

"See! Your girl's not a child any more, yet she still fools about. When *she* brings people here to wreck the place, how can I tell them off?"

Mother Ho's tiff with Fang-kuan still rankled, and Chun-yen's waywardness made her even angrier. Stepping forward she boxed her ears.

"You bitch!" she cried. "A few years in high society and

you imitate the ways of those loose women. I'll have to teach you a lesson. I may not be able to control my foster-child but you're my own spawn. I'm not afraid of *you*! Even if I can't go where you young bitches go, why don't you stay put there, waiting on your mistress? Why gad about outside so shamelessly?" Grabbing the osiers she brandished them in Chun-yen's face. "What's this you're making? Your mother's arse?"

"*We* made that," cut in Ying-erh. "Don't 'scold the locust while pointing at the mulberry.' "

Mother Ho was eaten up with jealousy of senior maids such as Hsi-jen and Ching-wen, who had more prestige and authority in the different compounds than she. Fearing them and forced to defer to them, she could only work off her rage and resentment on others. Now the sight of Ou-kuan, to whom her sister had such an aversion, added fuel to the fire of her anger.

Chun-yen set off in tears to Happy Red Court. Afraid that if questioned she would explain why she was crying and make Ching-wen angry again, her mother shouted frantically:

"Come back! I've something to tell you."

But Chun-yen kept right on. Her mother in desperation chased after her. When the girl turned and saw her, she broke into a run; then Mother Ho, in hot pursuit, slipped on the moss and fell — at which the other three girls burst out laughing.

In disgust, Ying-erh tossed all her flowers and twigs into the stream and went back to her room, while Chun-yen's aunt crossly invoked the aid of Buddha.

"May a thunderbolt strike the wicked little bitch, spoiling all those flowers!" she swore. She then picked more flowers to take to the various apartments.

Meanwhile Chun-yen, running into Happy Red Court, bumped into Hsi-jen setting off to call on Tai-yu. She caught hold of her, begging:

"Save me, miss! My mother's beating me again."

Annoyed to see Mother Ho close behind, Hsi-jen said, "You beat your foster-daughter one day, your own daughter the next. Are you showing off how many daughters you have? Or do you really not know the rules here?"

The woman, although only recently come to the Garden, had sized up Hsi-jen as quiet and good-tempered.

"You don't understand, miss, so don't meddle in our affairs," she retorted. "You're the ones who spoil them. Just mind your own business."

She chased after Chun-yen then to beat her again, while Hsi-jen indignantly turned back into the courtyard. Sheh-yueh, hanging up handkerchiefs under the crab-apple tree, had overheard the commotion.

"Never mind her, sister," she said. "What can *she* do?"

She signed to Chun-yen, who took the hint and ran straight to Pao-yu.

"Well, wonders will never cease!" declared the maids.

Sheh-yueh urged the woman, "Steady on. Do us a favour, won't you, and calm down."

Mother Ho saw that her daughter had darted up to Pao-yu, who had taken her hand.

"Don't be afraid; I'll protect you," he promised her.

Chun-yen told him tearfully all that had just happened to her and Ying-erh. This only made Pao-yu more exasperated.

"Why not simply fool about here?" he asked. "Why must you even annoy our relative?"

Sheh-yueh observed to the company at large, "We can't blame her for telling us not to meddle in their business. Not knowing the facts, we've no right to interfere. We'd better ask someone who *can* cope to come and deal with this. That's the only way to convince her and teach her manners." She turned and ordered a young maid, "Go and fetch Ping-erh here. If she's busy, ask Mrs. Lin to come."

As the little girl left on this errand, the older servant-maids gathered round Mother Ho.

"Quick, sister!" they urged. "Ask the young ladies to call that child back. If Miss Ping-erh comes, you're in for trouble."

"Whichever Miss Ping-erh comes I must have justice," blustered the woman. "No one has any right to stop a mother teaching her own daughter a lesson."

"Don't you know who this Miss Ping-erh is?" the others retorted. "She's the one in Madam Lien's household. If she's in a good mood she may let you off with a short scolding. If she's in a bad mood, sister, you're in for it!"

The little maid came back at this point to report, "Miss Ping-erh's busy just now. When she asked what had happened and I told her, she said: 'In that case drive her out, and tell Mrs. Lin to give her forty strokes with a cane at the side gate.'"

Dismissal was the last thing Mother Ho wanted. Tears streaming down her cheeks, she pleaded with Hsi-jen and the rest:

"It wasn't easy for me to get this job. I'm a lone widow doing my very best to serve you all faithfully here and save my family a little expense. If I leave, I shall have to fend for myself and won't be able to manage."

Seeing the state she was in, Hsi-jen relented.

"You want to stay yet won't keep the rules or do as you're told, beating people right and left," she said. "How did we come to take on someone so stupid? These endless rows make people laugh at us."

"Don't listen to her," put in Ching-wen. "Send her packing, that's the only thing to do. Who has the time to argue with her?"

"Be kind!" the woman pleaded. "Lay up virtue in heaven! I was wrong, but in future I'll do whatever you young ladies tell me." She prompted Chun-yen, "This comes of my beating you. Not really beating you either, yet now *I'm* the one smarting for it. Put in a good word for me too."

Pao-yu took pity on her then and agreed to let her stay on.

"But no more of these scenes!" he warned her.

After thanking them each in turn, Mother Ho left. And then Ping-erh arrived on the scene to ask what had happened.

"It's all over now," Hsi-jen told her. "We can forget it."

Ping-erh smiled.

"It's best to be easy on people — saves trouble," she approved. "The mistresses have been away for a few days only, yet we've heard of nothing but squabbles of all sorts in every household —

before one's over the next one crops up. I just don't know how I'm to cope."

"I thought we were the only ones," remarked Hsi-jen. "I didn't know there'd been other rows too."

"This business of yours is nothing," rejoined Ping-erh. "I was just listing to Madam Yu all the troubles there've been in the last three or four days — eight or nine of them big and small. This little tiff of yours is nothing — it doesn't count. There've been far more serious or ridiculous rows."

Hsi-jen asked what she was referring to. To know Ping-erh's answer you must read the next chapter.

CHAPTER 60

Jasmine Powder Is Substituted for Rose-Nitric Powder Rose Flavoured Juice Is Repaid with Pachyma Cocos

Hsi-jen asked Ping-erh what trouble there had been.

"Oh, a lot of nonsense that no one could conceive of!" was the reply. "I'll tell you some other day. Right now I'm too busy, and things aren't straightened out either."

As she was speaking, in came a maid sent by Li Wan.

"Is Sister Ping-erh here?" she asked. "My mistress is waiting for you. What's keeping you?"

"Coming, coming!" responded Ping-erh, hurrying out.

Hsi-jen and the others commented jokingly, "With her mistress ill she's in such great demand, everyone's trying to grab her."

Once Ping-erh had gone, Pao-yu suggested to Chun-yen, "Why not take your mother over to Miss Pao-chai's place to say a few kind words to Ying-erh, so that she doesn't feel too wronged."

Chun-yen agreed to this, going out with her mother, and Pao-yu called again to her through the window, "Mind you don't mention it in front of Miss Pao-chai, or Ying-erh may get scolded instead!"

Mother Ho and her daughter assented and left, chatting as they walked along.

"I kept *telling* you, ma, but you never believed me," said Chun-yen. "Why land yourself in trouble like this?"

"Go on, you little bitch," chuckled her mother. "As the proverb says: 'We learn from experience.' I understand now, so don't keep on at me."

"If you'd just know your place and mind your own business here, ma, in the long run you'd gain a whole lot by it," went on

Chun-yen. "Let me tell you something: Pao-yu often says that he's going to ask the mistress to send all of us working here — whether inside or outside — back to our own parents. Isn't that fine?"

"Did he really say that?" her mother asked eagerly.

"Why should anyone tell such a lie?" Chun-yen retorted.

"Buddha be praised! Buddha be praised!" cried her mother.

When they reached Alpinia Park, Pao-chai, Tai-yu and Aunt Hsueh were having a meal. As Ying-erh had gone to make tea, the two of them went straight to find her.

"I was talking too wildly just now," said Mother Ho ingratiatingly. "Please don't hold it against me, miss. I've come now specially to apologize."

Ying-erh, smiling, offered them seats and poured them some tea. But saying that they had business they took their leave and were starting back when Jui-kuan hurried out after them.

"Auntie! Sister!" she called. "Wait a minute."

Coming up to them she gave them a packet, explaining that this was some rose-nitric powder for Fang-kuan.

"How small-minded of you, really!" chuckled Chun-yen. "Do you imagine she can't get this in our place that you have to send her a packet?"

"What she gets there is one thing," retorted Jui-kuan, "but this is a present from *me*. Do take it back for her."

Chun-yen had to accept it then. When she and her mother got back, Chia Huan and Chia Tsung had just called to see Pao-yu.

"I'll go in by myself, ma," said Chun-yen. "You'd better keep out."

Her mother, now completely under her thumb, did not venture to oppose her.

When Pao-yu saw that Chun-yen was back he nodded to her and she took the hint, holding her tongue. After standing there for a few minutes she turned and went out, signalling to Fang-kuan to join her, then quietly told her what Jui-kuan had said and handed over the powder.

Pao-yu, having nothing to say to Tsung and Huan, asked

Fang-kuan presently what she had in her hand; and readily showing it to him she explained that it was rose-nitric powder for a spring rash.

"It was kind of her to think of it," he remarked.

Chia Huan hearing this craned his neck to have a look, and when he smelt how fragrant the powder was he stooped to pull a sheet of paper out of his boot.

"Give me half of it, won't you, good brother?" he wheedled.

Pao-yu felt obliged to comply, but Fang-kuan was unwilling to part with a gift from Jui-kuan.

"Don't you touch this!" she cried. "I'll fetch you some from elsewhere."

Pao-yu smiled understandingly as he wrapped the powder up again.

"Bring it quickly then," he said.

Fang-kuan took the packet and put it away, then went to her dressing-case to look for her own powder. When she opened the case, however, she found the box empty. "There was still some this morning. Where has it all gone?" she wondered. The other maids when questioned did not know.

"Why try to track it down just now?" asked Sheh-yueh. "Someone in this place must have run out of hers and taken it. Just give them something else, it doesn't matter what — they won't know the difference. Hurry up and get rid of those boys so that we can have our meal."

So Fang-kuan wrapped up a packet of jasmine powder and took it to Chia Huan; but when he eagerly held out his hand for it she tossed it on to the *kang*, forcing him to pick it up himself. Having put it in his pocket he took his leave.

In the absence of Chia Cheng, Lady Wang and the rest, Chia Huan had been playing truant from school for several days on the pretext of illness. Now that he had this powder he went off in high spirits to find Tsai-yun, who happened just then to be chatting with Concubine Chao. Beaming, he told the girl:

"I've got something good here for you to powder your face with. You've often said that rose-nitric powder is better for skin trouble than that nitric concoction bought outside. Have a look and see if this is the right stuff."

Tsai-yun opened the packet and promptly burst out laughing.

"Who gave you this?" she asked.

Chia Huan explained how he had acquired it.

"They were fooling you because you're such a bumpkin," she chuckled. "This isn't rose-nitric powder, it's jasmine powder."

Chia Huan examined it, and saw that it was pinker than the powder he had been shown, but equally fragrant.

"Well, it's good stuff just the same," he retorted. "Keep it to powder your face. It's better than anything you can get outside."

So Tsai-yun accepted it.

"How could she give *you* anything good?" sneered Concubine Chao at this point. "Who told you to go there begging? No wonder they made a fool of you. If *I* were you, I'd take it back and throw it in her face. Now's the time, while some have gone to the funeral and others are ill in bed, to raise a rumpus and let no one have any peace. This way we can get our own back. Two months from now they won't rake it up again. Even if they do, you can have an answer ready. Pao-yu is your elder brother, so if you don't dare tackle him, never mind; but are you afraid of those cats and dogs in his place too?"

Chia Huan hung his head.

"Why stir up more trouble?" put in Tsai-yun quickly. "Whatever happens, we'd better put up with it."

"Don't you barge in," retorted Concubine Chao. "This has nothing to do with *you*. Better seize this chance, while we've got a good excuse, to bawl out those dirty bitches." Pointing at Chia Huan she spat out, "You spineless wretch, you *deserve* to be bullied by that scum! If *I* say a word against you or give you the wrong thing by mistake, you toss your head in a rage and throw a tantrum, your eyes popping out of your head; but now that these sluts make fun of you, you take it lying down. Do you expect anyone in this family to have any respect for you in future? You're so useless, I blush for you."

Chia Huan, though ashamed and annoyed, was afraid to do as she said. He brushed it aside.

"You can talk, but *you* don't dare go either," he muttered. "You just want me to go and have a row with them. If they report me to our school and I get a beating, of course *you* won't feel the pain. Each time you've egged me on and trouble came of it so that I got beaten or cursed, you've always kept quiet. Now you're egging me on again to quarrel with those servant-girls. Aren't you afraid of Third Sister? If *you* have the guts to go, I'll have more respect for you."

This touched his mother on the raw.

"Why should I be afraid of a creature I spawned myself?" she snapped. "If I were, there'd be even more rows here."

She grabbed the packet and dashed off towards the Garden. Tsai-yun, unable to stop her no matter how hard she tried, made herself scarce while Chia Huan slipped out of the ceremonial gate and went off to amuse himself elsewhere.

Concubine Chao stormed straight into the Garden where she ran into Mother Hsia, Ou-kuan's foster-mother, who seeing the rage she was in asked where she was going.

"Just look at this household!" fumed the concubine. "Even those little singsong girls brought in to put on shows every other day treat some people better than others, taking advantage of those who have less weight. If it had been anyone else I wouldn't have minded, but how can I let that little whore get the upper hand of *us*?"

This struck a chord in Mother Hsia's heart. She hastily asked what had happened, and was told how Fang-kuan had made a fool of Chia Huan by giving him jasmine powder instead of rose-nitric powder.

"Is that all, madam?" exclaimed Mother Hsia. "Have you only just woken up to them? Why, that's nothing! Yesterday they were even burning paper money here on the sly, and Pao-yu stood up for them. But if other people bring something in they say it's forbidden, unclean or taboo. So isn't burning paper money taboo here? Just think, apart from the mistress, there's nobody higher than you in this house; only you won't use your authority, so nobody's afraid of you.

"Now what I suggest is this. As those young whores are low-class girls it won't matter offending them. So seize hold of these two things they've done to teach them a lesson, and I'll back you up as a witness. This way you can assert your authority, and other issues will be easier to handle. The mistresses and the young ladies can hardly side with those singsong girls against *you*."

This made Concubine Chao feel in a stronger position.

"I didn't know about that business of burning paper. Tell me the details," she said.

Mother Hsia accordingly told her all that had happened. "Just go ahead and trounce them," she concluded. "If there's a row, we'll back you up."

Emboldened by this, Concubine Chao made her way confidently to Happy Red Court. It so happened that Pao-yu had gone to call on Tai-yu, having heard that she was in, and Fang-kuan was having a meal with Hsi-jen and the others. When the concubine came in they all stood up to greet her and offer her a seat, after which they asked her her business. Instead of answering, she stepped forward and threw the powder in Fang-kuan's face.

"You trollop!" she swore, pointing a finger at her. "We bought you with our money to train as an actress. You're nothing but a painted whore. Even the lowest slave in our house ranks higher than *you*, yet you make up to some people and look down on others. When Pao-yu wants to give someone a present you stop him, as if it were *your* property. And you fob this stuff off on my son, imagining he doesn't know the difference. They're both sons of the house, young masters. Who are *you* to treat him like dirt?"

This was more than Fang-kuan could take.

"There was no rose powder left," she sobbed. "That's why I gave him this. If I'd told him there wasn't any more, he most likely wouldn't have believed me. Isn't this good powder too?

"Even if I did train as an actress, I never performed outside.

I'm only a girl; what do I know about painted whores? You've no call to swear at me, madam. *You* didn't buy me. We're all birds of a feather — all slaves here. Why go for me?"

Hsi-jen pulled her away, remonstrating, "Don't talk such nonsense!"

The concubine was so angry that she darted forward and slapped Fang-kuan on both cheeks. Hsi-jen hastily intervened.

"She's just a child with no sense, madam. Let her be! We'll give her a good talking to presently."

After being slapped, however, Fang-kuan would not keep quiet. She flew into a tantrum, wailing and screaming:

"Who are *you* to beat me? Take a look at yourself in the mirror first. I'd sooner die than let a hag like you beat me!"

She threw herself at Concubine Chao and dared her to slap her again. As the others tried to quiet her and pull her away, Ching-wen gently tugged at Hsi-jen's sleeve.

"Leave them alone," she whispered. "Let them make a row and see what comes of it. Everything's at sixes and sevens now, with so many people trying to have the whip hand, taking it in turn to throw their weight about. This sort of thing can't go on."

The attendants outside who had come with Concubine Chao were each and all delighted to hear this row.

"High time too!" they crowed. "Buddha be praised!"

As for the old women who had a grudge against the actresses, they all gloated too at the sight of Fang-kuan being beaten.

Meanwhile Ou-kuan and Jui-kuan were amusing themselves together. When Kuei-kuan, the "warrior" actress assigned to Hsiang-yun, and Tou-kuan assigned to Pao-chin heard of this fracas, they rushed to find the two of them.

"Fang-kuan's being bullied!" they cried. "How can we put up with that? Let's all go and have a first-class row to get our own back!"

Being all of them so childish, their one thought was to avenge their friend without worrying about the consequences, and so they ran together to Happy Red Court. First Tou-kuan butted Concubine Chao with her head, very nearly knocking her down.

The other three swarmed round as well, weeping and wailing, tearing at her and butting her, so that she was surrounded on all sides. Ching-wen and the other maids, laughing, only made a show of trying to intervene. As for Hsi-jen, she was frantic. But as she pulled one away another rushed forward.

"Are you out of your minds?" she demanded. "If you have some complaint, say so quietly. How can you carry on in this crazy way?"

Concubine Chao was helpless. All she could do was pour out a flood of abuse. Jui-kuan and Ou-kuan, one on each side of her, had pinioned both her arms while Kuei-kuan and Tou-kuan, one in front and one behind, were butting her with their heads.

"You'll have to kill all four of us!" they swore.

Fang-kuan, stretched out on the ground, was crying as if she were about to die.

During this hurly-burly, Ching-wen had sent Chun-yen to report it to Tan-chun. So now Madam Yu, Li Wan and Tan-chun came over with Ping-erh and some older serving-women. They ordered the four actresses to lay off, and asked what the trouble was. Concubine Chao, nearly bursting with rage, her eyes bulging, broke into an incoherent diatribe. Madam Yu and Li Wan paid no attention to her, simply ordering the four girls to keep quiet. Tan-chun sighed.

"What a fuss about nothing!" she said. "You lose your temper, madam, too easily. I was just wanting to consult you about something, and was surprised when the maids told me they couldn't find you. So you were here all the time in one of your rages. Please come along with me."

Madam Yu and Li Wan chimed in with a smile, "Please come to the hall, and we can talk things over."

Concubine Chao had no choice but to go with the three of them, still muttering and maundering.

"Those girls are playthings," said Tan-chun. "If we like them we can chat and joke with them; if we don't, we can ignore them. If they misbehave it's like being scratched by a cat or a puppy, and we should overlook it whenever possible. If it's something inexcusable, we should just tell the stewards' wives to punish them. Why lower ourselves to raise a hullabaloo? This is so undignified!

"Look at Concubine Chou. Why is it that no one takes advantage of *her*, and she doesn't go round hounding other people either? My advice to you, madam, is to go back to your rooms and get your temper under control. Don't listen to malicious trouble-makers, or you'll just make *yourself* a laughing-stock by doing other people's dirty work for nothing. Even if you're bursting with anger, put up with it for a few days. When the mistress comes back she'll straighten everything out."

Concubine Chao had nothing to say in reply to this lecture and had to go home. Then Tan-chun turned indignantly to Li Wan and Madam Yu.

"She's so old, yet the way she carries on makes it impossible for *anyone* to respect her. Was it worth rampaging in such an undignified fashion over such a trifle? She has no sense of dignity and is too gullible — she *never* uses her head. Those shameless slaves must have egged her on again to do this, using her — because she's a fool — to get their own back."

The more she thought about it, the angrier she felt. So she ordered the serving-women to find out who was at the bottom of this business. They had to agree, but once outside they smiled at each other and said:

"This is like looking for a needle in the ocean!"

They summoned Concubine Chao's maids and all those in the Garden for questioning, but each denied any knowledge of how this had started. At a loss, they had to report to Tan-chun their failure to find the culprit, but promised to make further investigations, to inform her of any irresponsible talk, and to have the offender punished. Tan-chun was gradually calming down when Ai-kuan slipped in to see her.

"It's Mother Hsia who's got her knife into us all and is always stirring up trouble," she confided. "The other day, she accused Ou-kuan of burning sacrificial paper; but luckily Pao-yu said he'd asked her to do it, and that silenced the old creature. Today, when I brought you your handkerchief, I noticed her gabbing away with Concubine Chao. She only **went** away when she saw me coming."

Although this sounded suspicious to Tan-chun, she knew that Ai-kuan and the other girls belonged to one set and were very mischievous too; so after hearing her out, she was unwilling to use this as proof.

Now Mother Hsia's grand-daughter Chan-chieh also served in Tan-chun's apartments and often bought things or ran errands for the maids there, all of whom liked her. After her meal that day, Tan-chun went to the hall to attend to some business; and Tsui-mo, left at home in charge, told Chan-chieh to go and send a page to buy some cakes.

"I've just swept a whole big courtyard and my legs and back are aching," objected Chan-chieh. "Can't you get someone else to go?"

"Who else is there?" countered Tsui-mo. "Go while it's still early. And let me give you a word of advice: on your way to the back gate, tell your grandma to be on her guard."

Then she explained how Ai-kuan had been telling tales about Mother Hsia.

Taking the money from her Chan-chieh snorted, "So that little bitch wants to get *us* into trouble too! Wait till I tell my grandma this."

With that she went off to the back gate. She found all the kitchen-maids, Mother Hsia among them, sitting chatting on the steps there, as they were free for a while. She asked one of the women to go and buy the cakes. Then, fulminating, she passed on to her grandmother what she had just been told. Mother Hsia, both angry and frightened, wanted to go and challenge Ai-kuan and to complain to Tan-chun. Chan-chieh quickly stopped her.

"What would you say if you went, grandma?" she asked. "How did you get to know about it? Carping and complaining would only cause more trouble. I'm just telling you so that you'll be on your guard. Don't go rushing off in such a hurry."

As she was speaking, along came Fang-kuan. Leaning on the gate she called pleasantly to Mrs. Liu in the kitchen:

"Mrs. Liu, Master Pao says he'd like a cool, vinegary vegetable dish for supper; but don't put in sesame oil — that would make it greasy."

"All right," answered Mrs. Liu. "How come you were sent on this errand today? If you don't think our place too dirty, come in and chat for a bit."

Fang-kuan had just entered the kitchen when a woman came along carrying a plate of cakes.

"Whose hot cakes are these?" asked the girl jokingly. "Let me try one."

Chan-chieh promptly took the plate.

"These were bought for other people," she said. "You wouldn't care for this stuff."

Mrs. Liu seeing this quickly put in, "If you like such things, miss, I've some here freshly bought for my daughter. She hasn't eaten any yet so they're still here, clean and untouched." She brought out another plate for Fang-kuan, adding, "Wait, I'll brew you some good tea."

While she went in to poke up the fire and make tea, Fang-kuan took a cake and thrust it under Chan-chieh's nose.

"Who wants your cake? Isn't this cake too?" she demanded. "I was only joking, but I wouldn't eat *yours* even if you kowtowed to me." She crumbled the cake into pieces then and tossed these to the sparrows, calling out, "You mustn't feel hurt, Mrs. Liu. I'll buy you another two catties presently."

Chan-chieh was first speechless with anger. Then she snorted:

"If the thunder god has eyes, why doesn't he strike such wicked people dead? She's deliberately needling me! Of course, I can't compare with the likes of *you* who have people sending you presents, offering to be your slaves and flattering you, in the hope that, if need be, you'll put in a good word for them."

The older women intervened, "Enough of that, you two. Why bicker every time you meet?"

A few of the more quick-witted, afraid this argument would lead to further trouble, quietly slipped away. Chan-chieh, however, dared not say any more. Grumbling to herself she went off.

When Mrs. Liu saw there was nobody about, she came out of the kitchen and asked Fang-kuan, "Did you mention that matter I spoke of the other day?"

"Yes, I did," was the answer. "And I'll bring it up again in a couple of days. But that old hag Chao would choose this time for another row with me. Did sister take that rose flavoured juice I brought the other day? Is she any better?"

"Oh yes, she drank it all and just loved it, but she doesn't like to ask you for more."

"That's nothing. I'll get her some more."

The fact was that Mrs. Liu had a daughter just turned sixteen. Although the daughter of a cook, she was just as good-looking as Ping-erh, Hsi-jen, Yuan-yang or Tzu-chuan. As she was the fifth child they called her Wu-erh; but being delicate, she had never been given a job. Recently Mrs. Liu had noticed that Pao-yu had many attendants, whose work was light; and she had heard that he meant to let all the girls in his service return to their own homes in future. She wanted to send Wu-erh there as a maid but had no one to recommend her. It so happened that she had worked in Pear Fragrance Court and been more assiduous than their foster-mothers in waiting on Fang-kuan and the other actresses, with the result that they were good to her too. So now she had mentioned this request to Fang-kuan, asking her to pass it on to Pao-yu. And he had agreed. Only, having been unwell recently and in view of all the troubles in the household, he had not yet referred the matter higher up. Enough, however, of this.

Fang-kuan returned now to Happy Red Court and broached the subject again to Pao-yu. He had been away when Concubine Chao made such a scene, and found himself in a difficult position, not knowing whether to intervene or not. After the uproar died down and he heard that Tan-chun had persuaded her to leave, he returned from Alpinia Park to comfort Fang-kuan, and at last everybody had calmed down again.

Now Fang-kuan came back and told him that she wanted some more rose flavoured juice for Liu Wu-erh.

He answered readily enough, "There's plenty.   I seldom drink it.   You can take her the whole lot."

He told Hsi-jen to fetch it.   And seeing that there was not much left, he gave the whole bottle to Fang-kuan who took it away.

Mrs. Liu had just taken her daughter into the Garden to amuse her.   After strolling for a while in an out-of-the-way corner, they went back to the kitchen to rest and have some tea. Now Fang-kuan came in with a small glass bottle about five inches high.   The light falling on it showed that it was almost half full of some red juice, which they assumed to be some of the Western port which Pao-yu drank.

"Sit down, while we fetch the pewter heater to warm it in a jiffy with hot water," they said.

"This is all there is left, so he's given it you with the bottle," Fang-kuan explained.

Wu-erh realized then that it was the juice and accepted it with profuse thanks.

Asked if she was better she said, "I do feel a bit more energetic today; that's why I came here for a stroll.   There's not much of interest at the back, though, only some big rocks and big trees and the back walls of the buildings.   I haven't seen any of the real beauty spots yet."

"Why didn't you go to the front?" asked Fang-kuan.

"I wouldn't let her," said Mrs. Liu.   "The young ladies don't know her.   If someone who has it in for us were to see her, that would lead to another row.   If in future, with your help, she gets a job, she'll have so many chances to stroll around she may even get tired of the place."

"Don't worry," replied Fang-kuan.   "You can count on me."

"*Aiya*, miss!" exclaimed Mrs. Liu.   "We're of no account, not like you."

With that she served tea.   But as it was not to Fang-kuan's taste, after just one sip she rose to take her leave.

"I have my hands full here," said Mrs. Liu. "Wu-erh will see you off."

So Wu-erh went out with Fang-kuan, and seeing there was nobody about she tugged at her sleeve.

"Did you really put in a word for me?" she asked.

Fang-kuan laughed.

"Why should I fool you? I've heard there are definitely two vacancies in our compound. One is Hung-yu's place: Madam Lien took her away but hasn't yet sent anyone to replace her. The other is Chui-erh's, which is still vacant too. So merely taking *you* on wouldn't count as too many. It's just that Ping-erh keeps telling Hsi-jen that any new requests for people or money shouldn't be raised yet awhile if possible, because Miss Tan-chun's looking for someone to make an example of. Even in her own quarters she's turned down two or three requests. Right now she's on the look-out for something in *our* place to make an issue of; so why should we jump into her trap? And if we were turned down now, it would be hard to get the decision changed later. Better wait for things to cool down. When the old lady and the mistress are free, if we approach *them* first, no matter how big a favour we ask they're bound to agree to it."

"Even so, I'm feeling too impatient to wait," said Wu-erh. "If I were to be chosen now, in the first place my mother'd be able to hold up her head and feel she hadn't brought me up for nothing; in the second, my monthly allowance would make things easier for our family; in the third, I'd feel happier myself and my health might well improve. Even if I still had to see doctors and buy medicine, I needn't spend the family's money on it."

"I understand," said Fang-kuan. "Just don't worry."

Then the two of them went their different ways.

Wu-erh, back home, told her mother how very grateful she was to Fang-kuan.

"I never thought we'd get all that juice," said Mrs. Liu. "Though this is expensive stuff, if you take too much it will increase the hot humours, so why not give some away? That would make a very handsome gift."

"Give it to whom?"

"To your cousin. He's been having a fever and was wanting something like this. I'll take him half a cup."

Wu-erh remained silent while her mother poured out half a cup and put the bottle with what was left in the cupboard. Then she said with a faint smile:

"If I were you, I wouldn't send it. If people asked where it came from there'd be more trouble."

"Why should we be afraid of that? After all our hard work, if our masters give us something it's only right. We didn't *steal* this, did we?"

So ignoring her daughter's advice, she went straight off to the house of her elder brother outside, where her nephew was lying in bed. When they saw what she had brought, her brother, sister-in-law and nephew were all delighted. Cold water was drawn from the well to mix with the tonic, and the invalid drinking a bowl of it found it extremely refreshing. What was left in the cup was covered with a piece of paper and put on the table.

Now it happened that a few of the Chia family pages who were friendly with the young patient called to see how he was. Among them was Chien Huai, a nephew of Concubine Chao, both of whose parents worked in the counting-house, and whose own job was escorting Chia Huan to school. No wife had yet been found for him and as he had taken a fancy to pretty Wu-erh he told his parents he would like to marry her. Time and again they had sent a go-between to propose the match; and as they were in easy circumstances and fairly well connected, Liu and his wife were quite willing, but they could not get Wu-erh's consent. Though she did not say so outright, her attitude was so clear that her parents could not accept the offer for her. Recently, moreover, since they hoped she would get a job in the Garden they had let the matter drop, assuming that after a few years when she was released from service she would choose someone else outside. And the Chien family, in view of this situation, had given up the idea too. Only Chien Huai, angry and mortified by his failure, had resolved that he must have his way and get Wu-erh as his wife. He had come with the others today to see his friend, never expecting to find Mrs. Liu there too.

When Mrs. Liu saw all these new arrivals, with Chien Huai among them, she rose on the pretext of business to take her leave.

"Have some tea first," her brother and sister-in-law urged her. "It was very good of you to think of your nephew."

"It'll soon be time to serve dinner in the Garden. I'll come to see him again when I'm free," she answered.

Then her sister-in-law took a packet from a drawer and saw her out. Having reached the corner of the wall, she gave the packet to Mrs. Liu.

"Yesterday your brother was on duty at the gate," she said. "For five days before that everything was so quiet that he didn't get any tips; only yesterday an official from Kwangtung called and presented two small baskets of *pachyma cocos* for the masters, and another basket for the men at the gate. This is your brother's share. Down south there they have so many ancient firs, they just extract the essence of the fungus on the roots and mix it with some kind of medicine to make this handsome snowy white *pachyma cocos* powder. They say if you mix it with human milk and drink a cup first thing every day, it's the best tonic you could have. If you haven't human milk, cow's milk is next best; or failing that even boiling water will do. We thought it would be just the thing for your daughter, and I sent a maid this morning to take it to you; but she said your door was locked and you'd taken Wu-erh with you into the Garden. I'd been meaning to call to see how she was and take it her myself. But knowing that with the mistresses away there's a strict watch everywhere, I thought as I'd no special business I'd better not go. Besides, I've heard that the last two days you've had a lot of upsets in the Garden; and I didn't want to get mixed up in anything. So I'm very glad you came. You can take this back now yourself."

Mrs. Liu thanked her, took her leave and went back. As she approached the side gate, a boy called out to her:

"Where have you been, auntie? They've been asking for you several times inside. Three or four of us have been looking for you everywhere — the others aren't back yet. But this isn't the way to your house. This seems rather suspicious."

"You monkey!" chuckled Mrs. Liu.

To know what followed, read the next chapter.

CHAPTER 61

Pao-yu Covers Up a Girl's Theft to Protect
His Sister
Ping-erh Wields Authority
to Right a Wrong

"You monkey!" chuckled Mrs. Liu. "If your aunt goes to find a lover that means one more uncle for you — what's wrong with that? Don't make me tear out that tuft of mangy hair stuck on your head like the lid of chamberpot. Hurry up! Open the gate and let me in."

Instead of doing so, the young rascal went on teasing.

"When you go in, auntie, do filch a few apricots for me. I'll wait for you here. If you forget, don't expect me to open the gate for you in future, when you want to buy wine or oil in the middle of the night. I won't even *answer* you, just leave you to shout yourself hoarse."

Mrs. Liu spat.

"You're crazy!" she scoffed. "This year's not like the old days. Everything here has been put in the care of different women, every single one of them spoiling for a fight. Just walk under a tree, and they glare like broody hens. How can you touch their fruit?

"The other day I was walking under a plùm tree when a bee brushed past my face, and just as I flapped it away that aunt of yours spotted me. She was too far away to see what I was doing and thought I was picking plums, so she let out a screech, then started squawking at the top of her voice that this fruit hadn't yet been offered to Buddha, that Their Ladyships being away hadn't tasted it yet, and that after the best had been sent to the mistress the rest of us would get *our* share, carrying on as if I were dying for her plums! I didn't take it too kindly, so I gave her tit for tat.

"But you have several aunts in charge of things here. Why not ask them for what you want? Why apply to *me*? This is like the rat in the barn who asked a crow for grain, as if a bird on the wing had some while the rat living in the barn had none."

"*Aiyaya!*" chortled the boy. "If you can't help, you can't. Why all this palaver? Think you won't need me in future? If your daughter *does* get a good post, seems to me she'll be wanting our help even more often, and only if we give it will she do all right."

"So you're up to monkey tricks again, little wretch! What good post is my daughter going to get?"

The boy laughed.

"Don't try to fool me. I know all about it. Think you're the only ones with connections inside? We have ours too. Though my own post's out here, I have a couple of sisters who count for something in the Garden too. So, how can any secret be kept from us?"

Just then another old woman inside called out, "Hurry up, you young rascals, and go and fetch your Aunt Liu before it's too late."

Not stopping to bandy any more words with the boy, Mrs. Liu hastily opened the gate and went in, saying:

"Don't worry, I'm coming."

She headed straight for the kitchen, where some other cooks shirking responsibility had been waiting for her to decide what dishes to send to the different apartments.

"Where's Wu-erh?" Mrs. Liu asked.

"She's just gone to the boiler-house to look for the other girls," they told her.

Mrs. Liu, having put the *pachyma* flour away, was busy allotting the dishes for different quarters when Ying-chun's little maid Lien-hua came in.

"Sister Ssu-chi says she wants a bowl of beaten eggs very lightly steamed," she announced.

"You *would* ask for a rarity!" remarked Mrs. Liu. "There's

such a shortage of eggs this year, goodness knows why, they cost ten cash each, and even at that price they're hard to get. Yesterday the order came down to send food to the families of relatives, and several purveyors went out yet only managed to get two thousand eggs. So where am I to find eggs? Go and tell her she can have them some other time."

"The other day when she asked for beancurd, you sent over some which was rancid," protested Lien-hua. "She gave me a scolding for that. Now she wants eggs and you say you haven't any. What's so precious about eggs? I don't believe you haven't even got eggs, I'll have a look."

She marched over to open the chest containing provisions, and sure enough found a dozen eggs in it.

"There you are!" she cried. "Why should you be so tight-fisted? What we eat is the share given us by our mistresses; why should it worry *you*? You didn't lay those eggs. Why take on so if people eat them?"

Mrs. Liu at once put down what she was holding and went over to confront her.

"Stop talking rubbish!" she cried. "Your mother's the one who lays eggs! These few are all we've got left for making sauce with. They're for emergencies. Unless the young ladies ask for some, I won't use them. If you've eaten them all up, there'll be a fine to do!

"You girls living shut away in the inner compounds take everything for granted. You may think eggs are easily come by, knowing nothing about conditions outside in the market. Not to say eggs, there are some days when there's not so much as a blade of grass to be had. Take my advice and be satisfied with the fine rice, fat hens and big ducks you get every day. You're so sated with all that rich food, though, that you pester us all the time for something different: eggs and beancurd, or gluten of wheat and salted turnips. You certainly know how to vary your menu! But it's not my job to cater specially for *you*. If each place asks for a different dish, that comes to over ten dishes. I'd better stop looking after our first-grade mistresses so as to devote myself to you second-grade mistresses."

"Who's been asking for new dishes every day?" shouted Lien-hua, her face scarlet. "Are you never going to stop ranting? If we get you a job here, of course we expect a little consideration. The other day when Hsiao-yen told you that Sister Ching-wen would like some artemisia, you immediately asked whether she wanted it fried with pork or with chicken. Hsiao-yen said anything with meat was no good; that was why she asked for artemisia fried with gluten of wheat with as little oil as possible. At once you cursed yourself for being so dense and hastily washed your hands to cook the dish, taking it there yourself — like a dog wagging its tail. Yet today you pick on me in front of all these people!"

"Gracious Buddha!" cried Mrs. Liu. "All those here can bear witness. Not to say the other day, but ever since this kitchen was set up last year, any apartment wanting something extra has always brought money to buy it. Sometimes we had what was wanted, sometimes we didn't. It may sound as if I've got a cushy job, with perks too, just catering for the young mistresses. Just work it out, though, and it's really sickening. The young ladies plus their maids come to forty or fifty people, yet each day we get only a couple of hens, a couple of ducks, some dozen catties of meat and one string of cash worth of vegetables. Figure it out for yourselves: how far will that go. It's not even enough for the two fixed meals, so how can it be stretched to cover extras ordered by you girls? And you won't take what we've bought but want us to go out and buy other things.

"The way things are, we'd better ask the mistress for more money so that we can do as they do in the big kitchen catering for the old lady: put down all the known dishes on the menu, prepare different dishes every day, and settle the accounts at the end of each month.

"The other day Miss Tan-chun and Miss Pao-chai took it into their heads to have some fried wolfberry sprouts, and sent over a maid with five hundred cash. I couldn't help laughing and told her, 'Even if the two young ladies had bellies as big as a

Buddha, they couldn't eat five hundred cash worth. It'll only cost twenty to thirty cash and that we can afford.'

"So I sent the money back, but they wouldn't take it, giving it me as a tip to buy wine with. And they said, 'Now that the kitchen's inside the Garden, some of our people may go and pester you for things like salt or bean-sauce, all of which cost money. You can hardly refuse them; but if you give them what they want you'll lose out. So take this money to make good the arrears they've let you in for.'

"They're such considerate, understanding young ladies, those two, we can only pray to Buddha in our hearts to bless such kind mistresses. But when Concubine Chao heard of this, she flew into a rage and fumed that I was getting too many perks. In less than ten days she kept sending over a maid to ask for this, that and the other. I laughed to myself: So you think this gives *you* the excuse to demand one thing after another. How can I afford so much?"

As they were arguing, Ssu-chi sent someone over to find Lien-hua. "Is she dead that she hasn't come back yet?" she asked.

Lien-hua went back then in a huff to tell Ssu-chi all that had been said, embroidering her account too. The result was that Ssu-chi flared up. As soon as she had finished serving Ying-chun's meal she took the young maids with her to the kitchen, where they found the kitchen-maids having their own meal. When Ssu-chi stormed in, the women stood up and asked her to take a seat, but she ordered the younger maids to ransack the place.

"Just throw all the eatables in their chests and cupboards to the dogs," she cried, "so that no one gets any perks."

At the word of command, the young maids crowded forward and started turning the whole place upside down. The kitchen-maids tried frantically to stop them.

"Don't believe what those children say, miss," they begged Ssu-chi. "Even if Mrs. Liu had nine lives she'd never dare offend you. Honestly, eggs are hard to buy this year. We've just been scolding her for being so stupid: whatever she's asked for, she ought to make shift to get it. Now she's realized her mistake and steamed the eggs. If you don't believe us, look on the stove."

This soft talk gradually mollified Ssu-chi, and the young maids were led away before they could smash everything. Having continued to make a scene for a while, Ssu-chi finally let herself be persuaded to leave. Mrs. Liu could only clatter bowls and dishes as she grumbled to herself; but when the bowl of eggs was steamed and sent over, Ssu-chi emptied it on the ground. However, the maid who had taken it kept silent about this on her return, for fear of causing fresh trouble.

Mrs. Liu now gave her daughter some soup and half a bowl of porridge, then explained to her about the *pachyma* flour. Wu-erh decided to share the gift with Fang-kuan; so she wrapped up half of it in a piece of paper and as it was now growing dark, with few people about, slipped through the flowers and willows to find her friend. Luckily she was challenged by no one on her way to Happy Red Court. Once there, however, she was afraid to go in. She stood waiting in front of a rose bush some distance away until, after the time it would take for a cup of tea, Hsiao-yen happened to come out. Wu-erh ran forward to call her. Hsiao-yen did not recognize who it was until Wu-erh came closer.

"What are *you* doing here?" she asked.

"Ask Fang-kuan to come out," urged Wu-erh. "I've something to tell her."

"You're too impatient, sister," Hsiao-yen whispered. "Just another ten days and you'll be here. Why keep on looking for her? She was sent off on an errand to the front just now. You can either wait for her, or let me pass on your message if you're in a hurry. The Garden gate may be closed soon."

Wu-erh handed her the *pachyma* flour then, telling her how it should be taken and what it was good for.

"I'm just giving her part of some that was given to me," she explained. "Please be good enough to let her have it."

With that she took her leave and started back. She had just reached Smartweed Bank when along came Lin Chih-hsiao's wife with a few serving-women. Having no time to hide, Wu-erh had to step forward to greet them.

"I heard you were ill," said Mrs. Lin. "What are you doing here?"

"The last couple of days I've felt better, so I came here with my mother for a little change. Just now she sent me to Happy Red Court to deliver something."

"I don't believe it," replied Mrs. Lin. "I just saw your mother go out, so I locked the gate. If she'd sent you on an errand, why didn't she tell me you were here? Why should she let me lock the gate? I really can't understand this. You must be lying."

Wu-erh had nothing to say to that, so she faltered, "My mother told me to send those things this morning, but I forgot and only just remembered. I suppose she imagined I'd already left; that's why she didn't tell you."

Mrs. Lin saw how flustered and guilty she looked, and remembered Yu-chuan telling her recently that things had disappeared from Lady Wang's rooms but the young maids there claimed to know nothing about it, and the culprit hadn't been found. All this made her suspicious. And just at this moment Chan-chieh and Lien-hua arrived with several serving-women. When they understood the situation, they said:

"You'd better cross-examine her, Mrs. Lin. She's been creeping in here the last couple of days in a very sneaky way. Goodness knows what she's up to."

"That's right," added Chan-chieh. "Yesterday Sister Yu-chuan told me that cupboard in the mistress' annex had been opened and quite a few odd things were missing. And when Madam Lien sent Ping-erh to get some rose flavoured juice from Yu-chuan, there was one bottle short. They wouldn't have known if they hadn't been looking for it."

"I didn't hear about that," put in Lien-hua. "But today I saw a bottle of juice."

Since Hsi-feng had been sending Ping-erh every day to press Mrs. Lin to track down the thief, as soon as she heard this she asked:

"Where did you see it?"

"In their kitchen," was Lien-hua's answer.

At once Mrs. Lin told them to light the lantern and set off at their head to make a search.

In desperation then Wu-erh confessed, "That was given me by Fang-kuan in Master Pao's place."

"I don't care who gave it you," snapped Mrs. Lin. "Now that we have evidence of the theft, I shall report it and you can explain it to the mistresses."

By this time they had entered the kitchen where Lien-hua showed her the bottle. Suspecting there might be other stolen goods there, they made a thorough search and found a packet of *pachyma* flour as well. Picking up these things and taking Wu-erh with them, they went to report the business to Li Wan and Tan-chun.

As Li Wan's son Lan was ill, she had stopped attending to household affairs and told them to go and see Tan-chun. The latter had returned to her quarters, where she was washing in her room while her maids rested in the courtyard. Tai-shu went in alone to report, coming out again after some time to say:

"I've told the young mistress. She wants you to get Ping-erh to report this to Madam Lien."

Mrs. Lin had to lead them all off then to Hsi-feng's quarters. First she found Ping-erh, who went in to report the business to her mistress. Hsi-feng had just retired for the night. Upon hearing this news she ordered:

"Give Wu-erh's mother forty strokes with the cane and throw her out. She's never to set foot inside the inner gate again. Give Wu-erh forty strokes too, and pack her off at once to the manor to be sold or married off."

When Ping-erh came out and passed on these instructions to Mrs. Lin, Wu-erh burst out weeping for terror. Kneeling to Ping-erh she told her all that she and Fang-kuan had done.

"That's easily checked on," said Ping-erh. "We shall find out whether she's telling the truth or not by questioning Fang-kuan tomorrow. But this *pachyma* flour was sent in as a present only the other day, and it shouldn't have been unpacked until after Their Ladyships had come back and inspected it. You shouldn't have stolen it."

Wu-erh hastily explained how the *pachyma* flour had been given them by her uncle.

"If that's the case," said Ping-erh with a smile, "then you've done nothing wrong but are being used as a scapegoat. Well, it's late now and my mistress has just taken her medicine and gone to bed; we mustn't disturb her again over such a trifle. Let the night-watchers keep an eye on Wu-erh tonight, and tomorrow after I've told my mistress this we'll decide what to do."

Not daring to object, Mrs. Lin took Wu-erh out and handed her over to the women keeping watch that night, after which she went home.

Wu-erh, kept under guard, did not dare to stir hand or foot. Some of the women on duty berated her for her bad conduct. Others complained:

"It's bad enough having to keep watch at night without having to guard a thief too; if she should kill herself or escape while we weren't looking, we'd get into trouble."

Other women who were on bad terms with Mrs. Liu were delighted by this development, and they came to jeer at the girl too. Wu-erh who had always been delicate, having no water to drink and nowhere to sleep that night, felt angry at being so unfairly treated, but there was nobody to whom to complain. She sobbed the whole night through. All those women who had it in for her and her mother were longing to have them thrown out straight away, for fear the decision might be changed the next day. They got up early and went secretly to try to win Ping-erh over to their side, taking her presents, complimenting her on her competence and good judgement, and telling her all kinds of tales about Mrs. Liu. Ping-erh heard them out in turn and sent them away. Then she slipped over to see Hsi-jen and find out whether it was true that Fang-kuan had given Wu-erh the rose flavoured juice.

"I did give Fang-kuan some," said Hsi-jen, "but I don't

know what she did with it." Fang-kuan, when questioned, was startled into admitting that she had indeed given it to Wu-erh. Then Fang-kuan told Pao-yu, and he was worried too.

"Though the rose juice business is cleared up," he said, "if the *pachyma* flour is brought into it she'll have to own up; and when they know that her uncle got it at the gate he'll be blamed. They meant well, but we'll be getting them into trouble."

He lost no time in talking it over with Ping-erh.

"The rose juice business is cleared up," he told her. "But they're still in the wrong over the *pachyma* flour. Why not just say, good sister, that this was given her by Fang-kuan too? Then it will be all right."

"That's all very well," smiled Ping-erh. "But yesterday evening Wu-erh already admitted that it was a gift from her uncle; so how can she say now that it was from *you*? Besides, before the thief who stole the juice has been found, how can we let off the one caught with evidence and go looking for other culprits? Who would own up? People wouldn't be convinced either."

Ching-wen joined in at this point, saying, "That rose juice from the mistress' place must obviously have been taken by Tsai-yun — no one else could have stolen it — to give Master Huan. So stop making all these wild guesses."

Ping-erh chuckled, "Of course, we know that's the case. But now Yu-chuan's so frantic, she's crying. If we asked Tsai-yun in confidence and she owned up, Yu-chuan could stop worrying and everybody would forget about it. Who wants to stir up trouble anyway? But that wretch Tsai-yun not only won't admit it, she's accused Yu-chuan of the theft. Because of their back-biting and bickering the whole mansion's heard of this business. So how can we pretend that nothing's happened? We shall have to make investigations. We all know that the one who reported the theft is the thief herself, but as there's no evidence how can we accuse her?"

"Never mind," said Pao-yu. "I'll take the blame for that

too. I'll say I filched it on the sly from my mother's place to frighten them for fun. Then both matters will be settled."

Hsi-jen commented, "Of course that would be a kind deed, clearing their reputations. When the mistress hears about it, though, she'll scold you again for having no sense and acting so childishly."

"That doesn't matter so much," said Ping-erh with a smile. "Actually, I could easily find the evidence in Concubine Chao's rooms, but I was afraid that would make another good person lose face. Other people wouldn't mind, but she'd certainly be angry. It was *her* I was thinking of. I didn't want to smash a jade vase to catch a rat." While saying this she held out three fingers to indicate to Hsi-jen and the others that it was the third young mistress, Tan-chun, whom she had in mind.

"Quite right," they said. "Better put the blame on us here."

"Even so," proposed Ping-erh, "we must call those two trouble-makers Tsai-yun and Yu-chuan over, and get them to agree to this arrangement. Otherwise they'll get off unscathed without knowing the reason, thinking instead that because I hadn't the gumption to get at the truth, I had to beg you people here to cover up the theft. That would encourage one of them to go on stealing with impunity, the other to let things drift."

"That's true," agreed Hsi-jen and the rest. "You must make it clear where we stand."

A messenger was sent by Ping-erh to fetch the two girls.

"You don't have to worry," they were told. "We've found the culprit."

"Where?" asked Yu-chuan.

"In Madam Lien's place," Ping-erh told her. "She admits to everything, but I know quite well that she didn't steal those things; the poor creature's confessed to it because she's frightened. Master Pao here is sorry for her and means to take half the blame. I could, of course, name the real thief, but it so happens that she's a good friend of mine. I don't care much what happens to the receiver of the stolen goods, only this would damage a good person's reputation too; so being in a quandary I'm going to ask Master Pao to take the blame, so as to keep the rest of us out of trouble.

"Now I want to know what *you* intend to do. If you both agree to be more careful in future, so that nobody loses face, I'll ask Master Pao to take the blame. If not, I'll report the truth to Madam Lien rather than wrong an innocent person."

Tsai-yun, at this, blushed with shame.

"Don't worry, sister," she said. "There's no need to wrong an innocent person, or to make a young lady who wasn't involved lose face. It was Concubine Chao who kept begging me to filch things, and I gave some of them· to Master Huan — that's the truth. Even when the mistress is at home, we often take this or that to give to friends. I thought after a couple of days this storm would blow over; but I can't stand seeing an innocent person accused. You'd better take me to the Second Mistress, and I'll make a clean breast of everything to her."

The others hearing this were impressed by her courage.

"That's very decent of Sister Tsai-yun," said Pao-yu. "But there's no need for you to admit it; I'll just say that I took it in secret to tease you all, and now that trouble's come of it I should own up. I simply ask you sisters to make less trouble in future. That would be best for us all."

"Why should you own up to something I did?" asked Tsai-yun. "I'm the one, if anyone, who deserves to be punished."

"That's not the way to look at it," interposed Ping-erh and Hsi-jen. "If you were to admit it you'd have to let on about Concubine Chao, and when Miss Tan-chun heard of it she'd feel bad again. Better let Master Pao take the blame to keep us all out of trouble. Apart from the few of us here, no one else need know about it — isn't that much neater? In future, though, we must all of us be more careful. If you want to take anything, at least wait till the mistress is back; then even if you give the whole *house* away, it'll be no concern of ours."

Tsai-yun lowered her head in thought and then agreed. After their plans were laid, Ping-erh took the two of them with Fang-kuan to the front where women kept watch at night and, having summoned Wu-erh, gave her secret instructions to say that the *pachyma* flour had also been a present from Fang-kuan. After Wu-erh had poured out her thanks Ping-erh took them to her own quarters, where Mrs. Lin and some other serving-women had long been waiting, holding Mrs. Liu.

Mrs. Lin told Ping-erh, "I brought her here first thing this morning. For fear nobody would see to the young ladies' morning meal, I sent Chin Hsien's wife to the Garden to take charge for the time being. Why not suggest to the Second Mistress that Mrs. Chin, being clean and painstaking, might as well be assigned the job for keeps?"

"Who is Chin Hsien's wife?" asked Ping-erh. "I don't seem to know her."

"She's one of those who keep watch at night at the south gate of the Garden," Mrs. Lin answered. "She has nothing to do in the day time; that's why you don't know her. She has high cheekbones and big eyes, and is very clean and spry."

"That's right," put in Yu-chuan. "How could you forget, sister? She's the aunt of Ssu-chi who serves Miss Ying-chun. Though Ssu-chi's parents belong to the Elder Master's household, her uncle works here."

Ping-erh recollected the woman then and smiled.

"Ah, if you'd said that before I'd have known," she said. "Still, you're in too much of a hurry to give her a job. The fact is, this business is more or less solved; we've even found out as well who took the things missing from the mistress' place the other day. It was Pao-yu who went over there and asked those two wretched girls for something. To tease him they said they dared not take anything with the mistress away; so when they weren't looking he went in and took the things. Those silly creatures didn't know, that's why they got scared. Now that Pao-yu knows this has involved other people, he's told me the whole story and shown me the things he took — there's nothing missing. He got that *pachyma* flour outside as well, and shared it out to a whole lot of people, not just the girls in the Garden. Even the nannies got some to take out for their relatives, some of whom passed it on to other people. Hsi-jen gave some to Fang-kuan and others too. This was just doing friends a favour, nothing unusual. As for those two baskets brought the other day, they're still in the hall and the seals on them haven't been broken; so how can we accuse people of pilfering them? Wait till I've reported this to my mistress and then we'll see."

She went into the bedroom to tell Hsi-feng the same story.

"That's all very well," said Hsi-feng, "but we know Pao-yu. He sticks up for those girls even if they're in the wrong. And if people appeal to him or flatter him — crowning him with a charcoal basket — he'll agree to anything. If we take *his* word for it and there's worse trouble of this kind in future, how are we to control these servants? We must go on making detailed investigations. My plan is to fetch all the maids from the mistress' house here. No need to torture or beat them; we can just make them kneel in the sun on shards of porcelain with nothing to eat or drink. If they don't come clean, they'll have to kneel all day. Then even if they're made of iron, in a day they're bound to confess."

She added, "Flies go for cracked eggs. Even if this Liu woman didn't steal anything, she must have been up to something or people wouldn't have accused her. Even if we don't punish her, we should dismiss her; that's the usual court procedure. It wouldn't be doing her an injustice."

"Why trouble yourself over this?" countered Ping-erh. "We should be lenient whenever we can. This isn't anything so important that you can't overlook it. What I feel is this: however hard you work over here, you'll be going back eventually to the other house; so why make enemies of the servants here, making them bear you a grudge? It's not as if you haven't troubles enough of your own. You managed after years to conceive a son but lost him in the seventh month through a miscarriage brought on, for all we know, by overworking and getting too upset and worked up over things. Wouldn't it be better, while it's not too late, to shut your eyes to half of what's going on?"

This advice made Hsi-feng smile.

"All right, you little bitch," she said. "Do whatever you like. I'm just feeling slightly better; I don't want to lose my temper."

"That's the right way to talk!" chuckled Ping-erh.

With that she went out to deal with the women outside one by one. To know what happened later, read the next chapter.

CHAPTER 62

Sweet Hsiang-yun Sleeps Tipsily
Among Peonies
Silly Hsiang-ling Coyly Takes Off
Her Pomegranate Skirt

Ping-erh, going out as we saw, told Lin Chih-hsiao's wife, "A prosperous family ought to minimize big scandals and overlook minor ones. It wouldn't look good if we were to ring bells, beat drums and raise a rumpus over a trifle. So take mother and daughter back now: they're to keep their jobs. And send Chin Hsien's wife back as well. There's no need to say any more about this business. Just make a careful inspection every day." With that she left.

Mrs. Liu and Wu-erh hastily stepped forward to kowtow their thanks, after which Mrs. Lin took them back to the Garden and reported the matter to Li Wan and Tan-chun, both of whom approved of the way it had been settled.

So Ssu-chi and the rest had worked themselves up for nothing. And Chin Hsien's wife, after this stroke of luck came her way, was able to gloat for no more than half a day. She had busily taken over and checked up on the utensils, rice, grain, charcoal and so forth in the kitchen, where she discovered serious shortages.

"There's two piculs of good rice short," she observed. "An extra month's supply of ordinary rice has been drawn in advance, and there's charcoal missing as well."

At the same time she prepared presents for Mrs. Lin, secretly getting ready a load of charcoal, five hundred catties of firewood and one picul of good rice outside the Garden for her nephew to take to the Lins' house. In addition, she prepared gifts to send the accountants and some dishes to treat her new colleagues.

"My coming here is all thanks to your help," she told them. "In future we shall be one family. If I overlook anything, please see to it for me."

As she was bustling frantically about, a messenger suddenly arrived to announce: "You're to leave after serving the morning meal. Mrs. Liu has been cleared and the job given back to her."

Thunderstruck and utterly cast down by this news, Chin Hsien's wife made haste to pack up and beat a retreat. She was badly out of pocket over the presents, and now she had to make good that sum herself. Ssu-chi too was completely taken aback, but fume as she might there was nothing she could do.

As for Concubine Chao, because Tsai-yun had given her so many things on the sly and Yu-chuan had raised such a fuss, she was afraid others would find out the truth. This kept her in a constant cold sweat as she waited to hear the upshot. When Tsai-yun assured her that there would be no further trouble as Pao-yu had taken the blame, this took a great load off her mind. It only made Chia Huan more suspicious, however. He fetched out all Tsai-yun's secret gifts to him and threw them at her face.

"Sneaky double-crosser!" he swore. "I don't want this trash of yours. If you weren't on good terms with Pao-yu, why should he cover up for you? If you had any guts, you wouldn't have let a single person know you'd given me these things. Now that you've blabbed about it I'd lose face if I kept them."

Tsai-yun frantically assured him that she was not on friendly terms with Pao-yu, nor had she told anyone. Sobbingly she tried in all sorts of ways to convince him, but Chia Huan stubbornly refused to believe her.

"If not for our past friendship," he cried, "I'd go and tell sister-in-law Hsi-feng that you stole these things and offered them to me, but I dared not take them. Just think what would happen then!" With that he stormed out.

By this time Concubine Chao was frantic too.

"Ungrateful brat!" she cursed. "Misbegotten monster!"

Tsai-yun, weeping her eyes out, looked quite heart-broken no matter how the concubine tried to comfort her.

"Good child, how ungrateful he is, after all your kindness!" she said. "But I know how it is. Let me put these things away, and in a couple of days he'll come to his senses again."

She wanted to take the things, but Tsai-yun in a fit of pique bundled them up together, and when no one was watching slipped into the Garden and threw them all into the stream, where some sank and some floated away. That night, under her quilt, she secretly wept with rage.

By now Pao-yu's birthday had come round again, and they found that Pao-chin's birthday happened to fall on the identical day. As Lady Wang was away from home, however, it was not as lively as in previous years. Still, the Taoist priest Chang sent over four gifts and a new charm with the boy's Buddhist name on it; then some monks and nuns from various abbeys, nunneries and temples brought sacrificial offerings of food, pictures of the God of Longevity, sacrificial paper for burning, the name of his own star god, the name of the star god presiding over that year, and lock-charms to safeguard Pao-yu throughout the year. Men and women story-tellers who frequented the house came to offer congratulations.

Wang Tzu-teng sent his nephew his usual gifts: a pair of shoes and socks, a suit of clothes, a hundred longevity cakes in the shape of peaches, and a hundred bundles of "silver-silk" noodles of the kind used in the Palace. From Aunt Hsueh the boy received half this amount, appropriate to her status. As for the rest of the family, Madam Yu gave him her usual gift of a pair of shoes and socks, and Hsi-feng a pouch symbolizing harmony embroidered in the Palace, in which were a golden God of Longevity, as well as a toy from Persia. Alms and gifts were dispatched to various temples, and there were presents for Pao-chin as well, but we need not enumerate these. The girls just sent whatever they pleased — a fan, some calligraphy, a painting or a poem — to mark the occasion.

Pao-yu got up early that morning and as soon as his toilet was finished put on ceremonial dress and went to the front court. There Li Kuei and four other stewards had set ready the incense

"This is rather intriguing," remarked Tan-chun. "There are twelve months in a year with several birthdays in each. On account of there being so many people here some birthdays coincide, with two or three of them falling on the same day. Even on New Year's Day we celebrate one — that's Elder Sister's birthday. No wonder she's had such good fortune, with her birthday coming before anyone else's. It was great-great-grandfather's birthday too. Then comes the birthday of the old lady and cousin Pao-chai; there's one coincidence for you. The first of the third month is the mistress' birthday; the ninth is Cousin Chia Lien's. There's none in the second month. . . ."

"The twelfth of the second month is Miss Lin's birthday," put in Hsi-jen. "Only she isn't one of our family."

"Of course!" chuckled Tan-chun. "What's wrong with my memory?"

Pao-yu pointed at Hsi-jen.

"She and Cousin Tai-yu have the same birthday, that's why she remembers it."

"The same birthday, do they?" cried Tan-chun. "But you've never even kowtowed to us each year. We didn't know when Ping-erh's birthday was either. We've only just now learned it."

"We're nobodies," rejoined Ping-erh. "We haven't the luck to be congratulated on our birthdays or the rank to receive presents, so why trumpet the day abroad? Naturally we keep quiet about it. Now that she's given me away, I shall call on you young ladies later to pay my respects."

"We mustn't put you to such trouble," Tan-chun demurred. "Instead we must celebrate your birthday too today, so as to make me feel better."

Pao-yu, Hsiang-yun and the rest approving this, Tan-chun sent a maid to report to Hsi-feng, "We've decided not to let Ping-erh go today, as we're all chipping in to celebrate her birthday."

The maid went off smiling, returning after some time with Hsi-feng's reply.

"Madam Lien thanks you young ladies for doing her such an

honour.　She wants to know what birthday treat you'll be giving Ping-erh, and says if you promise not to leave *her* out she won't come to plague her."

All laughed at this.

Tan-chun said, "As it happens, our meals today aren't being prepared by the kitchen in the Garden.　We're having noodles and dishes cooked outside.　So we can whip round for the money, and get Mrs. Liu to take charge and prepare something here."

The others all agreed to this.

Tan-chun then sent to invite Li Wan, Pao-chai and Tai-yu, while another maid summoned Mrs. Liu who was instructed to lose no time in preparing in her kitchen a feast for two tables. Mrs. Liu was puzzled by this.

"The outside kitchen's got everything ready," she said.

"You don't understand," Tan-chun told her.　"Today is Miss Ping-erh's birthday.　The meal prepared outside is provided by the chief accountant's office.　Now we've raised the money ourselves for a special party for Ping-erh.　You just choose and make some new appetizing dishes, and bring the bill to me later."

Mrs. Liu laughed.

"So it's Miss Ping-erh's birthday too, eh?　I didn't know that."　She approached Ping-erh to kowtow to her, and when Ping-erh stopped her went off to prepare the feast.

Tan-chun had already invited Pao-yu to have his noodles with them in the Council Hall; so as soon as Li Wan and Pao-chai had arrived, maids were sent to invite Aunt Hsueh and Tai-yu over.　As the day was mild and Tai-yu was feeling better, she accepted the invitation.　The hall was packed with people, gay with flowers and silks.　But now Hsueh Ko sent Pao-yu four birthday presents — a scarf, a fan, some scent and silk — so Pao-yu went over to eat noodles with him.　Both families had prepared feasts and exchanged gifts.　At noon Pao-yu drank a few cups of wine with Hsueh Ko, and Pao-chai took Pao-chin to pay her respects to him too.　After toasting Hsueh Ko, Pao-chai told him:

"There's no need to send a feast to the other house.　Better

dispense with those formalities and just invite the shop assistants to a meal. We're going to the Garden now with Cousin Pao-yu, as we have others to look after; so we can't keep you company."

"Don't let me keep you, cousins," replied Hsueh Ko. "The shop assistants will be here any time."

Then Pao-yu asked to be excused and left with the girls.

When they entered the side gate, Pao-chai ordered the women in charge there to lock it, and took the key herself.

"Why lock this gate?" asked Pao-yu. "Har lly anyone uses it; but now auntie and you two are inside and it will be awkward if you want something fetched from your home."

"One can never be too careful," was Pao-chai's reply. "There's been all sorts of trouble in your house these last few days, but our household wasn't involved: that shows the advantage of keeping the gate shut. If it were left open, people might take a short cut through here, and then which of them should we stop? Better lock it, even if that's less convenient for mother and me. Don't let anyone through. Then whatever trouble there may be, our household won't be implicated."

"So you knew we'd lost some things recently," remarked Pao-yu with a smile.

"You only heard about the rose flavoured juice and *pachyma* flour because of the girls involved," retorted Pao-chai. "If not for them, you wouldn't even have known of those two things. Actually there have been losses more serious than that. If it isn't noised abroad, so much the better for everyone; otherwise, goodness knows how many people in the Garden would be implicated. I'm telling you this because you pay no attention to what goes on. I told Ping-erh the other day, too, because she's an intelligent person and as her mistress isn't here I wanted her to know. If word doesn't get out, we may as well do nothing; if there's a scandal, she'll have been forewarned and know what it's all about, then she won't wrong innocent people. Take my advice and be more careful in future. And don't repeat what I've told you to anyone else."

They now reached Seeping Fragrance Pavilion where a dozen or so girls were amusing themselves by watching the fish. Among them were Hsi-jen, Hsiang-ling, Tai-shu, Su-yun, Ching-wen, Sheh-yueh, Fang-kuan, Ou-kuan and Jui-kuan. When they saw them approaching they said:

"Everything's ready in Peony Bower. Hurry up and go to the feast."

Pao-chai went with them to Peony Bower, a small three-frame hall in Red Fragrance Farm, where all the ladies of the house including even Madam Yu had assembled. Only Ping-erh was missing.

Ping-erh had gone out, as it happened, because the families of Lai Ta, Lin Chih-hsiao and the other stewards had been sending presents over in turn, and many of the servants of the first, second and third rank had also come one after another with gifts to offer their congratulations. Ping-erh was kept busy dispatching the messengers with tips and thanks, and she also had to report each case to Hsi-feng. Only a few of the gifts did she keep for herself; some she declined, and the rest she immediately made over to others. After occupying herself in this way for a while, she waited on Hsi-feng while she had her noodles, then changed her clothes and went back to the Garden. As soon as she entered it, she was met by several maids who had come to fetch her. They escorted her to Red Fragrance Farm where a sumptuous feast had been spread.

"Now all the birthday stars are here," cried the others laughingly. They insisted that these four must take the seats of honour, but this they declined to do.

Aunt Hsueh declared, "I'm too old to mix in your crowd, and I feel very boxed up here too. I'd rather lie down in comfort in the Council Hall. I can't eat anything or drink much either, so I'll leave my place to them and that will suit everybody."

At first Madam Yu and the rest would not hear of this, but Pao-chai said, "That's all right. Why not let mother lie down in the hall where she can relax? We can send over any dishes she likes. She'll feel freer. Besides, there's nobody in front today, and she can keep an eye on things."

"In that case," agreed Tan-chun, "we'd better do as she asks instead of standing on ceremony."

So they saw Aunt Hsueh to the hall, told the young maids to spread a silk mattress, back-rest and pillows for her, and instructed them:

"Mind you look after Madam Hsueh well. Massage her legs, serve her tea and don't shirk your work. We'll be sending food over later, and after she's eaten you can have what's left. But you mustn't leave this place."

The young maids promised to carry out these orders.

Then Tan-chun and the others went back. Finally they made Pao-chin and Hsiu-yen take the top seats at the first table with Ping-erh facing west and Pao-yu facing east, while Tan-chun got Yuan-yang to join her at the lower side of the table. At the table on the west side sat Pao-chai, Tai-yu, Hsiang-yun, Ying-chun and Hsi-chun in the same order, with Hsiang-ling and Yu-chuan on the fourth side. Madam Yu and Li Wan shared a third table with Hsi-jen and Tsai-yun. At a fourth sat Tzu-chuan, Ying-erh, Ching-wen, Hsiao-luo and Ssu-chi.

When all were in place, Tan-chun wanted to offer toasts, but Pao-chin and the other three declined.

"If you start that," they objected, "we'll be standing here all day toasting again and again — and still never finish."

At that she did not insist. Then two women story-tellers offered to perform a ballad for the occasion.

"No one here wants to hear your wild talk," everyone said. "Go to the hall to amuse Madam Hsueh." They picked various dishes and had them sent to her.

"Just feasting quietly is no fun. Let's play some drinking games," Pao-yu proposed.

All the rest agreed, and suggested different games.

"Let's write down the names of all sorts of games and draw lots to decide which one to play," said Tai-yu.

This met with general approval and writing-brush, inkstone and fancy note-paper were sent for.

Now Hsiang-ling had been learning to write poetry and practising her calligraphy every day. When the brush and inkstone arrived, she could not resist getting up at once and offering to act as amanuensis. As the others thought of and called out the names of a dozen games, she put them down on separate slips of paper, which were rolled into spills and put in a vase. Then Tan-chun told Ping-erh to take one. Ping-erh stepped forward to mix the lots and picked one out with her chopsticks. When she unfolded it, she found written there "*She-fu* conundrums."

"You've picked the ancestor of all drinking games," chuckled Pao-chai. "It was played in ancient times, but the original rules have been lost now. What we have is a later version, more difficult than all other drinking games. Half of us here wouldn't be able to play it. Better scrap this and pick one to suit all tastes."

"As this has already been picked," Tan-chun objected, "how can we scrap it? Pick another as well, and if that one's more popular let the others play that while we play this first one."

She told Hsi-jen to draw another lot, and this proved to be the finger-guessing game.

"This is simple and quick, it suits me!" chortled Hsiang-yun. "I shan't play conundrums; that's too boring and depressing. I shall guess fingers."

"She's broken the rules," cried Tan-chun. "Quick, Cousin Pao-chai, make her drink a cup as a forfeit."

Pao-chai laughingly forced Hsiang-yun to drain a cup.

"I'm taking charge so I'll drink a cup too," said Tan-chun. "There's no need for any announcement, just do as I say. Fetch a dice-bowl and throw the dice in turn, starting with Pao-chin. When two people throw the same number they must play conundrums."

Pao-chin cast a "three"; Hsiu-yen and Pao-yu threw different numbers; and Hsiang-ling when it came to her turn threw another "three."

"We must stick to objects in this room," said Pao-chin. "If things outside were chosen, we wouldn't have a clue."

"Right," agreed Tan-chun. "Anyone who makes three wrong guesses must drink a cup. Now give her a conundrum to guess."

Pao-chin thought for a moment then said, "Old."

Hsiang-ling, who was unfamiliar with this game, looked round the room and feasters but could see nothing fitting a classical allusion containing the word "old." But Hsiang-yun on hearing the clue had started staring around too. Catching sight of the name Red Fragrance Farm over the door, she realized that Pao-chin had in mind the line "I am not as good as the old gardener."[1] As Hsiang-ling could not guess the answer and they were beating the drum to hurry her, she quietly tugged at her sleeve.

"Say 'peony,'" she whispered.

Tai-yu saw this and cried, "Quick, punish her! She's cheating."

That gave the game away and Hsiang-yun, forced to drink a cup of wine, in a huff rapped Tai-yu's knuckles with her chopsticks. Then Hsiang-ling had to drink a cup as a forfeit too.

Now Pao-chai and Tan-chun threw the same number, and Tan-chun gave the word "man."

"That's too general," protested Pao-chai.

"I'll add another word then," said Tan-chun. "Two clues for one conundrum can't be considered too vague." This time she gave the word "window."

Pao-chai thought this over and, seeing chicken on the table, remembered the allusions "cock-window" and "cock-man," so she answered with the word "roost." Tan-chun knew that Pao-chai had guessed right and had in mind the allusion "Chickens come home to roost." Smiling at each other both girls took a sip of wine.

Meanwhile Hsiang-yun, too impatient to wait, had started playing the finger-guessing game with Pao-yu, shouting "three" or "five" at random. Madam Yu and Yuan-yang, facing each other across the table to play the same game, were shouting now "seven" now "eight." Ping-erh and Hsi-jen had paired off together too, and were indicating the numbers they guessed with their fingers, which set their bracelets tinkling. Hsiang-yun, beating Pao-yu, was entitled to make him pay forfeits before and after drinking.

---

[1] From the *Analects*.

She announced, "Before drinking, the loser must quote one line from a classical essay, one from an old poem, one domino's name, one name of a melody, and one line from the almanac. All these together must make up a sentence. The forfeit after drinking is to name some sweetmeat or dish and link it with human affairs."

The others hearing this laughed.

"Her forfeits are always more pernickety than other people's; still, they're fun," they remarked, then urged Pao-yu to speak up quickly.

"We've never done this before. Give me a chance to think first," he begged.

Tai-yu offered, "Drink an extra cup and I'll do it for you."

So Pao-yu drank while Tai-yu recited:

> "Sunset clouds float with the lone wild duck,
> The wild goose cries through the sky above wind-swept river;
> A wild goose with a broken leg,
> Its crying fills all hearts with sorrow.
> Such is the wild goose's return."

Amid general laughter the others commented, "Stringing lines together like this is rather fun."

Then Tai-yu picked up a hazel-nut to pay the after-drinking forfeit and said:

> "Hazel-nuts having nothing to do with neighbourhood
>   washing-blocks,
> Why with them comes the sound of clothes beaten by ten
>   thousand households?"

After these forfeits had been paid, Yuan-yang and Hsi-jen who had also lost each recited a proverb alluding to "long life," which we need not repeat.

They went on playing the finger-guessing game for some time, Hsiang-yun pairing off with Pao-chin. Then Li Wan and Hsiu-yen, casting dice, threw the same number. Li Wan gave the clue "gourd," which Hsiu-yen answered with "green," and as she had guessed correctly each took a sip of wine. By now Hsiang-yun had lost the finger-game and had to pay a forfeit.

Pao-chin quipped, "Please get into the jar, sir!"[1]

The rest laughed and cried, "Very apt!"

Then Hsiang-yun declaimed:

> "Leaping and rushing,
> The river's waves surge towards the sky;
> An iron chain is needed to fasten the lonely boat,
> Because there is wind on the river
> It is not expedient to make a journey."

Roaring with laughter the rest said, "How side-splitting! No wonder she made up this forfeit. It was so as to make us laugh."

They waited then to hear her final line; but having tossed off her wine Hsiang-yun helped herself to a piece of duck, noticing as she did so that there was half a duck's head in the bowl. She picked this out and started eating the brain.

"Don't just eat," they scolded. "Finish your forfeit first."

Then holding up her chopsticks Hsiang-yun said,

> "This duck's head is not that serving-maid,[2]
> How can its head be smeared with oil of osmanthus?"

At that the rest laughed even louder, while Ching-wen, Hsiao-luo, Ying-erh and the other maids came over to protest:

"Miss Hsiang-yun, you're making fun of us. You must drink a cup by way of penalty. Why should we be smeared with osmanthus oil? You'd better give us each a bottle of it."

Tai-yu chuckled, "She wouldn't mind giving you a bottle, if it weren't for fear of being suspected of theft!"

Most of the company paid no attention; but Pao-yu, understanding, lowered his head while Tsai-yun, having a guilty conscience, blushed. Pao-chai shot Tai-yu a warning glance, making her regret her indiscretion; for in her eagerness to tease Pao-yu she had forgotten until it was too late how sensitive Tsai-yun was. Dropping the subject then, they went on with their games.

Presently Pao-yu and Pao-chai threw dice with the same

---

[1] A quotation from Szuma Kuang's *Mirror of Governance*, meaning that injury is repaid in kind.

[2] "Duck's head" and "serving-maid" are both *yatou* in Chinese.

number. Pao-chai gave the clue "precious" and Pao-yu after a little thought knew that this was a playful reference to his magic jade.

"You're making fun of me, cousin, and I've guessed the answer," he told her with a smile. "Don't be annoyed if I break your taboo by saying your own name *chai* — 'hairpin.'"

Asked what he meant he explained, "When she said 'precious' she naturally meant 'jade'; so I answered 'hairpin.' An old poem has the line 'The jade hairpin is broken, the red candle cold.' Isn't that the answer?"

"You're not allowed topical references," Hsiang-yun cried. "Both of you should pay a forfeit."

"It's not just topical," objected Hsiang-ling. "There are classical sources too."

"Not for 'precious jade,'" retorted Hsiang-yun. "Only New Year congratulatory couplets pasted on gates may use it, but you won't find it in any classical records. This conundrum won't do."

Hsiang-ling insisted, "The other day reading Tsen Shen's poems I found the line 'There is much precious jade in these parts.' How could you have forgotten that? And then in one of Li Shang-yin's poems I found another line, 'The precious hairpin daily gathers dust.' I remarked at the time that apparently both their names appeared in Tang poetry."

"This will silence her!" the others laughed. "Drink up, quick!"

Hsiang-yun having no more to say had to drain her cup.

So they went on dicing and playing finger-guessing games. And as there was nobody to control them in the absence of the Lady Dowager and Lady Wang, they enjoyed themselves just as they pleased, shouting different numbers, the hall a scene of wild merriment filled as it was with the fluttering of red and green silk, the flashing of jade and pearl trinkets.

When at last the feast ended and they prepared to leave, they suddenly discovered that Hsiang-yun was missing. Thinking she had gone out to relieve herself and would soon be back, they waited and waited, but there was no sign of her. A general search was made, but she could not be found.

Presently the wife of Lin Chih-hsiao arrived with several old nannies. For fearing that the young ladies might want something, and that in the absence of Lady Wang the young maids might get out of hand or become tipsy and obstreperous, they had come to ask if they were needed. Tan-chun realized the reason for their coming.

"So you've come to check up on us, being worried again!" she chuckled. "We haven't drunk much; we were just having fun together on the pretext of drinking. You nannies can set your minds at rest."

Li Wan and Madam Yu also said, "Go and rest. We wouldn't dream of letting them drink too much."

"We know that," answered Mrs. Lin and the others. "Even when the old lady wants them to drink they won't, much less so now that the mistress is away; of course this is just in fun. We came to find out if you need anything. The days are long now, and after amusing themselves all this time the young ladies ought to have some extra snack. They don't usually eat between meals, but unless they have something after a few cups of wine it may not be good for them."

Tan-chun smiled.

"You're quite right. We were thinking of asking for something."

She turned to order some cakes. The maids standing on both sides assented and went off quickly to fetch them, while Tan-chun urged the old women, "Go and rest or have a chat with Madam Hsueh. We'll send you some wine."

Mrs. Lin and the others politely declined and after a while withdrew.

As soon as they had gone Ping-erh felt her cheeks.

"My face is so hot I didn't like to let them see me," she said. "I suggest we wind up now to stop them from coming again — that would be awkward."

"Never mind," said Tan-chun. "It's all right as long as we don't get really drunk."

As she was speaking a young maid came in, smiling.

"Go and have a look quick, miss, at Miss Hsiang-yun," she cried. "She's drunk, and she's picked a cool spot on a stone bench behind the rockery to sleep it off."

The rest laughed to hear this.

"Let's not make a noise," they said.

With that they went out to look, and sure enough found Hsiang-yun lying on a stone bench in a quiet spot behind an artificial mountain. She was sound asleep and covered with peony petals, which had floated over from all sides to scatter, red and fragrant, over her face and clothes. Her fan, dropped to the ground, was half buried in fallen blossoms too, while bees and butterflies were buzzing and flitting around her. And she had wrapped up some peony petals in her handkerchief to serve as a pillow. They all thought she looked both sweet and comical. As they crowded round to wake her, Hsiang-yun was still mumbling lines for forfeits in her sleep:

> "Sweet the fountain, cold the wine
> Gleaming like amber in a cup of jade;
> The drinking lasts till the moon rises over the plum trees,
> Then the drunkards help each other back —
> An appropriate time to meet relatives and friends."

Laughing, they nudged her.

"Hurry up and wake up! We're going to eat. You'll make yourself ill if you sleep on this damp bench."

Hsiang-yun slowly opened her eyes then and saw them all, then looked down at herself and realized she was tipsy. She had come here in search of coolness and quiet, but as she had drunk so much wine by way of forfeits, overcome by dreamy inertia she had dozed off. Rather sheepishly, she hastily sat up, straightened her clothes and went back with the others to Red Fragrance Farm. There she had a wash and two cups of strong tea, and Tan-chun sent for the "pebble to sober drunkards" for her to suck. Presently she made her drink some vinegar soup too, after which Hsiang-yun felt better.

Now they picked some sweetmeats and dishes to send to Hsi-feng, who sent them some food in return. After Pao-chai and

the others had eaten some cakes, some of them sat or stood about in the hall while others went outside to enjoy the flowers or lean over the balustrade to watch the fish, laughing and chatting or doing whatever each pleased. Tan-chun and Pao-chin played draughts, with Pao-chai and Hsiu-yen looking on, while Tai-yu and Pao-yu engaged in a conversation under a flowering tree.

Then Lin Chih-hsiao's wife and some other matrons brought in another woman looking most upset, who would not venture to enter the hall but knelt down at the foot of the steps to kowtow.

Now one of Tan-chun's positions on the draughtboard had been threatened, and although after putting up a struggle she had managed to win two spaces she was still losing the game. Her eyes intent on the board, she was thinking hard, toying with one hand with the draughtsmen in the box. When she finally turned her head to ask for tea and noticed Mrs. Lin, the latter had been standing there a long time. Asked her business, Mrs. Lin pointed at the woman.

"This is the mother of young Tsai-erh who works for Miss Hsi-chun," she reported. "She's one of those looking after the Garden, and a fearful gossip. Just now I overheard her saying something which I dare not repeat to you, miss. She ought to be dismissed."

"Why not report this to Madam Chu?" asked Tan-chun.

"I met her just now on her way to the Council Hall to see Madam Hsueh, and told her about it. She sent me to tell you."

"Why not go to Madam Lien?"

"There's no need for that," interposed Ping-erh. "I'll just tell her when I go back."

Tan-chun nodded.

"In that case, dismiss her now and wait until the mistress comes back to make a final decision." This said, she went on with her game, while Mrs. Lin took the woman away.

Tai-yu and Pao-yu standing under the blossoms had watched this from a distance.

"Your third sister's rather smart," remarked Tai-yu. "Although she's been put in charge of things, she never oversteps her authority. Most people would have given themselves big airs long ago."

"You don't know that while you were unwell she did quite a few things, putting different people in charge of various parts of the Garden, so that now you can't pick one extra blade of grass. She scrapped a few things too, taking me and Hsi-feng as her main targets. She's very calculating, not simply smart."

"So much the better," said Tai-yu. "This household of ours is too extravagant. Though I'm not in charge, when I've nothing to do and reckon things up I can see that the expenditure here exceeds the income. If expenses aren't cut down now, a time will come when there'll be nothing left."

Pao-yu chuckled. "Never mind. Whatever happens, the two of us won't go short."

Tai-yu hearing this turned and went to the hall to join Pao-chai.

Pao-yu was about to leave too when Hsi-jen came along carrying a small carved, double-circle foreign lacquer tray on which were two cups of newly brewed tea.

"Where has she gone?" she asked. "I noticed that the two of you had had no tea for a long time, so I specially brought you two cups — only to find her gone."

"She's over there; take it to her."

With that he took one of the cups. Hsi-jen, going off with the other, found Tai-yu with Pao-chai.

"I've only the one cup of tea," she said. "Whichever of you is thirsty can drink this first, and I'll go to fetch another."

"I'm not thirsty," answered Pao-chai. "I'll just take a sip."

She took the cup and drank one mouthful, leaving half a cup which she handed to Tai-yu.

"I'll get you some more," Hsi-jen offered.

But Tai-yu said, "You know the doctor won't let me drink too much tea on account of my illness, so this half cup is plenty. Thank you for bringing it."

She drained the cup and put it down, after which Hsi-jen went to collect Pao-yu's cup.

He asked her, "Where's Fang-kuan? I haven't seen her all this time."

Hsi-jen looked around as she answered, "She was here a moment ago. A few of them were playing the 'matching-herbs' game, but I don't see her now."

Then Pao-yu hurried back to his compound and found Fang-kuan lying on the bed with her face to the wall.

"Don't go to sleep," he said nudging her. "Let's amuse ourselves outside. It'll soon be time for dinner."

"You were all drinking and ignoring me; so having nothing to do all that time naturally I came to lie down," Fang-kuan retorted.

Pao-yu pulled her up.

"We'll have another drink later at home, and I'll tell Sister Hsi-jen to bring you to the dinner table. How's that?"

"If Ou-kuan and Jui-kuan aren't there, only me, that's no good. Besides, I don't like noodles. I didn't have a proper meal this morning and I'm hungry, so I've told Mrs. Liu to prepare me a bowl of soup and half a bowl of rice and send them here. I'll eat here. If we're drinking tonight you mustn't let anyone stop me — I mean to drink my fill. At home, in the old days, I used to be able to drink two or three catties of good Huichuan wine; but after I learned this wretched singing they said drinking might spoil my voice, so for the last few years I haven't so much as smelt a whiff of wine. I shall take the chance today to break my fast."

"That's simple," he said.

Now a maid arrived with a hamper from Mrs. Liu. Hsiao-yen took it and opened it, then put on the table one bowl of chicken-skin soup with shrimp balls, one bowl of steamed duck with wine sauce, one of salted goose and another of four pine-kernel cream puffs, as well as a big bowl of hot green rice. She then fetched pickles, bowls and chopsticks, and filled one small bowl with rice.

"Who wants such greasy stuff?" complained Fang-kuan, just ladling some soup on the rice and eating a bowlful with two pieces of goose.

To Pao-yu, the food smelled more appetizing than his usual fare, so first he ate one cream puff, then asked Hsiao-yen for half a bowl of rice which he ate with soup and found delicious, exactly to his taste, much to the two girls' amusement. After he had finished, Hsiao-yen prepared to take back what was left.

"You may as well finish it off," proposed Pao-yu. "If it's not enough ask for some more."

"There's no need for that; this is plenty for me," she answered. "Just now Sister Sheh-yueh brought us two plates of cakes. After eating this I'll have had enough and shan't need any more." So standing there by the table she finished all the food except two cream puffs, saying, "I'll keep these for my mother. If you're drinking tonight, give me a couple of bowls."

"So you like wine too?" exclaimed Pao-yu. "Wait till this evening then, and we'll have a good bout of drinking. Your sisters Hsi-jen and Ching-wen have a good capacity and enjoy drinking too, only normally they don't feel they should. Well, today everyone can break her fast. There's another thing I meant to tell you which I've only just remembered. In future you must take good care of Fang-kuan, and tell her if she does anything wrong. Hsi-jen hasn't time to look after so many girls."

"I know all that," said Hsiao-yen. "You don't have to worry. But what about Wu-erh?"

"Tell Mrs. Liu to send her here tomorrow. I'll inform them about it later and that will be that."

Fang-kuan hearing this exclaimed, "Now *that's* something really important!"

Hsiao-yen called in two young maids then to wait on them while they washed their hands and to pour them tea while she herself cleared the table, gave the dishes to a serving-woman, washed her hands and went to see Mrs. Liu.

Pao-yu started back then to Red Fragrance Farm to rejoin the girls, followed by Fang-kuan carrying his handkerchief and fan. As they went out of the gate they met Hsi-jen and Ching-wen, coming back hand in hand.

"What are you two doing?" Pao-yu asked them.

"The meal's on the table waiting for you," Hsi-jen said.

Smiling, Pao-yu told them what he had just eaten.

"I always say you're as bad as a cat," Hsi-jen laughed. "Whatever you smell takes your fancy. Other people's food tastes better to you than your own. Still, you'd better go and keep them company and make a show of eating."

Ching-wen stabbed at Fang-kuan's forehead with her finger.

"You vamp!" she cried. "When did you sneak off to have a meal? How did you two arrange it? Why didn't you let us know?"

"They just happened to meet," said Hsi-jen soothingly. "They certainly didn't arrange it in advance."

"If that's how it is, he doesn't need *us*," said Ching-wen. "Tomorrow we'll all clear out, leaving just Fang-kuan here to wait on him."

Hsi-jen chuckled, "All the rest of us can go, but not you."

Ching-wen retorted, "I should be the first to go, lazy, stupid, bad-tempered and useless as I am."

"Supposing that peacock-feather cape gets burned again, who can mend it if you're gone?" asked Hsi-jen. "Don't give me that silly talk. When *I* ask you to do anything, you're too lazy to thread a needle. And I never trouble you with sewing for me, only with things for *him*, yet you still refuse. How come then that when I was away for a few days and you were laid up, practically at death's door, you mended that cape for him with no thought of your health? What made you do that? Come on, speak up! Don't pretend not to understand and just keep on smiling."

While talking together they had reached the hall. Aunt Hsueh had already come, so all took their seats and started the meal, Pao-yu just eating half a bowl of rice steeped in tea to keep them company. Afterwards they sipped tea and chatted or amused themselves as they pleased.

Hsiao-luo, Hsiang-ling, Fang-kuan, Jui-kuan, Ou-kuan and Tou-kuan had been romping all over the Garden and picking flowers and herbs. Now they sat down on the grass holding these on their laps to play the game "matching herbs."

One said, "I've bodhisattva-willow."

This was capped by "I've arhat-pine."

Another said, "I've gentleman-bamboo."

Yet another answered, "I've lovely-lady plantain."

"I've starry-green."

"I've monthly-crimson."

"I've the peony of *Peony Pavilion*."

"I've the loquat of the *Romance of the Lute*."

Then Tou-kuan said, "I've a sister-flower," and nobody could match that until Hsiang-ling said:

"I've a husband-and-wife orchid."

"I've never heard of such an orchid," Tou-kuan protested.

"A stem bearing one flower is the *lan* orchid, and a stem bearing several flowers is the *hui* orchid," Hsiang-ling told them. "When there are flowers above and below that's a brothers-orchid; when two flowers bloom side by side that's a husband-and-wife orchid. This one of mine is like that, with two flowers side by side. How can you deny it?"

Unable to refute her, Tou-kuan rose to her feet and teased, "In that case, if one flower is large, the other small, it should be a father-and-son orchid. Two flowers confronting each other should be an enemy orchid. Your husband's been away for nearly a year and you're longing for him, so you dream up a husband-and-wife orchid. For shame!"

Blushing, Hsiang-ling got ready to spring up to pinch her.

"You foul-mouthed bitch!" she swore, laughing. "What drivel you talk!"

Seeing she was about to spring up, Tou-kuan promptly stooped to hold her down, turning to appeal to Jui-kuan and the rest:

"Come and help me pinch her foul mouth!"

The two of them rolled over on the grass while the others laughed and clapped.

"Look out!" cried one. "There's a puddle there. It would be a pity to dirty her new skirt."

Tou-kuan turned and saw just beside them a puddle of rain water which had already muddied half Hsiang-ling's skirt. Disconcerted, she let go of her and ran off. The others could not help laughing, but afraid Hsiang-ling might vent her annoyance on them they too scampered away giggling.

Hsiang-ling got up now and started cursing when she looked down and saw water dripping from her skirt. Just at this moment, along came Pao-yu with some herbs and flowers he had picked, intending to join in their game. He saw the rest running away leaving Hsiang-ling there, her head lowered, fingering her skirt.

"Why have they all gone?" he asked.

"I had a husband-and-wife orchid," she told him. "They'd never heard of it and said instead I was cheating, so we started squabbling and I've spoilt my new skirt."

"You have a husband-and-wife orchid and I've a neck-to-neck caltrop flower here," he answered, showing her the caltrop and taking the orchid from her.

"Never mind about husband-and-wife or neck-to-neck," she grumbled. "Look at my skirt."

Pao-yu bent to look, then exclaimed, "*Aiya*! How did you get it in the mud? It's too bad, this pomegranate-red silk shows the dirt so."

"This silk was brought the other day by Miss Pao-chin. Miss Pao-chai made one skirt and I made another, which I put on today for the first time."

Pao-yu stamped his foot.

"Your family can well afford to spoil a hundred skirts like that each day. Only this was given you by Miss Pao-chin, and you and Cousin Pao-chai both have one; if hers is still all right while yours gets dirtied first, that looks ungrateful. Besides, dear old Auntie's a fuss-pot. Even when you're careful, I've often heard her complaining that you're a poor manager and don't know how to save but just waste things all the time. If she sees this, you'll never hear the end of it."

Hsiang-ling was pleased and struck by his understanding.

"That's just it," she replied. "I have several new skirts, but none like this. If I had, I'd change it quickly and things would be all right for the time being."

"Better not move," Pao-yu warned her. "Just stay put, otherwise you'll muddy your underclothes and shoes as well. I have an idea. Last month Hsi-jen made a skirt exactly like this. As she's still in mourning she isn't wearing it. How about letting her give you hers instead?"

Hsiang-ling smiled and shook her head.

"No, if others heard about it, that would be worse."

"What would it matter? After her mourning ends, if she fancies something you can surely give it her, can't you? The way you're behaving isn't like your usual self. Besides, this isn't anything that need be kept secret; you can tell Cousin Pao-chai about it. We just don't want to vex dear old Auntie."

Hsiang-ling thought this made good sense.

Nodding she said, "All right then. To show how grateful I am to you I'll wait here. But be sure you get her to bring it here herself."

Pao-yu was delighted and agreed to this, musing as he hurried back with lowered head, "Poor girl, with no parents, not even knowing her family name after being kidnapped and sold to this Tyrant King." Then he thought, "What I did for Ping-erh last time was unexpected; now this is even more of a pleasant surprise." His thoughts wandering in this foolish way, he went back to his room and got hold of Hsi-jen to explain the situation. As Hsiang-ling was a general favourite and open-handed Hsi-jen was a good friend of hers, as soon as she knew what had happened she opened her case, took the skirt out and folded it, then went off with Pao-yu to find Hsiang-ling still standing in the same spot.

"I always said you were naughty," teased Hsi-jen. "Now see what a mess you've landed yourself in."

Hsiang-ling blushed and said, "Thank you, sister. I never thought those mischievous imps would play such a dirty trick on me." When she took the skirt and unfolded it, she found it was just like her own. She made Pao-yu look the other way and, turning her back on him, took off her skirt and slipped into the clean one.

"Give me the dirty one to take back," said Hsi-jen. "I'll have it cleaned, then return it. If you take it back, they may see it and ask questions."

"You take it and give it to one of the girls. Now that I've got this one, I don't need it any more."

"That's very generous of you," said Hsi-jen.

Then Hsiang-ling curtseyed her thanks, and Hsi-jen went off with the soiled skirt.

Now Hsiang-ling saw that Pao-yu was squatting on the ground using a twig to scrape a little pit in which to bury her orchid and his caltrop flower together. First he lined the bottom of the pit with fallen blossoms then laid the flowers in it, strewed them with more blossoms, then filled in the pit with earth.

Hsiang-ling pulled him by the hand saying, "What's the idea? No wonder people say you're always up to underhand tricks. Look, your hands are all muddy and filthy. Go and wash them, quick."

Pao-yu got up smiling and set off to wash his hands while Hsiang-ling walked away too. They had neither of them gone far when she turned back and called him to stop. Not knowing the reason, Pao-yu turned back grinning, holding his muddy hands away from himself.

"What is it?" he asked.

But Hsiang-ling simply giggled. Just then her young maid Chen-erh appeared.

"Miss Pao-chin wants you," she said.

Hsiang-ling urged Pao-yu then, "Just don't say anything about the skirt to your Cousin Pan. That's all." With that she turned and went off.

Pao-yu called laughingly after her, "Think I'm crazy? Why should I put my head in a tiger's mouth?" Then he went home to wash.

To know what happened later, read the next chapter.

CHAPTER 63

Girls Feast at Night to Celebrate
Pao-yu's Birthday
Chia Ching Dies of an Elixir and Madam Yu
Manages the Funeral Single-Handed

Pao-yu going back to his room to wash up told Hsi-jen, "We mustn't stand on ceremony tonight but drink and enjoy ourselves. Let them know in good time what dishes we want so that they'll have them ready."

"Don't worry," she replied. "Ching-wen, Sheh-yueh, Chiu-wen and I have contributed half a tael of silver each, which makes two taels; and Fang-kuan, Pi-heng, Hsiao-yen and Ssu-erh have each given thirty cents. So, apart from those who are away, we've raised three taels and twenty cents which we've already given to Mrs. Liu, who's preparing forty dishes. I've also arranged with Ping-erh to have a vat of good Shaohsing wine smuggled in. The eight of us are going to throw a birthday party for you."

Pao-yu was delighted but demurred, "How can they afford it? You shouldn't have made them chip in."

Ching-wen demanded, "Do we have money and not they? All of us are just showing our feeling. Never mind whether they can afford it. Even if they steal the money, just you accept it."

"That's right," said Pao-yu.

"It seems that you can't be satisfied unless she gives you a few digs every day," chuckled Hsi-jen.

"Now you're learning bad ways too," shot back Ching-wen. "Always goading others on to stir up trouble!"

At that all three laughed, after which Pao-yu proposed locking the courtyard gate. But Hsi-jen objected:

374

"No wonder people say you're for ever making a great ado about nothing. If we lock the gate now that will arouse suspicion. Better wait a bit."

Pao-yu nodded.

"I'll take a stroll outside then," he said, "while Ssu-erh fetches water. Hsiao-yen can come with me."

He went out, and as there was nobody else about asked when Wu-erh would be coming.

"I told Mrs. Liu just now, and of course she's very pleased," Hsiao-yen informed him. "Only Wu-erh got so worked up that night she was hauled over the coals that as soon as she got home she fell ill again. She can't come until she's better."

Pao-yu sighed in disappointment.

"Does Hsi-jen know this?" he asked.

"I didn't tell her," was the reply. "But Fang-kuan may have done for all I know."

"Well, *I* never told her. All right, I'll let her know now."

He went back inside on the pretext of washing his hands.

Now, as the time came to light the lamps, they heard people approaching the courtyard gate and when they peeped through the window saw Mrs. Lin with a few other stewards' wives, the one in front carrying a big lantern.

"They're making their nightly check-up of those on duty," whispered Ching-wen. "Once they've gone we can close the gate."

All the servants on night duty in Happy Red Court had gone out to meet these women. After checking that they were all present Mrs. Lin warned them:

"No gambling or drinking now, and no sleeping till morning! If I hear of such goings-on I'll have something to say."

"Which of us would dare?" they answered laughingly.

Then Mrs. Lin asked, "Is Master Pao in bed yet?"

As they replied that they did not know, Hsi-jen nudged Pao-yu, who put on slippers to go out to greet them.

"No, I'm not in bed yet," he called. "Come in and sit down." Looking towards the house, he ordered: "Serve tea, Hsi-jen."

Mrs. Lin entered then, smiling.

"Still up!" she exclaimed. "Now the days are long, the nights short, you should go to bed early so as to get up early tomorrow. Otherwise you may oversleep, and people will jeer that you don't behave like a scholarly young gentleman but like a common coolie." Having said this she laughed.

Pao-yu promptly agreed, "You're right, nanny. I do generally go to bed early, so that I don't know when you come every evening because I'm already asleep. But today after eating noodles I was afraid of getting indigestion; that's why I've stayed up a bit."

Mrs. Lin advised Hsi-jen and Ching-wen to brew him some *puerh* tea.

"We've made him some *nuerh* tea[1] and he's drunk two bowls. Won't you try some, madam?" they answered. "It's already brewed."

As Ching-wen poured a bowl Mrs. Lin observed, "Recently I've noticed that the Second Master always calls you girls by your names. Though you're working here you belong to Their Ladyships, so he should show more respect. If once in a while he happens to use your names, that doesn't matter; but if this becomes a habit then his cousins and nephews may follow suit, and then people will laugh at us and say we've no respect for elders in our household."

"You're right, nanny," agreed Pao-yu again. "Actually I only do that once in a while."

The two girls put in, "You must be fair to him. Even now he still refers to us as 'elder sisters,' only using our names occasionally in fun. In front of others he always addresses us as he did before."

"That's good," approved Mrs. Lin. "That's how someone with education and good manners ought to behave. The more modest you are, the more respected you'll be. Not to say

---

[1] *Puerh* tea, a green tea from Yunnan, is good for the digestion. *Nuerh* tea is not really tea but brewed from tender *wutung* leaves grown in the Taishan Mountains.

members of the staff of long standing or those transferred from
Their Ladyships' apartments, but even the dogs and cats from
there mustn't be badly treated. That's the way a well brought
up young gentleman should behave." She then drank up her
tea and said, "We must be off now. I'll wish you a good
night."

Pao-yu pressed them to stay, but Mrs. Lin had already led
her party off to finish making their rounds. At once Ching-wen
and others ordered the gate to be locked, and coming back
Ching-wen said:

"That grandame must have been drinking, gabbing away and
nagging at us like that."

"She means well anyway," remarked Sheh-yueh as she started
to lay the table. "She has to remind us from time to time to
be on our guard and not overstep the limits."

"We don't need that high table," put in Hsi-jen. "Let's put
that round low pear-wood one on the *kang*. There's room for
all of us at it, and it's more convenient."

So they carried the table over, after which Sheh-yueh and
Ssu-erh fetched the dishes, making four or five trips with two
big trays while two old women squatting outside by the brazier
warmed the wine.

"It's so hot, let's take off our outer clothes," Pao-yu suggested.

"You can if you want to," said the girls, "but we have to
take it in turns to offer toasts."

"If you do that it'll take all night," he objected. "You know
how much I dislike those vulgar conventions. We may have
to observe them in front of outsiders, but if *you* provoke me
like that it won't be nice."

"We'll do as you say," they agreed.

So before taking seats they first divested themselves of their
outer things and had soon laid aside their formal gowns and
trinkets, leaving their hair to hang free and wearing only long
skirts and bodices. Pao-yu himself stripped down to a scarlet
linen jacket and green dotted satin trousers, letting the ends
of the trouser legs hang loose. Leaning on a jade-coloured

gauze cushion filled with all sorts of fresh rose and peony petals, he started playing the finger-guessing game with Fang-kuan.

Fang-kuan, who had also been complaining of the heat, had on only a short lined satin jacket — a patchwork of red, blue and jade-coloured squares, a green sash, and pink trousers with a floral design left untied at her ankles. Her hair, woven in small plaits, was gathered on the crown of her head into a thick braid hanging down at the back. In her right ear she wore a jade stop no bigger than a grain of rice, in her left a ruby ear-ring set in gold the size of a gingko nut, making her face seem whiter than the full moon, her eyes clearer than water in autumn.

"The two of them look like twin brothers!" chuckled the others.

Hsi-jen and the rest poured wine for each.

"Wait a bit before you start the finger-guessing game," they said. "Though we're dispensing with the usual toasts, you must each take a sip from our cups."

Hsi-jen held the first cup to her lips and took a sip, to be followed by the others, after which all sat down in a circle. As there was insufficient room on the *kang*, Hsiao-yen and Ssu-erh set two chairs beside it. The forty white *Ting* ware dishes no bigger than saucers held all manner of sweetmeats and delicacies of land and sea, fresh or preserved, from every part of the country and from abroad. And now Pao-yu proposed playing some drinking games.

"Something quiet, not too rowdy," advised Hsi-jen. "We don't want people to hear us. And nothing too literary either, as we're no scholars."

"How about the dice game 'Grabbing the Red'?" said Sheh-yueh.

"That's no fun," objected Pao-yu. "Better play the 'Flower Game.'"

"Yes, do let's!" cried Ching-wen. "I've always wanted to play that."

"It's a good game," agreed Hsi-jen, "but no fun for just a few people."

"I've an idea," put in Hsiao-yen. "Let's quietly invite Miss Pao-chai and Miss Tai-yu over to play for a short time. It won't matter if we go on till the second watch."

"If we go around knocking different people up, we may run into some night-watchers," Hsi-jen pointed out.

"Don't be afraid," said Pao-yu. "My Third Sister likes drinking too; we should count her in. And Miss Pao-chin as well."

"Not Miss Pao-chin," the others demurred. "She's with Madam Chu, so that would make too much of a stir."

"Never mind," insisted Pao-yu. "Hurry up and invite them."

Hsiao-yen and Ssu-erh, who had been awaiting this order, immediately called for the gate to be unlocked and went off to the different apartments.

"They may not be able to get Miss Pao-chai and Miss Tai-yu," predicted the senior maids. "We'll have to go and drag them here by main force." So, telling an old woman to bring a lantern, Hsi-jen and Ching-wen went off as well.

Sure enough, Pao-chai objected that it was too late while Tai-yu pleaded poor health, but the two maids begged them:

"Do give us a little face. Just go and sit there for a while."

As for Tan-chun, she was eager to come but felt that if Li Wan were left out and came to hear of it later that wouldn't be good; so she told Tsui-mo and Hsiao-yen to insist that Li Wan and Pao-chin should both be invited. Presently they all arrived, one by one, at Happy Red Court, where Hsi-jen had dragged Hsiang-ling over as well. Another table had to be put on the *kang* before they could all sit down.

"Cousin Tai-yu feels the cold," said Pao-yu. "Come and sit by the partition."

She was given a cushion for her back while Hsi-jen and the other maids fetched chairs and seated themselves beside the *kang*.

Leaning against her back-rest some way from the table, Tai-yu teased Pao-chai, Li Wan and Tan-chun, "You're always accusing people of drinking and gambling at night, and now that's just what *we're* doing. How can we blame others in future?"

"It doesn't matter," replied Li Wan, "if we only do this on birthdays or festivals, not every night. There's nothing to be afraid of."

As she was speaking, Ching-wen brought in a carved bamboo container filled with ivory slips bearing the names of flowers. Having shaken this she put it down in the middle. Next she brought the dice-box and shook it, and upon opening the box saw that the number on the dice was five. She counted, starting from herself, and Pao-chai being the fifth was the one who should start.

"I'll draw," said Pao-chai. "I wonder what I shall get."

She shook the container and took out a slip on which they saw the picture of a peony with the words "Beauty surpassing all flowers." Inscribed in smaller characters beneath was the line of Tang poetry, "Though heartless she has charm." The instructions read, "All the feasters must drink a cup by way of congratulations, for this is the queen of the flowers. She can order anyone to compose a poem or tell a joke to enliven the drinking."

"What a coincidence!" all exclaimed laughingly. "A peony is just the flower for you." With that they drank a cup each.

After Pao-chai had drunk she decreed, "Let Fang-kuan sing us a song."

"In that case," said Fang-kuan, "you must all finish your cups."

When all had drained them, Fang-kuan started singing *The Birthday Feast Is Spread in a Fine Season.*

"Not that song," protested the others. "We don't want you, right now, to congratulate him on his birthday. Sing us your best song instead."

Then Fang-kuan had to give them a careful rendering of a verse set to the melody *The Season for Enjoying Flowers.*[1]

> With a broom of green phoenix feathers,
> I leisurely sweep fallen blossoms for immortals;
> Lo, a wind rising all of a sudden

---

[1] An aria from the third scene "Recommended to the World of Immortals" of *Story of Hantan,* by the Ming playwright Tang Hsien-tzu.

Swirls jade dust under the clouds,
So far removed though just outside the gate.
Do not miss by an inch again your slash at the yellow dragon,
Nor return to the poor wine-vendor in the east,
But let us turn our eyes to the roseate clouds.
Ah, Lu Tung-pin,
Hasten back when you have found one to replace me!
If you delay,
I shall nurse my grief for ever by the peach-blossom.

Pao-yu, holding the slip of ivory, had been softly repeating to himself, "Though heartless she has charm," gazing at Fang-kuan as she sang, lost in thought. Now Hsiang-yun snatched the slip from him and gave it to Pao-chai who threw sixteen, which made it Tan-chun's turn.

"I wonder what I'll get," she said with a smile.

But having drawn a slip out and seen what it was, she threw it down.

"We shouldn't play this game," she declared with a blush. "It's a game for those men outside, a whole lot of silly nonsense."

The others were wondering what she meant when Hsi-jen picked up the slip for all to see. Under the picture of an apricot-blossom were the words in red "Fairy flower from paradise" and the verse "A red apricot by the sun grows in the clouds." The directions were: "Whoever draws this will have a noble husband. All must drink to her, then drink another cup together."

"Is that all?" they laughed. "This is a game for the inner apartments. Apart from a couple of slips with mottoes like these, there's nothing improper; so what does it matter? Our family already has one Imperial Consort; are you going to be another? Congratulations!"

They all raised their cups, but Tan-chun would not drink this toast until compelled to by Hsiang-yun, Hsiang-ling and Li Wan.

When she protested, "Let's give up this game and play another," they would not agree, and Hsiang-yun held her hand, forcing her to throw the dice. The number nineteen coming up, it was Li Wan's turn. She shook the container, took out a slip, and smiled when she saw what it was. "Excellent!" she crowed. "Just see what I've got. This is fun."

They saw the picture of an old plum-tree with the motto

"Cold beauty in frosty dawn" and the line of verse "Content to stay by the bamboo fence and thatched hut." The instructions were: "Whoever draws this lot must drink a cup, then the one whose turn comes next must throw the dice."

"That's fine," said Li Wan. "You go on dicing while I just drink one cup without worrying how the rest of you get on."

She drained her cup and passed the dice to Tai-yu, who threw eighteen, making it Hsiang-yun's turn. Hsiang-yun rolled up her sleeves to draw her lot, a picture of crab-apple-blossom with the motto "Deep in a fragrant dream" and the line "So late at night the flower may fall asleep."

Tai-yu teased, "The words 'late at night' should be changed to 'cool on the stone.'"

At that everyone laughed, knowing that she was referring to how Hsiang-yun had fallen asleep earlier that day on a stone.

Giggling, Hsiang-yun pointed at the mechanical boat.

"Hurry up and leave by that boat, and stop talking nonsense!" she retorted.

Amid more laughter they read the instructions, "As she is deep in a fragrant sleep and cannot drink, the two next to her must each drink a cup instead."

Hsiang-yun clapped her hands.

"Amida Buddha!" she cried. "This is really a lucky dip!"

It so happened that Tai-yu and Pao-yu were on either side of her, so they both filled their cups. Pao-yu first drank half the cup, as no one was watching, then passed the rest to Fang-kuan, who drained the cup. As for Tai-yu, while chatting with the others she quietly poured her drink into a rinse-bowl. Hsiang-yun then threw a nine, which made it Sheh-yueh's turn. On the lot she drew they saw a rose with the motto "Flower of final splendour" and the line "When the rose blooms, spring flowers fade." Below was written, "All at the feast should drink three cups each to farewell the spring."

When Sheh-yueh asked what was written there, Pao-yu frowned and hid the slip, saying, "We must all drink." So they took three sips each to symbolize three cups.

Then Sheh-yueh threw nineteen and it was Hsiang-ling's turn.

She drew a picture of two flowers on one stem with the motto "Double beauty linked with good fortune" and the line "Double flowers bloom on a single stem." The instructions were: "All must congratulate the one who draws this lot and make her drink three cups, drinking one each themselves."

Hsiang-ling then threw a six, making it Tai-yu's turn. "I hope I get something good," she thought while drawing a lot. It showed a hibiscus flower with the motto "Quiet and sad in wind and dew" and the line "Blame not the east wind but yourself." The instruction was: "Both hibiscus and peony must drink a cup."

"Fine!" cried the others. "She's the only one here fit to be compared to a hibiscus."

Tai-yu smiled too as she drank, then threw a twenty which made it Hsi-jen's turn.

Hsi-jen drew a picture of peach-blossom with the motto "Exotic scene at Wuling" and the line "Another spring returns and the peach blooms red." The instructions were, "The apricot-blossom, as well as those born in the same year, on the same day and those with the same surname must drink one cup."

"This one is lively and good fun," cried the rest.

They worked it out that Hsiang-ling, Ching-wen and Pao-chai were the same age as Hsi-jen, while Tai-yu's birthday fell on the same day; but they could not think of anyone with the same name until Fang-kuan said:

"My family name is Hua. I'll drink with her."

As they filled their cups Tai-yu remarked to Tan-chun, "You're the apricot-blossom destined to have a noble husband. So drink up quickly and we'll follow suit."

"Stop talking nonsense!" retorted Tan-chun. "Sister-in-law, give her a slap."

"She hasn't got a noble husband and now you want me to beat her," teased Li Wan. "No, I can't bring myself to do it."

At that they all laughed.

Hsi-jen was about to throw the dice when they heard someone at the gate. An old woman went to see who was there and found it was a maid sent by Aunt Hsueh to fetch Tai-yu back.

"What time is it?" everyone asked.

"After the second watch," the maid informed them. "The clock's just struck eleven."

Pao-yu could not believe it was so late, but when he called for his watch and looked at the time it was ten past eleven.

"I can't stay up any longer," said Tai-yu getting up. "I have to take medicine too after I go back."

All agreed that it was time to disperse, so when Hsi-jen and Pao-yu tried to keep them Li Wan and Pao-chai demurred:

"It doesn't look right being so late. We've already made an exception to our rule."

"In that case," said Hsi-jen, "let's each have one final cup."

Ching-wen and the others filled the cups, and after drinking them they called for lanterns. Hsi-jen and the rest, having seen the visitors past Seeping Fragrance Pavilion to the other side of the stream, came back and locked the gate, then continued their game. They also filled several big goblets and selected several dishes for the old maid-servants waiting on them. And now, being slightly tipsy, they played the finger-guessing game and made the losers sing songs. By the time of the fourth watch, the old women in addition to drinking their share had stolen more wine on the sly so that the whole vat was empty. When they learned to their surprise that the wine was finished, they cleared the table, washed and made ready for bed.

Fang-kuan's cheeks after drinking were as red as rouge, making her look still more charming. Unable to hold herself steady she leaned on Hsi-jen.

"Dear sister," she murmured, "my heart's beating ever so fast!"

"Who gave you permission to drink so much?" Hsi-jen retorted.

Hsiao-yen and Ssu-erh, who had felt dizzy too, had already gone to bed. Only Ching-wen was still trying to rouse them.

"No need to wake them," Pao-yu remonstrated. "Let's just get some rest anyhow."

With that, lying back on his pillow of fragrant red petals, he curled up and went to sleep too.

Hsi-jen feared that Fang-kuan was so drunk that she might be sick, so she quietly helped her over to lie down next to Pao-yu, then sank down on the opposite couch herself. They all slept then, oblivious of everything around them.

When Hsi-jen next opened her eyes the day was bright.

"So late!" she exclaimed.

Seeing Fang-kuan still sleeping on the edge of the *kang* she got up quickly to wake her. But by this time Pao-yu had turned over and woken up.

"It *is* late!" he chuckled, nudging Fang-kuan to make her get up.

Fang-kuan sat up, still drowsy, rubbing her eyes.

"Aren't you ashamed?" Hsi-jen laughed. "You were so drunk you didn't care where you flopped down to sleep."

Fang-kuan stared round, and when she discovered that she had shared Pao-yu's bed she at once scrambled up.

"How is it that I don't remember a thing?" she answered laughingly.

"That goes for me too," rejoined Pao-yu. "If I'd known, I'd have blackened your face with ink."

Some young maids came in now to help them with their toilet.

"I gave you a lot of trouble yesterday," declared Pao-yu. "Tonight I'm going to throw a return party."

"No, we mustn't raise another rumpus today," said Hsi-jen. "If we did, people would complain."

"Why should we care?" he retorted. "It's only a couple of times. But we must be good drinkers if we managed to finish that whole vat of wine. Things were just getting lively when we ran out of wine."

"That's what made it so good," said Hsi-jen. "If we'd drunk to our full capacity, it wouldn't seem such fun looking back. Yesterday we all did fine, and Ching-wen actually forgot her scruples. I remember that she even sang a song."

"Have you forgotten, sister, that even *you* sang one too?" demanded Ssu-erh. "Everyone at the party sang."

They all blushed then, hiding their faces in their hands, and were giving way to fits of laughter when Ping-erh came in.

"I've come in person," she announced merrily, "to invite all the people at the party yesterday. Today I'm standing treat. Everybody must come."

They asked her to take a seat and drink some tea.

"It's a pity we didn't have her here last night," observed Ching-wen.

"What did you do last night?" she asked.

"We can't tell you," Hsi-jen replied. "Things were so lively, it was far more fun than even those times when Their Ladyships gave us parties. We finished up a whole vat of wine; then after drinking we all forgot ourselves and started singing, really let ourselves go! Finally — not till after the fourth watch — we lay down just anywhere to sleep it off."

"Fine goings-on!" exclaimed Ping-erh. "You asked me for the wine but didn't invite me, then tell me this to provoke me."

"He's giving a return party today and is sure to invite you," Ching-wen assured her. "Just wait."

" 'He'? Who is 'he'?" asked Ping-erh with a smile.

Ching-wen made as if to slap her, protesting laughingly, "Why do you have such sharp ears?"

"I'm too busy to bandy words with you now," Ping-erh told her. "I must be off to see to some business. Later on I'll send to invite you. If anyone fails to turn up, I'll come and knock down your door."

Pao-yu wanted to urge her to stay, but she was already gone. After he had finished his toilet and was drinking tea he suddenly caught sight of a piece of paper under the inkstone.

"It's no good," he scolded, "the way you stuff things carelessly just anywhere you please."

Hsi-jen and Ching-wen hastily asked what was wrong. Pao-yu pointed at the paper.

"What's this under the inkstone? One of you must have forgotten to put your patterns away."

Ching-wen took the paper from under the inkstone and saw it was a greeting card on a sheet of pink stationery. She passed it to Pao-yu who read: "Miao-yu, the one outside the threshold, sends respectful greetings on the young master's birthday."

At once he sprang to his feet.

"Who brought this in?" he demanded. "Why wasn't I told?"

The state he was in made Hsi-jen and Ching-wen suppose that this was a greeting from someone of consequence.

"Who accepted this card yesterday?" they both asked together.

Ssu-erh rushed in to explain, "Miao-yu didn't come herself but sent an old servant with this, so I put it there. But after all that drinking I forgot it."

When the other girls heard this they commented, "We thought it was someone who mattered, the way you were carrying on; but this isn't worth making such a fuss about."

Pao-yu, however, immediately asked for some paper and while spreading it out and grinding ink wondered how to word a reply matching that phrase "outside the threshold." Brush in hand he thought hard for a long time, but could not hit on anything appropriate. He reflected, "If I consult Pao-chai, she's bound to criticize this as eccentric. I'd better ask Tai-yu." So tucking the card up his sleeve he set off to find her and had just passed Seeping Fragrance Pavilion when he saw Hsiu-yen approaching with swaying steps.

"Where are you going, cousin?" he inquired.

"To have a chat with Miao-yu," was the answer.

In surprise he remarked, "She's so aloof and unconventional that she looks down on everybody. If she thinks so highly of *you*, this shows you're not vulgar like the rest of us."

"She may not really think highly of me," replied Hsiu-yen with a smile, "but we were next-door neighbours for ten years when she was practising asceticism in Curly Fragrance Nunnery. My family was poor, and we lived for ten years in a house rented from the nunnery; so I often went in to see her when I was free, and she's the one who taught me all the characters I know. Apart from being friends in poverty, she was half my teacher too. After we had left the nunnery to join our relatives, I heard that because she'd offended certain powerful people by her eccentric ways she had to come here for protection too. So as luck would have it we met again, and our old feeling for each other hadn't changed — in fact she's even kinder to me than before."

Much impressed by this account Pao-yu said with delight, "No wonder your own behaviour and conversation are as unworldly as a wild stork or floating clouds! So this is the reason. I'm stumped just now by something connected with her and was on my way to ask somebody's advice. Meeting you is a heaven-sent chance. You must tell me what to do."

Then he showed the card to Hsiu-yen.

"She hasn't changed in the least," observed Hsiu-yen with a smile. "She was born like this — headstrong and eccentric. I've never seen other people use appellations like this in greeting cards. Why, this, as the saying goes, is neither fish, flesh nor fowl! It doesn't make sense."

"But you see she's not one of us," Pao-yu put in. "She's outside the mundane crowd. She's only sent me this greeting because she thinks I have some slight discernment. But I'm at a loss as to how to word my reply. I was on my way to ask Cousin Tai-yu when luckily I met you."

Hearing this, Hsiu-yen looked him up and down for a while.

She then said cheerfully, "As the proverb says, 'To know someone by repute is not as good as meeting face to face.' No wonder Miao-yu sent you this greeting card; no wonder she gave you that plum-blossom last year. As even *she* shows you special consideration, I shall have to explain this to you. She often says that the only good poetry written by the ancients from the times of Han, Tsin, the Five Dynasties, Tang and Sung, was the two lines:

> For a thousand years you may have an iron threshold,
> But the end must be a mound of earth.

This is why she calls herself the one outside the threshold. She likes the writings of Chuang Tzu, from which she took that term 'the odd person.' If she called herself 'the odd person' in her card, you could call yourself 'the mundane person,' meaning you're one of the common herd, and that would please her. Now that she's called herself the 'one outside the threshold,' meaning she's outside the iron threshold, to fall in with her you should call yourself the 'one inside the threshold.'"

Pao-yu felt as if Buddha had suddenly shown him the light.

"*Aiya!*" he exclaimed. "No wonder our family temple is called Iron Threshold Temple. So that's the origin of the name. Well, cousin, I won't hold you up any longer. I must go and write a reply."

Then Hsiu-yen went on to Green Lattice Nunnery while Pao-yu went back to write on a card: "With the deepest respects of Pao-yu, the one inside the threshold." Taking this himself to the nunnery, he slipped it through a crack in the gate, then went back.

He found that Fang-kuan had finished doing her hair, which was fastened up in a knot, and she was wearing some trinkets. At once he insisted on her dressing in a different style. He urged her to shave off her fringe completely, exposing her bluish scalp, and to part her hair in the middle. He also said that in winter she should wear a sable cap in the shape of a crouching hare and small tiger-head battle boots decorated with multi-coloured curling clouds, or leave her trouser ends loose and wear white socks and thick-soled boots. He objected to the name Fang-kuan as well, saying it would be more original to take a man's name instead, and proposing the name Hsiung-nu.[1] Fang-kuan was delighted.

"In that case," she said, "when you go out you must take me along, and if anyone asks who I am just tell them I'm a page like Ming-yen."

"Still, people will be able to see who you are," he chuckled.

"How dense you are, I must say!" she retorted. "We have some families of tribesmen here — just say I'm from one of those. Besides, everyone tells me I look better with my hair plaited. Wouldn't that be the smart thing to do?"

---

[1] Literally, "male slave," and a homophone for "Hun."

"Splendid!" approved Pao-yu elatedly. "I've often seen officials with followers captured from abroad, as such people can stand wind and frost and are excellent horsemen. In that case, I'll give you a tribal name — Yali Hsiung-nu. Those are names used by the tribes who have been a scourge to China since the days of Yao and Shun, and who plagued us so much during the Tsin and Tang dynasties.

"We're lucky to be living now under the rule of an Emperor directly descended from the sage king Shun, an age when virtue, humanity and filial piety as vast as Heaven are manifest, and in a dynasty which will endure as long as the sun and moon. That's why all the unruly barbarians who made such trouble in previous dynasties now submit to us with folded hands and bowed heads, according to Heaven's will, without our having to resort to arms; and distant tribes have surrendered to our rule. So we *should* make fun of them to add to the glory of our sovereign."

"If that's how you feel," countered Fang-kuan, "you should go and practise archery and horsemanship and learn other martial arts, then set off to the border to capture some rebels! Wouldn't that show your loyalty better than using *us* to do it? You're simply wagging your tongue for your own amusement, on the pretext of praising the state's achievements and virtue."

"That's exactly what you don't understand," replied Pao-yu laughingly. "Now the Four Seas have submitted to our rule and peace reigns everywhere; so for ages to come there will be no need for arms. And even when having fun we should praise the court, so as not to be unworthy to enjoy the fruits of peace."

Fang-kuan agreed to this, and as both of them felt it quite appropriate he started addressing her as Yali Hsiung-nu. Actually the two Chia mansions had been presented by the court with slaves who had been captured by their ancestors; but these were only used as grooms, not being fit for other work.

Now Hsiang-yun was a madcap who loved to dress up as a warrior in a belted, tight-sleeved jacket. When she saw Pao-yu fit Fang-kuan out as a boy, she followed suit by dressing Kuei-kuan up as a page too. Kuei-kuan, who had played warriors, kept her hair shaved over her temples and forehead as that had made it easier to paint a warrior's face, and she was nimble too. So it was easy to dress her up as a page. Then Li Wan and Tan-chun, also thinking it a good idea, made Pao-chin's Tou-kuan dress up as a boy too in a short jacket and red shoes with her hair in two tufts. Had her face been painted, she would have been the spit of the Taoist priest's acolyte who carries his master's lyre on the stage.

Hsiang-yun changed Kuei-kuan's name to Ta-ying, and as her family name was Wei she was called Wei Ta-ying;[1] for in choosing this name Hsiang-yun had in mind the phrase "Only a true hero can keep his true colour." Why, to appear a man, should one resort to rouge or powder?

Tou-kuan[2] had been given that name because she was both small and young and a clever little imp. So in the Garden she was also called Ah-tou or Fried Pea. Thinking that to give her a name like "Lyre-boy" or "book-boy" would sound vulgar, and that "Tou" was more original, Pao-chin called her Tou-tung.[3]

That afternoon when Ping-erh gave a return feast she had several tables of new wine and good dishes set out in Elm Shade Hall, saying that it was too warm in Red Fragrance Farm. To everybody's delight, Madam Yu brought over her husband's two concubines Pei-feng and Hsieh-yuan, two attractive young women who seldom had a chance to enjoy themselves in the Garden. Coming here now and meeting Hsiang-yun, Hsiang-ling, Fang-kuan, Jui-kuan and the other girls, it was a genuine case of "like attracts like" or "birds of a feather flock together." Chatting and laughing with each other they paid no attention to Madam Yu, leaving it to the maids to wait on her while they amused themselves with the other girls.

When presently they went to Happy Red Court and heard Pao-yu call Yali Hsiung-nu, the two concubines and Hsiang-ling

---

[1] A homophone in Chinese for "only a true hero."

[2] *Tou* means "pea."

[3] This means "pea-boy."

burst out laughing and asked what language this was. They tried to say this name themselves but kept getting it wrong, sometimes forgetting one character or even calling her Yeh-lu,[1] which made all who heard them double up with mirth. Fearing that Fang-kuan might feel hurt, Pao-yu hastily interposed:

"I've heard that west of the ocean, in France, they've a type of precious golden-starred glass which in their language they call *venturina*. Suppose we compare you with that and change your name to Venturina?"

Fang-kuan was pleased and readily agreed. Accordingly they changed her name again. However, the others still found this a tongue-twister, so they translated it into Chinese and took to calling her Po-li.[2] But enough of this.

They returned now to Elm Shade Hall to amuse themselves there on the pretext of drinking. Some women story-tellers were told to beat the drum and Ping-erh plucked a spray of peony; then everyone — twenty or so in all — passed this round and the one who had it when the drumming stopped had to drink. They had been making merry for some time when it was announced that two serving-women had come with presents from the Chen family. Tan-chun, Li Wan and Madam Yu went to the hall to receive them, and the rest left Elm Shade Hall to stroll outside. Pei-feng and Hsieh-yuan went to take turns on the swing.

"Both get on together and I'll push you," offered Pao-yu.

"Oh no," said Pei-feng in dismay. "Don't get us into trouble. Better ask your Wild Ass to come and push us instead."

"Stop teasing, sister," he begged. "Otherwise other people will follow your example and make fun of her too."

"If you're limp from laughing, how can you swing?" warned Hsieh-yuan. "You'll fall off and get smashed like an egg!"

Pei-feng ran to catch her, and they were scuffling in fun when some servants from the Eastern Mansion came rushing up fran-

---

[1] "Wild Ass."
[2] "Glass."

tically. "The old master's ascended to Heaven!" they announced.

Everybody was consternated.

"He wasn't even ill, how could he pass away so suddenly?" they exclaimed.

The servants explained, "His Lordship took elixirs every day; now he must have achieved his aim and become an immortal."

Madam Yu was most worried by this news; for as her husband Chia Chen, their son Chia Jung, and Chia Lien too were all away, there was no man at home to take charge. She hurriedly took off her finery and sent a steward to Mysterious Truth Temple to have all the Taoist priests there locked up until her husband came back to question them. Then she hastily went by carriage out of the city with the wives of Lai Sheng and some other stewards, having also sent for doctors to see what illness her father-in-law had succumbed to.

As Chia Ching was dead it was no use for the doctors to feel his pulse. They knew, however, that for years he had been practising absurd Taoist breathing exercises. As for his yoga, worship of the stars, keeping vigil on certain nights, taking sulphide of mercury and wearing himself out with his senseless striving for immortality — these were what had carried him off. His belly after death was hard as iron, the skin of his face and lips parched, cracked and purple. They reported to the serving-women that he had died of excessive heat as a result of taking Taoist drugs.

The Taoist priests in their panic confessed, "His Lordship had just concocted a new elixir with some secret formula, and that was his undoing. We'd warned him not to take such things before achieving a certain potency; but last night, during his vigil, unknown to us he took some and became an immortal. Doubtless he has attained immortality owing to his piety, leaving this sea of woe and sloughing his earthly integument to fare forth at will."

Madam Yu, shutting her ears to this, ordered them to be immured until Chia Chen's return. And she sent messengers posthaste to take the news. Seeing that the temple was too cramped for the coffin to be left there, and as it could not be taken into the city, she had the corpse shrouded and conveyed by sedan-chair to Iron Threshold Temple. She reckoned that her husband could not be back for another fortnight at least, and as the weather was too hot for the funeral to be delayed she decided to get an astrologer to choose a day for it. As the coffin had been prepared many years ago, and kept ever since in the temple, the funeral was easily managed. Three days later a mourning service was held and further masses were performed while waiting for Chia Chen. Since Hsi-feng of the Jung Mansion could not leave home and Li Wan had to look after the girls, while Pao-yu knew nothing of practical affairs, the work outside was entrusted to a few second-rank stewards. Chia Pien, Chia Kuang, Chia Heng, Chia Ying, Chia Chang and Chia Ling also had their different assignments. Madam Yu, being unable to go home, invited her step-mother old Mrs. Yu to come and keep an eye on things in the Ning Mansion. And Mrs. Yu, to be easy in her mind, had to bring her two unmarried daughters with her.

When Chia Chen heard of his father's death he immediately asked for leave, as did Chia Jung who also had official duties. The Board of Ceremony, well aware that the Emperor set great store by filial piety, dared make no decision themselves but reported the request to the throne. The Emperor, with his transcendent benevolence and filial piety, always treated the descendants of meritorious ministers with special consideration. As soon as he saw the memorial he asked what official post Chia Ching had held, and the Board of Ceremony reported that he had been a Palace Graduate, whose ancestor's noble title had passed on to his son Chia Chen. Being old and infirm Chia Ching had retired to live quietly in Mysterious Truth Temple outside the city, where he had now died of illness. His son Chen and his grandson Jung were both at court on account of the state obsequies. They had therefore asked leave to return to attend to the funeral.

When the Emperor heard this, in his exceeding kindness he decreed: "Though Chia Ching was an ordinary citizen who performed no special service for the state, in view of his grandfather's merit he is to be promoted posthumously to the fifth rank. His son and grandson are to escort his coffin through the lower north gate into the capital for a funeral ceremony at his own home, so that his descendants can mourn for him as is fitting before escorting his remains to their ancestral district. Let the Office of Imperial Banquets bestow on the deceased a sacrificial feast of the first grade, and let all at court from princes and dukes downwards be granted leave to offer their condolences. By Imperial Decree!"

As soon as this decree was issued, not only did the Chia family express thanks for the Emperor's goodness, all the high ministers at court were loud in their praise.

Chia Chen and his son were speeding home posthaste when they saw Chia Pien and Chia Kuang galloping towards them, attended by some servants. At sight of Chia Chen they hastily dismounted to pay their respects.

Asked their errand Chia Pien reported, "Sister-in-law was afraid that after you and our nephew came back there would be nobody to travel with the old lady, so she sent us to escort Her Ladyship."

Chia Chen expressed full approval, then asked how matters had been arranged at home, and Chia Pien described how the Taoist priests had been detained and the corpse taken to the family temple; and how, as there was no one in charge at home, old Mrs. Yu and her two daughters had been invited to stay and accommodation found for them in the main building.

Chia Jung had also dismounted. When he heard of the arrival of his two young aunts, he grinned at his father who was reiterating:

"Well done, well done!"

They galloped on then, not stopping at any inns but changing horses at different post-houses as they sped back through the night. And upon reaching the capital they went straight to Iron Threshold Temple. It was then the fourth watch and the watchmen, hearing them, aroused everyone in the place. Chia Chen alighted and with Chia Jung wailed aloud, both advancing on their knees from outside the gate to where the coffin was resting, kowtowing and lamenting all the way. They went on wailing till dawn, by which time their voices were hoarse.

Madam Yu and the others all came to meet them. Then Chia Chen and his son, having changed into mourning according to the rites, prostrated themselves before the coffin. However, since they had business to attend to which they could not ignore, they had to curtail their mourning in order to issue instructions. Chia Chen read out the Imperial Decree to their relatives and friends, then sent Chia Jung home first to arrange for the removal of the coffin there.

Chia Jung had been eagerly awaiting this order. He rode swiftly home and hastily gave instructions for the tables and chairs to be cleared away from the front hall, the partitions removed, white mourning curtains hung up, and a shed for musicians as well as an arch erected in front of the gate. This done, he hurried in to greet his step-grandmother and two aunts.

Now Mrs. Yu, being old and fond of sleeping, often lay down on the couch to have a nap while her two daughters were sewing with the maids. When they saw Chia Jung they expressed their condolences. Beaming all over his face he said to his second aunt:

"So you're here again, Second Auntie. My father's been longing for you!"

Second Sister Yu blushed.

"You rascal!" she swore at him. "You can't get by if I don't curse you every other day! You're going from bad to worse, with absolutely no sense of what's proper. Imagine the son of a good family, who studies and is taught manners all the time, not even being up to low-class riffraff."

She picked up an iron and grabbed his head as if to hit him, whereupon, shielding his head, he nestled close to her and begged for mercy. Third Sister Yu reached out to pinch his lips.

"Wait till our elder sister hears of this," she scolded.

Chuckling, Chia Jung knelt on the *kang* to ask their pardon, at which both the sisters laughed. Then he tried to snatch some cardamom from his second aunt, who spat what she was chewing all over his face; but he just licked it off and ate it, shocking the maids who were there.

"You're wearing mourning and your grandmother is napping here," one of them remonstrated. "And after all they're your aunts, for all they're young. You really haven't much respect for your mother. Presently we shall tell the master, and then you'll be in big trouble."

Chia Jung let go of his aunt then and grabbing hold of the maid kissed her on the mouth.

"You're quite right, sweetheart," he cried. "Now let's make both their mouths water!"

The maids pushed him away. "You short-lived devil!" they cursed. "You've a wife and maids of your own just like anyone else — why come to plague *us*? Some people may know this is just fooling about; but there are other dirty-minded busybodies who like to gossip. They may spread so much talk that everyone in the other house hears about it. They'll be saying we're all fast and loose here."

"We're two different households," scoffed Chia Jung. "We should both mind our own business. Haven't we all enough troubles of our own? Since ancient times, even the Han and Tang dynasties have been described as 'filthy Tang and stinking Han,' to say nothing of families like ours. Which household hasn't its share of philanderers? Shall I give you a few examples? Even though the Elder Master over there is so strict, Uncle Lien carried on with his young concubines; and though Aunt Hsi-feng is so stern, Uncle Jui tried to make her. Neither affair was any secret to me. . . ."

As Chia Jung was rattling away so wildly he noticed that the old lady had woken up, and made haste to pay his respects.

"Sorry to have put you to so much trouble, Old Ancestress," he said. "And my two aunts as well. My father and I are most grateful. When this business is over, we shall take the whole family, young and old, to your place to kowtow our thanks."

Old Mrs. Yu nodded.

"It's good of you to say that, my child," she replied. "We're only acting as relatives should." Then she asked, "Is your-father well? When did you get the message and hurry back?"

"We've only just arrived,' he told her. "He sent me on ahead to see how you are, madam, and to beg you to stay till the whole business is finished." As he said this he winked at his second aunt.

Gritting her teeth and smiling, Second Sister Yu scolded softly, "You glib-tongued monkey! Are you keeping us here to be your father's mothers?"

"Don't worry, madam," said Chia Jung to old Mrs. Yu. "Not a day goes by but my father is thinking of my two aunts and looking for two well-born, handsome young gentlemen from rich and noble families to arrange two matches for them. For some years he couldn't find anyone suitable. Luckily, on his way home this time, he met just the right man."

Old Mrs. Yu was only too ready to believe him.

"What family is he from?" she promptly asked.

The two sisters put down their sewing at this to chase him playfully and pummel him.

"Don't you believe the rascal, mother," one of them cried.

Even the maids protested, "Old Man Heaven has eyes. Look out, or you'll be struck by a thunderbolt!"

Just then someone came in to announce, "We've made everything ready. Please go and have a look, Master Jung, and report it to His Lordship."

Then Chia Jung went out chuckling to himself. To know what happened later, read the next chapter.

CHAPTER 64

A Chaste Girl in Sad Seclusion Writes Poems
on Five Beauties
An Amorous Libertine Drops
His Nine-Dragon Pendant

Chia Jung hurried back to the temple to report to his father that all was ready at home; and that same night they assigned the various tasks and prepared all the pennons, poles and other essential paraphernalia. Five o'clock in the morning of the fourth day was fixed upon as the hour to have the coffin taken into the city, and all relatives and friends were informed of this.

When the time arrived, with its splendid funeral rites, a host of guests assembled, and tens of thousands of spectators lined the road all the way from Iron Threshold Temple to the Ning Mansion, some sighing in admiration, others in envy, while crabbed pedants argued that frugality in the funeral rites would have been better than such extravagance. Endless different comments were made as the cortège passed; and not till nearly three in the afternoon did it finally reach the Ning Mansion, where the coffin was deposited in the main hall. After the sacrifice and mourning ended, the relatives and friends gradually dispersed, leaving only members of the Chia clan to see to the entertaining of guests. The sole close relative to remain was Lady Hsing's elder brother.

Chia Chen and Chia Jung, by duty bound to keep vigil by the coffin and mourn, nevertheless seized the chance once the guests had gone to fool around with old Mrs. Yu's two daughters. Pao-yu, wearing mourning, also went every day to the Ning Mansion, not returning to the Garden till the evening after the guests had left. Hsi-feng was still not well enough to stay there all the time; but when Buddhist masses were held and sutras read, or when visitors came to offer sacrifices, she made the effort to come over to help Madam Yu cope.

One day after the morning sacrifice, at a time when the days were still long, Chia Chen worn out after his recent exertions was dozing by the coffin and Pao-yu, seeing that no guests had come, decided to go back to call on Tai-yu.

He went first to Happy Red Court. As he stepped through the gate he found the court quiet and empty except for a few old women and young maids resting in the shade of the verandah, some asleep and others nodding drowsily. He did not go to disturb them, and only Ssu-erh noticed his arrival. As she hurried over to lift the portière for him, Fang-kuan came dashing out, laughing, and nearly knocked full tilt into Pao-yu.

At sight of him she pulled up.

"Why are you here?" she asked. "Hurry up and stop Ching-wen from spanking me!"

As she was speaking they heard a clattering as if some things had fallen to the ground, and the next minute Ching-wen appeared.

"Where are you going, you bitch?" she swore. "You've lost, yet you want to escape a spanking. With Pao-yu out who's going to come to your rescue?"

Pao-yu hastily intercepted her.

"She's still young," he said with a smile. "If she's offended you in some way, do let her off for my sake."

Ching-wen had never expected him back so soon. Amused by his sudden appearance, she exclaimed, "Fang-kuan must be a fox-fairy! Why, not even a magic charm to conjure spirits could work so fast." She added, "But I'm not afraid, even if you've called in a god."

She made a grab at Fang-kuan, who had taken refuge behind Pao-yu. Holding each girl by the hand he led them inside. On the western *kang* there he found Sheh-yueh, Chiu-wen, Pi-heng and Tzu-hsiao playing knuckle-bones for melon-seeds. Apparently Fang-kuan had lost to Ching-wen, then refused to accept a spanking and run away; and Ching-wen, jumping up to chase her, had scattered the knuckle-bones on her lap all over the floor.

Pao-yu told them with a chuckle. "Now the days are so long, I was afraid you might all be bored while I was out and go to bed after your meal, which might make you fall ill. I'm glad you found a way to amuse yourselves." As there was no sign of Hsi-jen, he asked, "Where's your sister Hsi-jen?"

"Her?" said Ching-wen. "She's becoming more and more of a Confucian, sitting meditating alone with her face to the wall in the inner room. We haven't been in for some time and don't know what she's up to. She hasn't made a sound. Go on in, quick, and see if she's attained sainthood yet."

Laughing, Pao-yu went inside and saw Hsi-jen seated on the couch by the window, in her hand a skein of grey silk which she was netting. At sight of him she stood up. "What fibs has that creature Ching-wen been telling about me?" she asked. "I was in a hurry to finish this net and had no time to fool around with them, so I told them, 'You amuse yourselves. While the Second Master's out I want to sit quietly here for a while to rest.' Then she made up all that nonsense about me meditating and attaining sainthood. By and by I must go and pinch her lips!"

Pao-yu smiled as he sat down beside her to watch her at work.

"The days are so long, you should rest or amuse yourself with the others," he advised. "Or else go to see Cousin Tai-yu. Why work at this in such hot weather? What's it for?"

"I noticed that you're still using the fan case made that year when Madam Jung of the East Mansion died. As it's blue it should only be used while mourning in summer for one of our clan or for relatives and friends outside. It shouldn't normally be needed more than once or twice a year. Now there's mourning in the other house, of course you should wear it every day when you go over; so I'm hurrying to finish another for you to replace that old one. You don't care about such things, but if the old lady were to come back and see it, she'd scold us for being too lazy to fit you out properly."

"It's good of you to think of such things, but you mustn't

overwork," he answered. "We don't want you knocked out by the heat."

Now Fang-kuan brought in a cup of freshly brewed tea which had been cooled in cold water; for even in summer they dared not use ice, as Pao-yu was so delicate. Instead they immersed the tea-pot in water fresh from the well, changing the water from time to time until the tea was cool. Fang-kuan held the cup to Pao-yu's lips and he drank half of it.

Then he told Hsi-jen, "When I came, I left word with Pei-ming that if any important visitors come to Cousin Chia Chen's place he must let me know directly. If nothing urgent crops up I won't go back." As he turned to go out he instructed Pi-heng and the others, "If anything happens you can find me in Miss Lin's place." With that he set off for Bamboo Lodge to find Tai-yu.

As he was crossing Seeping Fragrance Bridge he saw Hsueh-yen approaching, behind her two old women who were carrying caltrops, lotus-root, melons and other fruit.

"Your mistress hardly ever eats cold things like these. What are you going to do with all this?" he asked. "Are you inviting some of the other young ladies?"

"If I tell you, you mustn't let her know," said Hsueh-yen.

Pao-yu nodded.

Then she told the two women, "Take this fruit to Sister Tzu-chuan. If she asks for me, tell her I've something to do and will soon be back."

The women assented and went on their way. "Our young lady's been feeling better the last few days," said Hsueh-yen when they had gone. "After lunch today Miss Tan-chun came to ask her to go with her to see Madam Lien, but she didn't go. And then — I don't know what she was thinking of — she had a fit of depression, after which she took up her brush and wrote something — whether poetry or something else I don't know. When she sent me to fetch this fruit I also heard her tell Tzu-chuan to clear away the things on the small lyre table and move it outside, then to put the tripod with dragon designs on the table ready for the melons and fruit. If she were going to entertain visitors, she wouldn't bother to set out an incense-burner first; if she were going to burn incense, she's not in the habit of scenting her clothes with it or having anything in the room except fresh flowers and fruit. Even when she *does* burn incense for the fragrance, it's usually in her sitting room or bedchamber. Could it be that she has to scent the place with incense because the old serving-women have made it smelly? I really don't know why else she's doing this." Having said this she hurried away.

Pao-yu involuntarily lowered his head to think this over.

"Judging by what Hsueh-yen said, there must be a reason," he thought. "If Tai-yu were expecting one of the girls to call, she'd hardly make such elaborate preparations. Can this be the anniversary of her father's or mother's death? But in the past, on those days, I remember the old lady always had dishes specially prepared for her to offer as a private sacrifice; and both those dates have passed. More likely, as the seventh month is the season for melons and fruit and every family is making an autumn sacrifice at its graves, she's felt moved to sacrifice privately in her own quarters, according to the precept in the *Book of Rites* that in autumn and spring one should offer the food in season. That may be it.

"But if I go there now and find her upset, I shall have to do my best to comfort her; then she may try to hide her unhappiness, so that it rankles. On the other hand, if I don't go, there'll be no one to stop her grieving too much. Either way, she may fall ill. The best thing would be to call on Hsi-feng first, just for a short while, then come back. If I find Tai-yu still upset I can try to console her. That way, she won't give way to grief too long, but by having a good cry she'll have vented her feelings without injuring her health."

Having reached this decision he left the Garden and went to Hsi-feng's place. A number of serving-women were coming out after having reported on the business in their charge, and Hsi-feng, leaning against the door, was chatting with Ping-erh. At sight of Pao-yu she smiled.

"So you're back," she said. "I've just told Lin Chih-hsiao's wife to send word to your pages that if there was nothing much to do you should take the chance to come back and rest a bit. Besides, with all that crowd there, the place is too stifling for you. Well, I'm glad you've come back of your own accord."

"Thank you for your concern," he answered. "It was because there was nothing to do today and I was wondering whether you were better, as you hadn't been over for a couple of days, that I came back to have a look."

"That's just the way it is with me," Hsi-feng told him. "I have my good days and my bad days. With Their Ladyships away from home, these women — *ai!* — not a single one of them behaves herself. Every day they either fight or squabble, and there've even been several cases of gambling and theft. Although Tan-chun's helping me see to things, she's an unmarried girl. There are some things I can tell her, others I can't. So I just have to bear up as best I can, and never have a moment's peace. Don't talk about getting better — if I don't get worse that's good enough for me."

"Even so, you must take good care of your health and worry less," he urged her.

After a little further chat he took his leave of Hsi-feng and went back to the Garden.

When he entered Bamboo Lodge, he saw that the incense in the burner was nearly burnt out and the libation had already been poured. Tzu-chuan was supervising the maids carrying the table inside and replacing the ornaments on it. Knowing that the sacrifice was over, Pao-yu went in and found Tai-yu reclining on the couch, her face to the wall. She looked ill and exhausted.

Tzu-chuan announced, "Master Pao is here."

Tai-yu got up slowly then and with a smile invited him to sit down.

"You seem much better recently," he remarked. "You look less flushed. But what's upset you again?"

"That's no way to talk," she retorted. "There's nothing wrong with me. Why should I be upset?"

"You've tear-stains on your face, why try to fool me? I just thought that being so delicate you should take things easy, not distress yourself for no purpose. If you spoil your health, I'll be. . . ." He broke off here, finding it difficult to go on.

Though he and Tai-yu had grown up side by side and were kindred spirits who longed to live and die together, this was simply tacitly understood by both but had never been put into words. Moreover Tai-yu was so sensitive that his careless way of talking always offended her or even reduced her to tears. Today he had come to comfort her; but again, without meaning to, had spoken too hastily so that he had to break off, desperately afraid that Tai-yu would be angry. And when he reflected that he had really meant well, he started shedding tears of distress. Tai-yu had been annoyed at first by Pao-yu's immoderate language. Now, touched by the state he was in, being prone to weeping herself, she started shedding tears in silence too.

Tzu-chuan, arriving with tea for them, supposed they were bickering over something again.

"Our young lady's just getting better, Master Pao," she said. "What do you mean by coming to provoke her again?"

Pao-yu wiped his tears and smiled.

"I wouldn't dream of provoking her," he protested, getting up to wander around.

He noticed a sheet of paper under the inkstone and reached out for it. At once Tai-yu started up to stop him, but he had already tucked it inside his clothes.

"Do let me see it, dear cousin," he begged with a smile.

"Regardless of when you come you ransack this place."

As Tai-yu was saying this Pao-chai dropped in.

"What is it that Cousin Pao wants to read?" she asked.

As Pao-yu had not yet seen what was on the paper and did

not know what Tai-yu's reaction would be, he dared not answer outright. Instead, he looked at Tai-yu with a smile.

Tai-yu offered Pao-chai a seat.

"I've read of many talented beauties in ancient history," she said, "whose lives were sometimes enviable, sometimes tragic. As I'd nothing to do today after my meal, I decided to choose a few of them and dash off some verses about them to express my feelings. Then Tan-chun came to ask me to call on Hsi-feng with her, but I felt too lazy to go. I'd just written half a dozen poems when I felt sleepy, so I tossed them aside, not expecting the Second Master to come in and see them. Actually I don't mind *him* reading them, but I don't want him to copy them out and go showing them to other people."

"When have I ever done such a thing?" asked Pao-yu. "As for that fan, because I liked those poems about white begonia I copied them out neatly on it just for my own convenience when I have it in my hands. Of course I know that the poems and calligraphy from our inner apartments mustn't be lightly taken outside. And remembering that time you ticked me off I've never taken it out of the Garden."

"Cousin Lin's right to have such scruples," said Pao-chai. "As you've written our poems on your fan, you may forget and take it to your study where the secretaries may see them and ask who wrote them. If word spread, it wouldn't look good. As the old saying goes, 'Lack of talent in a woman is a virtue.' The important thing for us is to be chaste and quiet, feminine accomplishments being secondary. As for versifying and the like, we simply do that for fun in the inner apartments; and whether we're good or not at it doesn't matter. Girls from families like ours don't want to have a reputation for brilliance." Then she said to Tai-yu with a smile, "Still it doesn't matter if you show them to *me*, provided Cousin Pao doesn't take them outside."

"In that case you needn't see them either," said Tai-yu. Pointing at Pao-yu she added, "He's already snatched them."

At that Pao-yu took the poems out of his pocket and stepped to Pao-chai's side to read them with her. The poems were as follows:

HSI SHIH[1]

Gone with the foam the beauty who felled cities,
Her longing for home in Wu's palace an empty dream,
Laugh not at the East Village girl who aped her ways,
White-haired, she still washed clothes beside the stream.

LADY YÜ[2]

Heart-broken as black steed neighing at night in the wind,
In silent grief she stayed beside her lord;
The renegades Ying Pu and Peng Yueh were doomed to be slaughtered;
Better, then, in Chu's tent to fall on her own sword.

WANG CHAO-CHUN[3]

A breath-taking beauty banished from the Han palace —
From of old lovely girls have shared a sorry fate;
Even if the sovereign set little store by his beauties,
Why give a painter the power to arbitrate?

GREEN PEARL[4]

Rubble and pearls alike were cast away,
Shih Chung used this fair maid so slightingly;
Predestined he was to good fortune —
Together they died, but still lonely in death was she.

RED WHISK[5]

From his low bows, proud talk and air of distinction

---

[1] Hsi Shih, a beauty of the Spring and Autumn Period (770-476 B.C.), was presented to Prince Fu Chai of Wu by Prince Kou Chien of Yueh to induce him to neglect affairs of state. Fu Chai lost his kingdom to Kou Chien, while Hsi Shih was drowned in a river by the people of Wu.

[2] A favourite of Hsiang Yu, the Conqueror of Chu, she cut her throat when he was besieged by Liu Pang so that Hsiang Yu could break out of the blockade unburdened. Ying Pu and Peng Yueh were former Chu generals who surrendered to Liu Pang, but were later killed for disobeying orders.

[3] A palace maid during the reign of the Han emperor Yuan-ti (48-33 B.C.). Because she refused to bribe the palace painter Mao Yen-shou, he painted an unflattering portrait of her and therefore the emperor never summoned her but decided to marry her to a Hunnish chieftain. When she left and he saw how beautiful she was, he regretted his mistake and had Mao Yen-shou killed. See Note 5 on p. 160.

[4] A favourite concubine bought by the Tsin official and plutocrat Shih Chung (249-300) with three pecks of pearls. After Shih Chung's fall from power his rival Sun Hsiu demanded Green Pearl from him. She killed herself by jumping from a tower, and Shih Chung's whole household was killed.

[5] According to a Tang romance, Li Ching while in obscurity visited Yang Su, Duke of Yueh. One of the duke's attendants, a girl holding a red

The discerning beauty his true worth foretold;
The grand duke Yang Su was a living corpse,
How could he keep a girl so staunch and bold?

Pao-yu having read these poems was loud in his praise. "You've written just five poems, cousin," he said. "So why not call the whole *An Ode to Five Beauties*?" Without giving her time to object, he picked up a brush and added this title.

Pao-chai observed, "In writing poetry, no matter what the subject, the important thing is to express some original ideas. If we tread in other people's footsteps, even if the lines are polished they're still second-rate and can't be considered good poetry.

"Take, for example, the poems on Wang Chao-chun, all expressing different opinions. Some lamented her fate, some blamed Mao Yen-shou the painter, and others reproached the Han emperor for making him paint portraits of palace beauties instead of good ministers. Then Wang An-shih[1] wrote:

A painting can never succeed in catching the spirit;
Unjust it was to execute Mao Yen-shou.

And Ouyang Hsiu[2] wrote:

If the Emperor treated those in his presence like this,
How could he control tribesmen ten thousand *li* away?

Both those poems were original, not mere plagiarizing. And these five Cousin Lin has written today can also be considered as fresh and original, a quite new approach to the subject."

She would have said more, but someone came in to announce Chia Lien's return. It had just been reported outside that he had gone to the East Mansion, and as he had now been there for some time he could be expected back soon. When Pao-yu

---

whisk, was so impressed by Li Ching that she sought him out in his inn that night and they made off together. Li Ching then entered the service of Li Shih-min (later Emperor Tai-tsung of Tang) to overthrow the declining Sui Dynasty. He subsequently became a prime minister and a duke.

[1] Wang An-shih (1021-86).

[2] Ouyang Hsiu (1007-72).

heard this he hastily got up and went to the main gate to wait for his cousin's arrival, just as Chia Lien, having dismounted outside, came in. Pao-yu knelt down and first asked after Their Ladyships' health, then inquired after Chia Lien's health. The two of them went hand in hand into the hall, where they found assembled Li Wan, Hsi-feng, Pao-chai, Tai-yu, Ying-chun, Tan-chun and Hsi-chun, and greetings were exchanged.

"The old lady will be back tomorrow morning," said Chia Lien. "She's kept very well all through the journey. Today she sent me back ahead to have a look, and I'm to go out of the city at the fifth watch tomorrow to meet her."

Next they questioned him about the journey and then, as he was just back from such a long trip, took their leave and left him to go home to rest. No need to go into details about that evening.

About noon the next day, sure enough, the old lady, Lady Wang and others arrived. After the whole family had paid their respects they sat down just long enough for a cup of tea, then escorted Lady Wang and the others to the Ning Mansion. They heard loud wailing inside; for as soon as Chia Pien and Chia Kuang had brought the Lady Dowager home they had come over, and Chia Sheh and other members of the clan had come out to meet the old lady, shedding tears. Chia Pien and Chia Kuang, each holding her by one arm, helped her to the shrine while Chia Chen and Chia Jung approached on their knees and threw themselves into her arms, wailing bitterly. At this sight the old lady clasped them to her and gave way to a storm of grief, until finally Chia Sheh, Chia Lien and the others prevailed on her to stop weeping. She then went to the right side of the shrine to see Madam Yu and her daughter-in-law, and inevitably as they embraced they started wailing again. When these lamentations were over, the others went forward to pay their respects in turn. As the Lady Dowager had just come home and had as yet had no time to rest, Chia Chen, afraid that sitting there watching this scene would distress her too much, urged her repeatedly to go back. Lady Wang and others added their persuasions, and the old lady had to comply.

Indeed, on account of her age, she succumbed to her grief and the fatigue of the journey. That night she had a headache, a pain in her chest and sore throat, and found difficulty in breathing. A doctor was hastily summoned to feel her pulse and prescribe medicine, so that everyone was kept busy half the night. Luckily the cold was staved off, and the viscera proved to have been unaffected. And when at midnight she perspired a little her temperature went down and her pulse returned to normal, to everybody's relief. The following day she took more medicine and rested.

A few days later it was time for Chia Ching's coffin to be taken to the temple. As the old lady was still not completely recovered, she kept Pao-yu at home to keep her company. And Hsi-feng, not being too well, did not go either. Chia Sheh, Chia Lien, Lady Hsing, Lady Wang and the rest, accompanied by their stewards and serving-women, escorted the coffin to Iron Threshold Temple, not getting home till the evening. As for Chia Chen, Madam Yu and Chia Jung, they stayed in the temple to keep vigil. After a hundred days the coffin would be taken to their ancestral district; in the meantime the Ning Mansion was left in the charge of old Mrs. Yu and her two daughters.

Now Chia Lien had long heard of Madam Yu's lovely stepsisters and longed to meet them. Recently, with Chia Ching's coffin in the house, he had been seeing Second Sister and Third Sister every day so that he was on familiar terms with them and had designs on them too. Knowing how free and easy both girls were with Chia Chen and Chia Jung, he tried in a hundred ways to convey his own feelings, casting arch glances at them. Third Sister only treated him coolly, however, while Second Sister appeared very interested; but since there were so many people about he could not make any advances. Fear of arousing Chia Chen's jealousy also kept him from acting too rashly. So the two of them had to be content with a secret understanding.

After the funeral, however, there were few people left in Chia Chen's house. The main quarters were occupied only by old Mrs. Yu and her two daughters attended by a few of the maids and serving-women who did the rough work, all the senior maids and concubines having gone to the temple. As for the female servants who lived outside, they simply kept watch at night and minded the gate in the daytime, and would not go inside unless they had business. So Chia Lien was eager to make good use of this chance. He spent the nights in the temple too, on the pretext of keeping Chia Chen company; but he often slipped back to the Ning Mansion to inveigle Second Sister, telling Chia Chen that he was going to see to the family affairs for him.

One day the young steward Yu Lu came to report to Chia Chen, "The funeral sheds, mourning clothes and blue uniforms for attendants and carriers cost a thousand taels in all, of which we've paid five hundred; so we're still five hundred short, and the tradesmen have sent to ask for payment. That's why I've come for your instructions, sir."

"Just get the money from the treasury. Why come and ask me for it?" said Chia Chen.

"I did go to the treasury yesterday," Yu Lu replied. "But since His Lordship's demise there have been all sorts of expenses, and the money on hand is being kept for the hundred days' masses and for use in the temple; so for the moment they can't issue me any. That's why I've come specially to report to you. Perhaps this sum could be taken from the inner treasury for the time being, or raised some other way. Just give me your orders and I'll carry them out."

"Do you think this is like the old days when we had silver lying idle?" retorted Chia Chen. "Go and borrow some for the time being, I don't care from where."

Yu Lu smiled.

"I can probably raise a couple of hundred taels somewhere," he said. "But how can I get hold of four or five hundred so fast?"

Chia Chen thought it over, then instructed Chia Jung, "Go and ask your mother for this sum. After the funeral the Chen family in the south sent us five hundred taels for a sacrifice. That money arrived yesterday, and we haven't sent it to the treasury yet. Get that first and give it to him."

Chia Jung assented and went over to tell his mother, coming back to report:

"We've already spent two hundred of the five that arrived yesterday. The remaining three hundred were sent home today to be kept by granny."

"In that case, take Yu Lu along and get it from her. You can also make sure that all's well at home and ask after your two aunts. Yu Lu can borrow the rest."

Chia Jung and Yu Lu agreed and were just starting out when Chia Lien came in. Yu Lu stepped forward to pay his respects. Chia Lien asked what he had come for, and Chia Chen told him. At once Chia Lien thought, "This is a chance for me to go to the Ning Mansion and see Second Sister."

"This is a small sum," he said. "Why borrow from others? Yesterday I received some silver which I haven't spent yet. Better give him that for this payment to save trouble."

"Fine," said Chia Chen. "Send Jung along and tell him how to get it."

"I shall have to get it myself," said Chia Lien hastily. "Besides, I haven't been home these last few days; I ought to go and pay my respects to the old lady and my other elders. Then I'll go to your place to make sure that the servants aren't making trouble, and call on old Mrs. Yu as well."

"I don't like putting you to so much trouble," objected Chia Chen.

"What does it matter between cousins?" Chia Lien answered.

So Chia Chen told his son, "Go with your uncle, and mind you go too to pay your respects to the old lady, master and mistresses of the other house. Give them our regards and ask if the old lady is better now or still taking medicine."

Chia Jung assented and went off with Chia Lien. Taking a few pages with them, they mounted their horses and rode back to the city, chatting idly on the way.

Then Chia Lien deliberately mentioned Second Sister Yu, praising her for her good looks and modest behaviour, her lady-like ways and gentle speech, as if she were a paragon admired and loved by all.

"Everyone praises your Aunt Hsi-feng," he said, "but to my mind she can't stand comparison with your Second Aunt."

Chia Jung, knowing his game, rejoined, "If you've taken such a fancy to her, uncle, I'll act as your go-between to make her your secondary wife. How about that?"

"That would be fine!" Chia Lien beamed. "I'm only afraid your Aunt Hsi-feng wouldn't agree, and neither might your grandmother. Besides, I heard that your Second Aunt is already engaged."

"That doesn't matter," Chia Jung assured him. "My second and third aunts aren't my grandfather's daughters but only step-daughters. I've been told that while old Mrs. Yu was in the other family she promised her second daughter, before the child was born, to the Chang family who managed the Imperial Farm. Later the Changs were ruined by a lawsuit, and she herself married again into the Yu family. Now, for the last ten years or so, the two families have lost touch completely. Old Mrs. Yu often complains that she'd like to break off the engagement, and my father also wants to find Second Aunt a different husband. As soon as they've picked a suitable family, all they need do is send someone to find the Changs, pay them a dozen or so taels of silver, and have a deed written breaking off the betrothal. The Changs are so hard up that when they see the silver they're bound to agree; on top of which they'll know that in dealing with a family like ours they can't do anything else. If a gentleman like you, uncle, wants her as a secondary wife, I guarantee both her mother and my father will be willing. The only problem is my Aunt Hsi-feng."

At this Chia Lien was too overjoyed to speak and could only grin foolishly.

After a little reflection Chia Jung continued, "If you have the nerve to do as I say, uncle, I guarantee it will be all right. It will simply mean spending a little extra money."

"What's your plan? Out with it quick! Of course I'll agree."

"Don't let on a word about this when you go home. Wait till I've told my father and settled it with my grandmother; then we'll buy a house and the furnishings for it somewhere near the back of our mansion, and install a couple of our servants and their wives there. That done, we'll choose a day and you can get married on the sly. We'll forbid the servants to tell anyone about it. As Aunt Hsi-feng lives tucked away inside the big mansion, how can she possibly get to know of it? Then you'll have *two* homes, uncle. After a year or so, if word does get out, at most you'll get reprimanded by your father; but you can say that as my aunt had no son you arranged this in secret outside, in the hope of having descendants. When Aunt Hsi-feng sees that the rice is already cooked, she'll have to put up with it; and if you ask the old lady then to put in a word for you, the whole thing will blow over."

As the old proverb says, "Lust befuddles the mind." Chia Lien was so infatuated by Second Sister's beauty that he felt Chia Jung's plan was foolproof, completely forgetting that he was in mourning and how inappropriate it was to have a concubine outside when he had a stern father and jealous wife at home.

As for Chia Jung, he had ulterior motives. He was attached to both his young aunts, but his father's presence at home cramped his style. If Chia Lien married Second Sister he would have to have a separate establishment outside, where Chia Jung could go to fool about in his absence.

Of course none of this occurred to Chia Lien, who thanked him saying, "Good nephew, if you fix this up I'll buy you two really ravishing maids."

By now they had reached the Ning Mansion and Chia Jung said, "Uncle, while you go in to get the silver from my grandmother and give it to Yu Lu, I'll go on ahead to call on the old lady."

Chia Lien nodded, then said with a smile, "Don't tell the old lady that I've come with you."

"I know." Chia Jung whispered then into his ear, "If you see Second Aunt today, don't act too rashly. If there's any trouble now, it will make things more difficult in future."

"Don't talk rot," chuckled Chia Lien. "Go on. I'll wait for you here."

Chia Jung accordingly went to pay his respects to the Lady Dowager.

When Chia Lien entered the Ning Mansion, some of the stewards stepped forward with other servants to pay their respects and followed him to the hall. Chia Lien questioned them briefly for appearance's sake, then dismissed them and went in alone. As he and Chia Chen were cousins and on a close footing, he was not subject to any restrictions here and did not need to wait to be announced. He went straight to the main apartment. The old woman on duty in the corridor lifted the portière as soon as she saw him; and on entering the room he saw Second Sister sewing with two maids on the couch on the south side, but of old Mrs. Yu and Third Sister there was no sign. Chia Lien went forward to greet Second Sister, who asked him to take a seat, and he sat down with his back to the east partition.

After an exchange of civilities he asked, "Where are your mother and Third Sister? Why aren't they here?"

"They just went to the back for something; they'll be here soon," she told him.

As the maids had gone to fetch tea and there was no one else present, Chia Lien kept darting smiling glances at Second Sister, who lowered her head to hide a smile but did not respond, and he dared not make any further advances. Seeing that she was toying with the handkerchief to which her pouch was fastened, he felt his waist as if groping for his own pouch.

"I've forgotten to bring my pouch of betel-nuts," he said. "Will you let me try one of yours, sister?"

"I have some, but I never give mine away."

Smiling, he approached her to take one; and afraid this would look bad if someone came in, she laughingly tossed him her pouch. Having caught it he emptied it out, chose one half-eaten nut which he popped into his mouth, then pocketed all the others. He was about to return the pouch when the two maids came back with the tea. As Chia Lien sipped his tea, he surreptitiously took off a Han-Dynasty jade pendant carved with nine dragons and tied this to her handkerchief. And when both maids were looking the other way, he tossed the handkerchief back. Second Sister just let it lie and went on drinking her tea, as if she had not noticed. Then the portière behind them swished and in came old Mrs. Yu and Third Sister with two young maids. With a wink Chia Lien signalled to Second Sister to pick up the handkerchief, but she simply paid no attention; and not knowing what she meant by this he felt frantic. He had to step forward to greet the newcomers. As he did so, he glanced back at Second Sister, who was still smiling as if nothing had happened. But looking again he noticed with relief that the handkerchief had vanished. They all sat down now and chatted for a while.

"My sister-in-law says she gave you some silver the other day to keep for her, madam," said Chia Lien. "Today they have to settle an account, so Cousin Chen sent me to fetch it and to see if everything is all right at home."

On hearing this old Mrs. Yu immediately sent Second Sister to fetch the key and get the silver.

Chia Lien went on, "I wanted to come anyway to pay my respects to you and see both the young ladies. It's good of you to have come here, madam, but we're sorry to be putting our two cousins to such trouble too."

"What way is that for close relatives to talk!" she protested. "We've made ourselves at home here. The truth is, sir, that since my husband died we've found it hard to make ends meet, and we've only managed thanks to my son-in-law's help. Now that they have their hands full, we can't help in any other way but at least we can keep an eye on things here for them — how can you talk of putting us to trouble?"

By now Second Sister had brought the silver and given it to her mother, who passed it to Chia Lien. He sent a young maid to fetch a serving-woman.

"Give this to Yu Lu," he ordered her. "Tell him to take it back to the other house and wait for me there."

As the old woman assented and left, they heard Chia Jung's

voice in the courtyard; and presently in he came to pay his respects to the ladies.

"Just now His Lordship your father was asking about you, uncle," he said. "He has some business he wants you to see to and was going to send to the temple to fetch you, but I told him you'd be coming presently. His Lordship told me, if I met you, to ask you to hurry."

As Chia Lien rose to leave he heard Chia Jung tell old Mrs. Yu, "The young man I told you about the other day, grandmother, the one my father has in mind for Second Aunt, has much the same features and build as this uncle of mine. How does he strike you, madam?"

As he said this he pointed slyly at Chia Lien and motioned with his lips at Second Sister. She was too embarrassed to say anything, but her sister scolded:

"What a devilish monkey you are! Have you nothing else to talk about? Just wait, I'm going to pull out that tongue of yours."

She ran towards him but Chia Jung had slipped out, laughing, and now Chia Lien took his leave of them with a smile. In the hall he cautioned the servants not to gamble and drink, then secretly urged Chia Jung to hurry back and take the matter up with his father. Next he took Yu Lu over to the other house to make up the sum of silver needed; and while the steward went off with this he paid his respects to his father and the Lady Dowager.

To return to Chia Jung, when he saw that Yu Lu and Chia Lien had gone for the money and he had nothing to do, he went in again to fool around with his two aunts before leaving.

It was evening by the time he got back to the temple and reported to his father, "The money's been given to Yu Lu. The old lady's much better now and has stopped taking medicine." He then took this opportunity to describe how Chia Lien had told him on the road of his wish to make Second Sister Yu his secondary wife and set up house outside, so that Hsi-feng should know nothing about it.

"This is just because he's worried at having no son," Chia Jung explained. "And as he's seen Second Aunt, who's already related to our family, marrying her would be better than getting some girl from a family about which we know nothing. So uncle repeatedly begged me to propose this to you, father." He omitted to say that this idea had originated with him.

Chia Chen thought it over.

"Actually, it would be just as well," he said finally. "But we don't know whether your Second Aunt would be willing. Go and talk it over first with your old granny tomorrow. Get her to make sure your Second Aunt agrees before we make any decision."

Then, having given his son some further instructions, he went to broach the matter to his wife. Madam Yu, knowing that this would be improper, did her best to dissuade him; but as Chia Chen had already made up his mind and she was in the habit of falling in with his wishes, and as Second Sister was only her step-sister and she was therefore not so responsible for her, she had to let them go ahead with this preposterous scheme.

Accordingly, the first thing the next day, Chia Jung went back to the city to see old Mrs. Yu and tell her his father's proposal. In addition, he expatiated on Chia Lien's good qualities and declared that Hsi-feng was mortally ill and, if they bought a house to live in outside for the time being, after a year or so when Hsi-feng died his Second Aunt could move in as the proper wife. He also described the betrothal presents his father would give, and the wedding ceremony Chia Lien would arrange.

"They'll take you in to live in comfort in your old age, madam," he assured her. "And later they'll see to Third Aunt's marriage too."

He painted such a glowing picture that naturally old Mrs. Yu agreed. Besides, she was wholly dependent on Chia Chen for money, and now that he had proposed this match she would not have to provide any dowry. Furthermore, Chia Lien was a young gentleman from a noble family, ten times better than the wretched Chang family. So she went straight to discuss it with her second daughter.

Second Sister was a coquette. She had already had an affair with Chia Chen, and it was her constant regret that her betrothal to Chang Hua prevented her from making a better marriage. Now that Chia Lien had taken a fancy to her and her brother-in-law himself had proposed the match, of course she was only too willing. She nodded in assent, and this was at once reported to Chia Jung, who went back to inform his father.

The next day they sent to invite Chia Lien to the temple. When Chia Chen told him that old Mrs. Yu had given her consent, he was so overjoyed that he could not thank Chia Chen and Chia Jung enough. They made plans then to send stewards to find a house, have trinkets made and the bride's trousseau prepared, as well as the bed, curtains and other furnishings for the bridal chamber.

Within a few days everything was ready. The house they bought was in Flower Sprig Lane about two *li* behind the Ning and Jung Street. It had over twenty rooms. They also bought two young maids. In addition, Chia Chen installed his own servant Pao Erh and his wife there to wait on Second Sister after she moved in. He then sent for Chang Hua and his father and ordered them to write a deed cancelling the betrothal for old Mrs. Yu.

Now Chang Hua's grandfather had been in charge of the Imperial Farm. After his death Chang Hua's father had taken his place, and as he was a good friend of old Mrs. Yu's first husband, Chang Hua and Second Sister Yu had been engaged to each other before they were born. Later the Changs became involved in a lawsuit which ruined their family, leaving them too poor to feed and clothe themselves well, to say nothing of bringing home a bride for their son. And as old Mrs. Yu had left her first husband's home, the two families had lost touch for more than ten years. When the Chia family's stewards summoned Chang Hua and ordered him to renounce his betrothal to Second Sister Yu, although unwilling he had to agree for fear of the power which Chia Chen and the others wielded. He accordingly wrote a deed cancelling the engagement, and old

Mrs. Yu gave him ten taels of silver, after which the matter was settled.

When Chia Lien saw that all preparations were ready, he chose the third of the next month, an auspicious day, for the wedding, of which more will be told in the next chapter.

Truly:

> Because he lusted after a kinswoman,
> Husband and wife fell out.

CHAPTER 65

A Hen-Pecked Young Profligate Takes
a Concubine in Secret
A Wanton Girl Mends Her Ways and Picks
Herself a Husband

Chia Lien, Chia Chen and Chia Jung, consulting together, soon had everything satisfactorily arranged. On the second of the month, old Mrs. Yu and Third Sister were escorted first to the new house. Old Mrs. Yu saw at a glance that it was not as grand as Chia Jung had claimed; still, it appeared quite respectable, and she and her daughter were both satisfied. Pao Erh and his wife gave them an effusive welcome, assiduously addressing old Mrs. Yu as "Old Madam" or "Old Lady" and Third Sister as "Third Aunt" or "Third Young Mistress."

The next day at dawn when Second Sister was brought over in a white sedan-chair, all the incense, candles and sacrificial paper as well as fine bedding, wine and food were ready. Presently Chia Lien, dressed in mourning, arrived in a small sedan-chair, after which they bowed to Heaven and Earth and burned sacrificial paper. And old Mrs. Yu was most gratified to see Second Sister's new finery, so unlike the trinkets and clothes she had worn at home. The bride was helped into the bridal chamber, where that night she and Chia Lien enjoyed the transports of love.

Chia Lien, more enamoured than ever of his new bride, did all in his power to please her in every way. He forbade Pao Erh and the other servants to refer to her as "Second Mistress." They must all call her the mistress just as he did, as if Hsi-feng had been blotted out of existence. Whenever he went home he merely claimed to have been detained by business in the East Mansion; and Hsi-feng, knowing how close he and Chia Chen were, thought it natural for them to talk things over together and never suspected the truth. As for the domestics, they never interfered in affairs of this kind. In fact, the idlers among them who made a point of learning all the gossip tried to profit by the situation, seizing this chance to make up to Chia Lien; thus none of them was willing to expose him. So Chia Lien's gratitude to Chia Chen knew no bounds.

Every month Chia Lien paid five taels of silver to defray the daily expenses of this new establishment. In his absence, the mother and two daughters ate together; if he came, husband and wife had their meal alone while old Mrs. Yu and Third Sister retired to their own room to eat. Chia Lien also made over to Second Sister the savings he had put aside in the last few years, and when in bed told her freely all about Hsi-feng and her behaviour, promising to take her into the family as soon as Hsi-feng died. This, of course, was what Second Sister hoped for. So their household of a dozen or so people managed very comfortably.

Two months passed in a flash. One evening when Chia Chen came home from Iron Threshold Temple, he decided to pay a visit to the two sisters whom he had not seen for so long. First he sent a page to find out whether Chia Lien was there, and was delighted when the boy reported that he was not. Having dismissed his attendants except for two trusted boys to lead his horse, he went straight to the new house. It was already lighting-up time when he slipped quietly in. The two pages tethered the horse in the stable, then went to the servants' quarters to await further orders.

When Chia Chen entered the house the lamps had just been lit. He first met old Mrs. Yu and Third Sister; then Second Sister came out to greet him, and he addressed her as before as Second Cousin. They sipped tea together and chatted.

"Well, how is the marriage I arranged for you?" asked Chia Chen with a smile. "If you'd missed this chance, you couldn't have found another such man, not even if you'd searched with a lantern! Your elder sister will be coming to call one of these days with presents."

Second Sister ordered wine and food to be prepared. And as they were members of one family now they closed the door and chatted without constraint until Pao Erh came in to pay his respects.

Chia Chen told him, "It's because you're an honest fellow that I sent you here to work. In future I shall give you more important jobs. Don't get drunk outside or make trouble, and I shall reward you well. Your Second Master Lien is busy and there are all sorts of people about in his place, so if you're short of anything here just let me know. After all, we're cousins — it's not as if I were an outsider."

"Yes, sir, I understand," answered Pao Erh. "If I don't do my best, you can cut off my head."

Chia Chen nodded.

"I just want you to understand."

The four of them drank together until Second Sister, sizing up the situation, said to her mother, "I'm afraid to go out alone. Will you come with me?"

Old Mrs. Yu took the hint and withdrew with her, leaving only two young maids there. Then Chia Chen and Third Sister nestled up to each other and flirted so outrageously that the maids were shocked and slipped out, leaving them to amuse themselves however they pleased.

Chia Chen's pages were drinking in the kitchen with Pao Erh, while his wife attended to the cooking, when the two maids burst in, giggling, and asked for drinks.

"Why aren't you waiting on them, sisters?" asked Pao Erh. "Why leave your post and come here? If they want something and nobody's at hand, there's bound to be more trouble."

"You stupid, befuddled turtle!" scolded his wife. "Why not drink yourself silly and pass out? Just keep your balls between your thighs and stretch your carcass out. Whether they call or whether they don't, it's nothing to do with *you*. I'll see to all that. Anyway no drop of rain will spatter *your* head."

Now Pao Erh owed all his good fortune to his wife, and his recent good luck was even more thanks to her, for in this cushy job he had nothing to do but make money and get drunk, yet

Chia Lien and the rest never reprimanded him. He therefore obeyed her implicitly, as if she were his mother. And so having drunk enough, he went to bed. His wife kept the maids and pages company drinking, and made up to them in the hope that they would speak well of her to Chia Chen. But as they were enjoying themselves they heard a sudden knocking on the gate; and when Pao Erh's wife hurried out to open it, she saw Chia Lien dismounting from his horse. He asked if all was well.

She quietly told him, "The Elder Master is here, in the west courtyard."

When Chia Lien heard that he went to his bedroom and found Second Sister there with her mother. At sight of him, they looked a little put out, but he pretended not to notice.

"Bring some wine, quick," he ordered. "After a couple of drinks we can go to bed. I'm tired out."

Second Sister at once stepped forward with a smile to take his outer garments and offer him tea, then asked about this and that. Chia Lien was so pleased that he itched to make love to her. Soon Pao Erh's wife brought in wine which the two of them drank, while his mother-in-law went back to her room, sending one of the young maids to wait on them.

When Chia Lien's trusted page Lung-erh went to stable the horse he discovered another there and, looking closely, recognized it as Chia Chen's. Understanding the situation, he too went to the kitchen where he found Hsi-erh and Shou-erh sitting drinking. At sight of him, they exchanged knowing glances.

"You've come just at the right time," they chortled. "We couldn't overtake the master's horse, and as we were afraid of being caught out after curfew, we came here to spend the night."

Lung-erh chuckled, "Well, there's plenty of room on the *kang*, just lie down as you like. Second Master sent me to bring the monthly allowance to the mistress, so I shan't be going back either."

"We've drunk too much," said Hsi-erh. "You must have a cup now."

But as Lung-erh sat down and raised his cup, they heard a sudden commotion in the stable where the two horses, unwilling to be tethered together, had started kicking each other. Lung-erh hastily put down his cup and rushed out to soothe them, coming back after he had managed to tie Chia Lien's horse up elsewhere.

"You three stay here," Pao Erh's wife told them. "There's tea ready made for you. I must leave you now." With that she left, closing the door behind her.

Hsi-erh after a few cups was already glassy-eyed. By the time Lung-erh and Shou-erh had locked the door they saw that he had passed out on the *kang*. They gave him a shove.

"Get up and move over, good brother," they urged. "If you hog all the space, where are *we* to sleep?"

"Must play fair tonight, each get a good fuck," Hsi-erh mumbled. "Anyone who poses as proper — I'll fuck his mother."

The other two seeing that he was drunk ignored him, simply putting out the light, then lying down to sleep as best they could.

The commotion made by the horses had alarmed Second Sister, who tried to distract Chia Lien with conversation. After a few cups, feeling randy, he ordered the maids to clear away the wine and dishes, then closed the door to undress. Second Sister was wearing nothing but a scarlet jacket. With her hair hanging loose, her cheeks flushed, she looked even lovelier than in the daytime.

Throwing his arms around her, Chia Lien declared, "Everyone calls that shrew of mine good-looking, but to me she isn't fit even to pick up your shoes."

"I may have good looks but I've got a bad name," she answered. "So it seems not to be good-looking would be better."

"Why do you say that?" he asked. "I don't understand."

"You all think me silly," she told him, shedding tears. "But I have my wits about me. Now I've been your wife for two months, and already in that short time I've learned that you're no fool either. I'll be yours dead or alive. Being married to you, I'll depend on you all my life, so of course I won't keep any secrets from you. *I'm* provided for, but what about my sister? Seems to me things can't go on the way they are now. We must think of some long-term plan."

"Don't worry," chuckled Chia Lien. "I'm not the jealous type. I know all that happened in the past, you don't have to be afraid. As your brother-in-law is my cousin, you naturally don't like to broach the subject. It would be better for me to make the proposal."

So he went to the west courtyard and saw through the window that the room was brightly lit and Chia Chen and Third Sister were drinking and enjoying themselves inside. Chia Lien opened the door and went in.

"So you're here, sir," he said with a smile. "I've come to pay my respects."

Chia Chen, too embarrassed to speak, simply stood up and waved him to a seat.

Chia Lien laughed. "Why look so worried? As cousins we've always been on the closest terms. I can't thank you enough for all you've done for me. If you take offence now, I shall be most upset. Please behave just as you did before. Otherwise I shall never dare come here again, not even if it means having no son." He made as if to kneel down.

Chia Chen hastily raised him.

"I'll do whatever you say, cousin," he assured him.

Then Chia Lien called for wine, saying, "I'll have a couple of drinks with Elder Cousin." Taking Third Sister by the hand he added, "Come and drink a cup with me too."

Chia Chen laughed.

"What a character you are! I shall have to empty this cup." And he tossed it off.

Third Sister jumped on to the *kang* then and pointed at Chia Lien.

"Don't try to get round me with your glib tongue!" she cried. "We'd better keep clear of each other. I've seen plenty of shadow-plays in my time; anyway don't tear the screen to show what's behind the scenes. You must be befuddled if you think we don't know what goes on in your house. Now after spending a bit of your stinking money, you two figure you can amuse yourselves with us as if we were prostitutes! Well, you're out in your calculations.

"I know your wife's such a termagant that you tricked my sister into coming here to be your second wife; but you can't beat a stolen gong. And I've a good mind to call on this Madam Hsi-feng, to see what sort of prodigy she is. If everyone treats us right we can all live at peace. But if anyone takes the least liberties, I'm quite capable of tearing out both your stinking guts, then fighting it out with that shrew. If I don't, I'm not Third Mistress Yu! Who's afraid of drinking? Let's go ahead and drink."

She picked up the wine-pot to fill a cup and drank half of this herself, then throwing one arm round Chia Lien's neck started pouring the rest down his throat.

"I've already drunk with your cousin," she said. "Now let's *us* play at being sweethearts."

This gave Chia Lien such a scare that he sobered up. Chia Chen, for his part, had never dreamed that Third Sister could act so brazenly. The two cousins, for all their experience of loose women, now found themselves struck dumb by this chit of a girl.

Then Third Sister cried out, "Ask my sister in! If you want fun, let's all *four* of us have fun together. As the saying goes, 'Perks should be kept inside the family.' You're cousins, we're sisters; none of us are outsiders — come on!"

Second Sister who had joined them began to feel embarrassed, and Chia Chen wanted to sneak away, but Third Sister would not let him. By now Chia Chen regretted having come. He had had no idea that Third Sister would behave like this, making it impossible for him and Chia Lien to have their way with her.

Now Third Sister wound her hair in a loose knot, her scarlet jacket, half unbuttoned, disclosing her leek-green bodice and snow-white skin. Below she was wearing green trousers and red slippers, and she now kicked her dainty feet against each other, now stretched them out side by side — never still for a moment — while her pendant eardrops swung this way and that. Under the lamplight her willowy eyebrows curved enticingly, her fragrant lips glowed red as cinnabar, and her eyes, bright as autumn pools, sparkled even more seductively after drinking. To Chia Chen and Chia Lien it seemed that not only did she surpass her elder sister but that none of the girls they had ever seen, whether high or low, noble or humble, had possessed such bewitching charm. Both were too dazed and too intoxicated even to lift a finger. Her wanton coquetting had deprived them of speech.

Gesticulating and making eyes at them, Third Sister Yu had not put herself out to excite them, yet already the two men were at a loss to know which way to look, and had not so much as a word to say for themselves, so befuddled were they both by wine and lust. Holding forth loudly and freely, she heaped abuse on them, taunting and teasing them just as she pleased, as if *they* were prostitutes called in by her instead of men who had wanted to seduce her. Finally, sated with wine, having worked off her high spirits she drove them out, closed the door behind them, and retired to bed.

After this, whenever the maids were remiss in any way, Third Sister would loose a flood of abuse against Chia Chen, Chia Lien and Chia Jung, accusing them of cheating a widow and her two fatherless daughters. Thereafter, Chia Chen hardly dared to come back unless Third Sister happened to be in the mood to send a page boy secretly to fetch him. And when he arrived he had to let her have her way.

Third Sister was in fact a born eccentric. Being good-looking and romantic, she liked to dress strikingly and behave more lasciviously and seductively than all other girls to infatuate men until they were fairly drooling, unable either to approach her or stay away. She delighted in keeping them on a string like this. Her mother and sister tried in vain to dissuade her.

"How silly you are, sister," she would retort. "Why let those two reincarnated apes defile our precious bodies? Why act so helpless? Besides, that wife of his is a real terror. As long as this is kept from her, we're all right. If she comes to hear of it one day, she won't take it lying down and there's bound to be a big row. Who knows which of you will survive? If I don't have some fun now treating them like dirt, by the time this breaks it'll be too late to regret it — I'll be left with nothing then but a bad name."

They realized then it was no use trying to persuade her, and gave up.

And now Third Sister started demanding the best of everything, whether food or clothing. When silver trinkets were made for her she wanted gold as well; when pearls were given her she asked for gems; if a fat goose was served her she demanded duck, and unless humoured would overturn the table. If her clothes were not just as she wanted, regardless of whether they were silk or satin, new or old, she would cut them up, swearing as she tore them to shreds. So not for a day did Chia Chen have any satisfaction. Instead, he squandered large sums of money for nothing.

Chia Lien when he went there just stayed in Second Sister's rooms, and he was beginning to regret this set-up. But Second Sister had an affectionate disposition. To her, Chia Lien was her lord and master for life, she doted on him. As regards gentleness and obedience, she was ten times better than Hsi-feng, for she would consult him on everything and never dared make any decisions herself or trust to her own better judgement. As regards her looks, conversation and behaviour, she was superior too. Yet although she had now reformed, because of her previous slip-ups she had been labelled a wanton, and so her other good qualities counted for nothing.

However, Chia Lien said, "Who's perfect? If you recognize your mistakes and correct them, that's all right." Thus he never mentioned her loose living in the past, content to dwell on her present goodness. And he stuck to her like glue, like a fish to water, vowing from his heart to be true to her his whole life long, having lost all interest in Hsi-feng and Ping-erh.

When they shared the same pillow and quilt, Second Sister often urged him, "Why not talk it over with your cousin Chen, and choose some man you know to marry my sister? It's no good keeping her here indefinitely, because sooner or later there's bound to be trouble, and then what shall we do?"

"I did mention this to him the other day," said Chia Lien.

"But he can't bear the idea of giving her up. I pointed out, 'What's the good of fat mutton if it's too hot to eat? The rose is lovely but prickly. How can we control her? We'd better find someone and marry her off.' He just hemmed and hawed, then changed the subject. So what do you expect me to do?"

"Don't worry," said Second Sister. "Tomorrow we'll first tackle my sister. If she's willing, we'll let her go on making rows until he has no choice but to marry her off."

"That's the idea," agreed Chia Lien.

The next day Second Sister prepared a feast and Chia Lien stayed in. At noon, they invited Third Sister and her mother over and made them take the seats of honour. Third Sister guessed their intention, and when their cups had been filled three times, without waiting for her sister to speak she said tearfully:

"You must have invited me today, sister, for some important reason. I'm no fool, and there's no need to harp on my shameful conduct in the past. I'm aware of it; it's no use talking about it. You've found yourself a good niche now, and so has mother, and it's only right and proper that I should look for a home of my own too. But marriage is a serious business; it's for life, not a joking matter. I've had a change of heart and mean to turn over a new leaf, but I must find someone congenial before I'll marry. If your choice, no matter how rich, talented and handsome, wasn't a man after my own heart then my whole life would be wasted."

"That's no problem," said Chia Lien. "You can make your own choice. And we'll provide the whole dowry, so that mother needn't worry about that either."

"Sister knows who I mean," sobbed Third Sister. "I don't have to name him."

"Who is he?" Chia Lien asked Second Sister, but she could not think who it could be.

While the others were wondering, Chia Lien, sure that he had guessed, clapped his hands.

"I know who it is! He's certainly not bad. You've made a good choice."

"Who is it?" asked Second Sister.

"It must be Pao-yu," he chuckled. "No one else would do for her."

Second Sister and old Mrs. Yu thought he had guessed right, but Third Sister spat in disgust.

"If there were ten of us sisters, would we all have to marry your brothers and cousins?" she asked. "Are there no men outside your family?"

This puzzled them all. Who else could it be? they wondered.

"Forget about the present, sister," said Third Sister. "Just think back five years and you'll know."

As they were talking, Chia Lien's trusted page Hsing-erh came in to report, "The old master wants you to go over at once, sir. I told him you'd gone to see your uncle, then came straight to fetch you."

"Did they ask about me at home yesterday?" demanded Chia Lien hastily.

"I told Madam that you were at the family temple making plans for the hundredth day sacrifice with Lord Chen, so you probably couldn't come home."

Chia Lien promptly called for his horse and rode off, accompanied by Lung-erh, leaving Hsing-erh behind to attend to other things. Second Sister ordered two dishes and made him drink a goblet of wine as he squatted by the *kang* while she questioned him about the Chia family. How old was Madam Lien? Was she really a terror? How old were the old lady and Lady Wang? How many girls were there in the household? Beaming as he ate and drank beside the *kang*, Hsing-erh regaled old Mrs. Yu and her daughters with a detailed account of the Jung Mansion.

"I keep watch at the inner gate," he said. "We have two shifts, four men in each, eight altogether. Some of us are trusted by Madam, some by the master. We're careful not to annoy *her* men, but they're always provoking *us*.

"You ask about our mistress. Well, I shouldn't really be telling you this, madam, but she's crafty and vicious with a sharp, quick tongue. Second Master is all right, but he's under her thumb. Still Miss Ping-erh in their apartments is good-natured; even though she's on Madam Lien's side, behind her back she often does people good turns. If we do anything wrong, Madam won't let us off; but if we beg Ping-erh for help she smooths things over.

"There's no one now in the whole household, barring Their Ladyships, who doesn't hate her. We just make a show of liking her out of fear. That's because she looks down on everyone and just sucks up to the old lady and mistress. Whatever she says goes, and no one dares stop her. She tries to save up piles of silver so that Their Ladyships will praise her for being a good manager; but of course we servants are the ones to suffer while she takes all the credit.

"If anything good happens, she rushes to take the credit before anyone else can report it. If anything bad happens, or if she herself makes some mistake, she ducks and shifts the blame on to other people, stirring up more trouble too on the side. Now even her own mother-in-law, the Elder Mistress, can't stand her, calling her a fair-weather sparrow, or a black hen that neglects her own nest but keeps butting in everywhere else. If not for the old lady's backing, her mother-in-law would have fetched her back long ago."

Second Sister smiled.

"The way you're talking behind her back makes me wonder what you'll say about *me* in future. As I'm lower in status you can lay it on even thicker!"

Hsing-erh hastily fell on his knees.

"If I do, may a thunderbolt strike me dead!" he swore. "If we'd had the luck from the start to have a mistress like you, we wouldn't have had to put up with so many beatings and cursings or to live in fear and trembling all the time. Why, all our master's servants keep praising you, behind your back as well, for your goodness and kindness to us. We've been talking of asking our master to let us come here to wait on you, madam."

"You monkey!" she laughed. "Get up quickly. I was only joking — you needn't be afraid. Why should you all come here? I've been meaning, actually, to call on your mistress."

Hsing-erh threw up his hands in dismay. "On *no* account

do that, madam. Take my word for it, it will be best for you never to meet her all your life. She'll give you sweet talk when there's hatred in her heart, she's so double-faced and tricky. All the time she's smiling she tries to trip you up, making a show of great warmth while she stabs you in the back. That's the way she is. I'm afraid not even Third Aunt could outtalk her, so how could a gentle, kindly lady like you be a match for her?"

"If I treat her politely what can she do to me?"

"It's not that I'm talking wildly because I'm drinking. Even if you treated her with respect, once she saw you were better looking and more popular with people, how could she let you off? If other women are jealous, she's a hundred times so. If the master happens to cast a second glance at any maid, she's liable to make a row then and there. Though Miss Ping-erh's part of their household, and the master may be allowed to sleep with her once a year, or once in two years, she keeps nagging until Ping-erh loses her temper and makes a scene. 'I didn't ask to be his concubine,' she says. 'When I was unwilling you called me disobedient. You forced me into it, yet now you treat me like this!' Then, generally, she pipes down and even asks Miss Ping-erh's pardon."

"There you're lying," said Second Sister with a laugh. "How could a hellion like that be afraid of a concubine?"

"As the proverb says," he retorted, " 'everyone has to listen to reason.' Miss Ping-erh has been her maid since she was a girl, being one of the four she brought here at the time of her marriage. The rest got married or died, leaving only this favourite maid, so she decided to make her a concubine. That was so as to show how broad-minded she was and also to stop the master from chasing after loose women outside.

"There's another reason too. It's a rule in our family that when the young gentlemen reach teen age, before they're married, two girls are always assigned to wait on them. Second Master had two, but within half a year of *her* arrival she picked fault with them and sent them both packing. Although no one could very well say anything, she knew it didn't look good, so she forced Ping-erh to become his concubine. Ping-erh's really a good sort. Instead of holding this against her or stirring up trouble between husband and wife, she's completely loyal to her mistress — that's why she's kept on."

"So that's the way it is," remarked Second Sister. "But I hear you've another mistress who's a widow, and several young ladies too. Why do they put up with her if she's such a shrew?"

Hsing-erh clapped his hands.

"You don't understand, I see. That widow, Madam Chu, is such a kindly soul that she's nicknamed Great Bodhisattva. Besides, the rule in our family is so strict that widows never attend to affairs: all that's expected of them is to live quietly and chastely. But as there happen to be so many young ladies, they've been put in her charge and it's her job to superintend their studies and teach them needlework and moral principles. She doesn't have to bother about anything else. It's only because of Madam Lien's recent illness and because there's so much to be done that Madam Chu's helping out for a few days. Still, there isn't much she can do, she simply sticks to the old ways, not throwing her weight about like Madam Lien to show how smart she is.

"As for our eldest young lady, it goes without saying, if she wasn't so fine in every way she wouldn't have been blessed with her present good fortune. Our second young lady, the one we call Dumbbell, won't let out a peep even if she's pricked with a needle. The third has the nickname Rose."

"Why's that?" asked the two Yu sisters.

Hsing-erh chuckled.

"Everyone loves roses, they're so red and fragrant. But they're prickly too. And she's wonderfully clever. The pity is she's not Lady Wang's own child but 'a phoenix from a crow's nest.' The fourth, who's still young, is actually Lord Chen's younger sister; but because she lost her mother when she was a child, the old lady made Lady Wang adopt her and bring her up; and she never bothers about family affairs either.

"Then, you may not know, madam, apart from our own young ladies we have two others, the likes of whom are seldom seen on earth or in heaven. One's Lin Tai-yu — her mother was the old lady's daughter. In looks and figure she's just as lovely as Third Aunt, with a bellyful of book learning besides; but she's always falling ill. Even in hot weather like this she wears lined clothes, and a puff of wind can blow her over. Being a disrespectful lot, behind her back we all call her the Sick Beauty.

"Then there's Aunt Hsueh's daughter Pao-chai, with a skin so white she looks as if made of snow. Whenever we catch a glimpse of them coming out of the gate or getting into a carriage, or in the courtyard, we all seem to be possessed by ghosts or gods! The sight of either of them takes our breath away."

Second Sister laughed.

"A big family like yours has strict rules. Even though you were taken into service there as children, when you happen to meet any of the young ladies you ought to make yourselves scarce."

Hsing-erh brushed this aside.

"It's not that. If you talk about the proper etiquette, it goes without saying we should keep out of the way. But even when we do we still hold our breath because, if we let out a gasp, it might blow Miss Lin over; or being warm, might melt Miss Hsueh."

Everybody in the room burst out laughing at this. To know what followed read the next chapter.

CHAPTER 66

A Girl in Love Is Rejected and
Kills Herself
A Cold-Hearted Man Repents and
Turns to Religion

Pao Erh's wife slapped Hsing-erh playfully.

"How you do twist the truth and exaggerate!" she teased. "The senseless way you talk sounds as if you were Pao-yu's servant, not Second Master's."

Before Second Sister could ask any other questions, Third Sister put in, "By the way, what does he do, that Pao-yu of yours, apart from studying?"

"Don't ask, aunt," Hsing-erh chuckled. "If I tell you, you won't believe me. Big as he is, he's unique in never having had any proper schooling. All earlier generations of our family right down to Second Master studied hard for years; he's the only one who won't study, and he's the old lady's pet. At first his father tried to discipline him, but he's long since given that up.

"Pao-yu carries on the whole time like a lunatic, talking in a way that no one understands, and what he gets up to goodness only knows. He's handsome and is taken for an intelligent boy, but for all he looks so smart he's actually muddle-headed, with nothing to say for himself in company. The only good thing about him is that though he's never been to a proper school he's managed to learn to read. He never studies books or practises military arts; and he doesn't like meeting strangers, instead he just loves to fool about with the maids.

"He has no sense of what's fitting either. When he sees *us*, if he's in the mood he'll play around with us quite forgetting his station; if he's not in the mood he'll go off by himself, ignoring everyone else. If we're sitting or lying about when he turns up, and we pay no attention to him, he never ticks us off. So nobody's afraid of him; we know we can behave just as we please."

"When your master's lenient you run him down; if he were strict you'd complain," said Third Sister with a smile. "That shows what a troublesome lot you are."

"He made a good impression on *us*," remarked Second Sister. "We didn't know he was like this. What a pity when he's such a handsome boy."

"Don't believe the nonsense he talks, sister," said Third Sister. "We've met Pao-yu several times. The way he behaves and speaks does seem rather effeminate, but that's because he spends all his time in the inner apartments. You can't call him muddle-headed. Remember when we were in mourning, that day the monks filed round the coffin? We girls were all standing there and he stepped in front of us, standing in our way. People said he had no manners and should know better; but later didn't he tell us in confidence, 'You know, sisters, it's not that I had no sense of respect, but those monks are so dirty I was afraid you'd find their stench overpowering.'

"Then he was drinking tea, and you wanted some too. When that old woman took his bowl to pour some for you, he said at once, 'I've dirtied that bowl; you must wash it first.' From these two incidents, viewed dispassionately, I saw how obliging he is towards us girls — he knows how to make himself agreeable to us. It just doesn't seem right to outsiders; that's why they can't understand him."

"It sounds as if the two of you are already of one mind," Second Sister chuckled. "How would it be if we were to betroth you to him?"

Inhibited by Hsing-erh's presence, Third Sister just lowered her head and went on cracking melon-seeds.

"As far as looks and behaviour go, they'd make a fine-couple," chortled Hsing-erh. "Only he's already made his choice, although it hasn't yet been announced. It's bound to be Miss Lin. Nothing has been done so far, as she's so delicate and they're both still young; but in another two or three years, as soon as the old lady says the word it will certainly be settled."

As they were chatting, Lung-erh came back to report, "The old master has some business, something extremely important and confidential, that he's sending Second Master to Pinganchou to attend to. He's to set out in a few days and the whole trip there and back will take more than a fortnight. So he can't come back today. He hopes the old mistress and Second Aunt will see to that matter right away, so that he can make the final decision when he comes tomorrow." This said, he went off with Hsing-erh.

Second Sister ordered the gate to be closed and they turned in early, but she spent most of the night questioning her sister.

The next day it was after noon before Chia Lien arrived.

"Why be in such a hurry to come when you've other important business?" Second Sister asked him. "You mustn't delay your journey on my account."

"It's not all that important," he told her. "The nuisance is I've got to make a long trip, starting early next month, and I shan't be back for a fortnight."

"Well, just go with an easy mind. You needn't worry about anything here. My sister's not the type that keeps changing her mind. She says she's going to turn over a new leaf, and she'll be as good as her word. She's already made her choice of a man. All you need do is to fall in with her wishes."

"Who is he?" asked Chia Lien.

"He's not here now, and there's no knowing when he'll come back. But she's made an intelligent choice. If he stays away for a year, she'll wait for a year, she says. If he doesn't return for ten years, she'll wait for ten years. If he's dead and never comes back, she'll gladly shave off her hair and become a nun, fasting and chanting sutras all her life."

"Who can the fellow be that has won her heart so completely?"

"It's a long story," said Second Sister with a smile. "Five

years ago, when it was our grandmother's birthday, my mother took us there to offer congratulations. They'd invited a troupe of amateur actors, among them a certain Liu Hsiang-lien who liked to play the young hero's part in operas. She took such a fancy to him, she now declares he's the only man for her. Last year we heard that he'd got into trouble and run away. We don't know whether he has ever come back."

"Well, I never!" exclaimed Chia Lien. "So that's who it is. I was wondering what sort of fellow he could be. Yes, she's made a good choice. But you know this Second Master Liu, for all he's so handsome, is cold and stand-offish. He has no time for most people but happens to get on splendidly with Pao-yu. Last year after he beat up that fool Hsueh Pan he left, feeling too embarrassed to see us, and we don't know where he's gone. Some people say he's returned. I suppose we can ask Pao-yu's pages to find out. If he hasn't come back and is still drifting about, Heaven knows how many years he may stay away. Your sister may wait in vain."

"No, my sister's always as good as her word," she assured him. "Just let her have her way."

At this point Third Sister joined them.

"Believe me, brother-in-law, I'm not one of those who don't say what they think," she declared. "I mean what I say. If Mr. Liu comes I'll marry him. Until then I'll fast, chant sutras and look after my mother while waiting for him to come and marry me, even if I have to wait a hundred years. If he never comes, I'll go and become a nun." Drawing a jade pin from her hair she broke it in two, exclaiming, "If I've said a single word that isn't true, may I end up like this pin!"

This said, she went back to her room. And after that she was, indeed, most correct in her speech and behaviour.

There was nothing Chia Lien could do. Having discussed some family business with Second Sister, he went home to tell Hsi-feng about his trip, then sent to ask Ming-yen whether Liu Hsiang-lien had returned or not.

"I don't know," said Ming-yen. "Probably not. Otherwise I would have heard."

And Liu's neighbours when questioned said he had never come back. So Chia Lien had to pass on this information to Second Sister.

As the time for his departure approached he announced that he was leaving two days early, but in fact he spent two nights in Second Sister's place, starting his journey secretly from there. He observed that Third Sister's behaviour had indeed changed out of all recognition, and as Second Sister was managing the house diligently and prudently he had no need to worry.

He left the city early in the morning and took the highway to Pinganchou. He travelled all day, stopping only to refresh himself when he was hungry or thirsty, staying in inns at night, and he had been three days on the way when a caravan of pack-horses came towards him escorted by a dozen or so men on horseback. As they drew near he saw to his astonishment that among them were Hsueh Pan and Liu Hsiang-lien. At once he spurred his horse forward to meet them, and after exchanging the usual courtesies they chose an inn in which to rest and chat.

Chia Lien said, "After the two of you fell out we were very eager to patch it up between you, but Brother Liu had vanished without a trace. How come you're together today?"

"Wonders never cease," said Hsueh Pan. "I and my assistants bought some goods and started back to the capital this spring. All went well till the other day when we reached Pinganchou and a band of brigands seized everything we had. Then along came Brother Liu in the nick of time to drive the brigands away, rescue our goods and save our lives into the bargain. When he wouldn't accept anything for his help, we became sworn brothers and have been travelling together. From now on we shall be like real blood-brothers. But we shall part company at the crossroad in front, as he has to go two hundred *li* farther south to visit an aunt of his. I shall go to the capital first to finish my business, then find a house for him and a suitable wife, so that we can all settle down there."

"If that's the case," exclaimed Chia Lien, "we've been worrying needlessly for several days." As Hsueh Pan had spoken of finding a wife for Hsiang-lien, he hastened to continue, "I've got the very bride for him, a splendid match for Brother Liu." He went on to explain how he had married Second Sister Yu and now wanted to find a husband for her younger sister, omitting only to add that Liu was Third Sister's own choice. He then cautioned Hsueh Pan, "Mind you don't tell the family. Just wait until she has a son, then of course they'll have to know."

Hsueh Pan was delighted.

"You should have done that long ago," he said. "It serves Cousin Hsi-feng right."

"You're talking nonsense again," put in Hsiang-lien with a smile. "You'd better shut up."

"In that case," said Hsueh Pan, changing the subject, "we must fix up this match."

"It's been my intention all along," Hsiang-lien told them, "to marry only an outstanding beauty. But as this proposal comes from my honourable elder brothers, I shan't insist on that. I'll agree to whatever you suggest."

"Words don't carry conviction," Chia Lien rejoined. "But once you see her, Brother Liu, you'll realize that this sister-in-law of mine is a matchless beauty."

Hsiang-lien was overjoyed by this assurance.

"If that's so," he said, "when I've called on my aunt, in less than a fortnight I'll come to the capital and we can settle everything then. How's that?"

"We're both men of our word," replied Chia Lien. "But you're such a rolling stone, always on the move, I don't like leaving it undecided. If you drift away now and don't come back, what's to become of her? You'd better let me have some betrothal token."

"A true man never goes back on his word. I'm not rich and I'm in the middle of a journey, so where would I get a betrothal token?"

"I've something suitable," Hsueh Pan cut in. "Just take it, Second Brother."

"I don't want gold or silk," said Chia Lien. "What I have

in mind is one of Brother Liu's personal possessions; it doesn't have to be anything valuable. I'll just take it as a pledge."

"Very well, then," agreed Hsiang-lien. "The only things I have with me, apart from this sword which I need in self-defence are a pair of 'duck and drake' swords in my luggage — they're a family heirloom which I never use but always keep with me. You can take them as a pledge. However much of a wanderer I am, I'd never give up these swords."

After that they drank a few more cups, then mounted their horses, took their leave of each other and went their different ways.

Truly:

> Generals, not dismounting from their horses,
> Gallop off to their destinations.

After Chia Lien reached Pinganchou he called on the governor to settle his business, and was told to come back again before the tenth month. The very next day he hurriedly started back, and as soon as he got home went to see Second Sister.

Since his departure Second Sister had been running her household most prudently, staying in every day behind closed doors and taking no interest in outside affairs. And Third Sister had proved her iron resolution: apart from waiting on her mother and sister she had kept to herself, doing her share of work every day and sleeping alone at night on her lonely pillow. Although unaccustomed to such a solitary life she avoided all company, simply longing for Liu Hsiang-lien's early return, so that the main affair of her life could be settled.

When Chia Lien saw how things were, he was very pleased with Second Sister's virtuous conduct. After the usual civilities had been exchanged, he described his encounter with Liu Hsiang-lien on the road and taking out the pair of swords passed them to Third Sister. She looked at the dragon and serpent designs on the sheath which was studded with bright pearls and jewels, then drew out the two swords, identical in size, one engraved with the word "duck," the other "drake." The blades had the cold gleam of two autumn streams. Overjoyed, she hastily took them to her chamber to hang them on the wall over her bed. Every day she would feast her eyes on them, happy that her future was provided for.

After Chia Lien had spent two days there, he went to report on his mission to his father, then returned home to see his family. By now Hsi-feng was well enough to attend to affairs and get about again. When Chia Lien told Chia Chen about Third Sister's engagement his cousin showed little interest, as he had recently found himself a new mistress and given up calling on the Yu sisters. He was willing to let Chia Lien do as he pleased. But suspecting that the latter might be unable to defray all the expenses, he gave him thirty taels of silver which Chia Lien passed on to Second Sister to prepare her sister's trousseau.

Liu Hsiang-lien did not come to the capital till the eighth month. When he called on Aunt Hsueh and Hsueh Ko he learned that Hsueh Pan, being unaccustomed to the rigours of travel and a different climate, had fallen ill as soon as he arrived home and was still being treated by doctors. Hearing of Hsiang-lien's arrival, he invited him into his bedroom.

Full of gratitude for the good turn Hsiang-lien had done them, Aunt Hsueh let bygones be bygones, both she and her son thanking him most profusely. They went on to speak of the wedding, all the preparations for which were complete except for the choice of an auspicious day. Hsiang-lien, in turn, was loud in his thanks.

The next day he called on Pao-yu, and meeting again they felt so at home with each other that Hsiang-lien asked for more details about Chia Lien's secret marriage to a second wife.

"I only heard about it from Ming-yen and the others," Pao-yu told him. "And it wasn't my business to interfere. I also heard from Ming-yen that Cousin Lien was very anxious to find you — I don't know what for."

Hsiang-lien explained all that had happened on the road.

"Congratulations!" cried Pao-yu. "You'd be hard put to it to find a lovelier girl. She's really ravishing, just the right match for you."

"If she's so lovely she ought to have lots of suitors; why should he single me out? It's not as if the two of us were close friends or he has any special concern for me. In our brief meeting on the road he kept pressing me to agree to this engagement. Why should the girl's family be in such a hurry? I couldn't help having misgivings, and soon started regretting having given him my swords as a pledge. That's why I thought of asking you just what's behind this."

"You're a smart fellow," answered Pao-yu. "Once you've given your pledge how can you start having second thoughts? You always said you wanted a ravishing beauty, and now you've got one. Isn't that good enough? Why be so suspicious?"

"If you didn't know about Chia Lien's secret marriage, how do you know that she's so beautiful?"

"She's one of the two daughters of Madam Yu's step-mother, old Mrs. Yu, by her first marriage. I saw a lot of them for a couple of months, so of course I know. She and her sister are really a pair of beauties."

Hsiang-lien stamped his foot.

"That's no good then! I can't go through with it. The only clean things in that East Mansion of yours are those two stone lions at the gate. Even the cats and dogs there are unclean. I don't want to be a cuckold and take someone else's leavings."

Pao-yu blushed. And Hsiang-lien, regretting his tactlessness, made haste to bow.

"I deserve death for talking such nonsense. But do at any rate tell me what her character's like."

"If you know so much already, why ask *me*? I may not be clean myself either."

"I forgot myself just now," said Hsiang-lien with a smile. "Please don't make such an issue of it."

"Why mention it again?" retorted Pao-yu. "This makes it seem that you take it seriously."

Hsiang-lien took his leave then with a bow and left. He thought of going to see Hsueh Pan, but reflected that as the latter was unwell and so irascible at the best of times he had better

up in nature, and the fortunes of men may change overnight.' They can't have been predestined to be husband and wife. You're upset, mother, because he rescued my brother, and if all had gone well between them of course it would have been only right for you to help with the wedding. Now that one of them is dead and the other's gone, it seems to me you'd better let things be. Don't grieve so much for them that you injure your health.

"Now quite a time's passed since brother came back from the south, and all the goods he brought ought to be disposed of. The assistants who went with him worked hard for several months. Why not talk it over with brother, and invite them to a meal to express our gratitude? Otherwise they may think we're lacking in manners."

In came Hsueh Pan then, tears still in his eyes. As he stepped through the door he clapped his hands together.

"Mother," he blurted out, "have you heard about Brother Liu and Third Sister Yu?"

"I heard talk of it in the Garden, and your sister and I were speaking about it just now."

"Isn't it extraordinary?"

"It certainly is. Why should a smart young man like Master Liu suddenly do such a foolish thing, going off with a Taoist priest? I suppose it's because he was pre-ordained in some former existence to become a saint that he was so ready to listen to the priest. As you were such good friends and he lived all alone here, with no parents or brothers, you ought to make a thorough search for him. How could that lame and crazy priest go very far? He must be hiding in one of the temples near by."

"That's exactly what I thought," replied Hsueh Pan. "As soon as I got this news I took my servants out to search high and low, but not a trace of him could we find. And everyone we asked said they hadn't seen them. I was so frantic that, before coming back, I faced northwest and burst out howling." As he said this his eyes brimmed with tears again.

"If you've made a search and failed to find him, you've done your duty as a friend," said his mother. "After all, his renouncing the world may not be a bad thing. You'd better not worry too much. For one thing, you've your business to attend to; and then you should make preparations in good time for your own wedding. Our family's short-handed and, as the proverb says, 'A slow sparrow should make an early start.' We don't want to find, when the time comes, that we've forgotten this, that and the other, so that people laugh at us.

"Another thing, your sister says you've been home nearly a month now, so presumably those goods are all disposed of. You ought to entertain the assistants who went on the trip with you to a feast, to thank them for their hard work. Of course, they're our employees and we pay them; still, they're our protégés too. And, after all, they accompanied you on a journey of one or two thousand *li*, working hard for four or five months and sharing your hardships and dangers on the road."

"You're quite right, mother," agreed Hsueh Pan. "Sister thinks of everything. It did occur to me too, but these days I've been so busy dispatching goods, my head's been in a whirl; and the last few days I've been rushing about arranging Brother Liu's wedding — not that anything's come of it — and that's held up our own business. Suppose we fix on tomorrow or the day after and send out invitations?"

"Just decide on any day you please," said his mother.

As she was speaking a servant came in to report, "Manager Chang's assistants have brought two cases. They say these are things the master bought for himself, not included in the bill of goods. They meant to bring them over earlier but couldn't get at them as they were beneath other cases. Yesterday they finished dispatching the goods; that's why they've only sent them over today."

Meanwhile two servant-boys had brought in two big palm-fibre cases, crated with spars.

"*Aiya!*" exclaimed Hsueh Pan. "How could I be so muddle-headed! These are things I bought specially for you, mother and sister, but as I forgot to bring them home they've had to send them."

Pao-chai teased, "You say these were bought specially, yet

you left them lying there for over a fortnight. If they had been something not specially bought, I suppose you wouldn't have given them to us until the end of the year. You're altogether too casual."

"I guess those brigands on the road scared the wits out of me, and they haven't come back to my noddle yet," he said, raising a laugh. Then turning to the servants, he ordered, "Go and tell the messengers I've received these cases and they can go back now."

Aunt Hsueh and Pao-chai now asked, "What good things are these, so carefully packed and crated?"

Hsueh Pan called servants to unfasten the ropes and remove the spars, then he unlocked the cases. They saw that one was filled with silks, satins, brocades, foreign imports and articles of daily use. The other, meant for Pao-chai, in addition to writing-brushes, ink-tablets, inkstones, stationery, perfume-sachets, scented beads, fans, fan-sheaths, powder, rouge and pomade, had in it all sorts of toys from Huchiu in Soochow. Among them were figurines with movable limbs, lots for drinking-games, toy tumblers weighted with quicksilver, earthen-ware lanterns, whole sets of clay opera figures in blue gauze boxes, and even a clay sculpture of Hsueh Pan done to the life by one of the Huchiu craftsmen.

Pao-chai was not interested in the other things, but she picked up the figurine of Hsueh Pan to examine it carefully; and comparing it with her brother, she burst out laughing.

She told her maids, "Take this case to the Garden, so that it'll be easier to distribute these presents to the different apartments there."

With that she stood up to ask leave from her mother, then went back to the Garden.

Aunt Hsueh, for her part, when she had unpacked her case, divided the things into different lots which she told her young maid Tung-hsi to take to the Lady Dowager, Lady Wang and others.

Pao-chai, who had followed her case back to her own rooms, looked through the things in it one by one. Some she kept for herself; the rest she divided into appropriate lots. To some people she would just give toys; to others, stationery; or sachets, fans and pendants; rouge and pomade. She gave careful thought :o what was a fair share for each, only making an exception in Tai-yu's case — she was to have twice as much as anyone else. After she had allotted all the shares, she sent Ying-erh with an old maid-servant to deliver them to the different apartments.

Li Wan, Pao-yu and the rest, on receiving these presents, tipped the messengers and told them that they would thank Pao-chai when next they saw her. Only Tai-yu was grief-stricken at the sight of these toys from her home in the south which reminded her of her parents. Gazing at them through tears she sighed:

"I come from south of the Yangtze, but my parents are dead and I'm all on my own, with no brothers; so I have to put up in my grandmother's house. My health is poor too, and though I'm well looked after by my grandmother, aunt and cousins, none of the Lin family ever calls to see me or brings me local products which I could gain face by distributing as presents. This shows how lonely it is, how utterly wretched, to have no family of one's own." These reflections made her feel her heart would break.

Tzu-chuan, having waited on Tai-yu for so long, knew just how her mind worked and that it was the sight of these gifts from her old home in the south that had upset her, making her feel homesick. But not daring to say so outright, she just tried to comfort her.

"You're so delicate, miss," she said, "that you're always taking medicine. These last few days you've just begun to re-cover your appetite and have a little more energy; but you're not completely well yet. Miss Pao-chai's gift of these things today shows how fond she is of you. They ought to make you happy instead of upsetting you. Doesn't it look as if her presents, which she hoped would please you, have vexed you instead? Wouldn't she feel bad if she knew this?

"And just think, miss, Their Ladyships are doing all they can to find good doctors to diagnose your illness and prescribe medicine, so that you'll be cured as soon as possible. You ve just taken a turn for the better, but by weeping again like this aren't you yourself injuring your health? Don't you want to please the old lady? You fell ill, didn't you, because you undermined your strength by worrying too much? Your health's as precious as gold, miss. Don't treat it so lightly!"

As Tzu-chuan was pleading like this with Tai-yu, a young maid in the courtyard announced, "Master Pao has come."

"Show him in at once," called Tzu-chuan.

Even as she was speaking Pao-yu walked in, and Tai-yu invited him to take a seat.

Seeing the tear-stains on her face he asked, "Who's been offending you again, cousin? Your eyes are red from weeping."

Tai-yu said nothing. Tzu-chuan, standing to one side, jerked her chin towards the bed, and Pao-yu taking the hint walked over to have a look. When he saw all the things piled up there he knew that these were presents from Pao-chai. "What nice things!" he exclaimed. "Are you starting a shop? Or why display them like this?"

Still Tai-yu ignored him.

"Don't mention them, Second Master," said Tzu-chuan. "They were sent by Miss Pao-chai, but at sight of them our young lady got upset and started weeping. I've been trying hard to console her, but it's no use. And she's missed a meal again. If she wears herself out with crying so that her illness comes back, the old lady's going to give us a fearful scolding. It's lucky you've come. Do talk her round for us."

Pao-yu was intelligent, and having always paid more attention to Tai-yu than anyone else he knew just how narrow-minded and hyper-sensitive she was, how eager to outshine others in every way. When she saw that Pao-chai's brother had brought all these things from the south, from her old home, to give away as presents, she must have been painfully reminded of her own loss and other causes for grief. But though he knew the real reason for her distress he refrained from speaking of it, for fear of making her feel worse.

"I know why your young lady cried," he said with a smile. "She's angry and upset because Miss Pao-chai didn't send her *more* things. Don't worry, cousin, next year when I go south I'll bring you back two *boatloads* of things to stop you crying all the time."

Tai-yu couldn't help chuckling at this.

But at once she protested, "However little I've seen of the world, I'm not such a fool as to get provoked because a present's too little. What do you take me for, a two-year-old? You really have too low an opinion of other people. I have my own reasons which you know nothing about." With that she started shedding tears again.

Pao-yu at once went to sit down on the bed beside her. He picked up the gifts one by one to examine them.

"What's this?" he asked. "What's it called? What's that cute thing made of? And this one, what's it used for? Look, cousin, you could put this one as an ornament on your book-case or on your cabinet as a curio." In the hope of distracting her he kept up this idle chatter for a while.

Seeing Pao-yu clowning like this to amuse her and asking all sorts of inconsequential questions, Tai-yu was mollified and cheered up a little.

Noticing this, he suggested, "Don't you think we should call on Pao-chai to thank her? Will you come with me?"

Tai-yu had not intended to make a special trip to thank Pao-chai — that could wait until next they met. But as Pao-yu's proposal was right she could hardly refuse, so she went off with him.

To return to Hsueh Pan. On his mother's advice he lost no time in sending out invitations and making preparations for a feast, which kept him busy all day.

The next day the three or four assistants invited arrived. After some talk about the dispatching of goods and the ac-counts, they were ushered to their seats. Hsueh Pan poured drinks for each in turn to thank them for their work, and Aunt

Hsueh sent a maid out from the inner room to express her thanks as well.

One of the men asked, "Why isn't Brother Liu here today? Did you forget to invite him, sir?"

Hsueh Pan knitted his brows.

"Don't bring up his name," he sighed. "None of you know, I suppose, what's happened to him. It's really tragic. Two days ago, out of the blue, some crazy Taoist priest persuaded him to renounce the world, and he went away with the priest. Don't you call that extraordinary?"

One of them answered, "In the shop we did hear a great hubbub outside about some Taoist priest, who with just a few words persuaded a young man to go away with him. Some said they disappeared in a gust of wind, others that they rode off on rainbow-coloured clouds — there were different accounts. But we were too busy dispatching goods to pay much attention, so we didn't make further inquiries. Besides, we were rather sceptical about it. Now you tell us that the convert was our Brother Liu. If we'd known that, we ought to have dissuaded him and never allowed him to leave. It's really too bad to have lost such an entertaining friend. No wonder you feel upset, sir.

"But would such an intelligent man really go off with the priest? Brother Liu can use arms, he's strong. He may have seen through the priest's black magic and just pretended to be taken in, so that he could do for the fellow somewhere else."

"One never knows," said Hsueh Pan. "If that's what happened, fine: there'll be one less sorcerer casting spells on people."

"But when you heard about it, didn't you go to make a search?" they asked.

"We searched high and low, inside and outside the city, but couldn't find him. And when I saw no sign of him — you may think me a fool for this — I broke down and blubbed."

As he kept sighing and looked very downcast, not urging them to drink in his usual cheerful way, though it was a sumptuous feast with chicken, duck, fish, meat and other delicacies of land and sea, in view of their host's low spirits the guests did not like to stay too long. After finishing a few cups of wine and a little food they left.

Meantime Pao-yu had taken Tai-yu to Pao-chai's place to thank her. After the usual exchange of civilities, Tai-yu said to Pao-chai:

"Your brother must have been to a lot of trouble bringing back all those things. Now you've given so many to us, you can't have anything left for yourself."

"Exactly. Why didn't you keep them?" asked Pao-yu.

"They weren't anything good," said Pao-chai, "just some local products from far away, some novelties to amuse us. Whether *I* keep any or not doesn't matter. If there's anything I fancy, next year when my brother makes another trip I can ask him to bring more; it's no trouble at all."

At once Pao-yu chuckled, "If he does, we'll expect you to give *us* some. You mustn't forget us."

"Speak for yourself," said Tai-yu. "Don't drag *me* in." Turning to Pao-chai she added, "You see he's not come to thank you, but to order things for next year."

Pao-yu laughed.

"If I get some, of course you'll get a share too. So you ought to back me up instead of making such sarcastic remarks."

Tai-yu just smiled.

"How did you two happen to arrive here at the same time?" Pao-chai asked. "Did one of you fetch the other?"

"Well, when you sent me those things, I knew Cousin Lin must have her share too," explained Pao-yu. "So if I wanted to thank you, so would she. I called to pick her up and come here together, but found her upset and in tears. I can't understand why she's so fond of crying."

Tai-yu shot him a repressive look.

Taking the hint he changed his tune and said, "Cousin Lin hasn't felt too well these last few days. She was crying for fear her illness might come back. I tried to comfort her for a while and then we came, partly to thank you, partly because she'd feel low sitting all alone in her room."

"It's only right to worry about one's health," replied Paochai. "But all one need do is to take extra care about food and sufficient rest, and wearing suitable clothes for different weather. Why should one feel upset? Don't you know, cousin, that grieving saps your spirits and energy? If you do yourself such serious harm you'll fall ill. Do remember that."

"You're quite right, cousin," agreed Tai-yu. "Of course I know that. But you've seen how it's been with me these last few years. Not one year's gone by without my falling ill once or twice; that's what unnerves me. The very sight of medicine, whether it does me any good or not, gives me a headache, and the smell nauseates me. How can I help being afraid of a relapse?"

"Even so, you shouldn't get too upset," urged Pao-chai. "Instead, whenever you don't feel too well you should make an effort to come out and stroll about to cheer yourself up. That would be better than sitting moping at home. Depression just makes your health worse, that's the trouble with it. A couple of days ago I felt so lazy and limp I longed to lie down, but knowing this is a treacherous time of the year I was afraid I might fall ill, so I forced myself to find something to do, and that way I got over it. You mustn't mind me saying this, cousin, but 'the more afraid you are the more likely the devil is to come.'"

"What devil, cousin? From where?" demanded Pao-yu. "Why have I never seen one?"

Everyone laughed.

"Silly lordling!" mocked Pao-chai. "That's just a figure of speech. There are no such things as devils. If there were, you'd be crying for fright."

"Well said, cousin," approved Tai-yu with a smile. "You're right to tick him off for blurting out whatever comes into his head."

"So you're pleased whenever people snub me," said Pao-yu.

"Well, now that you've stopped feeling sad we'd better be going."

After a little further chat they said goodbye to Pao-chai and left, Pao-yu seeing Tai-yu to Bamboo Lodge before going home himself.

Now when Concubine Chao saw the presents sent to Huan, she seized on them gleefully, loud in her praise of Pao-chai.

"Everyone speaks of Miss Pao-chai's good manners and generosity," she gushed, "and sure enough here's an example today. How much stuff could her brother bring back? Yet she sends some to every household, not missing one out or making any distinctions, even thinking of *us* who don't count for anything here. This really does her credit! Miss Lin, now, she's quite different. Of course nobody brings her anything; but even if they did, she'd only send presents to those who have power and big face. Would she ever think of me or of my son? This shows that good breeding is really exceptional."

As Concubine Chao gloated over these presents for Huan, picking them up to play with and examine, it occurred to her that as Pao-chai was Lady Wang's niece this was a good opportunity to go and make up to her mistress. So she hurried over with the presents to Lady Wang's room.

Standing to one side there she said, "These are things Miss Pao-chai just gave Huan, things brought her by her brother. She's so young yet she thinks of everybody! I gave the maid who brought them two hundred cash. I heard that Aunt Hsueh sent you some gifts too, madam. I wonder what they are? So their family's sending us two lots of presents! How many things could they have got? No wonder the old lady and you both praise Miss Pao-chai and make such a favourite of her. She's really most lovable."

While saying this she held out the things she had brought. But Lady Wang neither looked up nor reached out her hand.

"Good, let Huan play with them," was all she said, without so much as glancing at the toys.

Annoyed by this snub, the concubine trailed back dejectedly to her room where she threw the toys aside and started grumbling, scolding and complaining. As no one asked her what the matter was, she sat there muttering to herself, showing how petty-minded and stupid she was. Even when good things came her way, she would make so many tactless and irritating remarks that Tan-chun can hardly be blamed for being exasperated with her mother and despising her.

When the maid delivering the presents for Pao-chai returned, she reported how some of the recipients had thanked her and some had given her tips; only she had brought back the share for little Chiao-chieh.

"Didn't you take it or wouldn't she accept it?" asked Pao-chai in surprise.

"When I took the things to Master Huan," Ying-erh explained, "I saw Madam Lien going to the old lady's place. As she wouldn't be at home, I didn't know to whom to give Chiao-chieh's share, so I didn't go there."

"How silly of you," scolded Pao-chai. "Even if she were out, Ping-erh and Feng-erh would hardly be out as well. You could have given it to them, and they'd have told Madam Lien when she came back. Do you have to deliver it to her in person?"

So Ying-erh took the things out of the Garden again. On the way to Hsi-feng's quarters she told the old maid-servant carrying them for her:

"If I'd known that would be all right, I could have saved this trip."

"We've nothing to do at home, so this is a good chance for a stroll," said the old woman. "Only you're not used to much walking, and after going to so many places today I daresay you're tired out, miss. Still, after delivering this we shall be through, and then you can have a rest."

Still chatting they reached Hsi-feng's place and delivered the gift.

On their return, Pao-chai asked, "Did you see Madam Lien?"

"No, we didn't," Ying-erh answered.

"I suppose she wasn't back then?"

"She was back, but Feng-erh told me, 'Since coming back from the old lady's place she hasn't looked her usual cheerful self — her face is black as thunder. She called Ping-erh in for a whispered consultation which the rest of us weren't allowed to hear — she even sent *me* out. So you'd better not go in. I'll report that you've come.' Then Feng-erh took the present in. When she came out again she said, 'Our mistress sends her thanks to your young lady.' And she gave us a string of cash. Then we came back."

Pao-chai was puzzled by this account, unable to think why Hsi-feng should be so angry.

But let us return to Pao-yu. When Hsi-jen saw him come home she asked:

"Why didn't you amuse yourself outside a bit longer? You said you were going with Miss Lin to thank Miss Pao-chai. Did you do that?"

"Of course that's what I intended to do," said Pao-yu, "but when I got there I found her in her room weeping over those things. I understood the reason, but I couldn't very well ask her about it or scold her, so I pretended not to understand and chatted for a while about this and that so as to cheer her up; and as soon as she felt better I took her with me to thank Cousin Pao-chai. We chatted there for a bit, then I saw Tai-yu back before coming home myself."

"Did you notice," asked Hsi-jen, "whether Miss Lin got more things than we did or the same amount?"

"Her share was two or three times bigger."

"That shows real understanding and tact," approved Hsi-jen. "Miss Pao-chai knows that all her other cousins have close relatives at hand to send them presents; besides, she and Miss Lin aren't simply relatives but half-sisters too, for, as you know, last year Miss Lin became Aunt Hsueh's god-daughter. So it was only right to give her a bigger share."

Pao-yu chuckled, "You sound like an old judge reviewing a case." He called a young maid then to fetch him a pillow as he wanted to lie down for a while.

"If you're not going out," said Hsi-jen, "there's something I want to ask you."

"Well, what is it?"

"You know how good Madam Lien's always been to me. Now she's just getting over a serious illness and for some time I've been meaning to call on her, but it wasn't convenient while Master Lien was at home, so I never went. Now I hear he's out and you're not going over there today; besides, this early autumn weather is neither too hot nor too cold; so I'd like to go and pay my respects to her, to prevent her scolding me when next we meet. And this is a good excuse to take a stroll while you and the other girls keep an eye on things here. I shan't be gone long."

"Yes, that's what you should do," agreed Ching-wen, "as you happen to be free now."

"I was just saying what a good judge she was in her appraisal of Miss Pao-chai," Pao-yu remarked. "Now in this case she's showing real thoughtfulness too."

"There's no need to heap praise on me, my good young master," replied Hsi-jen with a smile. "Just amuse yourself with them here, but whatever happens don't go to sleep and catch a chill, or the blame will fall on me again."

"I know," he said. "You can go."

Hsi-jen went to her room to change into new clothes, then picked up the mirror to tidy her hair and dust her face with powder. Coming out, she gave Ching-wen and Sheh-yueh some further instructions before leaving Happy Red Court.

At Seeping Fragrance Bridge, she paused to look round and enjoy the early autumn scene. Cicadas were shrilling in the trees, insects chirping in the undergrowth; the pomegranate flowers were fading, the lotus leaves withering, but the hibiscus on the river bank had put out clusters of red buds which looked enchanting against the vivid green leaves. Crossing the bridge then she soon saw Li Wan's maid Su-yun approaching, followed by an old serving-woman with a lacquer hamper. Hsi-jen asked where they were taking the hamper and what was in it.

"These are caltrops and lotus seeds our mistress is sending Miss Tan-chun," Su-yun told her.

"Were they picked in the stream in our Garden or bought outside?"

"Mother Liu who works in our house asked leave to go and visit some relatives, then brought these back as a present for our mistress, and Miss Tan-chun saw them as she happened to be in our place. Our mistress had some peeled for her to taste, but she refused as she'd just been drinking hot tea and said she'd try some later. So now we're taking these to her house."

Then they went their different ways. In the distance Hsi-jen now saw someone flicking a whisk under a trellis of grapes, but as the sun was in her eyes she could not make out who it was. Drawing nearer she discovered it was old Mrs. Chu, who came forward, beaming, to greet her.

"How is it you have time to come out for a stroll today, miss?" she asked. "Where are you going?"

"I've no time to stroll about, I'm on my way to call on Madam Lien. What are you doing here?"

"I'm chasing away the wasps. This has been such a dry summer, all the trees are infested by insects who've been boring into the fruit so that lots of it has dropped — what a wretched waste! Look at the grapes, just forming such pretty clusters, but the wasps and bees keeping swarming round to bite them. Worse still, magpies and sparrows come to steal grapes too. The trouble is that once a sparrow or insect has made a hole in three or four grapes in one cluster, the juice dripping on to the good ones rots them too. These sparrows and wasps are such a pest, I'm here to shoo them away. Just look, miss, because I stopped for one minute to talk, another swarm of wasps has come."

"Even if you keep waving that whisk you'll never keep them all away. As soon as you drive one lot away from here, another will come over there. Better tell the purveyors to have a whole lot of small gauze bags made. If you put one bag over each cluster of grapes, the birds and insects won't be able to spoil them; and as gauze lets through the air, that won't hurt the grapes."

"That's a good idea," agreed the old woman. "This is my first year at this job, so I don't know these clever dodges."

"We have many different kinds of fruit in the Garden," remarked Hsi-jen. "Which kind ripens first?"

"This is the start of the seventh month. The grapes are only just turning red. They won't be really ripe and good to eat until the end of the month. If you don't believe me, miss, I'll pick one for you to taste."

"Even if they were ripe, the first fruits have to be sacrificed to Buddha and the next sent to the mistresses. How can *we* taste them first? As an old hand here, surely you know this rule?"

The old woman smiled sheepishly.

"You're right, miss. I only said that because of the question you asked." But while saying this she was thinking, "Drat it all! It's lucky I was chasing wasps just now. If I'd happened to pick a grape to taste and been spotted, what a to-do there'd have been!"

"Put in a request to Madam Lien for those bags I told you about," Hsi-jen advised her. "She'll get the stewards to have them made."

This said she left by the Garden gate and went straight to Hsi-feng's place.

Hsi-feng and Ping-erh were discussing Chia Lien's secret marriage. As Hsi-jen was a rare visitor and they did not know her errand, they broke off their conversation on her arrival.

With a forced smile Hsi-feng asked, "What wind's blown such a noble visitor to our humble place?"

Hsi-jen replied with a smile, "I knew you'd tease me when I came, madam, but never mind. While you were unwell I kept wanting to come and pay my respects, but when Master Lien was at home it wasn't convenient, and I didn't like to disturb you while you were ill, so I didn't venture to come. As you've always been so kind to me, I knew you'd overlook it and not be offended."

"Cousin Pao has plenty of maids in his place, but you're the only responsible one," said Hsi-feng. "Of course you couldn't get away. Ping-erh often told me that you were thinking of me and asking after my health, so I felt very pleased. Now that you're here it's I who should be thanking you for your concern. How could I tease you, my dear Miss Hsi-jen?"

"If you put it like that, my dear madam, you're really too kind."

Hsi-feng took Hsi-jen's hand and urged her to sit on the *kang*, but only after declining several times did she take a seat on a stool by it, while Ping-erh herself fetched in tea.

"Let the young maids attend to that," urged Hsi-jen. "I don't like to trouble you, miss."

As she stood up to take the tea, turning her head she noticed in a needlework basket on one side of the *kang* a small crimson apron of imported satin.

"Busy as you are every day, madam, do you still have time to do needlework?" she asked.

"I'm no needlewoman," said Hsi-feng. "And now that I've just got over my illness there are so many family affairs to see to I've naturally no time for such things — I've even given up doing what's most urgent. But when I went to pay my respects to the old lady, I saw the gay materials Aunt Hsueh had sent her, which would look cute made into little clothes for children; so I asked the old lady for some. That provoked our Old Ancestress into baiting me. She declared I was the bane of her life, the way I demanded and grabbed everything I saw in her place. She had everyone laughing at me. You know I'm too thick-skinned to mind being scolded, so I just let our Old Ancestress rattle on and pretended not to hear. I've given that material to Ping-erh to first make a small apron for Chiao-chieh. With what's left, when I've time, I'll make some other things."

"You're indeed the only one, madam, who can keep the old lady happy," rejoined Hsi-jen laughingly. She picked up the sewing to examine it, then commented admiringly, "It's really pretty with all these different colours. A good material needs someone with skilful fingers like this to embroider it. Especially for Chiao-chieh. Why, when she's carried out wearing this, people won't be able to take their eyes off her. Where *is* Chiao-chieh?" she added. "Why haven't I seen her all this time?"

Ping-erh told her, "Just now Miss Pao-chai sent over some toys, and she was so tickled with them that she went on playing with them till her wet-nurse carried her off. She must have gone to sleep now, tired out."

"Chiao-chieh must be growing more and more of a romp."

"Her plump little face is like a round silver plate. She smiles at everybody she sees and never offends anyone. She's truly a little darling who keeps our mistress amused."

"What is Cousin Pao doing at home?" Hsi-feng inquired.

"I begged him to keep an eye on things there with Ching-wen and the others, so that I could ask leave and come out," Hsi-jen told her. "But I've been so engrossed in talking, a long time's slipped by and I must be getting back now. I don't want to have him complaining that I'm so lazy, wherever I go I stay sitting there and won't move." With that she got up, took her leave of them, and went back to Happy Red Court.

After Ping-erh had seen Hsi-jen out, Hsi-feng called her back to cross-examine her further. The more she heard, the more furious she became.

"You say you heard from the pages at the inner gate that your Second Master had secretly married another wife outside. Who told you that?"

"Lai Wang."

At once Hsi-feng sent for him.

"Did you know that your Second Master had bought a house and married a concubine outside?" she demanded.

"I'm on duty all day long at the inner gate," stammered

Lai Wang. "How could I know about the Second Master's business? I heard this from Hsing-erh."

"When did Hsing-erh tell you?"

"Before the master left on that trip."

"Where is Hsing-erh now?"

"He's working in the new mistress' house."

In a furious temper Hsi-feng spat at him.

"You contemptible son of an ape," she swore. "Who are you to talk about a new mistress or an old mistress? How dare *you* confer the title of mistress on her. The nonsense you talk, you deserve to be slapped." Then she asked, "Isn't Hsing-erh supposed to wait on the Second Master? Why didn't he go with him?"

"He was specially left here to look after Second Sister Yu; that's why."

Hsi-feng at once ordered him to fetch Hsing-erh.

Lai Wang rushed off on this errand and, when he found Hsing-erh fooling about with some other pages outside he simply told him that Hsi-feng wanted him. When Hsing-erh heard this, without asking why he was wanted, he hurried with Lai Wang to the inner gate, where he announced his business and was admitted. Having bowed to Hsi-feng he stood respectfully to one side. At sight of him she glared.

"What fine goings-on have you, master and slave, been up to outside?" she snapped. "Did you take me for a fool who wouldn't know? As Second Master's personal attendant, you must know the whole story. I want the true facts from you. Any attempt to cover up or lie, and I'll have you beaten till your legs are broken!"

Hsing-erh fell on his knees to kowtow.

"What goings-on are these, madam, that you're asking about?"

"How dare you stall, you little bastard! I'm asking how your master fixed things up outside with Second Sister Yu. How did he buy the house and furnish it? How did the marriage take place? Tell me all these things clearly, you dog, and I may spare your life."

Hearing these explicit questions Hsing-erh reflected: Both mansions know about this business; the only ones kept in the dark were the old lady, Lord Sheh, Lady Hsing and Madam Lien. As the truth's bound to come out in the end, why should I try to cover it up? I may as well come clean to get off a beating and worse punishment. For one thing, I'm too young to be expected to know how serious this was; for another, I've always known that Madam's such a firebrand that even Master Lien's half afraid of her; and, besides, this business was arranged by Master Lien, Lord Chen and Master Jung between them — it had nothing to do with *me*.

His mind made up, he screwed up his courage.

"Have mercy on me, madam!" he begged on his knees. "I'll tell you everything. It started during our mourning for the Elder Master of the East Mansion. Second Master happened to meet Second Sister Yu there a few times, and I suppose he took a fancy to her and wanted to make her his concubine. So he first discussed it with Master Jung, asking him to act as go-between and arrange the match, and promising him presents if he pulled it off. Master Jung agreed readily and told Lord Chen, who broached it to Madam Yu and old Mrs. Yu.

"Old Mrs. Yu was quite willing but she said, 'Second Sister was engaged as a child to the son of the Chang family; so how can I marry her to Master Lien? If the Changs hear of it there may be trouble.'

" 'That's nothing serious,' said Lord Chen. 'Leave it to me. That fellow Chang's family has been beggared. If we just give him a few extra taels of silver, we can make him write a document cancelling the engagement and there'll be no further trouble.'

"Later they did fetch that man Chang and put it to him. When he'd written the document they paid him and off he went. Then Second Master felt safe enough to go boldly ahead. Only, for fear lest this came to your ears, madam, and you stopped him, he bought and furnished a small house outside at the back, then took her over. And Lord Chen gave him a married couple to work there.

"Often, when he says he has business to attend to for Lord Sheh or Lord Chen, that's a lie — an excuse for him to stay outside there.

"Originally the mother and the two sisters lived there, and they wanted to arrange a match for Third Sister Yu too, promising to give her a handsome dowry; but now Third Sister Yu's dead, so there's only old Mrs. Yu keeping Second Sister Yu company.

"All this is the truth, I haven't dared hide a thing." With that he kowtowed again.

This account had left Hsi-feng transfixed with rage, her face livid, her almond eyes squinting. For a while she trembled convulsively, unable to get a word out for stupefaction. Then, looking down suddenly, she saw that Hsing-erh was still kneeling there.

"You're not the one most to blame for this," she said. "But when Second Master carried on like that outside you ought to have told me about it earlier. For not doing that you fully deserve a beating. Still, since you've told me honestly now, without lying, I'll let you off this time."

"I deserve death, madam, for not telling you before." Again he thumped his head hard on the ground.

"Be off now."

As he rose to leave she added, "Next time I send for you, mind you come at once. Don't go far away."

Assenting repeatedly, Hsing-erh withdrew. Once outside he stuck out his tongue in dismay.

"That was touch and go!" he exclaimed. "I only just escaped a good beating." He regretted having passed on the news to Lai Wang, and was scared stiff for worrying what to say when Chia Lien returned. But no more of this.

After the page had left, Hsi-feng turned to Ping-erh and asked, "Did you hear what Hsing-erh said?"

"Yes, I heard it all."

"How can there be such a shameless man in the world? Guzzling what's in the bowl, he has his eyes on what's in the pan. He wants every woman he sees, the greedy dog. Talk about off with the old love and on with the new! It's a pity to give a lecher like him the insignia of the fifth or sixth rank. He may believe in the saying that the flowers at home aren't as sweet as flowers growing wild; but if he thinks that, he's making a big mistake. Sooner or later he'll cause such a scandal outside, he won't be able to face relatives and friends; and then only will he give up."

To mollify her Ping-erh said, "Of course you're right to be angry; but you've only just got over your illness, madam, you shouldn't let yourself be carried away. After that affair with Pao Erh's wife, the master seemed to be restraining himself and behaving much better. So why is he having affairs of this sort again? It must be Lord Chen's fault."

"Of course Lord Chen's to blame too. Still, it's because our master is so debauched that it's easy for people to tempt him. As the proverb says, 'If an ox doesn't want to drink, you can't force it to.'"

"Lord Chen's wife ought to have stopped him from doing such a thing."

"Exactly. How could Madam Yu let her sister be betrothed to two different families? First the Changs, then the Chias. Have all the other men in the world died out? Must all girls marry into our Chia family? Are we so well off, or what? It's lucky that slut Third Sister Yu had sense enough to kill herself first; otherwise they'd have married her to Pao-yu or Huan.

"Madam Yu doesn't seem to have cared about saving her sister's face — how could she ever have held up her head in future? But she wouldn't worry about that, as after all Second Sister was only her half-sister and, by all accounts, a loose-living, shameless bitch. But Cousin Chen's wife is a lady of rank; shouldn't she feel ashamed of having such a flighty sister at home? Yet instead of trying to keep her away she blatantly brings her here to carry on in that shocking way, not caring if people laugh.

"Besides, Lord Chen's an official. He may not know all the rules of propriety, but surely he knows that it's taboo for a man in mourning to marry, or to spurn his wife and take another woman. What I'm wondering is this: did he fix this up as a favour for his cousin or to harm him?"

"Yes, Lord Chen is too short-sighted," said Ping-erh. "He just wanted to please his cousin without worrying about the consequences."

"Please his cousin?" Hsi-feng snorted sarcastically. "No, this was giving him poison. Of all our cousins, he's the oldest and most experienced; but instead of setting the others a good example he teaches them bad ways to spoil their reputation. And when there's a public scandal he'll just stand aside watching the fun. Honestly, I can't find words strong enough to damn him. The scandalous goings-on in that East Mansion of his don't bear speaking of. And to cover up his own debauchery he must needs make his cousin follow his example. Is this the way an elder brother should behave? He should have drowned himself in his own piss and died in place of his father, for what's his life worth? Look how virtuous Lord Ching of the East Mansion was, fasting, chanting sutras and doing so many good deeds. How could he beget a son and grandson like these? I suppose all the family's good luck, generated by the auspicious geomancy of the ancestral tombs, was used up by the old man."

"That does seem to be the case. How else could they be so lacking in decency?"

"It's lucky the old lady, Lord Sheh and Lady Hsing haven't heard of it. If it came to their ears, not only would our good-for-nothing master get beaten and cursed, even Lord Chen and Madam Yu would certainly be made to smart for it."

Hsi-feng went on cursing and raging, refusing to go over for lunch on the excuse that her head ached. Seeing that she was working herself up into a greater fury, Ping-erh urged:

"You'd better calm down, madam. The thing's done, so there's no hurry. There'll be plenty of time to talk it over again after Second Master's return."

Hsi-feng gave a couple of snorts.

"After his return? No, that would be too late."

Ping-erh knelt down to reason with her and comfort her,

till at length Hsi-feng calmed down enough to sip some tea. Then, after taking some deep breaths, she asked for her pillow and lay down on the bed, her eyes closed as she considered what to do. When Ping-erh saw that she was resting, she withdrew. And when some people ignorant of what had happened arrived to report on their business, they were sent packing by Feng-erh. Then Ma-nao was sent by the Lady Dowager to ask:

"Why hasn't the Second Mistress gone over for lunch? The old lady's worried and sent me to see what's wrong."

As it was the Lady Dowager who had sent to inquire, Hsi-feng forced herself to get up.

"I've a bit of a headache, nothing serious," she said. "Tell the old lady not to worry. After lying down for a while I'm feeling better." With that she sent the maid back.

She then thought the whole business over carefully once more, and hit on a cunning plan to kill several birds with one stone, working out the safest measures to achieve this. This done, instead of disclosing her plan to Ping-erh, she behaved as cheerfully as if nothing had happened, giving no sign of her fury and jealousy. She sent a maid to fetch Lai Wang and ordered him to bring workers the next day to clean up, repaper and furnish the eastern rooms in their compound. Ping-erh and the others were nonplussed by this.

If you want to know the upshot, read the next chapter.

CHAPTER 68

Unhappy Second Sister Yu Is Decoyed
into Grand View Garden
Jealous Hsi-feng Makes a Scene
in the Ning Mansion

When Chia Lien left on his mission, it so happened that the
Governor of Pinganchou was away for a month inspecting
border areas. To get a definite reply, Chia Lien had to wait
in the hostel for his return. Thus by the time the governor
came back, received him and settled the matter, nearly two
months had passed.

Hsi-feng's plans were already laid. As soon as Chia Lien
left she ordered workmen to fix up the three rooms on the
eastern side, decorating and furnishing them just like her own.
On the fourteenth, she reported to the Lady Dowager and
Lady Wang that she wanted to go to the nunnery to offer
incense the next morning, taking only Ping-erh, Feng-erh and
the wives of Chou Jui and Lai Wang. Before setting out she
disclosed her true purpose to them and ordered them all to
wear mourning.

Then they set off, Hsing-erh leading the way, to the house
where Second Sister Yu lived. He knocked at the gate, which
was opened by Pao Erh's wife.

Hsing-erh announced with a grin, "Tell the Second Mistress
that Madam Lien is here. Quick!"

Frightened out of her wits, Pao Erh's wife flew in to report
this. Second Sister Yu, too, was taken aback; but since Hsi-
feng had come she had no choice but to receive her with be-
fitting respect. She hastily straightened her clothes and went
out to meet her as Hsi-feng dismounted from her carriage and
stepped through the gate.

Second Sister Yu saw that Hsi-feng had nothing but silver trinkets in her hair and was wearing a pale blue satin jacket, black satin cape and white silk skirt. Under eyebrows arched like willow leaves her almond eyes were as bright as those of a phoenix; she was pretty as peach-blossom in spring, simple and austere as chrysanthemums in autumn. As the wives of Chou Jui and Lai Wang helped her into the courtyard, Second Sister Yu stepped forward with a smile to curtsey to her, addressing her as "elder sister."

"I wasn't expecting the honour of this visit, so I didn't come out to meet you," she apologized. "Please overlook my negligence, elder sister." Again she curtseyed.

Smiling, Hsi-feng returned her greeting and hand in hand they entered the house, where Hsi-feng took the seat of honour while Second Sister ordered her maid to bring a cushion, then knelt to pay her respects.

"Your slave is young," she said. "Since coming here, I've left all decisions to my mother and my step-sister. Now that I've had the good fortune to meet you, elder sister, if you don't consider me too far beneath you I'd like to ask for your advice and instructions. I'll bare my heart to you, too, and wait upon you." She bowed low.

Hsi-feng left her seat to return the courtesy.

"This all comes of my behaving like a silly woman," she answered, "for ever advising my husband to take good care of his health and keep away from brothels, to spare his parents worry. We're both fond, foolish women. But he seems to have misunderstood me. If he'd taken a mistress outside and hidden it from me, that wouldn't have signified; but now he's taken you as his second wife, and that's an important matter, in accordance with the rules of propriety, yet he never told me about it.

"Actually, I'd advised him to take another wife, because if he begets a son I, too, shall have someone to rely on in future. But he seems to have thought me the jealous type, and so he took this important step in secret. That was really wronging me! And to whom can I complain but to Heaven and Earth?

"This came to my ears about ten days ago, but for fear of vexing my husband I didn't venture to take it up with him. Now that he happens to have gone on a long journey, I've come to call on you in person. I do hope you'll understand how much I take this to heart and agree to move into our house so that we can live together as sisters, both of one mind, to advise Second Master to pay careful attention to his business and to look after his health. This is only right and proper.

"Foolish and lowly as I am, and unworthy of your company, if we live in separate establishments like this, how do you suppose I can set my mind at rest? Besides, once outsiders know, it will reflect badly on both of our reputations. Not that gossip about *us* is so serious — it's Second Master's reputation that really counts. Besides, it's entirely up to you to save me from getting a bad name.

"I daresay you've heard talk about me from servants who think I run the household too strictly and most likely exaggerate behind my back. But how can someone as intelligent and broad-minded as you believe such disgruntled talk? If I were really so impossible, why have three generations of my seniors as well as all my cousins and in-laws — and don't forget that the Chias are a well-known old family — put up with me all this time? Anyone else would have been angry at his marrying you in secret like this outside, but I actually consider it a blessing which shows that the gods and Buddhas of Heaven and Earth don't want me to be defamed by those low creatures' slander.

"I've come today to beg you to move in and live with me, on the same footing, share and share alike to serve our father and mother-in-law and advise our husband together, and share the same griefs and joys like real sisters. Then those low types will be sorry they sized me up wrongly; and when Second Master comes back and sees this, he as our husband will regret his mistake. So, sister, you'll have become my benefactress, redeeming my reputation.

"If you won't agree to coming back with me, I'll gladly move out to live with you here and wait on you like a younger sister. All I beg of you is to put in a few good words for me to Second Master, so that he'll allow me somewhere to stay. Then I shall die content."

With that she started sobbing and weeping, moving Second Sister to tears too.

After this exchange they resumed their seats, and now Ping-erh came in to pay her respects. As she was unusually well-dressed and looked a cut above the other maids, Second Sister Yu realized who she was and hastily laid a restraining hand on her arm.

"Don't do that, sister!" she exclaimed. "You and I are of the same rank."

Hsi-feng rose with a smile to protest, "Don't overrate her — that would spoil what little good fortune she may have! Just let her pay her respects, sister. She's after all our maid. There's no need to stand on ceremony with her."

She then ordered Chou Jui's wife to unwrap four rolls of fine silk and four pairs of jewelled trinkets set in gold as her gift to Second Sister Yu at this first meeting, and these were accepted with thanks. Then, sipping tea, they spoke of what had happened.

"It was all my fault," Hsi-feng kept reiterating. "No one else is to blame. But do be good to me."

Second Sister, quite taken in by her protestations, thought it was only natural for disgruntled servants to run down their mistress. So she replied very frankly, treating Hsi-feng as a trusted friend. Moreover, Mrs. Chou and the other serving-women there praised Hsi-feng for her goodness, saying it was her being honest to a fault which had given rise to resentment. They announced too that the house had been made ready, as the new mistress would see for herself when she moved in. Second Sister had always thought it would be better for her to live in the Chia mansion, and hearing all this she naturally agreed.

"I ought to accompany you, sister," she said. "But what about this household here?"

"That's no problem," Hsi-feng assured her. "Just get the

servants to take over your personal belongings. The furniture here won't be needed. You can assign anyone you think fit to stay here so as to keep an eye on it."

"Since I've met you today, elder sister, I'll leave all the arrangements for the removal to you. I haven't been here long, and never having run a house before I'm too inexperienced to make decisions. These few cases can be taken. I've really nothing else here of my own, the other things belong to Second Master."

Hsi-feng ordered Chou Jui's wife to make a note of these cases and see to it that they were carried carefully to the eastern rooms. Then she urged Second Sister to put on her jewels and they went out hand in hand to mount the carriage, in which they sat side by side.

"Our family rules are strict," Hsi-feng now told her confidentially. "So far the old lady knows nothing about this business. If they learned that the Second Master married you while still in mourning, they'd have him beaten to death! So we can't present you yet to Their Ladyships. We have a very big garden where the girls of our family live, but other people hardly ever go there. Now that you're moving over, you can stay in the Garden for a couple of days till I've found some way to break this news, and then it will be all right to pay your respects."

"Do exactly as you think best, elder sister," acquiesced Second Sister.

As the pages accompanying the carriage had received their orders in advance, instead of entering the main gate they went straight to the one at the back; and as soon as the ladies alighted, everyone in the neighbourhood was chased away. Then Hsi-feng led Second Sister through the back gate of Grand View Garden to see Li Wan.

By this time most of the inmates of the Garden had heard the news. Now that they saw Hsi-feng bringing Second Sister in, they flocked over to see her and she greeted each in turn. Not one but was very favourably impressed by her beauty and her charm.

"Don't let word of this get out," Hsi-feng warned them all. "If it comes to the ears of Their Ladyships, I'll kill the lot of you!"

The matrons and maids in the Garden were all afraid of Hsi-feng. And as Chia Lien had taken this second wife while observing state mourning and family mourning too, they knew it was a most serious offence and took care not to speak of the matter.

Hsi-feng quietly asked Li Wan to put up the new arrival for a few days.

"Once this business is straightened out," she said, "of course she'll move over with me."

Knowing that rooms had been made ready in Chia Lien's quarters and that it would not be fitting to announce this marriage during the period of mourning, Li Wan agreed.

Hsi-feng then dismissed all Second Sister's maids, assigning some of her own to wait on her, and ordered the women in the Garden to look after her well.

"If she disappears or runs away, you'll have to answer for it!" she threatened them, after which she went off to make other secret arrangements.

Everyone in the household was amazed to see how benevolent Hsi-feng had become. As for Second Sister, now that she had found this niche and all the girls in the Garden treated her well, she was quite contented and happy, thinking her future assured.

After three days, however, Shan-chieh, the maid assigned to her, started showing signs of insubordination.

"There's no hair-oil left," Second Sister told her. "Go and ask Madam Lien for some."

"How can you be so inconsiderate, madam?" Shan-chieh retorted. "Madam Lien has to look after the old lady every day, as well as the mistresses of both mansions and all the young ladies. At the same time she has to give orders to several hundred men-servants and women-servants all told. Not a day goes by but she has ten or twenty important matters to attend to, besides dozens of minor ones. Outside, she has to see to sending gifts and returning the courtesies of so many noble families from Her Imperial Highness down to princess and marquises; on top of which she has to cope with countless relatives and friends, as well as receiving or sending out thousands of taels of silver every day. How can you trouble her with trifles like this? I wouldn't be so demanding if I were you. Yours isn't a proper marriage. She's treating you well because she's so exceptionally kind and generous. If not for that, hearing the way you talk, she could well storm at you and kick you out. And then what could you do? You'd really be stranded."

This harangue made Second Sister hang her head. She saw she would just have to stomach such slights. And things went from bad to worse: Shan-chieh even stopped fetching her meals, or served them unpunctually, bringing nothing but scraps. If Second Sister complained, the maid started screaming at her; but for fear others might scoff that she didn't know her place, she had to put up with it. Every week or so when she happened to see Hsi-feng, the latter was all smiles and sweetness, for ever addressing her as "my dear sister."

"If any servants are remiss and you can't control them, just let me know and I'll have them beaten," promised Hsi-feng. Then she scolded the maids and matrons, "I know the way you take advantage of those who are kind and fear only those who are hard on you. Once my back's turned you're not afraid of anyone. If I hear one word of complaint from the second mistress, I'll have your lives for it!"

Second Sister was taken in by this show of kindness.

"With her taking my side like this, I'd better not make any fuss," she reflected. "Some servants have no sense, that's only natural. If I report them and get them into trouble, I'm the one people will blame." So she covered up for the maids instead.

Meanwhile Hsi-feng had sent Lai Wang out to make detailed inquiries, and had now ascertained that Second Sister had indeed been engaged before to a certain Chang Hua now nineteen, a wastrel and loafer who spent his time gambling and whoring and had squandered his family's money. Having been driven out by his father, he now stayed in a gambling den. And his father, without telling him, had accepted ten taels of silver from old Mrs. Yu for cancelling the engagement.

After Hsi-feng had learned all these particulars, she gave Lai Wang a packet of twenty taels of silver and secretly ordered him to get Chang Hua to stay with him and bring a suit against Chia Lien. He was to accuse him of marrying during a period of state and family mourning, against Imperial decree and unknown to his parents; of relying on his wealth and power to force Chang Hua to renounce his engagement; and of taking a second wife without the consent of his first.

Chang Hua, however, only too well aware of the danger involved, dared not bring such a charge. When Lai Wang reported this to Hsi-feng she fumed:

"Damn him for a mangy cur that won't let itself be helped over a wall! Go and explain to him that it doesn't matter even if he accuses our family of *high treason*. I just want him to make a row so that everyone loses face. If big trouble comes of it, I can always smooth things over."

Lai Wang carried out her orders and explained this to Chang Hua.

Hsi-feng also instructed Lai Wang, "Get him to implicate *you*, then you can confront him in court — I'll tell you just what to say — and I guarantee everything will be all right."

When Lai Wang saw that he had Hsi-feng's backing, he told Chang Hua to include his name in his charge.

"Just accuse me of acting as the middleman and of putting Second Master up to this," he said.

Chang Hua, given this cue, acted on Lai Wang's advice and wrote out his plaint, taking it the next morning to the Court of Censors. When the judge took his seat in the court and saw that this charge against Chia Lien involved his servant Lai Wang, he had no choice but to send for the latter to answer the charge. The runners, not daring to enter the Chia mansion, meant to order a servant to deliver the summons. But Lai Wang had reckoned on their coming, and was already waiting out in the street. When he saw the runners he approached them with a smile.

"Sorry to have put you to this trouble, brothers," he said. "I must have done wrong. All right, put the chains round my neck."

Not venturing to do this, they replied, "Please just come quietly, sir, and stop joking."

Then Lai Wang went to the court and knelt down before the judge, who showed him the charge. He pretended to read it through and then kowtowed.

"I was in the know about this," he admitted. "My master did this all right. But this fellow Chang Hua has a grudge against me, that's why he's accused me of being the middleman. Actually, it was someone else. I beg Your Honour to make investigations."

Chang Hua, kowtowing too, said, "That's true; but it's someone I dared not mention, that's why I accused the servant instead."

"Silly fool!" Lai Wang made a show of desperation. "Hurry up and come clean. This is a government court. You must name him even if he's a gentleman."

Then Chang Hua named Chia Jung. And the judge had to have him served with a summons.

Hsi-feng had secretly sent Ching-erh to find out when this summons was issued. Now she promptly called for Wang Hsin, explained what had happened, and told him to go and bribe the judge with three hundred taels just to make a display of severity in order to frighten the culprits.

That evening Wang Hsin went to the judge's house and fixed things up. The judge, knowing the situation, accepted the bribe and the next day announced in court that Chang Hua was a scoundrel who had trumped up this charge against innocent people because he was in debt to the Chia family. For as this judge was on good terms with Wang Tzu-teng, after a word in private from Wang Hsin he was all for settling the matter without making trouble for the Chias. He therefore said no more, simply detained the plaintiff and the accused and summoned Chia Jung to court.

Chia Jung was seeing to some business for Chia Chen when someone brought him word of this charge against him and urged him to think of a way out at once. He made haste to report this to Chia Chen.

"I was prepared for this; but that fellow certainly has a nerve!" said Chia Chen.

At once he sealed two hundred taels in a packet to be sent to the judge, and ordered a servant to go and answer the charge. As they were discussing their next step, the arrival of Madam Lien from the West Mansion was announced. Both men started and wanted to slip away into hiding, but it was too late — Hsi-feng had already entered.

"A fine elder brother you are!" she cried. "A fine thing you got your younger brother to do!"

Chia Jung hastily stepped forward to pay his respects. Hsi-feng simply caught hold of him and went on in.

"Entertain your aunt well," said Chia Chen. "Order a good meal for her." He then called for his horse and made off.

Hsi-feng marched Chia Jung towards the inner rooms and Madam Yu came out to meet her.

"What's the matter?" she asked, seeing how furious she looked. "Why this hurry?"

Hsi-feng spat in her face.

"Couldn't you find husbands for the girls of your Yu family that you had to smuggle them into the Chia family?" she demanded. "Are all men of the Chias so wonderful? Have all the other men in the world died out? Even if you want to pawn off your sisters, there's a proper procedure for marriage and it should be announced in a decent way. Have you taken leave of your senses? How could you send her over during a time of state and family mourning? And now that someone's brought a charge against us, I'm all in a flurry. Even the court thinks me a jealous shrew and has summoned me to stand trial. My name will be mud! And I shall be divorced!

"What wrong have I done you since I've come to this house that you treat me so cruelly? Or did Their Ladyships tip you a hint to trap me like this so as to get rid of me? Let's go to face the judge now, both of us, to clear this up. Then we can put the case before the whole clan. If they give me a bill of divorce, I'll leave."

Sobbing and storming she caught hold of Madam Yu, insisting on going to court. Chia Jung knelt in desperation and kowtowed, begging her not to be angry.

"May lightning blast your skull!" she swore at him. "May five devils tear you apart, you heartless wretch! You fear nothing in heaven or on earth, playing such dirty tricks all the time and doing such shameless, lawless things to ruin our family. Even your dead mother's spirit will disown you, so will all our ancestors. How dare you appeal to me?"

After this tearful tirade she raised her hand to strike him. Chia Jung thumped his head on the ground again.

"Don't be angry, aunt!" he cried. "Don't hurt your hand — let me slap myself instead. Please don't be angry, auntie."

He raised his hands and slapped himself on both cheeks.

"Will you meddle in that thoughtless way again?" he asked himself. "Just listen to your uncle and not to your aunt?"

All present, repressing smiles, begged him to stop.

And now Hsi-feng threw herself into Madam Yu's arms to weep and wail, calling on Heaven and Earth.

"I wouldn't mind you finding another wife for your brother-in-law," she sobbed. "But why make him flout the Imperial decree and keep it secret from his parents? Why give *me* a bad name? We must go to find the judge before he sends police and runners to arrest me. After that we must go and see Their Ladyships and call the whole clan together to discuss this. If I've acted so badly, refusing to let my husband take a second wife or another concubine, just give me a bill of divorce and I'll leave at once.

"Actually, I've fetched your sister here myself, but didn't venture to report it to Their Ladyships for fear they'd be angry. She has maids in the Garden to wait on her hand and foot, and I've prepared rooms for her in our place exactly like my own, where I meant to take her as soon as the old lady knew. We could all have settled down then, minding our own business, and I'd have let bygones be bygones. How was I to know that she was engaged to another man before? How was I to know what you'd been up to?

"Yesterday, hearing that her betrothed had brought a charge against me, I was so desperate that I had to take five hundred taels of the mistress' silver to use as a bribe; because if I were summoned to court your Chia family would lose face. And my servant is still locked up by the police."

She went on storming and wailing, sobbingly invoking their ancestors and her parents, then tried to dash out her brains and kill herself. Madam Yu, reduced to a squelch, her clothes covered with tears and snot, could only round on Chia Jung.

"You degenerate!" she scolded. "You and your father are to blame for this. I warned you against it."

Hsi-feng let out another wail, clasping Madam Yu's face between both hands.

"Were you crazy?" she demanded. "Was your mouth stuffed with eggplant or with a bit and curb, that you couldn't let me know? If you had, I wouldn't be in such a fix, with this business so out of hand it's been taken to court. Yet you're still trying to shift the blame to *them*! As the saying goes, 'A good wife keeps her husband out of trouble — a sound woman counts for more than a sound man.' If you were any good, how could they do such things? You're as stupid and dumb as a gourd with its tip sawn off. All you care about, you fool, is getting a *name* for goodness. So they're not afraid of you and won't listen to what you say." She spat again and again in disgust.

"That's how it was, really," sobbed Madam Yu. "If you don't believe me, ask the servants. Of course I tried to stop them — they just wouldn't listen. So what could I do? I don't blame you for being angry, sister, but I simply couldn't help it."

The concubines and maids kneeling fearfully round them now pleaded with Hsi-feng, "You're so wise and understanding, madam, even if our mistress did wrong you've got even with her now. Usually, in front of us slaves, you're both on the best of terms. So please leave her some face!"

They brought Hsi-feng some tea, but she smashed the cup. However, she stopped crying and smoothed her hair.

"Fetch your father here!" she ordered Chia Jung. "I want to ask him why, with still a fortnight to go before the mourning for the uncle was over, he let the nephew take a wife. I've never heard of such a thing! I must learn the rules of propriety from him so as to pass them on later to the young people."

Still on his knees, Chia Jung kowtowed and protested, "This had nothing to do with my parents. It was I who put my uncle up to it — I must have eaten some shit. My father knew nothing about it. He's gone now to prepare for the funeral procession. If you make a scene, aunt, it will be the death of me. Whatever punishment you impose I'll accept it, but for pity's sake settle this court case — it's too serious for me to handle. You're so intelligent you know the saying: 'If your arm is broken, hide it in your sleeve.' I was an utter fool. As I've done such a despicable thing, I'm just like a cat or a dog. Now that you've given me this lesson, auntie, do please do your best to settle this with the court. Though I've been so undutiful and wronged you, aunt, by causing all this trouble, what else can I do but beg you to take pity on me!" He went on kowtowing as if he would never stop.

The behaviour of mother and son made it hard for Hsi-feng to go on storming at them. She had to adopt a different attitude now.

Apologizing to Madam Yu she said, "I'm too young and inexperienced. When I heard the case had been taken to court, I was frightened out of my wits. How could I have been so rude to you just now, sister! Still, Jung is right: 'If your arm is broken, hide it in your sleeve.' You must forgive me. And please ask Cousin Chen to lose no time in settling this lawsuit."

"Don't worry," Madam Yu and Chia Jung assured her.

"Uncle won't be involved at all," added Chia Jung. "You

said just now you'd spent five hundred taels, aunt. Of course we'll get together that sum and send it over to make it up to you. How can we make you out of pocket over us? That would be even more outrageous. But one thing, aunt, will you help see to it that no word of this reaches Their Ladyships?"

Hsi-feng smiled sarcastically at Madam Yu.

"First you stab me in the back and now you ask me to hush it up for you! I may be a fool but I'm not all *that* foolish. Your cousin happens to be my husband, sister. If you were worried because he had no son, wouldn't I be still more worried? I look on your younger sister as my own sister. When I heard about this I was too excited to sleep and made my people get ready rooms at once, to fetch her in to live with us. Actually the servants had more sense: they said, 'You're too kind-hearted, madam. It seems to us it would be better to wait till you've reported this to Their Ladyships and see what they have to say.' That made me rage at them, so they said no more.

"But nothing worked out as I wanted. Like a slap in the face or a bolt from the blue came this suit brought by Chang Hua. I had to beg people to find out who this Chang Hua was, that he had such a nerve; and two days later I was told he was a rascally beggar. Being young and ignorant, I laughed and asked what he'd accused us of. The servants told me, 'The new mistress was engaged to him. Now he's desperate, liable to starve or freeze to death anyway, so he's seized on this chance. Even if he dies for it, it's a better bet than dying of hunger and cold; so how can you blame him? After all, the master acted too hastily and was guilty of two offences by marrying during state mourning and family mourning. He was wrong, too, to keep it a secret from his parents and to take a new wife without his wife's consent. As the proverb says, "One who will risk being sliced to pieces dare unsaddle the Emperor." A man so desperately poor will go to any lengths. He's in the right too, so why not make an indictment?'

"So you see, sister, even if I'd been as wise as Han Hsin or Chang Liang,[1] such talk would have frightened me out of my wits. Besides, with my husband away, I had no one to consult; I could only try to patch things up with money. Yet the more I gave him, the more I was at his mercy and the more he blackmailed me. But how much can he squeeze out of *me*? No more than from a pimple on a rat's tail. That's why I panicked and flew into such a rage that I came looking for you. . . ."

Not waiting for her to finish, Madam Yu and her son said, "Don't worry. We'll see to it."

Chia Jung added, "It's Chang Hua's poverty that's made him so reckless he's risked his life to indict us. I know what to do. Promise him some money and get him to admit that he brought a false accusation; then we can settle the business. When he comes out, we'll give him some more silver and that will be that."

"What a clever boy!" said Hsi-feng derisively. "No wonder that you did this thing with no thought of the consequences. How stupid you are! Suppose he agreed to what you proposed and got money from us after the case was settled, of course that would be that — for the time being. But as such people are rascals, as soon as that silver was spent he'd start blackmailing us again. If he made further trouble what should we do? We may not be afraid of him, still it's something to worry about. And he can always say if we hadn't wronged him why should we give him money?"

Chia Jung had sense enough to understand this.

He said with a smile, "Well, I have another plan. Since I caused the trouble it's up to me to fix it. I'll go and sound Chang Hua out. Does he want her back, or will he give her up and settle for money with which he can marry another girl? If he insists on having her, I'll go and persuade my second aunt to leave here and marry him; if he wants money, we shall have to give him some."

---

[1] See Note 3 on p. 159 and Note 2 on p. 160.

"That's all very well," said Hsi-feng hastily. "I certainly don't want her to leave us, and I certainly won't let her. If you've any feeling for me, nephew, just give him a bigger sum in settlement."

Chia Jung knew very well that in spite of Hsi-feng's protestations she really wanted to get rid of Second Sister and was only posing as broad-minded. He had to agree, however, to whatever she said, at which she looked delighted.

"The problem outside is easy to handle, but what about the arrangement at home?" Hsi-feng now asked. "You must come back with me to report this."

This threw Madam Yu into another panic. She begged Hsi-feng to make up some story for her.

"If you can't talk your way out, why do this in the first place?" asked Hsi-feng sarcastically. "I've no patience with the way you're carrying on. But it wouldn't be like me to refuse to find a way out for you, as I'm so soft-hearted that even when people trick me I still act like a fool. All right then, I'll see to this. Both of you keep out of it.

"I'll take your sister to pay her respects to Their Ladyships, and tell them that I took a fancy to her, and because I have no son I was thinking of buying a couple of concubines. Finding your sister so charming, and as we're relatives too, I wanted her to be Lien's second wife. But because her parents and sister had died recently and she was finding it hard to manage, with no home of her own, how could she possibly wait till after the full hundred days' mourning? So I decided to bring her into our house, and I've made the side rooms ready for her to stay in for the time being. Once the mourning is over she can live with my husband.

"I shall brazen it out somehow in my shameless way. If anyone is blamed it won't be *you*. What do you think of this plan?"

Madam Yu and Chia Jung responded, "It's most generous and kind of you. How clever you are! Once it's settled, we'll certainly both come to thank you."

Madam Yu ordered her maids to help Hsi-feng wash her face

and comb her hair. Then the table was spread and she herself served the wine and food. Before long, however, Hsi-feng rose to go.

She went to the Garden and told Second Sister what had happened, explaining how worried she had been, how she had ascertained the facts, and what would have to be done to keep them all out of trouble. She promised to get them out of the dilemma.

To know what her plans really were, read the next chapter.

CHAPTER 69

Crafty Hsi-feng Kills Her Rival
by Proxy
And Second Sister Swallows Gold
and Dies

Unable to express all her gratitude, Second Sister went off with Hsi-feng. And propriety required Madam Yu to accompany them to report to the old lady.

"You needn't say anything," Hsi-feng assured her. "Leave all the talking to me."

"Of course," agreed Madam Yu. "If there's any blame we'll let you take it."

They went first to the Lady Dowager's room where she was chatting and laughing with the girls from the Garden. At sight of the pretty young woman Hsi-feng had brought in, the old lady looked at her searchingly. "Whose child is this?" she asked. "So charming!"

Hsi-feng stepped forward and said with a smile, "Take a good look, Old Ancestress. Isn't she sweet?" Pulling Second Sister forward too, she told her, "This is grandmother-in-law. Hurry up and kowtow to her."

At once Second Sister prostrated herself to pay her respects. Then Hsi-feng introduced the girls to her one by one.

"Now you know them," she said. "After the old lady's through with inspecting you, you can pay your respects to each other."

Second Sister pretended that this was the first time she had met them, then stood there with lowered head while the Lady Dowager looked her up and down.

"What is your name?" she inquired. "How old are you?"

489

"Never mind about that, Old Ancestress," Hsi-feng chuckled. "Just say, is she prettier than me?"

The old lady put on her spectacles, telling Yuan-yang and Hu-po, "Bring the child closer. I want to look at her skin."

Amid suppressed laughter, Second Sister was pushed forward and subjected to a carefully scrutiny. Then the Lady Dowager made Hu-po hold out her hands for inspection. Yuan-yang lifted Second Sister's skirt as well to show her feet. Her examination at an end, the old lady took off her spectacles.

"Perfect!" she pronounced. "She's even prettier than you."

Smiling, Hsi-feng promptly knelt down to relate in detail the story she had made up in Madam Yu's room. "Do take pity on her, Old Ancestress," she pleaded. "Let her move in now, and after a year they can be formally married."

"That's quite in order," the old lady conceded. "I'm glad you're so understanding and tolerant. But she mustn't live with Lien for a year."

Hsi-feng kowtowed, then got up and requested that two maids be sent to present Second Sister to Lady Hsing and Lady Wang and tell them this was the old lady's decision. The Lady Dowager agreed and this was done. Lady Wang had been worried because of Hsi-feng's bad name. Now that she was taking in a second wife for her husband, she was naturally pleased. So from now on Second Sister could come into the open, and she moved to Hsi-feng's side rooms.

Hsi-feng meanwhile sent a messenger in secret to urge Chang Hua to insist on claiming his bride, promising that in addition to a generous dowry he would be given money to set up house. For Chang Hua himself was too spineless to dare sue the Chia family.

Then Chia Jung sent a man to court to contend, "It was Chang Hua who first gave up the engagement. Being related to the Yu family we did, it is true, invite her to stay in our house; but there was no talk of marriage. Because Chang Hua owed us money and could not pay it, he trumped up this charge against our master."

As the judges were all connected with the Chia and Wang

families and had in addition accepted bribes from them, they condemned Chang Hua as a rascal whom poverty had driven to blackmail. His plea rejected, he was beaten and thrown out of court. But Ching-erh outside had fixed it with the runners not to beat him severely.

And now Ching-erh told Chang Hua, "As you were engaged to the girl first, if you demand her the court will have to give her to you."

Thereupon Chang Hua brought a new suit; but again Wang Hsin took a message to the judge, and the court's verdict was: "Chang Hua's debt to the Chia family must be repaid in full by a specified date. As for his betrothed, he can marry her when he has the means."

Chang Hua's father, summoned to court to hear this verdict after having been told the situation by Ching-erh, exulted that now he would get both the money and the girl. He went to the Chia mansion to fetch Second Sister.

Hsi-feng with a great show of alarm reported this to the Lady Dowager.

"This muddle is all my Sister-in-Law Chen's fault!" she complained. "Apparently the engagement was never really cancelled. That's why the Changs took the case to court, and now this decision's been made."

The old lady sent at once for Madam Yu.

"Because your sister was promised from childhood to the Chang family, and they never broke the engagement, they've brought this charge against us now," she scolded.

"But they took the money," protested Madam Yu. "How can they still claim her?"

Hsi-feng put in, "According to Chang Hua, he never saw any money, and no one contacted him. According to his father, Second Sister's mother did make such an offer but they turned it down; and after her mother died you took her in as a secondary wife. As we've no proof to the contrary, he can talk any nonsense he pleases. It's lucky Second Master Lien isn't at home and they haven't been formally married. Still, as she's already here, how can we send her back? Wouldn't that make us lose face?"

The old lady said, "They're not married yet, and it wouldn't look good to seize someone promised to another man. That would damage our reputation. We'd better send her back. It'll be easy enough to find some other nice girl."

When Second Sister heard this she exclaimed, "My mother really *did* give them ten taels of silver to cancel the engagement. Now in desperation because he's poor, he denies it. My sister did nothing wrong."

"That shows how troublesome such rascals are," said the Lady Dowager. "Well, I leave it to you, Hsi-feng, to sort this out."

Hsi-feng had to comply. On her return she sent for Chia Jung, who knew perfectly what she was aiming at. He realized what a great loss of face it would be if Second Sister were to be reclaimed by the Changs, so he reported this to Chia Chen and secretly sent Chang Hua the message: Now that you've got so much money, why must you have the girl back? If you insist, the gentlemen may get angry and find a way to kill you where no one will bury you. With money, you can go home and find a good bride. If you do that, we'll help with your travelling expenses.

Chang Hua on reflection thought this a good idea. He discussed it with his father, and they reckoned they were now the richer by about a hundred taels. So the next day at dawn, father and son started home.

When Chia Jung heard this he told the Lady Dowager and Hsi-feng, "Chang Hua and his father have fled for fear of being punished for bringing a false charge. The court knows of this but has decided to let the matter drop. The whole business is over!"

Hsi-feng reflected, "If I make Chang Hua reclaim Second Sister, Lien on his return will most likely offer more money to get her back, and Chang Hua's bound to agree. So I'd better keep her here with me until I've made other plans. The only snag is we don't know where Chang Hua will go, and whether he'll spread this story or come back later to re-open this case. If he does, I'll have cut my own throat! I should never have given other people this handle against me." She bitterly regretted what she had done.

Then she hit on another plan. She quietly ordered Lai Wang to send men to find Chang Hua, then either hale him to court on a charge of theft and have him done to death, or send assassins to kill him secretly. In this way the root of the trouble would be removed and her reputation assured.

Lai Wang went home and thought over these instructions.

"Since the man's gone and the matter's dropped, why do anything so drastic?" he asked himself. "Taking someone's life is a serious crime, no joke. I'll fool her into thinking it's done instead."

He lay low outside for a few days, then returned to report that Chang Hua, travelling with a fair amount of silver had been beaten and killed at dawn one day by some highwaymen in the Chingkou district, and his father had died of fright in the inn. A post-mortem had been held there and the bodies buried.

Hsi-feng did not believe him.

"If I find you've been lying, I'll knock out your teeth!" she threatened. But there the matter rested.

Meanwhile Hsi-feng and Second Sister were on the best of terms, to all appearances closer even than sisters.

When Chia Lien finally came home after completing his business, he went straight to the new house. But it was locked up and deserted, with only an old caretaker there who told him all that had happened. Chia Lien stamped his foot in the stirrup, then went to report on his mission to his parents. Chia Sheh, very pleased, praised his competence and rewarded him with a hundred taels of silver as well as a new concubine — a seventeen-year-old maid of his named Chiu-tung. Chia Lien kowtowed his thanks and left in high spirits. Having paid his respects to the Lady Dowager and other members of the family he went home somewhat sheepishly to see Hsi-feng, but found her less stern than usual. She came out with Second

Sister to welcome him and ask after his health. Then Chia Lien, telling her of his father's gift, could not help looking pleased and proud. Hsi-feng immediately sent two serving-women to fetch Chiu-tung by carriage. Before she had rid herself of one thorn in her side, here — out of the blue — was another! However, she had to watch her tongue and hide her anger by a show of complaisance, ordering a feast of welcome, then taking Chiu-tung to present her to the Lady Dowager and Lady Wang, much to her husband's amazement.

On the Double Twelfth, Chia Chen rose early to sacrifice to the ancestors, then took his leave of the Lady Dowager and other ladies of the family. Most of the men saw him off to the Pavilion of Tearful Parting, only Chia Lien and Chia Jung accompanying him all the way to the temple and back, a trip taking three days and three nights. On the road, Chia Chen admonished them on the need to run their households well, and they gave him the appropriate assurances — there is no need to dwell on their conversation.

To return to Hsi-feng at home. Outwardly, it goes without saying, she treated Second Sister well; but inwardly she plotted to destroy her.

When the two of them were alone she told Second Sister, "You have such a bad name, sister, even the old lady and the mistresses have heard about it. They say that while still a girl you were unchaste and intimate with your brother-in-law. 'You've picked someone nobody else wanted,' they scold me. 'Why not get rid of her and choose someone better.' Talk like that makes me furious. I've tried to find out who started this, but I can't. If this goes on, how are we to hold up our heads in front of these slaves? I seem to have landed myself in a foul mess." Having said this a couple of times, she pretended to fall ill with anger, refusing to eat or drink.

All the maids and servants, with the exception of Ping-erh, kept gossiping, making sarcastic remarks, and casting aspersions at Second Sister. As for Chiu-tung, having been given to Chia Lien by his father, she felt superior to everyone else including even Hsi-feng and Ping-erh, not to say a discarded wanton who had been Chia Lien's mistress before she became his wife. "How can she take precedence of *me*!" she thought. So she treated her with contempt. Hsi-feng was secretly pleased at this, and Second Sister had to swallow her indignation.

As Hsi-feng was shamming sickness she stopped having her meals with Second Sister, just ordering the servants to take food to her room every day — and the rice and dishes were always of the worst. Ping-erh took pity on her. She would spend her own money on extra dishes for her, or take her sometimes for a stroll in the Garden, getting special soups made for her in the kitchen there. No one else dared report this to Hsi-feng; but Chiu-tung, happening to find out, went to tell her.

"Ping-erh's spoiling your reputation, madam," she said. "The good dishes we have here are wasted on her — she won't eat them. Instead, she scrounges food in the Garden."

Hsi-feng swore at Ping-erh, "Other people's cats catch mice for them, but mine just steals my chickens!"

Ping-erh did not venture to talk back. After that she had to keep at a distance from Second Sister, and she bore Chiu-tung a grudge but could not speak out.

Li Wan, Ying-chun and Hsi-chun in the Garden thought Hsi-feng was uncommonly good to Second Sister. Others like Pao-yu and Tai-yu were worried for her, but did not like to meddle in their affairs. Second Sister looked so pathetic when she called that they sympathized with her, and when they were talking alone she would shed tears, but she never breathed a word against Hsi-feng who had shown her nothing of her vicious side.

When Chia Lien came home and observed Hsi-feng's irreproachable behaviour to Second Sister, he did not give the matter a second thought. Besides, he had long had designs on many of his father's concubines and young maids, including Chiu-tung, who for their part were disgusted because their senile old master, still lecherous, was virtually impotent. Why, then, should he keep them all there? So apart from a few with some sense of propriety, the rest played about with the pages at the inner gate or even made eyes at Chia Lien, who was only too ready to flirt with them but for fear of his father dared go no further than that.

Although Chiu-tung had been interested in Chia Lien, they had never had an affair. Now that as luck would have it she had been given to him, it was truly like throwing a dry faggot on a blazing fire. They clung to each other like glue, Chia Lien so enamoured of his new concubine that he never left her side. Little by little his affection for Second Sister lessened. Chiu-tung was the only one he cared for.

Hsi-feng, though hating Chiu-tung, was eager to use her first to rid herself of Second Sister by "killing with a borrowed sword" and "watching from a hilltop while two tigers fought." For once Chiu-tung had killed Second Sister, she could do this new concubine in. Her mind made up, when they were alone she often advised Chiu-tung:

"You're young and inexperienced. She's now the second mistress, your master's favourite. Even *I* have to yield to her to some extent, yet you keep provoking her. You're just looking for trouble."

Inflamed by such talk, Chiu-tung took to cursing and storming every day, "The mistress is too soft and weak; I haven't that kind of forbearance. What's happened to her? She used to be such a terror. Well, the mistress may be broad-minded, but I'm not going to put up with a mote in my eye. Just let me have it out with that bitch — then she'll see!"

Hsi-feng in her room pretended to be too frightened to say a word. Second Sister in her room wept for rage and could not eat, but she dared not tell Chia Lien. And the next day when the Lady Dowager asked why her eyes were so red and swollen, she dared not explain.

Chiu-tung seized every chance to score off her. She secretly told the old lady and Lady Wang, "She keeps making trouble, complaining and whining all day for no reason at all, besides cursing madam and me behind our backs. She hopes we'll both die early, so that she can live with Second Master and do just as she pleases."

"Imagine!" exclaimed the old lady. "When a girl's too pretty, she is bound to be jealous. Hsi-feng's been kind to her all along, yet she repays her by treating her like a rival! This shows she's a worthless creature."

Little by little she took a dislike to Second Sister. And when the others saw that she had lost favour with the old lady, they naturally bullied her too. Second Sister was in such a miserable dilemma, she could neither die nor live. Ping-erh was the only one who tried, behind Hsi-feng's back, to help her and divert her mind from her troubles.

How could Second Sister, fragile as snow, delicate as a flower, stand up to such cruel treatment? After suppressing her anger for just a month, she fell ill and lost her appetite. Too listless to move, she grew daily thinner and paler. One night when she closed her eyes, she saw her younger sister approaching, the duck-and-drake swords in her hands.

"You've always been too naive and soft-hearted," Third Sister told her. "That's why you're in trouble now. Don't trust that shrew's honeyed talk or her show of being such a virtuous wife — at heart she's crafty and cruel. She's made up her mind to kill you. If I'd been alive, I'd never have let you move into their house; even if you had, I'd not let her treat you like this. Still, we brought this on ourselves by our worthless lives and wanton ways, corrupting men and upsetting family relations. So this is just retribution. Now take my advice and kill that shrew with this sword, then go together to the Goddess of Disenchantment for her to decide the case. Otherwise you will die in vain and no one will pity you."

Second Sister sobbed, "I've already got a bad name, sister. As I deserve my present fate, why should I add to my crimes by killing her? Let me just put up with it. If Heaven takes pity on me, I may recover. Wouldn't that be better?"

"Still so naive, sister?" the other scoffed. "No one, since time immemorial, has escaped Heaven's far-flung net. The Way of Providence is retribution. Although you've repented and mended your ways, you've already made father, son and cousins guilty of incest; so how can Providence allow you to live at peace?"

"If I can't live at peace, that's only just," said Second Sister tearfully. "I bear no resentment."

Hearing this, Third Sister heaved a long sigh and withdrew. Second Sister woke with a start to find it was only a dream.

When Chia Lien came to see her, as no one else was about she told him with tears, "I shan't get over this illness. I've been with you for half a year and I'm with child, but don't know whether it will be a boy or a girl. If Heaven has pity and the child is born, well and good. Otherwise, I shan't be able to save myself, let alone the child."

"Don't you worry," Chia Lien, in tears himself, reassured her. "I'll get a good doctor for you."

He immediately went out to send for the doctor. However, Doctor Wang was busy manoeuvring to get a post in the army in order to acquire a noble title for his offspring. In his absence the servants fetched Doctor Hu Chun-jung. His diagnosis was that her menstruation was irregular and some tonic would set her right. When Chia Lien told him that she had missed three periods and was often sick, so it looked like a pregnancy, Hu Chun-jung asked the serving-women to show him the lady's hand, and Second Sister stretched out her hand from behind the curtains. After feeling the pulse for some time he declared:

"If it were a pregnancy, the liver humour should be strong. But the wood is in the ascendant, and that engenders the fire element which causes irregular menstruation. May I make so bold as to ask to have a glimpse of the lady's face, so that I can see how she looks before venturing to make out a prescription."

Chia Lien had to order the curtain to be raised. But the sight of Second Sister robbed Hu Chun-jung of his senses. He was too dazed to know what he was doing. Then the curtain was lowered and Chia Lien escorted him out. Asked what the trouble was he said:

"It's not a pregnancy, just congestion of the blood. To make her periods normal, we must get rid of the congestion." He then wrote a prescription and took his leave.

Chia Lien ordered servants to send over the doctor's fee and buy and prepare the medicine for the patient.

In the middle of the night, Second Sister had such a pain in her stomach that she miscarried — the foetus was male — and bled so copiously that she fainted. Chia Lien hearing this cursed Hu Chun-jung and had another doctor fetched at once. He also sent men to go and beat up Hu; but the latter heard of this in time to bundle together his things and run away.

The newly summoned doctor said, "She had a weak constitution to begin with, and after conceiving she seems to have been bottling up some resentment. That other gentleman made the mistake of using potent drugs which have undermined the lady's health completely. We cannot look for a speedy recovery. She will have to take both potions and pills, and must pay no attention to any malicious gossip; then we can only hope she may get well." This said, he left.

In a frenzy, Chia Lien asked who it was that had fetched that fellow Hu and had the man beaten within an inch of his life.

Hsi-feng showing ten times more anxiety exclaimed, "We seem fated to have no son! After going to such trouble to beget one, we come up against this bungling quack." She offered incense and kowtowed to Heaven and Earth, praying earnestly, "Let me fall ill if only Sister Yu can recover, conceive again and give birth to a boy. Then I'll gladly fast and chant sutras for the rest of my life."

Chia Lien and the others, seeing this, could not but praise her.

While Chia Lien stayed with Chiu-tung, Hsi-feng prepared soup and broth for the invalid.

She also berated Ping-erh, "You're just as luckless as me with my illness, because you're not ill, just barren! It must be our bad luck that's brought the Second Mistress to this pass — or may be someone's horoscope clashes with hers."

Thereupon she sent out to consult fortune-tellers, who returned the reply that the trouble had been caused by a woman born in the year of the rabbit. They checked, and as Chiu-tung was the only one in their household born in that year they laid the blame at her door.

Chiu-tung's jealousy had already been aroused by the care Chia Lien lavished on Second Sister, fetching doctors, giving her medicine, and having the servant who had blundered beaten. Now *she* was told that she was the one to blame, and Hsi-feng advised her to move out for a few months and make herself scarce.

Chiu-tung wept and stormed, "What's all this senseless talk from that blind rascal? I kept as clear of her as well water and river water. How could *my* horoscope clash with hers? She had all sorts of contacts outside, the slut. Why does the jinx have to be found here? Which of all those fine fellows she knew got her with child? It's only this credulous master of ours who's taken in by her. Even if she had a child, we wouldn't know whether its name should be Chang or Wang. *You* may treasure her bastard, madam, but not I! Who can't have a child? If I have one a year or so from now, at least there'll be no doubt who fathered it."

The maids were amused by this tirade but dared not laugh outright. And just then Lady Hsing called.

Chiu-tung told her, "The Second Master and Second Mistress want to throw me out. I've nowhere to go. Please take pity on me, madam!"

Lady Hsing first scolded Hsi-feng, then said sternly to Chia Lien:

"You ungrateful cur! Whatever her faults, she was given you by your father. How can you throw her out for the sake of a woman you brought in from outside? Have you no respect for your father? If you want to get rid of her, you can at least return her to him." She then left in a temper.

Emboldened by this, Chiu-tung went to Second Sister's window to scream abuse at her, making her feel even more wretched.

Chia Lien spent that night in Chiu-tung's room. And after Hsi-feng had gone to bed Ping-erh slipped in to see Second Sister and comfort her, advising her to rest well and not trouble about that bitch.

Second Sister took her hand and said through tears, "How good you've been to me, sister, since I came here! You've suffered a lot too on my account. If I come out of this alive, I'll repay your kindness. I'm afraid I'm done for, though, and can only pay you back in my next life."

Ping-erh was reduced to tears too.

"It was all *my* fault," she confessed. "I was too naive. I never kept anything from her, so when I heard of your marriage outside I felt I had to tell her. I had no idea such trouble would come of it."

"No, you're wrong," protested Second Sister. "If you hadn't told, she'd have found out anyway. You just happened to tell her first. At any rate, I *wanted* to move in for appearances' sake. So you're in no way to blame."

They both wept again and presently, after a few more words of advice, Ping-erh saw that it was late and went back to rest.

Left to herself Second Sister thought, "I'm so ill, and getting worse every day, I see no hope of recovery. And now that I've miscarried and haven't the child to worry about, why should I go on putting up with such taunts? Better die and be done with it! They say swallowing gold will kill you. Wouldn't that be a cleaner death than hanging myself or cutting my own throat?"

She struggled out of bed and opened her case, from which she took a piece of gold of a fair size. Weeping and cursing her fate, she put it in her mouth and after several desperate attempts succeeded in swallowing it. Then she hastily dressed herself neatly and put on her trinkets, after which she lay down on the *kang*. Not a soul had any suspicion of what she had done.

The next morning when she failed to call for her maids, they attended cheerfully to their own toilets while Hsi-feng and Chiu-tung went off to pay their respects to the senior mistresses.

Ping-erh was shocked by this and scolded the maids, "Don't be so heartless! You only obey harsh people who beat or curse you — and that's the treatment you deserve. Have you no pity at all for someone so ill? You might at least behave decently, instead of taking advantage of her good nature and kicking her when she's down."

The maids opened Second Sister's door then. At sight of her lying — neatly dressed — dead on her bed, they screamed with fright. Ping-erh running in wept bitterly when she saw this. And the maids, remembering now how gentle Second Sister had been and how much kinder to them than Hsi-feng, shed tears over her death as well, but took care to hide their grief from their dreaded mistress.

The news spread at once through the whole mansion. Chia Lien came in, clasped the corpse and wept without stop.

Hsi-feng put on a show of sobbing, "How cruel of you, sister, to leave me alone like this! What a poor return for my kindness!"

Madam Yu and Chia Jung also came to mourn and console Chia Lien. Then he reported the matter to Lady Wang, and obtained permission to leave the corpse for five days in Pear Fragrance Court before its removal to Iron Threshold Temple. Hasty orders were given to have the court gate opened and the three main rooms cleared for the coffin's resting place. Since it would be unbecoming to carry the bier through the back gate, Chia Lien had a new gate leading to the street made through the main wall facing Pear Fragrance Court; booths were set up on either side of this and an altar was erected for Buddhist masses. And there Second Sister was carried on a soft couch with a silken mattress and a coverlet shrouding her body. Eight pages and a few matrons escorted the bier from the inner wall to Pear Fragrance Court, where they had an astrologer waiting.

When Chia Lien lifted the coverlet and saw Second Sister

lying there as if alive, yet even lovelier than in life, he threw his arms around her.

"Wife, your death is a mystery," he wailed. "But I brought it on you."

Chia Jung hastily stepped forward to console him.

"Don't give way to such grief, uncle. This aunt of mine was ill-starred." As he spoke he pointed south at the wall of Grand View Garden.

Chia Lien caught his meaning and softly stamped his foot.

"Yes, I know. I shall get to the bottom of it and avenge you!"

The astrologer reported that as the lady had died at five in the morning she could not be carried to the temple on the fifth, but the third or the seventh would be appropriate, and the body should be coffined at three the next morning — an auspicious hour.

"The third won't do," said Chia Lien. "We'll make it the seventh. As my uncle and cousin are away, we mustn't leave her here too long as this is a minor funeral. After the coffin has been placed in the temple for five weeks, we'll have a big mass and then close the mourning shrine. Next year it can be taken south for burial."

The astrologer approved this and left after writing out the obituary. Pao-yu had already come to mourn, and now other members of the clan arrived. Chia Lien hurried back then to ask Hsi-feng for money for the coffin and funeral rites.

Meanwhile, after seeing the body carried away, Hsi-feng had shammed illness again and claimed that Their Ladyships would not let her attend any ceremonies while unwell. She did not put on mourning either. Going instead to the Garden, past the rockeries to the wall at the north end, she eavesdropped on her husband outside, then came back to report the few remarks she had caught to the Lady Dowager.

"Don't listen to his nonsense," said the old lady. "Girls who die of consumption are cremated, aren't they, and their ashes scattered? Why should she have a formal funeral and burial? Still, as she was a secondary wife, let her body be kept for five weeks in the temple before being carried out to be burnt or buried in some common graveyard."

Hsi-feng smiled.

"That's exactly what I think, but I dare not urge him to do that."

A maid came then to ask Hsi-feng to go back as Chia Lien had gone home to get some money from her, and so she had to return.

"What money do we have?" she asked him. "Don't you know how tight things have been here recently? We couldn't distribute each month's allowance on time. It's been like hens eating up next year's grain. Yesterday I pawned a gold necklace for three hundred taels, and that may have given you ideas; but now only about two dozen taels are left. If you want that you can have it."

She told Ping-erh to fetch this and gave it to Chia Lien, then went off again on the excuse that the old lady wanted her.

Chia Lien swallowing his resentment had to resort to opening Second Sister's cases to look for any savings; but all he found were some broken trinkets, soiled artificial flowers and some of her half worn silk clothes, the sight of which reduced him to tears again. He wrapped them up in a cloth and, not asking the maids or pages to carry the bundle, started out to burn it himself. Ping-erh, both touched and amused, filched a packet of loose silver — about two hundred taels — and going to the eastern rooms gave him this, warning him to keep it a secret.

"If you must cry, can't you cry as much as you want outside?" she scolded him. "Why do it here, attracting attention?"

"You're right," said Chia Lien as he took the silver. He then gave a skirt to Ping-erh saying, "This is one she was fond of wearing. Keep it for me as a memento."

Ping-erh accepted it and put it away.

Having taken the silver, Chia Lien came out with some others and ordered men to buy wood for the coffin. The best timber was expensive, but nothing inferior would satisfy him; so he

mounted his horse and went to make the choice himself.   By
evening some good timber had been delivered — as it cost five
hundred taels, he had to buy it on credit.   He had the coffin
made immediately, at the same time assigning mourners to
keep vigil, and he did not go home that night, but watched by
the coffin.

What happened later is recorded in the next chapter.

CHAPTER 70

Tai-yu Starts Another Poetry Club —
Peach-Blossom Society
Hsiang-yun Dashes Off a Poem
on Willow Catkins

Chia Lien attended the funeral ceremonies at Pear Fragrance Court for seven days and seven nights, during which monks and priests chanted sutras. Then the Lady Dowager summoned him and forbade him to send the coffin to the family temple, so all he could do was choose a spot near Third Sister's grave and arrange with Shih Chueh of the temple to have Second Sister buried there. Only members of the clan, Wang Hsin and his wife, Madam Yu and her daughter-in-law were present at the interment. Hsi-feng did not lift a finger to help, leaving Chia Lien to manage everything himself.

New Year was now approaching and, on top of the host of things that had to be seen to, Lin Chih-hsiao brought a list of eight men-servants who had reached the age of twenty-five and not yet married, to ask whether there were any maids due to leave who would make them suitable wives. Hsi-feng having read the list went to consult the old lady and Lady Wang, but although there were several maids in that category they found objections in the case of each. First, Yuan-yang since vowing never to leave their service had neither spoken to Pao-yu nor put on fine clothes or make up; and in view of her determination, they could hardly force her to marry. Then Hu-po was disqualified by illness. And Tsai-yun, since breaking with Chia Huan recently, had also contracted some unknown disease. Apart from them, only the older maid-servants doing rough work for Hsi-feng and Li Wan were due to leave. The others were too young. So the men had to look for wives outside.

While Hsi-feng was unwell, Li Wan and Tan-chun had been too occupied with domestic affairs to have time for anything else; and what with celebrating New Year and the Lantern Festival and miscellaneous business, the poetry club had been forgotten. Now, although there was a lull and it was mid-spring, a whole series of misfortunes — Pao-yu's loss of his friend Liu Hsiang-lien, the suicides of Third Sister and Second Sister, and Liu Wu-erh's illness brought on by mortification — had reduced Pao-yu to such a state of dejection that he appeared dazed and often raved like a madman. Hsi-jen and his other maids were alarmed but not daring to report this to the old lady they just did their best in every way to divert him.

One morning, as soon as he woke he heard giggling and muffled cries from the outer room.

"Go and rescue her, quick!" said Hsi-jen with a smile. "Ching-wen and Sheh-yueh have pinned Venturina down and are tickling her."

Pao-yu draped his squirrel-fur jacket over his shoulders and went out to have a look. The three girls had not folded their quilts or put on their outer clothes. Ching-wen in a leek-green silk bodice, red silk pants and red slippers, her hair tousled, was sitting astride Fang-kuan who was being tickled in the ribs by Sheh-yueh in a red silk chemise, an old jacket over her shoulders. Fang-kuan lying on her back in a flowered bodice, red pants and green socks was thrashing her legs wildly, quite out of breath from laughing.

"Two big girls bullying one small one!" chuckled Pao-yu. "I've come to the rescue."

He climbed on to the *kang* to tickle Ching-wen in the ribs. Being ticklish, she at once let go of Fang-kuan to grab him; and Fang-kuan seized this chance to pull her down and tickle her under the armpits.

"Mind you don't catch cold!" warned Hsi-jen, amused to see the four of them scuffling together.

Just then Li Wan's maid Pi-yueh came in.

"Last night my mistress left a handkerchief somewhere," she announced. "Is it here?"

Hsiao-yen answered, "Yes, it is. I picked it up from the floor and didn't know whose it was. I've just washed it and hung it out. It's not quite dry yet."

Pi-yueh smiled at sight of the scrimmage on the *kang*.

"You're lively here," she remarked, "starting your horseplay so early in the morning."

"Don't you play about in your place too?" asked Pao-yu. "There are plenty of you there."

"Our mistress is so serious that her two cousins and Miss Pao-chin hold themselves in check as well. And now that Miss Pao-chin's moved in with the old lady we're even quieter. By winter next year, when her cousins will have gone, it will be still quieter. Didn't you notice how lonely Miss Pao-chai's place seemed after Hsiang-ling went home, leaving Miss Hsiang-yun all on her own?"

Even as she was speaking, in came Tsui-lu sent by Hsiang-yun to invite Pao-yu over to read a fine poem. Asked where this good poem was, she said:

"The young ladies are all at Seeping Fragrance Pavilion. Go and see for yourself, young master."

Pao-yu hastily washed, dressed and left. Sure enough he found Tai-yu, Pao-chai, Hsiang-yun, Pao-chin and Tan-chun all there reading a poem.

"Why are you so late up?" they demanded. "For a year our poetry club's been broken up and no one's called it together again. Now it's early spring, a fresh start for all living things and high time to bestir ourselves to get it going again."

"We started the club in autumn," added Hsiang-yun. "That's why it didn't prosper. If we start it again now in spring when everything burgeons, it's bound to come to life. And this poem on peach-blossom is so good, why not change our Begonia Club into Peach-Blossom Club?"

Pao-yu nodded approvingly and asked to read the poem.

But the others proposed, "Let's go and find the Old Peasant of Sweet Paddy, to talk it over together and get things going."

With that they all got up and set off for Paddy-Sweet Cottage, Pao-yu reading the poem on the way. It was as follows:

PEACH-BLOSSOM

Outside the blind, peach-blossom, a soft spring breeze;
Within, a girl is languidly dressing her hair.
Outside, the peach-blossom; within the girl —
Not far apart the blossom and maid so fair.
Obligingly, the breeze blows back the blind
And holds it to afford a glimpse of her bower;
Outside, the peach is blooming as of old,
Frailer the girl within than any flower.
The flowers, knowing pity, grieve for her;
Their sighs gentle breezes express;
Breeze wafts through bamboo slats, blooms fill the court,
But this spring scene redoubles her distress.
The gate of the quiet, mossy courtyard is closed,
At sunset she leans alone on the balustrade;
Then, shedding tears in the soothing breeze,
Neath blossoming boughs slips the red-skirted maid.
Luxuriant the foliage and blooms
With petals a fresh red, leaves emerald green;
These myriad trees enwrapped in mist
Cast a rosy glow, as if of warmth, on her screen.
Duck-and-drake brocade from heaven's loom is burned,
While on coral pillow she wakes in balmy spring;
But chill to the touch of rouged cheeks,
Sweet spring water in golden basins her maids bring.
To what can the vividness of rouge be likened?
The colour of flowers? A girl's tears dropping slow?
If tears are likened to blossom,
Long as the blooms retain their charm they flow.
As she gazes at the blossom her tears run dry —
Her tears run dry, spring ends, blooms fade away;
The fading blossoms hide the fading maid;
Blossoms drift down, she tires, dusk follows day.
A cuckoo-call and spring is left behind,
Only faint moonlight falls on the lonely blind.

Pao-yu instead of praising this poem shed tears, for he knew it must be by Tai-yu. But not wanting the girls to see how moved he was, he hastily wiped his eyes.

"Where did you get this?" he asked.

"Guess who wrote it," challenged Pao-chin.

"The Queen of the Bamboos, of course."

"No, she didn't," giggled Pao-chin. "*I* did."

"I don't believe it. The style and spirit are definitely not yours."

"That just shows how little you know," put in Pao-chai.

"Were all Tu Fu's lines like 'clustered chrysanthemums have flowered twice in tears for other days'? He has other exquisite lines like 'Plums steeped in rain will wax crimson in days to come' and 'The waterweed in the breeze trails long emerald belts.'"

"Even so," Pao-yu retorted, "I know you'd never let your cousin write such sad lines. And even if she had the talent, she wouldn't want to. Cousin Tai-yu is different. She's known such grief that she writes mournful lines."

All laughing, they now reached Paddy-Sweet Cottage where they showed Tai-yu's poem to Li Wan, who was of course loud in her praise. Then they discussed the poetry club and decided to start it the following day, the second of the third month, and to change its name from Begonia Club to Peach-Blossom Society, electing Tai-yu as its president.

The next day after breakfast they all gathered in Bamboo Lodge. When the question arose of a subject for the first poem, Tai-yu suggested that each of them should write a hundred rhyming couplets on peach-blossom.

"That won't do," objected Pao-chai. "There have been so many poems since ancient times on peach-blossom, if we did that we'd be bound to produce something stereotyped, not to be compared with *your* poem. We must think of a different subject."

Just then the arrival of Lady Wang's sister-in-law was announced and they all had to go to the mansion to pay their respects. They chatted with Wang Tzu-teng's wife, and after lunch showed her round the Garden. Not till after dinner when the lamps were lit did she take her leave.

The day after that was Tan-chun's birthday. Yuan-chun sent two young eunuchs to present her with a few curios, and she received gifts which need not be enumerated from the rest of the family. After breakfast she changed into ceremonial costume and went to the different apartments to pay her respects.

Tai-yu observed laughingly, "I picked the wrong day again to start this club, forgetting that we'd be celebrating her birthday for the next two days. Though there won't be feasts and operas, we'll all have to go with her to spend the day amusing Their Ladyships, and that won't leave us any spare time." So the date was changed to the fifth.

That day, however, while the girls were waiting upon the old lady and Lady Wang at breakfast, a letter arrived from Chia Cheng. After paying his respects Pao-yu asked his grandmother's permission to open it and read it to her. Apart from the usual greetings, the letter said that Chia Cheng would definitely be back by the middle of the sixth month. Another letter on family affairs was opened and read by Chia Lien and Lady Wang.

The news of Chia Cheng's impending return by the sixth or seventh month threw them all into a flurry of excitement. On this same day, too, they heard that Wang Tzu-teng had arranged to marry his daughter to the son of Marquis Paoning on the tenth of the fifth month. Hsi-feng hastened to offer her services, and this took her away from home for days at a time. Then Wang Tzu-teng's wife came to invite Hsi-feng and the young people for a day's pleasure, and the Lady Dowager and Lady Wang told Pao-yu, Tan-chun, Tai-yu and Pao-chai to accompany Hsi-feng. Not daring to refuse, they had to go back to dress in formal costumes and then went out for the whole day, not returning till the evening.

Pao-yu, back in Happy Red Court, took a short rest. And Hsi-jen seized this chance to advise him to avoid distractions in future and spend his spare time revising the classics, ready for his father's return.

Pao-yu reckoned on his fingers. "There's still plenty of time," he expostulated.

"Reading's one thing, and there's writing too," she replied. "You may have read what's required, but how about your calligraphy exercises?"

"I've done quite a few. Haven't they been kept?"

"Of course. When you were out yesterday I got them out and counted them — there are only fifty to sixty sheets. Surely you should have written more than that in the last three or four years? I suggest that, starting tomorrow, you'd better put aside all other business and concentrate on writing a few sheets every day to make up. Then even if you haven't a sheet to show for each day, you'll have done enough to pass muster."

Pao-yu at once counted the sheets himself and found he had really procrastinated too long.

"From tomorrow on I'll write a hundred characters a day," he promised, after which they turned in for the night.

The next day as soon as he was dressed, he sat down by the window to grind ink and practise writing in real earnest, instead of going straight to his grandmother. Thinking he must be unwell she sent maids to make inquiries, whereupon he went over to pay his respects and explain that he was late because he had been practising calligraphy since first thing that morning.

The old lady was very gratified to hear this.

"As long as you're writing or studying, you needn't come here," she said. "You tell your mother that."

Pao-yu did so.

"It's no use sharpening your spear just before a battle," warned Lady Wang. "If you'd done some reading and writing every day, you'd have finished all that's expected and wouldn't feel so frantic. If you go at it too hard now you may fall ill again."

"No, I'll be all right," he assured her.

The old lady also expressed the fear that he might overwork and ruin his health.

"Don't you worry, madam," said Pao-chai and Tan-chun. "His reading we can't do for him, but writing we can. We'll each copy out one sheet for him every day to get him out of this fix; then His Lordship won't be angry when he comes home, and Pao-yu won't fret himself ill."

The old lady was delighted with this idea.

When Tai-yu heard that Chia Cheng was coming home, she knew he would certainly check on his son's studies and was afraid Pao-yu would get into trouble. So she pretended to have lost interest in re-starting the poetry society, in order not

to distract him. Tan-chun and Pao-chai each day neatly copied out a sheet of characters in the orthographic script for
Pao-yu, while he himself put on a spurt and wrote two or
three hundred characters a day. In this way, by the end of
the third month, he had amassed quite a number of exercises.
He reckoned that with another fifty sheets he could get by.

Then to his surprise Tzu-chuan came to give him a rolled-
up package. When he opened it he found a number of sheets
of old bamboo paper filled with small characters modelled on
those of Chung Yu and Wang Hsi-chih, exactly as he would
have written them himself. Pao-yu joyfully bowed his thanks
to Tzu-chuan, and went over in person to thank Tai-yu. Hsiang-
yun and Pao-chin also copied out some sheets for him. So
altogether, although less than was strictly required, he had
about enough. And once this was off his mind, Pao-yu started
re-reading the classics he had been set.

But it so happened that at this time some coastal regions
were devastated by tidal waves and the local officials reported
this to the court, whereupon the Emperor decreed that Chia
Cheng on his way back should inspect these areas and supervise
relief work. This meant that he would not be home till the
end of winter. When Pao-yu heard this, he put aside his books
and calligraphy exercises and started amusing himself again as
before.

It was then the end of spring. Hsiang-yun, feeling listless
one day, watched the swaying willow catkins and then dashed
off the following short poem to the melody *Ju-meng-ling*:

> Boughs with silk floss entwined
> Or sweet mist glimpsed through a half rolled-up blind?
> As slender fingers with the catkins play,
> Cuckoo and swallow cry out in dismay:
>   Stop, pray! Do stay!
>   Don't let spring steal away.

Feeling rather pleased with this verse she wrote it down and
showed it to Pao-chai, then went to find Tai-yu.

Tai-yu read it and pronounced, "Good. It's fresh and original. I can't write in this way myself."

"Our poetry club has never tried writing irregular metres,"

said Hsiang-yun. "Why don't you call a meeting tomorrow to do that? Wouldn't that make a change?"

Intrigued by this suggestion Tai-yu cried, "Of course! That's a wonderful idea. I'll send out invitations right away."

She gave orders for refreshments to be prepared, then sent her maids out to invite the others while she and Hsiang-yun fixed on willow catkins as the subject and on the different melodies to be used. They fastened a notice to this effect on the wall.

When the others arrived they read first this notice and then Hsiang-yun's poem, which they praised.

Pao-yu said: "I'm no good at irregular metres. Still, I shall have to write some sort of nonsense."

They drew lots for the different metres and Pao-chai got *Lin-chiang-hsien*; Pao-chin, *Hsi-chiang-yueh*; Tan-chun, *Nan-ko-tzu*; Tai-yu, *Tang-to-ling*; and Pao-yu, *Tieh-lien-hua*. Tzu-chuan lighted a stick of Sweet-Dream Incense then and they started. Very soon Tai-yu had finished and written her verse out. Then Pao-chin and Pao-chai completed theirs. They looked at each other's poem.

Pao-chai said with a smile, "Let me see yours first, and then you can see mine."

"How come the incense is burning so fast today?" exclaimed Tan-chun. "There's only one third left, yet I've just made up half." She asked Pao-yu, "How about you?"

Pao-yu did not think what he had written was any good, so he crossed it out meaning to start again, then looking round saw that the incense was nearly burnt up. The others laughed.

"Pao-yu's lost again," said Li Wan. "You'd better write out the half you've done, Tan-chun."

Tan-chun did so. Her lines to the melody *Nan-ko-tzu* were only half completed:

> In vain the willow trails long slender branches,
> Hanging strands of silk are they;
> They cannot curb the catkins
> And north, south, east and west these drift away....

Li Wan said, "That sounds easy. Why not finish it?"

Seeing that the incense was already burnt out, Pao-yu preferred to admit defeat rather than writing something inferior.
He put down his brush to read Tan-chun's unfinished poem,
and this gave him the idea for the following conclusion which
he wrote:

> Do not mourn their falling;
> Where they fly, only I have any idea;
> Orioles grieve, butterflies flag as flowers fade,
> But next spring, another year past, they will reappear.

The others teased, "You didn't do your own assignment, so
even if you've finished this off well it doesn't count."

Then they read Tai-yu's poem to the melody *Tang-to-ling*:

> Pink petals fall in Hundred Flowers Islet.
> By Swallow Tower their fragrance slowly fades;
> Catkins following in clusters
> Float off like ill-fated maids;
> Vain their close attachment and beauty.

> The willow too knows what it is to yearn;
> In early prime her head turns white,
> She laments her life but has no one to whom to turn.
> The spring breeze to whom she is wedded no pity will show,
> Leaving it to chance whether to stay or go.

As they read this they nodded and exclaimed, "Too sad! But
of course it's good."

Next they read Pao-chin's verse to the melody *Hsi-chiang-
yueh*:

> Few and far between in the Han garden,
> They make the whole Sui Dyke gleam!
> Their spring splendour gone with the wind,
> Moonlight and plum-blossom nothing but a dream.

> Here and there in the courtyard crimson petals fall —
> Beside whose curtain snow down these fragrant flakes?
> North and south of the Great River it is the same,
> The heart of every parted lover aches.

The others commented with a smile, "This is really in a
tragic vein. The fifth and sixth lines are the best."

"Still it's too mournful," objected Pao-chai. "Willow catkins
may be light and fickle, yet it seems to me, to be original, we
should praise what's good about them. That's what I've done,
but you may not approve."

"Don't be so modest," said the rest. "Yours is bound to be good, so let's hear it." Then they read her verse to the melody *Lin-chiang-hsien*:

> Dancing at ease in spring before white jade halls,
> Swirling gracefully in the spring breeze....

"That's the best line yet!" cried Hsiang-yun. "Swirling gracefully in the spring breeze."

> While whirling all around me
> Are butterflies and bees.
> I have never followed the flowing stream,
> Why then should I abandon myself to the dust?
> Constant to ten thousand boughs,
> Whether together or parted I keep trust.
> Do not jeer at me as rootless,
> But lend me strength, good wind,
> To soar up to the azure sky at last.

The others clapped the table and exclaimed with admiration. "There's real strength in this," they said. "It's the best of the lot. Less tender and poignant, though, than the Queen of Bamboo's poem; and Pillowed Iridescence's has charm and feeling. Today Little Hsueh and the Stranger Under the Plantain have fallen behind. They'll have to be penalized."

"We'll accept any penalty," cried Pao-chin gaily. "But how will you punish the one who handed in a blank paper?"

"Just wait," said Li Wan. "We'll deal with him strictly, you can be sure of that, to make an example of him."

As she was speaking something crashed against the bamboo outside — it sounded as if a window had fallen out. They all jumped with fright and maids ran out to investigate.

One of the girls outside called, "A big butterfly kite's got entangled in the bamboo."

"What a fine kite," remarked the other maids. "Whose can it be? Its string has snapped. Let's get it down."

Hearing this Pao-yu and the others went out to look.

"I know this kite," said Pao-yu. "It belongs to Yen-hung in the other house. Fetch it down and send it back to her."

"Is there only one kite like this in the world?" objected Tzu-chuan. "How can you be sure it's hers? I don't care if it is, I'm going to keep it."

"Don't be so greedy, Tzu-chuan," scolded Tan-chun. "You've kites of your own, so why filch somebody else's? That may bring you bad luck."

"Quite right," agreed Tai-yu. "Someone may have set it adrift to float away evil influences. Get rid of it, quick. And let's loose ours too to send away our bad luck."

Then Tzu-chuan told some younger maids to take the kite to the women on duty at the gate, who should give it to anyone who came asking for it.

When the younger maids heard they were going to fly kites, they hurried off eagerly to fetch a kite in the form of a beautiful girl, as well as high stools, cords and reels, and a pole with a stick tied to its top for launching the kite. Pao-chai and the others, standing by the gate, ordered the maids to fly this on the open ground outside.

Pao-chin remarked, "This of yours isn't as handsome as Cousin Tan-chun's big phoenix with flapping wings."

Pao-yu agreed and turned to tell Tsui-mo to fetch it, where-upon she went off cheerfully on this errand.

Pao-yu, in high spirits, sent a young maid home with the instructions, "Fetch that big fish kite Mrs. Lai brought us yesterday."

After a long interval the maid came back empty-handed.

"Ching-wen flew it yesterday and lost it," she announced.

"And I hadn't flown it even once!" exclaimed Pao-yu.

"Never mind," said Tan-chun. "She sent off your bad luck for you."

"In that case bring the big crab kite," ordered Pao-yu.

The maid came back presently with a few others carrying a beauty kite and reel. "Miss Hsi-jen says yesterday she gave the crab kite to Master Huan," she told him. "Here's one just brought by Mrs. Lin. She suggests you fly this instead."

Pao-yu examined the kite and was pleased to find it ex-quisitely made. He told them to fly it. By now Tan-chun's kite had come too, and Tsui-mo and some other maids were already flying it above a nearby slope. Pao-chin told her maids to fly a big red bat kite. Pao-chai, infected by the general enthusiasm, had sent up a kite in the shape of a formation of seven wild swans. Now all these kites were airborne except Pao-yu's beauty, making him so frantic that sweat poured down his face. When the others laughed at him, he angrily threw the kite to the ground and pointing at it swore:

"If you weren't a beauty, I'd trample you to bits!"

"It's the fault of the bridle," said Tai-yu soothingly. "If you adjust it, it'll be all right."

Pao-yu ordered this to be done and at the same time sent for another kite. They were all looking up and watching the kites sail through the air when the maids brought many others of different kinds and played with them for a while.

Then Tzu-chuan exclaimed, "It's pulling hard now, miss. Won't you take over?"

Tai-yu wrapped a handkerchief round her hand and pulled. Sure enough, the wind was blowing hard. She took the reel and paid out the cord. As the kite soared off, the reel whirred and all of a sudden the whole cord had run out. Then she urged the rest to let their kites drift away.

"We're all ready," they said. "You start first."

"Though it's fun to let it go, I haven't the heart to," she replied with a smile.

"Kite-flying is just for fun, that's why we call it 'sending off bad luck,'" said Li Wan. "You should do this more often, and then you might get rid of that illness of yours. Wouldn't that be a good thing?"

"Our young lady's getting more and more stingy," put in Tzu-chuan. "We always sent off a few kites every year, so why begrudge one today? If you won't do it, miss, I will." She took from Hsueh-yen a pair of small silver Western scissors, and clipped the cord tied to the reel.

"There!" she said with a laugh. "That'll carry off her illness."

The kite drifted away until soon it seemed no bigger than

Lady Hsing Feeling Wronged Puts Hsi-feng
in the Wrong
Yuan-yang Happens upon
Two Lovers

Upon Chia Cheng's return to the capital, after all his business was despatched, he was granted a month's home leave. Growing old now and worn out by his heavy responsibilities, he was so happy after this long time away to be reunited with his family that banishing all thought of business he passed the time reading, and when he was tired would play chess or drink with his protégés or enjoy the domesticity of the inner quarters with his mother, sons and wife.

The second of the eighth month that year would be the old lady's eightieth birthday, and all their relatives and friends were bound to come to offer congratulations. How were they to accommodate so many feasters? Chia Cheng talked it over with Chia Sheh, Chia Chen and Chia Lien, and they decided to hold feasts from the twenty-eighth of the seventh month to the fifth of the eighth in both mansions, the Ning entertaining the men, the Jung the ladies. Two of the larger buildings in Grand View Garden, Variegated Splendour Tower and Auspicious Shade Hall, could be prepared as retiring rooms. On the twenty-eighth they would invite the prince consorts, princes, princesses and dukes of the Imperial House together with their ladies; on the twenty-ninth, ministers, military governors and their titled wives; on the thirtieth, other officials with their titled wives, and relatives close and distant with their wives. Family feasts would be given on the first by Chia Sheh, on the second by Chia Cheng, on the third by Chia Chen and Chia Lien, on the fourth by the whole Chia family old and young. Finally, on the fifth, Lai Ta, Lin Chih-hsiao and the other chief stewards would give a feast.

From the start of the seventh month streams of messengers had been arriving with gifts. The Ministry of Rites by Imperial decree presented the old lady with one gold and jade *ju-yi* sceptre, four lengths of coloured satin, four gold and jade ear-rings, and five hundred taels of silver from the Imperial Treasury. The Imperial Consort Yuan-chun sent eunuchs with a golden image of the God of Longevity, an eaglewood cane, a string of scented beads, a box of rare incense, one pair of gold and four of silver ingots, twelve lengths of coloured satin and four jade cups. As for the gifts sent by all the princes and their consorts, as well as officials and officers high and low who had connections with the Chia family, these were too many to enumerate. A large table covered with a red felt was set in the hall to display all the best gifts for the old lady's inspection. The first two days she enjoyed examining them, but after that she lost interest.

"Let Hsi-feng put them away," she said. "I'll look at them some other time when I've nothing to do."

On the twenty-eighth, both mansions were hung with lanterns as decorations, phoenix screens were set up and lotus-patterned carpets spread, while the sound of fluting and drumming carried into the streets outside. The only guests that day in the Ning Mansion were the Prince of Peiching, the Prince of Nanan, Prince Consort Yungchang, the Prince of Loshan and a few young nobles. To the Jung Mansion came only the Dowager Princess of Nanan, the wife of the Prince of Peiching and a few other noble ladies.

The Lady Dowager and the rest received them in full court costume appropriate to their rank. After greetings had been exchanged the guests were invited to Auspicious Shade Hall in the Garden to drink tea and freshen up, after which they went to the Hall of Glorious Celebration to offer their congratulations and sit down to a feast. There was much polite deferring to each other before finally they sat down, the two princes' consorts in the seats of honour, then the other ladies according to

their rank. The wives of the Marquis of Chinhsiang and the
Earl of Linchang sat at the lower table on the left. The Lady
Dowager, as hostess, took a lower seat on the right and Madam
Yu, Hsi-feng and some other daughters-in-law, headed by Lady
Hsing and Lady Wang, ranged themselves behind her on both
sides to wait on the guests. Outside the bamboo portière matrons headed by the stewards' wives Mrs. Lin and Mrs. Lai
served the dishes and wine, while a few young maids supervised
by Mrs. Chou Jui stood behind the screens waiting for orders.
The servants who had come with the guests were entertained
elsewhere.

Presently, actors came on the stage to offer congratulations,
which signified that it was time for the performance to start.
At the foot of the stage stood twelve pages, still too young to
let their hair grow. One of these with both hands presented
a list of the repertoire to the woman in charge at the bottom
of the steps, who passed it to Mrs. Lin. She laid it on a
small tray and noiselessly raised the portière, then sidled up
to Madam Yu's maid, the concubine Pei-feng. Pei-feng presented
it to Madam Yu, who carried it over to the two highest seats.
The mother of the Prince of Nanan after first declining this
honour chose an auspicious item, then passed the list to the wife
of the Prince of Peiching who — after a show of modesty —
also selected one item. The rest after some deferring to each
other finally all said:

"Let them sing whatever they think best."

When dishes had been served four times followed by soup,
the servants who had accompanied their mistresses brought
forward tips which were given to the performers, after which
they all had a wash and returned to the Garden where fresh
tea was served. The mother of the Prince of Nanan, asking
after Pao-yu, was told by the Lady Dowager that he had gone
to worship in one of the temples where monks were chanting
sutras to pray for peace and longevity for her. Then she asked
after the girls.

"Some of them are unwell, others are delicate, and they're
so shy in company that I told them to keep an eye on my rooms

for me," said the old lady. "As we have plenty of actresses, I've sent a troupe to perform in my hall, and they're watching operas there with the girls in their aunt's family."

"In that case, do invite them over," urged the Dowager Princess.

The Lady Dowager turned to tell Hsi-feng, "Go and fetch Hsiang-yun, Pao-chai, Pao-chin and Tai-yu, and ask Tan-chun to come with them."

Hsi-feng assented and went off. She found the girls eating sweetmeats and watching an opera in the old lady's place with Pao-yu, just back from the temple. When she passed on her instructions, Pao-chai, Pao-chin, Tai-yu, Tan-chun and Hsiang-yun all went with her to the Garden where they were introduced and paid their respects. Some of the visitors had met them before. One or two had not, but all alike expressed their admiration. The mother of the Prince of Nanan knew Hsiang-yun best.

"When you heard I was here, why didn't you come out?" she teased. "Were you waiting for an invitation? I shall take your uncle to task for this some time."

Next she took Tan-chun and Pao-chai by the hand to ask them their age and exclaimed in delight, so impressed was she by them. Then letting them go she drew Tai-yu and Pao-chin to her, subjected them to a close scrutiny and praised them in the highest terms.

"They're all so charming," she said laughingly, "I don't know which to praise most."

A servant had already brought in the five sets of presents prepared: five gold and five jade rings and five bracelets of scented beads.

"Don't laugh at these gifts," said the mother of the prince. "Take them to give to your maids."

The five girls curtseyed their thanks, and then the wife of the Prince of Peiching also gave each of them a set of presents. There is no need to describe all the gifts presented them by the other guests.

After sipping tea the guests strolled for a while in the Garden. Then the Lady Dowager asked them to go back to feast, but the mother of the Prince of Nanan declined.

"I'm not feeling well today, but I simply had to come," she said. "So please excuse me if I leave early."

The old lady and others could not press her to stay, and after a further exchange of civilities they saw her to the Garden gate, where she mounted her sedan-chair and left. The wife of the Prince of Peiching stayed a little longer, then took her leave too. Some of the others withdrew early, some stayed till the end.

As the Lady Dowager had had a tiring day, the next day she did not receive any guests, leaving Lady Hsing and Lady Wang to entertain them for her. The sons of noble families simply came to the outer hall to pay their respects, and were received by Chia Sheh, Chia Cheng and Chia Chen, who then took them off to feast in the Ning Mansion. But no more of this.

During these celebrations, Madam Yu did not go home at night. She spent each day entertaining guests, and stayed on in the evening to amuse the Lady Dowager and help Hsi-feng to supervise the disposal of the various utensils, the putting away of presents and tipping of servants, then retired for the night in Li Wan's quarters in the Garden.

This evening after she had waited on the old lady during her meal, the latter said, "You must all be tired, I know *I* am. So eat early and go and rest. Tomorrow you have to get up early again."

Madam Yu assented and withdrew to have dinner in Hsi-feng's apartments; but Hsi-feng was in the upstairs storeroom overlooking the servants putting away the tapestry screens presented while Ping-erh, alone in the room, put away Hsi-feng's clothes.

"Has your mistress had her meal?" asked Madam Yu.

Ping-erh smiled.

"How could we omit to invite you, madam, if we were having a meal?"

"Well then, I'll go somewhere else to find something to eat. I'm ravenously hungry."

As she started off, Ping-erh called, "Do come back, madam! Here are some cakes for you to be going on with.   Then come for dinner later."

"No, you're all so busy here, I'll go and cadge a meal from the girls in the Garden."   With that she left and Ping-erh could not detain her.

Madam Yu went straight to the Garden.   As she found its main gate and the side gates still open and coloured lanterns still hanging there, she ordered her maid to fetch the women on duty, but the girl came back to report that not even the shadow of anyone was to be found in the gatehouse.   Told to fetch the stewards' wives in charge, she went to the corner house outside the inner gate where those women gathered to chat before work.   There she found only two matrons sharing out sweetmeats and dishes.

"Are none of the stewards' wives here?" she asked.   "My mistress from the East Mansion wants one of them immediately."

The two matrons, intent on the food, hearing that it was a mistress from the other mansion answered casually:

"They've just gone."

"Well then, go to their homes and fetch them," urged the maid.

"We're caretakers, not messengers.   If you want someone fetched, send a messenger."

"*Aiya,* this is mutiny! So you won't take orders!" the girl cried.   "And why can't you go yourselves? You may be able to fool newcomers but you can't fool *me*.   Who's to run errands if not you? Whenever you get wind of any perks or handouts to one of the stewards' wives, you dash off like dogs with wagging tails to announce it.   Have you no sense of respect? Would you respond like this to Madam Lien's instructions?"

The women had been drinking, and now that this maid had shown them up they retorted angrily:

"Shut your filthy mouth. Whether we run errands or not is none of your business. You've no right to nag at us. You know very well how that father and mother of yours toady to the stewards of your mansion — they're worse than any of *us*. People who live in glass houses shouldn't throw stones. *We* know what's what. We belong to different households. Go and impress your own people if you can, before you come here meddling in *our* affairs."

"Fine, fine," snapped the maid. "That's fine!"

Livid with anger she hurried back to report this.

Madam Yu, now in the Garden, had come across Hsi-jen, Pao-chin and Hsiang-yun exchanging stories and jokes with two nuns from the Ksitigarbha Nunnery. Explaining that she was hungry, she went on to Happy Red Court where Hsi-jen offered her some sweet and savoury pastries. The two nuns and Pao-chin and Hsiang-yun went on sipping tea and telling stories till the maid arrived, fuming, to report everything the women had said.

"Who were they?" asked Madam Yu grimly.

To spare her feelings, the nuns and Pao-chin and Hsiang-yun suggested that it must be a misunderstanding — the maid had heard wrongly.

The nuns nudged the maid.

"You lose your temper too easily, miss," they scolded. "Why pass on all the nonsense those silly old women talk? Madam's health is what's important. Here she's been wearing herself out for days, and not a bite to eat or a drop to drink has she had yet. The least we can do is try to keep her amused. Why should you tell such tales?"

Hsi-jen drew the maid aside.

"Good sister, just go out and have a rest," she coaxed. "I'll get someone to fetch them."

"No need," said Madam Yu. "Just send for those two women, then 'fetch Hsi-feng here."

"I'll go," offered Hsi-jen.

"No, not you," replied Madam Yu.

The two nuns rose respectfully to their feet to demur, "You're so magnanimous, madam, won't it make for talk if you lose your temper today of all days when our Old Ancestress is celebrating her birthday?"

Pao-chin and Hsiang-yun interceded too.

"All right then," said Madam Yu. "If it weren't for the old lady's birthday I'd certainly thrash this out. As it is, I'll overlook it for the time being."

Meanwhile the girl sent by Hsi-jen to find some woman in charge outside the Garden had met Chou Jui's wife and told her what had happened. Though Mrs. Chou was not in charge, as the maid who had attended Lady Wang to the Chia mansion at the time of her marriage she was a person of some consequence, and so quick-witted and ingratiating that all the mistresses liked her. She now hurried to Happy Red Court, exclaiming as she ran:

"The mistress's angry! That will never do. Things have come to a pretty pass. If only *I'd* been there! I'll slap their faces for them, and in a few days we'll deal with them properly."

When Madam Yu saw her she cried, "Come on, Sister Chou, let's hear what you think about this. The Garden gates are still wide open so late, with the lanterns alight and all sorts of people going in and out. What if anything happens? So I decided to tell the women on duty to put out the lights and lock up. But to my surprise there was no one there at all."

"How outrageous!" said Mrs. Chou. "The other day Madam Lien told them that with all sorts of people here these days they must lock up and put out the lights as soon as it gets dark, and not let any outsiders into the Garden. Yet today they leave their posts. When these celebrations are over, some of them must be given a good hiding!"

Madam Yu then told her what the maid had reported.

"Don't be angry, madam," urged Mrs. Chou. "After the merry-making I'll get the stewards to beat them within an inch of their lives, and we'll ask who told them to talk in that way about different households. Now I've ordered the lights to be put out and the main and the side gates closed."

Just then a maid arrived from Hsi-feng to invite Madam Yu to supper.

"I'm not hungry now," was the answer. "I've just had some pastries. Ask your mistress to start without me."

Mrs. Chou went off to report this to Hsi-feng.

"Those two women carry on like stewardesses," she said. "And when we speak to them they treat us like dirt. If you don't make an example of them, madam, Madam Yu is going to feel slighted."

"In that case," replied Hsi-feng, "remember those two women's names, and when this commotion is over have them tied up and sent to the other mansion for Madam Yu to beat or pardon as she thinks fit."

This was just what Mrs. Chou had been hoping for, as she had long been on bad terms with both women. On withdrawing she sent a page with this message to Lin Chih-hsiao's wife, and asked her to go straight to see Madam Yu. At the same time she sent people to have both those women tied up and kept under guard in the stable.

It was dark now and, not knowing what was afoot, Lin Chih-hsiao's wife took a carriage to the mansion. She went first to Hsi-feng's quarters. But when she announced herself at the inner gate some maids came out to tell her:

"The mistress has just gone to bed. Madam Yu is in the Garden. You can go and see her there."

So Mrs. Lin had to go to the Garden. When the maids at Paddy-Sweet Cottage announced her, Madam Yu regretted the trouble she had caused her. Inviting her in she said:

"I only asked for you because I couldn't find the women on duty. It isn't all that important. Since you'd left they shouldn't have called you back again, making a trip for nothing. It's a small matter and I've already set it aside."

Mrs. Lin responded with a smile, "Madam Lien sent to tell me you had some instructions for me, madam."

"The idea! I didn't know you'd left or I wouldn't have asked for you. Some busybody's been talking to Hsi-feng. I suppose it was Sister Chou. You go back and rest now. It's of no consequence."

Li Wan was on the point of explaining, but Madam Yu stopped her.

Seeing this, all Mrs. Lin could do was leave. But it so happened that on her way out of the Garden she ran into Concubine Chao.

"Well, well, sister!" cried the concubine with a smile. "Why are you running about here at this hour of the day instead of resting at home?"

Mrs. Lin explained that she had gone home and why she had returned, then gave a detailed account of what had happened.

Now the concubine was naturally officious, and as she kept on good terms with the stewards' wives, trading information with them, she had a fair idea of what had happened. She told Mrs. Lin what she knew of the whole story.

"So that's the way it was!" Mrs. Lin laughed. "What a storm in a teacup. If she's kind she'll forget it; if she's mean, at most she'll just give them a thrashing and have done with it."

"My dear sister-in-law," said the concubine, "this may not be serious but it shows how domineering they are, fetching you here for nothing to make an outright figure of fun of you. Go back and rest now; you'll be busy tomorrow, so I won't keep you for tea."

Then Mrs. Lin left and was approaching the side gate when the daughters of those two women came up to her in tears and begged her to help.

"You silly children," she scolded. "Who told your mothers to get drunk and talk nonsense, landing themselves in trouble? This had nothing to do with me. It was Madam Lien who had them tied up, and now people are holding *me* to blame too. I'm in no position to help you."

The two children, being only seven or eight, had no sense and just went on crying and pleading with her.

Unable to shake them off Mrs. Lin exclaimed, "Silly creatures! Why don't you approach the right people instead of pestering me?" She turned to one girl. "Your elder sister's mother-in-law Mrs. Fei came here with Lady Hsing at the time of her marriage. Get your sister to ask her mother-in-law to enlist Her Ladyship's help, then your problem will be solved, won't it?"

The little girl accepted this advice. The other went on pleading.

"How silly can you get?" snapped Mrs. Lin. "If she goes and asks, the whole business will blow over. They can't just let her mother off and have yours beaten, can they?" With that she went off in her carriage.

So one of the small girls went to ask her sister to speak to old Mrs. Fei. This Mrs. Fei, as Lady Hsing's personal maid at the time of her marriage, had once been of some consequence, but as Lady Hsing had recently lost favour with the Lady Dowager her servants had lost some of their authority too; thus they were always eager to find fault with the upper servants of Chia Cheng's household. Old Mrs. Fei, presuming on her age and Lady Hsing's backing, had taken to drinking and cursing people at random to work off her resentment. The Lady Dowager's grand birthday celebrations had filled her with envy as she watched other people showing off their administrative ability and ordering their underlings about; but no one in Chia Cheng's household paid much attention to her spiteful scolding and aspersions. The news now that Chou Jui's wife had had a relative of hers tied up added fuel to the fire of her indignation. Being in her cups, she pointed at the wall separating the two brothers' houses and loosed off a flood of abuse. She then went to find Lady Hsing.

"My son's mother-in-law has done nothing wrong," she complained. "She had a few words with one of the maids of Madam Yu over in the other mansion, and at the instigation of Chou Jui's wife Madam Lien has had her tied up in the stable. They're threatening to beat her after the celebrations, and her an old woman of more than seventy too! Please, Your Ladyship, ask Madam Lien to let her off this once."

Lady Hsing had felt snubbed after her request for Yuan-yang was turned down; and since then the old lady had treated her more coldly, showing much more consideration to Hsi-feng. Moreover, during the Dowager Princess of Nanan's recent visit, when she asked to see the girls the Lady Dowager had sent for Tan-chun but passed over Ying-chun. Lady Hsing's resentment had been rankling, only she had had no occasion to express it. And now these jealous and spiteful servants, not daring to avenge their own grievances, kept making up stories to provoke her, first simply denouncing servants of Chia Cheng's house, then by degrees throwing the blame on Hsi-feng herself. They said Hsi-feng just curried favour with the old lady and liked to throw her weight about, keeping her husband under her thumb, getting Lady Wang worked up, and showing no respect at all for the real mistress of the mansion. Later, they even brought charges against Lady Wang, alleging that she and Hsi-feng had set the old lady against Lady Hsing. So even if Lady Hsing had been strong-minded, as a woman she could not help bearing a grudge, and recently she had come to detest Hsi-feng. Still, when Mrs. Fei told her this tale she made no comment.

The next morning she went to pay her respects to the Lady Dowager. The whole family had come to feast and watch operas, and the old lady was in high spirits. As no distant relatives had been invited, only junior members of the family, she came out in informal dress to receive their salutations in the hall, reclining on a couch in the middle furnished with a pillow, back-rest and foot-stool. Seated on low stools around the couch were Pao-chai, Pao-chin, Tai-yu, Hsiang-yun, Ying-chun, Tan-chun and Hsi-chun. Chia Pien's mother had brought her daughter Hsi-luan too, Chia Chiung's mother her daughter Ssu-chieh, and about twenty other grand-nieces of different ages had assembled as well.

As Hsi-luan and Ssu-chieh were good-looking, well-spoken girls a cut above the others, the Lady Dowager was delighted

with them and made them also sit in front of her couch where
Pao-yu was massaging her legs. Aunt Hsueh had the seat of
honour, the others sitting down in a row on each side according
to their ages and the seniority of their family branch. In the
corridor outside the portière the male members of the clan
also sat in due order.

First the women of the clan, row by row, paid their respects;
then the men. By the time the old lady on her couch told
them to desist, they had all gone through the ceremonies.

Then Lai Ta led the other stewards and servants to kowtow,
kneeling from the ceremonial gate to the hall. They were
followed by their wives, then the maids from various apartments. This went on for the time it would take for two or
three meals, and after that many bird-cages were brought into
the courtyard and the birds let loose.[1] Chia Sheh and the
others burnt incense and paper money to sacrifice to Heaven,
Earth and the God of Longevity; and only then did they start
to watch operas and feast. Not until the interval did the old
lady retire to her room to rest, enjoining the others to enjoy
themselves. She also told Hsi-feng to keep Hsi-luan and Ssu-
chieh there to have a good time for a couple of days. Hsi-
feng went out to inform the girls' mothers, and as they owed
much to her they agreed with alacrity. And the girls were
only too glad to amuse themselves in the Garden, and spend
the night there.

That evening when the time came for the party to break up,
Lady Hsing in front of everyone approached Hsi-feng with a
smile to ask her a favour.

"Last night I heard you were angry and sent Steward Chou's
wife to have two old women tied up — I don't know what
they'd done wrong. By rights I shouldn't ask to have them
let off, but it seems to me the old lady's birthday is surely the
time to give alms to the poor and aged, yet here we are punish-
ing old folk instead. So if you won't give *me* this face, do

---

[1] It was believed that to set caged birds free on someone's birthday would
add years to that person's life.

at least let them off for the old lady's sake!" After this speech she went off in her carriage.

Mortified at being addressed like this in front of so many people, Hsi-feng flushed crimson, quite put out for a moment. Then she turned with a cold laugh to Mrs. Lai and the stewards' wives.

"How extraordinary!" she said. "Yesterday some of this household annoyed Madam Yu of the other mansion, and not wanting her to take offence I left her to deal with the culprits. It wasn't because they had offended *me*. Who's been telling tales again?"

Lady Wang asked what all this was about, and Hsi-feng reported what had happened the previous day.

Then Madam Yu said with a smile, "I had no idea of this. And you needn't have meddled."

"I wanted to save your face," retorted Hsi-feng. "That's why I left you to deal with them — that seemed only reasonable. Just as, if someone in your place offended me, stands to reason you'd send her to *me* to deal with, however much of a favourite that servant might be. I don't know what busybody went and reported this as if it was something of consequence, just to prove her loyalty."

"But what your mother-in-law said is right," put in Lady Wang. "Your cousin Chen's wife isn't an outsider, so such formalities are uncalled for. The old lady's birthday is the important thing. You'd better let them off." She turned and gave orders for both old women to be released.

More mortified than ever, in her frustration Hsi-feng could not hold back her tears. But not wanting anyone to see her weep, she went back in a pique to her room. However, it so happened that the Lady Dowager sent Hu-po to fetch her. When Hu-po saw her she exclaimed in surprise:

"What's come over you suddenly? The old lady wants you."

Hsi-feng hastily wiped her eyes, washed and powdered her face, then went over with Hu-po.

The Lady Dowager asked her, "How many of those families who sent presents the other day sent screens?"

"Sixteen families," replied Hsi-feng. "There are twelve big screens and four small ones for *kang*. The big screen sent by the Chens south of the Yangtze has twelve red tapestry scenes from the opera *Every Son a High Minister* on one side and on the other gilded depictions of the character 'Longevity' in various styles of calligraphy. That's the best of the lot. Then there's a glass screen from the family of Admiral Wu of Canton which isn't bad."

"In that case don't dispose of those two, but store them in a safe place," the old lady said. "I want to give them as presents."

As Hsi-feng assented, Yuan-yang suddenly stepped forward to stare at her.

"Don't you know her?" asked the old lady. "What are you staring for?"

"I'm wondering why her eyes are so swollen," answered Yuan-yang with a smile.

The Lady Dowager told Hsi-feng to come closer and looked at her hard.

Hsi-feng tried to laugh it off.

"My eyes were itching so I rubbed them," she said.

Yuan-yang chuckled, "Has someone been provoking you again?"

"Who would dare?" retorted Hsi-feng. "Even if someone did, I wouldn't dare cry on the old lady's birthday."

"Quite right," agreed the Lady Dowager. "I'm just going to have my supper. You can wait on me, then take what's left for yourself and Chen's wife. Then you two must help the two nuns to pick some Buddhist beans for me. That'll bring you long life too. The other day your girl cousins and Pao-yu did that; so I want you to do it too, and then you can't accuse me of favouritism."

As she was speaking a vegetarian meal was served for the two nuns, after which a meal with meat was brought for the old lady. When she had finished eating, the remainder was taken to the outer room for Madam Yu and Hsi-feng. They had

just started their meal when the old lady sent for Hsi-luan
and Ssu-chieh to join them.

After that they washed their hands and lit incense, and a
pint of beans was brought. First the two nuns chanted some
Buddhist incantations over it, then they picked out the beans
one by one and put them in a basket, chanting the name of
Buddha over each. These beans would be cooked and distributed at the crossroads to bring longevity. The old lady lay
down on her couch then and listened to the Buddhist tales of
karma told by the nuns.

Yuan-yang, having heard from Hu-po about Hsi-feng crying,
had found out the reason from Ping-erh. So that night after
the others had left she reported:

"Madam Lien did cry, because Lady Hsing made her lose
face in public."

Asked how it had happened, she told the old lady.

The Lady Dowager said, "This shows Hsi-feng has good
manners. How can she allow servants to offend each and every
mistress in our clan — and get away with it just because it's
my birthday? Lady Hsing's been sulking for some time but
didn't dare flare up. This gave her the excuse to shame Hsi-
feng in public."

Just then Pao-chin came in and they broke off, the old lady
asking Pao-chin where she had come from.

"We were chatting in Cousin Lin's place in the Garden,"
she answered.

This reminded the Lady Dowager of something, and she ordered an old woman to take her instructions to the servants in
the Garden.

"I've kept Hsi-luan and Ssu-chieh here," she said. "Though
they may be poor they're the same as our own young ladies, so
you must look after them well. I know all our servants, men
and women alike, are impressed only by riches and rank and
unlikely to think much of them; but if I hear of anyone showing
them the *least* disrespect, there's going to be trouble!"

The woman assented and was about to leave when Yuan-

yang said, "I'll go. The people there wouldn't pay any attention to her."

She went straight to the Garden, going first to Paddy-Sweet
Cottage. Finding neither Li Wan nor Madam Yu there, she
questioned the maids who told her that they were with Tan-
chun. Yuan-yang went on to Morning Emerald Hall and,
sure enough, found all the inmates of the Garden there chatting.
At sight of her they pressed her to take a seat.

"What brings you here at this hour?" they asked.

"Can't I come and enjoy myself as well?" Yuan-yang
chuckled before giving them the old lady's message.

Li Wan hastily stood up to hear it, then sent for the chief
servants from each household and ordered them to pass on
these instructions.

Madam Yu remarked, "The old lady really thinks of everything. Even ten of us healthy young people put together
aren't up to her."

Li Wan said, "Hsi-feng's devilish clever, she comes closest
to her; but the rest of us can't hold a candle to *her*."

"Don't talk about her, poor thing," put in Yuan-yang. "These
last few years she may have made no mistakes that the old lady
knows of, but she's offended goodness knows how many other
people. Well, it's hard to please everybody. If you're too
honest and don't know any tricks, your father and mother-in-
law will think you a simpleton and the household won't respect you. If you're full of tricks, you'll please some and
offend others. In our family especially, this new lot of 'mistresses' promoted from slaves are so puffed up they all think
they can do as they like. If they're in the least dissatisfied,
they gossip behind people's backs or stir up trouble. So as not
to upset the old lady, I haven't breathed a word about this
to her. If I did, none of us could have a single day of peace!
I shouldn't be saying this in front of you, Miss Tan-chun, but
when someone complains on the sly that the old lady dotes on
Pao-yu, that doesn't matter — it counts as natural partiality.
But when the old lady shows her fondness for *you*, I hear the
same person complain. Isn't that ridiculous?"

Tan-chun said with a smile, "There are plenty of silly people; don't take it so seriously. It seems to me humble households are better off having fewer people even though they're poorer, because parents and children enjoy themselves together, laughing and joking. In a big family like ours, outsiders think our wealthy young ladies must be very happy. Little do they know the unspeakable troubles we have here, much worse than anywhere else."

"Other people don't worry as much as you, third sister," said Pao-yu. "I'm always urging you not to listen to that vulgar talk or think about those vulgar matters. Just enjoy your wealth and high rank. You're luckier than us men who can't enjoy a quiet, leisurely life, but have to muck about."

"Who can compare with you, with not a care in the world?" asked Madam Yu. "All you do is play around with your girl cousins, eating when you're hungry, sleeping when you're tired and going on like this year after year, taking no thought at all for the future."

"Every day I spend with my cousins is all to the good," he answered. "When I die that'll be the end. Who cares about the future?"

The others laughed.

"You're talking nonsense again," teased Li Wan. "Even if you were good for nothing and stayed here all your life, these girls would get married and leave the family, wouldn't they?"

"No wonder people say you belie your handsome looks," chuckled Madam Yu. "You're really and truly a fool."

"A man's fate is uncertain," Pao-yu quipped. "Who knows when he will die? If I died today or tomorrow, this year or next, I'd die content."

The others hastily stopped him.

"He's raving again," they said. "We mustn't talk to him. If we do, he talks like a fool or a lunatic."

"Don't say such things, Cousin Pao," Hsi-luan put in. "When all your sisters and cousins here have left to get married, the old lady and the mistress are bound to feel lonely too; then I'll come and keep you company."

Li Wan and Madam Yu laughed.

"You're talking nonsense too, child. Are *you* never going to get married? Whom are you trying to fool?"

Hsi-luan blushed and lowered her head.

It was then already the first watch, so they all went back to their own rooms to rest.

Yuan-yang, when she reached the Garden gate, saw that the side gates were closed but not yet bolted. There was nobody about, and the only light apart from the faint moonlight was in the gatehouse. As she was all alone and had not brought a lantern, and as she walked quietly, no one in the gatehouse had noticed her approach. Happening just then to want to relieve herself, she left the path and walked across the grass to the back of a rockery under a large fragrant osmanthus. She had just skirted the rockery when the rustle of clothes made her start with fright, and looking in that direction she saw two people who at sight of her ducked behind some rocks under the trees. But Yuan-yang had seen in the moonlight that one of them, a tall, buxom maid in a red skirt with loosely tied hair, was Ssu-chi from Ying-chun's apartments. Assuming that she and another girl were also relieving themselves here and had dodged out of sight to frighten her for fun, she called out laughingly:

"Ssu-chi, if you don't come out quickly and try to scare me, I'll scream and have you caught as a thief. Fancy a big girl like you fooling about at this time of the night."

Yuan-yang was only teasing to get her to come out. But Ssu-chi, having a guilty conscience, thought she had been caught red-handed and was afraid Yuan-yang's shouts would alert other people, which would be even worse. As Yuan-yang had always treated her well, better than the other girls, she ran out from behind the tree to catch hold of her arm.

"Good sister." she begged, dropping to her knees. "Do keep quiet for goodness' sake."

Puzzled by this, Yuan-yang pulled her up to ask, "What do you mean?"

Ssu-chi blushed crimson and burst into tears. Then Yuan-yang remembered that the other figure had looked something like a young man, and she guessed more or less what had happened. She flushed up to her ears, quite consternated. Presently, taking a grip on herself, she asked softly:

"Who was he?"

Ssu-chi sank to her knees again.

"My cousin," she faltered.

Yuan-yang spat in disgust.

"How could you?"

Ssu-chi turned and hissed, "It's no use hiding. Sister's seen you. Come here quick and kowtow to her."

At that the page boy had to crawl out from behind the tree to thump his head vigorously on the ground. Yuan-yang wanted to hurry away, but Ssu-chi caught hold of her and begged through her sobs:

"Our lives are in your hands, sister. Do, please, let us off!"

"Don't worry," said Yuan-yang. "I won't tell a soul."

As she was speaking they heard someone at the side gate call, "Miss Chin's left. Lock the gate."

Yuan-yang, unable to shake off Ssu-chi's grip, promptly called out, "I'm still here. Just wait a bit, I'll be leaving in a minute."

Then Ssu-chi had to let her go.

To know what came of this, read on.

CHAPTER 72

Hsi-feng Puts up a Bold Front,
Ashamed to Admit Her Illness
Lai Wang's Wife Relies on Her Mistress' Power
to Force Through a Match for Her Son

Yuan-yang left the side gate still blushing, in a flutter after this shock. "This is serious!" she thought. "If it got out, the charge of lewdness linked with theft might even cost them their lives besides involving other people. Well, as it's no concern of mine, I'd better keep it to myself and not tell a soul." So on her return she simply reported that she had passed on the Lady Dowager's orders, after which they all went to bed. After this Yuan-yang seldom went to the Garden after dark; and reflecting that if even the Garden was the scene of such strange carryings-on, other places must be still worse, she went nowhere else either if she could avoid it.

Now Ssu-chi and her cousin had been playmates as children and vowed in fun to marry no one else. Both of them had now grown up good-looking, and whenever Ssu-chi went home they would exchange glances, recalling their former feeling for each other although neither could make open overtures. Besides, they feared their parents' disapproval. So they had bribed the women in charge of the Garden gate to leave it open, and taking advantage of today's confusion had had their first rendezvous. Although they had not made love, they had secretly exchanged solemn vows and pledges, baring their hearts to each other. Their sudden discovery by Yuan-yang had made the boy run off through the flowers and willows to slip out by the side gate.

Ssu-chi, repenting too late, could not sleep that night. The next day when she saw Yuan-yang she turned red and white by turns in an agony of embarrassment and guilt. She lost her appetite and grew quite bemused. But when two days passed without any repercussions she began to feel somewhat easier in her mind.

That evening, however, one of the matrons came to tell her in confidence, "Your cousin's skedaddled. He hasn't been home for three or four days and a search is being made for him everywhere."

Distraught by this news Ssu-chi thought, "Even if there's a scandal we ought to die together. Of course, being a man he can go anywhere he wants to. How heartless he is!" This embittered her so much that the next day she felt too upset to bear up. Ill with frustration she took to her bed.

When Yuan-yang learned that a page in the Chia household had fled and Ssu-chi was asking to go home on sick leave, she knew they were afraid of the consequences if she disclosed their secret. As this preyed on her mind, she went to see Ssu-chi. After sending everyone else out of the room, she gave the girl her solemn word:

"I'll die before I breathe a word about this. Just stop worrying and nurse your illness. Don't risk your little life like this, child!"

Ssu-chi caught her by the arm.

"Sister, we've been on good terms since we were children," she sobbed. "You've never treated me as an outsider, and I've always respected you. Now if you'll really keep my slip-up a secret, I shall look on you as my own mother — for I'll owe every day that I live to you. If I get well, I shall set up a shrine to you and burn incense and bow to it every day to pray for good fortune and long life for you. If I die, I'll become a donkey or a dog so as to repay your kindness. 'Even the longest feast must break up at last,' says the proverb. In two or three years we shall all be leaving this place. Still, even floating weeds may come together again, much more so human beings. And if we do meet again I shall try to repay your goodness." She shed tears as she spoke.

By now Yuan-yang was weeping in sympathy.

Nodding she said, "All right. I'm not in charge, so why should I spoil your good name? Why be so officious? In any case, I could never bring myself to speak of such a thing. So don't you worry. When you're better you must behave more circumspectly and not carry on like that."

Ssu-chi propped on her pillow nodded repeatedly, and after more reassurances Yuan-yang left.

As she knew that Chia Lien was away and these last few days Hsi-feng had looked out of sorts, quite unlike her usual self, on the way back she called to see her. When she entered the courtyard the servants at the inner gate stood up to let her in, and as she stepped into the hall Ping-erh came out of the bedroom and approached her.

"She's just had a bite to eat and is having a nap," Ping-erh whispered. "Won't you wait in the other room for a while?" She took her to the eastern room where a maid served tea.

"What's the matter with your mistress these days?" Yuan-yang asked in a low voice. "I've noticed she seems very listless."

As they were alone Ping-erh sighed, "She's been this way for some time, at least a month. And these last few days she's been kept on the go and provoked into the bargain, so that's brought on a relapse. As it's worse now than before, she can't put up a brave front and hide it."

"In that case why not get a doctor in good time?"

Again Ping-erh sighed.

"Don't you know the way she is, sister? She won't hear of fetching a doctor or taking medicine. When I simply asked out of concern how she felt, she swore crossly that my nagging was making her ill. Poorly as she is, she still insists on checking on this and that every day instead of taking things easy to get back her health."

"Even so, you ought to get a doctor to diagnose her illness and save us all worry."

"I'm afraid it's something serious."

"What do you mean?"

Ping-erh drew closer to whisper, "Since her period last month she's been having fluxions off and on non-stop. Wouldn't you call that serious?"

"*Aiya*! From what you say, it sounds like menorrhagia."

Ping-erh spat in disgust, then chuckled.

"What does a girl like you know about such things? It's unlucky to talk like that."

Yuan-yang blushed.

"I didn't know any such things to start with," she answered. "But have you forgotten that was how my sister died? I'd no idea what her illness was till I overheard my mother telling her mother-in-law, and the name meant nothing to me. Later I heard mother explain its cause and that gave me an inkling."

"Yes, I'd forgotten that," said Ping-erh gently.

As they were chatting a maid came in.

"Just now Mrs. Chu came again," she announced. "We told her the mistress is having a siesta, so she went to Lady Wang's place."

Ping-erh nodded.

Yuan-yang asked, "Which Mrs. Chu?"

"That professional go-between," Ping-erh explained. "The family of some official named Sun wants to arrange a match with us, so recently she's been turning up here every day with a card, making a regular nuisance of herself."

Before she had finished the maid returned to report, "The master's back."

By now Chia Lien was calling Ping-erh from the door of the hall, and before she could go to meet him he stepped through her doorway. At sight of Yuan-yang seated on the *kang* he halted.

"What brings our distinguished Sister Yuan-yang to our humble abode?" he asked smiling.

Remaining seated she answered, "I came to pay my respects to you and madam, but you were out and she was having a nap."

"You work so hard all the year round for the old lady, by rights I should call on you. How can we trouble you to come to see us?" He added, "Still, this is very opportune. I was meaning to go and see you, but felt so hot in this heavy gown that I came back first to change into a lighter one. Now Heaven has taken pity on me and saved me a trip by having you waiting here." He seated himself on a chair.

She asked what his business was.

"It's slipped my mind," Chia Lien chuckled, "but you may remember. On the old lady's birthday last year, an itinerant monk presented her with a Buddha's-hand made of soapstone; and as the old lady took a fancy to it, it was taken straight to her place for display. The other day on her birthday I checked our inventory of curios and found this listed there, but I don't know where it's got to now. The caretakers of the storeroom for antiques have mentioned it several times, as they want to record where it is. So I meant to ask you whether it's still in the old lady's place or whom she's given it to."

"The old lady had it out for a couple of days, then got tired of it and gave it to Madam Lien," was Yuan-yang's answer. "So now you are asking *me*! I even remember the day when I sent Old Wang's wife to bring it here. If you can't remember, ask Madam Lien or Ping-erh."

Ping-erh who was getting out clothes for Chia Lien came out on hearing this.

"Yes, it was delivered here. It's kept upstairs," she said. "Madam sent to tell them that it had been given to us, but the fools must have forgotten to record it. Now they're pestering us again over these trifles."

Chia Lien grinned.

"How come I didn't know it was given to your mistress? You two must have pocketed it."

"She told you, sir," Ping-erh retorted. "You wanted to give it to someone else, but she didn't agree, so we managed to hang on to it. Now you've forgotten and say we've kept it. What precious, priceless rarity is it, pray? We've never kept anything from you, not even things ten times better than this. Why should we value that worthless object now?"

Chia Lien lowered his head with a smile to think this over, then clapped his hands.

"Yes, I'm getting muddle-headed and forgetful," he exclaimed. "I don't wonder you scold me — my memory's not what it was."

Yuan-yang smiled.

"You're not to blame. You have so much to attend to, so many people coming to you with requests; and then when you drink a few cups of wine how can you remember every single thing?" While saying this she rose to take her leave.

Chia Lien stood up hastily too.

"Dear sister, please sit down for a while," he begged. "I've something else to ask you." He reprimanded the maid, "Why didn't you brew some better tea? Hurry up and fetch a clean bowl with a lid and brew some of that new tribute tea."

Turning back to Yuan-yang he went on, "These days, because of the old lady's birthday, I've spent the few thousand taels of silver I had. Our house rents and land rents from various places won't be coming in till the ninth month, so right now I'm rather hard up. Tomorrow I have to send presents to the Prince of Nanan and prepare Double-Ninth gifts for Her Imperial Highness; then there are weddings and funerals coming up in several other families too. I need at least two or three thousand taels, and I can't raise that sum quickly. As the proverb says, 'It's better to ask of one's own folk than of outsiders.' So I wonder, sister, if you'll stick your neck out and filch me a case of gold and silver utensils which the old lady isn't using for the time being. I can pawn them for some silver to tide over. In less than half a year, when my money comes in, I'll redeem them and return them. I promise not to land you in any trouble."

"You certainly know a trick or two," Yuan-yang laughed. "The idea!"

"I won't lie to you," he chuckled. "Apart from you, there are several others who have control of plenty of silver, but none of them is as sensible and plucky as you. If I approached them they'd take fright. So I'd rather strike the golden bell once instead of trying all the broken drums."

At this point one of the Lady Dowager's maids hurried in in search of Yuan-yang.

"The old lady wants you, miss," she said. "We've been looking everywhere, but here you were all the time."

Then Yuan-yang quickly went back.

As soon as she had gone Chia Lien went in to see Hsi-feng, who had woken up and heard him ask for a loan. Not liking to interpose, she just lay on the *kang* until Yuan-yang had left and Chia Lien entered her room.

"Did she agree?" she asked him.

"Not in so many words, but it looks hopeful," he answered cheerfully. "You must go and mention it again this evening, and that should fix it."

"I'll do nothing of the sort," retorted Hsi-feng. "If she agrees, once you get hold of the money you'll forget all your fine talk and promises now. Who's going to run such a risk for you? If it came to the old lady's ears, I'd lose all the face I've had the last few years."

"Be an angel," he begged. "If you fix this up, I'll make it worth your while — how's that?"

"What with?"

"Whatever you say."

Ping-erh beside them put in, "Don't ask for any other rewards, madam. Just yesterday you were saying you needed a couple of hundred taels. If you get this loan you can deduct them from that. Wouldn't that suit you both?"

"I'm glad you reminded me," cried Hsi-feng gaily. "All right then."

"What a hard bargain you drive," protested Chia Lien. "Don't talk about pawning things for a mere thousand taels when I know you could easily produce three to five thousand of ready cash here and now. You should be thankful I'm not borrowing from *you*, just asking you to put in a word; and yet you still demand interest. This is the limit. . . ."

Before he could go on, Hsi-feng sprang up.

"If I have three thousand or fifty thousand, I didn't earn it from *you*," she cried. "Nowadays everybody inside and out, high and low, keeps carping about me behind my back, so you may as well join in. Ghosts from outside don't come in unless they're invited by some family devils. Where did our Wang family's money come from, pray? Is it all from your Chia family? Don't make me vomit. You think you're as rich as a mint-master. The sweepings from the cracks in our Wang family's floor are enough to last you a lifetime. Aren't you ashamed talking like that? There's evidence to prove it. Just look at the dowries Lady Wang and I brought and compare them with yours. In what way are we inferior to you?"

"Why take a joke so seriously?" he asked, smiling. "This is nothing to get so worked up about. If you want a couple of hundred taels, that's nothing. More than that I can't manage, but this I can afford. Suppose you take that to be going on with before you raise this loan?"

"I'm not waiting for that to pay for my funeral, so what's the hurry?"

"Why carry on like that? There's no need to flare up."

"Don't accuse me of temper. But your words cut me to the heart. I was thinking that the day after tomorrow is the anniversary of Second Sister Yu's death; and as she and I were good friends, the least I can do is burn some paper money at her grave for friendship's sake. Though she didn't leave any children, we shouldn't forget her now that she's turned to dust."

Chia Lien lowered his head and was silent for some time.

"I'd forgotten," he admitted. "It's good of you to remember. If you don't need the money till the day after tomorrow, wait till we raise this loan tomorrow, then you can take as much as you want from it."

Just then Lai Wang's wife came in.

"Is it settled?" Hsi-feng asked her.

"No, nothing doing," answered Mrs. Lai. "But I think if *you* sponsor it, madam, it should come off."

Chia Lien wanted to know what they were talking about.

"It's of no great consequence," Hsi-feng told him. "Lai Wang has a son who's seventeen this year and not yet married. They want Tsai-hsia who waits on Lady Wang, but don't know whether Her Ladyship will agree. The other day she kindly said that as Tsai-hsia is grown up and so delicate she can be given her freedom and sent home, so that her parents can arrange for her marriage. Then Mrs. Lai approached me. I thought the two families being fairly well matched, once the request was made it was bound to be granted. Yet here she comes now saying nothing doing!"

"What does that matter?" he rejoined. "There are plenty of better girls than Tsai-hsia."

Mrs. Lai put in with a smile, "You may look at it that way, sir; but her family turning us down like that will make others look down on us even more. It's not so easy to find a suitable girl. I thought with your help we could fix it up — that at a word from madam they'd surely agree. So I troubled someone to go and sound them out, but to my surprise we got snubbed. The girl herself is agreeable and never seemed to be against the match, but those two old creatures have grander ideas for their daughter."

This was a challenge to Hsi-feng and Chia Lien; but as her husband was there the former said nothing, just waited to see his reaction. Chia Lien having other things on his mind did not take this seriously. However, as Mrs. Lai had accompanied Hsi-feng here at the time of her wedding and served them well, he could hardly ignore her request.

"It's not all that important," he said. "Why keep on about it? Don't worry, you can go now. Tomorrow I'll act as go-between and send two respectable fellows with betrothal gifts to tell them it's *my* proposal. If they still hold out, we'll get them to come and see me."

At a sign from Hsi-feng, Mrs. Lai fell on her knees to kowtow her thanks to Chia Lien.

"It's your mistress you should be kowtowing to," he said. "Even though I'll do what I can, it would be best for her to send for Tsai-hsia's mother and put it to her nicely.   Otherwise even if they agree, we'll seem too overbearing."

"If you're willing to go to this trouble for her," put in Hsi-feng, "how can I just stand watching? Well, Mrs. Lai, you've heard that.   After this is settled, you must hurry up and see to my business for me.   Tell your husband to collect all the money lent out before the end of this year — not a single cash short.   I've a bad enough reputation as it is.   I don't want to make it worse by going on lending out money."

Lai Wang's wife laughed.

"You needn't worry, madam.   Who would dare say a word against you? But, honestly speaking, if you stopped lending out that money we'd save ourselves trouble and offend fewer people."

Hsi-feng snorted.

"I've acted like a fool all for nothing.   What did *I* need money for? Only for daily expenses, as we're overspending our income and our household is always short.   My monthly allowance and his, plus those of our four maids, come to only some twenty taels a month — not enough to last three or five days. If I hadn't raised more by hook or by crook, we'd long ago have had to move into some tumble-down cave.   But all I've got for my pains is the reputation of a moneylender.   So I may as well call in all those loans.   I can spend money as well as anyone else.   In future let's all sit here spending, without worrying how long the money will last.   Isn't that the idea?

"Before the old lady's birthday the other day, Lady Wang worried for two months, not knowing how to raise funds, till I reminded her that in the back upstairs storeroom there were four or five cases of big copper and pewter vessels lying useless.   By pawning these for three hundred taels she managed to make her contribution.   As for me, as you know, I sold that gold striking-clock for five hundred and sixty-four taels. But in less than half a month it all went on some ten outlays big and small.   Now that even our treasury is short, someone's had the bright idea of milking the old lady.   A few more years and we'll be reduced to selling our clothes and jewellery, and won't that be fine!"

Lai Wang's wife chuckled.

"The clothes and jewels of any single one of our mistresses would raise enough to last *us* a whole lifetime. But of course that would never do."

"It's not that I've got cold feet," Hsi-feng insisted. "But if things go on this way I really can't cope. Last night I suddenly had a very odd dream. I dreamed that someone with a familiar face, but whose name I couldn't recollect, came to see me. When I asked her business, she said Her Imperial Highness had sent her to fetch a hundred rolls of silk from me. I asked which Imperial Highness. She told me it wasn't the one from our family, so I refused. Then she tried to take the silk by force. We were scuffling when I woke up."

Lai Wang's wife said with a smile, "That's because you'd been worrying all day about presents for the Palace."

Just then it was announced that the eunuch Hsia had sent a young eunuch to see them.

Chia Lien frowned.

"What is it *this* time?" he exclaimed. "Haven't they squeezed enough out of us this year?"

"You keep out of sight and let me handle this," suggested Hsi-feng. "If it's some small matter, all right. If it's something important I know how to ward him off."

Chia Lien withdrew then to the annex.

Hsi-feng ordered the young eunuch to be brought in and offered him a seat, after which tea was served. She then asked his business.

"His Excellency Hsia saw a house today which he'd like to buy, but he's two hundred taels short," was the answer. "He sent me to ask you, madam, if you have ready money at home and can lend him a couple of hundred for the time being. He'll pay you back in a few days."

Hsi-feng replied with a smile, "Don't speak of paying us back. We've plenty of silver here; just take any amount you need. If ever we're short of funds, we'll apply to you."

"His Excellency also said he still hasn't repaid the twelve hundred taels he borrowed the last two times. He will definitely return it all before the end of the year."

"His Excellency is too scrupulous." Hsi-feng laughed. "He may as well forget it. At the risk of offending him I'd like to say that if he remembered to pay us back all he's borrowed, goodness knows how much that would come to. The only thing that worries us is that we may not have money when he needs it. As long as we have, he can take it." She called for Lai Wang's wife and told her, "Go and get hold of two hundred taels from somewhere."

Taking the hint, Mrs. Lai replied, "I came to borrow from *you*, madam, because I couldn't raise money anywhere else."

"You just come in asking *us* for money," scolded Hsi-feng. "When I ask you to get some outside, you say you can't." She told Ping-erh, "Take those two gold necklets of mine and have them pawned for four hundred taels."

Ping-erh went off, returning after some lapse of time with a brocade-covered box containing two silk wrappers. In one was a gold filigree necklet studded with pearls as large as lotus seeds; in the other, a jewelled green enamel necklet. Both were similar to those made for the Palace. She took these away and soon brought back four hundred taels, half of which on Hsi-feng's instructions she gave to the young eunuch, the other half to Lai Wang's wife to meet expenses for the Moon Festival. Then the young eunuch took his leave, and a servant was ordered to carry the silver for him and see him out of the main gate.

Chia Lien returned now demanding, "When will those scoundrels outside stop plaguing us?"

Hsi-feng chuckled, "It's a case of 'talk of the devil.'"

"Yesterday the eunuch Chou came and asked straight out for a thousand taels. When I hedged, he looked put out. In future we're bound to offend them even more often. I only wish we could come into another two or three million taels."

While he was speaking Ping-erh helped her mistress with

her toilet, and then Hsi-feng went to wait upon the Lady Dowager at dinner.

Chia Lien had barely gone to his outside study when Lin Chih-hsiao appeared.

"Just now I heard that Chia Yu-tsun has lost his post," he reported. "I don't know why. Of course, it may not be true."

"Whether it's true or not, he's not likely to keep his present post for long," replied Chia Lien. "If he gets into trouble, I'm afraid we'll be involved. It would be better to keep clear of him."

"Quite so," agreed Lin. "But that's easier said than done. At the moment he's very thick with the master of the East Mansion, and our master Lord Sheh likes him too. Everybody knows that he's a frequent visitor here."

"Provided we don't get involved in any of his schemes, it doesn't matter. Go and check up to find out what's really happened."

Lin Chih-hsiao assented, but instead of leaving he sat there chatting until the subject of their financial straits came up again. He took this chance to advise:

"We should cut down on our household — it's too large. Why not ask the old lady and the master to release some old servants who have served the family well but are no longer useful? They all have independent means, and that would save us some money and grain each year. We have too many maids as well. Now that times have changed we can't follow the old rules but should tighten up a bit! Those used to eight maids can make do with six, those used to four with two. By cutting down like this in all our apartments we'd save a good deal of money and grain every year. And then half the girls in the household, who are grown up anyway, should get married. With them married, our household would increase. Wouldn't that be a good thing?"

"I've had the same idea," agreed Chia Lien. "But the master is only just back, and there are quite a few important matters I haven't yet reported to him; so there's been no time to bring this up. The other day when the professional matchmaker came with a horoscope to propose a match, Her Ladyship told us not to mention it as His Lordship is just home, enjoying this family reunion, and a sudden proposal of this sort might upset him."

"Quite right and proper too. You think of everything, sir."

"Yes, but this reminds me of something. Our man Lai Wang wants Tsai-hsia in Her Ladyship's place for his son. Yesterday he asked my help. As it's nothing important, I don't think it matters which of you goes to propose it. Just send anyone who's free and say I approve of the match."

Lin Chih-hsiao could not but assent. After a pause, however, he smiled.

"Actually, sir, if I were you I'd have nothing to do with this. That son of Lai Wang's, for all he's so young, drinks and gambles and gets up to all sorts of devilry outside. They may both be bond-servants; still, marriage is for life. Though I haven't seen Tsai-hsia these last few years, I hear she's grown up a nice-looking girl. Why ruin her life for her?"

"So that young fellow's a dissolute drunkard, eh?"

"He not only drinks and gambles but carries on outrageously outside. We've turned a blind eye because his mother worked for madam."

"I didn't know that," said Chia Lien. "In that case we certainly won't give him a wife. We'll give him a good beating instead, then have him locked up and take his parents to task."

"This isn't the time for that." The steward smiled. "I shouldn't have brought it up. Wait till he makes trouble again and we'll report it to you, sir, for you to handle. Better let him off for the time being."

Chia Lien said nothing to this, and soon Lin Chih-hsiao withdrew.

That evening Hsi-feng sent for Tsai-hsia's mother and proposed the match. Although the woman did not like the idea, as Hsi-feng had done her the honour of proposing it in person she had to agree out of hand. After she had left, Hsi-feng asked Chia Lien whether he had broached the matter.

"I was meaning to," he said, "but then I heard that the boy is a worthless wretch. I thought: if he's really no good, we'd better discipline him for a couple of days before giving him a wife."

"Who told you he's no good?"

"One of our servants, of course."

"You think nothing of us Wangs, not even of me, much less our servants. I've spoken to Tsai-hsia's mother and she's consented gladly. Am I to call her back now and tell her it's off?"

"There's no need for that if you've already made the proposal. I'll just tell the boy's father tomorrow to give him a good dressing-down."

The rest of their conversation need not concern us.

Now Tsai-hsia after being released from service was waiting for her parents to choose her a husband. Although she had been on friendly terms with Chia Huan, nothing had come of it; and now she saw Lai Wang coming repeatedly to ask for her hand. As she had heard that his son was a drunkard and gambler and ugly into the bargain, she felt all the more upset — for if Lai Wang fixed up this match with Hsi-feng's backing her whole life would be ruined. This prospect made her so frantic that that evening she secretly sent her younger sister Hsiao-hsia to Concubine Chao, to find out the situation.

Concubine Chao had always been on good terms with Tsai-hsia and was all for giving her to Chia Huan, for then she would have an ally in the house. She had never expected Lady Wang to discharge her. Day after day she urged Chia Huan to go and ask for her, but he was too shy to speak and not too attracted by Tsai-hsia in any case. To him, she was only a maid and he would have others in future; so he procrastinated, quite willing to give her up. His mother was reluctant to do this, however. After the younger sister came for news, as she was free that evening she went to enlist Chia Cheng's help.

"What's the hurry?" he asked. "Wait till the boys have studied a year or two more before we get concubines for them.

I've already got two suitable maids in mind, one for Pao-yu, one for Huan. But they're still young and it might hold up their studies; so let's wait a couple of years."

"Pao-yu's had one for two years already. Didn't you know that, sir?" asked Concubine Chao.

At once Chia Cheng demanded, "Who made the decision?"

Before she could answer they heard a crash outside. To know what had happened, read the following chapter.

CHAPTER 73

A Foolish Maid by Chance Picks up
a Pornographic Pouch
A Timid Young Lady Ignores the Loss
of Her Gold Phoenix Tiara

Concubine Chao's conversation with Chia Cheng was interrupted by a crash outside. Upon inquiry they found that one
of the shutters of the outer room, not being properly secured,
had clattered to the ground. Concubine Chao reprimanded
the maids and got them to fix it in place, then helped Chia
Cheng to bed.

Meanwhile, in Happy Red Court, Pao-yu had just gone to
bed and his maids were thinking of turning in themselves when
someone knocked at the gate. An old woman opened it to
admit Hsiao-chueh, a girl working for Concubine Chao, who
would not state her business but went straight in to find Pao-
yu already in bed, with Ching-wen and some other maids sitting
chatting beside him.

"What's happened?" they asked. "What brings you here at
this hour?"

Addressing herself to Pao-yu, Hsiao-chueh announced, "I've
got some news for you. Just now my mistress was talking to
Lord Cheng and I heard your name. So look out tomorrow
if he sends for you."

This said, she turned to leave.

Hsi-jen urged her to stay for some tea, but for fear that the
Garden gate would be closed she went off.

Pao-yu instantly felt as distraught as Monkey King on hearing

the incantation to tighten the magic band around his head.[1]
Staggered, he racked his brains but could think of no way out
except to cram in readiness for a test the following day. He
fancied that if he could give correct answers from his books,
other lapses would be overlooked and he might muddle through.
Throwing a jacket round his shoulders he got up to study,
thinking remorsefully, "I was sure he wouldn't test me these
first few days, so I let things slide and got rusty. If I'd known,
I'd have done some revising every day."

Now, the only ones of the *Four Books* he knew by heart
together with the commentaries were the *Great Learning,* the
Doctrine of the Mean and the *Analects.* His knowledge of
the first half of *Mencius* was so sketchy that if suddenly give
one sentence from it he would be unable to recite what followed,
and the whole of the second half had slipped his mind. When
it came to the *Five Classics,* while writing poems himself he
had browsed quite often through the *Book of Songs* and if
questioned on that should be able to get by. It did not matter
that he had forgotten the rest, as his father had never told him
to study them. As for classical prose, in the past few years
he had read several dozen works including the *Chou Annals,
Anecdotes of the Warring States,* the commentaries of Kung-
yang and Kuliang, and some writings of the Han and Tang
dynasties — no more than a few score works in all; but he was
quite unable to quote from them, for he had only glanced at
them when at a loose end and in the mood. Never having
studied them hard, he had since forgotten them and if tested
on them now would be floored.

Then there were the fashionable eight-section essays which
he had always loathed, taking the view that as these were not
written by sages or worthies they could not expound the wisdom
of sages or worthies and were simply ladders by which later
examination candidates climbed up to bureaucratic advance-

---

[1] It is related in *Pilgrimage to the West* that Kuan-yin had a gold band
put on Monkey King's head to subdue him. If he became unruly, the Incantation of the Magic Band would be recited to cause him an unbearable
headache.

ment. Chia Cheng before his departure had set him over a hundred essays of this kind to study. Pao-yu had skipped through these, noting here and there a well-written paragraph or argument or certain digressions, amusing anecdotes or poignant sentiments. But this again was only when the mood took him. He had never given his mind to studying whole essays. If he prepared one now, tomorrow he might be examined on quite another; and it was out of the question to revise the whole lot in one night. These reflections made him more and more frantic.

While Pao-yu was dilly-dallying over his studies, none of the girls in his place could go to bed either. It goes without saying that his chief maids Hsi-jen, Sheh-yueh and Ching-wen trimmed candles and poured tea for him. The younger ones, however, were all so sleepy that they kept dozing off.

"Little bitches!" Ching-wen scolded. "You all sleep like the dead every day — are you so short of sleep that you can't even sit up late for once? If you drowse off again I'll jab you with a needle."

Just then they heard a thump in the outer room and rushing out to look found that one young maid, falling asleep in her chair, had banged her head on the wall. She woke up with a start to hear this scolding and in her dazed state imagined that Ching-wen had struck her.

"Good sister," she cried tearfully, "I promise not to do it again!"

The others burst out laughing.

"Don't punish her," put in Pao-yu hastily. "You should have sent them all to bed. And you must be tired yourselves. You'd better take it in turns to get some sleep."

"Just get on with your work, Little Ancestor," urged Hsi-jen. "You've only this one night; so give your mind to those books for the time being. You'll have plenty of time once you've passed this test to attend to other things."

As she spoke in such earnest Pao-yu had to comply. He went on reading. But presently when Sheh-yueh poured him more tea to moisten his throat, he noticed that she was wearing a short jacket but had taken off her skirt.

"It's cold so late at night," he warned. "You should put on a gown."

With a smile she pointed at his books.

"Just forget us for the moment and concentrate on those."

At this point Venturina dashed in through the back door declaring excitedly that someone had just jumped down from the top of the wall.

"Gracious! Where?" cried the others.

At once they called people out to search everywhere.

Ching-wen saw how wearisome Pao-yu found this cramming, and knew that if he wore himself out tonight he was likely to make a poor showing the next day. She had been wanting to find some way out for him and this alarm provided her with a pretext.

"Take this chance to sham ill," she advised him. "Just pretend you've had a fright."

Pao-yu snatched eagerly at this suggestion.

The matrons on night duty were summoned to search everywhere with lanterns.

When they failed to find anyone they said, "The girls, going out half asleep, must have taken some branches tossed by the wind for a man."

"Stop farting!" retorted Ching-wen. "You're trying to shift the blame for not making a proper search. More than one person saw someone break in. Some of us had gone out with Pao-yu, and we *all* saw it. It gave him such a fright that he turned white and now he's feverish. I'm going to the mistress to get a sedative for him, and when she asks what's happened I'll have to report it in full. So how can you give up searching?"

At this the matrons dared not raise any further objections. They made a more thorough search while Ching-wen and Venturina went off to fetch medicine, loudly spreading the news that Pao-yu had fallen ill as a result of a shock. At once Lady Wang sent some of her own attendants to give him medicine, besides ordering those on night duty to search every nook and cranny of the Garden and check on the men on duty at the inner gate outside it. So they ransacked the Garden all night with lanterns and torches, and when dawn came the stewards were instructed to make careful investigations. They questioned all the matrons and men-servants who had been on night duty.

When the Lady Dowager heard of Pao-yu's fright and asked the reason they dared not hide it from her.

"I guessed as much," said the old lady. "It shows how careless they are on the night watch nowadays. And what's more serious is that some of them may even be thieves themselves. You can never tell."

Lady Hsing and Madam Yu had come over to pay their respects and were waiting on her with Hsi-feng, Li Wan and the girls. They all remained silent after this remark until Tan-chun stepped forward.

"It's true that with Cousin Hsi-feng unwell the servants in the Garden have become much more disorderly," she said. "At first, they used to gather in threes or fours to dice or play cards for small stakes in their spare time, or to keep themselves awake when on night duty. But recently they've grown bolder. They've actually formed gambling clubs with someone acting as banker, and the stakes are as high as thirty, fifty or a hundred strings of cash. A fortnight ago they even started a fight."

"If you knew this why didn't you report it before?" demanded the old lady.

"As Her Ladyship was busy and out of sorts and Cousin Hsi-feng was ill, I just told my sister-in-law and the stewardesses. I also reprimanded the servants several times, and lately they've behaved better."

"You unmarried young girls can't be expected to know how serious this is. To *you* gambling is nothing much; you're only afraid that it may lead to quarrels. But this gambling night after night leads to drinking and unlocking the gates to buy this, that and the other or send to look for someone. At the dead of night when few people are about, thieves may hide themselves there and debauchees and bandits can easily be smuggled in, and then *anything* could happen! Besides, in those places where you girls live in the Garden the maids are a mixed lot, some good and some bad. Pilfering isn't of much consequence, but if worse trouble came of it there could be a scandal! This isn't something we can pass over lightly."

After this harangue Tan-chun resumed her seat in silence.

Hsi-feng, though not fully recovered, was feeling a little better today. Having heard what the old lady said, she remarked, "It's too bad my falling ill again at this time."

She sent at once to summon Lin Chih-hsiao's wife and three other stewardesses in charge of the maids and reprimanded them in the presence of the Lady Dowager, who ordered them to fetch the culprits forthwith, promising rewards to those who voluntarily gave information and threatening to punish any who withheld it. Seeing how angry she was, Mrs. Lin and the others dared not shelter their friends. They hurried to the Garden to summon and question all the servants in turn. Though at first everyone denied ever having gambled, in the end inevitably they arrived at the truth: there were three main bankers, eight minor ones, and more than twenty people involved in the gaming.

Haled before the Lady Dowager they all knelt down in the courtyard, kowtowing to beg for mercy. First she ascertained the names of the chief bankers and the sums of money involved. One was no other than a relative of Lin Chih-hsiao; another was the younger sister of Mrs. Liu the cook in the Garden; the third was Ying-chun's nurse. These three were the ringleaders. The rest need not be enumerated here. The Lady Dowager ordered all the dice and cards to be burned and all the winnings confiscated and distributed among the other servants. The chief culprits were given forty strokes of the bastinado apiece then dismissed from service, with orders never to set foot there again. Their followers received twenty strokes apiece, were fined three months' wages and demoted to clean the privies. Lin Chih-hsiao's wife was also reprimanded.

Her relative's disgrace mortified Mrs. Lin, and Ying-chun too was embarrassed. Tai-yu, Pao-chai and Tan-chun sympathizing with her rose to beg the old lady to forgive her nurse.

"That nanny never used to gamble," they pleaded. "She must have been drawn in accidentally. Do let her off for Cousin Ying-chun's sake."

"You don't understand," said the Lady Dowager. "Those nannies are privileged because they nursed you. As a result they're worse than anyone else when it comes to making trouble, setting their mistresses against each other and covering up the faults of their favourites. I've experience enough of that. I've been meaning to make an example of one of them and now, luckily, she's presented me with the chance. So don't interfere. I know what I'm doing."

Then Pao-chai and the others could say no more.

Presently the old lady lay down to have a nap and the others withdrew; but knowing how angry she was they did not go straight home. Madam Yu chatted for a while in Hsi-feng's place, and when Hsi-feng looked tired she left to pass the time with the girls in the Garden. Lady Hsing after sitting a little with Lady Wang decided to take a stroll in the Garden too. She had just reached the gate when Sister Numskull, one of the Lady Dowager's maids, came along chortling to herself over some gaudy object in her hands, and as her head was lowered bumped into Lady Hsing. She looked up then and halted.

"What outlandish toy have you got there that you're so pleased, silly creature?" asked Lady Hsing. "Let me see it."

This Sister Numskull, who was fourteen or fifteen, had recently been chosen to do rough jobs — fetching water or sweeping the yard — for the Lady Dowager. She was plump with a round face and big feet, a good, fast worker. And being ignorant and simple-minded she behaved and talked quite unconventionally. Since the old lady liked her rough-and-ready ways and her ability to make people laugh, she gave her the nickname Numskull and when she felt bored would make fun of her, letting her behave in any way she liked. For this reason she also called Numskull her crazy maid. So when the girl did anything wrong no one took her to task for it, knowing the old lady's partiality to her. And this emboldened her when she was free to go and play in the Garden.

Today she had been catching crickets there when she saw behind a rock a gaily embroidered sachet. It was exquisitely made and very charming, but on it in place of the usual flowers or birds were two naked figures locked in embrace, and on the other side some characters.

Not knowing that this was pornography the silly girl wondered, "Are these two monsters fighting? Or maybe a husband and wife tussling together?" Unable to make it out she had started back, chuckling to herself, to show it to the Lady Dowager. In reply to Lady Hsing's question she said:

"Yes, this really is very strange, madam. Do have a look." She handed her the pouch.

One glance at it so horrified Lady Hsing that she clutched it tight.

"Where did you find this?"

"Behind a rock when I was catching crickets."

"Mind you don't tell anybody! It's something very wicked. You'd be beaten to death for picking it up if you weren't such a fool. But you mustn't mention it to anyone else."

Numskull turned pale with fright.

"I won't!" she promised, then kowtowed several times and went off quite bewildered.

Lady Hsing looked round and saw some girls about. She stuffed the pouch into her sleeve to conceal it from them, wondering where it could have come from, then hiding her consternation went on to see Ying-chun.

Ying-chun was vexed and depressed by her nurse's disgrace. When Lady Hsing was announced she invited her in and tea was served.

"You're no longer a child," scolded Lady Hsing. "Why didn't you take your nurse to task for carrying on in that way? Other people's servants don't misbehave, only ours — how do you account for that?"

Ying-chun lowered her head to play with her sash.

"I did speak to her twice but she paid no attention," she

muttered after a pause. "What more could I do? Besides, she's my nanny. It's for *her* to scold *me*, not for me to speak sharply to *her*."

"Nonsense. If you do wrong, of course she should pull you up; but when she breaks the rules like this you should assert your authority as mistress. If she wouldn't obey you, why not report it to me? Once outsiders hear about this what fools we shall look!

"Another thing, to raise money for her bank I daresay she wheedled you, soft and spineless as you are, into lending her some trinkets and clothes to pawn. If she's swindled you I haven't a cent to help you redeem your trinkets and clothes for the coming festival."

Ying-chun, her head lowered, just fingered her clothes in silence.

Lady Hsing laughed scornfully.

"Your fine brother and sister-in-law, Master Lien and Madam Lien, are high and mighty. They control this household and run everything but pay no attention to you, their only younger sister. If you were a child of my own and discriminated against, there'd be nothing we could do about it. Yet you're not my own child. But even though you and Lien didn't have the same mother, at least you have the same father; so he ought to show a little consideration instead of making people laugh at you.

"It's a mystery to me the way things turn out. Your mother was Lord Sheh's concubine, Tan-chun's mother Lord Cheng's concubine, and by rights you two should have the same status. When your mother was alive she was ten times better than Concubine Chao, so you should be superior to Tan-chun. How come, then, you're not half as good? Isn't it strange? Well, I'm thankful I've no children of my own to make a laughing-stock of me."

Some servants waiting on them interposed, "Our young lady's good-hearted and honest, not like Miss Tan-chun who talks so glibly and likes to score off her cousins. She knows very well how it is with our young mistress but never shows the least concern for her."

"What can you expect when her own brother and sister-in-law treat her like that?"

Just then the arrival of Hsi-feng was announced.

Lady Hsing snorted.

"Ask her to go back and rest to get over her illness. I don't need her services here."

Then another maid came to report that the old lady had woken up, whereupon Lady Hsing took her leave.

"Now what's to be done?" asked Hsiu-chu when Ying-chun came back from seeing off Lady Hsing. "The other day I told you, miss, that gold filigree phoenix tiara inlaid with pearls was missing, but you wouldn't even ask what had happened to it. When I said nanny must have pawned it to raise money for gambling, you didn't believe me and told us to ask Ssu-chi where she had put it. I did. And though she was ill she remembered quite distinctly that it hadn't been put away but left in a case on the bookshelf for you to wear during the Moon Festival. You should have asked nanny about it, only you're too soft and afraid of offending people. Now it's missing, won't it look odd if you're the only young lady not wearing one tomorrow?"

"There was no need to ask," said Ying-chun. "Of course she took it to tide her over. I thought she'd smuggled it out and would smuggle it back again in a day or two, but apparently she forgot. It's no use asking her now that she's in trouble."

"How could she have forgotten? She knows you too well and was simply taking advantage of you, miss. I've just had an idea. Why not let me go and report this to Madam Lien? She can either send to demand it back or just get it out of hock for her with a few strings of cash. What do you think?"

"Don't do that," demurred Ying-chun hastily. "Let's not make any fuss. I'd rather lose it than stir up more trouble."

"How can you be so soft, miss?" protested Hsiu-chu. "If you'll never stand up for your rights, some day you'll be spirited away yourself! Better let me go." She started off and Ying-chun had no way to stop her.

Now the wife of Wang Chu the old nurse's son had come to beg Ying-chun to intercede for her mother-in-law, but she stayed outside when she heard this talk about the gold phoenix tiara. Ying-chun was so weak that none of the servants were afraid of her. If Hsiu-chu reported this to Hsi-feng, however, it would be serious. So Mrs. Wang came in, with an ingratiating smile, to make her appeal.

First she begged Hsiu-chu, "Please don't go, miss, to stir up trouble. My mother-in-law, being old and muddle-headed, borrowed your young lady's phoenix tiara because she'd lost some money and had no means of winning it back. She meant to redeem it in a day or two, but she didn't recoup her losses and that delayed her. Then, as ill luck would have it, someone told tales and landed her in trouble. Still, we can't keep something belonging to your mistress. We'll redeem it without fail." She turned to Ying-chun. "Do us a favour, miss. As she nursed you at her breast when you were small, go and ask the old lady to let your old nanny off."

"It's out of the question, sister," replied Ying-chun. "Even if I pleaded for a year it wouldn't be any use. Just now Cousin Pao-chai, Cousin Tai-yu and the other girls tried to beg her off, but the old lady wouldn't hear of it. How much more could I do alone? Besides I've been humiliated enough. Why should I go asking for another snub?"

Hsiu-chu put in, "Redeeming the tiara and asking a favour are two quite different things. Don't mix them up. Or do you mean you won't give it back if our young lady doesn't get her off? Go and fetch the tiara first."

Ying-chun's refusal and Hsiu-chu's taunt left Wang Chu's wife at a momentary loss. Then, in her mortification, she took advantage of Ying-chun's good temper to round on her maid.

"Don't be so smug, miss!" she cried. "In all the different young masters' and mistresses' households, which nurse or nanny doesn't get certain perks. Why expect *us* to be so scrupulous? Are you maids the only ones allowed to filch things on the sly? After Lady Hsing's niece came here, Her Ladyship ordered us to save one tael of silver a month for her sister-in-law; so here we are spending more on Miss Hsiu-yen while getting one tael less. And when you're short of this or that we have to provide it. Who goes to ask for more money? We just make do somehow. We're out of pocket by at least thirty taels. Now it seems we've been spending our money all for nothing. . . ."

Not waiting for her to finish, Hsiu-chu spat in disgust.

"On what have you spent thirty taels for us? Let's work it out. What has our young lady asked you for?"

As the woman had cast aspersions on Lady Hsing, Ying-chun hastily interrupted, "That's enough. If you can't produce my tiara, at least don't drag in other things and raise this rumpus. I don't want that tiara. If Their Ladyships ask about it I'll tell them I've lost it, so as not to involve you. Better go back and rest now." She told Hsiu-chu to bring her some tea.

Instead the girl exploded, "You may not mind, miss, but how about us who are supposed to be looking after you? After filching your things they even accuse you of sponging on them and want their money back! If Her Ladyship asks you why and how so much was spent, people may think *we've* been squeezing you! That would be dreadful!" She burst into tears.

Ssu-chi could not let this pass either and dragged herself out of bed to take Hsiu-chu's side. Unable to stop their dispute, Ying-chun picked up *Retribution for Good and Evil* and started reading it.

It so happened that Pao-chai, Tai-yu, Pao-chin and Tan-chun had agreed to come together to cheer Ying-chun up, guessing that she must be moping. They reached the courtyard as the three servants were squabbling. And Tan-chun peeping through the window was amused to see Ying-chun sitting on the couch reading, oblivious of the row. A small maid hastily raised the portière and announced the young ladies' arrival. Ying-chun put down her book and got up while Mrs. Wang, seeing Tan-chun among the visitors, quieted down of her own accord and prepared to slip out.

Tan-chun sat down and asked, "Who were talking in here just now? It sounded like a quarrel."

"Not really," Ying-chun told her. "They were making a mountain out of a molehill. It's nothing to worry about."

Tan-chun smiled.

"I heard something about a gold phoenix and 'sponging on us servants.' Who's been asking the servants for money? Have you, cousin? Don't you get your monthly allowance just like the rest of us?"

"Of course she does," cried Ssu-chi and Hsiu-chu. "All the young mistresses get the same and their nurses and nannies make free with their money, never keeping any account, just asking for what they need. But now she claims that our young lady overspent and they had to make it up. When did our mistress ever ask them for anything?"

"If my cousin hasn't, they must mean *we* have. Call her in. I want to get this clear."

"Don't be ridiculous," protested Ying-chun. "This doesn't concern you, so why involve yourself with her?"

"That's not so," retorted Tan-chun. "We're in the same boat, cousin, so your business is mine too. If she's rude to you, she's rude to me as well. You'd feel the same if you heard someone in my place complaining about me. Of course, as mistresses we don't worry about trifling expenses, just ask for whatever we want — yes, that does happen. But what was that about your gold phoenix tiara?"

Wang Chu's wife hurried in now to defend herself before Hsiu-chu and Ssu-chi could accuse her. And Tan-chun seeing this smiled.

"How stupid you are!" she sneered. "As your mother-in-law's in trouble you should beg Madam Lien to redeem the tiara with some of the winnings still left, to settle the matte.. It's not as if we don't know about this, so we could have covered it up to save her face. Since she's already lost face, whatever crimes she's charged with she can only be punished once — nobody has two heads to be chopped off. So if I were you I'd appeal to Madam Lien. It's outrageous to make a scene here."

The woman could not deny the truth of this, but she dared not go to confess the theft to Hsi-feng.

"If I hadn't heard about it that would be different," Tan-chun continued. "But now that I know about this I shall have to help you out."

She signalled to Tai-shu, who slipped out of the room. And the others went on talking until suddenly Ping-erh came in.

"Cousin Tan-chun must have magic powers," giggled Pao-chin clapping her hands. "She can summon goddesses."

"This isn't Taoist magic," Tai-yu chuckled. "It's the first-rate military tactic called 'guarded as a virgin, swift as a hare' to catch your opponent off guard."

Pao-chai shot them a warning glance and they dropped the subject.

"Is your mistress any better?" Tan-chun asked Ping-erh. "Her illness has really made her lose her wits. She's let everything slide, and we're the ones who suffer."

"What do you mean, miss?" asked Ping-erh hastily. "Tell me who's dared to offend you."

Wang Chu's wife stepped forward, very flustered, to urge her, "Please take a seat, miss, and let me explain."

"Who are you to butt in when the young ladies are talking?" demanded Ping-erh sternly. "If you had any manners, you'd wait outside till you were sent for. It's unheard of for servants from outside to enter the young ladies' rooms without any reason."

"You should know we have no manners here," put in Hsiu-chu. "People barge in whenever they please."

"That's your fault," retorted Ping-erh. "Your young lady is good-natured, but you should put people out and then report them to Her Ladyship."

Seeing that Ping-erh was red in the face with anger, Mrs. Wang finally withdrew.

Tan-chun resumed, "Let me tell you: if anyone else offended me I'd not make an issue of it. But this woman and her mother-in-law, because Ying-chun's so sweet-tempered and she's her nanny, smuggled out her trinkets so that she could gamble and then cooked up a false account to blackmail Ying-chun into getting her off. Wang Chu's wife had a big row with these two maids in the bedroom, and Ying-chun couldn't control her. It was too much for me: that's why I asked you over. Tell me, has that woman, coming from another planet, no sense at all? Or has someone put her up to this to get Ying-chun to knuckle under first, and after that Hsi-chun and me?"

"What an idea, miss!" declared Ping-erh with a smile. "How could our mistress stand up to such a charge?"

Tan-chun smiled cynically.

"As the proverb says, 'Everyone feels for his fellow creatures.' And 'When the lips are gone the teeth will feel the cold.' How can I help being alarmed?"

Ping-erh asked Ying-chun, "What's your opinion, miss? A little business like this is easy to handle, but she's your nanny's daughter-in-law after all."

Ying-chun, reading *Retribution for Good and Evil* with Pao-chai, had not even heard what Tan-chun was saying.

"Why ask me?" she replied. "There's nothing I can do. They brought this on themselves. I can't get them off but I shan't blame them either. If they bring back the tiara I'll take it; if not I won't demand it. If the mistresses ask about it and I'm able to cover up for them, they'll be in luck; if I can't, there's no more I can do. I can't lie to the mistresses for their sake — I have to tell the truth. If you say I'm too soft and can't make up my mind, while you have a good plan to please all parties without annoying the mistresses, just go ahead with it — I don't need to know it."

This answer amused them all.

Tai-yu chuckled, "This is really a case of 'descanting upon religion while tigers and wolves gather at one's gate.' What would happen to this household if you were a man and had to keep it in order?"

"Many men are the same, so why laugh at me?" answered Ying-chun.

As she was speaking a new arrival walked in. If you want to know who it was read the following chapter.

CHAPTER 74

Malicious Talk Makes Lady Wang Have
a Search Made of the Garden
To Guard Her Integrity Hsi-chun Breaks with
the Ning Mansion

As Ping-erh was smiling over Ying-chun's answer they were
suddenly joined by Pao-yu. It turned out that enemies of
Mrs. Liu in charge of the Garden's kitchen had reported that
she had organized gambling parties in her younger sister's
name, and they had divided the winnings equally. Alarmed
by the news that Hsi-feng had decided to have her punished
too, Mrs. Liu had hurried to Happy Red Court, being on
the best of terms with the maids there, and secretly got Ching-
wen and Venturina to enlist Pao-yu's help. And as Ying-
chun's nurse was also incriminated, he thought it better to go
with Ying-chun to intercede for both women instead of going
alone for Mrs. Liu.

When he found so much company there and was asked about
his health and why he had come, he replied evasively that he
had simply dropped in to see Ying-chun. The others accepted
this and went on chatting. Presently Ping-erh took her leave
to attend to Hsi-feng's business, and Mrs. Wang followed her
out.

"Do put in a good word for us, miss," she begged. "We're
going to redeem the tiara anyhow, I promise you."

"You'll have to sooner or later," retorted Ping-erh. "So
why make such a scene today? You expect us to get you off,
don't you? Well, if you're truly repentant I haven't the heart
to report this, not if you bring the tiara straight back to me
as soon as possible."

"I will," promised Mrs. Wang, reassured by this. "I won't

keep you from your work, miss. I'll get it out of hock this evening and report to you before returning it."

"Mind you do, or you'll have to take the consequences!"

Then they went their different ways, Ping-erh rejoining Hsi-feng who asked her what Tan-chun had wanted her for.

"She was afraid you were angry," Ping-erh prevaricated. "She urged me to soothe you and asked how your appetite was."

"That was kind of her. Just now something else cropped up. It's been reported to me that Liu Erh's wife and her younger sister ran gambling parties together, but Mrs. Liu was really the one behind it. You've always advised me to let things slide whenever possible, to get more rest and keep fit. Because I ignored your advice, I've had to pay for it — to start with, I've offended my mother-in-law and ruined my own health. Well, now I know better. Let them raise any rumpus they please; at any rate there are plenty of other people to control them. Why should I worry for nothing, just getting myself disliked by everyone? It's more important for me to take care of my health. And even after I'm better I mean to take things easy — leave all responsibility to them and have a good time myself. So I'm paying no attention, as I said, to that report."

"If you take that line, madam, so much the better for us," Ping-erh approved.

Just then Chia Lien came in. With a clap of his hands he sighed.

"Here's fresh trouble out of the blue! How did my mother come to hear of Yuan-yang's loan to me the other day? Just now she sent for me and asked me to raise two hundred taels — no matter where — for her Moon Festival expenses. When I told her I'd nowhere to raise it she retorted, 'When you're short yourself you can get a loan, but when I ask your help you fob me off saying you've nowhere to turn. Where did you get stuff the other day to pawn for a thousand taels? You can even spirit away the old lady's things, yet you boggle now at a mere two hundred taels. It's lucky for you I haven't told anyone else.'

"I can't believe she's really short of money. Why should she pick on me like this for nothing?"

"There were no outsiders here that day. How did the news leak out?" wondered Hsi-feng.

Ping-erh thought back carefully, then cried, "I know! That evening the things were brought over, the mother of the old lady's girl Numskull came to deliver the laundry and stayed chatting for a while in the servants' quarters. She must have asked what was in the big case, and one of our maids, not knowing any better, told her."

She called in the maids and asked which of them had blabbed to Numskull's mother. In fright the girls dropped to their knees, swearing that none of them dared say a word out of turn: whenever questioned about anything they denied all knowledge of it, so how could they have let this secret out?

Hsi-feng saw they were telling the truth.

"No, they wouldn't dare," she agreed. "We mustn't wrong them. Let's not worry about this now but find a way to satisfy Her Ladyship. However short we are ourselves, we mustn't get into her bad books again." She told Ping-erh to pawn her gold necklace for two hundred taels and have the money sent to Lady Hsing.

"Let's pawn it for *four* while we're at it," suggested Chia Lien. "We need money ourselves as well."

"No, I don't need any," she answered. "And we don't know yet how to raise two hundred to redeem it."

Ping-erh sent Lai Wang's wife with the necklace to the pawnshop. And on her return, Chia Lien himself took the money to Lady Hsing while Hsi-feng and Ping-erh went on trying to guess who had let the cat out of the bag.

"Her Ladyship knowing doesn't matter much," Hsi-feng observed. "The danger is that her servants may take this chance to gossip and stir up fresh trouble. Those greedy gluttons in the other house, who are always throwing dirt, bear Yuan-yang a grudge. If they hear that she's secretly lent things to Master Lien, they may make a commotion and spread outrageous talk. Master Lien can take it, but Yuan-yang's a good girl and if she's involved in trouble it will be our fault."

"Don't worry," Ping-erh laughed. "Yuan-yang lent us those things for *your* sake, not for our master's. Though it sounds like a secret favour, in fact she'll have got the old lady's permission first. The old lady only pretends not to know because she has so many grandchildren, and if all of them borrow her things to pawn but then make a scene saying that they can't replace them, how is she to cope? So even if this gets out it won't hurt Yuan-yang."

"Even so, *we* know Yuan-yang's all right, but those who don't know her are bound to think the worst."

Just then Lady Wang was announced. Surprised by this unexpected visit, they hurried out to welcome her. They saw that her face was stern and she was accompanied by her confidential maid only. Without a word she went into the inner room and sat down, while Hsi-feng poured her some tea.

"You must be in good spirits," Hsi-feng remarked, "to stroll over here today, madam."

Lady Wang sharply ordered Ping-erh to leave the room. Hastily assenting she withdrew with all the other maids, wondering what this foreboded. Having closed the door behind her, she sat on the steps to stop anyone else going in. Hsi-feng was flustered too and quite bewildered.

Then Lady Wang with tears in her eyes produced a sachet from her sleeve.

"Look at this!"

Hsi-feng took it and saw the indecent embroidery on it.

Very shocked she exclaimed, "Where did you find this, madam?"

Tears streaming down her cheeks Lady Wang quavered, "Are you asking *me*? I've been in the dark all this time. Relying on your discretion, I took things easy. I'd no idea you were just as careless as me. Fancy leaving a thing like this on a rock in the Garden, openly, in broad daylight too! One of the old lady's maids picked it up. Luckily your mother-in-law found her with it; otherwise she'd have taken it to the old lady. How could you be so thoughtless as to leave this lying around?"

"What makes you think it's mine, madam?" asked Hsi-feng, changing colour.

"Whose else could it be?" Lady Wang sobbed. "Just think, you're the only young couple in our household. What would older women be doing with such a thing? And where could the girls get hold of it? No, it must be that dissolute wretch of a husband of yours who picked it up somewhere. And intimate as you are, it's natural that you young people keep playthings of this kind in your bedroom. Don't try to deny it. It's a mercy that nobody else in the Garden knows. If one of the maids there had found it and your girl cousins saw it, that would have been terrible! Or suppose some little maids picked it up and took it outside, telling people they had found it in the Garden, how could we ever hold up our heads again?"

Red in the face with pique and mortification, Hsi-feng knelt down by the *kang*.

"Of course your reasoning is logical, madam," she said tearfully. "I daren't contradict you. Still, do think more carefully, madam.

"In the first place, this sachet was made by craftsmen outside. See, the belt and tassels are the kind sold in the market. If they'd been made by embroiderers of our house they'd certainly be finer. However young and flighty I may be, I wouldn't want such trash.

"In the second place, this isn't the sort of thing I'd carry around with me. Even if I had one I'd have to keep it indoors, not take it everywhere with me. Besides, when I'm in the Garden with the girls we often scuffle in fun, and think how ashamed I'd feel if it was seen, not only by my cousins but even by the servants! However young and flighty I may be, I wouldn't be as foolish as all that.

"In the third place, of all the ladies of our house I'm the only young married woman, but there are plenty of servants' wives younger than me who are for ever dropping into the

Garden then going home again at night. Couldn't this belong to one of them?

"Fourthly, I'm not the only visitor to the Garden. Lady Hsing of the other house often takes Yen-hung, Tsui-yun and other young concubines there. They're all more likely than me to have such things. Cousin Chen's wife isn't too old either, and she often brings along Pei-feng and others; so this could equally well belong to them.

"Fifthly, with so many maids in the Garden, can we guarantee that they all behave properly? Isn't it possible that one of the older girls, who knows the facts of life, sneaked out unchecked or made some pretext to gossip with the pages at the inner gate, and smuggled this in from outside?

"This not only isn't mine, I can assure you that Ping-erh has never had such a thing either. Please reconsider the matter carefully, madam."

This made good sense to Lady Wang.

"Get up," she said with a sigh. "I should have known that a girl of good family like you couldn't be so frivolous. I just challenged you because I was so angry. But what's to be done? Your mother-in-law sent this over just now in a sealed package with word that she got it from Numskull the day before yesterday. I nearly choked with rage!"

"Don't be angry, madam. If this gets out, it may come to the old lady's ears. We must calm down and investigate this on the quiet to get to the bottom of it. And even if we fail to find the culprit, we mustn't let outsiders know about it but 'hide our broken arm in our sleeve.' Now let's take this gambling as a pretext to dismiss a good few servants. Let's choose four or five stewardesses like the wives of Chou Jui and Lai Wang, whose discretion we can count on, and put them in the Garden ostensibly to check up on the gambling.

"We have too many young maids now. As they grow up they start getting ideas and cause trouble. If we wait till there's a scandal, we shall regret it too late. Now if we send some of them packing for no reason, it'll not only vex the girls but will make us seem unreasonable, madam. So let's take this

chance to find fault with some of the older and more obstreperous ones, and send them home to get married. This will
prevent any scandals here and save us money too. What do
you think, madam?"

Lady Wang sighed again.

"You are right, of course. But to be fair to your cousins,
I pity the poor girls. We needn't go further back, but just
look at Tai-yu's mother — how cosseted she was before she
married, treasured like gold or jade! She lived in real style
like a fine young lady. But our girls today are only slightly
better off than other people's servants, with merely two or three
presentable maids apiece and four or five younger ones who
look like scarecrows. I haven't the heart to cut down their
attendants, and I doubt if the old lady would agree to it either.
Difficult as things are, we're not all that poor. I never lived
in real luxury and style, yet as a girl I was better off than you.
I'd sooner skimp a little myself rather than see them go short.
If we're to save money I'm willing to make a start.

"Now, send for Chou Jui's wife and the others and order
them — in strict confidence, mind — to hurry up and get to
the bottom of this."

Hsi-feng called Ping-erh in to pass on these orders. And
soon the wives of Chou Jui, Wu Hsing, Cheng Hua, Lai Wang
and Lai Hsi arrived, these being the only five couples here who
had accompanied Lady Wang or Hsi-feng to the Chia mansion
at the time of their marriage, the others having gone south on
business. Lady Wang was just thinking five too few to make
a careful check when they were joined by Lady Hsing's personal maid, wife of the steward Wang Shan-pao who had
brought over the pouch. As Lady Wang treated Lady Hsing's
trusted maids on the same footing as her own, and this woman
had come with a great show of concern to ask about this matter,
she said to her:

"Go and tell your mistress I want you to move into the
Garden for a while to keep an eye on things there. That would
be better than my finding other people."

Now Wang Shan-pao's wife, disgruntled by the lack of respect shown her by the maids in the Garden, had long been looking — unsuccessfully — for some grounds to fault them. To her mind, this pouch provided a handle against them, while Lady Wang's proposal gave her a welcome chance to settle scores with them.

She promptly answered, "That's easy. If you'll excuse your slave saying so, discipline should have been tightened up there long ago. You don't go to the Garden very often, madam. The maids there all behave as if they'd become fine young ladies of noble rank. They turn things upside-down, and nobody dares say a word for fear they'll work their young mistresses up to accuse people of insulting them. Who's willing to take such a risk?"

"Well, that's only to be expected," said Lady Wang. "Our young ladies' maids are a cut above the rest, but you should teach them manners. Not to correct the young mistresses would be wrong, how much more so in the case of their maids."

"The others aren't so bad," continued Mrs. Wang. "But do you know that minx Ching-wen in Pao-yu's place, madam? Because she's prettier than most and has the gift of the gab, she makes herself up every day like Hsi Shih and is very pert and forward, jabbering away all the time and showing off. She scolds and carries on in a shocking way on the least provocation. A regular vamp she is — it's scandalous!"

Thus reminded, Lady Wang remarked to Hsi-feng, "Last time we went for a stroll with the old lady in the Garden, I noticed a girl with a willowy waist, sloping shoulders and eyes and eyebrows rather like Tai-yu's. She was scolding one of the younger maids and I didn't at all like the wild look of her, but being with the old lady I said nothing. I meant to ask later who she was, but I forgot. She seems to fit this description of Ching-wen."

"Ching-wen's the prettiest among the maids," Hsi-feng replied. "She does act and talk rather flippantly too. Your description sounds like her, but I can't remember exactly what happened that day."

"That's easily remedied," said Wang Shan-pao's wife. "Just fetch her now for Your Ladyship to see."

Lady Wang observed, "The girls from Pao-yu's place whom I see most often are Hsi-jen and Sheh-yueh. They're not too smart and that's all to the good. If she's there, *she* naturally wouldn't dare come. She's just the sort of girl I've always disliked. And now that this has happened, think how dreadful it would be if this bitch were to lead our precious Pao-yu astray!"

She told her maid to go to the Garden.

"Just give them this message: I want Hsi-jen and Sheh-yueh to stay to look after Pao-yu, but that clever girl Ching-wen is to come here at once. Don't tell her why I want her."

The maid assented and went off to Happy Red Court.

Ching-wen happened to be unwell that day and had just got up from a nap, feeling out of sorts. She had no choice now but to obey this summons. As all the maids were well aware that Lady Wang disliked finery and pertness, Ching-wen had taken care to keep out of her way. Now as she had been unwell for a couple of days and not paid much attention to her toilet, she had no special misgivings. When she entered Hsi-feng's room with her hair dishevelled and her costume rumpled, like a frail beauty just aroused from sleep, Lady Wang immediately recognized her as the girl she had seen. This rekindled her anger. And being genuinely outraged and already prejudiced, she was too outspoken to conceal her feelings. She smiled sarcastically.

"What a beauty!" she sneered. "Really like an ailing Hsi Shih. Whom are you trying to vamp, going about like this? Don't think I'm ignorant of your goings-on. I'll let you off now, but very soon I'll have you skinned alive. How is Pao-yu today?"

Ching-wen knew that someone must have been running her down, but did not venture to express her resentment. And quickly recovering from her surprise she was intelligent enough not to give a truthful answer.

"I seldom go into Pao-yu's rooms or spend much time with

him," she lied. "So I can't say just how he is. You'll have to ask Hsi-jen or Sheh-yueh, madam."

"You deserve a slap on your mouth," fumed Lady Wang. "Are you dead? What are you paid for?"

"I used to serve the old lady," answered Ching-wen. "Then she said there were too few older maids in the Garden and Pao-yu was nervous because it was so empty, so I was to go and keep watch at night in the outer rooms, just to keep an eye on the place. When I said I was too clumsy to wait on the young master, the old lady scolded, 'I'm not asking you to look after him, you don't have to be smart.' So I had to go. It's only two or three times a month, when Pao-yu's bored, that we all have a game together. His personal needs are attended to by his old nurses and the matrons with Hsi-jen, Sheh-yueh and Chiu-wen under them. In my spare time I still do some sewing for the old lady, so I've never paid much attention to Pao-yu's affairs. But if you wish, madam, I shall be more attentive in future."

"Amida Buddha! Don't trouble!" exclaimed Lady Wang, quite taken in by this. "The less you have to do with Pao-yu, the better. Since you were assigned to him by the old lady, I'll get her permission tomorrow to have you dismissed."

She turned and told Wang Shan-pao's wife, "You people move into the Garden and keep a good watch on her for a few days. Don't let her sleep in Pao-yu's quarters. We'll deal with her after I've spoken to the old lady. Get out!" she rapped at Ching-wen. "What are you standing there for? I can't bear the sight of such a vamp. Who let you dress in those gaudy reds and greens?"

Ching-wen had to withdraw, so outraged that once out of the door she covered her face with her handkerchief and wept all the way back to the Garden.

Meanwhile Lady Wang was reproaching herself to Hsi-feng.

"These last few years I haven't had the energy to see to things," she lamented. "I never set eyes on such a fox-fairy! I suppose there are others like her too. Tomorrow I must make a thorough investigation."

Seeing how enraged she was, and knowing that Wang Shan-pao's wife often told tales to Lady Hsing and incited her to make trouble, Hsi-feng could not defend Ching-wen even had she had good reasons for doing so. She just lowered her head and assented.

"You must look after your health, madam," urged Mrs. Wang. "Just leave trifling matters like this to your slaves. It should be very easy to find the culprit. This evening after the Garden gates are locked and no news can get in or out, we'll take them by surprise and have a thorough search made of all the maids' rooms. I'm positive that whoever had that pouch will have other things of the same kind. When we find them we'll know whose it is."

"That's a good idea," approved Lady Wang. "We can't let innocent people take the blame." She asked Hsi-feng her opinion.

"Of course you're right, madam," Hsi-feng had to acquiesce. "That's the way to do it."

"This is an excellent plan," added Lady Wang. "Otherwise we could search for a year and still get nowhere."

So they agreed on it. After supper when the old lady had gone to bed and Pao-chai and the rest had returned to the Garden, Wang Shan-pao's wife accompanied Hsi-feng there. They ordered all the gates to be locked and started their search in the rooms of the servants on night duty, but discovered nothing more incriminating than some left-over candles and a jar or two of oil.

"These count as stolen property too," declared Wang Shan-pao's wife. "They mustn't be moved till we've made our report to Her Ladyship tomorrow."

Then they went first to Happy Red Court and had the courtyard gate locked. Pao-yu was rather unhappy on Ching-wen's account. When he saw these matrons marching into the maids' rooms, he asked Hsi-feng what they were doing.

"Something important is missing," she told him. "As people are accusing each other and we think one of the maids may have stolen it, we're making a general search to clear up suspicion."

She sat down to sip tea while Mrs. Wang and the others set about searching. They asked whose the different cases were and told the owners to open them themselves. Hsi-jen had already guessed from what had happened to Ching-wen that something was amiss. Now she was the first to step forward and open her cases and boxes for them to examine. Finding nothing out of the way, the women went on to search the other maids' cases one by one. When they came to Ching-wen's they asked:

"Whose is this? Why doesn't anyone open it for us?"

Hsi-jen was about to open it when Ching-wen rushed in, her hair loosely knotted. Crash! She flung the lid back and raised the case bottom upwards in both hands to empty all its contents on the floor. Wang Shan-pao's wife was disconcerted. She had a look and, finding nothing improper, suggested to Hsi-feng that they should move on.

"You'd better make a careful search," warned Hsi-feng. "If you fail to find anything, what are we going to say to Her Ladyship?"

The stewardesses assured her, "We've been through everything carefully, and there's nothing that shouldn't be here except a few objects used by boys; but these must have belonged to Pao-yu when he was small. There's nothing of consequence."

Hsi-feng smiled.

"In that case we can go to another house."

As they went out she said to Mrs. Wang, "I have a suggestion, if you agree to it, and that is to restrict the search to our own family. We mustn't raid Miss Pao-chai's quarters."

"Of course not. How can we search our relatives?"

"Exactly."

By now they had reached Bamboo Lodge where Tai-yu was already in bed. When visitors were announced, not knowing their errand she prepared to get up, but Hsi-feng came in and made her lie down again.

"Go back to sleep," she said. "We won't stay long."

She chatted with Tai-yu while Mrs. Wang took the others to the maids' quarters and searched their cases and baskets one by one. In Tzu-chuan s room they discovered two amulets which Pao-yu had often worn, two tassels from a boy's belt, two pouches and a fan in a sheath — all Pao-yu's old belongings. Wang Shan-pao's wife thought she had made a find and hastily called Hsi-feng over to have a look.

"Where do these things come from?" she asked.

Hsi-feng told her with a smile, "Pao-yu's been thick with them ever since he was a child, so naturally these are some of his old things. This is nothing extraordinary. Better put them back and try somewhere else."

"Our two apartments' accounts are so muddled," put in Tzu-chuan gaily, "I can't even remember the day, the month or the year when these things were left here."

In view of what Hsi-feng had said, Mrs. Wang had to let this pass and they went on to Tan-chun's place.

Apparently someone had sent Tan-chun word of their coming, and she knew there must be some reason for this indignity. She had ordered her maids to open all the doors and light candles in readiness. When the women arrived she deliberately asked them their business.

"Something's missing, and we don't know who took it," Hsi-feng told her. "For fear people may put the blame on these girls, we're making a general search to disarm suspicion. This seems the best way to clear them."

Tan-chun laughed scornfully.

"Naturally, all our maids are thieves and I'm their brigand chief. So search my cases first. They've given me all their stolen goods for safe-keeping."

She ordered her maids to open up all her chests as well as her mirror-stand, dressing-case, bedding, wrappers and bundles large and small for Hsi-feng's inspection.

"I'm simply carrying out Her Ladyship's orders," said Hsi-feng with a mollifying smile. "You've no call to blame *me*, cousin. Don't be angry."

answered soothingly, "We've made a thorough search, even including your things."

"Are you all satisfied?" Tan-chun challenged the others.

Chou Jui's wife and the rest assured her that they were.

But Wang Shan-pao's wife was tactless. She had heard that Tan-chun was difficult to handle, but thought this was because others were afraid to stand up to her. How could a young girl have her own way like this? Besides, the mere daughter of a concubine would hardly dare cross *her*, Lady Hsing's personal maid whom even Lady Wang treated with respect, to say nothing of younger members of the household. Tan-chun's behaviour had led her to believe that she was simply annoyed with Hsi-feng, not with the rest of them. So she decided to assert herself and stepping forward through the crowd she pulled up the girl's lapel.

"Yes," she sniggered. "I've searched even the young lady's person. There's really nothing."

"Let's go, nurse," interposed Hsi-feng. "Stop this fooling."

Even as she was speaking — slap! — Tan-chun boxed Mrs. Wang's ears.

"Who do you think you are?" she fumed, pointing one finger at her. "How *dare* you paw me? It's only for Her Ladyship's sake and because you're old that I call you 'nurse,' but like a dog counting on its master's backing you're always making trouble. Today you've gone too far. If you think I'm as good-natured as your young mistress, whom you bully just as you please, you're making a big mistake. I didn't scold you for coming to raid our place, but you've no right to take liberties with me."

She started taking off her clothes and insisted that, instead of letting a slave maul her, Hsi-feng must search her carefully herself.

Hsi-feng and Ping-erh hurriedly helped to dress her again. "A few cups of wine and you play the fool," they scolded Mrs. Wang. "The other day you offended Her Ladyship too. Be off with you now, and not another word."

They tried to placate Tan-chun.

"If I'd any pride," scoffed Tan-chun, "I should have dashed my brains out long ago. How can I let a slave search my person for stolen goods? Tomorrow I'll report this to Their Ladyships, then go to apologize to Lady Hsing and accept whatever punishment she thinks fit."

Wang Shan-pao's wife, thoroughly abashed, started grumbling outside the window, "This is too much! I've never been struck before in all my life. Tomorrow I'll ask Her Ladyship's leave to go home. What's there left for me to live for?"

"Hear that?" Tan-chun snapped at her maids. "Are you waiting for *me* to go out and argue with her?"

At once Tai-shu darted out.

"If you get leave to go home, that's our good fortune!" she cried. "We're only afraid you won't ask."

"Well!" laughed Hsi-feng. "Here's truly a case of 'like mistress like maid.' "

"We thieves all have ready tongues," retorted Tan-chun. "But she isn't clever enough to tell tales to her mistress."

Ping-erh tried to smooth things over and fetched Tai-shu back while Chou Jui's wife and the others soothed Tan-chun. And Hsi-feng waited till she had gone to bed before leading her search party to Warm Spring Village opposite, for as this lay just between Hsi-chun's and Tan-chun's quarters it was the next place to visit before Hsi-chun's. Li Wan, ill in bed, had just taken medicine and gone to sleep, so without disturbing her they searched her maids' rooms. Not finding anything there they went on to Hsi-chun's place.

Hsi-chun being little more than a child was frightened, and Hsi-feng had to soothe her. However, in Ju-hua's case they discovered a big package of thirty to forty gold and silver ingots: so instead of evidence of immoral conduct they had found stolen goods! There was also a set of jade ornaments for a man's belt and a bundle containing a man's sandals and socks. Ju-hua turned pale. And asked where these things came from she knelt down and sobbed.

"They were given my brother by Lord Chen," she faltered. "Now that our parents are down south he lives with our uncle.

And because my uncle and aunt are fond of drinking and gambling, for fear they'd squander anything he gets my brother always gives it to an old nurse to bring to me for safe-keeping."

Hsi-chun was naturally timid and this disclosure appalled her

"I'd no idea!" she cried. "How disgraceful! If you want to have her beaten, sister-in-law, do take her away so that I don't have to hear it."

"If what you say is true, it's forgivable," said Hsi-feng to Ju-hua. "But you shouldn't smuggle things in here in secret. If you had *these* smuggled in, you can smuggle in other things too; so whoever brought them in here is to blame. If you're lying and these are stolen goods, don't expect to get off alive!"

Kneeling before her Ju-hua sobbed, "I dare not lie to you, madam. You can check with Her Ladyship and His Lordship tomorrow. If they say these weren't gifts, I won't complain if you have me and my brother beaten to death."

"Naturally I shall check. But even if these were gifts you still did wrong. Who gave you permission to bring things here in secret? Tell me who your intermediary was and I'll let you off. But mind you never do such a thing again."

"Don't let her off, sister-in-law," cried Hsi-chun. "We have so many people here, if we don't make an example of one of them the bigger offenders will get quite out of hand. Even if you're willing to forgive her, I'm not."

"She's usually quite well behaved, isn't she? We all make mistakes, and this is her first offence. If she does it again we'll punish her for both. But I wonder who smuggled the things in for her?"

"As for that, it must be Mrs. Chang at the back gate. She's always whispering with the maids and they all do her little favours."

Hsi-feng told the stewardesses to make a note of this name, and the things were entrusted to Chou Jui's wife for temporary custody till a check had been made the next day. Then they took their leave of Hsi-chun and went on to Ying-chun's place.

Ying-chun was already asleep. They knocked for some time before the gate was opened. Hsi-feng gave orders not to disturb the young lady and went with the others to the maids' quarters. As Ssu-chi there was Mrs. Wang's grand-daughter, Hsi-feng was curious to know whether or not she was biased by family ties and she therefore paid special attention to this search. Mrs. Wang started with the other girls' cases and, finding nothing exceptionable, went on to open Ssu-chi's case. After a perfunctory search she declared there was nothing there and started to close it.

"Wait!" cried Chou Jui's wife. "What's this?"

She reached to pick out a man's silk socks and slippers as well as a small bundle. When they opened this, they found inside a love-knot and a letter. These were handed to Hsi-feng for her inspection, for as she was in charge of the household and had to read letters and go through accounts, she knew quite a few characters. Hsi-feng saw that this stationery was red with double happy-life designs. On it was written:

> After your visit home last month my parents found out about our understanding, but we can't have our wish until after your young lady's marriage. If it's possible to meet in the Garden, get Mrs. Chang to send me word. That would be more convenient than your coming here. Do, do arrange it! Also, I've received the two pouches you sent me, and I'm sending you a string of scented beads as a token of my love. Please keep them safely. Your cousin, Pan Yu-an.

This letter, far from angering Hsi-feng, amused her. As none of the others could read and Mrs. Wang had no inkling of this romance between her grand-daughter and young Pan, the sight of the slippers and socks had made her uneasy. When Hsi-feng started laughing at what was written on the red paper she said:

"I suppose this is some account and you're amused by their poor writing, madam?"

"Quite. This account takes some working out. As Ssu-chi's maternal grandmother, tell me how her cousin comes to have the name Pan instead of Wang?"

In some surprise Mrs. Wang stammered, "Her paternal aunt

married a Pan, so she has a cousin named Pan — the Pan Yu-an who ran away the other day."

"That explains it," chuckled Hsi-feng. "I'll read it for you."

She read the letter, and everybody was shocked. It had never occurred to Wang Shan-pao's wife, so intent had she been on exposing others, that her grand-daughter would be caught out. She was quite overwhelmed by shame and vexation.

Chou Jui's wife and the other stewardesses asked her, "Well, what have you to say to that? How should we deal with her in your opinion?"

Mrs. Wang wished she could sink into the ground, and Hsi-feng laughed at her.

"This is just as well," she remarked to Mrs. Chou. "She's saved her granny and everyone trouble by quietly picking a fine young man for herself."

Chou Jui's wife chuckled too and made some caustic comments.

Unable to vent her anger on anyone else, Mrs. Wang slapped her own face.

"You old bitch who's lived beyond your time!" she swore. "This is retribution for your sins. You brought this on yourself."

The others burst out laughing, then while making a show of consoling her flung a few taunts at her. Only Ssu-chi stood silent with lowered head, but to Hsi-feng's surprise she showed no sign of fear. It was too late to question the girl, but for fear she might do away with herself that night Hsi-feng detailed two matrons to keep an eye on her. Then she had the evidence they had discovered taken back to her place and retired, meaning to settle the matter the next day.

During the night, however, Hsi-feng had to get up several times and lost a good deal of blood. The next morning she kept to her bed, feeling weak and dizzy. The court physician summoned to examine her reported:

"The young mistress suffers from lack of vital blood and

a hot humour in the spleen caused by worry and undue exertion. This has resulted in listlessness, drowsiness, indigestion and lack of appetite. A tonic to restore her strength and cool the hot humour is recommended."

Having made out a prescription including ginseng, angelica, astragalus and the like, he took his leave.

Some old nurses took the prescription to Lady Wang, and this so added to her worries that for the time being she set Ssu-chi's business aside.

That day Madam Yu happened to call first on Hsi-feng and then on Li Wan in the Garden. She was meaning to visit the girls when Hsi-chun sent a maid to invite her over. Hsi-chun told her all that had happened the night before and showed her the ingots found among Ju-hua's things.

"These really were gifts to her brother from Chen," Madam Yu confirmed. "His giving them was above-board, but she shouldn't have smuggled them in here on the sly — that's turned state traffic in salt into contraband." She scolded Ju-hua for her stupidity, saying eating too much rich food had addled her wits.

"As master and mistress you weren't strict enough with your servants, yet now you blame the maid," protested Hsi-chun. "Of all us girls here I'm the only one to lose face through my maid. How am I to face people in future? Last night I urged Hsi-feng to take her away, but she wouldn't. That's natural, I suppose, as Ju-hua comes from the East Mansion. But today I meant to take her there myself, so I'm glad you've come. Do take her away quickly. You can beat her, kill her or sell her — I shan't care in the least."

Ju-hua fell on her knees weeping.

"I won't do such a thing again. But please, miss, for old time's sake, let me die here with you!" she pleaded.

Madam Yu and the nurses interceded too.

"This was just a momentary slip-up, and she won't dare do it again," they said. "She's been waiting on you since childhood. You'd better allow her to stay."

But Hsi-chun although young had a will of her own and

was most uncompromising and eccentric. However hard they pleaded, she was adamant as she felt the maid had disgraced her.

"I don't want Ju-hua," she insisted. "Not only that, now that I'm growing up I think it best not to visit you people over there myself. Especially as these last few days I've been hearing a lot of gossip. I don't want to be mixed up in any scandal."

"Who's been gossipping?" asked Madam Yu. "What about? Aren't we all one family? If you hear talk about us, you should ask the gossips why they spread such rumours."

Hsi-chun smiled scornfully.

"A fine way to talk! A young girl like me should just steer clear of scandals. What sort of creature would I be if instead I sought them out? And at the risk of offending you I must say: Your reputation's known, so I don't have to ask what it is. As the ancients said: 'Where good and evil, life and death are concerned, even fathers and sons are unable to help each other.' That's even truer of us. What I care about is *my* good name, not yours. If you get involved in scandals in future, don't drag me in."

Madam Yu did not know whether to laugh or be angry.

She said to the servants, "No wonder they all call her young and foolish. I didn't believe them, but you heard the unreasonable way she talked just now — showing no judgement or sense of proportion at all. It's childish talk, but it cuts people to the quick."

"She's young, madam," the nurses rejoined. "You must make allowances."

"I may be young," Hsi-chun retorted. "All the same I'm speaking from experience. You don't know enough characters to read, so you're all so benighted that when I talk sense you call me young and foolish."

"You're the Number One Scholar, the greatest talent of all times," quipped Madam Yu. "Stupid people like us don't have your sense. How's that?"

"Even Number One scholars can be foolish. In fact they're most likely to lack enlightenment."

"Fine!" Madam Yu crowed. "A moment ago you were a talented scholar; now you've become a chief monk holding forth on enlightenment."

"If I weren't enlightened, I wouldn't have the heart to give up Ju-hua."

"But that proves you heartless and cold."

"As the ancients said: 'One must be ruthless to keep out of trouble.' I'm pure and spotless. Why should I spoil my integrity by letting you involve me in your affairs?"

Being sensitive on this point, Madam Yu disliked such talk. She had been mortified to hear that there had been gossip, but had controlled herself in front of Hsi-chun. This last thrust was more than she could take, however.

"In what way have we involved you?" she demanded. "Your maid does wrong, and for no reason you round on *me*. I've put up with it for some time, but that's only emboldened you to keep on like this. If you're such a fine young lady, we won't venture to approach you in future for fear of spoiling your good reputation." She ordered her servants to take Ju-hua away and got up in a temper to leave.

"If you do stay away that will save us bickering and trouble, and we can all have a quiet life," cried Hsi-chun.

Madam Yu did not answer this but went straight out. To know what happened later, read the next chapter.

CHAPTER 75

At a Feast One Night Portentous Sighing
Is Heard
New Poems on the Moon Festival Are Taken
as Good Omens

Madam Yu left Hsi-chun in a huff to call on Lady Wang, but the nurses accompanying her quietly warned her, "Better not go there, madam. The Chen family have just sent people with some things and they seem to want it kept quiet, so this may not be a good time to call."

"Only yesterday your master told me that, according to the *Court Gazette*, the Chens have been charged with crimes," said Madam Yu. "Their house has been raided, their property confiscated, and they've been fetched to the capital to stand trial. So why have these people come?"

"Why indeed?" answered the nurses. "The few women who arrived just now looked flustered and agitated. They must be up to something they don't want to be known."

In view of this, Madam Yu called instead on Li Wan. The court physician treating her had just left, and as her health had recently improved she was sitting propped up against her pillow in bed with a quilt around her, just hoping someone would drop in for a chat. She soon noticed, however, that Madam Yu was not her usual amiable self, simply sitting there lost in thought.

"It was good of you to come," said Li Wan. "Have you eaten anything in your round of calls? You must be hungry." She told Su-yun to try to find some delicacies for her.

"No need, no need," Madam Yu at once demurred. "Ill as you've been, you can't have any delicacies here. Besides, I'm not hungry."

"Lan's aunt has sent me some good fried flour; let's mix a bowl for you to taste." She ordered a maid to prepare this, while Madam Yu remained silent in a brown study.

The attendants who had come with her suggested, "You didn't wash at noon, madam. Would you like to freshen up now?"

When she nodded, Li Wan told Su-yun to fetch her dressing-case, and with it the girl brought some of her own rouge and powder.

"Our mistress doesn't use cosmetics, so please make do with these of mine if you don't think them dirty, madam," she said with a smile.

"The idea!" scolded Li Wan. "Although I haven't got such things, you should have fetched some from one of the young ladies, instead of producing your own. You're lucky it's her and not anybody else — or they'd have taken offence at your impudence."

"What does it matter?" said Madam Yu. "I use all your servants' things each time I come here. Why should I be fussy today?"

She sat cross-legged on the *kang* while Yin-tieh took off her bracelets and rings, then spread a large handkerchief on her lap to protect her clothing. A large basin of warm water was brought in by Tsao-tou, one of the younger maids, who stooped to hold it out for Madam Yu.

"Will you never learn to adapt yourself to circumstances?" cried Yin-tieh. "Once given an instruction, you stick to it, regardless. Because our mistress is lenient and not particular about etiquette at home, you get the idea you can be equally casual in a relative's house, carrying on in public the way you do in private."

"Never mind," said Madam Yu. "All I want is a wash."

Tsao-tou hastily knelt down.

"In our family," went on Madam Yu with a smile, "high and low alike all observe the outward forms of etiquette but actually carry on in a scandalous way."

Li Wan knew from this that she had heard about the last night's happenings.

"Why do you say that?" she laughed. "Who's been carrying on in a scandalous way?"

"Why ask *me*? You may have been ill but you weren't dead. . . ."

Before she could say more, Pao-chai was announced and she entered even as Li Wan was asking her in. Madam Yu quickly wiped her face and got up to offer her a seat.

"All by yourself?" she asked. "Where are the other girls?"

"I haven't seen them," said Pao-chai. "I've come because mother's unwell, and our only two reliable maids are ill in bed; so I must go back to keep her company tonight. I meant to ask leave from Their Ladyships, but then I thought that as it's not really serious there's no need to mention it; and anyway I'll come back as soon as she's better. So I've just come to let you know."

Li Wan and Madam Yu exchanged smiles at this. And now that the latter had cleaned up they all had some fried-flour "tea."

Li Wan remarked, "We must send to inquire after Aunt Hsueh's illness, as I'm not well enough to go myself. Yes, just go along home, dear cousin. I'll assign people to keep an eye on your rooms for you while you're away. But mind you come back after a day or two, otherwise I'll be held to blame."

"Why should you be? This is just for the time being and perfectly natural. It's not as if you were taking a bribe to let a thief escape! And I see no reason for you to send people over. Why not invite Hsiang-yun here to stay with you for a few days? Wouldn't that be simpler?"

"Where is she?" asked Madam Yu.

"I just sent her to find Tan-chun and bring her here, so that I can let her know too."

That same moment Hsiang-yun and Tan-chun were announced, and after they had been offered seats Pao-chai explained why she was leaving the Garden.

"Very good," commented Tan-chun. "So you'll come back when auntie's better. And even if you don't, that won't matter either."

"That's a strange way to talk!" exclaimed Madam Yu. "Are we driving our relatives away?"

"That's the idea." Tan-chun smiled mockingly. "Better drive them out before getting thrown out by others. In any case, there's no need for relatives to live together all the time. We're a happy family of kith and kin I must say, all like game-cocks fighting to finish each other off."

"I'm certainly out of luck today," Madam Yu laughed, "finding so many of you girls in a bad temper."

"Who told you to come and burn yourself on the stove?" Tan-chun retorted. "And who else has offended you?" She went on thoughtfully, "Hsi-chun has no reason to scold you, so who else could it be?"

Madam Yu just muttered an evasive reply.

Knowing she was reluctant to speak out for fear of trouble, Tan-chun teased, "Don't pretend to be so simple. People don't get their heads chopped off except for crimes against the state, so what are you so afraid of? I'll tell you the truth: I slapped that old wife of Wang Shan-pao's yesterday, and I'm quite willing to take the consequences. But apart from calling me names behind my back, nobody's likely to give me a beating for it."

Asked by Pao-chai what had provoked her, Tan-chun described in detail the search made the night before and why she had struck Mrs. Wang. Since Tan-chun had come out with it, Madam Yu told them how Hsi-chun had just treated her.

"She's like that," observed Tan-chun, "so eccentric and stubborn there's just no talking her round." Then she informed them, "When no action was taken this morning and I heard that our peppery Hsi-feng was ill again, I sent my nanny to find out what had happened to Wang Shan-pao's wife. She came back to report that the old creature got a thrashing for being too meddlesome."

"Serves her right too," approved Madam Yu and Li Wan.

Tan-chun laughed caustically.

"Who can't see through that trick? Just wait and see. . . ."

Madam Yu and Li Wan made no answer to this. And presently,

thinking it time for the Lady Dowager's meal, Hsiang-yun and Pao-chai went back to pack their things while Madam Yu took her leave of Li Wan and went straight to the old lady's place. She found her sitting on her couch listening to Lady Wang's disturbing account of how the Chen family had got into trouble, had their property confiscated and been fetched to the capital for punishment. She asked Madam Yu where she had come from and if Hsi-feng and Li Wan were any better.

"They're both better today," Madam Yu made haste to assure her.

The old lady nodded and sighed.

"Well, let's not trouble ourselves about other people's affairs but consider how to celebrate the Moon Festival."

"We've got everything ready," said Lady Wang. "But we don't know where you'd like to have the feast. Only the wind may be cold at night in the empty Garden."

"That doesn't matter. We can dress more warmly. That's just the place to enjoy the moon, of course."

While they were chatting tables had been brought in, and Lady Wang and Madam Yu at once helped to serve the food. The Lady Dowager saw that in addition to the dishes prepared for her there were two big hampers of others, it being the custom for the two mansions to present her with extra dishes every day. She asked what they were.

"I've told you several times to stop this, but you never listen," she complained. "We're not as well off as we used to be."

"I've passed on your instructions more than once, but this goes on as usual," Yuan-yang said. "So I had to let it go."

"This is only everyday family fare," put in Lady Wang. "As today is one of my fast days we haven't got much, and knowing that you're not too fond of gluten of wheat and beancurd I just chose minced water-mallow with pepper sauce."

"That's good. Just what I fancy."

At once Yuan-yang set this dish before her. Pao-chin and the other girls after deferring to each other took seats too. And Tan-chun, told by the old lady to join them, after first declining the honour sat down opposite Pao-chin. Tai-shu then brought out a bowl and chopsticks. Pointing at two dishes in a hamper Yuan-yang remarked:

"We don't know what these are, they're from the Elder Master. This bowl of bamboo-shoots with chicken marrow is from Lord Chen." She placed it on the table.

The old lady simply tasted a couple of dishes, then ordered those two to be returned to the senders.

"Tell them I've tried them," she said. "In future there's no need to send over every day. If I fancy anything I'll ask for it."

The matrons assented and went off with the dishes.

"Is there any congee?" the Lady Dowager asked.

Madam Yu, who had a bowl ready, remarked that it was made of special red rice. The old lady took it and ate half a bowl, then had some sent to Hsi-feng. She also had a bowl of bamboo-shoots and a dish of salted raccoon sent to Tai-yu and Pao-yu, and another bowl of meat sent to Chia Lan. Then she urged Madam Yu to come and eat. The latter assented but waited till the old lady had washed her hands, rinsed her mouth and left the table to chat with Lady Wang. And as she took a seat, Tan-chun and Pao-chin got up and asked to be excused.

"What, leave me all alone at this big table!" cried Madam Yu. "I'm not used to it."

"Yuan-yang and Hu-po!" called the old lady, chuckling. "Here's your chance to tuck in. Come and keep her company."

"Fine, fine." Madam Yu smiled. "Just what I was hoping for."

"It's great fun watching a whole lot of people eating together." The old lady pointed at Yin-tieh. "That's a good child too. Come and join your mistress. You can stick to the rules again after leaving me."

"Come on, quick," Madam Yu cried. "No need to put on an act."

The Lady Dowager, her hands behind her as she looked on with amusement, noticed one of the maids offer Madam Yu a bowl of the ordinary white rice for the servants.

"Are you out of your mind, serving your mistress that rice?" she demanded.

"Your rice is finished, madam," said the maid. "And as there's an extra young lady today, we're short."

"We have to cut our coat according to our cloth," Yuan-yang put in. "Nowadays there's no margin at all."

Lady Wang explained, "The last couple of years, what with floods and drought, our farms haven't been able to produce their quota, especially of the rice of the finer kind. So we only issue as much as we think will be needed, for fear of running out. The rice you buy outside isn't to our taste."

The old lady chortled, "As the proverb says: 'Even a clever wife can't make congee without rice.'"

Amid general laughter Yuan-yang asked the servant, "In that case, why not fetch Miss Tan-chun's rice here to make up? Wouldn't that be the same? Why be so stupid?"

"No, I've had enough," said Madam Yu with a smile. "There's no need to fetch more."

"You may have had enough, but what about me?" Yuan-yang parried.

Then the serving-women hurried off to fetch more. Presently Lady Wang went off to have her meal leaving Madam Yu to chat with the old lady till about nine, when she was told:

"It's late now. You'd better go back."

Madam Yu took her leave then and went out to the gate to mount her carriage. Yin-tieh took a place at one side of the carriage. The serving-women, having let down the curtain, led the young maids to wait at the Ning Mansion's gate; for as the two mansions were less than a bowshot apart, no elaborate preparations had to be made when the members of both exchanged visits, especially at night when many of them went out and returned. So the old nurses just led the young maids the short distance over, the men-servants at both gates having already cordoned off the east and west ends of the street. Madam Yu's carriage was not drawn by a mule. Instead, seven or eight pages pulled it gently along to the steps of the Ning Mansion, then withdrew behind the stone lions flanking the gate while the serving-women raised the curtain and Yin-tieh alighted to help her mistress down. Seven or eight lanterns large and small shed a bright light, and noticing four or five carriages drawn up by the stone lions Madam Yu inferred that visitors had arrived for another gambling party.

"Look at all those carriages," she said to Yin-tieh. "And how many more came on horseback we've no means of knowing, as their horses will all be tethered in the stables. How much money can those young fellows' parents give them to throw away like this?"

By now she had reached the front hall, where Chia Jung's wife was waiting to welcome her at the head of serving-women and maids with candles.

"I've always wanted to take a peep at them," remarked Madam Yu. "Here's our chance at last! Suppose we walk past their windows?"

The matrons assented and led the way with lanterns, one of them going quietly ahead to warn the pages in attendance not to make any commotion. When Madam Yu and the rest tiptoed up to the windows they heard quite a noise inside — jokes and compliments interspersed with complaints and curses.

The fact is that Chia Chen, being in mourning and unable to go out to amuse himself or listen to operas or music, had thought of a way to while away the time. In the day-time, under the pretext of practising archery, he invited young lordlings and other wealthy relatives and friends to archery contests. Arguing that shooting at random could not improve their skill and might even spoil their style, he imposed certain penalties and set stakes as an incentive to all to do their best. They had set up a target in the shooting-range under Heavenly Fragrance Pavilion and made it the rule to assemble there every morning after breakfast. Chia Chen, not wanting his name to be used, made Chia Jung act as the banker.

The young hereditary nobles from wealthy families whom they invited were a set of profligates who enjoyed cock-fights, dog-racing and playing about with singsong girls and young actors. They agreed to take it in turn every day after the shooting contest to stand treat, so that Chia Jung need not defray all the expenses. And so day after day they had pigs, sheep and poultry killed and vied to show off their wealth, the skill of their chefs and the sumptuousness of their feasts.

Chia Sheh and Chia Cheng did not hear about this until it had gone on for a fortnight or so, and not realizing what was involved they judged it quite right and proper for these young men not versed in literature to practise military arts, the more so as they belonged to families of hereditary generals of noble ranks. They even ordered Chia Huan, Chia Tsung, Pao-yu and Chia Lan to come over too after breakfast every day to practise archery with Chia Chen for a while.

But since Chia Chen had other ends in view, alleging the need to relax after their exertions he soon started arranging card games in the evenings and they laid wagers while drinking. So little by little these turned into gambling parties. Now, after three or four months, gambling had priority over archery and they played cards, diced and gambled quite openly day and night. The servants, getting more perks, encouraged this and so it was now routine — quite unknown to people outside the family.

Recently their group had been joined by Lady Hsing's younger brother Hsing Teh-chuan, an inveterate wastrel, as well as the confirmed prodigal Hsueh Pan who naturally thought this a splendid scheme.

Hsing Teh-chuan although Lady Hsing's brother had totally different interests, being a credulous fool who spent money like water and found all his pleasure in drinking, gambling and debauchery. He liked good drinkers and shunned those who did not drink, no matter whether they were high or low, making no distinction between master and slave; hence everybody called him Foolish Uncle.

Hsueh Pan, who had long been dubbed the Stupid Lordling, naturally found Hsing a man after his own heart. As both of them liked dicing because it was fast, they had got two fellows to dice with them on the *kang* in the outer room where a few other men were playing cards at a big table, while in the inner room a less uncouth party were in the middle of a game of dominoes. Most of their attendants were pages of less than fifteen, all grown men-servants being debarred from the place. This was why Lady Yu dared peep through the window.

She saw that wine was being served by two young actors of seventeen or eighteen, strikingly handsome in their fine clothes and make up. Hsueh Pan was scowling after a losing throw, but now with a lucky toss he recouped his losses and won, which restored his good humour.

"Let's stop for a while," proposed Chia Chen, "and have some refreshments before going on."

He asked how the two other tables were getting on. The domino players in the inner room had also finished and were waiting for supper; but the card players were in the middle of a game and reluctant to stop. Without waiting for them they had one table set first, and Chia Chen sat down to dine with those who were ready, instructing Chia Jung to wait for the rest.

Hsueh Pan, in exuberation, fondling one of the actors as he drank, ordered him to toast Foolish Uncle. But Hsing was in a bad mood, after losing. Tipsy after two bowls of wine, he complained that the actors simply made up to the winners, ignoring the losers.

"You pansies are all the same," he swore. "We've been together all these days and you've had favours from us all, but now as soon as I lose a few taels of silver you start cold-shouldering me. Do you think you'll never need my help again?"

Seeing that he was half drunk, the others tried to humour him.

"Quite right, quite right," they said. "That's a bad way they have." They sternly ordered the two boys, "Hurry up and offer him wine to apologize."

The two young actors, accustomed to such scenes, knelt down to offer Hsing a drink.

"In our profession our masters train us all, no matter how generous or close our patrons may be, just to make up to the rich and powerful. A man may be a living Buddha or saint, but so long as he has no money or influence we have to ignore him. Besides, sir, we're young and in this low profession, so please overlook it this time and let us off."

They raised a cup of wine and fell on their knees.

Though Foolish Uncle was mollified he kept up a show of anger.

"They're telling the truth, that's how it is," said the others. "You've always had a soft spot in your heart for actors; why be like this today? If you refuse to drink how dare they get up?"

Hsing gave in at that and growled, "If it weren't for all these gentlemen interceding, I'd have nothing more to do with you." Then only did he take the cup and drain it.

Another bowl was poured. And now the wine went to his head, making him hark back to earlier grievances. Pounding the table he said to Chia Chen with a sigh:

"We can't blame these boys, my worthy nephew, for being so grasping. Why, where money and power are concerned, many people from big official families will forget even their own flesh and blood. Did you hear about the row I had yesterday with your respected aunt?"

"No, I didn't," was Chia Chen's reply.

Hsing Teh-chuan sighed again.

"It was all over filthy lucre."

Chia Chen knew he was on bad terms with Lady Hsing, who thoroughly disapproved of him and often complained about him.

"You're rather too improvident, uncle," he said. "If you go on spending at this rate, you'll never have enough."

"My dear worthy nephew, you don't know how it is in our family," Hsing retorted. "At the time of my mother's death I was still small and knew nothing of affairs. Of my three sisters your respected aunt is the oldest. She grabbed all our family property and brought it over with her at the time of her marriage. Now my second sister's married too, but also in straitened circumstances. My third is still at home. All our expenses are doled out to us by your aunt's personal maid here, the wife of your steward Wang Shan-pao. When I come to ask for money I'm not cadging from you Chias. Our Hsing family has quite enough for me to spend — if only I could get my hands on it. It's grossly unjust, but what can I do about it?"

Afraid this maudlin talk would make a bad impression on

in a row in the lower seats at their table to play the finger-guessing game and drink. Then Chia Chen, in high spirits after wine, sent a servant to fetch a purple bamboo flute and asked Pei-feng to play it while Wen-hua sang. Her voice was so clear and tender that the listeners were entranced.

After that they played more drinking games until nearly midnight, by when Chia Chen was eight-tenths drunk. Tea was served, and they had just been brought fresh wine cups when they heard long-drawn-out sighing from the direction of the garden wall. Everyone heard it distinctly and they were fearfully startled.

"Who is there?" demanded Chia Chen sternly.

But though he called out several times there was no answer.

"It may be one of our servants behind the wall," suggested Madam Yu.

"Nonsense," her husband retorted. "The servant's quarters are nowhere near the wall. Besides, that part is just by the ancestral temple. Who could be there at this hour?"

That same instant they heard a gust of wind on the other side of the wall and the sound as if of partition windows slamming inside the temple. The air struck them as colder, and the moon just now so bright and clear seemed suddenly dimmed. All the girls and women shivered. Chia Chen half sobered up, but though more in control of himself than the women he was most amazed and apprehensive too. This cast a gloom over the party. Still, they felt constrained to sit there a little longer before retiring to their rooms to rest.

The next morning being the fifteenth, Chia Chen rose early and led the whole family to open the ancestral temple to perform the usual rites for the first and the fifteenth of every month. Looking round carefully, he observed that everything in the temple was undisturbed with no sign of anything amiss. He therefore made no mention of the strange occurrence the previous night, thinking he must have imagined it in his cups. The ceremony at an end, he had the temple locked up as before.

After supper Chia Chen and his wife went over to the Jung Mansion. He found Chia Sheh and Chia Cheng sitting chatting with the Lady Dowager while the younger men and boys of the family stood around in attendance. Chia Chen greeted each in turn, and after a few remarks the old lady invited him to take a seat, which he did on a stool near the door.

"How is your cousin Pao-yu getting on with his archery these days?" she asked him.

"He's making great progress, not only in his form. He's now able to use a stronger bow as well."

"That's good. But don't let him overtax his strength."

When Chia Chen had agreed to this she remarked, "The mooncakes you sent us yesterday were good. The melons looked all right but were disappointing."

"The cakes were made by a new pastry cook. Finding them good I ventured to have some made for you, madam, as a token of respect. It's strange that this year's melons aren't up to the usual standard."

"There was too much rain this summer," remarked Chia Cheng.

"Well, the moon has risen now. Let's go and offer incense."

The old lady rose and leaning on Pao-yu's shoulder led the way to the Garden. By now all the Garden's main gates were wide open, big horn-lanterns hanging above. On the terrace in front of the Hall of Auspicious Shade where incense was burning in screened containers, shielded candles were alight, and melons, cakes and sweetmeats had been set out, Lady Hsing and the other ladies were waiting for them. The bright moonlight, coloured lanterns, scents and incense evoked an ethereal splendour defying description.

The terrace was spread with carpets and silk cushions. The Lady Dowager washed her hands, burned incense and kowtowed; then all the rest followed suit. After that she said it would be better to enjoy the view of the moon from a height, and ordered the feast to be served in the big pavilion on the ridge of the hill. Attendants hurried there to make preparations while she had a short rest in the Hall of Auspicious Shade, sipping tea and chatting with her family. When presently it was announced that all was ready she started up the hill, leaning on some maids' shoulders.

"The mossy stones may be slippery," warned Lady Wang. "Why not go up in a bamboo chair?"

"The path is swept every day and it's very smooth and wide," countered the old lady. "I may as well walk to loosen up my old bones."

Chia Sheh and Chia Cheng led the way, followed by two old nurses with horn-lanterns. Yuan-yang, Hu-po and Madam Yu kept beside the old lady to help her along while Lady Hsing and the rest clustered behind, and a mere hundred paces brought them to the summit on which stood Convex Emerald Hall, so called because it was built on a promontory. On its front terrace, partitioned into two by a large screen, were tables and chairs all round in shape to symbolize perfect reunion. The old lady took the centre seat with Chia Sheh, Chia Chen, Chia Lien and Chia Jung on her left, on her right Chia Cheng, Pao-yu, Chia Huan and Chia Lan. The circle, however, was only half complete, the other half being conspicuously vacant.

"I don't usually feel there are too few of us, yet tonight I do," observed the old lady. "Why, in the old days, on an evening like this there'd have been thirty to forty menfolk and womenfolk and it would have been ever so lively. This is too small a party. We can't ask others to join us, as they're all celebrating at home with their own parents, so let's get some of the girls to fill up the gap on the other side."

Ying-chun, Tan-chun and Hsi-chun were fetched, and Chia Lien, Pao-yu and the other boys stood up to offer them seats, taking lower places themselves. Then the Lady Dowager called for a twig of osmanthus and ordered a serving-woman to beat a drum on the other side of the screen as the twig passed from hand to hand. Whoever had it when the drumming stopped had to drink a cup of wine and tell a joke as forfeit. The game started with the old lady passing the twig to Chia Sheh, and so on in turn. After two rounds Chia Cheng was left with it in his hand and had to drink up, while his children, nephews and nieces nudged or tugged at each other meaningly as they waited, smiling, to hear what joke he would tell. As his mother was in high spirits he felt constrained to do his best to please her.

"If you can't make us laugh," she warned, "we shall punish you by making you tell another."

"I have only the one joke, madam. If you don't find it funny I'll accept the penalty. . . . There was a man who was hen-pecked. . . ."

He was interrupted here by a burst of laughter, as Chia Cheng had never told jokes of this type before.

"This must be a good one," said the old lady, laughing.

"If you think it good, you must drink another cup, madam."

"Agreed."

He went on, "This hen-pecked husband never dared go any-where without his wife's permission. But on the Moon Festival, going out to do some shopping, he met friends who dragged him home to drink with them. He got drunk and slept in their house. The next day when he woke up, quite conscience-stricken, he had to go home to apologize. It happened that his wife was washing her feet.

"She said to him, 'Well, if you lick my feet I'll forgive you.'

"So the man had to lick her feet. But he couldn't help retch-ing, and this so enraged his wife that she threatened to beat him.

" 'What insolence!' she cried.

"He fell on his knees in fright and explained, 'It's not that your feet stink, madam, but all the rice-wine and mooncakes I had yesterday have turned my stomach today.' "

The whole company laughed, and Chia Cheng at once poured a cup of wine for the old lady.

"If that's how you feel, let's replace this wine with spirits," she proposed. "We don't want you to be sick."

Amid general mirth the drumming started once more, stopping this time when Pao-yu had the osmanthus. His father's presence made him feel on edge, but here he was caught with the twig in his hand. If I fail to tell a good joke I'll be scolded for being too stupid even to tell a joke, he thought. If I tell an amusing one he'll say I'm no good at studying, only able to gab, and blame me all the more. So I'd better get out of it.

He stood up and pleaded, "I'm no good at telling jokes. Please set me some other forfeit."

"Well then," said Chia Cheng, "write an occasional poem with 'autumn' as the rhyme. If it's good you'll get a reward. If not, look out tomorrow!"

"We're just playing a drinking game," objected the old lady. "Why make him write a poem?"

"He can do it," Chia Cheng assured her.

At once she sent for paper and a brush.

Chia Cheng warned, "Mind you don't use ornate phrases like 'frozen jade,' 'silver crystal,' 'bright splendour' or 'shining purity.' Your poem must be original. I want to test your ability after these years of study."

This was just what Pao-yu had been hoping for. He promptly made up four lines and wrote them out, presenting the poem to Chia Cheng who nodded without any comment. The Lady Dowager took this as a good sign.

"How is it?" she asked.

To please her Chia Cheng answered, "Quite a good effort. But because he hasn't been studying the right books the language lacks distinction."

"That's good enough. After all, how old is he? Do you expect him to be a prodigy? You should encourage him, to make him pay more attention to study in future."

"Very well." Chia Cheng turned to order a nurse, "Go and tell the pages in my study to bring two of those fans I brought back from Hainan to give him."

Pao-yu having bowed his thanks sat down again, and they went on with the game.

This prize given to Pao-yu made Lan now leave his seat to write a poem too, which he handed to his grandfather. Chia Cheng, very pleased with it, explained the contents of both poems to the old lady. And she was so delighted that she ordered a prize to be given to Lan too, after which they resumed their seats to continue the game. This time the drumming stopped when the osmanthus was in Chia Sheh's hand, and he had to drink a cup and tell a joke.

"The son of a certain family was most filial," he began. "One day his mother fell ill, and unable to find physicians able to cure her they called in an old woman who practised acupuncture. As she knew nothing of the principles of pulse-taking, she diagnosed the illness as fire in the heart which a few acupuncture treatments would set right.

"The son asked in alarm, 'How can you needle her heart? Won't that kill her?'

"The old woman said, 'There's no need to needle the heart. Just needling the ribs will do.'

"He protested, 'But the heart isn't anywhere near the ribs.'

"She said, 'That doesn't matter. Don't you know that all parents are biased, so that their hearts always incline to one side?' "

Amid general laughter his mother had to sip some wine.

After a short silence she said, "I suppose I should get that old woman to give me some acupuncture treatment too."

Chia Sheh realized then that she took the joke personally and he had offended her by his tactlessness. At once he stood up to pour her wine and tried to pass it off, and the old lady let the matter drop.

The game went on and this time Huan was caught holding the flower. Recently he had paid more attention to his studies; but, like Pao-yu, instead of studying the orthodox classics he preferred to read poems, especially those dealing with the bizarre and supernatural. When he saw Pao-yu awarded a prize for his poem he wanted to show off too, but in his father's presence dared not suggest it. Now that his turn had come to pay a forfeit, he also took paper and brush and wrote a four-lined verse which he handed to Chia Cheng. His father, although quite impressed, could read between the lines a lack of interest in study.

"You brothers are alike," he rebuked them both. "All the ideas you express are heterodox. You'll both turn out undisciplined reprobates. The ancients spoke of a 'matchless pair,' and that's what you two are; only in your case 'matchless' means 'incorrigible.' The elder brother shamelessly compares himself to Wen Ting-yun, and now the younger considers himself another Tsao Tang."

Chia Sheh and the others laughed, and Chia Sheh asked to see the poem and was full of praise for it.

"This seems to me to show character," he observed. "In our family we're not like those poor pedants who must 'study by the light of reflected snow or glow-worms' to pass the examination for the highest degree in order to climb up to exalted positions. Our sons should study too; but if they're a bit more intelligent than average and look all right, they can hardly fail to get some official post. There's no need for them to pore over tomes and become bookworms. That's why I like this poem of his — it shows the spirit of our noble house."

Thereupon he ordered a servant to fetch some novelties from his room as a reward. And patting Huan on the head he said with a laugh, "Just go on writing like this — it's our family's style. I'm sure you'll inherit our noble ranks in future."

Chia Cheng protested, "He was just writing nonsense. How can these lines foretell the future?" He poured a cup of wine for the old lady and the game went on.

Then the Lady Dowager suggested, "You gentlemen can take your leave now. There must be friends waiting for you outside. It won't do to neglect them. Besides, it's already past the second watch. Once you've gone, our girls will be able to enjoy themselves more freely for a while before we retire for the night."

Chia Sheh and the others stopped the game then and after a final toast took the younger men away. If you want to know the sequel, read the next chapter.

CHAPTER 76

By Convex Emerald Hall Fluting
Fills an Old Lady with Grief
In Concave Crystal Lodge Girls Composing
a Poem Lament Their Loneliness

When Chia Sheh and Chia Cheng had led Chia Chen and the
other men away, the Lady Dowager ordered serving-women to
remove the screen and turn the two feasts into one. This they
did by clearing the tables, replenishing the refreshments and
bringing clean cups and chopsticks while the ladies put on
warmer clothes, washed their faces and sipped tea. As they
took seats again around one table the old lady noticed that Pao-
chai and Pao-chin were missing — they were celebrating the
festival at home. In addition, Li Wan and Hsi-feng were unwell and the absence of these four made things seem rather quiet.

"In the past," she remarked, "when the master was away we
used to invite Aunt Hsueh over to enjoy the moon with us and
had great fun, until suddenly the thought of his absence, parting
husband from wife, mother from son and father from children
took away a bit from our pleasure.

"This year with the master back our family's reunited, but that
means we couldn't ask Aunt Hsueh and her children over to have
a good time with us. Besides, they've two relatives staying
there this year and couldn't leave them to come over here. And
on top of that, Hsi-feng's unwell. If she were here joking and
laughing, she'd make up for *ten* other people. This shows
nothing can ever be perfect in this world." She sighed and
called for a big cup of heated wine.

"This year you and your son are together," said Lady Wang.
"That's an improvement on the past. Though you had more

young people around you then, it still wasn't as good as having
your own son back."

"True," agreed the old lady.   "That's why I'm in such good
spirits that I want to drink from a big cup.   You should switch
to big cups too."

Lady Hsing and the others had to comply.   It was late now,
they were tired, and as none of them were good drinkers they
were flagging; but since the old lady was still in the mood for
fun they had no choice but to keep her company.   She ordered
rugs to be spread on the steps and mooncakes, water-melons and
other refreshments set out there so that the maids could sit down
in a circle and enjoy the moon as well.

The moon, now in mid sky, was more dazzlingly lovely than
ever.

"With such a fine moon we must listen to some fluting," decided the Lady Dowager.   She sent for the girl musicians, telling
them, "Too many instruments would break the spell.   One flute
played in the distance will be enough."

The flutist was just going off when one of Lady Hsing's matrons brought her a message.   The old lady asked what it was,
and the matron answered:

"Just now, on his way home, the Elder Master tripped over
a stone and sprained his ankle."

At once the Lady Dowager sent two women to see how he
was and urged Lady Hsing to hurry back.   As she was taking
her leave the old lady added, "Chen's wife may as well go with
you.   I'll soon be turning in."

Madam Yu countered gaily, "I'm not going back today.   I
mean to sit up drinking the whole night with our Old Ancestress."

"No, that won't do.   A young couple like you ought to be
united tonight.   How can you desert your husband for my
sake?"

Madam Yu flushed crimson and tittered, "What do you take
us for, Old Ancestress? We aren't as young as all that — we've
been married for over a dozen years and are getting on for
forty.   Besides, we're still in mourning.   There's no harm in

my keeping you company tonight. How can you ask me to spend it with my husband?"

"Quite right," chuckled the old lady. "I'd forgotten you were still in mourning. Yes, your poor father-in-law has been dead two years and more — how time does fly! I must drink a big cup as a forfeit for forgetting. Well, don't go then but stay and keep me company. Jung's wife can go back with her great-aunt."

So Madam Yu told her daughter-in-law to accompany Lady Hsing, and they mounted their carriages at the gate, then left.

In the Garden, the Lady Dowager led her party to enjoy the osmanthus in bloom, after which they returned to the feast and fresh wine was heated. They were chatting when, all of a sudden, from under the osmanthus came wafting the sweet, dulcet, mellifluous sound of fluting. In the bright moonlight and fresh breeze, with the sky above a void, the earth utterly still, this music dispelled all care and anxiety. Every voice hushed, they sat appreciating it in silence.

The fluting went on for the time it takes to drink two cups of tea. When it stopped, everyone exclaimed in admiration. Then warm wine was poured again.

"Wasn't that delightful?" asked the old lady, beaming.

"Really lovely, madam!" they replied. "We'd never have thought of such a thing. We need *you* to show us how to enjoy ourselves."

"This still isn't good enough. What's needed is slow music, the slower the better."

They had been eating melon-seed oil mooncakes stuffed with pine-kernals from the Palace, and the old lady now ordered one of these to be sent with a big cup of warm wine to the flutist, with instructions to drink it slowly then play another melody to the very best of her ability. Some serving-women had just gone off on this errand when back came the two matrons sent to ask after Chia Sheh.

"We saw His Lordship," they reported. "His right instep is a bit swollen, but he's taken some medicine and the pain is less now. It's nothing serious."

The Lady Dowager nodded.

"I worry too much about my children," she sighed. "He calls me biased, yet I feel such concern for him." She repeated Chia Sheh's joke to Lady Wang and Madam Yu.

"It was only a joke after drinking," said Lady Wang soothingly. "Anyone can make a slip. He can't possibly have had you in mind, madam. Why take it to heart?"

Yuan-yang had now brought a soft hood and a cape. "It's late," she said. "There'll be dew, and you may catch cold in the wind unless you put more on. After a little while you should go and rest."

"Why hurry me when I'm in high spirits?" asked the old lady. "I'm not drunk, am I? I'm going to sit up till dawn."

She called for more wine, put on the hood and the cape, and went on drinking and joking with the rest.

Now from the shade of the osmanthus trees they heard the melodious strains of fluting again, sadder this time than before, and all kept silent. The old lady was under the influence of wine, and in the still night, under the bright moon, the plaintive music touched her heart and she could not hold back her tears. The others were painfully affected too; but after some time, noticing her distress, they began to talk gaily to cheer her up and called for more wine, directing the flutist to stop.

"I've learned one joke," announced Madam Yu. "Let me tell it to amuse our Old Ancestress."

The old lady forced a smile.

"So much the better."

"A family had four sons. The eldest had only one eye, the second only one ear, the third only one nostril, the fourth had all his organs but was dumb. . . ."

Seeing that the Lady Dowager had closed her eyes, she broke off and with Lady Wang softly asked if she was awake. The old lady opened her eyes.

"I'm not sleepy, just closing my eyes to rest them a bit. Go on with your joke, I'm listening."

Lady Wang demurred, "It's already the fourth watch, madam, windy and with heavy dew. Won't you go and rest? You can enjoy the moon again tomorrow; it's still bright on the sixteenth."

"How can it be so late?"

"It really is. The girls couldn't stay up any longer; they've all gone off to sleep."

The Lady Dowager looked around and found only Tan-chun there — the rest had slipped away.

"All right," she said with a smile. "You're not used to staying up all night either. And we shouldn't tire the girls, weak and delicate as they are. So poor Tan-chun's the only one still here. You'd better go too. It's time the party broke up."

She rose, took a sip of tea, then wrapped the cape around her and was carried off by two women in a small bamboo sedan-chair which they had ready. The others followed her out of the Garden.

The serving-women clearing up discovered that one fine porcelain cup was missing.

They asked the others, "Did one of you break a cup? If so, bring us the pieces to hand in as evidence. Otherwise we may be accused of stealing it."

The others denied having broken anything.

"But one of the maids attending the young ladies may have dropped a cup," they suggested. "Try to remember, or just go and ask them."

"That's right," cried the woman in charge of the tea-services. "I remember Tsui-lu taking a cup. I'll ask her."

She went to look for Tsui-lu, who happened to come towards her along the covered walk accompanied by Tzu-chuan.

Tsui-lu called out, "Has the old lady left? And do you know where our young ladies are?"

"I've come to ask you for a cup, but you ask me for your mistresses instead."

"I'd just taken Miss Hsiang-yun some tea when she suddenly disappeared."

"Her Ladyship said just now they'd all gone to bed. You must have been playing about somewhere not to notice."

"They can't have slipped off quietly to bed. They must be strolling about. Maybe, seeing the old 'ady leave, they went ahead to see her off. Let's go to her place to look for them. Once we find them your teacup will turn up too. You can fetch it first thing tomorrow. What's the hurry?"

"Provided I know where it is, there's no hurry. I'll come for it tomorrow."

The woman went back then to clear away while Tzu-chuan and Tsui-lu made for the old lady's quarters.

Tai-yu and Hsiang-yun had not gone to bed. This big family reunion in the Chia mansion, which the Lady Dowager still complained was less lively than in the old days, as well as her reference to Pao-chai and Pao-chin celebrating at home with their own family, had made Tai-yu feel so disconsolate that she had slipped out to the corridor to shed tears. As Pao-yu was listless and distraught these days because Ching-wen's illness had taken a turn for the worse, when his mother urged him to go to bed off he went. Tan-chun was in no mood for enjoyment either, with family troubles weighing on her mind. And as neither Ying-chun nor Hsi-chun was too intimate with Tai-yu, that left only Hsiang-yun to comfort her.

"You should have more sense," Hsiang-yun told her, "than to let this scene upset you. I have no family either, but I don't take it to heart the way you do. With your poor health you ought to look after yourself. It's too bad of Pao-chai and Pao-chin. They kept saying our club must meet to celebrate the Moon Festival this year by writing a poem together; but now they've abandoned us and gone off to celebrate it on their own. Instead of our meeting to write a poem, the men and boys of the house have had things all their own way. As the old saying goes: 'How can an outsider be allowed to sleep beside one's bed?' Well, if they won't join in, why don't the two of us write a poem together? Tomorrow we can shame them with it."

As Hsiang-yun was trying to cheer her up, not wanting to spoil her fun Tai-yu replied, "All right. But it's too noisy here to have any poetic inspiration."

"Enjoying the moonlight on this hill is good, but it's better still by the water. You know that lake at the foot of this hill and Concave Crystal Lodge by the inlet there? A lot of thought went into designing this Garden. The crest of the hill is called Convex Emerald, and the creek in the lake below Concave Crystal. 'Convex' and 'concave,' so seldom used before, make fresh, original names. And these two places — one above, one below; one bright, one dark; one hill, one water — seem specially designed for enjoying the moonlight. Those who like to look at the moon from a height can come here; those who prefer to see its reflection in water can go there. But as these two words are usually pronounced *wa* and *tieh*[1] they're considered rather uncouth. That's why Lu Yu's line 'The old inkstone, slightly concave, brims with ink' was scoffed at as vulgar. Ridiculous, isn't it?"

"Lu Yu wasn't the only one to use this word. So did many other writers of old — Chiang Yen in his poetic essay *On Green Moss,* Tungfang Shuo in his *Miraculous and Strange Records,* and Chang Yen-yuan in his *Anecdotes on Painting* when he described the frescoes Chang Seng-yu[2] painted in a monastery. Why, there are too many instances to quote. But nowadays people not knowing this think these vulgar words.

"To tell you the truth," Tai-yu continued, "I'm the one who suggested both names. It was when we proposed names for places which hadn't yet been given any and marked their localities. They were taken to the Palace and shown to Elder Sister who sent them to uncle, and he was delighted. He said if only he'd known he'd have asked us girls to help with the names, and he accepted them all without changing a word. Well, let's go to Concave Crystal Lodge."

They walked down the hill, round a bend, and reached the lake. A path by the bamboo railings along its bank led to Lotus Fragrance Pavilion. The little building here, nestling

---

[1] *Wa*, concave or 凹 in Chinese; *tieh*, convex, is 凸 in Chinese.

[2] Chiang Yen (444-505); Tungfang Shuo (154-93 B.C.); Chang Yen-yuan lived in the Tang Dynasty (618-907), and Chang Seng-yu in the Southern and Northern Dynasties (420-589).

at the foot of the hill on which stood Convex Emerald Hall, had been given the name Concave Crystal because it was on low ground close to the water. As it was so small, with few rooms, there were only two serving-women on night duty; and knowing that the ladies at Convex Emerald Hall would not be requiring their services, after enjoying their share of moon-cakes, sweetmeats, wine and dishes, they had put out the lights and gone to bed.

"So they're asleep — good," said Hsiang-yun when they saw that the place was dark. "Let's enjoy the water and moon-light under this awning."

Sitting on two bamboo stools they gazed at the bright moon in the sky and then at its reflection in the lake, the moon above and its reflection below rivalling each other in magnificence. It was like being in some mermaids' crystal palace. As a breeze ruffled the green water of the lake they felt thoroughly refreshed.

"What fun it would be to drink now in a boat on the lake!" exclaimed Hsiang-yun. "If we were at my home I'd take a boat out."

"As the ancients often said: 'What enjoyment can there be if everything is perfect?'" remarked Tai-yu. "To my mind this is quite good enough."

"It's only natural for men to hanker for more. Didn't the old people often say: The poor think the rich have all their hearts' desire. Try to disabuse them and they won't believe you — not unless they grow rich themselves. Take the two of us for instance. Although we've lost our parents we're living in luxury, yet we have a lot to upset us."

"We aren't the only ones. Even Their Ladyships, Pao-yu, Tan-chun and the others can't have their way in everything big and small, even if they have good reason for wanting some-thing. That applies to everyone. Especially girls like us who are living with other families, not our own. . . ."

Afraid Tai-yu would start grieving again, Hsiang-yun in-terposed, "Well, enough of this idle talk. Let's get on with our poem."

As she was talking they heard melodious fluting.

"Their Ladyships are in high spirits today," Tai-yu remarked. "This fluting is pleasant and should give us inspiration. As we both like five-character lines, let's make regulated couplets in that metre."

"What rhymes shall we use?"

"Suppose we count the bars from this end of the railing to the other to decide which category of rhymes to choose. For example, if it's sixteen we'll use the *hsien* rhymes. Wouldn't that make a change?"

"That's certainly original."

So they got up to count the bars and found there were thirteen in all.

Hsiang-yun chuckled, "It *would* be thirteen! That means the *yuan* group of rhymes. There aren't too many for a long poem of couplets, so it may be awkward. Still, you must make a start."

"We'll see which of us does better. But we ought to have paper and a brush to write it down."

"We can copy it out tomorrow. There's no danger of forgetting it before then."

"All right then. I'll start with a pat phrase." Tai-yu declaimed:

> "Mid-autumn's fifteenth night is here again. . . ."

Hsiang-yun reflected, then said:

> "As on the Feast of Lanterns we stroll round.
> The sky above is sprinkled with bright stars. . . ."

Tai-yu continued:

> "And everywhere sweet strings and pipes resound.
> Goblets fly here and there as men carouse. . . ."

"I like that last line," Hsiang-yun approved. "I must find something good to match it." After a moment's thought she said:

> "No house but has its windows opened wide.
> The breeze that softly fans the air is chill. . . ,"

"You've capped my attempt," admitted Tai-yu. "But your second line is trite. You should go from strength to strength."

"A long poem with tricky rhymes has to be padded out a bit. We can use some good lines later."

"If you don't, you should be ashamed!" Tai-yu went on:

> "But bright as day the fine night scene outside.
> The greybeard grabbing for a cake is mocked...."

"That's no good," laughed Hsiang-yun. "It's not classical. You're putting me on the spot by using an everyday incident like that."

"I'd say you hadn't read many books. This reference to cakes is a classical allusion. You should read the Tang Dynasty records before you talk."

"Well, you haven't foxed me. I've got it." Hsiang-yun capped the verse:

> "Green girls share melons laughing themselves silly.
> How fresh the scent of jade osmanthus bloom...."

"That really has no classical source," protested Tai-yu.

"Tomorrow we'll look it up for everyone to see. Let's not waste time now."

"Anyway your second line is no good, padded out with expressions like 'jade osmanthus.'" She continued:

> "How bright the regal gold of the day-lily.[1]
> Wax candles set the sumptuous feast aglow...."

"You got off cheap with 'day-lily,'" observed Hsiang-yun. "That ready-made rhyme saved you a lot of trouble. But there was no need to drag in praise of the sovereign on their behalf. Besides, the line after that is mediocre."

"If you hadn't used jade osmanthus, I wouldn't have had to match it with day-lily, would I? And we have to bring in some opulent images to make it true to life."

Then Hsiang-yun continued:

> "Wild drinking games the splendid park confuse.
> Opposing sides obey the self-same rule...."

---

[1] Day-lily stands for mother or maternal authority, here referring to Imperial Consort Yuan-chun.

"That last line's good but rather hard to match." Tai-yu thought for a little then said:

> "Those guessing riddles hear three different clues.
> The dice is thrown and wins — the dots are red. . . ."

Hsiang-yun said, "I like your 'three clues,' making something colloquial poetic. But you shouldn't have brought in dice again in the next line." She continued:

> "Drums speed the blossom passed from hand to hand.
> The courtyard scintillates with limpid light. . . ."

Tai-yu commented, "You capped my line all right but fell down again on the next. Why keep padding it out with the 'breeze' and the 'moon' all the time?"

"I haven't brought in the moon yet. And anyway a subject like this can do with some purple patches."

"Well, we'll let it go for the time being. We can consider it again tomorrow." Tai-yu went on:

> "A silver splendour merges sky and land.
> For hosts and guests alike the same requital. . . ."

"Why go on referring to others? Why not speak about us?" Hsiang-yun resumed:

> "Verses are written turn and turn about.
> One leaning on the barricade to think. . . ."

"Yes, this is where we come in," Tai-yu remarked, then continued:

> "One 'tapping the door'[1] to make the scene stand out.
> Engrossed as ever, though the wine is drunk. . . ."

"Now we're getting somewhere!" Hsiang-yun went on:

> "They savour the last watches of the night.
> Then comes a gradual end to talk and laughter. . . ."

"Here's where each line gets more difficult," observed Tai-yu, continuing:

---

[1] According to a Tang anecdote, Chia Tao, a famous poet of that dynasty, could not make up his mind whether to use "tap" or "push" in the line — The monk taps the door under the moonlight. Later, "tap and push" came to mean a careful choice of words in composition.

Tai-yu simply nodded, then capped this:

"The goddess flies towards the Palace of Cold Void.[1]
One soars on high to greet Weaving Maid and Cowherd. . . ."[2]

Hsiang-yun looking up at the moon nodded and continued:

"One sails a barque to the heavenly maiden fair.
The orb, for ever changing, wanes and waxes. . . ."

"You're using the same image again," objected Tai-yu, but
went on:

"At each month's start and end but its ghost is there.
Clepsydra's water has wellnigh run dry. . . ."

Before Hsiang-yun could continue, Tai-yu pointed at a dark
shadow in the pool and exclaimed, "Look there! That looks
like a man in the dark. Could it be a ghost?"

"You're imagining things again. I'm not afraid of ghosts.
I'll hit it."

Hsiang-yun bent to pick up a stone and threw it into the
pool. Splash! Ripples radiated out to shatter the moon's reflection, which then rounded out again. When this had happened several times, they heard a cry in the dark shadows and
a white stork took wing straight towards Lotus Fragrance
Pavilion.

"So that's all it was," chuckled Tai-yu. "I didn't think it
could be a stork. It gave me quite a fright."

"How amusing — it's given me an idea." And Hsiang-yun
declaimed:

"The lamp by the window is no longer bright.
A stork's shadow flits across the chilly pool. . . ."

Tai-yu exclaimed in admiration again, stamping her foot.
"This confounded stork has helped her! This line is even

---

[1] Chang Ngo was said to have stealthily eaten her husband's elixir then
flown to the Palace of Cold Void — the moon — becoming the goddess
there.

[2] According to Chinese folklore, Weaving Maid (Vega of Lyra) and
Cowherd (Altair of Aquila) neglected their duty after their marriage so that
the God of Heaven, grandfather of the former, separated them with the
Milky Way, allowing them to meet only once every year on the evening of
the seventh of the seventh month across a bridge made up of magpies.

more original than the one about 'autumn rapids.' How am I going to match it? The only parallel for 'shadow' is 'spirit.' A stork flitting across the chilly pool sounds so natural, apt, vivid and original too! I shall have to give up."

"We can find something if we both think hard; or else leave it till tomorrow."

Tai-yu still looking up at the sky ignored her.

After a while she suddenly laughed and said, "You needn't gloat. I've got it. Listen.

> "The poet's spirit is buried in cold moonlight."

Hsiang-yun clapped her hands.

"Very good indeed! The only possible parallel. Burying the poet's spirit — wonderful." She added with a sigh, "Of course that line's distinctive, but it's rather too melancholy. Now that you're unwell you shouldn't make such strangely sad and depressing lines which sound ill-omened."

Tai-yu chuckled, "If I hadn't, how was I to beat you? But I worked so hard on it, I haven't got the next line yet. . . ."

Just then someone stepped out from behind the rocks on the other side of the balustrade and laughed.

"A fine poem, a fine poem!" she cried. "But it *is* too melancholy. You'd better not go on. If you continue in this way, these two lines won't stand out so well and the poem may seem padded and forced."

Tai-yu and Hsiang-yun, caught unawares, were startled to see Miao-yu.

"Where did *you* spring from?" they asked.

"Knowing you were all enjoying the moon and listening to fine fluting, I came out to admire this clear lake and bright moonlight too and on my way here suddenly heard the two of you poeticizing, which seemed the height of refinement. So I stopped to listen. You've made some good lines but as a whole it's too mournful — or was that fated? That's why I stepped out to stop you.

"The party broke up long ago and the old lady's left the Garden. Most of the others here must be asleep, and your maids will be wondering what's become of you. Aren't you afraid of catching cold? Come back to my place now for a cup of tea. The day will break any minute."

"I'd no idea it was so late," said Tai-yu.

The three girls went to Green Lattice Nunnery. They found the lamp before the shrine still lit and the incense in the censer not yet burnt out, but the few old nuns there had gone to bed leaving only one young maid dozing on a hassock. Miao-yu roused her to brew tea. Then came a sudden knocking on the gate, and the maid opened it to admit Tzu-chuan and Tsui-lu with some old nurses come to look for Tai-yu and Hsiang-yun.

Seeing them drinking tea they said laughingly, "You had us searching the whole Garden — even Madam Hsueh's place — for you. We were looking just now in that small pavilion at the foot of the hill, and luckily the night-watchers were awake. They told us two people had been talking under the awning outside. Someone else joined them and they spoke of going to the nunnery. That's how we've tracked you down."

Miao-yu told the maid to take them to another room to have a rest and some tea. She herself brought out a brush, inkstone, paper and ink and asked the girls to recite their composition, which she wrote down from start to finish.

Finding her in such a good mood Tai-yu said, "I've never seen you before in such high spirits. If not for that I wouldn't presume to ask for your opinion. Is this poem worth polishing? If you think not, we'll burn it; but if it is, will you please make some corrections?"

"I won't venture to make rash comments, but as you've already used twenty-two rhymes I expect you've produced your most striking images and if you go on you may tire yourselves out. I'd like to round it off, only I'm afraid I may spoil it."

Tai-yu had never read any poems by Miao-yu, and as the young nun was so eager she urged her, "Please do! That may make our feeble attempts seem passable."

"We must wind up the poem by reverting to the present situation. If we pass over true feelings and incidents and simply search for striking images and expressions, we'll be losing our identity and departing from the main theme."

"Quite right," they concurred.

Miao-yu picked up her brush and wrote her addition straight off, then showed it to the other two, saying:

"Don't laugh at me! I feel this is the only way to get back to the theme. Then a few sad lines earlier on won't matter."

They took what she had written and read:

> The incense in gold tripods has burnt out,
> And ice-white oil in the jade basin forms;
> Fluting recalls a widow's lamentations
> As a small serving-maid the silk quilt warms.
> On empty curtains a bright phoenix hangs,
> The idle screens gay ducks and drakes enfold;
> Thick dew has made the moss more slippery,
> And heavy frost makes bamboo hard to hold.
> Strolling again beside the winding lake,
> Climbing once more the solitary hill,
> The rugged boulders seem contending ghosts,
> The gnarled trees wolves and tigers crouching still.
> Dawn lights the tortoise pedestal of stone,
> On outer trellis now the thick dew falls.
> A thousand woodland birds begin to stir,
> In vales below a single gibbon calls.
> How can we stray on a familiar road?
> Why ask the way to fountain-heads we know?
> The bells chime in Green Lattice Nunnery,
> The cocks in Paddy-Sweet Cottage start to crow.
> With cause for joy why grieve excessively,
> Or needlessly display anxiety?
> A maiden's feelings none but she can vent —
> To whom can she confide her nicety?
> Speak not of weariness though night is done,
> Over fresh tea let us talk on and on.

She then appended the title "A Poem Written Collectively with Thirty-five Rhymes While Celebrating the Mid-Autumn Festival in Grand View Garden."

Tai-yu and Hsiang-yun heaped praise on this ending.

"We've been ignoring a talent right under our eyes, yet trying to seek what is far away!" they exclaimed. "We have such a superior poetess here, yet every day we pretend to be able to write."

"We can polish it tomorrow," suggested Miao-yu. "It'll soon be light, and after all we must get some rest."

Then the other two took their leave and went off with their maids. Miao-yu saw them out of the gate and watched until they were out of sight before closing the gate and returning to her room.

Meanwhile Tsui-lu had told Hsiang-yun, "They're sitting up waiting for us in Madam Chu's place. Let's go back now."

"You can call in there on the way and tell them to go to bed," replied Hsiang-yun. "If I go, I'll only disturb them. I'd better raise a rumpus in Miss Lin's place instead."

In Bamboo Lodge half the maids were already asleep. Having undressed and washed, Tai-yu and Hsiang-yun went to bed; Tzu-chuan put down the gauze bed-curtain and took away the lamp, closing the door behind her. However, Hsiang-yun could not sleep in a strange bed. As for Tai-yu, being anaemic she often suffered from insomnia too, and having stayed up past her usual hour she now felt wide-awake. So the two of them tossed and turned.

Tai-yu asked, "Why aren't you asleep yet?"

"I can't sleep well in a strange bed — that's my trouble. And I'm no longer sleepy, so I'm just resting. What about you?"

"I've had insomnia a long time now," Tai-yu sighed. "In a whole year I probably have only ten nights of good sleep."

"No wonder you're unwell then!"

If you want to know what followed, read the next chapter.

CHAPTER 77

A Pretty Maid Wrongly Accused
Dies an Untimely Death
Lovely Actresses Sever Worldly Ties
and Join a Nunnery

After the Moon Festival, as Hsi-feng though well enough to leave her bed was not yet fully recovered, Lady Wang continued to summon the doctor to attend her every day as before. The fortifying pills he prescribed required, among other ingredients, two ounces of the best ginseng. Lady Wang sent for some. But after a long search, all her maids could find was a small box of roots no thicker than hairpins, of such poor quality that she made them look again. Presently they came back with a packet of ginseng rootlets.

"When we don't want it there's plenty; when we do there's none," she exclaimed in exasperation. "Time and again I've told you to make sure to put things back in the right place, but you never listen, just dumping them anywhere. You don't know the value of ginseng. When we need it we have to pay through the nose, and what's bought outside may not be efficacious."

Tsai-yun explained, "This seems to be all we have. Last time Lady Hsing came to ask for some, you gave her our whole stock."

"Nonsense. Go and make a more careful search."

This time Tsai-yun brought back a few packets of herbs.

"What these are I don't know," she said. "Please have a look, madam. There isn't anything else."

Lady Wang opened the packets but could not recall what they were, and there was no ginseng among them. She sent to ask Hsi-feng whether she had any. A few rootlets only, was the reply, not of the best quality either, and she needed these for her medicine every day.   Lady Wang then applied to Lady Hsing, who said it was because she had run out that she had asked her for ginseng the other day.

Then Lady Wang had no other recourse but to apply in person to the old lady.   The latter at once ordered Yuan-yang to fetch all she had, and this proved to be quite a large packet of ginseng roots each as thick as a man's finger.   Yuan-yang weighed out two ounces.   Lady Wang gave these to Chou Jui's wife, instructing her to send them to the doctor along with the herbs which they could not identify, and get him to label these.

Before long Mrs. Chou brought them back.

"All the herbs have been properly wrapped up and labelled," she said.   "But as for this ginseng, madam, although it's of the best quality and costs more than thirty taels of silver an ounce now, it's too old.   Ginseng isn't like other medicines.   No matter how fine the roots, after a hundred years they turn to ashes.   These haven't turned to ashes yet, but they have dried up and lost their potency.   So the doctor hopes you'll take this back and get him some fresher, whatever the quality."

Lady Wang lowered her head in thought.

"There's nothing for it then," she concluded at last, "but to go and buy two ounces."   Not interested in examining the other packets she had them put away, then told Chou Jui's wife, "Get the servants outside to buy two ounces of good ginseng.   If the old lady happens to ask, just tell her we used hers — no need to say any more."

Pao-chai who was present put in, "One moment, aunt.   There's no good ginseng to be bought outside.   Whenever they get a whole root they cut it into two or three pieces and graft other rootlets on to these to be sold, with others, as if they were whole roots; so the size is nothing to go by.   Our shop often does business with those ginseng dealers.   I can easily ask mother to get my brother to send an assistant to approach one of them and buy two ounces of good whole roots.   It's worth spending a few taels extra to get the best."

"That's a splendid idea!" exclaimed Lady Wang.   "It's good of you to take the trouble."

Pao-chai came back some time later to report that someone had been sent, and they should have the ginseng that evening — in time to prepare the medicine the next morning. Lady Wang was greatly relieved.

"This is like the proverb: 'The pomade-vendor uses water for her own hair,'" she sighed. "Goodness knows how much we've given away, but when we need any ourselves we have to ask for help right and left!"

"Ginseng's expensive," rejoined Pao-chai with a smile. "After all, it's only medicine, and such things should be given away to help others. We shouldn't hoard them the way vulgar people do."

Lady Wang nodded.

"Quite right."

Pao-chai left then, and as no one else was about Lady Wang summoned Chou Jui's wife to ask the result of their recent search of the Garden. Mrs. Chou had discussed this with Hsi-feng and agreed to keep nothing back. Her description of all that had happened shocked and enraged Lady Wang. But she was in a quandary too, as Ssu-chi was Ying-chun's maid and both of them belonged to Lady Hsing's house. She proposed reporting the matter to her.

Mrs. Chou demurred, "The other day she scolded Wang Shan-pao's wife and boxed her ears for being too officious. So now Mrs. Wang's shamming ill and won't leave home — especially as Ssu-chi's her grand-daughter and she fell into her own trap. All she can do now is pretend it never happened and hope things will quiet down. If we report this to Her Ladyship, she may suspect us of trying to stir up more trouble. Better take Ssu-chi to her with the evidence, and after seeing it they'll at most give her a beating and assign a different maid here. Wouldn't that be simpler?

"If instead of that we just report it, Lady Hsing may make excuses in order to shift the responsibility. 'Why doesn't your mistress deal with it, then?' she may ask. 'Why report it to me?' That would cause delay. And if Ssu-chi took this chance to kill herself, that would make matters worse. The women who've been watching over her the last few days are liable to grow slack. Suppose they do, and something happens — what then?"

After some thought Lady Wang decided, "You're right. We must hurry up and see to this before dealing with those vixens in our own house."

Thereupon Mrs. Chou called together some of her colleagues and led them to Ying-chun's compound.

She told Ying-chun, "The mistress says Ssu-chi has grown up and her mother keeps coming to ask to have her back, so Her Ladyship's giving her back to be married off. She's to leave today. Another good maid will be chosen to wait on you, miss."

She ordered Ssu-chi to pack up her things and leave.

Ying-chun's eyes filled with tears, for she hated to part with the girl. But as other maids had told her in confidence about the events of that evening, fond as she was of Ssu-chi there was nothing she could do where the question of morality was concerned. Ssu-chi had begged her to intervene on her behalf and let her stay on; however, Ying-chun did not have a ready tongue and was too weak to reach a decision.

"How cruel you are, miss!" sobbed Ssu-chi, seeing that her fate was sealed. "You've kept me hoping the last two days, yet won't say a good word for me now."

Chou Jui's wife demanded, "You don't expect the young lady to keep you, do you? Even if she did, how could you face the others in the Garden? Take my advice and pack up quickly to slip away without anyone noticing. That'll look better for us all."

Ying-chun said tearfully, "I don't know what wicked thing you've done, but asking to keep you would spoil my reputation too. Just look at Ju-hua: she was here for some years as well, but she left when she was told to. And you're not the only two. All the girls in the Garden will have to leave, I suppose, when they're grown up. Since we have to part sooner or later, you may as well go now."

"After all, the young lady sees things more clearly," agreed Mrs. Chou. "Others will be sent away later, don't you worry."

Ssu-chi had no alternative but to kowtow to Ying-chun and take her leave of the other maids.

In tears she whispered, "If you hear that I'm in bad trouble, miss, do put in a good word for me for old time's sake."

Ying-chun with tears in her own eyes promised, "I will."

Then Chou Jui's wife and her colleagues led Ssu-chi out, instructing two serving-women to carry away all her things. They had not gone far when Hsiu-chu overtook them and, wiping her tears, handed Ssu-chi a silk package.

"This is from our young lady," she said. "Now that mistress and maid are parting, she wants you to have this keepsake."

This gift reduced Ssu-chi to tears again. She and Hsiu-chu wept together until Mrs. Chou lost patience and insisted that they must be on their way.

"Please be kind and wait a little, aunties," Ssu-chi sobbed. "Let me say goodbye to the others here who've been like sisters to me all these years."

Mrs. Chou and the rest had business of their own to attend to and felt this task an extra imposition, in addition to which they bitterly resented the airs these maids put on. Naturally they had no patience with such talk.

"Get a move on and stop dilly-dallying," they scoffed. "We've more important things to see to. Are you one flesh and blood that you have to say goodbye? They'd only laugh at you. Shilly-shallying won't get you anywhere. So come along."

With that they marched straight on to the back side gate, and Ssu-chi afraid to say more had no choice but to follow.

It so happened that Pao-yu came back just then from outside. When he saw Ssu-chi being led off, followed by women carrying things, he guessed that she had been dismissed for good. He had heard of the commotion that night and the happenings earlier in the day which had led to Ching-wen's relapse; but though carefully questioned, she herself could not tell what had given rise to it all. The day before he had seen Ju-hua leave, and now it was Ssu-chi's turn. In consternation he barred the way and asked where they were going. The stewards' wives knew Pao-yu's quirky ways and did not want him to pester and delay them.

"This is none of your business," said Mrs. Chou with a smile. "Get back to your books."

"Good sisters, please wait a moment," he begged. "I have something to say."

"The mistress ordered us not to lose any time. And what can you have to say? We are just carrying out Her Ladyship's orders. That's our only concern."

Ssu-chi caught hold of his sleeve.

"They can't disobey orders," she sobbed. "But please go and beg Her Ladyship to let me off."

Pao-yu's heart bled for her. Tears started to his eyes.

"I don't know what dreadful thing you've done," he cried. "Ching-wen's fallen ill with anger, and now you're leaving. All of you are leaving! What's to become of me?"

At this Mrs. Chou scolded Ssu-chi, "You're no longer a deputy young mistress now. I'll beat you if you don't do as you're told. Don't think you still have your young mistress to protect you and can go on making any trouble you please. So come along quietly instead of tugging at Master Pao. What way is that to behave?"

They dragged Ssu-chi off before she could say any more; and Pao-yu, afraid they might report this, could only glare after them. When they had gone some distance he shook a finger at them and swore:

"How strange! How is it that once girls marry they get contaminated by men and become so obnoxious — even worse than men!"

The matrons on duty at the gate burst out laughing.

"Whatever is Master Pao talking about?" they cried. "Goodness knows where he gets hold of such nonsense." To tease him they asked, "Do you mean that all girls are good and all married women bad?"

"That's right." Pao-yu nodded. "Of course."

"We're so stupid," they chuckled, "there's something else we'd like you to explain. . . ."

Before they could finish some nurses came along.

"Watch out!" they cried. "Mind you gather together all those on duty and stay at your posts. Her Ladyship's come to the Garden on a tour of inspection. She may very well come here. . . ."

Then one of them ordered someone to fetch the relatives of that girl Ching-wen in Happy Red Court and wait here to take her away.

"Buddha be praised!" they chortled. "At last Heaven has opened its eyes. ·Once this pest is gone we shall have a little peace."

Pao-yu, as soon as he heard that his mother was coming to make a check-up, guessed that it boded trouble for Ching-wen. So he dashed off too soon to hear the nurses' jubilation.

He found Happy Red Court packed with people. His mother, sitting there with a face like thunder, ignored him.

Ching-wen was wasting away, having touched no food for four or five days; but now with dishevelled hair she was dragged from the *kang* and two women carried her off.

"She's only to take the clothes she has on," ordered Lady Wang. "The finer ones are to be kept for better maids."

She then summoned all the maids for her inspection.

This was because Wang Shan-pao's wife had taken advantage of Lady Wang's anger a few days previously to slander Ching-wen, as well as others in the Garden whom she disliked. And Lady Wang had taken all this to heart. As she was busy during the festival she let things slide for a couple of days, but now she had come to inspect all the maids in the Garden, not only to dismiss Ching-wen, but also because it had reached her ears that as Pao-yu was growing up, his maids who were hussies were teaching him bad ways. As this was more serious than Ching-wen's case, Lady Wang meant to examine all the maids from Hsi-jen down to the girls assigned rough work.

"Which is the one," she asked, "born on the same day as Pao-yu?"

Since the girl in question dared not answer, an old nurse pointed her out.

"Hui-hsiang here, also called Ssu-erh."

Lady Wang looked at her closely. She saw that this maid, while by no means half as pretty as Ching-wen, was not unattractive and looked intelligent. She dressed rather conspicuously too. Lady Wang smiled scornfully.

"Another shameless slut! She said in secret that a boy and girl born on the same day, at the same hour, are destined to marry. It was *you* who told him that. Do you think because we live apart I don't know? Though I don't often come to the Garden, I keep a close watch on what you're up to here. Pao-yu is my only son. How can I allow hussies like you to lead him astray?"

At mention of what she had said in confidence to Pao-yu, Ssu-erh blushed and hung her head, weeping.

Having ordered her to be fetched away by her parents and married off, Lady Wang asked:

"Which is the creature called Yali Hsiung-nu?"

The nurses pointed out Fang-kuan.

"Oh, an actress? No wonder she's a vamp. When we offered last time to release you, you wouldn't go. Well then, you should have behaved yourself, instead of making mischief and getting Pao-yu to carry on so wildly."

"I'd never dare!" pleaded Fang-kuan with a smile.

"So you're talking back! Tell me this: The year before last when we went to the Imperial Sepulchre, who coaxed Pao-yu to bring that girl Liu Wu-erh here? Luckily she died a premature death; otherwise, if you'd got her in, you'd have ganged up to make more trouble in the Garden. You even bully your own foster-mother, to say nothing of other people."

She sent for this woman to take Fang-kuan away and find her a husband outside, saying she could keep all her things. She also ordered all the young actresses assigned to the different girls' quarters the previous year to clear out of the Garden, be fetched away and married off. This naturally delighted their foster-mothers, who came to kowtow their thanks.

Then Lady Wang had the whole house searched. Any of Pao-yu's things which looked suspicious were to be confiscated and taken to her quarters.

"This will clean things up," she said, "and save gossip in future." She also warned Hsi-jen and Sheh-yueh, "Be careful now. If you overstep the mark I shan't let you off either."

She had them look up an almanac, which indicated that it would be inauspicious to move that year. So Pao-yu had to stay in the Garden for the time being.

"Next year we'll move him out," declared Lady Wang. "That will stop further trouble."

This said, she led her attendants off to inspect other compounds, not even waiting for tea.

But to revert to Pao-yu: He had expected nothing more than a perfunctory check-up, little dreaming that his mother would come down on them like a thunderbolt, taking them to task for things they had said in secret — which she had got word for word. He knew there was no saving the situation and wished he could die then and there; but as she was in such a rage he dared not make a false move or utter a word. He followed her to Seeping Fragrance Pavilion, where she told him:

"Go back and apply yourself to your books. You may be questioned tomorrow. Your father was fuming just now."

On his way back he wondered who had been telling tales. No outsiders knew what went on in his house, so how could his mother be so well informed? In a quandary, he returned to his room and found Hsi-jen weeping there. Distressed by the loss of his favourite maid, he threw himself on the bed to start weeping too.

Hsi-jen knew that Ching-wen's dismissal was the only thing that really mattered to him. She nudged him.

"It's no use crying. Get up and listen to me. Ching-wen's on the mend, and going home like this she'll be able to rest quietly for a few days. If you really don't want to let her go, wait till your mother has got over her anger then go and beg the old lady to recall her. That shouldn't be difficult. The mistress did this in a fit of anger, just because she was taken in by some spiteful talk."

"I can't imagine what her crime was," he sobbed.

"The mistress just feels that someone with her good looks is bound to be rather flighty, and there can't be any peace with such a beauty here — that's why she dislikes her.   She prefers plain, ungainly girls like us."

"Even so, how could she know our secret jokes?   No outsiders could have passed them on.   That's what's so odd."

"Have you ever shown any discretion?   When you get worked up you don't care who's about.   Many's the time I've tipped you a wink or signalled to you on the sly, but before you took the hint others had already noticed."

"How is it my mother knows all the faults of the other girls but not those of you, Sheh-yueh and Chiu-wen?"

Touched on the raw Hsi-jen lowered her head for a while, at a loss for an answer.

"Yes, that's odd," she agreed presently.   "We three have spoken carelessly in fun too, but the mistress seems to have forgotten that.   Maybe she has other things on her mind and won't send us away until she's dealt with them."

"You're known as a paragon of virtue," he retorted.   "And those two are influenced by you.   So how could you slip up so as to deserve punishment?   Fang-kuan now, being so young and a bit too smart, can't help bullying people and offending them.   In Ssu-erh's case, it's my fault.   It started that day when I quarrelled with you and called her in to wait on me. That made her uppish and led to this trouble today.

"But Ching-wen's like you, she was transferred here as a child from the old lady's quarters.   She may be better-looking, but what does that matter?   And though she's outspoken and has a sharp tongue she's never done *you* any harm.   I suppose it's her good looks that were her undoing."   He burst into tears again.

Inferring from this that Pao-yu suspected *her* of telling tales, Hsi-jen did not like to pursue the subject further.

"Only Heaven knows the truth," she sighed. "We can't find out now who told, so it's no use crying. Take it easy till the old lady's in a good mood, then you can tell her about it and ask to have Ching-wen back."

"Don't hold out false hopes," he snorted. "If I wait till my mother calms down it'll be too late, because Ching-wen's illness won't wait. She's always lived in comfort, never had to put up with a single day's bad treatment. Even I, who know her so well, often offended her. Dismissing her *now*," he went on more bitterly, "seriously ill as she is and with all that resentment bottled up inside her, is like throwing a delicate orchid just coming into bloom into a pigsty. Besides, she has no parents, only an elder cousin who's a drunkard. How can she stand it there? How can you talk of waiting for a few days? Who knows whether I'll ever see her again or not?"

Hsi-jen laughed.

"You're like 'the magistrate who goes in for arson but won't allow common people to light a lamp.' If we let slip some tactless remark you say it's unlucky, but it's all right for *you* to talk about her dying. She may be extra delicate, still it shouldn't come to that."

"I didn't speak at random. There was an omen this spring."

"What omen?"

"That begonia at the foot of the steps was thriving, but then for no reason half its branches withered. I knew that was a portent, and now see what's happened to her."

Hsi-jen laughed again.

"I shouldn't say this, but I must. You're a regular old woman. How can an educated young gentleman talk that way? What have plants to do with human fate? If you're not an old woman you really are a fool."

"You don't understand," Pao-yu sighed. "Not only plants and trees but all things in the world are just as sentient and rational as human beings. When in rapport with someone, they're specially sensitive. Some outstanding examples are the juniper tree before Confucius' temple and the yarrow before his tomb, as well as the cypress before Chuko Liang's[1] temple and the pine before Yueh Fei's[2] tomb. All these stately plants embodying these men's fine spirit have endured for centuries, withering when the world is in confusion and flourishing again when it is well governed. They have withered and revived again several times in all these thousands of years. Aren't they sure signs?

"Minor examples are the peony before Lady Yang's Scented Pavilion, the tree of longing before her Upright Tower, or the grass on Wang Chao-chun's tomb. They all had divine sensibility, didn't they? It's because she's going to die that half the begonia withered."

Hearing this senseless talk, Hsi-jen did not know whether to laugh or cry.

"You're getting more and more outrageous," she protested. "How can you rack your brains to compare Ching-wen, a mere nobody, with those great figures? Besides, however good she may be, she's lower in status than I am. You should compare *me*, not her, with the begonia. I suppose this means I'm going to die very soon."

Pao-yu clapped a hand over her mouth.

"What a thing to say! Before one death's taken place you're talking of another. All right, let's drop the subject. I've already lost three of you, I don't want to lose one more."

Secretly pleased, Hsi-jen told herself: If they hadn't gone, how far would you have let yourself go?

"From now on," he continued, "let's say no more about it, just consider the three of them as dead and gone. Others have died before without it mattering much to me anyway. It's all the same. But let's talk about practical matters. We must secretly send her things to her without letting the mistresses

---

[1] Chuko Liang (181-234), chief minister of the Kingdom of Shu of the Three Kingdoms Period. Intelligent and utterly loyal, he was considered an exemplary minister.

[2] Yueh Fei (1103-42), a Southern Sung general, was falsely accused and murdered in prison by order of the traitorous prime minister Chin Kuei (1090-1155).

know, as well as a few strings of cash from our savings to help cure her illness. We owe her that for old times' sake."

"How heartless and stingy you think us!" Hsi-jen exclaimed. "We don't need a reminder from *you*. I've already sorted out all her clothes and things and put them aside. In the daytime there are too many busybodies around, all eager to make trouble; but as soon as it's dark we'll quietly get Mrs. Sung to take them over. I've saved a few strings of cash too, which I'm giving her."

Pao-yu expressed grateful thanks.

"I'm already known as 'a paragon of virtue,' " she said sarcastically. "Surely this is a cheap way to add to my reputation."

At once he apologized and tried to mollify her.

That evening, in strict confidence, they sent Mrs. Sung off on this errand. And after settling his maids down, Pao-yu slipped out of the back gate alone and begged an old woman to take him to see Ching-wen. At first she most resolutely refused, saying that if it was found out and reported to the mistress she'd lose her job; but after he pleaded hard and promised her a tip she finally took him.

Now Ching-wen had been sold into bondage to Lai Ta's family at the age of ten, before she had grown her hair. Old Mrs. Lai used to take her to the Jung Mansion, and the Lady Dowager took a fancy to her because of her intelligence and good looks, whereupon Mrs. Lai presented her to the old lady, and that was how she had later become Pao-yu's maid. Having come here as a child, she had no recollection of her old home and parents. Her only relative was a cousin on her father's side, a good cook but without any steady employment. She had asked Mrs. Lai to take him into service in the Jung Mansion. By that time Ching-wen was waiting on the old lady and had turned out a smart, sharp-tongued girl with a hot temper; but touched by her remembering her kinsman, Mrs. Lai bought him too and gave him one of the bondmaids as his wife.

However, once living in comfort, the fellow forgot his hard life as a vagrant and took to drinking heavily, paying no attention to his wife who happened to be a good-looking, amorous woman. When he drank so recklessly, ignoring her, she felt as disconsolate as a piece of jade tossed among brambles or a beauty immured in solitude. Then, finding him so easygoing that he was never jealous, she started dispensing her favours to all the stout fellows and men of parts in the mansion until soon she had tried out half the men, masters as well as servants. If, Reader, you wish to know her name, she was that "Miss Teng," the wife of "To the Muddy Worm" with whom Chia Lien had once had an affair.

As these were Ching-wen's only relatives, she had to stay with them. Her cousin was away at this time and Miss Teng had gone out after supper to call on friends, leaving Ching-wen lying alone in the outer room. Pao-yu told the old woman to keep watch in the courtyard, then lifted the matting portière and went in. There was Ching-wen on an earthen *kang* covered with a coarse mat, although at least she had her own pillow and bedding. Not knowing what to do, he approached her with tears in his eyes and gently took her hand, softly calling her name.

Ching-wen had caught a chill and this, combined with her relatives' reproaches, had made her illness worse. After coughing for a whole day she had just dozed off, but hearing her name called she opened her eyes with an effort. When she saw it was Pao-yu, she was so overwhelmed with pleased surprise mingled with grief and anguish that she promptly burst out sobbing. Grasping his hand with all her might, she managed at last to gasp between fits of coughing:

"I never thought to see you again. . . ."

Pao-yu too could only weep.

"Merciful Buddha!" cried Ching-wen. "You've come just in time. Pour me half a cup of tea. I've been parched all this time, but when I call no one comes."

"Where is the tea?" he asked, wiping his eyes.

"On the stove."

Pao-yu saw a black earthenware pot which he would never have recognized as a teapot. He took from the table a bowl, so large and coarse that it bore no resemblance to a teacup either and when he had it in his hand it smelled of rancid oil. He washed and rinsed it several times, after which he picked up the pot and poured out half a bowl. The dark red brew was unlike any tea he had seen.

Ching-wen leaning on her pillow urged, "Pass it over, quick, for me to take a sip. You can't expect them here to have the kind of tea we're used to."

Pao-yu first took a sip himself. The brew had no fragrance, only a bitter taste slightly reminiscent of tea. But when he passed her the bowl she gulped it all down as if it were sweet dew. He reflected: In the past the best tea couldn't satisfy her, yet now she likes this! It shows the truth of the old saying: "The well-fed turn away from cooked meats, while the famished enjoy dregs of wine and husks of rice." And again: "One glutted with rice prefers thin gruel."

Shedding tears he asked, "Have you anything to tell me while nobody's about?"

"What is there to say?" she sobbed. "I'm just dragging on from day to day, from hour to hour. I shall be gone in a few days at most, I know. But I can't die content. I may have been born with more than my share of good looks, but there's been no secret understanding between us and I've never tried to lead you astray, yet they insist I'm a vamp. That I *do* resent! Now I've got this bad name for nothing and I'm dying. If only I'd known how things would. end I'd have acted differently; but I was fool enough to think we'd always be together. How could I guess there'd be this sudden scandal and I'd have nowhere to plead my innocence?" She burst into tears again.

Pao-yu took her hand. On her wrists, thin as sticks, were four silver bracelets.

"Better take these off," he advised. "You can wear them when you're better." As he drew off the bracelets and put them under her pillow he remarked, "You took such care to grow those finger-nails two inches long; now your illness is going to spoil them."

Ching-wen dried her tears and reached for a pair of scissors to cut off the tapering nails of the last two fingers of her left

hand.   Then, under the quilt, she took off her worn red silk
bodice and gave this to him together with the nails.

"Take these keepsakes to remind you of me," she said. "And
now take off your inner jacket and help me put it on, so that
lying in my coffin I shall feel as if I were still in Happy Red
Court.   I shouldn't do such a thing, of course, but as I've already
got a bad name — why not?"

At once Pao-yu took off his inner jacket, put on her bodice,
and concealed the finger-nails.

"If they see these when you go back and question you," she
sobbed, "there's no need to lie.   Just tell them these are mine.
Since I've been falsely accused, why shouldn't I at least have
this satisfaction?"

While she was still speaking her cousin's wife lifted the portière and burst in, smirking.

"Fine, I heard all you two said!" She turned to Pao-yu.
"What is a young master doing in a servant's room?   Have you
come to seduce me, thinking me young and pretty?"

"Hush, good sister! Not so loud!" he begged.   "She's
worked for me all these years, so I slipped in to see her."

Miss Teng hustled him into the inner room.

"You don't want me to shout," she chortled.   "All right —
if you'll be nice to me."

She plumped down on the edge of the *kang* hugging Pao-yu
to her.   He had never seen such behaviour as this before.   His
heart beating fast he blushed all over his face.

"Good sister, don't tease me!" he pleaded.

Miss Teng laughed tipsily.

"Bah!   I've always heard that you were a lady's man.   What
makes you so bashful today?"

Flushing crimson he implored, "Do let go of me, then we
can talk properly.   If the old woman outside hears — how
awful!"

"I came back long ago and sent her to wait for you at the
Garden gate," she laughed.   "I've been waiting and waiting for
a chance like this, but now that you're here I've discovered
you're a fraud.   For all you're so handsome, you're nothing but

a fire-cracker without powder — good only for show. Why, you're much shyer than I am. This shows it's no use listening to gossip. For instance, when my cousin came home I was sure you two must have been up to some monkey business; that's why I came back to listen outside the window. If there'd been some goings-on between you, as you were alone you would have talked about it; but to my surprise there'd been nothing of the sort. So it's clear lots of people get wrongly accused in this world. I'm sorry I misjudged you. Well, as this is the case, you've nothing to worry about. You can come whenever you like and I won't pester you."

Feeling very relieved he got up and straightened his clothes.

"Good sister, please take good care of her for a couple of days," he urged her. "I must be off now."

He went out then to say goodbye to Ching-wen. Both were reluctant to part, but part they must; and knowing how hard he found it, she covered her face with the quilt and ignored him until he left.

Pao-yu had wanted to call on Fang-kuan and Ssu-erh too, but as it was dark and he had been out for some time he was afraid he would be missed and a search might be made for him, leading to more trouble. He had better return to the Garden and go out again the next day. When he reached the back gate, pages were bringing out bedding while nurses inside were checking up on people. A minute later and he would have been locked out. Luckily he was able to slip in unobserved.

Home again, he simply told Hsi-jen that he had been with Aunt Hsueh and left it at that. Presently, when preparing his bed, she had to ask him how they should sleep that night.

"Any way you like," was his answer.

Now for the last couple of years, since Hsi-jen got into the good books of Lady Wang, she had begun to stand on her dignity and broken off her intimacy with Pao-yu even in private or at night, behaving more distantly than when they were young. And though she had no major business to attend to, all the needlework of the household, as well as the accounts and seeing to the clothing and shoes of Pao-yu and the young maids kept her fully occupied. Moreover, though she no longer suffered from fluxions, when she was tired or caught cold she sometimes coughed blood; and for this reason she had avoided sleeping in the same room as Pao-yu. However, he often woke up in the night and being very timid would always call for someone; so Ching-wen, who was a light sleeper and soft-footed, had been given the task of pouring him tea and attending him at night and had slept on a bed near his.

Now Hsi-jen had to ask who should sleep on the bed near his, as she considered this work at night more important than any daytime tasks. Told to do as she thought fit, she could only move in her own bedding to sleep in Pao-yu's room as in the old days.

That evening he was lost in thought. Finally she persuaded him to go to bed, but after she and the others had turned in she heard him groaning and tossing about in bed till after midnight, when finally he calmed down and started snoring. In relief she dozed off herself, but in less time than it takes to drink half a cup of tea he called for Ching-wen. Hsi-jen woke with a start and asked what he wanted. Some tea, he said. She got up, rinsed her hands in a basin of water, then poured him half a cup from the warm pot.

After sipping some tea Pao-yu said with an apologetic smile, "I'm so used to calling her, I forgot it was you."

"You were used to calling me in your sleep when she first took over. It took you months to get out of the habit. So I knew that though Ching-wen's gone her name would still be on your lips."

They lay down again. Pao-yu tossed and turned for another hour or two, not falling asleep till the fifth watch. Then he saw Ching-wen come in, looking her usual self. Having entered the room, she told him with a smile:

"Take good care of yourselves. I must leave you now." With that she turned and vanished.

Pao-yu called her, waking Hsi-jen again. She thought it was another slip of the tongue, but he sobbed:

"Ching-wen is dead!"

"What a thing to say! How could you know? Don't let other people hear you talk such nonsense."

Pao-yu insisted that he was right and could hardly wait till dawn to send to find out. Just at daybreak, however, a young maid sent by Lady Wang came to the Garden and called out asking to have the front side gate opened, as the mistress had instructions to be passed on.

"Pao-yu must wash and dress quickly!" she cried. "The master has been invited out to enjoy the autumn scenery and the osmanthus in bloom. He is pleased with Pao-yu because he wrote a good poem the other day, so he means to take him along. That's what Her Ladyship said, so don't get a word wrong. Hurry up and tell him to come as fast as he can. The master's waiting in the principal apartments for the boys to come and have breakfast. Master Huan has already arrived, and someone's been sent to fetch Master Lan as he's to go as well."

As she delivered this message, the serving-woman inside assented sentence by sentence while buttoning her clothes, then opened the gate. Several other maids, hastily dressing themselves, had run to pass on these instructions.

When Hsi-jen heard knocking at the gate, she got up at once and sent to ask what was so pressing. This summons relayed to her, she quickly called for hot water and urged Pao-yu to get up and wash while she fetched his clothes. Since he was going out with his father, instead of choosing his most splendid new clothes she selected a less conspicuous outfit.

Pao-yu had no choice but to go as fast as he could. He found his father drinking tea, obviously in a good humour. Having paid his morning respects he was greeted by Chia Huan and Chia Lan in turn, and then Chia Cheng ordered him to sit down to breakfast.

"Pao-yu doesn't study as hard as you," he told the other boys. "But when it comes to writing inscriptions or capping verses you haven't got his flair. Today our hosts are bound to make you write poems, and Pao-yu must help you both out."

Lady Wang, who had never heard such praise from him, was both surprised and pleased. After father and sons had left, she was thinking of going over to see the old lady when the foster-mothers of Fang-kuan, Ou-kuan and Jui-kuan were announced.

"Ever since Your Ladyship kindly allowed Fang-kuan to come home she's behaved like a crazy creature," one of them reported. "She'll neither eat nor drink. And now the three of them — she's got Ou-kuan and Jui-kuan to do the same — insist on cutting their hair and becoming nuns. They threaten to kill themselves if we won't let them. At first I thought the child was just unused to the way we live outside, and would get over this whim in a couple of days. But they're carrying on worse and worse. We've scolded and beaten them, but it's no use. We're really at our wits' end: that's why we've come to beg Your Ladyship's help. We'll either have to allow them to become nuns or give them a good talking to and let other families take them. We haven't the fortune to keep them!"

"Nonsense!" exclaimed Lady Wang. "How can you let them have their own way? How can anyone enter a nunnery for fun? Give them a thrashing and they'll show more sense."

Now as this was just after the mid-autumn sacrifices, nuns from various nunneries had come to present sacrificial offerings, and Lady Wang had kept Abbess Chih-tung of Water Moon Convent and Abbess Yuan-hsin of Ksitigarbha Nunnery to stay for a couple of days. When they heard this news, they thought it a chance to get two girls for nothing to work for them.

"After all," they told Lady Wang, "it's because your house is a virtuous one and you yourself do so many good deeds that these young girls have been influenced in this way. Though the house of Buddha isn't easy to enter, we should remember that the law of Buddha extends to all alike. Our Buddha's wish is to save all living creatures, yes, even chickens and dogs; but, alas, those who are deluded are hard to awaken. Anyone who has the root of goodness in her and can attain enlightenment can transcend transmigration. Why, even a number of tigers, wolves, snakes and insects have now entered Nirvana.

"These three orphan girls far from their native places lived here amid wealth and splendour; but now they remember their early poverty which forced them to take to a despised profession, and they have no idea what will become of them in future. So turning away from this sea of sufferings they have decided to renounce the world and cultivate virtue, in the hope of doing better in their next life. This is a good and noble resolve. Please don't stand in their way, madam."

Now Lady Wang was fond of doing good deeds. She had not allowed Fang-kuan and the other girls to have their way because, to her mind, they were only children who had made this proposal in a fit of anger; they might prove unable to stand austerity, leading to more trouble in future. The speech of these two swindlers struck her as reasonable. Besides, she was quite distracted these days with a host of family problems, in addition to which Lady Hsing had sent word that she intended to fetch Ying-chun back tomorrow for a couple of days so that her prospective in-laws could inspect her, and official go-betweens had also come to propose a match for Tan-chun. Unable to give much thought to these minor matters, she consented willingly.

"Well then, since that's how you feel, why not take these girls away as your acolytes?"

"Merciful Buddha!" the abbesses exclaimed. "How good of you, madam! This is a most virtuous deed." They forthwith bowed their thanks.

"They'd better be questioned first," said Lady Wang. "If they are really in earnest they can come and, in my presence, pay their respects to you now as their Mothers Superior."

The three foster-mothers fetched the three girls, and Lady Wang sounded them out carefully. As their minds were made up, they kowtowed to the two abbesses and then to Lady Wang by way of farewell. Seeing that they were determined and not to be dissuaded, she could not help feeling a pang of pity and sent for gifts for them as well as for the abbesses. Then Fang-kuan went off with Chih-tung of Water Moon Convent, and the other two erstwhile actresses with Yuan-hsin of Ksitigarbha Nunnery.

To know what followed, read on.

CHAPTER 78

An Old Scholar at Leisure
Has Eulogies Composed
His Unorthodox, Witless Son
Laments the Hibiscus

After the two abbesses had taken the young actresses away, Lady Wang called to pay her morning respects to the Lady Dowager. And finding her in a good mood she reported:

"Pao-yu's maid Ching-wen has grown up now, and this last year or so she's kept falling ill. I've noticed too that she's saucier and lazier than the others. Recently she was ill again for over ten days, and the doctor diagnosed it as consumption; so then and there I dismissed her with instructions not to come back when she's better, giving her to her family to marry off. I also took it on myself to send away those few young actresses. Because, on account of their theatrical training, they talked in a wild way we don't want our girls to hear; and as they performed for us here for a time, it wouldn't have been right to ask for money for them. In any case, we have too many maids. If we need more in future, we can always pick a few others."

"Quite right and proper." The old lady nodded approval. "Exactly what I had in mind myself. But I always thought Ching-wen a very nice girl. How could she have turned out so badly? She struck me as smarter than the other maids, with a ready tongue too and better at needlework — the best choice as a concubine for Pao-yu in future. Who could have dreamed that she'd change for the worse?"

"You made the right choice, madam, only she wasn't fated to have such good fortune. That's why she contracted this illness. As the saying goes, 'A girl changes eighteen times before reaching womanhood.' And the smarter the girl, the more out of hand she'll get.   You must have seen many such cases.

"Three years ago when I thought about this question too, she was my first choice.   No one's a match for her in other ways, it's just that she's a bit flighty.   For steadiness and propriety, Hsi-jen comes first.   Though what's wanted in a wife is virtue, they say, and in a concubine beauty, still it's better to choose a girl with a sweet disposition and steady character.   Hsi-jen may not be up to Ching-wen in looks, yet she's the best for Pao-yu's chamber.   Trustworthy, too, and honest.   These last few years she's never once led Pao-yu into mischief.   In fact, whenever he does wrong she tries her best to dissuade him — after watching her for two years I know this for certain.   That's why I secretly stopped her pay as a maid and gave her two taels a month from my own allowance, so that she'd understand and look after him even better.   I didn't make it public for two reasons: partly because Pao-yu's young, and if his father knew of this he might think it bad for his studies; partly because if she was known to be his concubine she wouldn't dare gainsay him, and Pao-yu would carry on more wildly than ever.   This is why I didn't report it to you earlier."

The Lady Dowager smiled.

"If that's the case, so much the better.   Hsi-jen's always been so quiet I felt she was rather stupid; but as you know her so well you can't be wrong.   I'm all in favour, too, of not letting Pao-yu know.   None of us must mention this, just let it be understood.   I'm well aware that in future Pao-yu won't listen to his wife's or concubines' advice.   I can't understand him either.   I've never known another child like him.   One expects a boy to be mischievous, but this extraordinary liking he has for maids has been preying on my mind.   I'm for ever finding him fooling about with them.   At first I thought this intimacy was because he'd grown big enough to know about sex; but watching him more closely I realized that wasn't the reason, which makes it even odder.   Could it be that he was really meant to be born a girl?. . ."

This set everybody laughing.   Then Lady Wang went on to describe how Chia Cheng had praised Pao-yu today and taken the boys out with him to pay a call. This pleased the old lady still more.

Soon Ying-chun, dressed to go out, came to take her leave. Then Hsi-feng arrived to pay her respects and wait upon the old lady as she had breakfast. They chatted till it was time for her siesta, when Lady Wang called Hsi-feng over to ask her whether she had prepared her pills.

"Not yet," was the answer. "I'm still taking herb-cordials. But don't you worry, madam. I'm much better."

Lady Wang believed her, having seen that she looked more energetic. She told her of Ching-wen's dismissal.

"How come you didn't know that Pao-chai — of her own accord — had moved home to sleep with her mother?" she continued. "A couple of days ago I made a search of all the other apartments in the Garden. And, just imagine, I found young Lan's new nurse a regular vamp! I didn't like the look of her at all. So I urged your sister-in-law to send her packing, as in any case he's big enough now not to need so many nurses. And I asked her, 'Surely you knew about Pao-chai's leaving?'

"She said yes, but Pao-chai had told her she'd be coming back in a few days, once Aunt Hsueh was better. Actually, there's nothing much the matter with Aunt Hsueh apart from that chronic cough and backache of hers which she gets every year. So Pao-chai must have moved out for some other reason. Do you think somebody offended her? She's a sensitive child, and it would be too bad if we offended her after living together for so long."

"Why should anyone offend them for no reason?" asked Hsi-feng cheerfully. "They spend all their time in the Garden, so if there *has* been any misunderstanding it must be among themselves."

"Can Pao-yu have been tactless?" wondered his mother. "He's such a simpleton, so lacking in scruples, that in a fit of excitement he may have spoken wildly."

"Don't worry so much about him, madam. When Pao-yu goes out on business, he may talk and behave like a simpleton. But when he's at home with all these girl cousins of his, or even with the maids, he's most considerate to them, afraid of giving offence. So no one could possibly be annoyed by *him*.

"I think Pao-chai must have left because of the search the other night, naturally concluding that we didn't trust certain people in the Garden. As she's a relative, we could hardly search *her* servants. But for rear that her household might be suspected, being sensitive as she is she took herself off so as to avoid suspicion. And quite right, too."

Convinced by this estimate, Lady Wang lowered her head and after some reflection told a maid to invite Pao-chai over. She explained about the recent search to set her niece's mind at rest, then urged her to move back into the Garden.

"I'd been meaning to move out for some time," said Pao-chai with a smile. "Only I didn't find the occasion to ask you, as you have so much important business to attend to. But that day, as it happened, my mother was unwell again and our only two reliable maids were ill; so I took the chance to move out. Now that you know about it, I can explain the reason and ask leave today to move my things out too."

Neither Lady Wang nor Hsi-feng would hear of this.

"Don't be so stubborn!" they cried laughingly. "What you should really do is move in again, not let something so inconsequential come between us."

"I don't understand what you mean," Pao-chai rejoined. "I didn't leave because of anything that happened here, but because my mother'd been feeling less energetic and at night she had nobody to rely on but me. Besides, my brother will soon be getting married. There's a lot of needlework to do, his rooms still have to be furnished, and I have to help her with all the preparations. *You* know, aunt and Cousin Hsi-feng, how it is in our family and that I'm not fibbing.

"For another thing, after I moved into the Garden that small side gate in the southeast corner was kept open for me to go through; but other people wanting to take a short cut could use it too, and there was nobody to make a check there. If trouble had come of it, it would have been awkward for both families.

"Besides, my moving into the Garden to sleep was of no great consequence. A few years ago we were all young and I had no business at home, so I was better off here than outside, able to do needlework with the other girls and amuse myself with them — that was better than sitting idly at home by myself. Now we've all grown up and have our different tasks. Moreover, these years you've had various troubles, aunt. And the Garden is too big for you to keep an eye on everything. The fewer the people there, the less you need worry. So now I've not only made up my mind to move out, but I'll venture to advise you, aunt, to cut down as far as possible, for that won't make us lose face. It seems to me that much of this expenditure in the Garden could be avoided. After all, times have changed. You know our family well, aunt — we weren't as badly off as this in the old days!"

Hsi-feng after hearing this said to Lady Wang, "She's right. We needn't insist."

Lady Wang nodded.

"I've no answer to that. Just do as you think fit."

At this point Pao-yu came back with the other boys.

"My father is still feasting," he said. "As it will soon be growing dark, he told us to come home first."

Lady Wang hastily asked, "Did you make any gaffes today?"

"No," he answered with a smile. "Not only that, but I've brought back a lot of loot."

Then some old serving-women fetched in from the pages at the inner gate the presents the young masters had received. Lady Wang saw these were three fans, three fan-pendants, six boxes of writing brushes and ink-tablets, three strings of scented beads and three jade rings, which Pao-yu explained had been given them by Academician Mei, Vice-Minister Yang and Secretary Li — one set apiece. He then pulled a talisman, a small sandalwood Buddha, from his pocket.

"This was a gift just for me from the Duke of Chingkuo."

Lady Wang asked what guests had been there and what poems they had written, then took the three boys to pay their duty visit to the old lady, ordering the servant carrying Pao-yu's presents to accompany them.

The Lady Dowager, delighted, inevitably cross-examined them too. Pao-yu was so worried about Ching-wen, however, that after answering her questions he told her that his bones ached after riding.

"Go back quickly then," urged the old lady. "Once you've changed your clothes and rested, you'll feel better. But mind you don't lie down."

Thereupon Pao-yu hurried back to the Garden.

Sheh-yueh and Chiu-wen had been waiting in the old lady's place with two younger maids. When Pao-yu left they followed him, Chiu-wen carrying his presents.

"How hot it is!" he kept complaining.

While walking he took off his hat, belt and outer garment, which Sheh-yueh carried for him. Pao-yu was now wearing only a green satin jacket above a pair of blood-red trousers, and Chiu-wen noticing that these were trousers which Ching-wen had made for him heaved a sigh.

"Better keep those trousers as a memento," she said. "Really, though she's gone her handiwork is still here."

"Yes, that's Ching-wen's work," said Sheh-yueh, then quoted the saying: "'The handiwork remains though the maker's gone.'"

Chiu-wen nudged her, saying more cheerfully:

"Those trousers, with that green jacket and the blue boots make a vivid foil for black hair and a snow-white complexion."

Pao-yu in front pretended not to have heard them and walked on a few paces, then stopped.

"Is it all right if I take a stroll?" he asked.

"What are you afraid of in broad daylight?" Sheh-yueh answered. "You can't get lost." She told the two young maids to accompany him. "We'll join you after we've put these things away."

"Won't you wait for me here, good sister?"

"We'll be back soon," Sheh-yueh promised. "With both our hands full we're like a regular retinue, one carrying the 'four treasures of the study,' one a hat, belt and garments — it looks so ridiculous!"

As this was what Pao-yu had hoped for, he let them go. He then led the two young maids behind a rockery. Without further ado he asked:

"After I left, did Sister Hsi-jen send anyone to see Sister Ching-wen?"

"She sent Mrs. Sung," one girl told him.

"What did she say after she came back?"

"She said Sister Ching-wen was crying out all night. First thing this morning, she closed her eyes and stopped calling because she'd fainted away and couldn't get a sound out, just gasping for breath."

"Whom was she calling all night?" he hastily asked.

"Her mother."

Pao-yu wiped his tears.

"Who else?"

"Nobody else."

"You silly thing, you can't have heard her clearly."

The other girl by him was smarter. When she heard this she stepped forward.

"She really is silly," she told Pao-yu. "*I* not only heard her clearly, I went over on the sly to see Ching-wen."

"Why did you do that?"

"Because I remembered how good Sister Ching-wen always was to us — not like other people. Though she'd been unfairly treated and left, if we couldn't find any other way to help her, we should at least go to see her to repay her former kindness. Even if we were found out and reported to the mistress, and if we got beaten for it, we'd gladly put up with that. That's why, at the risk of a beating, I slipped over to see her. She always had intelligence, and was clear in her head right up to the time of her death. She only closed her eyes because she didn't want to talk to those vulgar people. When she saw me, she opened her eyes and took my hand.

" 'Where is Pao-yu?' she asked me.

"I told her where you'd gone.

"She sighed, 'I shan't be able to see him again then.'

" 'Why not wait till he's back?' I asked. 'Then he can see you once more, which is what you both want.'

"She smiled and told me, 'You don't understand. I'm not going to die. There's a vacancy now in heaven for a flower goddess, and the Jade Emperor has appointed me. I have orders to go to my new post at half past two; but Pao-yu won't be back till a quarter to three — too late by a quarter of an hour to see me. When people are fated to die and the King of Hell summons them, he sends small devils to fetch their spirits away. If someone wants to delay a bit, he can burn paper money and serve some porridge; then while the devils are scrambling for the money, the one who's dying can have a short reprieve. But now I mustn't delay, as I've been *invited* by the gods in heaven.'

"At the time, I didn't quite believe her. But when I got back and looked carefully at the clock, it was true that she died at half past two, and at a quarter to three *your* return was announced. So she'd got both the times right."

"You don't understand because you can't read," Pao-yu answered. "This is absolutely true. Every single flower has its goddess, and there's also a goddess in charge of all the flowers. I wonder whether she's gone to take charge of them all, or of one particular flower."

The maid had no ready answer. As it happened to be the eighth month and hibiscus was blooming beside the pond in the Garden, she took her cue from that.

"I asked her to let us know what flower she'd be in charge of," she said, "so that in future we can sacrifice to her. She told me, 'Heaven's secrets can't be disclosed; but as you are so pious I'll tell you. You can let Pao-yu know, but no one else — if you do, you'll be struck dead by a thunderbolt!' Then she told me she was in charge of the hibiscus."

Pao-yu, far from being surprised, felt his grief turn into pleasure. He pointed at the hibiscus.

"This flower needs a girl like her to care for it," he observed, "I always thought that someone with her talents was bound to be given a responsible task."

But although Ching-wen had departed this sea of woe, the thought that they could never meet again inevitably filled him with grief and longing.

"Though I didn't see her at the end," he reflected, "I must go and sacrifice now at her shrine, for the sake of our friendship these last half dozen years."

Accordingly, he went straight back to change his clothes and, on the pretext of going to see Tai-yu, went out of the Garden alone to the house where he had last visited Ching-wen, assuming that her coffin would be there.

However, as soon as Ching-wen died, her cousin and his wife had reported this in the hope of getting some money at once for the funeral. Lady Wang on hearing this news gave them ten taels of silver and ordered them to have the body taken out of town immediately to be cremated, for as Ching-wen had died of consumption it must not be kept in the vicinity. The cousin and his wife took the money, then lost no time in having her body coffined and taken to the crematorium outside the city. Her clothes and trinkets, which were worth some three or four hundred taels, they kept for future use. Then they locked up the place and went to attend her funeral.

Pao-yu, finding no one there, stood outside the door for a while; then, as there was nothing he could do, he had to return to the Garden. Back in his own rooms, he felt so depressed that he decided to call on Tai-yu. However, he found she was out. When he asked where she had gone, her maids told him:

"To Miss Pao-chai's place."

Pao-yu went then to Alpinia Park, only to find it quiet and deserted — even the furnishings had been removed. He was very much taken aback. He inquired of an old serving-woman who chanced to come along just then what had happened.

"Miss Pao-chai has gone," she informed him. "We've been told to look after the place until everything's been moved away. After we've cleared these things away, the compound will be locked up. You'd better go now, young master, so that we can sweep up the dust. You won't have to make any more trips here, sir, in future."

For a while Pao-yu stood there stupefied. He saw that the fragrant herbs and creepers in the courtyard were as green and luxuriant as ever, but they suddenly seemed to have grown disconsolate too, and the sight added to his grief. He left in silence. It had struck him that for some time no one had passed the tree-lined dyke outside the gate, whereas in the old days a whole succession of maids from different quarters had kept coming here all of their own accord. Looking down, and seeing that the stream at the foot of the dyke was still flowing smoothly past, he marvelled that nature could be so lacking in feeling. After grieving awhile he reflected:

"Five girls have gone, among them Ssu-chi, Ju-hua and Fang-kuan; and now Ching-wen is dead, and Pao-chai's household has left. Though Ying-chun hasn't gone yet, she's been away these days and match-makers keep coming to arrange her marriage. It probably won't be long before all the girls in the Garden disperse. Still, it's no use moping over this. I may as well call on Tai-yu and keep her company for a while before coming back to pass the time with Hsi-jen. Most likely only the two or three of us will remain together till our dying day."

Thinking in this way, he went to Bamboo Lodge; but Tai-yu was still out. He thought next of attending Ching-wen's funeral, then decided against this, guessing that it would only make him feel sadder. So he returned dejectedly to his rooms.

He was just wondering what to do when a maid from Lady Wang came to find him.

"The master's back and wants you," she announced. "He has another good subject for poetry. Go quickly. Hurry!"

Pao-yu had to accompany her to Lady Wang's place, only to find that his father had left already. His mother ordered the servants to take him to his father's study.

Chia Cheng was discoursing with his secretaries on the beauty of the autumn scenery.

"Before the last party broke up," he remarked, "we spoke of an incident which was surely the most enchanting tale of all times. 'Gallantry and sublimity, loyalty and magnanimity' —

not one quality was missing. So it should make a fine subject for an elegiac poem. Suppose we write one?"

His protégés promptly asked what wonderful story this was.

"There was a certain Prince Heng who governed Ching-chow,"[1] Chia Cheng told them. "What he loved most was feminine beauty, and when at leisure he liked to practise the military arts. So he selected a number of beautiful girls and made them train for battle every day. When at a loose end, he would feast his beauties for days and ask them to display their swordsmanship or to seize or defend a bastion. One of these girls named Lin, the fourth child of her family, was a surpassing beauty and expert too in military arts. She was known as Fourth Mistress Lin. The prince, delighted with her, put her in command of all the other girls and called her his 'Lovely General.' "

The secretaries all exclaimed in wonder.

" 'Lovely' followed by 'General' — what a very gallant and romantic title! This is really miraculous. Prince Heng himself must have been the most romantic figure of all time!"

Chia Cheng smiled.

"Quite so. But what followed is even more amazing and heart-rending."

His protégés all asked eagerly, "What was that?"

"The next year the Yellow Turbans, Red Brows[2] and other rebels joined forces to raid the region east of the Taihang Mountains. The prince, thinking them rabble who did not need to be taken seriously, led a light force to wipe them out. However, those rebels were crafty. His forces lost two battles, and the prince was killed by the rebels. Then all the civil and military officers in the provincial capital said to each other:

" 'If even the prince could not beat them, what can *we* do?'

"They wanted to surrender. But Fourth Mistress Lin hearing this bad news assembled her women soldiers and announced:

" 'We were shown such favour by the prince in the past that we shall never be able to repay a fraction of it. Now that he

---

[1] The region around Yitu in present-day Shantung.

[2] The Yellow Turbans rose in 184 A.D., the Red Brows early in the first century.

has fallen in defence of the royal cause, I want to die for him too. Any of you who wish to follow me may — the rest are free to leave.'

"When the other women saw how determined she was, they all volunteered to join her. So that same night Fourth Mistress Lin led them out of the city to attack the rebels' camp. The rebels were caught unawares and several of their chieftains were killed. Then, seeing that their opponents were only a few women whom they reckoned couldn't amount to much, they counter-attacked and after some hard fighting killed them all, including Fourth Mistress Lin. And so she succeeded in proving her loyalty. When this was reported to the capital, the Emperor and all his ministers were shocked and moved and naturally sent troops to crush the rebels. As soon as the Imperial troops arrived, the rebellion was suppressed — we need not go into that.

"But, gentlemen, after hearing this story of Fourth Mistress Lin, don't you think it admirable!"

"Truly admirable and amazing!" exclaimed his secretaries. "This is really a wonderful subject. We should all write something to commemorate her."

One of them had already picked up a brush and written a short preface based on Chia Cheng's account, simply changing a few words. He now handed this to his patron to read.

"That's the idea," said Chia Cheng. "Actually, a short account has already been written. The other day an Imperial Decree was issued ordering a search to be made for all those who should have been commended but were left out of past records, whether monks, nuns, beggars or women, as long as they had performed some worthy deed. The accounts were to be sent to the Board of Rites for the Emperor's approval. So this account was sent to the Board of Rites. And after hearing this story, you should all write a poem on the Lovely General's loyalty and sense of honour."

"So we should," they all agreed, laughing. "And what's still more admirable is the fact that our dynasty is showing such unprecedented kindness, unmatched in earlier times. The men of Tang said, 'Our sagacious court overlooks nothing,' and this has come true today. Our dynasty lives up to this prediction."

Chia Cheng nodded.

"Exactly."

As they were speaking, Huan and Lan arrived, and Chia Cheng told them to look at the subject. Though both of them, like Pao-yu, could write poetry, this was not their special line. When it came to writing examination papers, Huan and Lan might surpass Pao-yu; but when it came to literature in general, they were much inferior. Besides, they lacked Pao-yu's literary brilliance and poetic flair. Thus the poems they wrote were like eight-section essays, inevitably stereotyped and pedantic.

Pao-yu, though not to be reckoned a good scholar, had innate intelligence and loved to browse on literature of all kinds. He believed that some ancient classics were apocryphal and contained errors too, thus they should not be taken for gospel; moreover, if one had too many scruples and just stuck together phrases from old books, such writing would be most uninteresting. These being his views, when he saw a subject for poetry — whether difficult or easy — he would write on it effortlessly, just as glib talkers having nothing to go on rely on their ready tongues to hold forth at random, spinning lengthy yarns which though they have no basis in fact delight all those who hear them. Even strict sticklers for the truth cannot beat such entertaining fantasies.

Chia Cheng, growing old now, no longer hankered after fame and profit; besides, by temperament, he was fond of poetry, wine and liberal talk. Although he felt constrained to guide his sons and nephews along the right path, when he saw that Pao-yu albeit not fond of study had some understanding of poetry, he decided that this did not really disgrace their ancestors; for they themselves, he recalled, had been the same and though working hard for the examinations had never distinguished themselves — apparently this was the Chia family's destiny. Moreover, his mother doted on this grandson. So Chia Cheng did not insist too much on Pao-yu working for the examinations and had recently treated him more leniently. And he wished that Huan and Lan, apart from writing eight-section essays, would follow Pao-yu's example. This was why, whenever they were composing poetry, he would summon all three boys together to write. But enough of this.

Now Chia Cheng told them to write a poem apiece, promising to reward the one who finished first and to give an additional prize for the best poem. As Huan and Lan had recently written several poems in company, they no longer lacked confidence. After reading the topic, they went off to think it over. Before long, Lan was the first one to finish. And Huan, afraid to be left behind, finished his too. By the time both had copied their verses out, Pao-yu was still lost in thought. Chia Cheng and his secretaries read the two younger boys' verses. Lan's heptasyllabic quatrain read as follows:

> Fourth Mistress Lin, Lovely General,
> Had jade-like beauty but an iron will;
> Because she gave her life to requite Prince Heng
> Today the soil of her district is fragrant still.

The secretaries said admiringly, "When a boy of thirteen can write like this, it truly shows the influence of a scholarly family."

Chia Cheng smiled.

"The language is childish, but it's quite a good effort."

Then they read Huan's eight-line pentameter, which was as follows:

> Fair young ladies know no sorrow,
> But a general has no relief;
> Wiping her tears she left her broidered hangings
> And took the battlefield, her heart filled with grief.
> She wanted to requite the prince's kindness —
> Who else would wreak vengeance on the enemy?
> Let us, at her grave, eulogize her loyalty
> And her eternal, peerless gallantry.

"This is even better!" the secretaries exclaimed. "Being a few years older after all, he is more original."

"It's not too bad," said Chia Cheng, "but it still lacks real feeling."

"It's quite good enough," they protested. "The Third Young

Master is only a couple of years older — he's not reached manhood yet. If they go on working hard like this, in a few years they'll be like the poets Yuan Chi and Yuan Hsien."

Chia Cheng laughed.

"You're praising them too highly. The trouble with them is that they don't study hard." Then he asked Pao-yu how he was getting on.

His protégés said, "The Second Young Master is composing his carefully. It's bound to be more stylish and poignant than the others."

Pao-yu said with a smile, "This subject seems unsuitable for a poem in the later style. Only a long poem in the old style — some song or ballad — can convey the spirit."

The secretaries rose to their feet, nodding and clapping.

"We knew he'd come out with something original," they said. "When presented with a subject, the first thing to consider is what is the most suitable form for it. This shows he's an old hand at versifying. This is like tailoring — you must measure your customer before cutting out a gown. As this is a eulogy of the Lovely General and there is a preface to it, it should be a longish ballad something like Wen Ting-yun's *The Pitcher Song*[1] or some other old ballad, or like Pai Chu-yi's *Song of Eternal Sorrow*,[2] half narrative and half lyrical, lively and graceful. That's the only way to do justice to such a good subject."

Chia Cheng, approving this, took up the brush ready to write the poem down.

"Very well then," he said to Pao-yu, smiling. "Dictate it to me. If it's no good, I'll give you a thrashing for making such a shameless boast."

Pao-yu started off with one line:

"Prince Heng loved martial arts, the fair sex too...."

Chia Cheng having written this down shook his head.
"Crude!"

---

[1] A descriptive poem in a florid style.

[2] About the Tang Emperor Hsuan Tsung and Lady Yang. See Note 1 on p. 161.

"That's the classical style. Surely not crude," one of his protégés remonstrated. "Let's see how he continues."

"We'll keep it for the time being," Chia Cheng conceded.

Pao-yu resumed:

> "He taught girls horsemanship and archery,
> Taking no joy in splendid song or dance,
> Only in spearmanship and soldiery."

When Chia Cheng had written this out, the secretaries said, "The third line has a classical flavour and is vigorous too — excellent. And these four lines are apt, fitting the narrative style."

"Don't overdo your praise," demurred Chia Cheng. "Let's see how he turns the subject."

Pao-yu went on:

> "No dust was seen to rise by watching eyes,
> By the red lantern stood the general fair."

After these two lines the rest exclaimed in approval.

"Wonderful — 'No dust was seen to rise' followed by 'the red lantern' and 'general fair.' The choice of words and images is superb."

Pao-yu resumed:

> "Her sweet breath scented every battle-cry,
> Hard for one so frail to wield cold sword and spear."

All clapped their hands and laughed.

"It's drawn to the life! Was Master Pao there at the time to see her delicate form and smell her sweet breath? If not, how could he have conjured it up like this?"

"When ladies practise fighting," Pao-yu explained, "however fearless they are they're no match for men. It goes without saying they'll appear rather delicate."

"Stop blethering," said his father, "and go on quickly."

After a moment's reflection Pao-yu recited:

> "Her knots of clove and her hibiscus belt. . . ."

The secretaries commented, "A change of rhyme here is excellent, showing flexibility and fluency. Besides, this line is charming in itself."

Chia Cheng wrote it down, observing, "This line is no good. He's already given us 'sweet breath' and 'hard for one so frail to wield.' Why go on like this? It's lack of substance that makes him pad out his lines in this way."

"A long poem needs certain ornate images to add some touches of colour," ventured Pao-yu.

"If you just hunt for images," said his father, "how can you move on to the fighting? Another couple of lines like this will be superfluous."

"In that case, I suppose I can revert to the subject in the next line."

Chia Cheng smiled scornfully.

"What great skill have you got? You've just made a fresh opening by bringing in something irrelevant. If now in one line you try to round it off and revert to the main theme, you'll find you've bitten off more than you can chew."

Pao-yu lowered his head to think, and then continued:

"Enchain no pearls but a keen blade enchain."

He asked hastily, "Will this line do?"

All the secretaries applauded.

Chia Cheng having copied this out said with a smile, "We'll let it go. Carry on."

"If this is all right, I'll go straight on; if it's not, I'll scrap it and think up something else."

"Be quiet!" snapped his father. "If it's no good you'll have to do it again. If you had to write a few dozen poems, would you complain it was hard work?"

Pao-yu had to rack his brains and then declaimed:

"After a night's manoeuvres she is exhausted,
Powder and rouge her silken headscarf stain."

Chia Cheng said, "This is another stanza. What follows?" Pao-yu resumed:

"The next year rebels rampaged east of the mountains,
Fierce tigers and leopards, swarming hornets were they."

Again the others exclaimed, "That fine word 'rampaged'

shows skill, and the turn in the narrative is natural too."
Pao-yu went on:

> "The prince led Imperial troops to wipe them out;
> One battle, then another — they lost the day.
> A reeking wind swept down the fields of wheat,
> Flags and empty commander's tent the sun did gild;
> Green hills were silent, the stream gurgled on;
> Now, in the heat of battle, Prince Heng was killed.
> Rain drenched the bones of the dead, blood stained the grass;
> Moonlight fell cold on the sand, ghosts hovered around."

"Wonderful, wonderful!" cried the secretaries. "Composition, narration and imagery — all are perfect. Let's see how he proceeds now to the Fourth Mistress. There's bound to be another skilful transition and more remarkable lines."
Pao-yu continued:

> "Commanders and men thought only of fleeing to safety,
> The city must speedily be razed to the ground.
> Who would have looked in a boudoir for loyalty?
> The prince's favourite rose up wrathfully."

All commented, "A good narrative style."
"Too wordy," said Chia Cheng. "It may grow tedious."
Then Pao-yu resumed:

> "Who might that be, the favourite of Prince Heng?
> Fourth Mistress Lin the fair general — none but she!
> She gave the order to her lovely troops,
> Fair as peach and plum-blossom they set off to fight;
> Tears stained their embroidered saddles, heavy their grief,
> No clank from their armour in the chilly night.
> None could know the outcome — victory or defeat —
> But they vowed at all costs their lord's kindness to repay;
> The rebels were too powerful to rout,
> They crushed these willows and blooms — alack the day!
> Their ghosts stayed by the city, close to home;
> Steeds trampled their sweet rouged corpses where they lay;
> This news, sent posthaste to the capital,
> Filled every family with sore dismay.
> The city's loss appalled the Emperor,
> Generals and ministers hung their heads in shame,
> For not one of the court officials could compare
> With lovely Fourth Mistress Lin of deathless fame.
> For this fair lady I sigh and sigh again
> And, my song ended, my thoughts with her remain."

After Pao-yu had finished, all the secretaries heaped praise on him and read through the poem once more.

Chia Cheng observed with a smile, "Well, though there are some good lines it's not moving enough."

Then he dismissed the three boys. They left like prisoners reprieved to return to their different quarters.

We need not concern ourselves with all the others, who went to bed as usual when night fell. Only Pao-yu, whose heart was heavy as he went back to the Garden, suddenly noticed the hibiscus in bloom and remembered the young maid's account of Ching-wen's appointment as the goddess in charge of this flower. Imperceptibly, his spirits rose again as he gazed at the hibiscus, sighing. All of a sudden it occurred to him that he had not yet paid his respects by her coffin, and it would be only fitting to sacrifice now before the flower — this would be more original than the vulgar ceremonies before the bier.

He was on the verge of bowing to the flowers when he had second thoughts. "Even if I do this, I mustn't be too casual about it," he told himself. "I'll have to dress properly and have the sacrifice well prepared to show my sincere respect."

Then he reflected, "It definitely wouldn't do to sacrifice to her in the usual vulgar manner. I must do something different and create a new ceremony which is romantic and original with nothing mundane about it — only then will it be worthy of the two of us. Besides, the men of old said: Objects as humble as ditch-water and water-weeds can be offered to princes and deities. It's not the value of the objects that counts, but only the heart's sincerity and reverence. That's the first thing.

"And secondly, the eulogy and elegy must be original too and unconventional. It's no good following the beaten track and padding the writing with high-sounding phrases; one should shed tears of blood, making each word a sob, each phrase a groan. It's better to show grief and to spare, even if that makes for an unpolished style. At no cost must genuine feeling be sacrificed to meretricious writing. Besides, this was deprecated by many of the ancients too — it's not a new idea of mine today. Unfortunately, men today are so keen on official advancement that they have completely discarded this classical style, for fear of not conforming to the fashion and damaging their chances of winning merit and fame. As I'm neither interested in rank or honour, nor writing something for others to read and admire, why shouldn't I follow the style of such poetic essays as *The Talk of the Great, Summoning the Soul, The Lament* and *The Nine Arguments* of the ancient Chu people, or *The Withering Tree, The Queries, The Autumn Flood* and *Life of the Great Gentleman*? I can intersperse the writing with solitary phrases or occasional short couplets, using allusions from real life as well as metaphors, and writing whatever I feel like. If merry, I can write playfully; if sad, I can record my anguish, until I've conveyed my ideas fully and clearly. Why should I be restricted by vulgar rules and conventions?"

Pao-yu had never been a good student, and now as he entertained such perverse ideas how could he produce any good poems or essays? Yet he wrote purely for his own enjoyment, not for others to read or admire. So giving free rein to his absurd imagination, he made up a long lament, and he copied this out neatly on a white translucent silk kerchief which Ching-wen had fancied, entitling it *Elegy for the Hibiscus Maid* and giving it a preface and a concluding song. He also had four of the things which Ching-wen had liked best provided. When it was dark and the moon was up, he told the young maid to place these before the hibiscus. First he bowed, then hung the elegy on a spray of flowers and, shedding tears, recited:

> "In this year of lasting peace, this month when hibiscus and osmanthus bloom, and on this hapless day, loutish Pao-yu of Happy Red Court presents fresh flowers, icy mermaid's silk, water from Seeping Fragrance Fountain and maple-dew tea, mere trifles to convey his sincere feelings and to sacrifice to:
>
> The Hibiscus Maid in charge of this autumn flower in the Palace of the White Emperor.
>
> The dedication:
>
> Pensively, I reflect that sixteen years have passed since this girl came into the dusty world, and her former name and home district have long been lost beyond recall. Only for little more than five years and eight months did I have her together with me as a dear companion in my bed-chamber to help me with my toilet and to

share my recreations. In life, neither gold nor jade could compare with her character; neither ice nor snow with her purity; neither sun nor stars with her fine spirit; neither flowers nor moon with her beauty. All the maids admired her goodness, all the nurses praised her kindness.

Who could know that the eagle would be trapped in a net because pigeons and falcons hated its soaring spirit, that the orchid would be cut down because weeds envied its fragrance? How could such a delicate flower withstand a fierce gale, or the care-stricken willow endure torrential rain? Slandered by poisonous pests, she fell mortally ill: her cherry lips lost their redness as she moaned, her apricot cheeks became wan and faded. Slanderous accusations came from behind screens and curtains; brambles and thorns choked doors and windows. It was not that she asked for trouble, but refuting false charges she was fated to die. She was trampled down without cease, endlessly accused. Like Chia Yi,[1] she was attacked by those jealous of her noble character; and, like Kun,[2] imperilled by her integrity. She hid her bitterness in her heart, and who is there to lament her life cut short?

Now the fairy clouds have scattered; no trace of her can be found. No search can be made for the incense that revives the dead, as the way to the Fairy Isles is lost. No medicine that restores life can be obtained, as the Magic Barge[3] is gone. Only yesterday I was painting those bluish eyebrows; today, who will warm her cold fingers with the jade rings? Medicine remains in the tripod on the stove; the tear-stains on my gown are still wet. Sad it is to open the mirror-case, for the phoenixes on its back have parted company with the broken mirror. Her comb has broken, alas, and flown off like a vanishing dragon; her gold hair-pin has dropped in the grass; her emerald hair clasp is in the dust; the magpies[4] are gone, the needle of the Double Seventh Festival rests idle; the love belt is broken, and who is there to weave the multi-coloured silk thread?

In this autumn season ruled over by the White Emperor, I dream in my lonely bed in a deserted room. In the dim moonlight under the plane tree, her charming image and sweet spirit have vanished; fragrance clings to the lotus curtain, but her scented breath and easy talk are no more. Withered grass stretches to the horizon, and everywhere crickets keep up a mournful chirping. In the evening the mossy steps are wet with dew, but no sound of pounding clothes comes through the portière. As rain patters down on the vine-covered wall, one hardly hears fluting from the other court. The

---

[1] Chia Yi (200-168 B.C.).

[2] A legendary figure, said to have been killed by the Heavenly Emperor for failing to curb floods.

[3] A Chinese legend said this belonged to the immortals and sailed in the Sky River, the Milky Way.

[4] See Note 2 on p. 626.

cockatoo before the eaves still remembers her sweet name; the begonia withering outside the balustrade foretold her death. No more games of hide-and-seek behind the screen, her dainty footsteps are silent; no more matching-herbs contests in the court where orchids burgeon in vain. The embroidery thread cast aside, who is there to decide the coloured patterns on silk? Linen crumpled, who is there to iron and scent it? Yesterday, on my father's orders, I was borne far off in a carriage to another garden; today, offending my mother, I wept over the removal of her lonely bier. When I heard that her coffin was to be cremated, I blushed with shame at breaking my vow to die, be buried and reduced to ashes together with her!

By the old temple in the autumn wind, will-o'-the-wisps are lingering; on the desolate mount in the setting sun, a few scattered bones only remain; elm trees rustle; tangled artemisia sighs; gibbons wail beyond the misty wilderness; ghosts weep around the foggy graveyard pathways. The young lordling behind red gauze curtains is filled with longing for the ill-fated maid in her mound of yellow earth. Facing the west wind, for you I shed tears of blood, while the master of Tzu Tse[1] pours out his grief to the cold moon in silence.

Alas! This calamity was caused by evil spirits, not because the gods were jealous. Slashing the slanderer's mouth would be too good for her! Cutting out the shrew's heart could not vent my anger! Though you had a short stay on earth, so deep was my feeling for you that I took careful thought and made detailed inquiries. Then I learned that the Heavenly Emperor had graciously summoned you to the Palace of Flowers; for in life you were like an orchid, and in death you are in charge of the hibiscus. Though the young maid's words seemed fantastic, in my humble opinion there are good grounds for them. Of old, Yeh Fa-shan[2] summoned a spirit to write an epitaph for him, and Li Ho[3] was ordered by Heaven to make a record — different happenings but the same in principle. For suitable tasks are selected for different talents, and the wrong choice of person would do the flowers injustice. This convinces me that the Heavenly Emperor makes most fitting use of his power, appointing those best suited to each post.

In the hope that her immortal spirit may descend here, I offer my poor composition for her compassionate ears. And here is the song to summon her spirit:

> Grey, grey is the sky!
> Are you riding a jade dragon in the void?

---

[1] Where Shih Chung's Golden Dell Garden had been. For Shih Chung, see Note 4 on p. 407.

[2] A magician said to have summoned the spirit of Li Yung, Tang poet and calligrapher, to write an epitaph for his grandfather.

[3] A great Tang poet who died young, reputedly because he was summoned to heaven to write an inscription.

Vast, vast is the earth!
Are you descending in jade and ivory carriage?
So bright and sparkling your canopy —
Is it the radiance from the zodiac's tail?
Are there coloured plumes leading the way
And on either side constellations?
Are you escorted by the God of Clouds,
Approaching with the Courier God of the Moon?
I hear the creaking of your carriage wheels —
Are you coming in a phoenix equipage?
I smell a subtle fragrance —
Are you wearing scented herbs?
Sparkling the light from your skirt —
Have you carved the bright moon for your pendant?
On an altar of luxuriant orchid leaves
I burn scented oil in lotus lamps,
And pour you osmanthus wine
In goblets of gourds.
Gazing intently through the cloudy air
I seem to glimpse some vision;
Bending over the depth to listen,
Methinks I catch a sound.
Can you, roaming through boundless space,
Bear abandoning me in the dust?
If I beg the God of Wind to drive my carriage,
May I hope to ride with you?
Wrathful is my heart,
But what use is it lamenting?
You are resting now in peace;
Is it destiny that has thus changed my life?
Tranquil you sleep in your secluded vault;
Can you leave it to change once more?
I remain enfettered here.
Ah, spirit, will you come at my call?
Are you approaching or tarrying?
Come, I implore you!

Since you live in the silent unknown, even if you approach me
my eyes cannot see you. With ivy as your screen, rush-swords as
your retinue, you rouse the willows to open their drowsy eyes and
dispel the bitterness in lotus seeds. Met by the Goddess of Music
at Cassia Cliff, you are welcomed by the Goddess of the River Lo[1]
at Orchid Isle; Nung Yu[2] plays the flute and Han Huang[3] sounds

---

[1] Known as Princess Fu, daughter of the legendary Emperor Fu Hsi, she
was drowned in the River Lo.

[2] The daughter of Duke Mu of Chin in the Spring and Autumn Period
(770-476 B.C.), she was a good flutist, said to have become a goddess.

[3] A serving-maid and a musician in the moon according to Chinese
mythology.

has fallen in defence of the royal cause, I want to die for him too. Any of you who wish to follow me may — the rest are free to leave.'

"When the other women saw how determined she was, they all volunteered to join her. So that same night Fourth Mistress Lin led them out of the city to attack the rebels' camp. The rebels were caught unawares and several of their chieftains were killed. Then, seeing that their opponents were only a few women whom they reckoned couldn't amount to much, they counter-attacked and after some hard fighting killed them all, including Fourth Mistress Lin. And so she succeeded in proving her loyalty. When this was reported to the capital, the Emperor and all his ministers were shocked and moved and naturally sent troops to crush the rebels. As soon as the Imperial troops arrived, the rebellion was suppressed — we need not go into that.

"But, gentlemen, after hearing this story of Fourth Mistress Lin, don't you think it admirable!"

"Truly admirable and amazing!" exclaimed his secretaries. "This is really a wonderful subject. We should all write something to commemorate her."

One of them had already picked up a brush and written a short preface based on Chia Cheng's account, simply changing a few words. He now handed this to his patron to read.

"That's the idea," said Chia Cheng. "Actually, a short account has already been written. The other day an Imperial Decree was issued ordering a search to be made for all those who should have been commended but were left out of past records, whether monks, nuns, beggars or women, as long as they had performed some worthy deed. The accounts were to be sent to the Board of Rites for the Emperor's approval. So this account was sent to the Board of Rites. And after hearing this story, you should all write a poem on the Lovely General's loyalty and sense of honour."

"So we should," they all agreed, laughing. "And what's still more admirable is the fact that our dynasty is showing such unprecedented kindness, unmatched in earlier times. The men of Tang said, 'Our sagacious court overlooks nothing,' and this has come true today. Our dynasty lives up to this prediction."

Chia Cheng nodded.

"Exactly."

As they were speaking, Huan and Lan arrived, and Chia Cheng told them to look at the subject. Though both of them, like Pao-yu, could write poetry, this was not their special line. When it came to writing examination papers, Huan and Lan might surpass Pao-yu; but when it came to literature in general, they were much inferior. Besides, they lacked Pao-yu's literary brilliance and poetic flair. Thus the poems they wrote were like eight-section essays, inevitably stereotyped and pedantic.

Pao-yu, though not to be reckoned a good scholar, had innate intelligence and loved to browse on literature of all kinds. He believed that some ancient classics were apocryphal and contained errors too, thus they should not be taken for gospel; moreover, if one had too many scruples and just stuck together phrases from old books, such writing would be most uninteresting. These being his views, when he saw a subject for poetry — whether difficult or easy — he would write on it effortlessly, just as glib talkers having nothing to go on rely on their ready tongues to hold forth at random, spinning lengthy yarns which though they have no basis in fact delight all those who hear them. Even strict sticklers for the truth cannot beat such entertaining fantasies.

Chia Cheng, growing old now, no longer hankered after fame and profit; besides, by temperament, he was fond of poetry, wine and liberal talk. Although he felt constrained to guide his sons and nephews along the right path, when he saw that Pao-yu albeit not fond of study had some understanding of poetry, he decided that this did not really disgrace their ancestors; for they themselves, he recalled, had been the same and though working hard for the examinations had never distinguished themselves — apparently this was the Chia family's destiny. Moreover, his mother doted on this grandson. So Chia Cheng did not insist too much on Pao-yu working for the examinations and had recently treated him more leniently. And he wished that Huan and Lan, apart from writing eight-section essays, would follow Pao-yu's example. This was why, whenever they were composing poetry, he would summon all three boys together to write. But enough of this.

Now Chia Cheng told them to write a poem apiece, promising to reward the one who finished first and to give an additional prize for the best poem. As Huan and Lan had recently written several poems in company, they no longer lacked confidence. After reading the topic, they went off to think it over. Before long, Lan was the first one to finish. And Huan, afraid to be left behind, finished his too. By the time both had copied their verses out, Pao-yu was still lost in thought. Chia Cheng and his secretaries read the two younger boys' verses. Lan's heptasyllabic quatrain read as follows:

> Fourth Mistress Lin, Lovely General,
> Had jade-like beauty but an iron will;
> Because she gave her life to requite Prince Heng
> Today the soil of her district is fragrant still.

The secretaries said admiringly, "When a boy of thirteen can write like this, it truly shows the influence of a scholarly family."

Chia Cheng smiled.

"The language is childish, but it's quite a good effort."

Then they read Huan's eight-line pentameter, which was as follows:

> Fair young ladies know no sorrow,
> But a general has no relief;
> Wiping her tears she left her broidered hangings
> And took the battlefield, her heart filled with grief.
> She wanted to requite the prince's kindness —
> Who else would wreak vengeance on the enemy?
> Let us, at her grave, eulogize her loyalty
> And her eternal, peerless gallantry.

"This is even better!" the secretaries exclaimed. "Being a few years older after all, he is more original."

"It's not too bad," said Chia Cheng, "but it still lacks real feeling."

"It's quite good enough," they protested. "The Third Young

Master is only a couple of years older — he's not reached manhood yet. If they go on working hard like this, in a few years they'll be like the poets Yuan Chi and Yuan Hsien."

Chia Cheng laughed.

"You're praising them too highly. The trouble with them is that they don't study hard." Then he asked Pao-yu how he was getting on.

His protégés said, "The Second Young Master is composing his carefully. It's bound to be more stylish and poignant than the others."

Pao-yu said with a smile, "This subject seems unsuitable for a poem in the later style. Only a long poem in the old style — some song or ballad — can convey the spirit."

The secretaries rose to their feet, nodding and clapping.

"We knew he'd come out with something original," they said. "When presented with a subject, the first thing to consider is what is the most suitable form for it. This shows he's an old hand at versifying. This is like tailoring — you must measure your customer before cutting out a gown. As this is a eulogy of the Lovely General and there is a preface to it, it should be a longish ballad something like Wen Ting-yun's *The Pitcher Song*[1] or some other old ballad, or like Pai Chu-yi's *Song of Eternal Sorrow*,[2] half narrative and half lyrical, lively and graceful. That's the only way to do justice to such a good subject."

Chia Cheng, approving this, took up the brush ready to write the poem down.

"Very well then," he said to Pao-yu, smiling. "Dictate it to me. If it's no good, I'll give you a thrashing for making such a shameless boast."

Pao-yu started off with one line:

"Prince Heng loved martial arts, the fair sex too. . . ."

Chia Cheng having written this down shook his head. "Crude!"

---

[1] A descriptive poem in a florid style.

[2] About the Tang Emperor Hsuan Tsung and Lady Yang. See Note 1 on p. 161.

"That's the classical style. Surely not crude," one of his protégés remonstrated. "Let's see how he continues."

"We'll keep it for the time being," Chia Cheng conceded.

Pao-yu resumed:

> "He taught girls horsemanship and archery,
> Taking no joy in splendid song or dance,
> Only in spearmanship and soldiery."

When Chia Cheng had written this out, the secretaries said, "The third line has a classical flavour and is vigorous too — excellent. And these four lines are apt, fitting the narrative style."

"Don't overdo your praise," demurred Chia Cheng. "Let's see how he turns the subject."

Pao-yu went on:

> "No dust was seen to rise by watching eyes,
> By the red lantern stood the general fair."

After these two lines the rest exclaimed in approval.

"Wonderful — 'No dust was seen to rise' followed by 'the red lantern' and 'general fair.' The choice of words and images is superb."

Pao-yu resumed:

> "Her sweet breath scented every battle-cry,
> Hard for one so frail to wield cold sword and spear."

All clapped their hands and laughed.

"It's drawn to the life! Was Master Pao there at the time to see her delicate form and smell her sweet breath? If not, how could he have conjured it up like this?"

"When ladies practise fighting," Pao-yu explained, "however fearless they are they're no match for men. It goes without saying they'll appear rather delicate."

"Stop blethering," said his father, "and go on quickly."

After a moment's reflection Pao-yu recited:

> "Her knots of clove and her hibiscus belt. . . ."

The secretaries commented, "A change of rhyme here is excellent, showing flexibility and fluency. Besides, this line is charming in itself."

After Pao-yu had finished, all the secretaries heaped praise on him and read through the poem once more.

Chia Cheng observed with a smile, "Well, though there are some good lines it's not moving enough."

Then he dismissed the three boys. They left like prisoners reprieved to return to their different quarters.

We need not concern ourselves with all the others, who went to bed as usual when night fell. Only Pao-yu, whose heart was heavy as he went back to the Garden, suddenly noticed the hibiscus in bloom and remembered the young maid's account of Ching-wen's appointment as the goddess in charge of this flower. Imperceptibly, his spirits rose again as he gazed at the hibiscus, sighing. All of a sudden it occurred to him that he had not yet paid his respects by her coffin, and it would be only fitting to sacrifice now before the flower — this would be more original than the vulgar ceremonies before the bier.

He was on the verge of bowing to the flowers when he had second thoughts. "Even if I do this, I mustn't be too casual about it," he told himself. "I'll have to dress properly and have the sacrifice well prepared to show my sincere respect."

Then he reflected, "It definitely wouldn't do to sacrifice to her in the usual vulgar manner. I must do something different and create a new ceremony which is romantic and original with nothing mundane about it — only then will it be worthy of the two of us. Besides, the men of old said: Objects as humble as ditch-water and water-weeds can be offered to princes and deities. It's not the value of the objects that counts, but only the heart's sincerity and reverence. That's the first thing.

"And secondly, the eulogy and elegy must be original too and unconventional. It's no good following the beaten track and padding the writing with high-sounding phrases; one should shed tears of blood, making each word a sob, each phrase a groan. It's better to show grief and to spare, even if that makes for an unpolished style. At no cost must genuine feeling be sacrificed to meretricious writing. Besides, this was deprecated by many of the ancients too — it's not a new idea of mine today. Unfortunately, men today are so keen on official advancement that they have completely discarded this classical style, for fear of not conforming to the fashion and damaging their chances of winning merit and fame. As I'm neither interested in rank or honour, nor writing something for others to read and admire, why shouldn't I follow the style of such poetic essays as *The Talk of the Great, Summoning the Soul, The Lament* and *The Nine Arguments* of the ancient Chu people, or *The Withering Tree, The Queries, The Autumn Flood* and *Life of the Great Gentleman*? I can intersperse the writing with solitary phrases or occasional short couplets, using allusions from real life as well as metaphors, and writing whatever I feel like. If merry, I can write playfully; if sad, I can record my anguish, until I've conveyed my ideas fully and clearly. Why should I be restricted by vulgar rules and conventions?"

Pao-yu had never been a good student, and now as he entertained such perverse ideas how could he produce any good poems or essays? Yet he wrote purely for his own enjoyment, not for others to read or admire. So giving free rein to his absurd imagination, he made up a long lament, and he copied this out neatly on a white translucent silk kerchief which Ching-wen had fancied, entitling it *Elegy for the Hibiscus Maid* and giving it a preface and a concluding song. He also had four of the things which Ching-wen had liked best provided. When it was dark and the moon was up, he told the young maid to place these before the hibiscus. First he bowed, then hung the elegy on a spray of flowers and, shedding tears, recited:

"In this year of lasting peace, this month when hibiscus and osmanthus bloom, and on this hapless day, loutish Pao-yu of Happy Red Court presents fresh flowers, icy mermaid's silk, water from Seeping Fragrance Fountain and maple-dew tea, mere trifles to convey his sincere feelings and to sacrifice to:

The Hibiscus Maid in charge of this autumn flower in the Palace of the White Emperor.

The dedication:

Pensively, I reflect that sixteen years have passed since this girl came into the dusty world, and her former name and home district have long been lost beyond recall. Only for little more than five years and eight months did I have her together with me as a dear companion in my bed-chamber to help me with my toilet and to share my recreations. In life, neither gold nor jade could compare with her character; neither ice nor snow with her purity; neither sun nor stars with her fine spirit; neither flowers nor moon with her beauty. All the maids admired her goodness, all the nurses praised her kindness.

Who could know that the eagle would be trapped in a net because pigeons and falcons hated its soaring spirit, that the orchid would be cut down because weeds envied its fragrance? How could such a delicate flower withstand a fierce gale, or the care-stricken willow endure torrential rain? Slandered by poisonous pests, she fell mortally ill: her cherry lips lost their redness as she moaned, her apricot cheeks became wan and faded. Slanderous accusations came from behind screens and curtains; brambles and thorns choked doors and windows. It was not that she asked for trouble, but refuting false charges she was fated to die. She was trampled down without cease, endlessly accused. Like Chia Yi,[1] she was attacked by those jealous of her noble character; and, like Kun,[2] imperilled by her integrity. She hid her bitterness in her heart, and who is there to lament her life cut short?

Now the fairy clouds have scattered; no trace of her can be found. No search can be made for the incense that revives the dead, as the way to the Fairy Isles is lost. No medicine that restores life can be obtained, as the Magic Barge[3] is gone. Only yesterday I was painting those bluish eyebrows; today, who will warm her cold fingers with the jade rings? Medicine remains in the tripod on the stove; the tear-stains on my gown are still wet. Sad it is to open the mirror-case, for the phoenixes on its back have parted company with the broken mirror. Her comb has broken, alas, and flown off like a vanishing dragon; her gold hair-pin has dropped in the grass; her emerald hair clasp is in the dust; the magpies[4] are gone, the needle of the Double Seventh Festival rests idle; the love belt is broken, and who is there to weave the multi-coloured silk thread?

In this autumn season ruled over by the White Emperor, I dream in my lonely bed in a deserted room. In the dim moonlight under the plane tree, her charming image and sweet spirit have vanished; fragrance clings to the lotus curtain, but her scented breath and easy talk are no more. Withered grass stretches to the horizon, and everywhere crickets keep up a mournful chirping. In the evening the mossy steps are wet with dew, but no sound of pounding clothes comes through the portière. As rain patters down on the vine-covered wall, one hardly hears fluting from the other court. The

---

[1] Chia Yi (200-168 B.C.).

[2] A legendary figure, said to have been killed by the Heavenly Emperor for failing to curb floods.

[3] A Chinese legend said this belonged to the immortals and sailed in the Sky River, the Milky Way.

[4] See Note 2 on p. 626.

cockatoo before the eaves still remembers her sweet name; the begonia withering outside the balustrade foretold her death. No more games of hide-and-seek behind the screen, her dainty footsteps are silent; no more matching-herbs contests in the court where orchids burgeon in vain. The embroidery thread cast aside, who is there to decide the coloured patterns on silk? Linen crumpled, who is there to iron and scent it? Yesterday, on my father's orders, I was borne far off in a carriage to another garden; today, offending my mother, I wept over the removal of her lonely bier. When I heard that her coffin was to be cremated, I blushed with shame at breaking my vow to die, be buried and reduced to ashes together with her!

By the old temple in the autumn wind, will-o'-the-wisps are lingering; on the desolate mount in the setting sun, a few scattered bones only remain; elm trees rustle; tangled artemisia sighs; gibbons wail beyond the misty wilderness; ghosts weep around the foggy graveyard pathways. The young lordling behind red gauze curtains is filled with longing for the ill-fated maid in her mound of yellow earth. Facing the west wind, for you I shed tears of blood, while the master of Tzu Tse[1] pours out his grief to the cold moon in silence.

Alas! This calamity was caused by evil spirits, not because the gods were jealous. Slashing the slanderer's mouth would be too good for her! Cutting out the shrew's heart could not vent my anger! Though you had a short stay on earth, so deep was my feeling for you that I took careful thought and made detailed inquiries. Then I learned that the Heavenly Emperor had graciously summoned you to the Palace of Flowers; for in life you were like an orchid, and in death you are in charge of the hibiscus. Though the young maid's words seemed fantastic, in my humble opinion there are good grounds for them. Of old, Yeh Fa-shan[2] summoned a spirit to write an epitaph for him, and Li Ho[3] was ordered by Heaven to make a record — different happenings but the same in principle. For suitable tasks are selected for different talents, and the wrong choice of person would do the flowers injustice. This convinces me that the Heavenly Emperor makes most fitting use of his power, appointing those best suited to each post.

In the hope that her immortal spirit may descend here, I offer my poor composition for her compassionate ears. And here is the song to summon her spirit:

> Grey, grey is the sky!
> Are you riding a jade dragon in the void?

---

[1] Where Shih Chung's Golden Dell Garden had been. For Shih Chung, see Note 4 on p. 407.

[2] A magician said to have summoned the spirit of Li Yung, Tang poet and calligrapher, to write an epitaph for his grandfather.

[3] A great Tang poet who died young, reputedly because he was summoned to heaven to write an inscription.

Vast, vast is the earth!
Are you descending in jade and ivory carriage?
So bright and sparkling your canopy —
Is it the radiance from the zodiac's tail?
Are there coloured plumes leading the way
And on either side constellations?
Are you escorted by the God of Clouds,
Approaching with the Courier God of the Moon?
I hear the creaking of your carriage wheels —
Are you coming in a phoenix equipage?
I smell a subtle fragrance —
Are you wearing scented herbs?
Sparkling the light from your skirt —
Have you carved the bright moon for your pendant?
On an altar of luxuriant orchid leaves
I burn scented oil in lotus lamps,
And pour you osmanthus wine
In goblets of gourds.
Gazing intently through the cloudy air
I seem to glimpse some vision;
Bending over the depth to listen,
Methinks I catch a sound.
Can you, roaming through boundless space,
Bear abandoning me in the dust?
If I beg the God of Wind to drive my carriage,
May I hope to ride with you?
Wrathful is my heart,
But what use is it lamenting?
You are resting now in peace;
Is it destiny that has thus changed my life?
Tranquil you sleep in your secluded vault;
Can you leave it to change once more?
I remain enfettered here.
Ah, spirit, will you come at my call?
Are you approaching or tarrying?
Come, I implore you!

Since you live in the silent unknown, even if you approach me my eyes cannot see you. With ivy as your screen, rush-swords as your retinue, you rouse the willows to open their drowsy eyes and dispel the bitterness in lotus seeds. Met by the Goddess of Music at Cassia Cliff, you are welcomed by the Goddess of the River Lo[1] at Orchid Isle; Nung Yu[2] plays the flute and Han Huang[3] sounds

---

[1] Known as Princess Fu, daughter of the legendary Emperor Fu Hsi, she was drowned in the River Lo.

[2] The daughter of Duke Mu of Chin in the Spring and Autumn Period (770-476 B.C.), she was a good flutist, said to have become a goddess.

[3] A serving-maid and a musician in the moon according to Chinese mythology.

the clapper to summon the Queen of Mount Sung and the Dowager of Mount Li.[1] The Divine Tortoise manifests itself in the River Lo, wild beasts dance to the melody *Hsienchih*,[2] dragons sing below the Red Stream, and phoenixes alight at the Pearl Forest.

I am sacrificing with sincerity, caring little what sacrificial vessels I am using.

Setting out in your chariot from the City of Bright Morning Clouds,[3] you return with your banners to the Hanging Garden.[4] One moment your form seems faintly visible, the next it is suddenly blotted out by mist. The clouds and mist converge, then part again; fog and rain obscure the sky; then the mist withdraws, high above gleam stars, and the moon in mid sky brightens the hills and streams.

My heart is beating fast, like one just waking from a dream. I weep with longing and shed tears, not knowing where to go. All human voices are hushed; the only sounds are the rustling of bamboo, birds taking wing in fright, fish blowing bubbles....

In my grief I invoke you and, these rites at an end, look for some sign.

Ah, may your spirit come to the sacrifice!"

After chanting this he burned the silk and poured a libation of tea, still reluctant to leave the place. The young maid had to urge him several times before he turned away. Then, abruptly, they heard laughter behind some rocks.

"Please wait a bit!" cried a voice.

The two of them gave a start. And the maid, looking back, saw a figure emerging from behind the hibiscus blooms.

"Help! A ghost!" she cried. "Ching-wen's spirit has really come!"

Pao-yu in fright turned to look too.

To know whether or not it was a ghost, read the next chapter.

---

[1] Both were immortals.

[2] It is said that when the Divine Tortoise showed its back with a magic sign on it, there was peace and prosperity in the world; and when the *Hsienchih* melody composed by the Yellow Emperor was played, all the wild beasts danced to it.

[3] Where the Cardinal God of Heaven of Taoism was believed to live.

[4] A fairy mountain said to be in the Kunlun Range.

CHAPTER 79

Hsueh Pan Marries a Fierce Lioness
and Repents Too Late
Ying-chun Is Wrongly Wedded
to an Ungrateful Wolf

Pao-yu, after sacrificing to Ching-wen, was startled to hear a voice from the shade of the flowers. Stepping forward to investigate, he found it was no other than Tai-yu.

"What an original funeral ode!" she teased, smiling all over her face. "It deserves to be passed down with that epitaph commemorating Tsao Ngo,[1] the filial daughter."

Pao-yu blushed.

"The usual run of funeral odes seem to me so stereotyped," he explained, "I tried to use a new form. It was just for fun; I never thought you'd hear it. If it won't do, why don't you suggest some improvements?"

"Where is your draft? I must read it carefully. I didn't hear the whole long piece, only the two lines:

> The young lordling behind red gauze curtains is filled with longing
> For the ill-fated maid in her mound of yellow earth.

That's a felicitous couplet, except that 'red gauze curtains' is rather trite. There are real-life images ready at hand — why not use one of those?"

He hastily asked what she meant.

"We all have rosy-cloud gauze pasted on latticed windows nowadays," she replied. "Why not say 'Under madder-gauze window, a young lordling filled with longing'?"

---

[1] Of Eastern Han who jumped into the river where her father was drowned and surfaced five days later with his body in her arms.

around. When the mistresses were chatting the other day, it turned out that your two mansions know this family too. The whole capital, from nobles down to tradesmen, all call that family the Osmanthus Hsias."

"How did they get that name?"

"Well, their surname is Hsia, and they are rolling in wealth. Apart from other landed property, they have several hundred acres growing nothing but osmanthus trees. They own all the shops in the capital selling osmanthus, and they supply the Palace too with all those needed for display. That's how they came by this name. Now old Mr. Hsia is dead; his widow lives with her daughter and there are no sons — it's too bad that their male branch has died out."

"Never mind that," said Pao-yu. "What's the girl like? How did he come to take a fancy to her?"

"It's partly fate, and partly a case of 'Beauty is in the eye of the beholder.' In the old days the two families were on close terms and as children they played together. Since they rank as cousins, they didn't have to avoid each other according to the rules of propriety. And though they hadn't met for so many years, as soon as he visited her family old Mrs. Hsia, having no son herself, struck by your cousin's good looks shed tears of joy, more delighted than if he had been her own son. She presented the two young people to each other. Well, the girl who'd grown up as pretty as a flower was taught to read and write at home; so your cousin made up his mind then and there. The Hsia family entertained him for three or four days, and those old pawnshop assistants of his as well, pressing them to stay even longer, and only letting them leave when they absolutely insisted.

"As soon as your cousin got home, he pestered our mistress to ask for the girl's hand. As she had seen the girl and the two families were well matched, she agreed. She talked it over with your mother and Madam Lien, then sent someone to propose the marriage, and it was immediately settled. Only there's so little time left before the wedding that we're rushed off our feet. The

Aunt Hsueh and Pao-chai paid no attention to her. And by now Hsueh Pan too was helpless, only regretting day and night that he had married this monster. They were all at their wits' end. High and low in the Ning and Jung Mansions knew of this, and none of them but deplored it.

By this time Pao-yu's hundred days' confinement was up and he was allowed out of doors. Coming over to call on Chin-kuei, he found nothing outrageous in her looks or behaviour — she seemed just as lovely as the other girls — so he was mystified and amazed by her bad reputation.

One day when he went to pay his respects to his mother, he found Ying-chun's nanny there too, telling Lady Wang what a reprobate Sun Shao-tsu was.

"All our young lady can do is to cry in secret," she said. "She's longing to be fetched home, to have a few days' respite."

"The last couple of days I've been thinking of sending for her," answered Lady Wang. "But so many troubles cropped up that it slipped my mind. The other day Pao-yu called there, and when he came back he made the same suggestion. Well, tomorrow's an auspicious day; we'll send to fetch her."

Just then a servant arrived from the Lady Dowager to tell Pao-yu to go first thing the next day to Tienchi Temple, in order to offer thanks for his recovery. As Pao-yu was only too eager for any outing, these instructions so delighted him that he could hardly close his eyes all night as he waited for day to break.

The next morning after he had washed and dressed, accompanied by two or three old nurses he went by carriage out of the West Gate to burn incense and offer thanks in Tienchi Temple, where all the preparations for this had been made the previous day. Pao-yu, being naturally timid, kept away from the fierce-looking images of gods and demons there. For this magnificent temple had been built in an earlier dynasty but then neglected for so many years that all the clay sculptures there struck him as monstrous and left him aghast.

After hastily burning the sacrificial paper, Pao-yu retired to a quiet room to rest. When he had been served a meal, the old nurses, Li Kuei and others strolled with him through the

each other just as do a prince and his ministers, and co-operate with each other just as do a host and his guests. Some of them are heating, some cooling, some costly, some cheap. Inwardly, they fortify the humours, build up the patient's strength, improve the appetite, increase resistance, tranquillize the nerves, expel cold and heat, and eliminate indigestion and phlegm. Outwardly, they regulate the blood, relax the muscles, remove dead tissues and help new ones to grow, cure chills and act as an antidote to poison. They are marvellously effective, as you'd know, sir, if you'd tried one."

"I can hardly believe that one plaster cures so many different ailments," Pao-yu answered. "I'd like to know if it's any good for a malady I have in mind."

"It cures *all* diseases," One-Plaster Wang asserted. "If it does you no good, you can tweak my beard, slap my old face and pull down my temple — how's that? Just tell me the symptoms of this malady."

"Have a guess. If you guess right, I'll believe in your medicine."

One-Plaster Wang thought for a while.

"This is quite a poser," he said at last with a smile. "I'm afraid my plaster may not work in this case."

Then Pao-yu told Li Kuei and the other servants, "Go out and have a stroll. There are too many people in here, it's getting stuffy."

The servants withdrew, leaving only Ming-yen in attendance. After he had lighted a stick of Sweet-Dream Incense, Pao-yu told him to sit down beside him so that he could lean against him. At this point, One-Plaster Wang had a sudden idea. Smiling all over his face, he drew closer to whisper:

"I've guessed it! Now that the young gentleman is growing up, I suppose he wants some drug to increase his virility — right?"

Cutting him short, Ming-yen snapped, "Shut up, you idiot!"

"What did he say?" asked Pao-yu in bewilderment.

"Never mind. He was talking rot."

One-Plaster Wang was appalled and dared not ask any more questions.

"Better tell me outright, sir," he said.

"What I wanted to know was this: have you a prescription to cure a jealous shrew?"

The priest clapped his hands and laughed.

"I give up! Not only have I no such prescription, I've never even heard of one either."

"In that case," Pao-yu teased, "your plaster doesn't amount to much."

"Though I've no plaster to cure a shrew, there *is* a potion which might. Only it takes time — it doesn't work overnight."

"What potion is that? And how should it be taken?"

"It's called Cure for Jealousy. Take one top-quality pear, one fifth of an ounce of crystal sugar, one tenth of orange peel and three bowls of water. Boil these till the pear is soft, and let the shrew take one dose first thing each day. Then in due course she'll be cured."

"That wouldn't cost much, but I doubt whether it would work."

"If one dose doesn't do the trick, give ten. If she's not cured today, repeat the treatment tomorrow. If it doesn't work this year, go on with it next year. At any rate, these ingredients aren't injurious but good for the lungs and digestion. This sweet potion cures coughs and tastes delicious too. If she takes it for a hundred years she'll die in any case, and once dead how can she go on being jealous? So in the end it will prove efficacious."

By now Pao-yu and Ming-yen were roaring with laughter. "You oily-mouthed ox!" they cried.

"What does it matter?" chuckled One-Plaster Wang. "I was just whiling away the time to stop you from feeling sleepy. It's worth money, making you laugh. To tell you the truth, even my plasters are bogus. If I had some really good medicine, I'd take it myself so as to become an immortal instead of coming here to fool around."

By this time it was the hour for the sacrifice, and they asked

Pao-yu to go out to burn sacrificial paper, pour a libation of wine and distribute alms. The sacrifice ended, he went back to the city.

By now Ying-chun had already been home for some time. When the women from the Sun family who had come with her had been entertained to dinner and sent home, Ying-chun, shedding tears in Lady Wang's room, described her wretchedness.

"Sun Shao-tsu cares for nothing but women, gambling and drinking," she sobbed. "He's had affairs with practically all our maids and young servants' wives. When I remonstrated mildly two or three times, he cursed me for being jealous, saying I must have been steeped in vinegar. He also says he put five thousand taels in father's safe-keeping and he shouldn't have spent it. He's come here several times to ask for it back, and when he fails to get it he points at me and scolds, 'Don't put on those ladified airs with me! Your old man has spent five thousand taels of mine; so he's *sold* you to me. If you don't behave yourself, I'll beat you up and send you to sleep with the servants. When your grandfather was alive, seeing how rich and influential our family was, he went to great trouble to get connected with us. Actually, I belong to your *father*'s generation. It was a mistake my marrying you because that's made me step down one generation, as if *I* were the one chasing after power and profit.'"

She wept as she spoke, and Lady Wang and all the girls shed tears too.

Lady Wang said soothingly, "You've already married this oaf, so it can't be helped. Your uncle did advise your father against it, but he wouldn't listen — he'd set his heart on this match. And now it's turned out badly. Well, child, this is fate."

"I can't believe I was fated to suffer like this," sobbed Ying-chun. "I lost my mother when I was a child, and was lucky to have a few peaceful years here with you, auntie. But now see what's become of me!"

CHAPTER 80

Lady Wang, trying to console her, asked where she would like to stay.

"Being snatched away so suddenly from my cousins, I dream of them all the time," Ying-chun replied. "I long for my old rooms too. If I can spend a few more days in my old quarters in the Garden, then I shall die content. Who knows if I'll ever have such a chance again."

"Don't talk so wildly," interposed Lady Wang. "Little squabbles between young couples are quite common. Why speak in that ill-omened way?"

She ordered the house at Purple Caltrop Isle to be made ready at once, and told the girls to keep Ying-chun company and cheer her up.

To Pao-yu she said, "Mind you don't breathe a word about this to the old lady! If she gets to hear of it, I'll hold you to blame."

Pao-yu promised to keep quiet.

That evening Ying-chun stayed in her old quarters, and her girl cousins and the maids lavished affection on her. After three days, however, she had to go to stay with Lady Hsing. First she took her leave of the Lady Dowager and Lady Wang. When it came to saying goodbye to the girls, she was prostrated by grief. It was Lady Wang and Aunt Hsueh who soothed her and finally persuaded her to stop weeping and go over to the other mansion, where she spent a couple of days with Lady Hsing. Then Sun Shao-tsu sent to fetch her back and, though Ying-chun dreaded returning, for fear of her cruel husband she had to hold back her grief and take her leave.

As for Lady Hsing, she was so callous that she had not even asked Ying-chun how she got on with her husband, or whether her household was difficult to manage, simply entertaining her in the most perfunctory manner.

To know what the outcome was, read the next chapter.